FIAT
Strada
Owners
Workshop
Manual

Peter G Strasman

Models covered
All FIAT Strada and Strada II (Ritmo) models, including 105 TC, Abarth 130 TC and special/limited editions
1116 cc, 1299 cc, 1301 cc, 1498 cc, 1585 cc & 1995 cc

Covers most features of Cabrio models

ISBN 1 85010 497 2

Printed in England *(479-6P8)*

AB

THE BOOK ®

Haynes Publishing Group
Sparkford Nr Yeovil
Somerset BA22 7JJ England

Haynes Publications, Inc
861 Lawrence Drive
Newbury Park
California 91320 USA

British Library Cataloguing in Publication Data
Strasman, Peter G., *1923–* Fiat Strada owners workshop manual. – 4th ed. 1. Cars. Maintenance & repair – Amateurs' manuals I. Title   .II. Series 629.28'722 ISBN 1-85010-497-2

Acknowledgements

Thanks are due to FIAT for the supply of technical information and the use of certain illustrations. The Champion Sparking Plug Company supplied the illustrations showing the various spark plug conditions. Duckhams Oils provided lubrication data.

Thanks are also due to all those people at Sparkford who helped in the production of this manual, and to Mr. Whittock of Shapwick for the loan of a Strada 105 TC.

About this manual

Its aim

The aim of this manual is to help you get the best value from your car. It can do so in several ways. It can help you decide what work must be done (even should you choose to get it done by a garage), provide information on routine maintenance and servicing, and give a logical course of action and diagnosis when random faults occur. However, it is hoped that you will use the manual by tackling the work yourself. On simpler jobs it may even be quicker than booking the car into a garage and going there twice to leave and collect it. Perhaps most important, a lot of money can be saved by avoiding the costs the garage must charge to cover its labour and overheads.

The manual has drawings and descriptions to show the function of the various components so that their layout can be understood. Then the tasks are described and photographed in a step-by-step sequence so that even a novice can do the work.

Its arrangement

The manual is divided into thirteen Chapters, each covering a logical sub-division of the vehicle. The Chapters are each divided into Sections, numbered with single figures, eg 5; and the Sections into paragraphs (or sub-sections), with decimal numbers following on from the Section they are in, eg 5.1, 5.2, 5.3 etc.

It is freely illustrated, especially in those parts where there is a detailed sequence of operations to be carried out. There are two forms of illustration: figures and photographs. The figures are numbered in sequence with decimal numbers, according to their position in the Chapter – eg Fig. 6.4 is the fourth drawing/illustration in Chapter 6. Photographs carry the same number (either individually or in related groups) as the Section or sub-section to which they relate.

There is an alphabetical index at the back of the manual as well as a contents list at the front. Each Chapter is also preceded by its own individual contents list.

References to the 'left' or 'right' of the vehicle are in the sense of a person in the driver's seat facing forwards.

Unless otherwise stated, nuts and bolts are removed by turning anti-clockwise, and tightened by turning clockwise.

Vehicle manufacturers continually make changes to specifications and recommendations, and these, when notified, are incorporated into our manuals at the earliest opportunity.

Whilst every care is taken to ensure that the information in this manual is correct, no liability can be accepted by the authors or publishers for loss, damage or injury caused by any errors in, or omissions from the information given.

Introduction to the FIAT Strada

The Strada is a compact, economical car, designed in the current hatchback style.

Mechanically, the use of proven components and assemblies should provide this model with a long and reliable operating life.

Maintenance and overhaul tasks can be carried out with the minimum use of special tools, 75 models being perhaps slightly easier when it comes to major dismantling such as engine and driveshaft removal.

Standard equipment is adequate and gives the car a rugged appearance. In fact, the car soon impresses the driver and owner as being one of the few smaller present day models where design and production engineers have together devised the correct formula and got everything 'just right.'

Information on later models will be found in the Supplement at the end of this manual.

Contents

FIAT Strada 75CL 3-door

General dimensions, weights and capacities

For modifications, and information applicable to later models, see Supplement at end of manual

Dimensions
Overall length:
    All models except North American .... 3937 mm (155 in)
    North American models .... 4089 mm (161 in)
Overall width .... 1651 mm (65 in)
Overall height .... 1403 mm (55.24 in)
Wheelbase .... 2449 mm (96.40 in)
Ground clearance .... 165 mm (6.50 in)

Weights (kerb)
3-door models
All models except North American .... 895 kg (1971 lb)
North American models .... 919 kg (2025 lb)
Note: *Add 4.50 kg (10 lb) for California models*

5-door models*
All models except North American .... 911 kg (2006 lb)
North American models .... 935 kg (2060 lb)
Note: *Add 4.50 kg (10 lb) for California models*

*Add 36 kg (80 lb) for models with automatic transmission and 49 kg (108 lb) for those with air conditioning

Capacities
Fuel tank .... 11.2 gals (13 US gals, 51 litres)
Cooling system:
    65 models .... 13.9 pints (16.7 US pints, 7.9 litres)
    75 models .... 14.1 pints (16.9 US pints, 8.0 litres)
Engine oil including filter renewal .... 7.7 pints (9.2 US pints, 4.40 litres)
Manual transmission (including final drive):
    4-speed gearbox .... 5.5 pints (6.6 US pints, 3.15 litres)
    5-speed gearbox (65 models) .... 5.7 pints (6.8 US pints, 3.26 litres)
    5-speed gearbox (75 models) .... 5.2 pints (6.2 US pints, 2.93 litres)
Automatic transmission:
    From dry .... 10.4 pints (12.5 US pints, 5.9 litres)
    At fluid renewal .... 5.3 pints (6.4 US pints, 3.0 litres)
Final drive (automatic transmission models only) .... 1.3 pints (1.6 US pints, 0.75 litres)
Steering gear:
    Oil .... 0.25 pints (0.31 US pints, 0.14 litres)
    Grease .... 5 fl oz (5 fl oz, 140 cc)
Driveshaft joints .... 4.5 fl oz (4.5 fl oz, 125 cc)
Windscreen washer reservoir .... 5.1 pints (6.1 US pints, 2.9 litres)
Rear screen washer reservoir .... 7.0 pints (8.4 US pints, 4.0 litres)

Use of English

As this book has been written in England, it uses the appropriate English component names, phrases, and spelling. Some of these differ from those used in America. Normally, these cause no difficulty, but to make sure, a glossary is printed below. In ordering spare parts remember the parts list may use some of these words:

English	American	English	American
Accelerator	Gas pedal	Leading shoe (of brake)	Primary shoe
Aerial	Antenna	Locks	Latches
Anti-roll bar	Stabiliser or sway bar	Methylated spirit	Denatured alcohol
Big-end bearing	Rod bearing	Motorway	Freeway, turnpike etc
Bonnet (engine cover)	Hood	Number plate	License plate
Boot (luggage compartment)	Trunk	Paraffin	Kerosene
Bulkhead	Firewall	Petrol	Gasoline (gas)
Bush	Bushing	Petrol tank	Gas tank
Cam follower or tappet	Valve lifter or tappet	'Pinking'	'Pinging'
Carburettor	Carburetor	Prise (force apart)	Pry
Catch	Latch	Propeller shaft	Driveshaft
Choke/venturi	Barrel	Quarterlight	Quarter window
Circlip	Snap-ring	Retread	Recap
Clearance	Lash	Reverse	Back-up
Crownwheel	Ring gear (of differential)	Rocker cover	Valve cover
Damper	Shock absorber, shock	Saloon	Sedan
Disc (brake)	Rotor/disk	Seized	Frozen
Distance piece	Spacer	Sidelight	Parking light
Drop arm	Pitman arm	Silencer	Muffler
Drop head coupe	Convertible	Sill panel (beneath doors)	Rocker panel
Dynamo	Generator (DC)	Small end, little end	Piston pin or wrist pin
Earth (electrical)	Ground	Spanner	Wrench
Engineer's blue	Prussian blue	Split cotter (for valve spring cap)	Lock (for valve spring retainer)
Estate car	Station wagon	Split pin	Cotter pin
Exhaust manifold	Header	Steering arm	Spindle arm
Fault finding/diagnosis	Troubleshooting	Sump	Oil pan
Float chamber	Float bowl	Swarf	Metal chips or debris
Free-play	Lash	Tab washer	Tang or lock
Freewheel	Coast	Tappet	Valve lifter
Gearbox	Transmission	Thrust bearing	Throw-out bearing
Gearchange	Shift	Top gear	High
Grub screw	Setscrew, Allen screw	Trackrod (of steering)	Tie-rod (or connecting rod)
Gudgeon pin	Piston pin or wrist pin	Trailing shoe (of brake)	Secondary shoe
Halfshaft	Axleshaft	Transmission	Whole drive line
Handbrake	Parking brake	Tyre	Tire
Hood	Soft top	Van	Panel wagon/van
Hot spot	Heat riser	Vice	Vise
Indicator	Turn signal	Wheel nut	Lug nut
Interior light	Dome lamp	Windscreen	Windshield
Layshaft (of gearbox)	Countershaft	Wing/mudguard	Fender

Buying spare parts and vehicle identification numbers

Buying spare parts

Spare parts are available from many sources, for example, FIAT garages, other accessory shops, and motor factors. Our advice regarding spare parts is as follows:

Officially appointed FIAT garages – This is the best source of parts which are peculiar to your car and otherwise not generally available (eg complete cylinder heads, internal gearbox components, badges, interior trim etc). It is also the only place at which you should buy parts if your car is still under warranty; non-FIAT parts may invalidate the warranty. To be sure of obtaining the correct parts it will always be

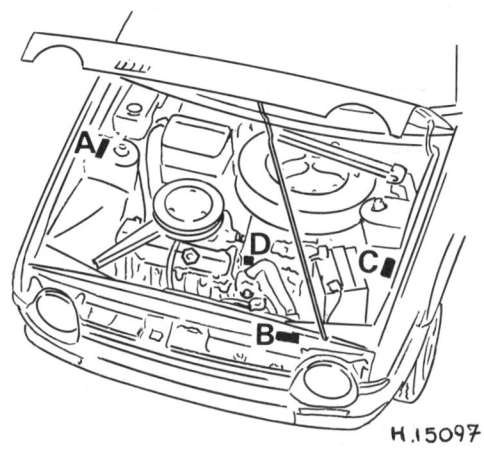

Typical locations of under-bonnet numbers and plates

A   Chassis type and number
B   Identification plate
C   Homologation plate (car type, country of manufacture and tests performed)
D   Engine type

necessary to give the partsman your car's engine number, chassis number and number for spares, and if possible, to take the old part along for positive identification. Many parts are available under a factory exchange scheme – any parts returned should always be clean. It obviously makes good sense to go straight to the specialists on your car for this type of part for they are best equipped to supply you. They will also be able to provide their own Fiat service manual for your car should you require one.

Other garages and accessory shops – These are often very good places to buy material and components needed for the maintenance of your car (eg oil filters, spark plugs, bulbs, drivebelts, oils and grease, touch-up paint, filler paste etc). They also sell accessories, usually have convenient opening hours, charge lower prices and can often be found not far from home.

Motor factors – Good factors stock all of the more important components which wear out relatively quickly (eg clutch components, pinions, valves, exhaust systems, brake pipes/seals and pads, etc). Motor factors will often provide new or reconditioned components on a part exchange basis – this can save a considerable amount of money.

Vehicle identification numbers

Modifications are a continuing and unpublished process in vehicle manufacture quite apart from major model changes. Spare parts manuals and lists are compiled upon a numerical basis, the individual vehicle numbers being essential to correct identification of the component required.

The *chassis type and number plate* is located on the wing valance under the bonnet. The *identification data plate* is located on the radiator top rail. The *ECE homologation plate* is located on the wing valance under the bonnet. The *engine type and number* is stamped on the cylinder block. On North American models, the vehicle number is repeated on the top of the facia panel, just inside the windscreen. A tune-up decal is also affixed to the car, along with other labels and certificates as required to comply with local regulations. The *paintwork colour code* is given on a label stuck to the inner surface of the tailgate.

Identification plate

Engine number

Tools and working facilities

Introduction

A selection of good tools is a fundamental requirement for anyone contemplating the maintenance and repair of a motor vehicle. For the owner who does not possess any, their purchase will prove a considerable expense, offsetting some of the savings made by doing-it-yourself. However, provided that the tools purchased are of good quality, they will last for many years and prove an extremely worthwhile investment.

To help the average owner to decide which tools are needed to carry out the various tasks detailed in this manual, we have compiled three lists of tools under the following headings: *Maintenance and minor repair, Repair and overhaul,* and *Special.* The newcomer to practical mechanics should start off with the *Maintenance and minor repair* tool kit and confine himself to the simpler jobs around the vehicle. Then, as his confidence and experience grow, he can undertake more difficult tasks, buying extra tools as, and when, they are needed. In this way, a *Maintenance and minor repair* tool kit can be built-up into a *Repair and overhaul* tool kit over a considerable period of time without any major cash outlays. The experienced do-it-yourselfer will have a tool kit good enough for most repair and overhaul procedures and will add tools from the *Special* category when he feels the expense is justified by the amount of use these tools will be put to.

It is obviously not possible to cover the subject of tools fully here. For those who wish to learn more about tools and their use there is a book entitled *How to Choose and Use Car Tools* available from the publishers of this manual.

Maintenance and minor repair tool kit

The tools given in this list should be considered as a minimum requirement if routine maintenance, servicing and minor repair operations are to be undertaken. We recommend the purchase of combination spanners (ring one end, open-ended the other); although more expensive than open-ended ones, they do give the advantages of both types of spanner.

Combination spanners - 10, 11, 12, 13, 14 & 17 mm
Adjustable spanner - 9 inch
Spark plug spanner (with rubber insert)
Spark plug gap adjustment tool
Set of feeler gauges
Brake bleed nipple spanner
Screwdriver - 4 in long x $\frac{1}{4}$ in dia (flat blade)
Screwdriver - 4 in long x $\frac{1}{4}$ in dia (cross blade)
Combination pliers - 6 inch
Hacksaw (junior)
Tyre pump
Tyre pressure gauge
Oil can
Fine emery cloth (1 sheet)
Wire brush (small)
Funnel (medium size)

Repair and overhaul tool kit

These tools are virtually essential for anyone undertaking any major repairs to a motor vehicle, and are additional to those given in the *Maintenance and minor repair* list. Included in this list is a comprehensive set of sockets. Although these are expensive they will be found invaluable as they are so versatile - particularly if various drives are included in the set. We recommend the $\frac{1}{2}$ in square-drive type, as this can be used with most proprietary torque spanners. If you cannot afford a socket set, even bought piecemeal, then inexpensive tubular box wrenches are a useful alternative.

The tools in this list will occasionally need to be supplemented by tools from the *Special* list.

Sockets (or box spanners) to cover range in previous list
Reversible ratchet drive (for use with sockets)
Extension piece, 10 inch (for use with sockets)
Universal joint (for use with sockets)
Torque wrench (for use with sockets)
Mole wrench - 8 inch
Ball pein hammer
Soft-faced hammer, plastic or rubber
Screwdriver - 6 in long x $\frac{5}{16}$ in dia (flat blade)
Screwdriver - 2 in long x $\frac{5}{16}$ in square (flat blade)
Screwdriver - 1$\frac{1}{2}$ in long x $\frac{1}{4}$ in dia (cross blade)
Screwdriver - 3 in long x $\frac{1}{8}$ in dia (electricians)
Pliers - electricians side cutters
Pliers - needle nosed
Pliers - circlip (internal and external)
Cold chisel - $\frac{1}{2}$ inch
Scriber
Scraper
Centre punch
Pin punch
Hacksaw
Valve grinding tool
Steel rule/straight-edge
Allen keys
Selection of files
Wire brush (large)
Axle-stands
Jack (strong scissor or hydraulic type)

Special tools

The tools in this list are those which are not used regularly, are expensive to buy, or which need to be used in accordance with their manufacturers' instructions. Unless relatively difficult mechanical jobs are undertaken frequently, it will not be economic to buy many of these tools. Where this is the case, you could consider clubbing together with friends (or joining a motorists' club) to make a joint purchase, or borrowing the tools against a deposit from a local garage or tool hire specialist.

The following list contains only those tools and instruments freely available to the public, and not those special tools produced by the vehicle manufacturer specifically for its dealer network. You will find occasional references to these manufacturers' special tools in the text of this manual. Generally, an alternative method of doing the job without the vehicle manufacturers' special tool is given. However, sometimes, there is no alternative to using them. Where this is the case and the relevant tool cannot be bought or borrowed you will have to entrust the work to a franchised garage.

Valve spring compressor
Piston ring compressor
Balljoint separator
Universal hub/bearing puller
Impact screwdriver
Micrometer and/or vernier gauge
Dial gauge
Stroboscopic timing light
Dwell angle meter/tachometer
Universal electrical multi-meter
Cylinder compression gauge
Lifting tackle
Trolley jack
Light with extension lead

Buying tools

For practically all tools, a tool dealer is the best source since he will have a very comprehensive range compared with the average garage or accessory shop. Having said that, accessory shops often offer excellent quality tools at discount prices, so it pays to shop around.

Remember, you don't have to buy the most expensive items on the shelf, but it is always advisable to steer clear of the very cheap tools. There are plenty of good tools around at reasonable prices, so ask the proprietor or manager of the shop for advice before making a purchase.

Care and maintenance of tools

Having purchased a reasonable tool kit, it is necessary to keep the tools in a clean serviceable condition. After use, always wipe off any dirt, grease and metal particles using a clean, dry cloth, before putting the tools away. Never leave them lying around after they have been used. A simple tool rack on the garage or workshop wall, for items such as screwdrivers and pliers is a good idea. Store all normal spanners and sockets in a metal box. Any measuring instruments, gauges, meters, etc, must be carefully stored where they cannot be damaged or become rusty.

Take a little care when tools are used. Hammer heads inevitably become marked and screwdrivers lose the keen edge on their blades from time to time. A little timely attention with emery cloth or a file will soon restore items like this to a good serviceable finish.

Working facilities

Not to be forgotten when discussing tools, is the workshop itself. If anything more than routine maintenance is to be carried out, some form of suitable working area becomes essential.

It is appreciated that many an owner mechanic is forced by circumstances to remove an engine or similar item, without the benefit of a garage or workshop. Having done this, any repairs should always be done under the cover of a roof.

Wherever possible, any dismantling should be done on a clean flat workbench or table at a suitable working height.

Any workbench needs a vice: one with a jaw opening of 4 in (100 mm) is suitable for most jobs. As mentioned previously, some clean dry storage space is also required for tools, as well as the lubricants, cleaning fluids, touch-up paints and so on which become necessary.

Another item which may be required, and which has a much more general usage, is an electric drill with a chuck capacity of at least $\frac{5}{16}$ in (8 mm). This, together with a good range of twist drills, is virtually essential for fitting accessories such as wing mirrors and reversing lights.

Last, but not least, always keep a supply of old newspapers and clean, lint-free rags available, and try to keep any working area as clean as possible.

Spanner jaw gap comparison table

Jaw gap (in)	Spanner size
0.250	$\frac{1}{4}$ in AF
0.276	7 mm
0.313	$\frac{5}{16}$ in AF
0.315	8 mm
0.344	$\frac{11}{32}$ in AF; $\frac{1}{8}$ in Whitworth
0.354	9 mm
0.375	$\frac{3}{8}$ in AF
0.394	10 mm
0.433	11 mm
0.438	$\frac{7}{16}$ in AF
0.445	$\frac{3}{16}$ in Whitworth; $\frac{1}{4}$ in BSF
0.472	12 mm
0.500	$\frac{1}{2}$ in AF
0.512	13 mm
0.525	$\frac{1}{4}$ in Whitworth; $\frac{5}{16}$ in BSF
0.551	14 mm
0.562	$\frac{9}{16}$ in AF
0.591	15 mm
0.600	$\frac{5}{16}$ in Whitworth; $\frac{3}{8}$ in BSF
0.625	$\frac{5}{8}$ in AF
0.630	16 mm
0.669	17 mm
0.686	$\frac{11}{16}$ in AF
0.709	18 mm
0.710	$\frac{3}{8}$ in Whitworth; $\frac{7}{16}$ in BSF
0.748	19 mm
0.750	$\frac{3}{4}$ in AF
0.813	$\frac{13}{16}$ in AF
0.820	$\frac{7}{16}$ in Whitworth; $\frac{1}{2}$ in BSF
0.866	22 mm
0.875	$\frac{7}{8}$ in AF
0.920	$\frac{1}{2}$ in Whitworth; $\frac{9}{16}$ in BSF
0.937	$\frac{15}{16}$ in AF
0.945	24 mm
1.000	1 in AF
1.010	$\frac{9}{16}$ in Whitworth; $\frac{5}{8}$ in BSF
1.024	26 mm
1.063	$1\frac{1}{16}$ in AF; 27 mm
1.100	$\frac{5}{8}$ in Whitworth; $\frac{11}{16}$ in BSF
1.125	$1\frac{1}{8}$ in AF
1.181	30 mm
1.200	$\frac{11}{16}$ in Whitworth; $\frac{3}{4}$ in BSF
1.250	$1\frac{1}{4}$ in AF
1.260	32 mm
1.300	$\frac{3}{4}$ in Whitworth; $\frac{7}{8}$ in BSF
1.313	$1\frac{5}{16}$ in AF
1.390	$\frac{13}{16}$ in Whitworth; $\frac{15}{16}$ in BSF
1.417	36 mm
1.438	$1\frac{7}{16}$ in AF
1.480	$\frac{7}{8}$ in Whitworth; 1 in BSF
1.500	$1\frac{1}{2}$ in AF
1.575	40 mm; $\frac{15}{16}$ in Whitworth
1.614	41 mm
1.625	$1\frac{5}{8}$ in AF
1.670	1 in Whitworth; $1\frac{1}{8}$ in BSF
1.688	$1\frac{11}{16}$ in AF
1.811	46 mm
1.813	$1\frac{13}{16}$ in AF
1.860	$1\frac{1}{8}$ in Whitworth; $1\frac{1}{4}$ in BSF
1.875	$1\frac{7}{8}$ in AF
1.969	50 mm
2.000	2 in AF
2.050	$1\frac{1}{4}$ in Whitworth; $1\frac{3}{8}$ in BSF
2.165	55 mm
2.362	60 mm

General repair procedures

Whenever servicing, repair or overhaul work is carried out on the car or its components, it is necessary to observe the following procedures and instructions. This will assist in carrying out the operation efficiently and to a professional standard of workmanship.

Joint mating faces and gaskets

Where a gasket is used between the mating faces of two components, ensure that it is renewed on reassembly, and fit it dry unless otherwise stated in the repair procedure. Make sure that the mating faces are clean and dry with all traces of old gasket removed. When cleaning a joint face, use a tool which is not likely to score or damage the face, and remove any burrs or nicks with an oilstone or fine file.

Make sure that tapped holes are cleaned, and keep them free of jointing compound if this is being used unless specifically instructed otherwise.

Ensure that all orifices, channels or pipes are clear and blow through them, preferably using compressed air.

Oil seals

Whenever an oil seal is removed from its working location, either individually or as part of an assembly, it should be renewed.

The very fine sealing lip of the seal is easily damaged and will not seal if the surface it contacts is not completely clean and free from scratches, nicks or grooves. If the original sealing surface of the component cannot be restored, the component should be renewed.

Protect the lips of the seal from any surface which may damage them in the course of fitting. Use tape or a conical sleeve where possible. Lubricate the seal lips with oil before fitting and, on dual lipped seals, fill the space between the lips with grease.

Unless otherwise stated, oil seals must be fitted with their sealing lips toward the lubricant to be sealed.

Use a tubular drift or block of wood of the appropriate size to install the seal and, if the seal housing is shouldered, drive the seal down to the shoulder. If the seal housing is unshouldered, the seal should be fitted with its face flush with the housing top face.

Screw threads and fastenings

Always ensure that a blind tapped hole is completely free from oil, grease, water or other fluid before installing the bolt or stud. Failure to do this could cause the housing to crack due to the hydraulic action of the bolt or stud as it is screwed in.

When tightening a castellated nut to accept a split pin, tighten the nut to the specified torque, where applicable, and then tighten further to the next split pin hole. Never slacken the nut to align a split pin hole unless stated in the repair procedure.

When checking or retightening a nut or bolt to a specified torque setting, slacken the nut or bolt by a quarter of a turn, and then retighten to the specified setting.

Locknuts, locktabs and washers

Any fastening which will rotate against a component or housing in the course of tightening should always have a washer between it and the relevant component or housing.

Spring or split washers should always be renewed when they are used to lock a critical component such as a big-end bearing retaining nut or bolt.

Locktabs which are folded over to retain a nut or bolt should always be renewed.

Self-locking nuts can be reused in non-critical areas, providing resistance can be felt when the locking portion passes over the bolt or stud thread.

Split pins must always be replaced with new ones of the correct size for the hole.

Special tools

Some repair procedures in this manual entail the use of special tools such as a press, two or three-legged pullers, spring compressors etc. Wherever possible, suitable readily available alternatives to the manufacturer's special tools are described, and are shown in use. In some instances, where no alternative is possible, it has been necessary to resort to the use of a manufacturer's tool and this has been done for reasons of safety as well as the efficient completion of the repair operation. Unless you are highly skilled and have a thorough understanding of the procedure described, never attempt to bypass the use of any special tool when the procedure described specifies its use. Not only is there a very great risk of personal injury, but expensive damage could be caused to the components involved.

Jacking and towing

For modifications, and information applicable to later models, see Supplement at end of manual

Jacking

The jack supplied with the car should only be used to change a wheel. Do not use this jack when overhaul or repair work is being carried out; employ a hydraulic or screw jack and supplement it with axle stands.

Jacking points are located under the sills for use with the jack supplied.

To raise the front of the car for repair, place a jack under the bracket beneath the radiator lower air intake grille.

To raise the rear of the car, place a jack under the bracket at the centre of the rear panel.

Towing

The towing hooks fitted at front and rear may be used for being towed or for towing another vehicle.

If a car being towed is equipped with automatic transmission, restrict the distance being towed to 30 miles (50 km) and the speed to 30 mph (50 kph). If these figures are likely to be exceeded, the front roadwheels will have to be raised; the transmission will otherwise be damaged due to starvation of lubricant.

Front jacking position (A)

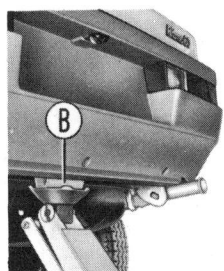

Rear jacking position (B)

Location of jack and spare wheel

Spare wheel, showing tubular support bracket

Sill jacking point with jack inserted

Towing hook

Safety first!

Professional motor mechanics are trained in safe working procedures. However enthusiastic you may be about getting on with the job in hand, do take the time to ensure that your safety is not put at risk. A moment's lack of attention can result in an accident, as can failure to observe certain elementary precautions.

There will always be new ways of having accidents, and the following points do not pretend to be a comprehensive list of all dangers; they are intended rather to make you aware of the risks and to encourage a safety-conscious approach to all work you carry out on your vehicle.

Essential DOs and DON'Ts

DON'T rely on a single jack when working underneath the vehicle. Always use reliable additional means of support, such as axle stands, securely placed under a part of the vehicle that you know will not give way.

DON'T attempt to loosen or tighten high-torque nuts (e.g. wheel hub nuts) while the vehicle is on a jack; it may be pulled off.

DON'T start the engine without first ascertaining that the transmission is in neutral (or 'Park' where applicable) and the parking brake applied.

DON'T suddenly remove the filler cap from a hot cooling system – cover it with a cloth and release the pressure gradually first, or you may get scalded by escaping coolant.

DON'T attempt to drain oil until you are sure it has cooled sufficiently to avoid scalding you.

DON'T grasp any part of the engine, exhaust or catalytic converter without first ascertaining that it is sufficiently cool to avoid burning you.

DON'T allow brake fluid or antifreeze to contact vehicle paintwork.

DON'T syphon toxic liquids such as fuel, brake fluid or antifreeze by mouth, or allow them to remain on your skin.

DON'T inhale dust – it may be injurious to health (see *Asbestos* below).

DON'T allow any spilt oil or grease to remain on the floor – wipe it up straight away, before someone slips on it.

DON'T use ill-fitting spanners or other tools which may slip and cause injury.

DON'T attempt to lift a heavy component which may be beyond your capability – get assistance.

DON'T rush to finish a job, or take unverified short cuts.

DON'T allow children or animals in or around an unattended vehicle.

DO wear eye protection when using power tools such as drill, sander, bench grinder etc, and when working under the vehicle.

DO use a barrier cream on your hands prior to undertaking dirty jobs – it will protect your skin from infection as well as making the dirt easier to remove afterwards; but make sure your hands aren't left slippery. Note that long-term contact with used engine oil can be a health hazard.

DO keep loose clothing (cuffs, tie etc) and long hair well out of the way of moving mechanical parts.

DO remove rings, wristwatch etc, before working on the vehicle – especially the electrical system.

DO ensure that any lifting tackle used has a safe working load rating adequate for the job.

DO keep your work area tidy – it is only too easy to fall over articles left lying around.

DO get someone to check periodically that all is well, when working alone on the vehicle.

DO carry out work in a logical sequence and check that everything is correctly assembled and tightened afterwards.

DO remember that your vehicle's safety affects that of yourself and others. If in doubt on any point, get specialist advice.

IF, in spite of following these precautions, you are unfortunate enough to injure yourself, seek medical attention as soon as possible.

Asbestos

Certain friction, insulating, sealing, and other products – such as brake linings, brake bands, clutch linings, torque converters, gaskets, etc – contain asbestos. *Extreme care must be taken to avoid inhalation of dust from such products since it is hazardous to health.* If in doubt, assume that they *do* contain asbestos.

Fire

Remember at all times that petrol (gasoline) is highly flammable. Never smoke, or have any kind of naked flame around, when working on the vehicle. But the risk does not end there – a spark caused by an electrical short-circuit, by two metal surfaces contacting each other, by careless use of tools, or even by static electricity built up in your body under certain conditions, can ignite petrol vapour, which in a confined space is highly explosive.

Always disconnect the battery earth (ground) terminal before working on any part of the fuel or electrical system, and never risk spilling fuel on to a hot engine or exhaust.

It is recommended that a fire extinguisher of a type suitable for fuel and electrical fires is kept handy in the garage or workplace at all times. Never try to extinguish a fuel or electrical fire with water.

Fumes

Certain fumes are highly toxic and can quickly cause unconsciousness and even death if inhaled to any extent. Petrol (gasoline) vapour comes into this category, as do the vapours from certain solvents such as trichloroethylene. Any draining or pouring of such volatile fluids should be done in a well ventilated area.

When using cleaning fluids and solvents, read the instructions carefully. Never use materials from unmarked containers – they may give off poisonous vapours.

Never run the engine of a motor vehicle in an enclosed space such as a garage. Exhaust fumes contain carbon monoxide which is extremely poisonous; if you need to run the engine, always do so in the open air or at least have the rear of the vehicle outside the workplace.

If you are fortunate enough to have the use of an inspection pit, never drain or pour petrol, and never run the engine, while the vehicle is standing over it; the fumes, being heavier than air, will concentrate in the pit with possibly lethal results.

The battery

Never cause a spark, or allow a naked light, near the vehicle's battery. It will normally be giving off a certain amount of hydrogen gas, which is highly explosive.

Always disconnect the battery earth (ground) terminal before working on the fuel or electrical systems.

If possible, loosen the filler plugs or cover when charging the battery from an external source. Do not charge at an excessive rate or the battery may burst.

Take care when topping up and when carrying the battery. The acid electrolyte, even when diluted, is very corrosive and should not be allowed to contact the eyes or skin.

If you ever need to prepare electrolyte yourself, always add the acid slowly to the water, and never the other way round. Protect against splashes by wearing rubber gloves and goggles.

When jump starting a car using a booster battery, for negative earth (ground) vehicles, connect the jump leads in the following sequence: First connect one jump lead between the positive (+) terminals of the two batteries. Then connect the other jump lead first to the negative (–) terminal of the booster battery, and then to a good earthing (ground) point on the vehicle to be started, at least 18 in (45 cm) from the battery if possible. Ensure that hands and jump leads are clear of any moving parts, and that the two vehicles do not touch. Disconnect the leads in the reverse order.

Mains electricity

When using an electric power tool, inspection light etc, which works from the mains, always ensure that the appliance is correctly connected to its plug and that, where necessary, it is properly earthed (grounded). Do not use such appliances in damp conditions and, again, beware of creating a spark or applying excessive heat in the vicinity of fuel or fuel vapour.

Ignition HT voltage

A severe electric shock can result from touching certain parts of the ignition system, such as the HT leads, when the engine is running or being cranked, particularly if components are damp or the insulation is defective. Where an electronic ignition system is fitted, the HT voltage is much higher and could prove fatal.

Routine maintenance

For modifications, and information applicable to later models, see Supplement at end of manual

Maintenance is essential for ensuring safety and desirable for the purpose of getting the best in terms of performance and economy from the car. Over the years the need for periodic lubrication has been greatly reduced if not totally eliminated. This has unfortunately tended to lead some owners to think that because no such action is required the items either no longer exist or will last forever. This is certainly not the case; it is essential to carry out regular visual examinations as comprehensively as possible in order to spot any possible defects at an early stage before they develop into major and expensive repairs.

When the vehicle covers less than 12 000 miles per year, use the time intervals instead of mileage to determine when maintenance is due. This is necessary because some fluids and systems deteriorate with time as well as with use.

Weekly, before a long journey or every 250 miles (400 km)

Check engine oil level
Check brake reservoir fluid level
Check tyre pressures and tread wear
Check operation of all lights
Top up washer fluid reservoirs and check operation of washers and wipers
Check coolant level
Check battery electrolyte level

At 3000 mile (4800 km) or three-monthly intervals

Check transmission fluid level
Check final drive fluid level (automatic transmission models only)
Lubricate all hinges, locks and controls
Check disc pads and brake shoes for lining wear
Check steering and suspension linkage, pivots and balljoints for wear

At 6000 mile (9600 km) or six-monthly intervals

Renew engine oil and filter (every six months if mileage not reached)
Clean air filter element by tapping on hard surface
Check tension of drivebelts
Check tightness of roadwheel bolts
Check clutch cable adjustment
Clean carburettor and fuel pump filter (not applicable to a sealed type pump)
Clean crankcase ventilation connecting pipes and flame trap

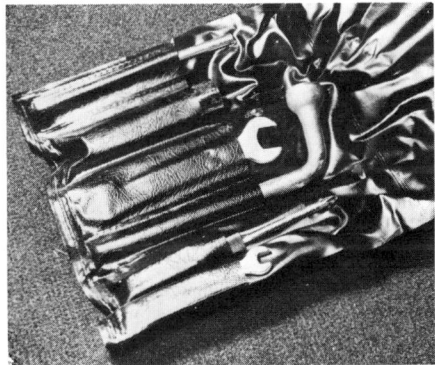
Tool kit supplied with car

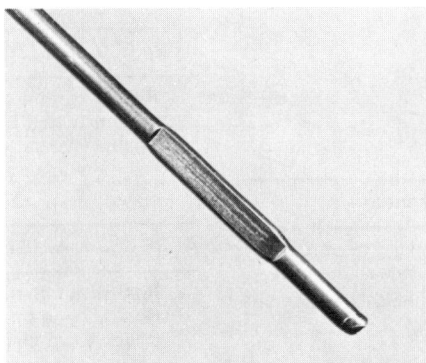
Engine oil dipstick

Topping-up the engine oil

Topping-up the brake fluid

Headlamp washer fluid reservoir

Windscreen washer fluid reservoir

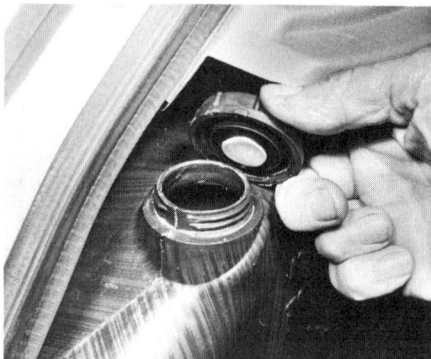
Tailgate washer fluid reservoir

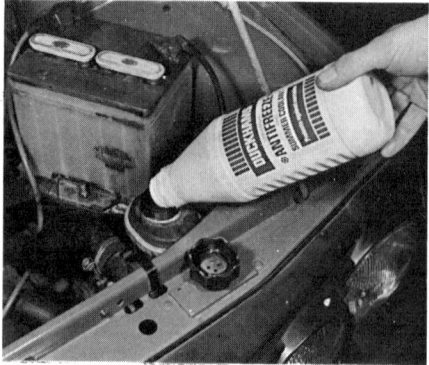
Topping-up the coolant

Manual transmission oil drain plug (arrowed)

Topping-up the manual transmission

Checking a front wheel for steering and suspension wear

Engine oil drain plug

Inspect exhaust system for corrosion
Clean and re-gap spark plugs
Adjust slow running
Check driveshaft flexible gaiters for splits
Clear door and body sill drain holes

At 12 000 mile (19 000 km) or twelve-monthly intervals

Renew air cleaner element
Renew in-line fuel filter (if fitted)
Clean , adjust or renew distributor points (mechanical breaker type only)
Check and adjust ignition timing
Renew spark plugs
Clean EGR valve
Check all emission control system connecting hoses and wires for security (if fitted)
Check front and rear wheel alignment

At 24 000 mile (38 000 km) or two-yearly intervals

Renew carbon canister on fuel evaporative emission control system (when fitted)
Renew manual gearbox oil
Renew engine coolant

At 36 000 mile (57 000 km) or three-yearly intervals

Renew automatic transmission fluid, clean or renew filter
Renew oil in final drive unit (automatic transmission)
Check valve clearances and adjust if necessary

Every two years, regardless of mileage

Renew brake hydraulic fluid

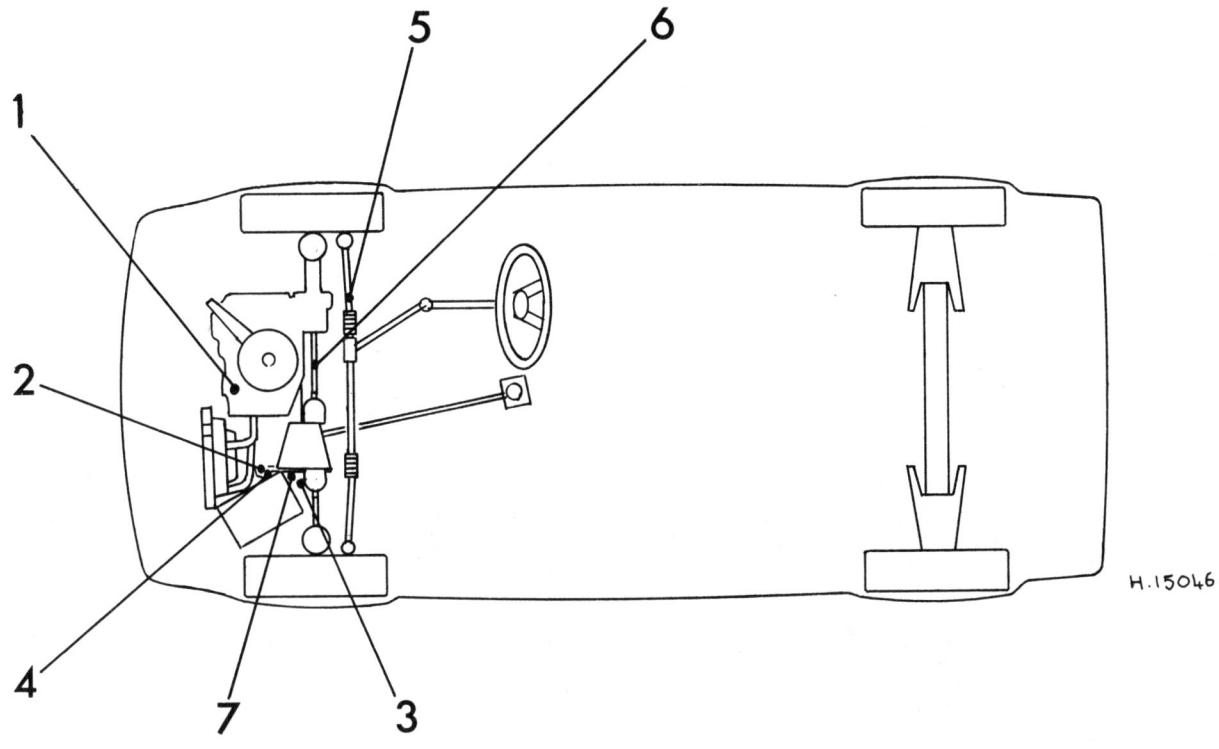

H.15046

Recommended lubricants and fluids

Component or system	Lubricant type/specification	Duckhams recommendation
Engine (1)	Multigrade engine oil, viscosity SAE 15W/40, to API SE	Duckhams QXR or Hypergrade
Manual transmission and final drive (2)	Multigrade engine oil, viscosity SAE 15W/40, to API SE	Duckhams Hypergrade
Automatic transmission (3)	Dexron II type ATF	Duckhams D-Matic
Final drive (with automatic transmission) (4)	Hypoid gear oil, viscosity SAE 80W/90, to MIL-L-2105 C	Duckhams Hypoid 75W/90S
Steering (5): Early type	Hypoid gear oil, viscosity SAE 80W/90, to MIL-L-2105 C	Duckhams Hypoid 75W/90S
Later type	Lithium-based grease with molybdenum disulphide (FIAT K854)	
Driveshaft CV joints (6)	Multi-purpose lithium-based grease with molybdenum disulphide, to NLGI No 2	Duckhams LBM 10
Braking system (7)	Hydraulic fluid to FMVSS 116 DOT 3	Duckhams Universal Brake and Clutch Fluid

Fault Diagnosis

Introduction

The car owner who does his or her own maintenance according to the recommended schedules should not have to use this section of the manual very often. Modern component reliability is such that, provided those items subject to wear or deterioration are inspected or renewed at the specified intervals, sudden failure is comparatively rare. Faults do not usually just happen as a result of sudden failure, but develop over a period of time. Major mechanical failures in particular are usually preceded by characteristic symptoms over hundreds or even thousands of miles. Those components which do occasionally fail without warning are often small and easily carried in the car.

With any fault finding, the first step is to decide where to begin investigations. Sometimes this is obvious, but on other occasions a little detective work will be necessary. The owner who makes half a dozen haphazard adjustments or replacements may be successful in curing a fault (or its symptoms), but he will be none the wiser if the fault recurs and he may well have spent more time and money than was necessary. A calm and logical approach will be found to be more satisfactory in the long run. Always take into account any warning signs or abnormalities that may have been noticed in the period preceding the fault – power loss, high or low gauge readings, unusual noises or smells, etc – and remember that failure of components such as fuses or spark plugs may only be pointers to some underlying fault.

The pages which follow here are intended to help in cases of failure to start or breakdown on the road. There is also a Fault Diagnosis Section at the end of each Chapter which should be consulted if the preliminary checks prove unfruitful. Whatever the fault, certain basic principles apply. These are as follows:

Verify the fault. This is simply a matter of being sure that you know what the symptoms are before starting work. This is particularly important if you are investigating a fault for someone else who may not have described it very accurately.

Don't overlook the obvious: For example, if the car won't start, is there petrol in the tank? (Don't take anyone else's word on this particular point, and don't trust the fuel gauge either!) If an electrical fault is indicated, look for loose or broken wires before digging out the test gear.

Cure the disease, not the symptom. Substituting a flat battery with a fully charged one will get you off the hard shoulder, but if the underlying cause is not attended to, the new battery will go the same way. Similarly, changing oil-fouled spark plugs for a new set will get you moving again, but remember that the reason for the fouling (if it wasn't simply an incorrect grade of plug) will have to be established and corrected.

Don't take anything for granted. Particularly, don't forget that a 'new' component may itself be defective (especially if it's been rattling round in the boot for months), and don't leave components out of a fault diagnosis sequence just because they are new or recently fitted. When you do finally diagnose a difficult fault, you'll probably realise that all the evidence was there from the start.

Electrical faults

Electrical faults can be more puzzling than straightforward mechanical failures, but they are no less susceptible to logical analysis if the basic principles of operation are understood. Car electrical wiring exists in extremely unfavourable conditions – heat, vibration and chemical attack – and the first things to look for are loose or corroded connections, and broken or chafed wires, especially where the wires pass through holes in the bodywork or are subject to vibration.

All metal-bodied cars in current production have one pole of the battery 'earthed', ie connected to the car bodywork, and in nearly all modern cars it is the negative (–) terminal. The various electrical components – motors, bulb holders etc – are also connected to earth, either by means of a lead or directly by their mountings. Electric current flows through the component and then back to the battery via the car bodywork. If the component mounting is loose or corroded, or if a good path back to the battery is not available, the circuit will be incomplete and malfunction will result. The engine and/or gearbox are also earthed by means of flexible metal straps to the body or subframe; if these straps are loose or missing, starter motor, generator and ignition trouble may result.

Assuming the earth return to be satisfactory, electrical faults will be due either to component malfunction or to defects in the current supply. Individual components are dealt with in Chapter 9. If supply wires are broken or cracked internally this results in an open-circuit, and the easiest way to check for this is to bypass the suspect wire temporarily with a length of wire having a crocodile clip or suitable connector at each end. Alternatively, a 12V test lamp can be used to verify the presence of supply voltage at various points along the wire and the break can be thus isolated.

If a bare portion of a live wire touches the car bodywork or other earthed metal part, the electricity will take the low-resistance path thus formed back to the battery: this is known as a short-circuit. Hopefully, a short-circuit will blow a fuse, but otherwise it may cause burning of the insulation (and possibly further short-circuits) or even a fire. This is why it is inadvisable to bypass persistently blowing fuses with silver foil or wire.

Spares and tool kit

Most cars are only supplied with sufficient tools for wheel changing; the *Maintenance and minor repair* tool kit detailed in *Tools and working facilities,* with the addition of a hammer, is probably sufficient for those repairs that most motorists would consider attempting at the roadside. In addition, a few items which can be fitted without too much trouble in the event of breakdown should be carried. Experience and available space will modify the list below, but the following may save having to call on professional assistance:

Spark plugs, clean and correctly gapped
HT lead and plug cap – long enough to reach the plug furthest from the distributor
Distributor rotor, condenser and contact breaker points (if applicable)
Drivebelt(s) – emergency type may suffice
Spare fuses
Set of principal light bulbs
Tin of radiator sealer and hose bandage
Exhaust bandage
Roll of insulating tape
Length of soft iron wire
Length of electrical flex
Torch or inspection lamp (can double as test lamp)
Battery jump leads
Tow-rope
Ignition waterproofing aerosol
Litre of engine oil
Sealed can of hydraulic fluid
Emergency windscreen
Worm drive hose clips
Tube of filler paste

If spare fuel is carried, a can designed for the purpose should be used to minimise risks of leakage and collision damage. A first aid kit and a warning triangle, whilst not at present compulsory in the UK, are obviously sensible items to carry in addition to the above.

When touring abroad, it may be advisable to carry additional spares which, even if you cannot fit them yourself, could save having to wait while parts are obtained. The items below may be worth considering:

Clutch and throttle cables
Cylinder head gasket
Alternator brushes
Fuel pump repair kit
Tyre valve core

One of the motoring organisations will be able to advise on availability of fuel etc in foreign countries.

Engine will not start

Engine fails to turn when starter operated
Flat battery (recharge, use jump leads, or push start)
Battery terminals loose or corroded
Battery earth to body defective
Engine earth strap loose or broken
Starter motor (or solenoid) wiring loose or broken
Automatic transmission selector in wrong position, or inhibitor switch faulty
Ignition/starter switch faulty
Major mechanical failure (seizure) or long disuse (piston rings rusted to bores)
Starter or solenoid internal fault (see Chapter 9)

Starter motor turns engine slowly
Partially discharged battery (recharge, use jump leads, or push start)
Battery terminals loose or corroded
Battery earth to body defective
Engine earth strap loose
Starter motor (or solenoid) wiring loose
Starter motor internal fault (see Chapter 9)

Starter motor spins without turning engine
Flat battery
Starter motor pinion sticking on sleeve
Flywheel gear teeth damaged or worn
Starter motor mounting bolts loose

Engine turns normally but fails to start
Damp or dirty HT leads and distributor cap (crank engine and check for spark)
Dirty or incorrectly gapped CB points (if applicable)
No fuel in tank (check for delivery at carburettor)
Excessive choke (hot engine) or insufficient choke (cold engine)
Fouled or incorrectly gapped spark plugs (remove, clean and regap)
Other ignition system fault (see Chapter 4)
Other fuel system fault (see Chapter 3)
Poor compression (see Chapter 1)
Major mechanical failure (eg camshaft drive)

Engine fires but will not run
Insufficient choke (cold engine)
Air leaks at carburettor or inlet manifold
Fuel starvation (see Chapter 3)
Ballast resistor defective, or other ignition fault (see Chapter 4)

Engine cuts out and will not restart

Engine cuts out suddenly – ignition fault
Loose or disconnected LT wires
Wet HT leads or distributor cap (after traversing water splash)
Coil or condenser failure (check for spark)
Other ignition fault (see Chapter 4)

Engine misfires before cutting out – fuel fault
Fuel tank empty
Fuel pump defective or filter block (check for delivery)
Fuel tank filler vent block (suction will be evident on releasing cap)
Carburettor needle valve sticking
Carburettor jets blocked (fuel contaminated)
Other fuel system fault (see Chapter 3)

Engine cuts out – other causes
Serious overheating
Major mechanical failure (eg camshaft drive)

Engine overheats

Ignition (no-charge) warning light illuminated
Slack or broken drivebelt – retension or renew (Chapter 2)

Ignition warning light not illuminated
Coolant loss due to internal or external leakage (see Chapter 2)
Thermostat defective
Low oil level
Brakes binding
Radiator clogged externally or internally
Electric cooling fan not operating correctly
Engine waterways clogged
Ignition timing incorrect or automatic advance malfunctioning
Mixture too weak
Note: *Do not add cold water to an overheated engine or damage may result*

Low engine oil pressure

Gauge reads low or warning light illuminated with engine running
Oil level low or incorrect grade
Defective gauge or sender unit
Wire to sender unit earthed
Engine overheating
Oil filter clogged or bypass valve defective
Oil pressure relief valve defective
Oil pick-up strainer clogged
Oil pump worn or mountings loose
Worn main or big-end bearings
Note: *Low oil pressure in a high-mileage engine at tickover is not necessarily a cause for concern. Sudden pressure loss at speed is far more significant. In any event, check the gauge or warning light sender before condemning the engine.*

Engine noises

Pre-ignition (pinking) on acceleration

Incorrect grade of fuel
Ignition timing incorrect
Distributor faulty or worn
Worn or maladjusted carburettor
Excessive carbon build-up in engine

Whistling or wheezing noises

Leaking vacuum hose
Leaking carburettor or manifold gasket
Blowing head gasket

Tapping or rattling

Incorrect valve clearances
Worn valve gear
Worn timing chain or belt
Broken piston ring (ticking noise)

Knocking or thumping

Unintentional mechanical contact (eg fan blades)
Worn fanbelt
Peripheral component fault (generator, water pump etc)
Worn big-end bearings (regular heavy knocking, perhaps less under load)
Worn main bearings (rumbling and knocking, perhaps worsening under load)
Piston slap (most noticeable when cold)

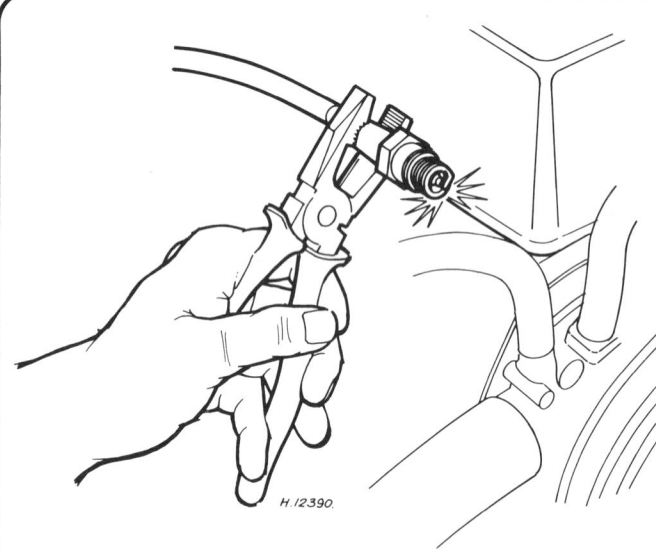

H.12390.

Crank engine and check for spark. Note use of insulated tool to hold plug lead

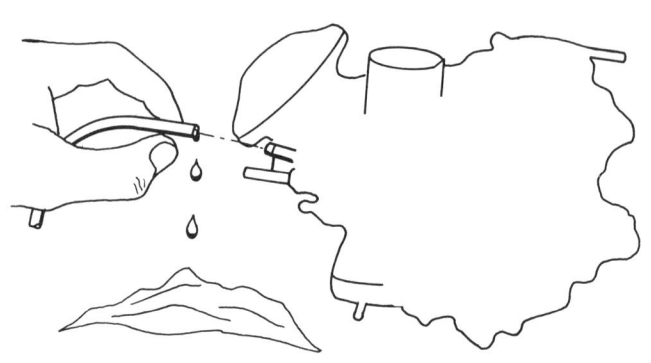

Remove fuel pipe from carburettor and check fuel delivery

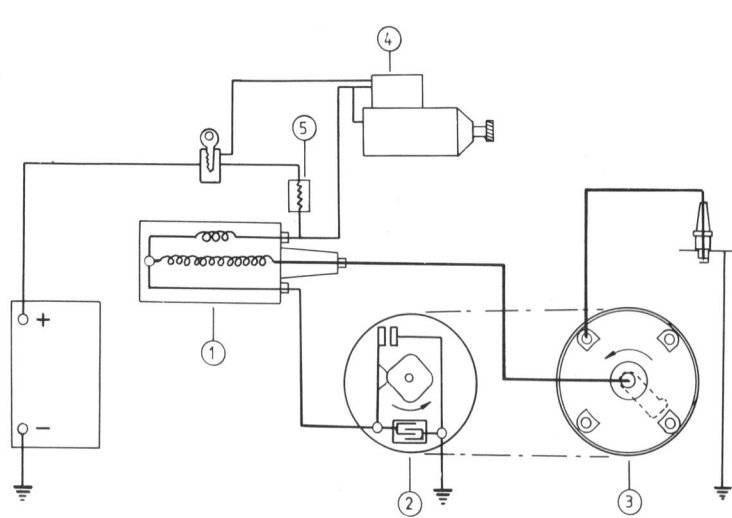

Ignition system schematic diagram. Ballast resistor is bypassed when starter motor operates

1 Coil	4 Starter motor
2 Distributor (LT section)	5 Ballast resistor
3 Distributor (HT section)	

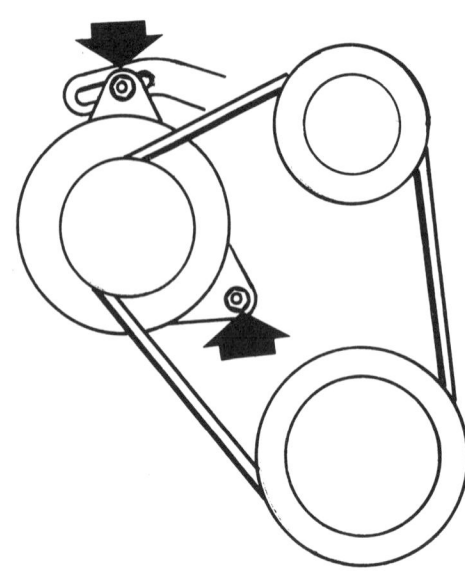

A slack drivebelt can cause overheating and battery charging problems. Adjustment bolts are arrowed

Chapter 1 Engine

For modifications, and information applicable to later models, see Supplement at end of manual

Contents

Specifications

All except North America models

Engine type	4 cylinder, in-line, single overhead camshaft, mounted transversely at front of car

Identification code

65 models (1301 cc)	138 A1.000
75 models (1498 cc)	138 A2.000

Model

	65	**75**
Bore	86.4 mm (3.40 in)	86.4 mm (3.40 in)
Stroke	55.5 mm (2.19 in)	63.9 mm (2.52 in)
Displacement	1301 cc (79.39 cu in)	1498 cc (91.44 cu in)
Compression ratio	9.1 : 1	9.0 : 1
Firing order	1-3-4-2 (No 1 at timing belt end)	1-3-4-2 (No 1 at timing belt end)
Power output	65 BHP (48 kW) at 5800 rpm	75 BHP (55 kW) at 5800 rpm
Maximum torque	98 NM (72 lbf ft) at 3500 rpm	118 Nm (87 lbf ft) at 3000 rpm

Crankcase and cylinder block

Material	Cast iron
Cylinder bore diameter (standard)	86.400 to 86.450 mm (3.401 to 3.403 in)

Crankshaft and bearings

Rotational direction	Clockwise (viewed from timing belt)
Main bearing shell seat diameter	54.507 to 54.520 mm (2.145 to 2.146 in)
Main bearing journal diameter:	
Model 65	50.785 to 50.805 mm (1.9994 to 2.0002 in)
Model 75	50.775 to 50.795 mm (1.9990 to 1.9998 in)

Main bearing shell thickness (standard):

Model 65 .... 1.825 to 1.831 mm (0.0718 to 0.0720 in)

Model 75 .... 1.834 to 1.840 mm (0.0722 to 0.0724 in)

Main bearing undersizes .... 0.254 mm (0.010 in)

0.508 mm (0.020 in)

0.762 mm (0.030 in)

1.016 mm (0.040 in)

Main bearing running clearance:

Model 65 .... 0.040 to 0.085 mm (0.0015 to 0.0033 in)

Model 75 .... 0.032 to 0.077 mm (0.0012 to 0.0030 in)

Thrust washer thickness (standard) .... 2.310 to 2.360 mm (0.0909 to 0.0929 in)

Thrust washer oversizes .... 2.437 to 2.487 mm (0.0959 to 0.0979 in)

Crankshaft endfloat .... 0.055 to 0.265 mm (0.0022 to 0.0104 in)

Maximum ovality of crankpins and journals .... 0.005 mm (0.0002 in)

Maximum taper of crankpins and journals .... 0.005 mm (0.0002 in)

Crankpin diameter (standard) .... 45.498 to 45.518 mm (1.791 to 1.792 in)

Connecting rods and gudgeon pins

Connecting rod big-end diameter .... 48.630 to 48.646 mm (1.914 to 1.915 in)

Connecting rod small-end diameter .... 23.939 to 23.972 mm (0.942 to 0.944 in)

Small-end bush outside diameter .... 24.016 to 24.041 mm (0.945 to 0.946 in)

Big-end bearing shell undersizes .... 0.254 mm (0.010 in)

0.508 mm (0.020 in)

0.762 mm (0.030 in)

1.016 mm (0.040 in)

Small-end bush interference fit .... 0.044 to 0.102 mm (0.0017 to 0.0040 in)

Gudgeon pin fit in small-end bush (running clearance) .... 0.010 to 0.016 mm (0.0004 to 0.0006 in)

Big-end bearing running clearance .... 0.036 to 0.086 mm (0.0014 to 0.0034 in)

Pistons and rings

	Model 65	Model 75
Standard piston diameters:		
Grade A	86.320 to 86.330 mm (3.3984 to 3.3990 in)	86.360 to 86.370 mm (3.4000 to 3.4004 in)
Grade C	86.340 to 86.350 mm (3.3992 to 3.3996 in)	86.380 to 86.390 mm (3.4008 to 3.4012 in)
Grade E	86.360 to 86.370 mm (3.4000 to 3.4004 in)	86.400 to 86.410 mm (3.4016 to 3.4020 in)
Oversize piston availability	0.2, 0.4 and 0.6 mm (0.008, 0.016 and 0.024 in)	
Piston to cylinder bore clearance	0.070 to 0.090 mm (0.0027 to 0.0035 in)	0.030 to 0.050 mm (0.0012 to 0.0020 in)

Piston boss diameter:

Grade 1 .... 21.996 to 21.999 mm (0.8660 to 0.8661 in)

Grade 2 .... 21.999 to 22.002 mm (0.8661 to 0.8662 in)

Piston groove width:

Top .... 1.535 to 1.555 mm (0.0604 to 0.0612 in)

Second .... 2.030 to 2.050 mm (0.0799 to 0.0807 in)

Lower .... 3.967 to 3.987 mm (0.1562 to 0.1570 in)

Piston ring thickness:

Top compression .... 1.478 to 1.490 mm (0.0582 to 0.0587 in)

Second oil control .... 1.978 to 1.990 mm (0.0779 to 0.0783 in)

Lower oil scraper .... 3.925 to 3.937 mm (0.1545 to 0.1550 in)

Piston ring clearance in groove:

Top compression .... 0.045 to 0.077 mm (0.0020 to 0.0030 in)

Second oil control .... 0.040 to 0.072 mm (0.0016 to 0.0028 in)

Lower oil scraper .... 0.030 to 0.062 mm (0.0012 to 0.0024 in)

Piston ring end gap:

Top compression .... 0.30 to 0.45 mm (0.012 to 0.018 in)

Second oil control .... 0.30 to 0.45 mm (0.012 to 0.018 in)

Lower oil scraper .... 0.25 to 0.40 mm (0.010 to 0.016 in)

Piston ring oversizes .... 0.2, 0.4 and 0.6 mm (0.008, 0.016 and 0.024 in)

Gudgeon pin diameters:

Grade 1 .... 21.991 to 21.994 mm (0.8658 to 0.8659 in)

Grade 2 .... 21.994 to 21.997 mm (0.8659 to 0.8660 in)

Oversize .... 0.2 mm (0.008 in)

Camshaft

Journal diameters:

Timing belt end .... 29.944 to 29.960 mm (1.1789 to 1.1795 in)

Intermediate .... 47.935 to 47.950 mm (1.8872 to 1.8878 in)

Centre .... 48.135 to 48.150 mm (1.8951 to 1.8957 in)

Intermediate .... 48.335 to 48.350 mm (1.9029 to 1.9035 in)

Flywheel end .... 48.535 to 48.550 mm (1.9110 to 1.9114 in)

Camshaft bearing bores in camshaft carrier:	
Timing belt end	29.989 to 30.014 mm (1.1810 to 1.1820 in)
Intermediate	47.980 to 48.005 mm (1.8890 to 1.8900 in)
Centre	48.180 to 48.205 mm (1.8968 to 1.8978 in)
Intermediate	48.380 to 48.405 mm (1.9050 to 1.9060 in)
Flywheel end	48.580 to 48.605 mm (1.9126 to 1.9136 in)
Camshaft bearing running clearance	0.030 to 0.070 mm (0.0012 to 0.0027 in)
Cam lift:	
Inlet	9.20 mm (0.362 in)
Exhaust	9.25 mm (0.364 in)

Valve timing

Inlet opens	12° BTDC
Inlet closes	52° ABDC
Exhaust opens	52° BBDC
Exhaust closes	12° ATDC

Camshaft carrier

Tappet bore diameter (standard)	37.000 to 37.025 mm (1.4567 to 1.4577 in)
Tappet outside diameter (standard)	36.975 to 36.995 mm (1.4557 to 1.4565 in)
Tappet clearance in bore	0.005 to 0.050 mm (0.0002 to 0.002 in)
Valve clearance adjusting shim thickness	3.70 to 4.70 mm (0.146 to 0.185 in) in increments of 0.05 mm (0.002 in)

Valve clearances (cold)

	UK models	US models
Inlet	0.4 mm (0.016 in)	0.28 to 0.36 mm (0.011 to 0.014 in)
Exhaust	0.5 mm (0.020 in)	0.38 to 0.46 mm (0.015 to 0.018 in)

Auxiliary shaft

Diameter of bush recess in crankcase:	
Front	38.700 to 38.730 mm (1.5236 to 1.5248 in)
Rear	35.036 to 35.066 mm (1.3794 to 1.3805 in)
Shaft bush internal diameter (fitted):	
Front	35.664 to 35.684 mm (1.4041 to 1.4049 in)
Rear	32.000 to 32.020 mm (1.2598 to 1.2606 in)
Shaft journal diameters:	
Front	35.593 to 35.618 mm (1.4013 to 1.4023 in)
Rear	31.940 to 31.960 mm (1.2575 to 1.2583 in)
Shaft running clearance:	
Front	0.044 to 0.091 mm (0.0017 to 0.0036 in)
Rear	0.040 to 0.080 mm (0.0016 to 0.0031 in)

Cylinder head

Material	Light alloy
Valve guide bore (standard) in cylinder head	13.950 to 13.977 mm (0.5492 to 0.5503 in)
Valve guide outside diameter	14.040 to 14.058 mm (0.5527 to 0.5535 in)
Valve guide oversize outside diameter	+0.20 mm (0.008 in)
Valve guide interference fit	0.063 to 0.108 mm (0.0025 to 0.0043 in)
Valve guide internal diameter (fitted)	8.022 to 8.040 mm (0.3158 to 0.3165 in)
Valve seat angle	45° ± 5'
Valve face angle	45° 30' ± 5'
Valve seat width	Not exceeding 2.0 mm (0.079 in)
Valve seat internal diameter:	
Inlet	30.00 mm (1.181 in)
Exhaust	26.75 mm (1.053 in)

Valves and springs

Valve stem diameter	7.974 to 7.992 mm (0.314 to 0.315 in)
Valve stem clearance in guide	0.030 to 0.066 mm (0.001 to 0.003 in)
Valve head diameter:	
Inlet	36.0 mm (1.417 in)
Exhaust	30.50 mm (1.200 in) (65 models)
	33.10 mm (1.303 in) (75 models)
Valve spring type	Coil, inner and outer

Lubrication system

Type	Oil pump driven from auxiliary shaft. Pressure relief valve in pump. Full flow oil filter
Pump gear end float	0.05 to 0.20 mm (0.002 to 0.008 in)
Pump gear to body clearance	0.08 to 0.11 mm (0.003 to 0.004 in)
Backlash between gears	0.15 mm (0.006 in)
Oil pressure at 212°F (100°C)	50 to 70 lbf/in² (3.4 to 4.8 kgf/cm²)
Engine oil capacity (with filter change)	7.7 Imp pints (9.2 US pints, 4.4 litres)
Engine oil type/specification	Multigrade engine oil, viscosity SAE 15W/40, to API SE (Duckhams QXR or Hypergrade)

Torque wrench settings

	lbf ft	Nm
Main bearing cap bolts	59	80
Cylinder head bolts and nuts (oiled threads):		
M12 (19 mm hexagon):		
Stage 1	30	41
Stage 2	44	60
Stage 3	68	92
M10 (17 mm hexagon):		
Stage 1	15	20
Stage 2	30	41
Tighten a further 180° in 2 stages		
Camshaft carrier bolts	15	20
Manifold nuts	20	27
Big-end cap nuts	37	50
Driveplate bolts (automatic transmission)	40	54
Flywheel bolts	61	83
Camshaft sprocket bolt	61	83
Timing belt tensioner	32	44
Auxiliary shaft sprocket bolt	61	83
Crankshaft pulley nut	100	137
Alternator mounting bolts	36	49
Spark plugs	27	37
Mounting bracket to engine bolts	43	58
Mounting bracket to body bolts	36	49
Rear mounting self-locking nut:		
M12	72	98
M8	18	24
Flexible mounting nuts and bolts to engine and transmission (M12) ..	65	88
Flexible mounting-to-body bolt (M8)	18	24

North American models only

Specifications are as for 75 models, except the following

Identification code	
All except California models	138AS.040
California models	138AS.031
Compression ratio	8.5 : 1
Power output:	
All except California models	69 SAE net horsepower at 5100 rpm
California models	65 SAE net horsepower at 5100 rpm
SAE net torque:	
All except California models	105 Nm (77.4 lbf ft) at 2500 rpm
California models	103 Nm (75.9 lbf ft) at 2500 rpm

1 General description

The engine is of the four-cylinder in-line type, mounted transversely at the front of the car in conjunction with the transmission and final drive.

The valvegear is operated by means of a single overhead camshaft, driven by a toothed belt.

The cylinder block is of cast iron, the cylinder head being of light alloy construction.

The crankshaft runs in five main bearings; the camshaft is also supported in five bearings, machined directly into the camshaft carrier.

An auxiliary shaft, driven by the timing belt, is used to drive the distributor, oil pump and fuel pump on all except air conditioned models, where the distributor is driven from the front of the camshaft.

The coolant pump and alternator are belt-driven by the crankshaft pulley, but the radiator cooling fan is electrically driven.

The engine oil is retained independently of the transmission and final drive lubricants.

On North American versions, emission control equipment is extensive and on the larger engined 1498 cc model, air conditioning is optionally available.

2 Major operations possible with engine in car

The following work can be carried out without the need to remove the engine from the car:

Removal and refitting of the camshaft carrier
Removal and refitting of the timing belt
Removal and refitting of the cylinder head

Removal and refitting of engine ancillaries (distributor, alternator, water pump)
Removal of the sump, oil pump, connecting rods and pistons

3 Major operations only possible with engine removed

To remove the crankshaft, flywheel (or driveplate on automatic transmission models), or to renew the main bearings, the engine/transmission must be removed from the car and separated.

4 Camshaft and camshaft carrier – removal and refitting (engine in car)

1   Disconnect the battery.
2   Remove the air cleaner (see Chapter 3).
3   Disconnect the fuel filter hose from the fuel pump and tie it back, out of the way.
4   Identify and then disconnect any electrical leads which must be moved away to enable the camshaft cover to be withdrawn.
5   Identify and disconnect any vacuum hoses which must be moved away to enable the camshaft cover to be withdrawn. These vary according to the vehicle model and the complexity of the emission control system fitted.
6   On air conditioned 75 CL models, remove the distributor from the end of the camshaft carrier, as described in Chapter 4.
7   Unscrew the securing nuts and remove the camshaft cover.
8   Using a socket on the crankshaft pulley nut, rotate the crankshaft until the notch in the pulley rim is aligned with the TDC mark on the timing belt cover, or the index plate (75 CL models), with No 4 piston at its firing position. This can be checked by observing whether both No 4 cylinder valves are closed with the pointed ends of the camshaft

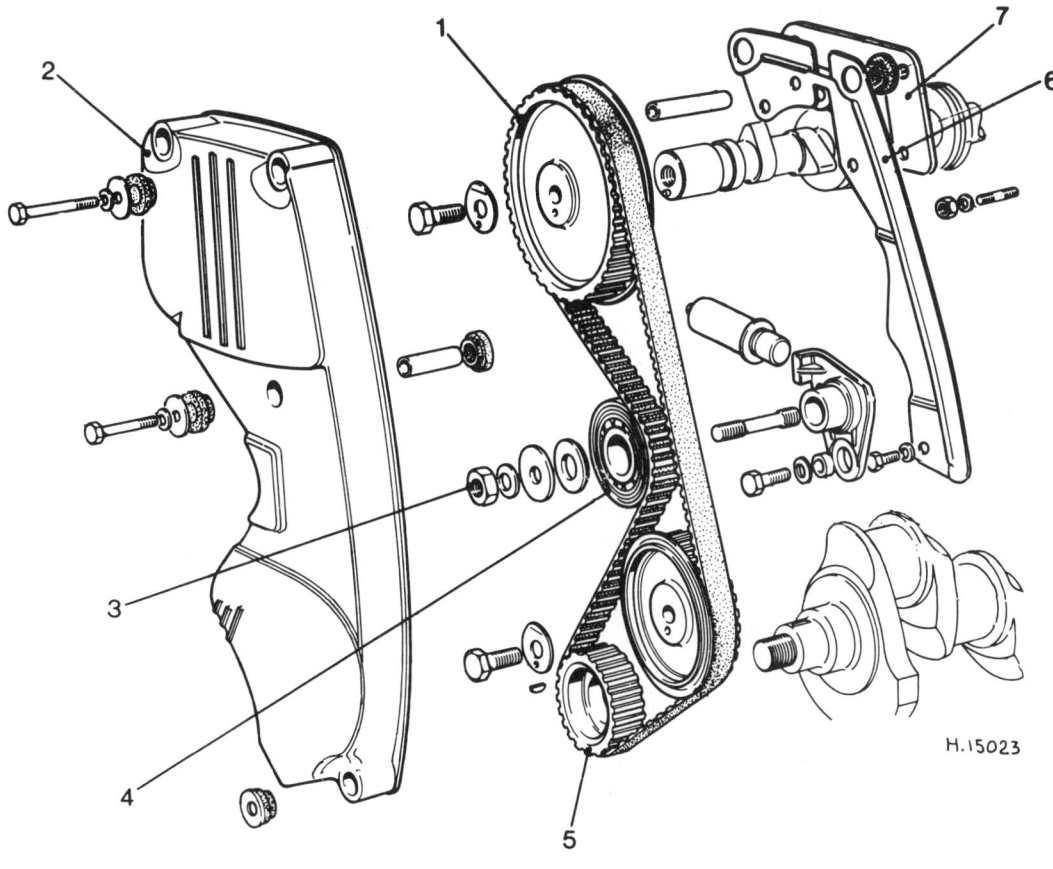

Fig. 1.1 Timing belt and cover (65 models) (Sec 4)

1	Belt	3	Tensioner pulley locknut
2	Cover	4	Tensioner pulley

5	Crankshaft sprocket	7	Bracket
6	Guard		

lobes pointing upwards. No 4 cylinder is the one furthest from the timing belt. If No 1 piston is at TDC, simply rotate the crankshaft through 360°.

9   Unbolt and remove the timing belt cover.

10 Check that the timing mark on the camshaft sprocket is aligned with the pointer on the belt cover backplate. The mark is a notch at the edge of the sprocket and will be positioned at the highest point of the sprocket when the engine is correctly timed.

11 Restrain the timing belt with the hand and release, but do not remove, the camshaft sprocket bolt. Release the belt tensioner pulley by slackening the pulley centre nut. Push the timing belt evenly from the sprockets, noting which way round the belt is fitted if it is to be completely removed. The lettering on the belt is normally legible from the crankshaft pulley end of the engine when the belt is as originally fitted.

12 Unbolt the camshaft carrier and lift it sufficiently from the cylinder head to break the seal of the mating faces. **Note:** *It is important not to allow the tappets (cam followers) to fall out;* they must be retained in their original locations. This can be done if the carrier is raised very slowly, until the fingers can be inserted to prise the tappets downwards onto their respective valve spring retainers. It is unlikely that the valve clearance adjusting shims will be displaced from their recesses in the tappets because of the suction of the lubricating oil, but watch that this does not happen; the shims must also be retained in their originally fitted sequence.

13 Removal of the camshaft sprocket and the camshaft is as described in Chapter 13, Section 5.

14 Refitting is a reversal of the removal process, but observe the following points.

15 Use new gaskets.

16 Retain the tappets and shims in their bores in the camshaft carrier with thick grease; they must not be allowed to drop out when the carrier is lowered onto the cylinder head.

Fig. 1.2A Timing mark alignment (Sec 4)

1	Camshaft sprocket mark	4	Crankshaft pulley notch
2	Pointer on backplate	5	TDC mark on cover
3	Tensioner pulley		

17 If the crankshaft or camshaft have been moved from their set position, align the timing marks as described in paragraphs 8 and 10; the valves may otherwise impinge upon the piston crowns when the camshaft lobes compress any of the valve springs during bolting down of the carrier.
18 Refit and tension the timing belt as described in Section 5.
19 Tighten all nuts and bolts evenly and progressively to the specified torque.

5 Timing belt – renewal (engine in car)

1 Using a socket wrench, turn the crankshaft pulley until the notch in the pulley flange is in alignment with the TDC mark on the timing belt cover (65 models) or on the index plate (75 models), with No 4 piston at firing position. This may be established by removing No 4 spark plug and feeling the compression generated by placing a finger over the plug hole.
2 Remove the alternator drivebelt (Chapter 2, Section 10) and any other auxiliary drivebelts. Unbolt and remove the timing belt cover.
3 Check that the camshaft sprocket timing mark is in correct alignment (refer to Section 4, paragraph 10).
4 Slacken the nut in the centre of the tensioner pulley and push in on the support to release the tension on the belt, then retighten the nut. Slide the drivebelt off the pulleys.
5 Check that the crankshaft and camshaft pulleys have not been moved from their previously aligned positions. Also check that the distributor rotor arm is still pointing to No 4 cylinder contact in the cap.
6 Fit the new belt. Start at the crankshaft drive pulley and, taking care not to kink or strain the belt, slip it over the camshaft pulley. The camshaft may have to be turned slightly to mesh the pulley with the teeth on the belt. Fit the belt on the tensioner pulley last; if this is difficult, do not lever or force the belt on, recheck the belt.
7 Slacken the tensioner pulley locknut to tension the belt, then retighten the nut.

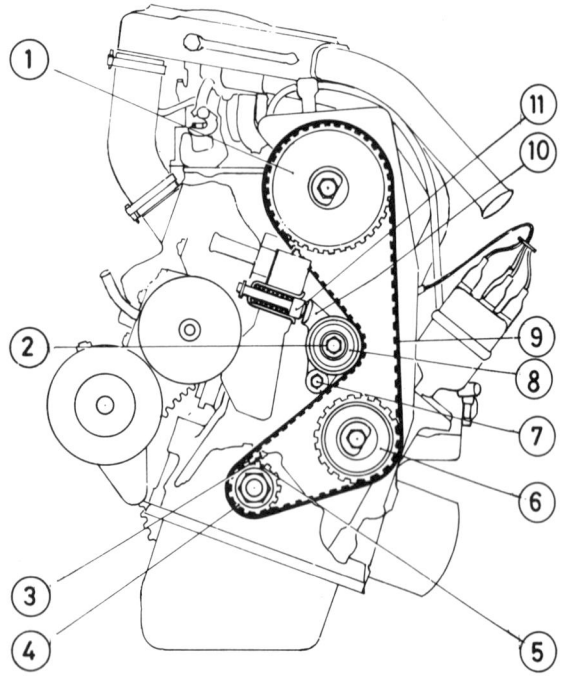

Fig. 1.2B Timing belt arrangement (Sec 5)

1	Camshaft sprocket	6	Auxiliary shaft sprocket
2	Tensioner pulley locknut	7	Tensioner bracket bolt
3	Timing mark on crankshaft front oil seal retainer	8	Tensioner pulley
4	Crankshaft sprocket	9	Timing belt
5	Crankshaft sprocket timing mark	10	Tensioner bracket
		11	Tensioner spring

8 Rotate the engine through half a turn. Slacken the tensioner pulley nut, to remove any slack on the belt, and then retighten the nut to 44 Nm (32.5 lbf ft). When tensioning the belt, never turn the engine backwards or rock the crankshaft as slack will develop in the belt and it may jump a tooth.
9 Refit the timing belt cover. Refit and tension the auxiliary drivebelt(s) and check the ignition timing.

6 Cylinder head – removal and refitting (engine in car)

1 Drain the cooling system (see Chapter 2) and remove the air cleaner (see Chapter 3).
2 Disconnect the battery.
3 Disconnect and plug the fuel flow and return hoses from the carburettor.
4 Disconnect the throttle linkage and the choke cable or automatic choke coolant hoses (North American models) from the carburettor.
5 Disconnect the high tension (HT) cables from the spark plugs. On air conditioned 75 CL models, remove the distributor cap and leads from the camshaft-driven distributor.
6 Disconnect the brake servo vacuum hose from the inlet manifold.
7 Disconnect the coolant hoses from the thermostat housing.
8 On cars with emission control systems, identify the hoses and disconnect them as necessary to clear the cylinder head for removal.
9 Unbolt and remove the timing belt cover.
10 Release the timing belt tensioner by unscrewing the tensioner pulley bolt. Lever the pulley against the spring plunger and retighten the pulley bolt. Slip the belt from the camshaft sprocket.
11 Disconnect the coolant pipes from the inlet manifold/carburettor.
12 Unbolt the exhaust downpipes from the manifold.
13 If a crowfoot wrench is available, the cylinder head, complete with camshaft and camshaft carrier, can be removed as an assembly – the cylinder head nuts can also be unscrewed with this type of wrench.
14 Where this type of wrench is not available, the camshaft carrier will have to be removed first, as described in Section 4.
15 Unscrew the cylinder head nuts and bolts evenly and progressively, working from those in the centre towards those at both ends.
16 Rock the cylinder head by gripping the manifolds. **Note:** *Do not insert a lever in the gasket joint to prise the head from the block.*
17 Pull the head off the studs and remove it to the bench. Remove and discard the old cylinder head gasket.
18 Unbolt and remove the hot air collecting shield for the air cleaner from the exhaust manifold. The exhaust and inlet manifolds can now be unbolted. The carburettor may remain on the inlet manifold.
19 Overhaul and decarbonising of the cylinder head is described in Section 15.
20 Refitting is a reversal of the removal process, but make sure the crankshaft and camshaft timing marks are set as described in Section 33, to avoid the valve heads digging into the piston crowns when the head is refitted.
21 Always use new gaskets. The cylinder head gasket must be fitted so that the oil pressure hole in the block is central in the copper ringed cut-out in the gasket.
22 Tighten the cylinder head nuts and bolts to the specified torque, in the sequence shown in Fig. 1.8.
23 Fit the timing belt (see Section 5) and check the valve clearances (see Section 34) after fitting the camshaft carrier (see Section 4).

7 Engine ancillaries – removal

1 These are all readily accessible and removable once the bonnet is raised.
2 The ancillary components include the following; reference should be made to the Chapters indicated for detailed descriptions of removal and refitting;

Distributor	Chapter 4
Carburettor	Chapter 3
Fuel pump	Chapter 3
Emission control devices	Chapter 3
Alternator	Chapter 9
Starter motor	Chapter 9
Coolant pump	Chapter 2

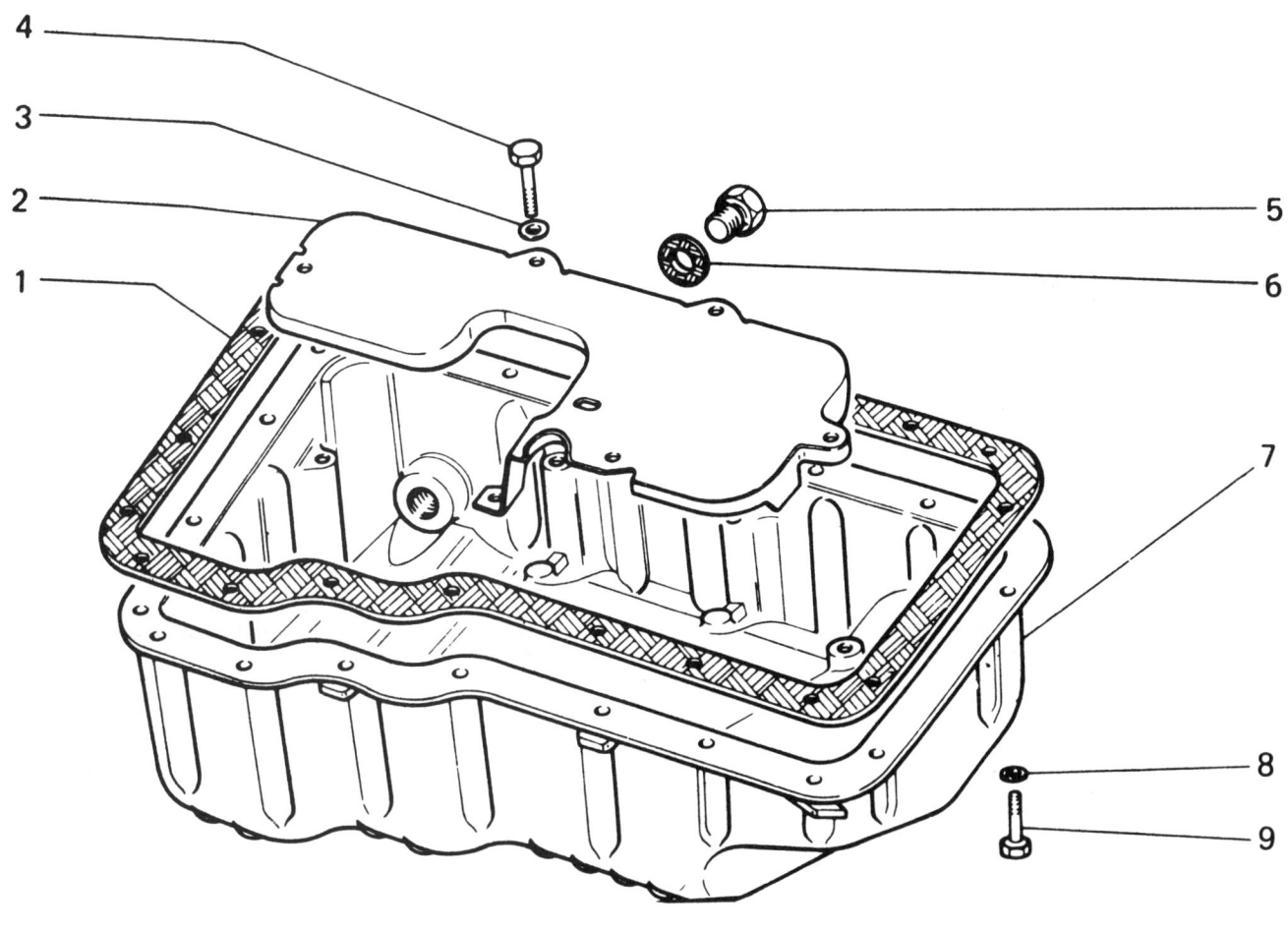

Fig.1.3 Engine sump and gasket (Sec 8)

1	Gasket	4	Bolt	7	Sump
2	Cover	5	Drain plug	8	Washer
3	Washer	6	Gasket	9	Bolt

3   Where the engine/transmission is being removed from the car, the ancillaries can be removed before the power train is lifted out. Alternatively, provided the connecting leads and hoses are disconnected, they can remain in position on the engine for removal later.

8   Sump, oil pump, pistons and connecting rods – removal and refitting (engine in car)

1   Position the front of the car over an inspection pit (or up on ramps) to provide working clearance under the engine. Disconnect the battery and drain the coolant. Drain the engine oil.
2   Support the base of the transmission securely and remove the engine centre mounting bracket. Unbolt the lower cover plate from the face of the clutch bellhousing.
3   Unscrew and remove the sump retaining bolts then remove the sump and gasket.
4   Remove the breather return drain, which is adjacent to No 3 main bearing.
5   Unbolt and remove the oil pump/pick-up assembly.
6   If it is intended to remove the piston/connecting rod assemblies, the cylinder head must be lifted from the engine as described in Section 6.
7   The big-end bearing shells can be renewed without having to remove the cylinder head if the caps are unbolted and the piston/connecting rod pushed gently about one inch up the bore (the crankpin being at its lowest point). If these shells are worn, however, the main bearing shells will almost certainly be worn as well. In this

case, the engine should be removed for complete overhaul including crankshaft removal.
8   Removal and dismantling of the piston/connecting rods is as described in later Sections of this Chapter, for engine dismantling when the engine has been removed from the car.
9   Refitting is a reversal of the removal process and is fully described in later engine component reassembly Sections of this Chapter.

9   Engine – method of removal

Note: *The engine should be removed complete with the transmission*

65 models
1   On 65 models, the method of removal is to lower the engine/transmission, complete with driveshafts attached to the final drive, to the floor or into an inspection pit. The front of the car can then be raised so that the engine/transmission can be withdrawn from under the engine compartment.

75 models
2   On 75 models, the engine/manual transmission with driveshafts disconnected from the final drive or support flanges, may be removed either downwards or by the preferred method of lifting it upwards out of the engine compartment.
3   On 75 models with automatic transmission, the engine, complete with automatic transmission, should be removed from beneath the car as described in Chapter 6, Section 18. It should then be separated.

10 Engine/manual transmission – removal

To remove the engine with automatic transmission, refer to Chapter 6, Section 18.

1 Place the front roadwheels on ramps or place the car over an inspection pit. Raise the bonnet and unbolt the hinges then remove the bonnet to a safe place.
2 Disconnect and remove the battery.
3 Remove the spare wheel.
4 Drain the cooling system (see Chapter 2).
5 Remove the air cleaner (see Chapter 3).
6 Disconnect the accelerator and choke controls from the carburettor; tie them back out of the way.
7 Disconnect the fuel hoses from the fuel pump and plug their open ends. Disconnect the fuel return hose from the carburettor.
8 Disconnect the radiator hoses.
9 Disconnect the heater hoses from the engine.
10 Disconnect the electrical leads from the alternator and the starter motor.
11 Pull the leads from the oil pressure and coolant temperature sender units.
12 Disconnect the coil-to-distributor HT and LT leads, then remove the distributor cap, complete with spark plug leads.
13 Disconnect the brake servo vacuum hose from the inlet manifold.
14 Unbolt the exhaust downpipes from the exhaust manifold. It is now preferable to remove the one-piece exhaust system from the car. Simply slip off the rubber support rings and remove it.
15 Disconnect the clutch operating cable from the clutch release lever.
16 A suitable hoist should be attached to the engine lifting lugs and the weight of the engine/transmission taken on the hoist. Disconnect the engine right-hand mounting.
17 Working underneath the car, disconnect the leads from the electronic type speedometer sender unit on the final drive housing.
18 Disconnect the gearchange control rod from the universally jointed selector shaft on the gearbox. Swivel the control rod to one side of the car and tie it up, out of the way.
19 Disconnect the electrical leads from the reversing lamp switch on the transmission.
20 Remove the engine centre torque control/mounting. To do this, make sure that the weight of the power unit is taken by the hoist, then unbolt the mounting from the transmission studs. Now extract the two small setscrews which hold the flexible mounting pad to the floor pan. Do not attempt to unscrew the flexible mounting centre bolt; its nut will only keep turning and cannot be held stationary as it is inaccessible with the mounting pad in position.

65 models
21 Support the body underframe securely on jacks and axle stands, remove the front wheels and slacken the driveshaft-to-hub nuts. These nuts are very tight and will require a spanner of good length to release them. Have an assistant apply the footbrake to hold the hub stationary.
22 The front end of the car should now be raised and supported so that there is sufficient clearance for the engine to pass under it. This will mean that the engine hoist must also be raised in conjunction with the body jacks.
23 Once the car is raised, make sure that it is really securely supported again on axle stands.
24 Unscrew and remove the previously slackened driveshaft-to-hub nuts.
25 Disconnect both front suspension track control arms from their inboard body brackets. Pull the arms downward.
26 Using a suitable balljoint separator, disconnect the left-hand steering tie-rod from the suspension strut.
27 Disconnect the radius rods from the track control arms. Unbolt the brake calipers and tie them up, out of the way.
28 Unbolt the engine mounting brackets from the engine/transmission.
29 From the lower ends of the suspension struts, remove the two pinch bolts and tap the steering knuckles downward. The driveshafts can now be pressed or knocked out of the hubs. Tie the disconnected shafts to the upper part of the engine.
30 Make a final check in case any wires or hoses have been overlooked and still require disconnecting, then lower the engine/transmission from the engine compartment.

75 models
31 Disconnect the driveshafts from their inboard flanges by extracting their socket-headed screws. The screws should be renewed and not used again. The left-hand driveshaft comes away from the final drive, complete with constant velocity (CV) joint; the right-hand shaft is separated at the bearing support, which is bolted to the engine crankcase. It also serves as the alternator mounting. Tie the driveshafts up and out of the way, then cover the joints at their inboard ends with plastic bags to prevent the entry of dirt. Refer to Chapter 7 for detailed removal operations for the driveshafts.
32 Disconnect the battery earth lead from its clip and the terminal bolt on the (left-hand) cover plate of the transmission.
33 Disconnect the electrical leads from the radiator fan and its thermostatic switch in the lower tank. Unbolt the radiator/fan assembly and remove it upwards from the engine compartment.
34 Unbolt the engine mountings and, using the hoist, lift the engine/transmission until the transmission end can be turned towards the radiator grille to clear the battery mounting platform. Carefully, raise the engine/transmission further and swing it out of the engine compartment.

North American models – emission controls
35 Disconnect any vacuum hoses and remove any system valves or other components which are likely to impede removal of the engine transmission. The hoses and valves involved are dependent upon the system used; refer to Chapter 3.

Air conditioning
36 Where air conditioning is fitted as an option on certain North American versions, the compressor and other adjacent components will have to be unbolted and moved as far away from the engine as their flexible hoses will allow. **Note**: *On no account disconnect any part of the refrigerant circuit as dangerous gas will be released.* If necessary, have the air conditioning system discharged by your dealer or a competent refrigeration engineer before starting to remove the engine/transmission.

11 Engine/manual transmission – separation and reconnection

1 With the engine/transmission withdrawn from the car, remove the driveshafts from the final drive (according to model) as described in Chapter 7.
2 Unbolt and remove the starter motor.
3 Unbolt and remove the engine mounting brackets.

11.6A Fixed driveshaft oil seal in differential (75 models)

11.6B Connecting engine and transmission (75 models)

11.6C Fixed driveshaft entering differential (75 models)

4   From the lower face of the flywheel bellhousing, unbolt and remove the cover plate.

5   Unscrew and remove the bolts and nuts which hold the clutch bellhousing to the engine. Support the weight of the transmission and withdraw it in a straight line from the engine.

6   Reconnection is a reversal of the separation process but if the clutch has been disturbed, the driven plate must be centralised (see Chapter 5) before attempting to reconnect the engine/transmission. Take care that the fixed right-hand driveshaft splines do not damage the oil seal in the differential as the shaft enters the final drive housing (on 75 models) (photos).

12   Engine/automatic transmission – separation and reconnection

1   Carry out the operations described in Section 11, paras 1 to 3.

2   Remove the starter motor and, working through the aperture left by its removal, unscrew and remove the bolts which hold the torque converter and the driveplate together. It will be necessary to turn the crankshaft pulley in order to bring each of the bolts into view within the aperture.

3   Remove the engine-to-transmission securing bolts and nuts.

4   Support the transmission on a trolley jack and withdraw it slowly from the engine. As soon as a small gap is evident, insert a lever right across the face of the torque converter to press the torque converter into full engagement with the fluid pump drive tangs. Keep it this way while the transmission is removed, then fix the lever so that it retains the converter fully into the transmission while the latter is out of the car.

5   Reconnection is a reversal of the separation process.

6   There is no need to mark the relationship of the torque converter to the driveplate as the torque converter is very carefully balanced during production.

7   Take care that the fixed right-hand driveshaft splines do not damage the oil seal in the differential as the shaft enters the final drive housing.

13   Engine dismantling – general

1   Before starting work, cover any openings with plastic sheet and masking tape. Clean away all external dirt, using paraffin and a stiff brush, or one of the water-soluble solvents which are commonly available.

2   If possible, have the engine on a bench or strong table. Where dismantling must be carried out on the floor, at least have a sheet of hardboard to work on; grit and dust will otherwise soon prevent the maintenance of the necessary clean working conditions essential to a successful overhaul. Rag used for cleaning out oilways and other components should be of the non-fluffy variety. If an air line is available, so much the better for final cleaning off. Paraffin, which could possibly remain in oilways, would dilute the oil for initial lubrication after reassembly.

3   Where components are fitted with seals and gaskets it is always best to fit new ones – but *do not* throw the old ones away until you have the new ones to hand. A pattern is then available if they have to be made specially. Hang them on a convenient hook.

4   In general, it is best to work from the top of the engine downwards. In any case, support the engine firmly so that it does not topple over when you are undoing stubborn nuts and bolts.

5   Always place nuts and bolts back with their components or place of attachment if possible – it saves so much confusion later. Otherwise put them in small, separate pots or jars so that their groups are easily identified.

6   If you are lucky enough to have an area where parts can be laid out on sheets of paper, do so – putting the nuts and bolts with them. If you are able to look at all the components in this way it helps to avoid missing something on reassembly.

14   Engine – complete dismantling

1   With the engine removed from the car, separated from the transmission, cleaned externally and resting securely on its work surface, remove the ancillaries (see Section 7) if they were not removed earlier.

2   Unbolt and remove the timing belt cover.

3   Grip the now exposed timing belt with the hands and loosen the camshaft sprocket bolt.

4   Release the timing belt tensioner pulley centre bolt, then slip the belt from the pulley and sprockets to remove it. Note which way round the belt is fitted, usually so that the lettering on the belt can be read from the crankshaft pulley end of the engine.

5   Remove the camshaft sprocket.

6   Unbolt and remove the camshaft timing belt cover backing plate.

7   Unbolt and remove the camshaft carrier cover.

8   Unbolt the camshaft carrier and lift it off very slowly, at the same time pushing the tappets and their shims down with the fingers securely onto their respective valve springs. It is easy to remove the camshaft carrier too quickly with some of the tappets stuck in it and as the carrier is lifted away, the tappets will fall out. If this happens, the valve clearances will be upset as the tappets and shims cannot be returned, with any certainty, to their original positions. The valve clearances will have to be adjusted as described in Section 34 even if the valves have not been dismantled or ground in.

9   Unscrew and remove the cylinder head bolts and nuts, grip the manifold, rock the head and remove the complete cylinder head/manifold/carburettor assembly. Remove and discard the cylinder head gasket.

10 Unbolt the coolant pump from the side of the cylinder block and remove it complete with coolant distribution pipe. Remove the crankcase breather.

11 Remove the distributor/oil pump driveshaft. This is simply carried out by inserting a finger into the hole vacated by the distributor and wedging it in the hole in the end of the driveshaft. Lift the shaft out of mesh with the auxiliary shaft. Where the distributor is driven by the camshaft, a cover plate retains the oil pump driveshaft in position.

12 Unbolt and remove the sprocket from the end of the auxiliary shaft. The sprocket is held to the shaft with a Woodruff key.

13 Unscrew and remove the crankshaft pulley nut. This is very tight and the flywheel (or driveplate) starter ring gear will have to be jammed with a cold chisel or a suitable bent piece of steel to prevent the crankshaft rotating.

14 Withdraw the crankshaft sprocket, which is located by a Woodruff key.

15 Unbolt the auxiliary shaft retainer and withdraw the shaft from the crankcase.

16 Unbolt and remove the clutch from the flywheel, if not already done. Mark the flywheel-to-crankshaft mounting flange relationship.

17 Unscrew the flywheel securing bolts. The starter ring gear will again have to be jammed to prevent the crankshaft rotating as the bolts are unscrewed. Mark the flywheel position in relation to the crankshaft mounting flange, then remove it.

18 Unbolt the front and rear crankshaft oil seal retainer bolts from the crankcase and the sump. Remove the oil seal retainers.

19 Turn the engine on its side, extract the remaining sump bolts and remove the sump. If it is stuck, try tapping it gently with a soft faced hammer. If this fails, cut all round the sump-to-gasket flange with a sharp knife. Do not try prising with a large screwdriver; this will only distort the sump mating flange.

20 With the sump removed, unbolt and remove the oil pump.

21 Grip the oil drain pipe and twist or rock it from its hole in the crankcase. It is an interference fit in the hole.

22 Unscrew the nuts from the big-end caps, then remove the caps with their bearing shells. The caps and their connecting rods are numbered 1, 2, 3 and 4 from the timing cover end of the engine. The numbers are adjacent at the big-end cap joint and on the side of the crankcase furthest from the auxiliary shaft.

23 If the bearing shells are to be used again, tape them to their respective big-end caps.

24 Push each connecting rod/piston assembly up the bore and out of the cylinder block. There is one reservation; if a wear ridge has developed at the top of the bores, remove this by careful scraping before trying to remove the piston/rod assemblies. The ridge will otherwise prevent removal or break the piston rings during the attempt.

25 If the connecting rod bearing shells are to be used again, tape the shells to their respective rods.

26 Before unbolting the main bearing caps, note that they are marked with one, two, three or four notches. No 5 main bearing cap is unmarked. Note to which side of the crankcase the notches are nearer; the fuel pump side.

27 Unbolt and remove the main bearing caps. If the bearing shells are to be used again, tape them to their respective caps. The bearing shell at the centre position is plain, the others have a lubrication groove.

28 Carefully, lift the crankshaft from the crankcase, noting the thrust washers at No 5 main bearing. These control the crankshaft endfloat.

---

15 Cylinder head and valves – servicing and valve clearance adjustment

1 With the cylinder head removed from the engine, unbolt and remove the exhaust manifold shield for the air cleaner hot air collection. Unbolt and remove the inlet and exhaust manifolds.

2 Prepare a box for the valves and their retainers. The lid of a cardboard box can have eight holes punched in it to hold the valves. All the valves must be identified so that they can be refitted in the same location from which they are removed.

3 Using a valve spring compressor round the head, compress the valve spring enough to permit removal of the split collets. Remove the spring compressor. Take off the spring cap, the outer and inner valve springs, the two spring seats and the rubber sealing ring.

4 Examine the valve seats for bad pitting and, in the case of the

exhaust valve seats, burning. Check the mating surface of the head to the cylinder block for signs of gasket blowing. With the carbon still on the head, the marks of leaks should be apparent. If the carbon deposit is thick, damp, and soft, it indicates too much oil is getting into the cylinders, either up past the piston rings or down through the inlet valve guides.

5 If the cylinder head gasket has been blowing, the head will need refacing. Either your FIAT agent or a local engineering works will get this done for you. The minimum amount necessary to get a clean, flat surface should be removed.

6 If the valve seats are badly pitted or burned they will need refacing. Again, your Fiat garage or any large repairer will have the cutters. If you try to do it by lengthy valve grinding, the valve will get badly worn, and the seating contact area will be too wide.

7 If the valve seats are being faced, the valves could be refaced too by the same firm at the same time. However, if the head is all right but the exhaust valves are bad, the most convenient and economical thing to do is to buy new exhaust valves. The inlet valves are usually in quite a good condition.

8 The valve guides will be worn. It is very difficult to measure the wear. A useful yardstick is that if you need the crankshaft regrinding,

15.21 Inserting valve into its guide

15.22A Valve oil stem seals with spring washer and seat

15.22B Fitting double valve springs

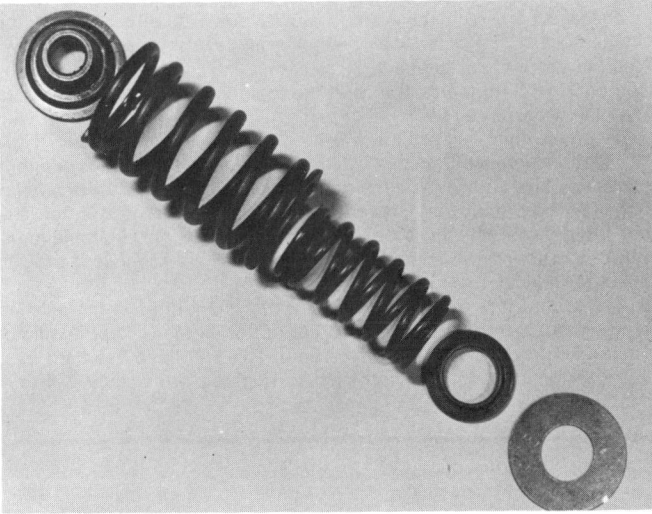

15.23 Valve springs and components

15.25 Inserting collets with valve springs compressed

you will need new valve guides. It is tricky pressing the old ones out and the new in. It is recommended you get the FIAT agent to do it. He also will have the experience on which to judge the wear. The guides wear more than the valve stems, so fitting new valves will not help this much.

9 Having decided what work must be done by a professional, now clean up the head. Scrape off all the carbon. Be careful not to scratch the valve seats. These are hard inserts, but a small scratch will be difficult to grind out. The head is made of aluminium, so soft, and easily cut when scraping. The combustion chambers, and inlet and exhaust ports, must be cleaned. A blunt screwdriver and flat paint scraper are useful. If using a wire brush on an electric drill, wear goggles.

10 It is after this that the head should be taken for any machining. Also during the cleaning any cracks will be found. Should this unlikely event occur, the only solution is another head.

11 Clean all carbon off the valves. It is convenient to do their heads by putting them (unfixed) in their seat in the cylinder head. Scrape off all deposits under the head, and down the valve stem. The rubbing surface (where the stem runs in the guide) should be highly polished by wear; do not touch this, but the part of the stem nearer the head may have lacquered deposits that can be removed with a wire brush. At this stage, do not touch the valve's seating surface.

12 Now grind in the valves. Even new ones will need grinding in, to bed them to their actual seat. If the seats and valves or just the one, have been recut, the hand grinding must still be done.

13 The idea is to rub the valve to-and-fro, to mate valve and seat, and give a smooth, flat, perfectly circular sealing surface, which should be matt grey. The seating surface should be about midway up the valve's 45° surface; not at the top, which happens if a valve is refaced so often its head diameter is reduced, and sits too deep in the seat.

14 The best tool is a rubber sucker on the end of a stick. Unless the sucker is good, and the valve absolutely oil free, it keeps coming off. Handles that clamp to the stem overcome this, but they are clumsy to hold. *On no account use an electric drill;* the rotational clockwise and anti-clockwise action is essential.

15 If the valves and seats have been refaced, you will only need fine grinding paste. If cleaning up worn seats, start with coarse paste.

16 Smear a little of the paste all round the seat, being very careful to get none on the valve stem. Insert the valve in its place. Put the valve grinding handle on the valve, and, pushing it lightly down onto its seat, rotate one way then the other. Every now and then, lift the valve clear on the seat, turn it about half a turn and then carry on. By altering the position the grinding paste is redistributed, and also the valve will work all round the seat and make it circular.

17 If coarse paste is used, try to judge the change to fine just before all marks have disappeared so that they and the large grain of the coarse paste are ground out at the same time; the less metal rubbed off the better, otherwise the seat will get too broad.

18 The seat should be a uniform pale grey. Rings are a sign that the valve has not been lifted and turned enough. If protracted grinding is required, the paste will lose its effectiveness, so wipe off the old and apply fresh paste periodically.

19 Clean off all traces of valve grinding paste thoroughly. Wipe out the valve guides by pushing a clean rag through a number of times. Engine oil makes a good detergent for this, particularly if squirted through hard with a good oil can. Leave everything oily to prevent rust.

20 The valve springs should be renewed if they fail to meet the load/length specifications in Chapter 13, if they are obviously distorted, or if they have been in use for 30 000 miles or more.

21 Reassemble the valves to the head. Make sure the valve goes into the correct seat, into which it was ground. Oil the guides and the valves all over, before assembly (photo).

22 Insert the valve in its seat, then fit the new oil seal, and push it down into place on the valve guide. Put the spring seats over the stem followed by the springs. If the springs used have a varying spiral, put the end which has the spring coils closest together next to the cylinder head (photo).

23 Put the cap on the spring (photo).

24 Put the valve spring compressing clamp round the head and compress the spring. It needs to go just so far that the groove in the end of the stem is about half clear of the cap.

25 Put in the two split collets. Undo the clamp gradually, if necessary moving the spring cap about to let it slide up the cotters to settle into position and clamp them properly. Repeat this procedure on the remaining seven valves (photo).

26 The original valve clearance adjusting shims will no longer provide the correct clearances if the valves have been ground in or the seats recut. Only where dismantling of a valve was carried out to renew a spring is there any purpose in returning the shims to their original locations. Try to obtain the loan of eight thin shims from your dealer and insert them into the tappets (cam followers) before assembling the tappets onto the carrier, where they should be retained with thick grease.

27 Fit the camshaft carrier, complete with tappets and shims, into the cylinder head.

28 Using feeler gauges inserted between the heel of each cam lobe and the tappet, check and record each clearance. Turn the camshaft as necessary to bring each cam into its correct checking position with the cam peak at its highest point.

29 Once all the clearances have been checked and recorded, remove the camshaft carrier and the tappets with their shims, keeping the latter in their fitted sequence.

30 The thickness of the individual shims can be established by the engraved number on them (or, if this has worn off, by using a micrometer).

31 By simple calculation, using the measured clearance and the shim thickness from each valve position, it can be found whether a thicker or thinner shim is required to bring the clearance within the specified tolerance.

32 Where no clearance can be measured, even with the thinnest available shim in position, the valve will have to be removed and the end of its stem ground off squarely. This will reduce its overall length by the minimum amount to provide a clearance. This job should be entrusted to your dealer as it is important to keep the end of the valve stem square.

33 Now that the thickness of the shims required to provide the correct valve clearances is known, the shims used or borrowed for testing should be exchanged for thicker or thinner ones as necessary. In practice, it is often found that some of the original shims can be interchanged between tappets to provide the specified clearances.

34 Keep the tappets with their respective shims ready for final reassembly, noting that the engraved numeral on the shim should not be visible when fitted; it will otherwise gradually be obliterated by the rubbing of the cam lobe.

35 If the cylinder head face was remachined, it will bring the valve down nearer the pistons. If the machining was done by a FIAT agent he should have checked the height with the FIAT gauge to ensure that

there will be no possibility of the piston crowns making contact with the valve heads when the engine is running, particularly at high revs.

16 Cylinders, pistons and connecting rods – overhaul

1 The oil consumption and exhaust oil smoke will have given some indication as to the wear of the bores and pistons. Once the cylinder head has been removed, they can be measured properly.

2 Scrape the carbon off the unworn lip at the top of the bore so that its original size can be compared with the worn lip.

3 Measure the bore diameters. They will be worn more near to the top than the bottom, and more across than fore and aft. If the difference between the largest and smallest dimension exceeds 0.15 mm (0.006 in), the ovality is excessive and a rebore is necessary. If the bores have any scores, they should be rebored.

4 Even if the cylinders may not need reboring, it is possible the pistons and rings will need renewing. They will have worn on their outer circumferential surfaces, and where the ring contacts the piston land in its groove.

5 Slide an appropriate feeler sideways into the piston groove to measure the clearance between each ring and its neighbouring land.

6 Carefully, expand the rings and lift them off the piston. Insert the piston into the cylinder at its correct axis (valve cut-outs away from the auxiliary shaft). Use the thickest feeler gauge that will pass between piston and bore with the piston halfway down its stroke, to get the widest part of the bore. Also, measure opposite the ridge at the top. You have now got the actual clearance at the worn bit, and by comparing it with the clearance at the top, the cylinder wear. Take out the pistons. Insert a piston ring. Push it halfway down the cylinder with a piston, so that it is square. Measure the gap in the ring (Fig. 1.5).

7 If the clearance between cylinder and piston or piston and ring is excessive (see Specifications), new components must be fitted. New rings can be fitted to old pistons by specialist firms who will machine out the groove, which will be worn conical, and supply suitable rings. But this is not really economic. The wear limits are listed separately in the Specifications.

8 Note that it is most important, if fitting new rings in the existing bores, that the top ring has a step cut out of its top so that it will not hit the ridge left at the top of the bore. This will have been left by a worn piston ring. Should normal new rings be fitted, they will foul,

16.12 Gudgeon pin circlip

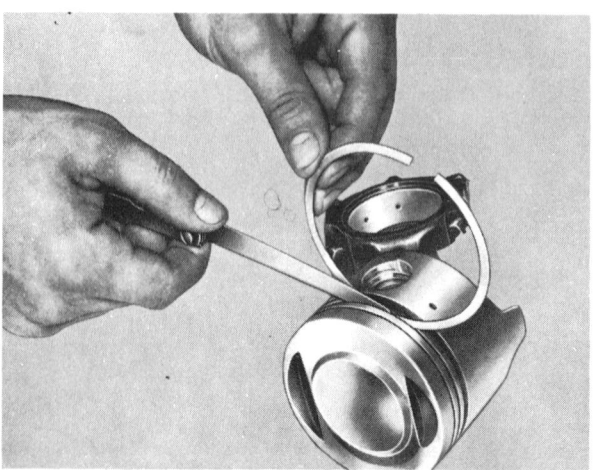

Fig. 1.4 Checking piston ring groove clearance (Sec 16)

Fig. 1.5 Checking piston ring end gap (Sec 16)

1 Feeler gauge   *2 Piston ring*

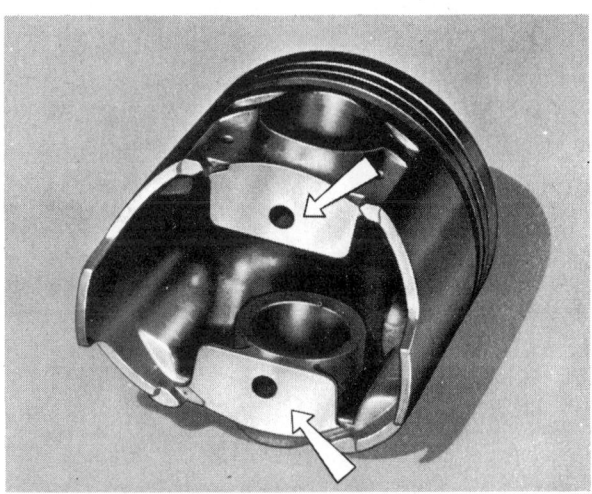

Fig. 1.6 Metal removing area for piston weight balancing (Sec 16)

13 Before fitting the pistons to their connecting rods, weigh each piston and check that their weights are all the same. If not, see paragraph 17.

14 Before fitting the new rings to the pistons, check the size of the ring gap. Insert the ring into its cylinder, and push it halfway down the bore, using a piston so that it is square. Measure the gap with feeler gauges. If the gap is too small, file it with a fine file, being careful, as the rings are brittle.

15 Check, when fitting, that all the rings are the right way up. They must be expanded only the minimum amount to get them over the piston lands. It is useful to cut a guide out of an old tin, and wrap this round the top of the piston.

16 The gaps in the three rings should all be equally spaced out, at 120° to each other.

17 The pistons' weight must all be within 2.5 grams, the same. If the spread is wider than this, the heavier ones must be lightened by milling metal off the underside of the small-end bosses.

18 Where cylinder bores have already been bored out to their maximum oversize, it is possible to have cylinder liners fitted.

17 Crankshaft and bearings – overhaul

1   The bearing surfaces of the crankshaft journals and pins should be bright and smooth. If there are scratches or scoring they will need regrinding. Measure the diameters of the bearings in a number of directions, looking for ovality. If the ovality exceeds the maximum specified then this is excessive purely as ovality, but also implies that overall wear will be too much. Take it to a FIAT agent, who can arrange the regrinding simultaneously with the supply of the main and big-end shells to the suitable undersize. Otherwise, you must take it to a machine shop, who could regrind it for you to the journal sizes, less undersize, given in the Specifications. Then order the new bearing shells from FIAT.

2   If the crankshaft ovality seems all right, you may be able to measure the clearance to confirm overall wear is within the condemnation limit. It is difficult to measure, and difficult to measure the shaft accurately enough, to know how much of the wear is from the shaft, and how much off the shells. But ovality is easier to measure as it is only a comparison. No ovality means negligible shaft wear. It can be assumed the shells will have worn. One way to measure the clearance is to use 'Plastigage', a crushable plastic strip. The bearings are reassembled with the gauge strip inside, and the amount it is squashed is measured.

3   Unless the engine has done a very low mileage, and the shells appear of an even, matt colour, they should be renewed anyway, if events have made the engine require dismantling. Remove the shells from their caps. If they are stubborn, just slide them round by pressure at the end. Confirm that the crankshaft is standard by looking at the markings on the backs of the shells. Because the shells are so easily fitted, and are relatively cheap, it is false economy to try and make do with the old ones.

18 Flywheel and starter ring gear – overhaul

1   There are two things to check; the clutch pressure surface, and the starter ring.

2   If the clutch has been badly worn, or badly overheated by slipping, the surface on which the clutch presses may be scored or cracked. This would wear a new clutch plate rapidly. The flywheel should not be skimmed to remove these, but renewed.

3   Wear on the starter ring gear should not be bad, as the starter is the pre-engaged type. Check that there are no broken teeth, or burrs. Minor blemishes can be filed off. If there is a bad defect, a new starter ring is required, though it may prove cheaper in the long run (and will certainly be easier) to buy a complete new flywheel.

4   To remove the old ring, it must be split by cutting with a cold chisel. Take care not to damage the flywheel, though again, minor burrs can be filed off.

5   To fit a new ring gear, it will be necessary to heat it gently and evenly until a temperature of approximately 230°C (510°F) is reached. With the ring gear at this temperature, fit it to the flywheel with the chamfered lead-in of the teeth facing the clutch fitting end of the flywheel. The ring gear should be either pressed or lightly tapped onto

which would anyway cause a knock, but probably also break the rings. Note also that the second and third rings have a special scraping bottom edge. The bores have three sizes, and the piston matching size is marked on it.

9   FIAT supply new pistons (and oversize ones) complete with rings and gudgeon pins; but not ones with the stepped top ring necessary if not reboring. This may persuade you to have the cylinder rebored, which would make a thorough job anyway.

10 The gudgeon pins are fully floating and can be removed after taking out one of the circlips.

11 The smallends should last the life of the pistons. If new pistons are being fitted, new gudgeon pins should also be fitted. This involves a replacement bush for the connecting rod. There should be no discernible free movement in the smallends.

12 When renewing the gudgeon pins, first check the fit in the piston. It should be fitted by hand pressure, but be such a good fit that it will not drop out under its own weight. After fitting the gudgeon pin, do not forget to fit the retaining circlip (photo).

its register and left to cool naturally, when the contraction of the metal on cooling will ensure that it is a secure and permanent fit. Great care must be taken not to overheat the ring gear, for if this happens, the temper of the ring gear will be lost.

19 Driveplate and starter ring gear (automatic transmission) – overhaul

1   On cars equipped with automatic transmission, a driveplate is used instead of a flywheel to transmit the power from the crankshaft to the torque converter.
2   The starter ring gear is an integral part of the driveplate and if worn or damaged the complete assembly should be renewed.

20 Oil pump – overhaul

1   Carefully, clamp the pump housing in a vice, shaft downwards..
2   Take off the pump cover, with the suction pipe. This will release the oil pressure relief valve inside. Also inside is a filter (photo).
3   Remove the internal cover plate.
4   Take out the driveshaft and the gears (photo).
5   Clean and examine all the parts. Measure the clearances against the Specifications. The end clearance is measured by putting a straight-edge across the cover face.
6   The oil pump should only need replacements after very long mileage, when the rest of the engine is showing great signs of wear.
7   The length of a new gear is given in the Specifications, so that the effect of just renewing that can be judged, to see if it will restore the end clearance to the Specifications. Otherwise the housing must be changed.
8   The driven gear shaft is mounted in the housing with an interference fit. If there is any slackness, a new housing (which will come with shaft fitted) must be used.
9   The pump shares its drive with the distributor on all models except the 75 CL with air conditioning, where the distributor is mounted on the end of the camshaft carrier and driven from the end of the camshaft.

21 Camshaft, tappets and shims – inspection

1   The camshaft journals and cams should be smooth, without grooves or scores.
2   Wear in the camshaft carrier bearings can only be rectified by renewal of the carrier.
3   Tappet wear is usually very small and when they show slackness in their bores, it is probably the light alloy of the camshaft carrier which has worn.
4   Always measure the thickness of the valve clearance shims using a metric micrometer. Any grooving or wear marks in the shims should be rectified by renewal with ones of similar thickness.

22 Auxiliary shaft – inspection

1   The shaft journals, the fuel pump eccentric, and the drivegear for the distributor and oil pump should be smooth and shiny. If not, the shaft will have to be renewed.
2   The bushes should still be tight in the cylinder block, their oil holes lined up with those in the block.
3   Measure the bearing clearance. If excessive, the bushes will have to be renewed. They are a press fit, and require reaming with a special reamer after fitting. This is a job best done by a FIAT agent with the special tools.
4   Ensure the new bushes are fitted with the oil holes lined up.
5   Also check the driven gear and its bush.
6   It is recommended a new oil seal is fitted in the endplate. Hold the shaft in a vice, and remove the pulley. Fit the new oil seal in the endplate, lips inwards.

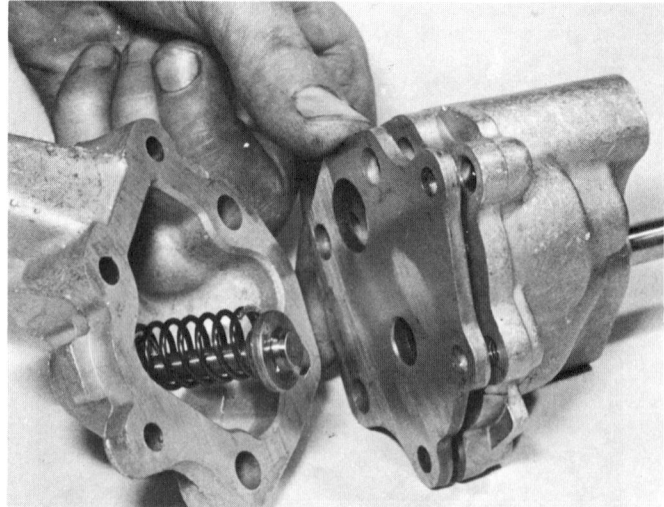
20.2 Oil pump dismantled

20.4 Oil pump driveshaft and gears

24.2 Engine mounting bracket circlip

23 Timing belt tensioner – servicing

1 Check the bearing revolves smoothly and freely, and has no play. Do not immerse it in cleaning fluid, as it is partially sealed. Wipe the outside, and then smear in some new general purpose grease.
2 The action of the spring will have been felt when the belt was taken off. It should be cleaned, and oiled, to prevent seizure through dirt and rust.

24 Engine/transmission mountings – inspection

1 Check the rubber of the mountings. If they are deformed or soft through oil contamination, or badly perished, they should be renewed.
2 Note the circlip on the engine right-hand mounting bracket (photo). This retains the timing belt tensioner plunger.

25 Lubrication system – general description

The oil pump is driven by the auxiliary shaft and is of the gear type. Incorporated in the pump is a pressure relief valve which opens when the oil pressure in the lubrication system is in excess of the normal operating pressure. The oil filter is of the disposable cartridge type and is located on the front of the engine. Incorporated in the filter mounting is a small, spring-loaded bypass valve which opens if the flow of oil through the filter drops due to severe contamination of the filter element.

The oil pump draws oil from the sump via a pick-up pipe and wire mesh filter, and it passes the oil, under pressure, through the filter element.

The crankshaft main bearings are supplied under pressure from drillings in the crankcase from the main oil gallery whilst the connecting rod big-end bearings are lubricated from the main bearings by oil forced through the crankshaft oilways. The camshaft bearings are fed from a drilling from the main oil gallery. The cams and tappets are lubricated by oil mist from outlets in the camshaft bearings.

The cylinder walls, pistons and gudgeon pins are lubricated by oil splashed up by the crankshaft webs. An oil pressure warning light is fitted to indicate when the pressure is too low.

26 Engine reassembly – general

Cleanliness is vital. Particles of grit in components, particularly when starting up, will score them, the situation being aggravated by the good new tight fit, and the time taken for the oil pump to circulate oil to wash them clean.

All parts must be liberally oiled, with engine oil. This oil must serve the component till the oilways are all filled by the pump, after which proper circulation will start. The oiling is also a final protection against dirt, as it washes as well as lubricating.

All parts must be tightened evenly and gradually. New gaskets and oil seals must be used to ensure an oil-tight engine. And they must only be fitted to clean surfaces, with the remains of old gaskets removed.

Lay out the parts in order, checking you know where everything goes before starting. Sheets of clean newspaper should be laid out on the working surface. Prevent wind blowing dust over the parts.

27.1A Crankcase main bearing shell

27.1B Crankcase main bearing shells correctly located

27.1C Main bearing cap and shell

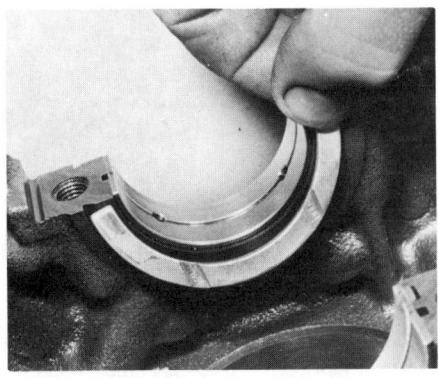

27.2 Fitting crankshaft thrust washer

27.3A Oiling the crankcase main bearing shells

27.3B Fitting the crankshaft

27 Crankshaft and main bearings – refitting

1   Fit the bearing shells to their crankcase seats and to their caps. The seatings and backs of the shells must be spotlessly clean, otherwise tight spots will occur when the crankshaft is fitted (photo).

2   Fit the thrust washer halves to their locations at No 5 bearing, noting that the oil grooves in the washers face outwards (photo).

3   Oil the surfaces of the bearing shells liberally and lower the crankshaft into position (photos).

4   Fit the main bearing caps to their correct locations, the correct way round (numerical chisel marks towards the auxiliary shaft). Tighten the cap bolts to the specified torque (photo).

5   Check that the crankshaft rotates smoothly and freely.

6   At this stage, the crankshaft endfloat should be checked. Prise the crankshaft fully in one direction and measure the gap between the machined face of the flywheel mounting flange and the crankcase.

Now push the shaft in the opposite direction and measure again (photo). Ideally, a dial gauge should be used for these measurements, but feeler blades will serve as a reasonable alternative. The difference between the two dimensions (feeler blades) or the total movement of the crankshaft (dial gauge) should be within the specified tolerance. If it is not, the thrust washers at No 5 main bearing will have to be changed for thicker ones; this will require taking out the crankshaft again to reach them.

7   Fit new oil seals to the retainers and, using new gaskets, bolt the retainers to the front and rear ends of the crankshaft, having first filled the oil seal lips with grease (photos).

28 Pistons and connecting rods – reassembly and refitting

1   Fit the new shells into the connecting rod and caps, ensuring the surfaces on which the shells seat, are clean and dry (photos).

27.4A Fitting the main bearing cap

27.4B Main bearing caps fitted

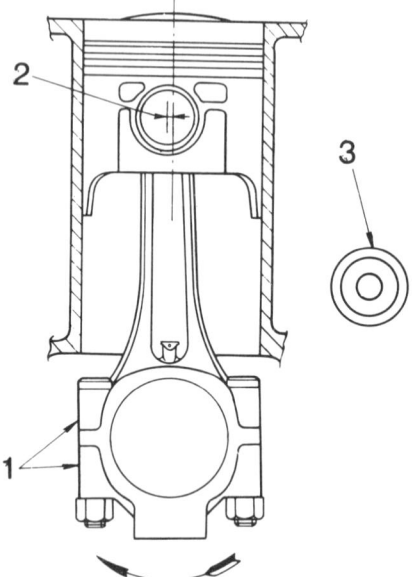

Fig. 1.7 Piston/connecting rod assembly diagram (Sec 28)

1   Matching numbers
2   Gudgeon pin offset
3   Auxiliary shaft
      Arrow indicates direction of
      rotation of crankshaft viewed from
      timing belt

27.6 Measuring crankshaft end float

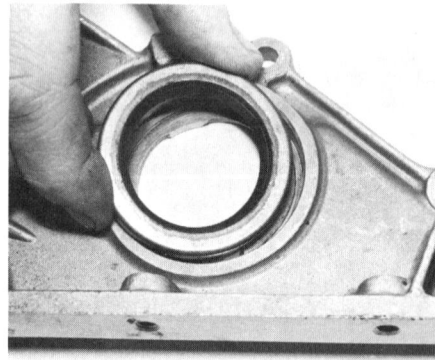

27.7A Crankshaft front oil seal

27.7B Crankshaft front oil seal retainer and gasket

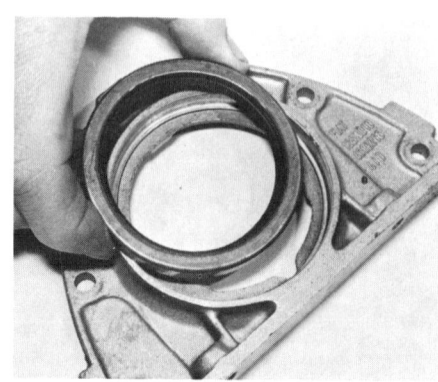

27.7C Crankshaft rear oil seal

27.7D Crankshaft rear oil seal retainer and gasket

2   Check that the piston ring gaps are evenly spaced at 120° intervals. Oil them liberally.
3   Fit a piston ring clamp to compress the rings.
4   Insert the piston/connecting rod into the cylinder bore, checking that the rod assembly is correct for that particular bore. The cap and rod matching numbers must be to the side of the piston crown which incorporates the deeper valve head clearance cut-outs. The cut-outs on the crown must have their deeper sections to the water pump side of the cylinder block (photos).
5   Push the piston into the bore until the piston ring clamp is against the cylinder block and then tap the crown of the piston lightly to push it out of the ring clamp and into the bore (photo).
6   Oil the crankshaft journal and fit the big-end of the connecting rod to the journal. Fit the big-end cap and nuts, checking that the cap is the right way round (photo).
7   Tighten the big-end nuts to the specified torque. The correct torque is important as the nuts have no locking arrangement. After tightening each big-end, check that the crankshaft rotates smoothly (photo).

29 Auxiliary shaft – refitting

1   Lubricate the auxiliary shaft bearings and fit the shaft into the crankcase (photos).
2   Fit a new seal to the endplate and fit the plate to the crankcase, using a new gasket (photos).
3   Fit the belt sprocket and partially tighten its bolt. Then, using an oil filter strap wrench or similar device to hold the sprocket against rotation, tighten the bolt to the specified torque. Take care not to damage the teeth of the sprocket, which is of fibre construction (photos).

30 Oil pump, sump and breather – refitting

1   Fit the oil drain pipe by tapping it into place, squarely in its hole in the crankcase. Tighten its retaining nut (photo).

28.1A Big-end cap and bearing shell

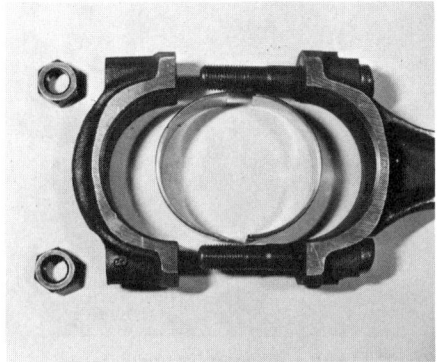
28.1B Connecting rod big-end components

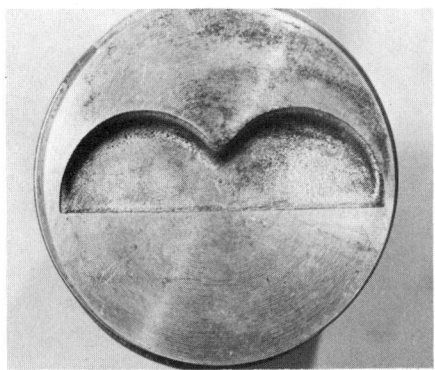
28.4A Piston crown recesses

28.4B Connecting rod big-end numbers

28.5 Fitting piston/connecting rod

28.6 Connecting rod big-end pulled onto crankshaft

28.7 Tightening big-end cap nut

29.1A Auxiliary shaft bearing

29.1B Fitting auxiliary shaft

2   Bolt up the oil pump, using a new gasket at its mounting flange (photos).

3   Fit the sump (using a new gasket) and tighten the securing screws to the specified torque (photos).

4   Insert the oil pump/driveshaft into the distributor hole. This does not have to be specially positioned as the distributor is splined to the shaft and can be set by moving its location in the splines (refer to Chapter 4) (photo). Where a camshaft-driven distributor is fitted, fit the oil pump driveshaft coverplate.

5   Fit the breather into its crankcase recess and tighten its securing bolt (photo).

31 Flywheel, clutch and crankshaft pulley – refitting

1   Make sure that the flywheel-to-crankshaft mounting flange sur-faces are clean. Although the bolt holes have unequal distances between them, it is possible to fit the flywheel in one of two alternative positions at 180° difference. Therefore if the original flywheel is being refitted, align the marks made before removal (photos).

2   Insert the bolts and tighten them to the specified torque, jamming the ring gear to prevent the flywheel turning. Fit the engine endplate (photos).

3   Fit the timing belt sprocket to the front end of the crankshaft (photo).

4   Fit the crankshaft pulley and the nut; tighten it to the specified torque, again jamming the starter ring gear to prevent the crankshaft from rotating (photos).

5   Fit the clutch assembly as described in Chapter 5.

6   A spigot bush is *not* fitted in the centre of the flywheel-to-crankshaft mounting flange (as is usually the case) to accept the transmission input shaft.

29.2A Auxiliary shaft endplate oil seal

29.2B Fitting auxiliary shaft endplate

29.3A Fitting auxiliary shaft belt sprocket

29.3B Tightening auxiliary shaft sprocket bolt

30.1 Fitting oil drain pipe

30.2 Oil pump and gasket

30.3A Locating new sump gasket

30.3B Fitting the sump

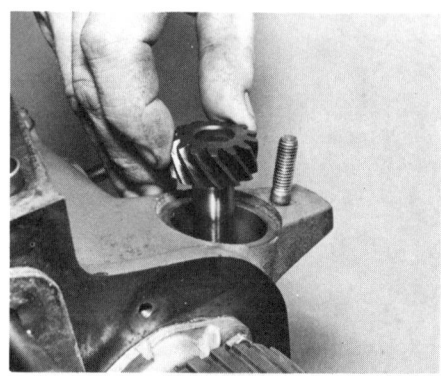

30.4 Fitting oil pump/distributor driveshaft to mesh with auxiliary shaft

32 Driveplate (automatic transmission) and crankshaft pulley – refitting

The operations are similar to those described in the preceding Section; tighten the driveplate bolts to their specified torque.

33 Cylinder head and camshaft carrier – refitting

1   Thoroughly clean the mating surfaces of the cylinder head and block.
2   To avoid the possibility of any valve heads impinging upon the piston crowns as the camshaft carrier is bolted down, turn the crankshaft by means of its pulley nut until No 4 piston is at TDC. If the timing index marks are embossed on the timing belt cover (and not on a separate right-angled plate), the belt cover will either have to be held

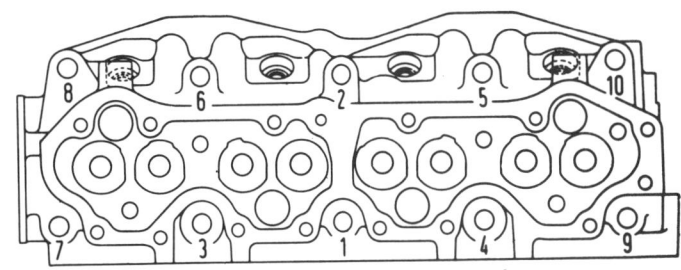

Fig. 1.8 Cylinder head bolt and nut tightening sequence (Sec 33)

30.5 Fitting crankcase breather housing

31.1 Fitting the flywheel

31.2A Tightening a flywheel bolt

31.2B Flywheel ring gear jamming device

31.2C Engine endplate

31.3 Fitting crankshaft belt sprocket

31.4A Crankshaft pulley nut

31.4B Tightening crankshaft pulley nut

33.4A Locating a cylinder head gasket

33.4B Cylinder head gasket upper surface marking

33.5 Lowering cylinder head into position

33.6 Tightening a cylinder head nut

33.8A Camshaft carrier oil seal

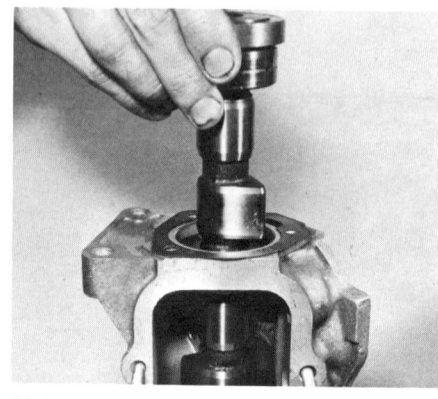

33.8B Fitting camshaft into carrier

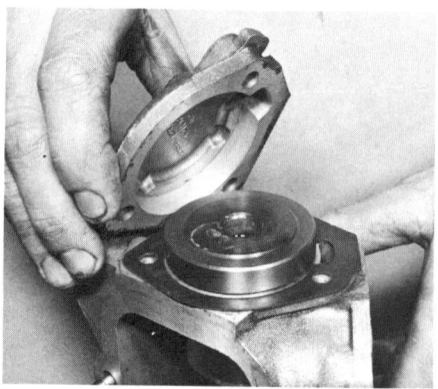

33.8C Fitting camshaft end cover and gasket

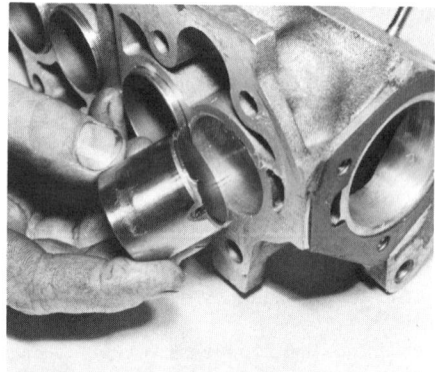

33.9 Fitting tappet to camshaft carrier

33.10 Camshaft sprocket timing aligned with pointer on belt backing plate

33.11A Fitting the camshaft carrier

33.11B Tightening the camshaft carrier bolts

33.14A Timing belt tensioner fitted

33.14B Fitting the timing belt

33.15A Tightening the camshaft sprocket bolt

33.15B Timing belt cover fitted

33.16A Fitting exhaust manifold

33.16B Fitting intake manifold

33.16C Fitting camshaft carrier top cover and gasket

34.4 Checking valve clearance

temporarily in position until the pulley notch is opposite the TDC mark or the vertical reference mark on the crankshaft front oil seal retainer used.

3   Fit the two dowels in the cylinder block (photo).
4   Fit the cylinder head gasket with the word 'ALTO' facing upwards (photos).
5   Fit the cylinder head on the cylinder block (photo).
6   Fit the large thick washers which spread the load on the aluminium head. Fit the cylinder head nuts and bolts. Using a torque wrench tighten them gradually (photo) and in the sequence shown in Fig. 1.8.
7   Tighten the cylinder head nuts and bolts progressively in stages until the specified torque is reached.
8   Fit a new oil seal to the end of the camshaft carrier, then oil the camshaft bearings and fit the camshaft. Fit a new gasket and bolt the end cover to the carrier (photo).
9   Fit the tappets and shims into their original bores in the carrier, holding them in position with a dab of thick grease (photo).
10 Set the camshaft so that the notch at the edge of the sprocket is aligned with the peak on the timing belt cover backing plate when fitted (photo).
11 Place a new gasket on the cylinder head, lower the carrier into position and tighten the securing bolts progressively and evenly to prevent distortion as some of the valve springs are compressed by the camshaft lobes. A socket will probably need grinding down in diameter slightly to reach the inner bolts (photos).
12 Fit the camshaft sprocket. Final tightening of the sprocket bolt can be left until after the belt is fitted and then gripped to prevent the sprocket rotating.
13 Fit the timing belt cover backing plate and check that the timing is set as described in paragraphs 2 and 10.
14 Fit the tensioner and timing belt. Tension it as described in Section 5 (photos).
15 Tighten the camshaft sprocket bolt to the specified torque and then fit the timing belt cover (photos).
16 Check the valve clearances, then bolt on the manifolds and the

camshaft carrier cover plate using new gaskets. Fit the exhaust manifold heat shield and throttle swivel plate (photos).

34 Valve clearance – adjustment

This should only be required if the valves have been renewed or ground in, or at high mileages when noise or poor engine performance indicates that a check is necessary.

It is important that the clearance is set correctly, otherwise the timing will be wrong and engine performance poor. If there is no clearance at all, the valves and their seats will soon burn. Always set the clearance with the engine cold.

1   Remove the camshaft cover. Jack-up a front wheel and engage top gear so that by turning the wheel, the crankshaft can be rotated.
2   Each tappet must be checked when the high point of the cam is pointing directly upward, away from the tappet.
3   Check the clearances in the firing order 1-3-4-2, No 1 cylinder being at the timing belt end of the engine. This will minimise the amount of crankshaft rotation required.
4   Insert the appropriate feeler blade between the heel of the cam and the tappet shim of the first valve. If necessary, increase or reduce the thickness of the feeler blade until it is a stiff, sliding fit. Record the thickness, which will, of course represent the valve clearance for this particular valve (photo).
5   Turn the crankshaft, check the second valve clearance and record it.
6   Repeat the operations on all the remaining valves, recording their respective clearances.
7   Remember that the clearance for inlet and exhaust valves differs – see Specifications. Counting from the timing cover end of the engine, the valve sequence is:

Inlet	*2-3-6-7*
Exhaust	*1-4-5-8*

8   Clearances which are incorrect will mean that the particular tappet shim will have to be changed. To remove the shim, turn the crankshaft until the cam high point is pointing directly upward. The tappet will now have to be depressed so that the shim can be extracted. A special tool (A60421) is available from your FIAT dealer for this job. Otherwise, you will have to make up a forked lever to locate on the rim of the tappet, but leaving room for the shim to be prised out by means of the cut-outs provided in the tappet rim.

9   Once the shim is extracted, establish its thickness and change it for a thicker or thinner one to bring the previously recorded clearance within specification. For example, if the measured valve clearance was 1.27 mm (0.05 in) too great, a shim *thicker* by this amount will be required. Conversely, if the clearance was 1.27 mm (0.05 in) too small, a shim *thinner* by this amount will be required.

10   Shims have their thickness (mm) engraved on them; although the engraved side should be fitted so as not to be visible, wear still occurs and often obliterates the number. In this case, measuring their thickness with a metric micrometer is the only method to establish their thickness (photo).

11   In practice, if several shims have to be changed, they can often be interchanged, so avoiding the necessity of having to buy more new shims than is necessary.

12   If more than two or three valve clearances are found to be incorrect, it will be more convenient to remove the camshaft carrier (see Section 4) for easier removal of the shims.

35 Engine ancillaries – refitting

With the engine reassembled, the ancillaries can be refitted before the engine/transmission is reconnected or fitted in the car.

1   Apply grease to the rubber sealing ring of a new oil filter canister and screw it on, using hand pressure only (photo).

2   Screw in the oil pressure and coolant temperature sender switches (photo).

3   Fit the fuel pump (see Chapter 3).

4   Fit the coolant pump and the thermostat housing (see Chapter 2) (photo).

5   Fit the intermediate flange plate, the carburettor and connect the coolant hoses which run between the flange plate and the thermostat housing.

6   Fit the distributor (see Chapter 4). On models with air conditioning (where the distributor is located on the end of the camshaft carrier), make sure that the blanking plate is fitted to the normal distributor hole in the side of the crankcase.

7   Fit the alternator and the drivebelts; tension the belts.

8   Fit the starter motor (photo).

36 Engine/manual transmission – fitting

Fitting the engine/automatic transmission is described in Chapter 6, Part B. With the engine/transmission reconnected (see Section 11), the engine should be fitted according to model type; 65 models from underneath, 75 and North American models from above.

65 models

1   Have the engine/transmission resting on the floor under the front end of the car which is raised sufficiently high for the assembly to pass underneath.

2   The driveshafts should be connected to the final drive and tied up to the upper part of the engine.

3   Raise the engine/transmission on a trolley jack or hoist until the driveshafts can be inserted into their wheel hubs and the lower parts of the suspension struts reconnected to the steering knuckles.

4   Continue to raise the engine until the engine left and right-hand mountings can be reconnected.

5   Reconnect the radius rods and bolt the brake calipers into position.

6   Reconnect the steering tie-rod balljoints and the track control arms.

34.10 Valve tappet and shim

35.1 Fitting oil filter

35.2A Oil pressure sender switch

35.2B Coolant temperature sender switch

35.4 Coolant pump and water distribution tube fitted

35.8 Starter motor

7 Screw on the driveshaft/hub nuts. Have an assistant apply the footbrake while these nuts are tightened to the specified torque, and staked.

8 Raise and simultaneously tilt the engine forward, to enable the centre mounting and crossmember to be fitted.

75 and North American models

9 With the engine/transmission resting on the floor, attach a suitable hoist to it and lift it so that the assembly hangs transversely over the engine compartment.

10 Check that the left and right-hand mounting pad nuts are not tight, but will allow the mountings to be swivelled (photo).

11 Lower the assembly carefully into the engine compartment, adjusting its position as necessary to avoid the various attachments to the engine wing valances (photos).

12 Align the engine mountings and bolt them in position (photos).

13 Now tilt the engine forward by repositioning the hoist or using a jack and a block of wood as an insulator until the centre mounting and crossmember can be bolted in position. Remove the jack or hoist (photos).

14 Reconnect the driveshafts and tighten the new socket headed flange bolts.

All models

15 Working underneath the car, connect the gearchange control rod linkage, adjusting it if necessary, as described in Chapter 6.

16 Fit the exhaust pipe. Use a new copper gasket at the manifold-to-downpipe flange joint, tighten the nuts using a socket and a long extension bar, then bend up the lockplate tabs (photos).

17 Working within the engine compartment, connect the clutch control cable to the release lever and adjust the cable if necessary, as described in Chapter 5.

18 Connect the throttle cable to the carburettor. Check that the throttle valve plate moves from fully closed to fully open during the stroke of the accelerator pedal. If it does not, adjust the throttle cable at the carburettor (photos).

36.10 Tightening engine mounting pad nuts

36.11A Fitting engine and manual transmission (75 models)

36.11B Engine front face (75 models)

36.12A Engine right-hand mounting

36.12B Engine left-hand mounting

36.13A Engine centre crossmember

13.13B Engine centre crossmember mounting to body

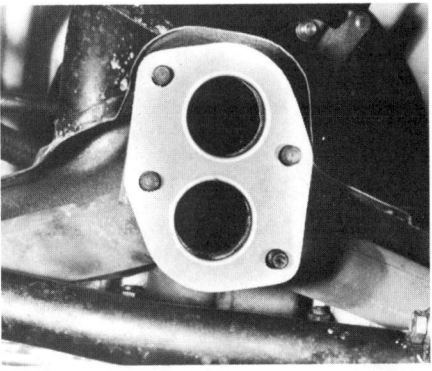
36.16A Exhaust manifold-to-downpipe flange gasket

36.16B Exhaust downpipe flange nuts

19 Attach the choke control cable or the automatic choke hoses, according to model (photo).
20 Connect the brake vacuum servo hose to the inlet manifold.
21 Connect the speedometer electric leads at the plug (photo).
22 Connect the fuel pipes to the carburettor. The fuel return pipe has no clips (photo).
23 Connect the coolant pipe to the carburettor lower housing (photo).
24 Connect the heater hoses (photo).
25 Reconnect the electrical leads, including those to the following:

> *Starter solenoid*
> *Oil pressure switch*
> *Coolant temperature switch (photo)*
> *The alternator (connector plugs located at right-hand side of heater assembly)*

26 Fit the distributor and set the static timing as described in Chapter 4.
27 Fit the distributor rotor and the cap; connect the high tension (HT) leads to the coil centre and the spark plugs and low tension (LT) lead to the coil negative terminal.
28 Connect the battery positive lead to the starter solenoid terminal and clamp the negative lead under the battery tray (photo).
29 Lower the radiator/fan assembly into position so that the rubber insulated lugs at its base engage in their slots. Fit the top retaining bracket.
30 Connect the radiator coolant hoses and the electrical leads to the fan thermostatic switch.
31 Connect the reverse lamp switch leads.
32 Lower the battery onto its tray and fit the heat deflecting shield and retaining clamp.

36.18A Throttle linkage swivel plate

36.18B Connecting throttle link rod balljoint

36.19 Choke cable connection to carburettor (Weber 34 ICEV type)

36.21 Speedometer electric leads

36.22 Carburettor fuel inlet hose (1) and return (2) (arrowed)

36.23 Carburettor coolant heater pipe at thermostat housing

36.24 Heater hose connection

36.25 Coolant temperature switch lead

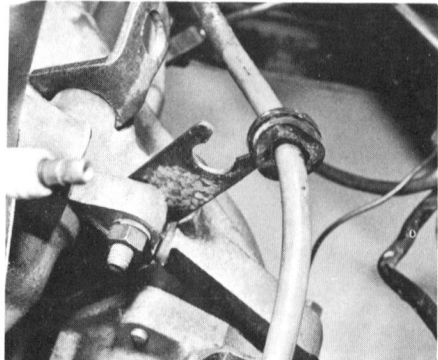
36.28A Battery positive lead grommet and support bracket

36.28B Battery negative lead clamp under battery tray

36.34A Air cleaner lower mounting plate

36.34B Hose connections on underside of air cleaner

36.34C Air cleaner, casing, element and upper mounting plate

36.34D Air cleaner bracket on camshaft carrier

36.35 Tightening air cleaner lid nuts

33 Connect the battery leads to the battery terminals.

34 Fit the air cleaner and connect the flexible hoses to the underside of its casing. Note the reinforcement plates above and below the casing at the carburettor throat (photo).

35 Insert a new air cleaner element and bolt on the cleaner lid. Set the air intake for 'winter' or 'summer' (not temperature controlled type) (photos).

36 With the help of an assistant, refit the bonnet.

37 Fill the engine, transmission and cooling system. Refit the spare wheel and tools.

38 Make a final visual check to see that everything has been connected; remove any rags or tools from the engine compartment.

Cars with emission control systems

39 Reconnect all hoses and electrical leads according to the system fitted (refer to Chapter 3).

Cars with air conditioning

40 Once the condenser and compressor have been refitted and reconnected, have the system charged with refrigerant by your dealer or a refrigeration engineer.

37 Engine – initial start-up after major overhaul

1 If new bearings and rings have been fitted, it is likely that the engine will be stiff to turn so make sure the battery is well charged.

2 Switch on the ignition and check that appropriate warning lights come on.

3 Start up the engine. If it refuses to start, refer to the Fault Diagnosis Section in the Introduction to this manual.

4 Watch the oil pressure warning light and alternator charging indicator light. If there is no charge or if the oil pressure warning light does not go out after a second or two, having had time to fill the new oil filter switch off and recheck.

5 If the warning lights go out, set the engine to run on fast idle and check the engine for leaks.

6 Check the coolant level; it will probably go down as air locks are filled.

7 Keep the engine running at a fast idle and bring it up to normal working temperature. As the engine warms up, there will be some odd smells and smoke from parts getting hot and burning off oil deposits.

8 When the engine running temperature has been reached, adjust the idling speed, as described in Chapter 3. Check and, if necessary, adjust the ignition timing using a stroboscope (see Chapter 4).

9 Stop the engine and wait a few minutes; check to see if there are any coolant or oil leaks.

10 Road test the car to check that the engine is running with the correct smoothness and power. If it does not, refer to the Fault Diagnosis Section in the Introduction of this manual. Do not race the engine. If new bearings and/or pistons and rings have been fitted, it should be treated as a new engine and run it at reduced speed for at least 500 miles (800 km).

11 After 500 miles (800 km), change the engine oil and filter.

38 Fault diagnosis – engine

Symptom	Reason(s)
Engine fails to turn when starter operated	Battery discharged Battery terminals loose or corroded Battery earth to body defective Engine/transmission earth strap broken or loose Disconnected or broken wire in starter circuit Ignition/starter switch defective Starter pinion jammed in mesh with flywheel gear Automatic transmission inhibitor switch defective or maladjusted Starter motor or solenoid defective (see Chapter 9) Major mechanical failure (seizure) or long disuse (piston rings rusted to bores)
Engine turns slowly and fails to start	Battery discharged Battery terminals loose or corroded Battery or engine earth strap loose Starter motor connections loose Oil in engine/transmission too thick Starter motor defective
Engine turns normally but will not start	Fuel tank empty Damp or dirty HT leads, distributor cap or plug bodies Broken, loose or disconnected LT leads Contact breaker points dirty or incorrectly gapped Other ignition fault (see Chapter 4) Other fuel system fault (see Chapter 3) Valve timing incorrect (after rebuild)
Engine fires but will not run	Insufficient choke (cold engine) or defective automatic choke Fuel starvation or tank empty Ignition fault (see Chapter 4) Other fuel system fault (see Chapter 3)
Difficult starting when cold	Insufficient choke or defective automatic choke Fouled or incorrectly gapped spark plugs Damp or dirty HT leads, distributor cap or spark plug bodies Dirty or maladjusted contact breaker points Other ignition fault or timing maladjustment (see Chapter 4) Fuel system or emission control fault (see Chapter 3) Poor compression (may be due to incorrect valve clearances, burnt or sticking valves, blown head gasket, worn or damaged pistons, rings or bores) Incorrect valve timing (after rebuild)
Difficult starting when hot	Incorrect use of manual choke or defective automatic choke Fuel line vapour lock (especially in hot weather or at high altitudes) Incorrect ignition timing Other fuel system or emission control fault (see Chapter 3) Poor compression (see above)
Engine slow to warm up	Choke linkage maladjusted or automatic choke defective Air cleaner temperature control unit defective Thermostat stuck open (see Chapter 2) Other fuel system fault (see Chapter 3)
Engine idles roughly	Carburettor incorrectly adjusted Other fuel system fault (see Chapter 3) Spark plugs fouled or incorrectly gapped. Ignition timing incorrect Incorrect valve clearances Widely differing cylinder compressions Other ignition fault (see Chapter 4) Low battery voltage (charging fault)
Engine lacks power	Ignition timing incorrect Air cleaner choked Valve clearances incorrect Brakes binding Poor compression Other fuel system fault (see Chapter 3) Other ignition system fault (see Chapter 4) Carbon build-up in cylinder head

Symptom	Reason(s)
Engine misfires throughout speed range	Defective or fouled spark plug Loose, cracked or defective HT lead Maladjusted, sticking or burnt valves Ignition timing incorrect Blown head gasket Fuel contaminated Other ignition fault (see Chapter 4) Other fuel system fault (see Chapter 3)
Poor engine braking	Throttle opener dashpot not operating correctly. Other fuel system fault (see Chapter 3) Low compression
Pre-ignition (pinking) during acceleration	Incorrect grade of fuel being used Ignition timing overadvanced Engine overheated Excessive carbon build-up Other ignition fault (see Chapter 4) Fuel system fault (see Chapter 3)
Engine runs on after switching off	Idle speed too high Incorrect type of spark plug Overheating Excessive carbon build-up Anti-diesel solenoid defective Other emission control fault (see Chapter 3)
Low oil pressure (verify accuracy of sender before dismantling engine!)	Level low Engine overheating Incorrect grade of oil in use Oil filter clogged or bypass valve stuck Pressure relief valve stuck or defective Oil pick-up strainer clogged or loose Main or big-end bearings worn Oil pump worn or mountings loose
Excessive oil consumption	Overfilling Leaking gaskets or drain plug washer Valve stem oil seals worn, damaged or missing after rebuild Valve stems and/or guides worn Piston rings and/or bores worn Piston oil return holes clogged
Oil contaminated with water	Excessive cold running Leaking head gasket Cracked block or head
Oil contaminated with fuel	Excessive use of choke or defective automatic choke Worn piston rings and/or bores
Unusual mechanical noises	Unintentional mechanical contact (eg fan blades) Worn drivebelt Worn valvegear (tapping noises from top of engine) or incorrect clearance Peripheral component fault (generator, water pump etc) Worn big-end bearings (regular heavy knocking, perhaps less under load) Worn main bearings (rumbling and knocking, perhaps worsening under load) Small-end bushes or gudgeon pins worn (light metallic tapping) Piston slap (most noticeable when engine cold)

Note: When investigating starting and uneven running faults, do not be tempted into snap diagnosis. Start from the beginning of the check procedure and follow it through. It will take less time in the long run. Poor performance from an engine in terms of power and economy is not normally diagnosed quickly. In any event, the ignition and fuel systems must be checked first before assuming any further investigation needs to be made.

Chapter 2
Cooling, heating and air conditioning system

For modifications, and information applicable to later models, see Supplement at end ot manual

Contents

Specifications

System type .... Pressurised, front mounted radiator with remote expansion tank. Belt-driven coolant pump, electric radiator fan.

Thermostat
Opening temperature .... 172.4 to 183.2°F (78 to 84°C)
Fully open .... 194 to 201°F (90 to 94°C)

Radiator cap pressure rating .... 11 lbf/in² (0.8 kgf/cm²)

Electric fan operating temperatures
Cut-in .... 194 to 201°F (90 to 94°C)
Cut-out .... 185 to 192°F (85 to 89°C)

Coolant capacity
65 models .... 13.9 Imp pints (16.7 US pints, 7.9 litres)
75 and North American models .... 14.1 Imp pints (16.9 US pints, 8.0 litres)

Antifreeze type/specification .... Ethylene glycol based antifreeze to BS 3151, 3152 or 6580 (Duckhams Universal Antifreeze and Summer Coolant)

1 General description

The cooling system comprises a front mounted radiator with remote expansion tank, a coolant pump (belt-driven from the crankshaft pulley), and a thermostatically controlled electric radiator cooling fan.

In order to assist rapid warm-up, a thermostat is located in a housing at the left-hand end of the cylinder head. The hose connections to the thermostat housing vary according to model, due to the fact that on models with air conditioning, the ignition distributor is mounted at the left-hand end of the camshaft carrier. On some emission controlled models, an air pump is mounted at the right-hand end of the camshaft carrier.

On air conditioned models, the drivebelt that drives the alternator and the coolant pump also drives the compressor. The condensor for the air conditioning system is located at the front of the engine compartment, on the right-hand side of the radiator.

The heater is connected to the engine cooling system. The heater casing, which incorporates the matrix and blower, is bolted to the right-hand side of the engine compartment rear bulkhead.

The heater control panel is located under the instrument panel. Stale air is exhausted through extractor grilles, located on either side of the rear window.

Coolant system connecting hoses also heat the lower housing of the carburettor; on North American models with a Weber two barrel carburettor, the coolant is used to heat the automatic choke.

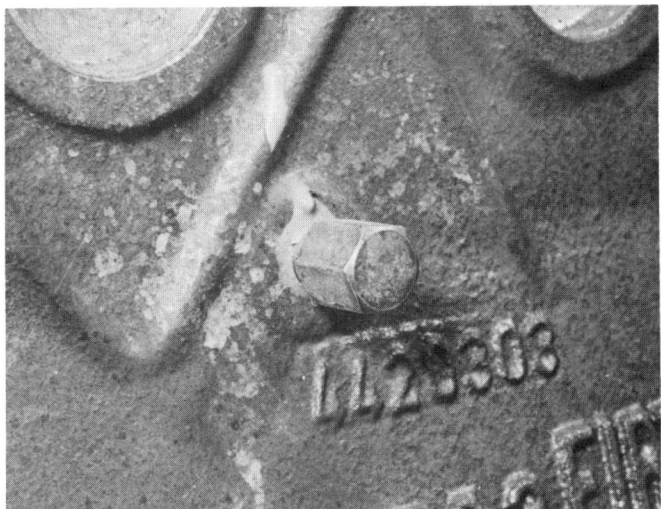

2.3 Cylinder block drain plug

3.5 Radiator cap

3.6 Radiator expansion pipe and upper mounting bracket

2 Cooling system – draining

1   Turn the heater temperature control fully clockwise.
2   Open the bonnet, then remove the caps from the radiator and the expansion tank.
3   If the cooling system is being drained in order to carry out repair or overhaul, and the coolant is to be re-used, place large containers under the radiator drain tap and the cylinder block drain plug (photo).
4   Open the drain taps and allow all the coolant to run out. If either drain hole is restricted due to sludge or rust, use a piece of wire to probe it.
5   To drain the expansion tank, disconnect the outlet hose from the tank. Be very careful not to let antifreeze mixture come into contact with the paintwork; it acts as a paint stripper!
6   Where necessary, place a cold water hose in the neck of the radiator and let it run until the water comes out of the drain holes quite clean.
7   In extreme cases of neglect, the radiator can be removed, the hose placed in the return stub and the radiator reverse flushed.
8   Provided the correct antifreeze or corrosion inhibiting mixture is always used in the cooling system, and is renewed at the specified intervals, rust, corrosion or sludge will rarely occur and flushing will never be required.
9   The use of radiator cleansers is not recommended. It seldom proves effective if the fine tubes of the matrix have been clogged as a result of neglect, causing the formation of rust or scale by using hard plain water in the system.

3 Cooling system – filling

1   Close the radiator and cylinder block drain taps.
2   Check that the heater temperature control is still set in the fully clockwise position.
3   Fill the radiator slowly with the correct coolant mixture (see Section 4) to the level of the filler neck.
4   Reconnect the hose to the expansion tank and fill the tank to the level mark with the same coolant mixture.
5   Refit the radiator cap (photo).
6   Start the engine and run it at a fast idle speed until air bubbles cease to appear in the coolant in the expansion tank (photo).
7   On some 75 models (without air conditioning), a bleed valve is located at the side of the heater air intake. Release any trapped air at this point, closing the bleed valve as soon as coolant is ejected.
8   When the engine has cooled down, top-up the expansion tank to the correct level.
9   The addition of coolant during normal operation should seldom if ever be required. If it is, always fill through the expansion tank. *Never release the radiator cap as a means of filling, especially if the engine is hot, scalding may result from the pressurised system.*
10 The need for frequent topping-up will indicate a leak in the system. An internal leak, caused by a blown gasket or cracked cylinder head or block, can be detected by a rise in the engine oil level or water being blown out of the exhaust in greater quantities than can be expected from the condensation during the initial engine warm-up period.

4 Anti-freeze and corrosion inhibitors

1   In cold climates, antifreeze is needed for two reasons. In extreme cases, if the coolant in the engine freezes solid it could crack the cylinder block or head. But also in cold weather, with the circulation restricted by the thermostat, and any warm water that *is* getting to the radiator being at the top, the bottom of the radiator could freeze, and so block circulation completely, making the coolant trapped in the engine boil.
2   The antifreeze should be mixed in the proportions advocated by the makers, according to the climate. There are two levels of protection. The first cuts risk of damage, as the antifreeze goes mushy before freezing. The second, valid all year round, is the corrosion protection it offers – see below. The normal proportion in a temperate climate is 25% antifreeze by volume, with 33 1/3% for a colder one. This mix should be used for topping-up too, otherwise the mixture will gradually get weaker.

3   Antifreeze should be left in through the summer. It has an important secondary function, to act as an inhibitor against corrosion. In the cooling system are many different metals, in particular the aluminium of the cylinder head. In contact with the coolant this sets up electrolytic corrosion, accentuated by any dirt in the system. This corrosion can be catastrophically fast. Reputable antifreeze of a suitable formula must be used.

4   After about two years, the effectiveness of the antifreeze's inhibitor is used up. It must then be discarded, and the system flushed as described earlier and then refilled with new coolant.

5   In warm climates free from frost, an inhibitor should be used. Again, a reputable make giving full protection must be chosen and renewed every two years. Inhibitors with dyes are useful for finding leaks, and on some makes the dye shows when the inhibiting ability is finished.

5   Thermostat housing – removal, testing and refitting

1   The thermostat assembly is mounted on the flywheel end of the cylinder block.

2   The housing accepts connections for three large coolant hoses and a small diameter hose which connects to the carburettor lower housing adaptor flange (photo).

3   Unfortunately, the thermostat/housing is a complete unit and failure of the thermostat will necessitate the purchase of the complete component.

4   If the thermostat/housing is removed from the engine, it can be suspended in water and the water heated to check out its opening temperature. Movement of the thermostat valve can be observed to some extent through the openings in the housing.

5   When refitting, always use a new gasket at its mounting face (photo).

6   Radiator fan thermostatic switch – removal, checking and refitting

1   Partially drain the cooling system to bring the coolant level below the thermostatic switch in the radiator bottom tank.

2   If the thermostatic switch is being removed because the fan is not operating and the switch is suspect, check the fan fuse and the relay fuse first, before removing the switch.

3   To remove the switch, disconnect the leads from the terminals and unscrew the switch (photo).

4   Connect a test bulb across the switch terminals and immerse the sensing part of the switch in a container of water. Heat the water and, using a thermometer, check the temperature of the water when the bulb lights up, indicating the switch is functioning. The switch should operate at approximately 194°F (90°C). Allow the water to cool and check that the switch cuts out at 185°F (85°C). Renew a faulty switch.

5   Refitting of the switch is the reverse of the removal procedure. Always fit a new O-ring on the switch.

7   Radiator fan, motor and relay – checking

1   If the fan is not operating, and the fuses and thermoswitch have been checked and found serviceable, check the fan motor and relay by connecting the two thick wires to the relay together. If the fan motor operates, the relay is at fault and must be renewed. If the fan motor does not operate, that is where the fault lies and the motor must be renewed.

2   If the cut-out, cut-in system fails, this can be temporarily overcome as follows:

    (a)   Connect both thermoswitch leads to the same terminal. If it is the switch which is faulty the fan will operate and run all the time the ignition is switched on. If the fan does not operate reconnect the leads in the normal way

    (b)   Connect the two thick wires to the relay together, if the relay is at fault the fan will operate and run all the time even when the ignition is switched off

Note: *Only the switch circuit at the relay is controlled by the ignition switch. The main feed through the relay is direct. If the relay leads are*

5.2 Thermostat housing

5.5 Fitting thermostat housing and gasket

6.3 Radiator fan thermostatic switch

8.4 Removing radiator/fan assembly

8.5 Radiator/fan assembly removed

8.6 Radiator lower mounting spigot and rubber insulator

connected together, they must be disconnected when the engine is switched off or the battery will be discharged.

8 Radiator/fan assembly – removal and refitting

1   Drain the cooling system as previously described.
2   Disconnect the hoses from the radiator.
3   Disconnect the electrical leads from the thermostatic switch on the radiator and from the fan plug.
4   Extract the radiator bracket mounting bolts and lift the radiator out of the engine compartment (photo).
5   The radiator cooling fins can be cleaned with compressed air or a jet of water from a hose to remove flies and dirt (photo).
6   Refitting is a reversal of the removal process, but make sure the radiator bottom positioning spigots engage correctly (photo)

9 Coolant pump – removal, overhaul and refitting

1   To gain access to the coolant pump, open the bonnet and remove the air cleaner.
2   Slacken the alternator pivot and adjustment strap bolts, push the alternator in towards the engine and slip the drivebelt from the coolant pump pulley.
3   On models using an air pump mounted at the timing belt end of the camshaft carrier, this is belt-driven from the inner groove of a double pulley on the coolant pump. Slip off this belt by slackening the air pump mounting bolts and adjuster, and moving the pump as necessary.
4   Drain the cooling system as previously described.
5   Disconnect the hoses from the coolant pump.
6   Unscrew and remove the coolant pump securing bolts, and lift the pump from the engine. Peel away and discard the old gasket.

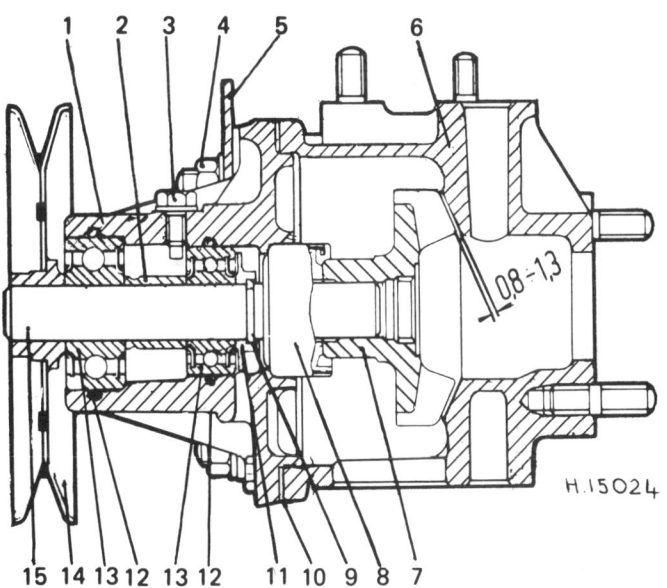

Fig. 2.1 Sectional view of the coolant pump (Sec 9)

1 Pump cover	9 Circlip
2 Bearing spacer	10 Gasket
3 Bearing stop screw	11 Shouldered ring
4 Cover nuts	12 Grommets
5 Lifting bracket	13 Bearing
6 Housing	14 Pulley
7 Impeller	15 Shaft
8 Gland (seal)	

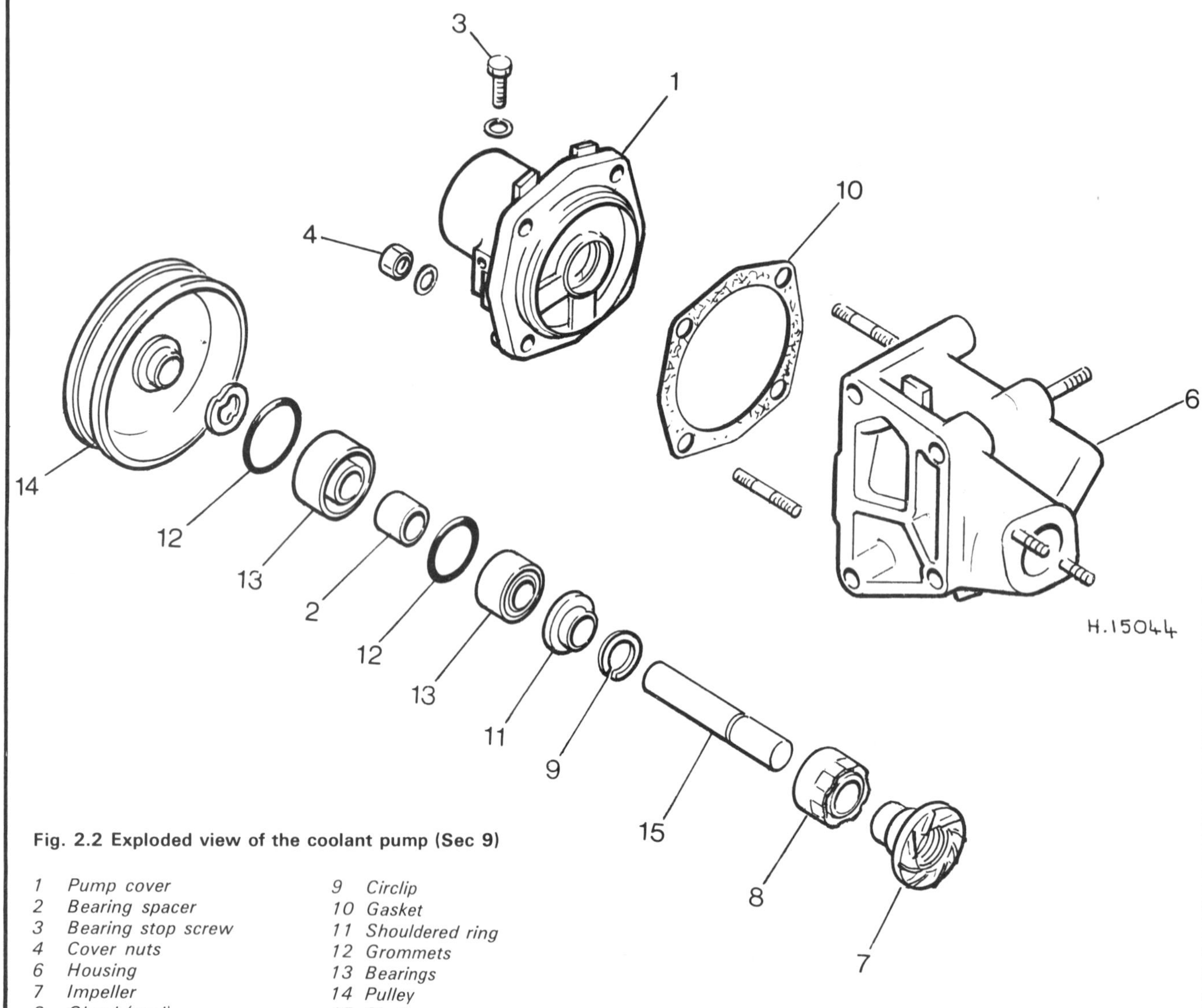

Fig. 2.2 Exploded view of the coolant pump (Sec 9)

1	Pump cover	9	Circlip
2	Bearing spacer	10	Gasket
3	Bearing stop screw	11	Shouldered ring
4	Cover nuts	12	Grommets
6	Housing	13	Bearings
7	Impeller	14	Pulley
8	Gland (seal)	15	Shaft

H.15044

9.10 Both halves of coolant pump separated

9.21 Fitting coolant pump

Fig. 2.3 Single drivebelt arrangement (Sec 10)

A   Adjuster bolt
B   Mounting bolt
Tensioning point arrowed

7   The pump is likely to need overhaul for worn or noisy bearings, or if the gland is leaking. There is a drain hole between the gland and the bearings to prevent contamination of the bearing grease by leaks, and possible damage to the bearings. Gland leaks are usually worse when the engine is not running. Once started, a leak is likely to get worse quickly, so should be dealt with soon. Worn bearings are likely to be noted first due to noise. To check them, the pulley should be rocked firmly, when any free movement can be felt despite the belt. But if the bearings are noisy, yet there is not apparently any free play, then the belt should be removed so the pump can be rotated by hand to check the smoothness of the bearings.
8   Dismantling and assembly of the pump requires the use of a press, and it is preferable to fit a new pump.
9   For those having the necessary facilities, overhaul can be carried out as follows.
10 Remove the retaining nuts and separate the two halves of the pump (photo).
11 The pump shaft is an interference fit in the impeller, bearings, and pulley boss. How the pump is dismantled depends on whether only the gland needs renewing or the bearings as well, and what puller or press is available to get everything apart.
12 Assuming complete dismantling is required, proceed as follows. Supporting it close in at the boss, press the shaft out of the pulley. Pull the impeller off the other end of the shaft.
13 Take out the bearing stop screw.
14 From the impeller end, press the shaft with the bearings out of the cover half of the housing.
15 Press the shaft out of the bearings, take off the spacer, the circlip, and the shouldered ring.
16 Do not immerse the bearings in cleaning fluid. They are 'sealed'. Liquid will get in, but a thorough clean will be impracticable, and it will be impossible to get new grease in.
17 Check all the parts, get a new gland, two new grommets, and a new gasket. Scrape all deposits out of the housing and off the impeller.
18 To reassemble, start by inserting the new grommets in their grooves by each bearing. Fit the circlip to the shaft, then the shouldered ring, bearings and spacer. Fit the shaft and bearing assembly into the cover. Fit the stop screw. Press on the pulley.
19 Fit the new gland (seal), seating it in its location in the cover. Press the impeller onto the shaft. The impeller must be put on part way, and then the housing held in place to see how far the impeller must go down the shaft to give the correct clearance, which is 0.8 to 1.3 mm (0.03 to 0.05 in) as shown in Fig. 2.1.
20 The impeller clearance can be checked through the coolant passage in the side of the pump.
21 Refitting is a reversal of the removal process, but use a new flange gasket and tension the drivebelts as described in the next Section (photo).
22 Refill the cooling system.

10.8A Tightening adjuster link bolt after tensioning the drivebelt

10 Drivebelts – removal, refitting and tensioning

1   The number of drivebelts and their arrangement depends upon the car model and its equipment.
2   All models have a single drivebelt which is driven from the crankshaft pulley, to drive in turn the alternator and the coolant pump.
3   On cars equipped with an air pump for the exhaust emission control system, the pump is mounted on the end of the camshaft carrier (above the coolant pump), and is driven by a second belt from the inner groove of a twin coolant pump pulley.
4   On cars equipped with air conditioning, the compressor is located above the alternator on the right-hand end of the engine.
5   Removal of the drivebelt on cars having only one belt is simply a matter of releasing the alternator mounting and adjustment link bolts, pushing the alternator in towards the engine and slipping the belt from the pulleys.
6   On cars with two belts, to remove the inner belt, the outer one must first be removed as described in the preceding paragraphs. Then the air pump or compressor mounting and adjuster must be released and moved to release tension on the belt for it to be slipped off its pulleys.
7   The correct tensioning of the drivebelts is essential to prevent slipping, or, conversely to avoid wear in the bearings of the driven units by over-tensioning.

10.8B Checking drivebelt tension

8   The correct tension of a drivebelt is obtained when it can be depressed at the centre of its longest run by 9.5 mm (0.375 in) using moderate thumb pressure. Adjustment is made by releasing the mounting and adjuster link bolts, then moving the alternator or other unit towards or away from the engine as necessary (photos).

11 Heater controls – general description

The description below relates to left-hand drive cars. On right-hand drive cars the left-hand and right-hand control knobs are reversed.

The heater and ventilation system control panel, together with the air duct assembly, is mounted under the facia panel and has connections to the air intake on the bonnet lid, the engine cooling system, blower fan wiring and the outlet ducts for fresh, cold or warm air for interior heating, demisting or defrosting of the windscreen.

The heater controls are somewhat complicated. The left-hand circular control knob regulates the volume of air passing through the heater. If the knob is turned clockwise until the needle in the indicator moves, the booster fan is brought into operation. Further movement of the control knob will increase the speed of the booster fan through 1 (low) 2 (medium) and 3 (high speed) settings.

The right-hand circular control knob adjusts the temperature of the heater air. As the knob is rotated clockwise, the needle in the right-hand indicator moves into the red sector. The higher it goes, the warmer the air.

The slide switch on the extreme right-hand side directs the airflow from the heater. In the 'up' position, air is ejected from the windscreen demister slots and in the 'down' position, all outlet vents are open.

The air from the facia side and centre vents is controlled for direction by the levers integral in the outlet grilles.

12 Heater – removal, dismantling, reassembly and refitting

1   Turn the heater temperature control knob fully clockwise, then drain the cooling system as described in Section 2 of this Chapter.
2   Working within the engine compartment, disconnect the cooling hoses from the pipe stubs on the heater casing.
3   Unscrew and remove the three nuts which hold the heater casing to the engine compartment rear bulkhead.
4   Disconnect the battery, then disconnect the leads from the coiled element type resistance unit on the side of the heater casing (photo).
5   Withdraw these disconnected leads through the grommet, into the heater casing interior.
6   Reach down into the heater casing air intake and release the control cable clips, then pull the heater casing forward until a gap of about 54 mm (2 in) appears between the heater and the bulkhead. The control and electrical cables will now be clearly visible, routed under the facia panel from the control panel within the car (photo).
7   Working within the car, unscrew and remove the four screws which secure the heater control panel housing to the facia panel. Lower the housing, which may be stuck and require prising from the sound deadening felt (photo).
8   The heater (or the control panel) may now be removed independently, once the fan motor leads and the control cables for the flap valves are disconnected.
9   The heater casing can be dismantled if the spring securing clips are prised off and the two screws at the rear extracted.

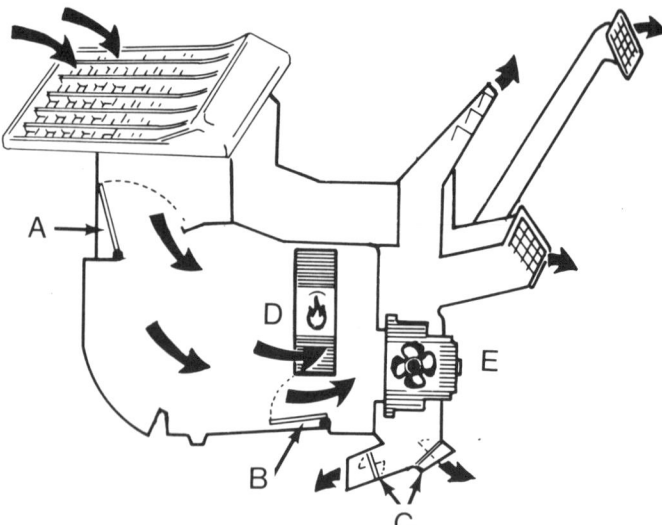

Fig. 2.4 Diagrammatic view of heater (Sec 12)

A   Air intake flap valve
B   Bypass flap valve
C   Air outlet deflectors
D   Matrix
E   Blower motor

10   If removal has been necessary because of a faulty coolant valve, motor or leaking matrix, the heater can be dismantled and either or both components removed for renewal. **Note:** *Soldering a leaking heater matrix seldom proves satisfactory.*
11   When reassembling the heater, refer to the diagram and adjust the controls in accordance with the following arrangement.
12   With the right-hand circular control knob (temperature) in the COLD position, the coolant valve on the heater should be closed and the flap (B) fully open (see Fig. 2.4). As the knob is turned in a clockwise direction, the coolant valve begins to open and the flap to close. When the knob is in the HOT position, the flap is fully closed and all incoming air must be directed through the matrix to absorb maximum heat.
13   The left-hand circular control knob not only controls the speed of the blower motor but simultaneously adjusts the position of the flap (A) (seeFig. 2.4). The flap should be closed when the control knob in in the OFF position and fully open when the knob is in the HIGH SPEED setting.
14   The extreme right-hand knurled control wheel should close the flaps (C) (see Fig. 2.4) when the wheel is in the fully up position or open them when it is down.
15   Adjust the linkage as necessary to achieve the foregoing conditions.
16   Refitting is a reversal of the removal process. Make sure that all joints between the heater casing and the engine compartment are thoroughly sealed with mastic to prevent the entry of fumes to the car interior.
17   Fill the cooling system as described in Section 3.
18   Reconnect the battery.

12.4 Heater resistance unit

12.6 Heater withdrawn from bulkhead

12.7 Heater control panel detached

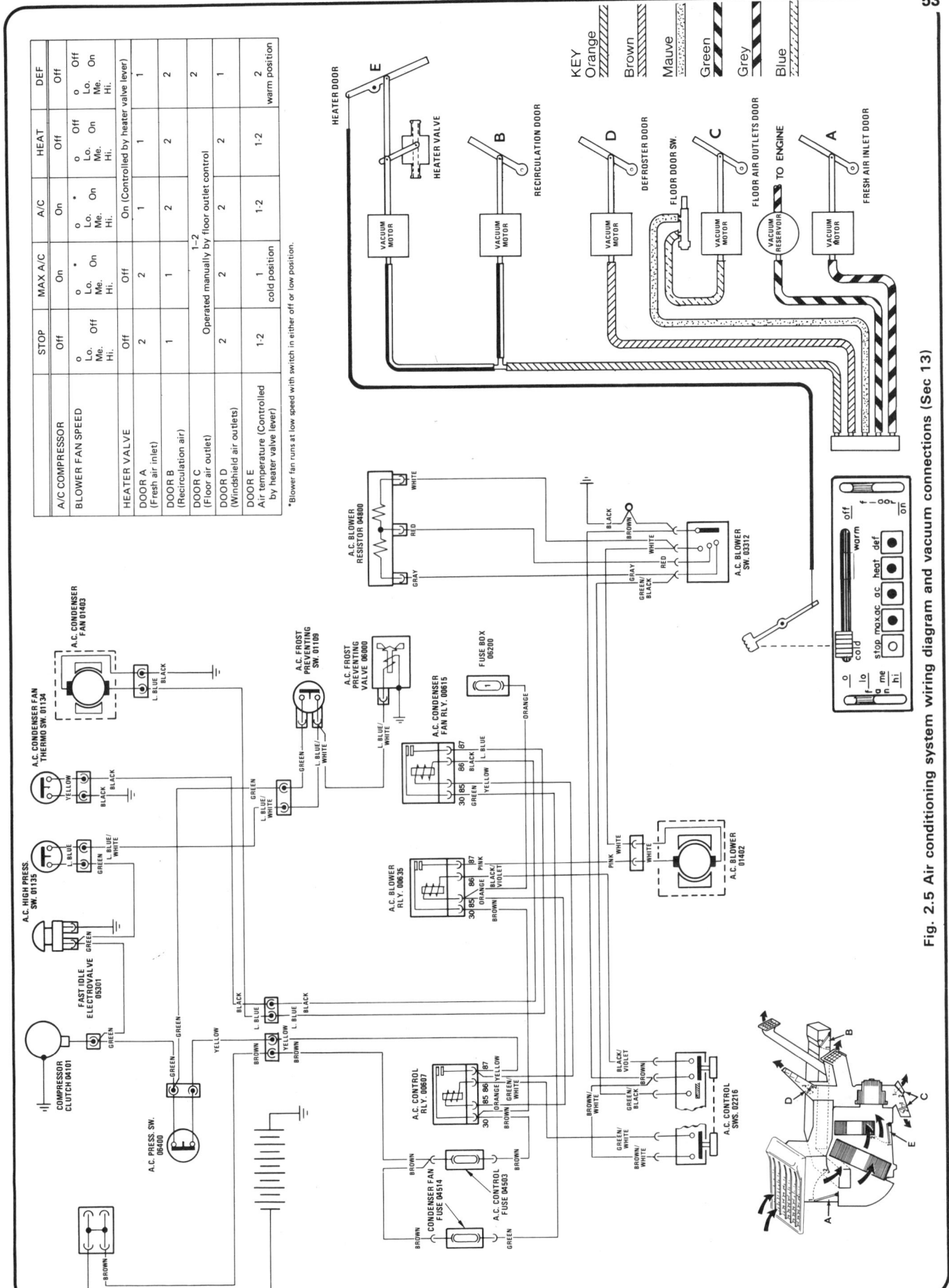

A/C COMPRESSOR		STOP	MAX A/C	A/C	HEAT	DEF
BLOWER FAN SPEED	o. Lo. Me. Hi.	Off	On	On	o. Lo. Me. Hi. Off On	o. Lo. Me. Hi. Off On
HEATER VALVE		Off	Off	On (Controlled by heater valve lever)		
DOOR A (Fresh air inlet)		2	*	o. Lo. Me. Hi.	1	1
DOOR B (Recirculation air)		1	2	1	2	2
DOOR C (Floor air outlet)		Operated manually by floor outlet control	1–2	On 1 2		2
DOOR D (Windshield air outlets)		2	2	2	2	1
DOOR E Air temperature (Controlled by heater valve lever)		1–2	cold position	1–2	1–2	warm position

*Blower fan runs at low speed with switch in either of off or low position.

KEY
Orange
Brown
Mauve
Green
Grey
Blue

Fig. 2.5 Air conditioning system wiring diagram and vacuum connections (Sec 13)

13 Air conditioning system – description, maintenance and precautions

On all models, a compact heater/air conditioning system is available as an option.

The system comprises a compressor, belt-driven from the crankshaft pulley, or condenser mounted adjacent to the radiator at the front of the car, a receiver dryer and an evaporator within the heater casing.

An expansion valve and a vacuum reservoir are located at the right-hand rearmost corner of the engine compartment.

Due to the thickness of the condenser, the ignition distributor is moved from its normal crankcase location (on cars without air conditioning) to the left-hand end of the camshaft carrier.

Normal maintenance should be confined to compressor belt adjustment and regular cleaning of the condenser fins with a soft brush or compressed air.

Frequently inspect the condition of the system flexible hoses. If they have deteriorated, the system must be discharged before renewing them.

In winter, when the air conditioner is not in use, run the system for a few minutes each week in order to circulate the compressor oil.

Whichever overhaul or repair operations require the removal of any component of the refrigeration circuit – unless they can be unbolted and lifted away far enough within the limits of their flexible connecting hoses to enable the work to be carried out – the system must be discharged by your dealer or a professional refrigeration engineer.

Never disconnect any part of the system yourself without it first having been discharged; dangerous refrigerant gas (Freon 12) will otherwise escape.

Whenever any part of the system is disconnected, cap or plug the open ends of pipes (and the holes in the components) to prevent the admission of moisture from the atmosphere.

14 Air conditioning system components – removal and refitting

1   Prior to removing any of the following components (except those marked *) the refrigerant in the system *must* be discharged by your dealer or by a competent refrigeration engineer. **Note:** *Disconnecting any part of the system refrigerant lines with the consequent escape of gas can cause personal injury.*

2   The reason for removal of a component may be due to the fact that it is faulty or to move it out of the way for engine/transmission removal.

Compressor

3   Disconnect the battery negative lead.

4   Raise the car sufficiently to give access underneath, then with the car safely jacked, remove the right-hand front wheel.

5   Unbolt and remove the compressor drivebelt guards.

6   Slacken the compressor mounting bracket bolts, move the compressor until the drivebelts can be slipped from their pulley grooves.

7   Release the connecting hose couplings on the compressor and plug their open ends.

8   Disconnect the electrical leads from the compressor.

9   Remove the previously released mounting bolts and lift the compressor from the engine compartment.

10   Refitting is a reversal of the removal process. Move the position of the compressor on its mountings until the tension of the drivebelts is correct at 9.5 mm ($\frac{3}{8}$ in) using moderate thumb pressure at the mid-point of the longest run of the belt.

Fig. 2.7 Compressor mounting bolts (Sec 14)

1	Compressor	4	Mounting bracket slot
2	Nut	5	Mounting bracket
3	Nut	6	Crankshaft pulley

Fig. 2.6 Compressor drivebelt guards (Sec 14)

1	Compressor	3	Belt guard securing bolts
2	Belt guard		

Fig. 2.8 Removing the condenser (Sec 14)

1   Condenser
2   Pipeline – condenser to receiver/dryer
3   Pipeline – condenser to compressor
4   Mounting bracket
5   Condenser cooling fan connector plug

Condenser

11 Disconnect the pipelines from the condenser and plug them immediately.
12 Unbolt the condenser from the upper crossmember.
13 Disconnect the electrical leads from the condenser cooling fan.
14 Lift the condenser upwards, withdrawing the locating pegs at its base out of their rubber bushes. Remove it from the engine compartment.
15 The fan assembly can be unbolted and removed if necessary.
16 Refitting is a reversal of the removal process.

Receiver/dryer

17 Unscrew the pipeline fittings from the receiver/dryer and plug their ends.
18 Remove the single securing bolt and withdraw the receiver/dryer from the side of the engine compartment.
19 Refitting is a reversal of the removal process.

Fig. 2.9 Condenser with cooling fan (Sec 14)

1　Condenser　　　　3　Fan mounting nuts
2　Fan

Fig. 2.10 Receiver/dryer (Sec 14)

1　Receiver/dryer
2　To condenser
3　To expansion valve
Receiver/dryer mounting bolts (arrowed)

Valves

20 These are located adjacent to the air intake plenum chamber on the engine compartment rear bulkhead. The individual valves and switches are identified in Fig. 2.11.

*Thermal switches *

21 There are two thermal switches in the system. One is located on the evaporator outlet pipe and energises the solenoid for the safety and frost prevention valve when the evaporation temperature falls and freezing of the condenser could occur. Then, by means of its second phase, it again energises the valve solenoid when excessive temperatures are signalled, even though the condenser cooling fan is operating.

Fig. 2.11 Valve block on right-hand side of plenum chamber (Sec 14)

1　Expansion valve
2　Outlet union
3　Low pressure switch
4　Safety and frost prevention valve thermal switch
5　Safety and frost prevention valve

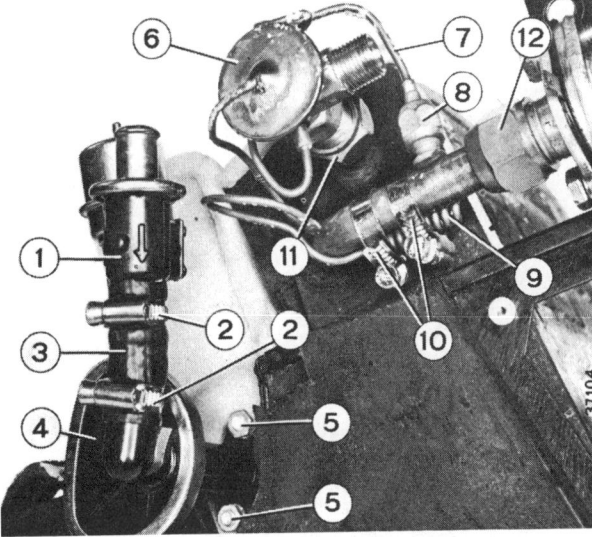

Fig. 2.12 Valve block details (Sec 14)

1　Coolant valve
2　Hose clip
3　Hose (coolant cock to valve)
4　Coolant cock
5　Coolant cock mounting nuts
6　Expansion valve
7　Expansion valve equaliser pipeline
8　Union
9　Temperature sensing bulb
10　Clips
11　Union (expansion valve to evaporator inlet)
12　Union (evaporator outlet to safety/frost prevention valve)

22 A second thermal switch is fitted to the condenser outlet and actuates the condenser cooling fan when the car is stationary or is moving slowly.

23 To remove a thermal switch, take off the insulating material and disconnect the electrical leads and holding clips.

24 The thermal switch operating temperatures are as follows. The switches can be tested by holding the metal part of the switch in water heated to the specified temperature and connecting a test battery and lamp across the switch terminals.

Safety/frost prevention valve thermal switch
Contacts open	Contacts closed
181 to 188°F (83 to 87°C)	168 to 176°F (76 to 80°C)

Condenser fan control thermal switch
Contacts open	Contacts closed
129 to 136°F (54 to 58°C)	118 to 125°F (48 to 52°C)

25 Refitting a switch is a reversal of the removal process.

Expansion valve

26 The valve is located in the valve block (refer to Figs. 2.11 and 2.12).

27 Remove the insulating material.

28 Remove the equalising line from the evaporator outlet pipe.

29 Remove the clamp bolts which hold the spirally wound tube to the temperature sensing bulb in contact with the evaporator outlet pipe.

30 Disconnect the pipes and fittings, then remove the expansion valve.

31 Failure of this valve may be due to a clogged filter.

32 Refitting is a reversal of the removal process, but make sure the contact surfaces between the sensing bulb and the outlet pipe are clean.

Coolant valve *

33 This is located on the heater inlet line.

34 Disconnect the heater pipe from the cylinder head, having first partially drained the cooling system.

35 Disconnect the vacuum pipe from the actuator which controls the coolant valve.

36 Release the coolant valve hose clamp and remove the valve and actuator.

37 Refitting is a reversal of the removal process, but make sure the flow directional arrow points downward.

Coolant cock

38 This cannot be removed until the evaporator/heater has first been withdrawn (refer to Section 15).

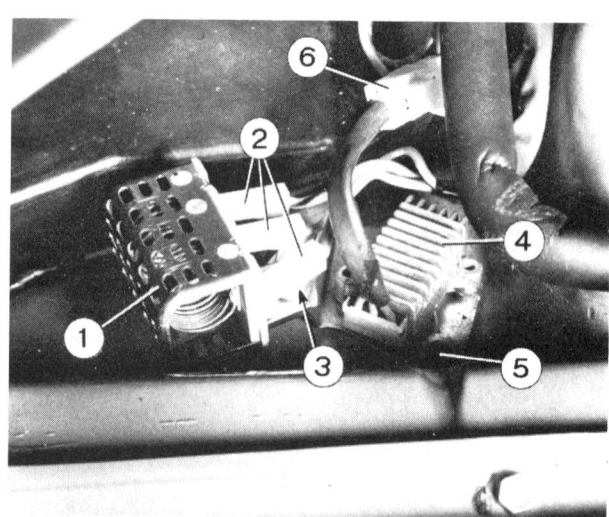

Fig. 2.13 Air conditioner voltage regulator/resistor unit (Sec 14)

1 Resistor for evaporator/ heater fan	4 Voltage regulator
2 Electrical connectors	5 Voltage regulator mounting nut
3 Resistor mounting nuts	6 Electrical connector

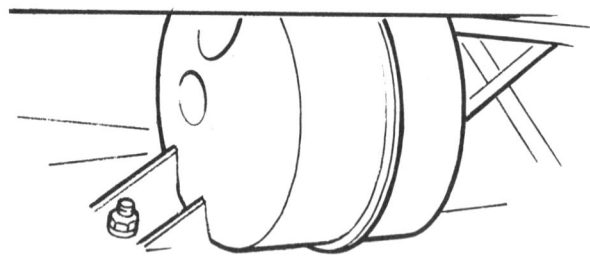

H.15027

Fig. 2.15 Vacuum reservoir tank (Sec 15)

Fig. 2.14 Air conditioner under bonnet location (Sec 15)

1 Heater return pipe	5 Mounting nut
2 Flexible hose	6 Mounting bolt
3 Clip	7 Casing
4 Vacuum pipe (vacuum reservoir to solenoid)	

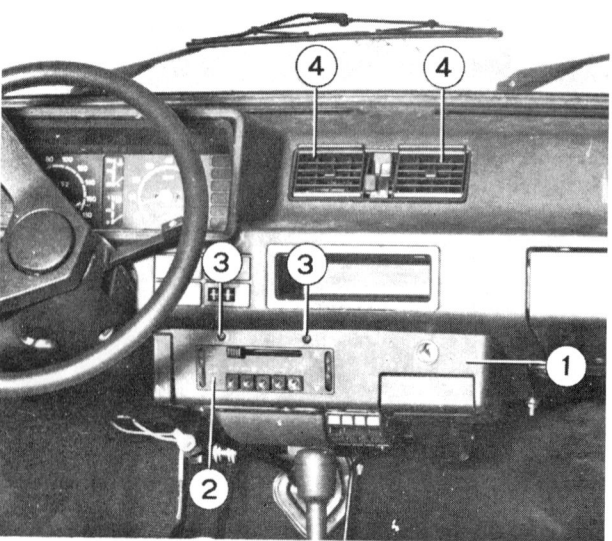

Fig. 2.16 Instrument panel and controls (Sec 15)

1 Control panel housing	3 Mounting screws
2 Air conditioner control panel	4 Air outlet grille

Safety/frost prevention valve

39 Disconnect the electrical lead from the valve.
40 Disconnect the pipes from the valve.
41 Unbolt the valve bracket from the evaporator/heater unit, then unbolt the bracket from the valve. Withdraw the valve.

Voltage regulator/resistor

42 The voltage regulator and resistor unit are mounted side by side. The resistor must be removed before the voltage regulator can be unbolted.
43 Identify the terminals and connecting leads before separating them.

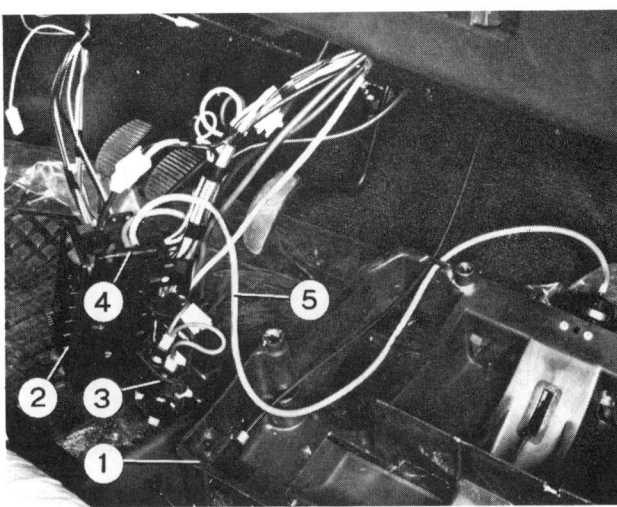

Fig. 2.17 Control panel housing removed (Sec 15)

1 Control panel housing	4 Air distribution control
2 Control panel	cylinder
3 Fuses	5 Vacuum pipes

15 Air conditioner (evaporator/heater) – removal, dismantling, reassembly and refitting

1 *Have the system discharged by your dealer or refrigeration engineer.* Drain the cooling system.
2 Working on the right-hand side of the air conditioner unit, within the engine compartment, disconnect the heater inlet hose from the coolant valve.
3 Working on the left-hand side of the unit, disconnect the heater return hose.
4 Returning to the right-hand side, disconnect the compressor hose from the frost prevention valve.
5 Unscrew the union nut on the forward face of the expansion valve to release the outlet fitting with the low pressure switch. Pull the leads from the low pressure switch.
6 Disconnect the pipes from the vacuum reservoir and from the air flap actuator, which is located behind the reservoir and controls air recirculation.
7 Disconnect the remaining leads from the front of the evaporator heater unit.
8 Working inside the car, release the nuts which hold the control panel housing to the underside of the instrument panel. Lower the housing, then extract the two screws which secure the control panel to the housing. Disconnect the electrical leads.
9 Disconnect the pipe which controls the windscreen outlet flap.
10 Disconnect the blue hose (5) from the air distribution control cylinder. See Fig. 2.17.
11 Unscrew and remove the nuts and bolts which hold the air conditioner to the engine compartment rear bulkhead.
12 Remove the air conditioner from the engine compartment, drawing the control unit through from the car interior.
13 To dismantle the air conditioner, first unbolt the frost prevention valve bracket.
14 Peel away the upper part of the sealing strip, taking care to cause as little damage as possible!
15 Disconnect the fan-to-control unit electrical lead at the plug.
16 Unscrew and remove the three screws (3) which hold the fan to the casing. See Fig. 2.18.
17 Remove the bolts (4) and spring clips (5) then separate the upper and lower halves of the casing. See Fig. 2.18.
18 Remove the fan and the air distribution ring.
19 Detach the coolant cock control lever from its bracket and withdraw the evaporator and heater matrix from the casing.

Fig. 2.18 Air conditioner removed (Sec 15)

1 Sealing strip	4 Half section securing
2 Lead connecting plug	bolts
3 Fan mounting bolts	5 Spring clips

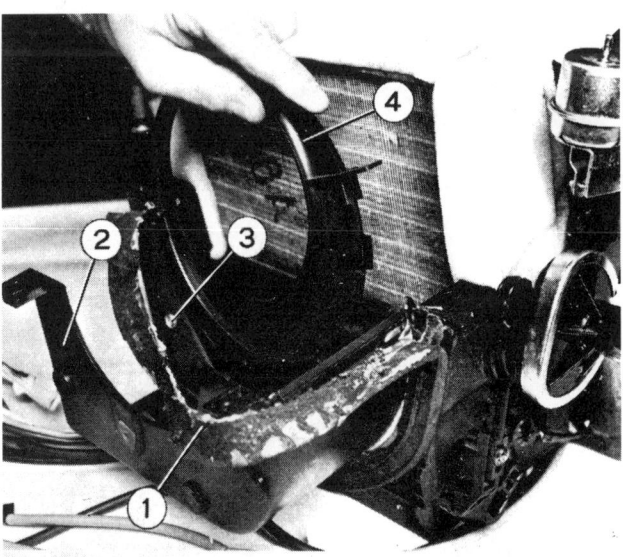

Fig. 2.19 Removing fan air deflector ring (Sec 15)

1 Sealing strip	3 Securing screw
2 Lower section	4 Deflector ring

20 Do not attempt to repair a heater matrix or air conditioner evaporator; renew them complete. Reassemble by reversing the dismantling process.

21 Refitting is a reversal of the removal process; make good the casing sealing strip.

16 Air conditioner control unit – removal, dismantling, reassembly and refitting

1 The control unit can be removed independently of the air conditioner.

2 Disconnect the battery negative lead.

3 Remove the nuts which hold the control panel housing to the underside of the instrument panel and lower the housing. Extract the two screws which hold the control panel to the housing.

4 Pull out the pushbuttons, then remove the screws which hold the lower plate to the control unit. Withdraw the plate.

5 If the pushbutton panel must be removed, first pull off the leads connected to its spade terminals and also disengage the vacuum pipe holder.

6 The air distribution control cylinder can be removed from the right-hand side, after extracting the two retainers.

7 The satisfactory operation of the control switches can be checked in the following way.

8 Connect a test bulb (A) to the centre spade terminal (marked 'verde-bianco').

9 Connect separate test bulbs to each of the side spade terminals (B – 'nero-verde' C – 'viola-nero').

10 The three test bulb leads which are still free should now be connected to the battery negative terminal.

11 Using jump leads, connect the remaining two spade terminals (marked 'marrone-bianco') to the battery positive terminal.

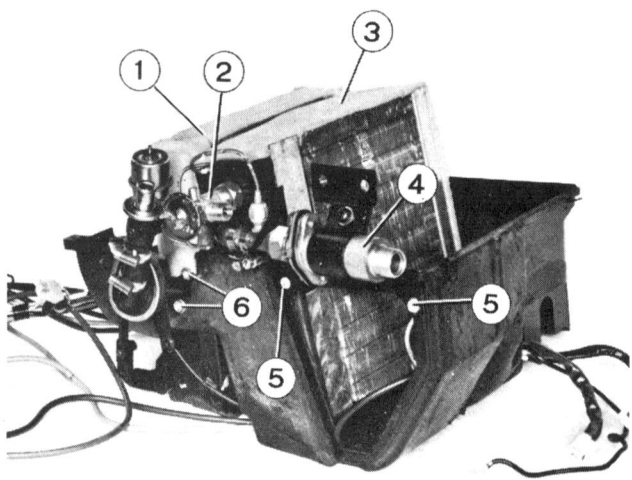

Fig. 2.20 Casing partially dismantled (Sec 15)

1 Heater matrix	4 Safety and frost prevention
2 Expansion valve	valve
3 Evaporator	5 Fixing plugs
	6 Coolant cock mounting nuts

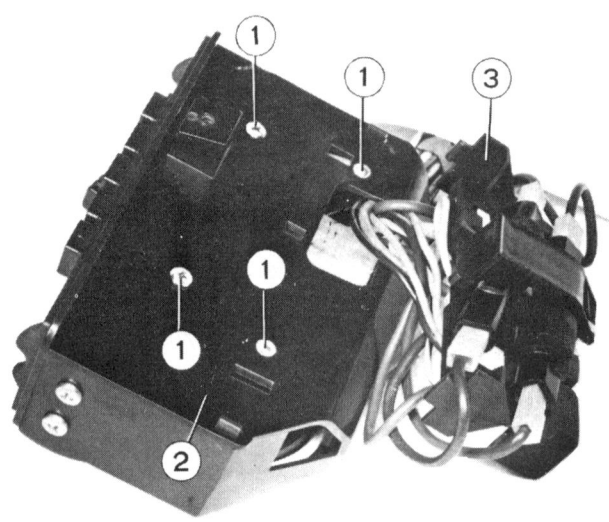

Fig. 2.21 Air conditioner control unit (Sec 16)

1 Lower plate fixing screws	3 Fuses
2 Lower plate	

Fig. 2.22 Interior view of control panel housing (Sec 17)

1 Air flap actuator	Air outlet grille
6 Air flap link	fixing tangs (arrowed)
7 Front air flap	

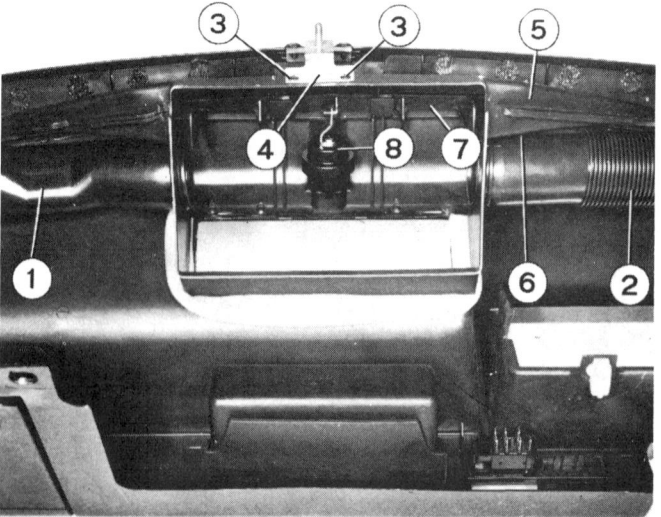

Fig. 2.23 Interior view of air outlet vents (Sec 17)

1 Duct to right-hand screen vent	4 Bracket
2 Duct to left-hand screen vent	5 Screen vent outlet
3 Fixing rivets	6 Screen vent inlet
	7 Screen vent air flap
	8 Screen vent air flap actuator

12 The individual push buttons should now be depressed in sequence; if the test bulbs light up according to the following pattern, the controls are in satisfactory condition:

Button depressed	Test bulb ON	Test bulb OFF
Stop	–	A, B and C
Max A/C	A, B and C	–
A/C	A, B and C	–
Temp	C	A and B
Def	C	A and B

13 The vacuum pipes can be disconnected from the control panel and the engine started; if a vacuum can be felt at the open end of the pipes, it can be assumed that the vacuum controls for the system are operating correctly.

14 The flexible control cables to the coolant valve and the air distribution flap can only be removed after the air conditioner has been withdrawn (see Section 15).

15 When fitting the new cable, adjust its inner and outer securing clamps so that the valve or flap opens and closes *fully* during complete movement of the control

17 Air outlet vents – removal and refitting

1 The vents under the instrument panel are accessible once the heater or air conditioner control panel housing is released by unscrewing its securing nuts and lowering it to the floor.

2 Access to the windscreen demister vents (and to the side vents) can be obtained if the instrument panel or the instrument cluster is first withdrawn (see Chapters 10 or 12).

3 The vents, actuators or distribution valve plates can be detached as necessary, some being held in place with rivets which will have to be drilled out.

18 Fault diagnosis – cooling system

Symptom	Reason(s)
Overheatng	Low coolant level due to leakage
	Drivebelt slipping or broken
	Inoperative fan or fan thermostatic switch
	Thermostat stuck closed
	Radiator fins clogged
	Pressure cap defective or of incorrect rating
	Ignition timing incorrect or distributor faulty (auto advance inoperative)
	Weak mixture
	Water pump defective
	Brakes binding
	Blown head gasket
	Internal blockage of radiator or engine waterways
	Hoses collapsed
Overcooling	Thermostat defective, missing or incorrect grade
	Fan operating all the time
Water loss – external	Loose hose clips
	Perished or cracked hoses
	Boiling due to overheating
	Pressure cap defective
	Radiator matrix or heater core leaking
	Water pump or thermostat housing leaking
Water loss – internal	Cylinder head gasket blown
	Cylinder head cracked or warped
	Cylinder block cracked
Corrosion	Infrequent draining and flushing
	Incorrect antifreeze mixture or inappropriate type
	Combustion gases contaminating coolant

Chapter 3
Fuel system, carburation and emission control

For modifications, and information applicable to later models, see Supplement at end of manual

Contents

Specifications

System type .... Rear mounted fuel tank, mechanically operated fuel pump and single or dual barrel downdraught carburettor

Carburettor

All 65 models and certain 75 models (except North America)	Weber 32 ICV 22/250 *or* Solex C32 DISA/2
Other 75 models (except North America):	
Manual transmission	Weber 34 ICEV 23/250
Manual or automatic transmission	Solex C34 DISA/3
Automatic transmission	Weber 34 ICEV 23/450
North American models:	
Except California:	
Manual transmission with air conditioning	Weber 28/30 DHTA 5/179
Manual transmission without air conditioning	Weber 28/30 DHTA 5/279
Automatic transmission with air conditioning	Weber 28/30 DHTA 6/179
Automatic transmission without air conditioning	Weber 28/30 DHTA 6/279
California:	
Manual transmission with air conditioning	Weber 28/30 DHTA 8/179
Manual transmission without air conditioning	Weber 28/30 DHTA 8/279
Automatic transmission with air conditioning	Weber 28/30 DHTA 9/179
Automatic transmission without air conditioning	Weber 28/30 DHTA 9/279

Calibration

Weber 32 ICEV 22/250

Venturi diameter	24 mm (0.945 in)
Auxiliary venturi diameter	3.50 mm (0.138 in)
Main jet	1.22 mm (0.048 in)
Air correction jet	1.55 mm (0.061 in)
Emulsion tube	F73
Slow running jet	0.50 mm (0.020 in)
Slow running air bleed	1.40 mm (0.055 in)
Accelerator pump jet	0.40 mm (0.016 in)
Accelerator pump excess fuel discharge orifice	0.70 mm (0.027 in)
Power fuel jet	1.30 mm (0.051 in)
Power air jet	1.40 mm (0.055 in)
Power mixture outlet	2.00 mm (0.079 in)
Needle valve	1.50 mm (0.059 in)
Anti-syphon bleed	1.00 mm (0.039 in)

Float level setting (gasket face to cover):
    Metal float .... 10.75 mm (0.423 in)
    Plastic float .... 35.85 mm (1.411 in)
Throttle valve opening for fast idle .... 0.75 to 0.80 mm (0.029 to 0.031 in)
Choke valve plate opening at cold start .... 4.75 to 5.25 mm (0.187 to 0.207 in)

Solex C32 DISA/2

Venturi diameter .... 24 mm (0.945 in)
Auxiliary venturi diameter .... 3.40 mm (0.134 in)
Main jet .... 1.325 mm (0.052 in)
Air correction .... 1.80 mm (0.071 in)
Emulsion tube N77
Slow running jet .... 0.55 mm (0.022 in)
Slow running air bleed .... 1.00 mm (0.039 in)
Accelerator pump jet .... 0.50 mm (0.020 in)
Accelerator pump excess fuel discharge orifice .... 0.40 mm (0.016 in)
Power fuel jet .... 0.90 mm (0.035 in)
Power mixture outlet .... 2.00 mm (0.079 in)
Needle valve seat .... 1.60 mm (0.063 in)
Anti-syphon bleed .... 1.60 mm (0.063 in)

Weber 34 ICEV 23/250

Venturi diameter .... 26 mm (1.024 in)
Auxiliary venturi diameter .... 4 mm (0.157 in)
Main jet .... 1.32 mm (0.052 in)
Air correction jet .... 1.70 mm (0.067 in)
Emulsion tube F86
Slow running jet .... 0.52 mm (0.020 in)
Slow running air bleed .... 1.45 mm (0.057 in)
Accelerator pump jet size .... 0.40 mm (0.016 in)
Accelerator pump excess fuel discharge orifice .... 0.40 mm (0.016 in)
Needle valve seat .... 1.50 mm (0.039 in)
Float level setting (gasket face to cover):
    Metal float .... 10.75 mm (0.423 in)
    Plastic float .... 35.85 mm (1.411 in)
Throttle valve opening for fast idle .... 0.80 mm (0.031 in)
Choke valve plate opening for fast idle .... 3.25 to 3.75 mm (0.128 to 0.148 in)

Solex C34 DISA/3

Venturi diameter .... 26 mm (1.024 in)
Auxiliary venturi diameter .... 3.40 mm (0.134 in)
Main jet .... 1.50 mm (0.059 in)
Air correction jet .... 2 mm (0.079 in)
Emulsion tube N82
Slow running jet .... 0.52 mm (0.020 in)
Slow running air bleed .... 0.80 mm (0.031 in)
Accelerator pump jet .... 0.70 mm (0.027 in)
Accelerator pump excess fuel discharge orifice .... 0.40 mm (0.016 in)
Needle valve .... 1.60 mm (0.063 in)
Anti-syphon bleed .... 1.60 mm (0.063 in)

Weber 28/30 DHTA

	Primary	Secondary
Barrel diameter	28 mm (1.102 in)	30 mm (1.181 in)
Venturi diameter	21 mm (0.827 in)	22 mm (0.866 in)
Main jet (except automatic transmission, California models)	1.05 mm (0.0413 in)	1.10 mm (0.0433 in)
Main jet (automatic transmission, California models)	1.10 mm (0.0433 in)	1.05 mm (0.0413 in)
Float level	6.75 to 7.25 mm (0.266 to 0.285 in)	

Idle speeds

Engines without exhaust emission control systems .... 750 rpm
Engines with exhaust emission control systems:
    Manual transmission .... 800 to 900 rpm
    Automatic transmission .... 700 to 800 rpm with speed selector lever in 'D'.
On North American models (except California), set the idle speed with the hose to the emission control reed valve clamped shut. On Californian models, set the idle speed with the hose to the emission control non-return valve clamped shut.

CO level at idle speed .... 1.0 to 2.0%

Fuel tank capacity (including reserve) .... 11.2 Imp gals (13 US gals, 51 litres)

Fuel grade .... Minimum 97 octane

Note: *On North American versions, use unleaded fuel only*

Torque wrench settings

	lbf ft	Nm
Manifold nuts	20	27
Carburettor mounting nuts	25	34
Fuel pump mounting nuts	28	38

1 General description

The fuel system comprises a rear mounted fuel tank, a mechanically operated fuel pump (driven from a cam on the camshaft or from the auxiliary shaft) and a Solex or Weber single or dual barrel downdraught carburettor (dependent upon engine capacity and operating territory).

The carburettor flange adaptor is coolant heated on all models; on models equipped with an exhaust emission control system, a temperature controlled type of air cleaner and an automatic choke (cold starting device) are also fitted.

One or more of several types of emission control system may be fitted; on models destined for operation in California, a catalytic converter and air injection system are usually fitted.

2 Air cleaner – element renewal

1 The filter element should be renewed at the intervals specified in 'Routine Maintenance' or earlier if operating the car in very dusty territories.

2 Open the bonnet, then unscrew and remove the nuts which hold the air cleaner cover in position.

3 Lift off the cover and extract the filter element.

4 Before fitting the new element, wipe the casing out.

5 The air cleaner intake spout is adjustable so that in winter, air is drawn from the vicinity of the exhaust manifold.

6 If the air cleaner casing must be removed, release its clamp plate to the carburettor throat, disconnect the crankcase ventilation hose and the hot air intake duct; remove the casing from the carburettor.

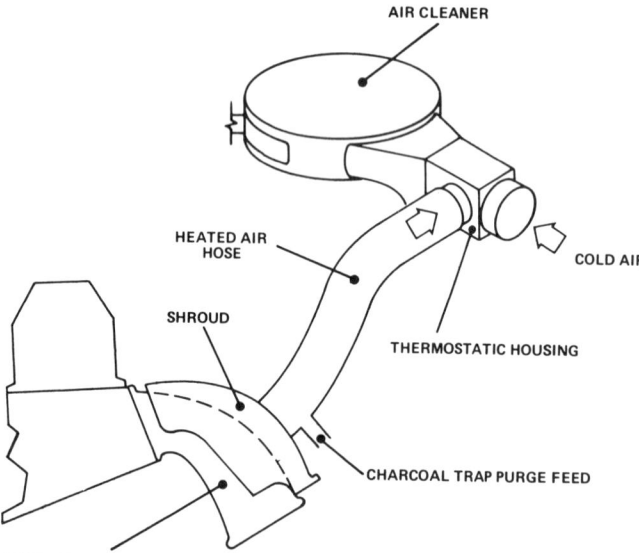

Fig. 3.1 Temperature controlled type air cleaner and intake ducts (Sec 3)

3 Air cleaner (temperature controlled type) – element renewal

1 With this type of air cleaner, air is drawn simultaneously from the engine compartment and from a shroud on the exhaust manifold.

2 The relatively cool and the heated air are then mixed by a deflector plate to provide the carburettor with intake air at a constant temperature of between 73° and 82°F (23° and 28°C).

3 Control of the deflector plate (to ensure the correct mix of cool and heated air) is arranged by a wax type thermostat.

4 Renewal of the filter element is as described for the non-temperature controlled air cleaner in the preceding Section.

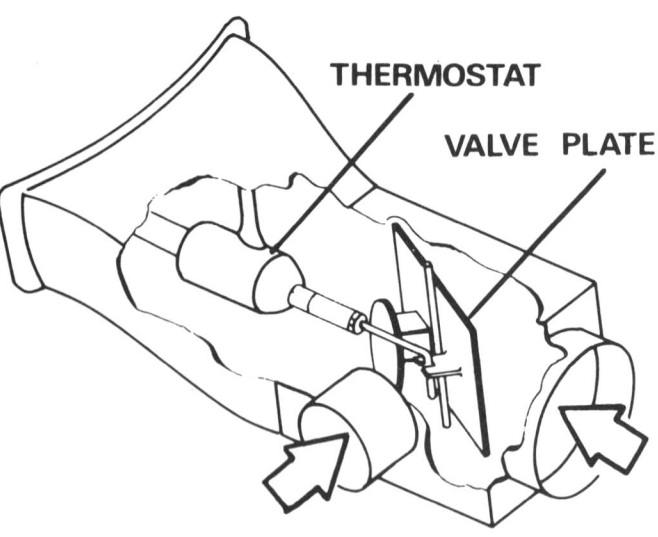

Fig. 3.2 Air mixing chamber on temperature controlled air cleaner (Sec 3)

4 Fuel pump – description and servicing

1 The fuel pump, fitted to the crankcase (most models, except North American versions), is a sealed unit and cannot be serviced or overhauled in any way (photo).

2 Occasionally, check the security of the pump connecting hoses and mounting bolts.

3 The fuel pump, located adjacent to the carburettor on North American models, is driven from a cam on the camshaft. It is possible to overhaul this type of pump, but servicing as such is not required as a separate in-line filter is located alongside it.

4.1 Fuel pump mounted on crankcase

5 Fuel pump – removal and refitting

1   Disconnect the flexible hoses from the fuel pump and plug them immediately.

2   Unscrew and remove the pump mounting nuts. The pump may have to be partially withdrawn to enable the mounting nuts to be fully unscrewed (photo).

3   Lift the pump away, followed by the insulator block and the gasket on either side of it.

4   If necessary, withdraw the pump operating pushrod.

5   Refitting is a reversal of the removal process, but renew the gaskets with ones of identical thickness; the purpose of the insulator block and gaskets is not only to seal the crankcase against loss of oil (and to insulate the pump from the heat of the engine), but also to determine the stroke of the pump by controlling the projection of the operating rod (photo).

6 Fuel filters – cleaning and renewal

1   On most carburettors, a gauze filter is located in the fuel inlet. The filter can be extracted and cleaned if the hexagonal plug is unscrewed or the fuel inlet pipe stub is unscrewed, dependent upon carburettor design (photo).

2   On cars fitted with an in-line fuel filter, at the intervals specified in 'Routine Maintenance', disconnect and plug the flexible hoses from each end of the filter.

3   Discard the filter and fit the new one, making sure the fuel flow directional arrow is pointing toward the carburettor.

7 Fuel pump (camshaft driven type) – overhaul

1   Obtain the appropriate repair kit.

2   Remove the pump as described in Section 5.

3   Scribe a line across the flange joints before dismantling so that the relationship of the upper and lower bodies can be maintained on reassembly.

4   Unscrew and remove the circle of flange screws, then remove the upper body.

5   Renew all components for which parts are included in the repair kit.

6   Reassembly is a reversal of the dismantling process.

8 Fuel tank – removal and refitting

1   Drain the fuel tank by syphoning with a length of flexible tubing. A drain plug is not fitted.

2   Working from below the car, disconnect the fuel filter hose from the left-hand side of the fuel tank. Release the hose clips and slide the rubber section up the metal pipe to achieve this.

3   Support the tank on a jack, with a block of wood as an insulator; otherwise obtain the help of an assistant and unbolt the tank; lower it until the leads from the tank transmitter unit and the vent or fuel evaporative system hoses can be detached (photo).

4   Lower the tank fully and withdraw it from under the back end of the car.

5   Refitting is a reversal of the removal process.

Warning: *Never attempt to solder or weld a fuel tank yourself; always leave fuel tank repairs to the experts. Never syphon fuel into a container in an inspection pit. Fuel vapour is heavier than air and can remain in the pit for a considerable time.*

9 Fuel contents gauge, transmitter and low reserve lamp – checking and renewal

1   The fuel level transmitter is accessible by peeling back the carpet within the luggage compartment and prising out the plastic panel. If the fuel reserve indicator warning lamp does not come on when the

Fig. 3.3 Typical fuel pump and filter (Sec 4)

5.2 Removing crankcase mounted fuel pump

5.5 Fuel pump, insulator block and pump operating pushrod

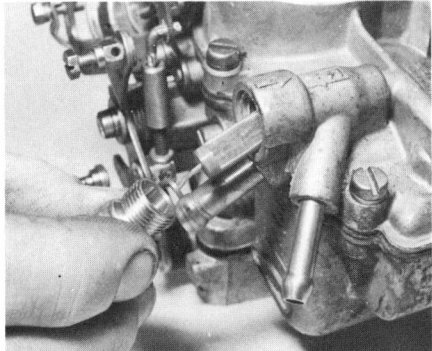

6.1 Carburettor fuel inlet filter

8.3 Fuel tank flange mounting nut

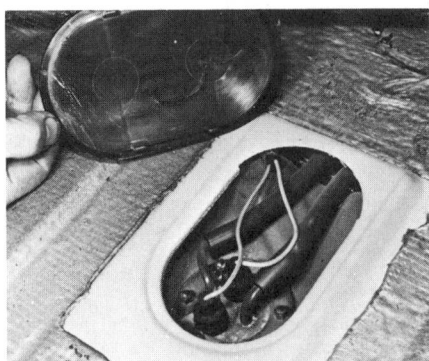

9.1 Fuel tank level transmitter

fuel level in the tank is low, first check the bulb in the instrument panel warning cluster (see Chapter 9) (photo).

2   If this is satisfactory, disconnect the electrical lead (W) from the fuel tank transmitter unit and connect it to earth. Switch on the ignition; if the warning lamp comes on, the contact inside the transmitter unit is not making a good earth connection.

3   If the fuel contents gauge always shows FULL when the ignition is switched on, check the security of the connecting lead (T) at the gauge and at the transmitter. If these are satisfactory, it is the transmitter which is most probably at fault.

4   If the fuel gauge shows no reading at all, a connecting lead from the transmitter is almost certainly broken. To check this out, disconnect the electrical lead (T). If the gauge now shows FULL with the ignition on, the fault lies in the transmitter. If the gauge shows EMPTY the fault is in the wiring or the gauge.

5   To remove the fuel gauge transmitter, first disconnect the battery earth lead. Disconnect the electrical leads from the transmitter, noting which goes where. Disconnect and plug the fuel line(s), again noting their location.

6   Undo the retaining nuts or bolts and lift the unit from the tank, taking care not to damage the float or bend its arm.

7   A defective transmitter unit must be renewed, no repair being possible. If the new unit looks different from the old one, make sure that its float can operate over its full range inside the tank without fouling any internal baffles.

8   Refitting is the reverse of the removal procedure. Use a new gasket if necessary. Make sure that the fuel lines are securely connected and check for leaks on completion.

10 Carburettor – idle adjustment

1   On all carburettors, the mixture adjusting screw is sealed with a plug or limiter cap. Any adjustment should normally be restricted to turning the throttle speed screw in or out to set the idle speed to the specified range with the engine at normal operating temperature (photos).

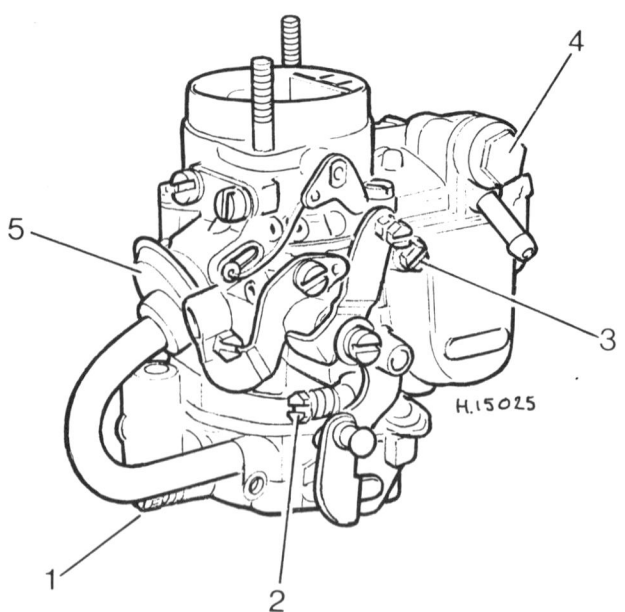

Fig. 3.4 Weber 32 ICEV carburettor (Sec 10)

1 Idle mixture screw	4 Gauze filter plug
2 Throttle speed screw	5 Choke unloader vacuum
3 Idle jet	capsule

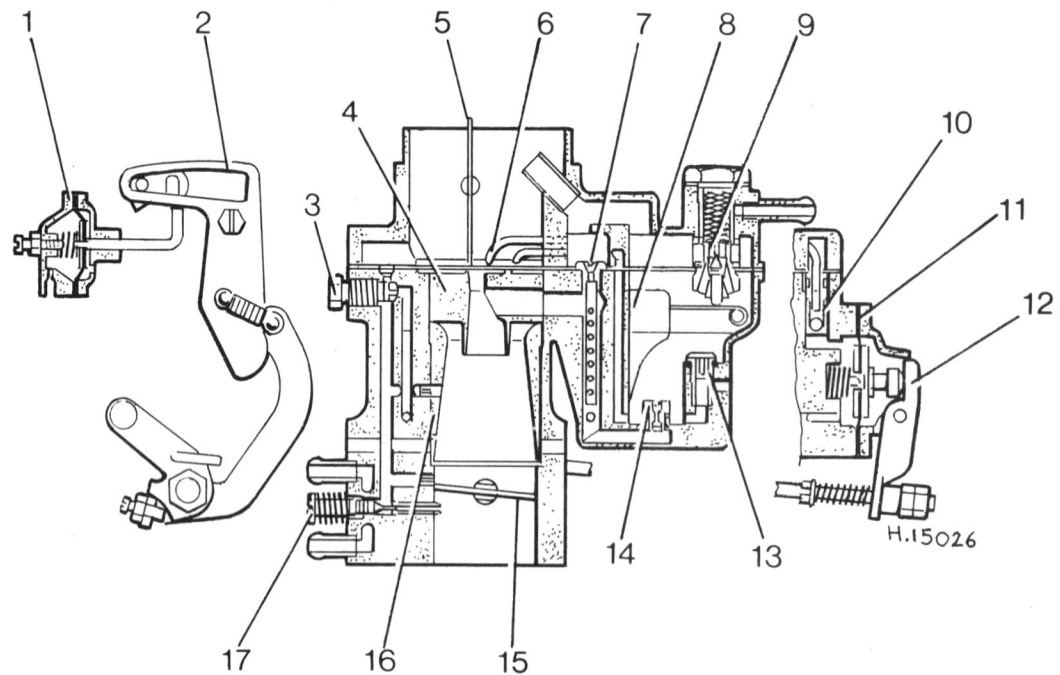

Fig. 3.5 Solex C32 DISA carburettor, diagrammatic view (Sec 10)

1 Choke unloader device	6 Accelerator pump discharge	10 Accelerator pump jet	14 Main jet
2 Cold start control lever	nozzle	11 Accelerator pump diaphragm	15 Throttle valve plate
3 Idle jet	7 Emulsion tube	12 Accelerator pump diaphragm	16 Main venturi
4 Auxiliary venturi	8 Float	control lever	17 Idle mixture adjusting
5 Choke valve plate	9 Needle valve	13 Accelerator pump valve	screw

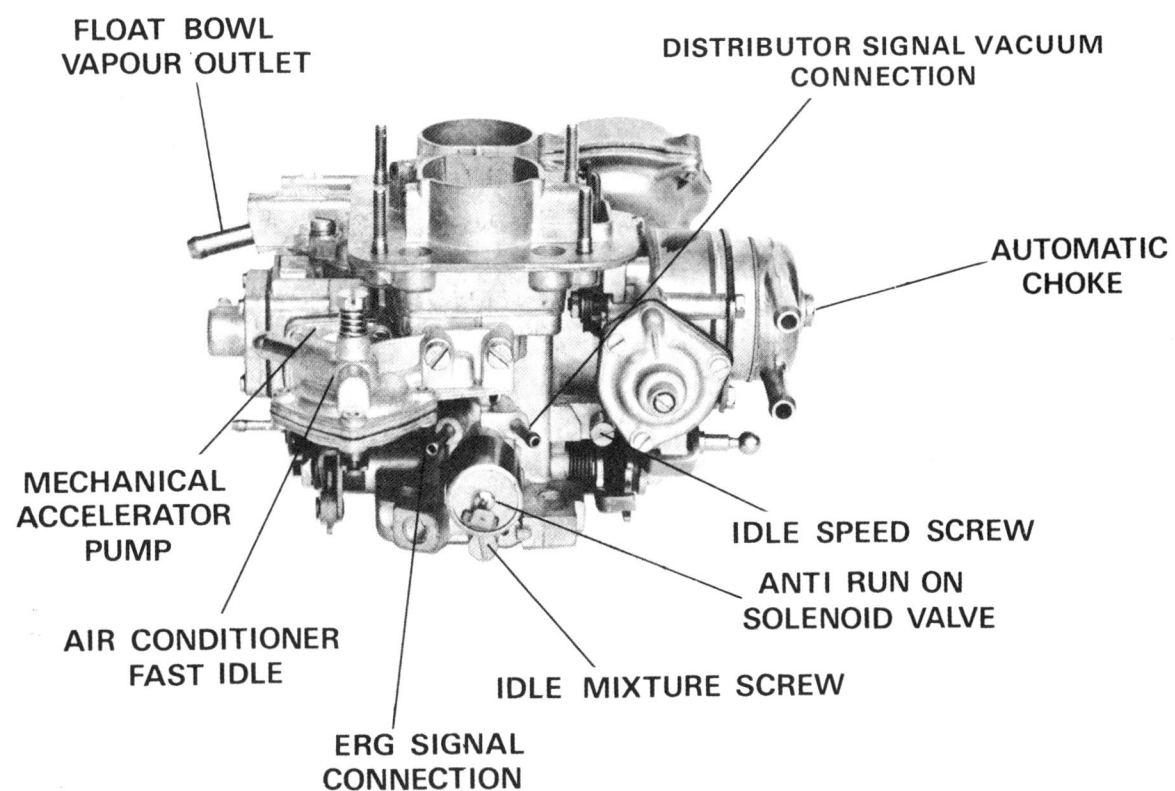

FLOAT BOWL
VAPOUR OUTLET

DISTRIBUTOR SIGNAL VACUUM
CONNECTION

AUTOMATIC
CHOKE

MECHANICAL
ACCELERATOR
PUMP

IDLE SPEED SCREW

ANTI RUN ON
SOLENOID VALVE

AIR CONDITIONER
FAST IDLE

IDLE MIXTURE SCREW

ERG SIGNAL
CONNECTION

Fig. 3.6 Weber 28/30 DHTA carburettor showing mechanical accelerator pump (Sec 10)

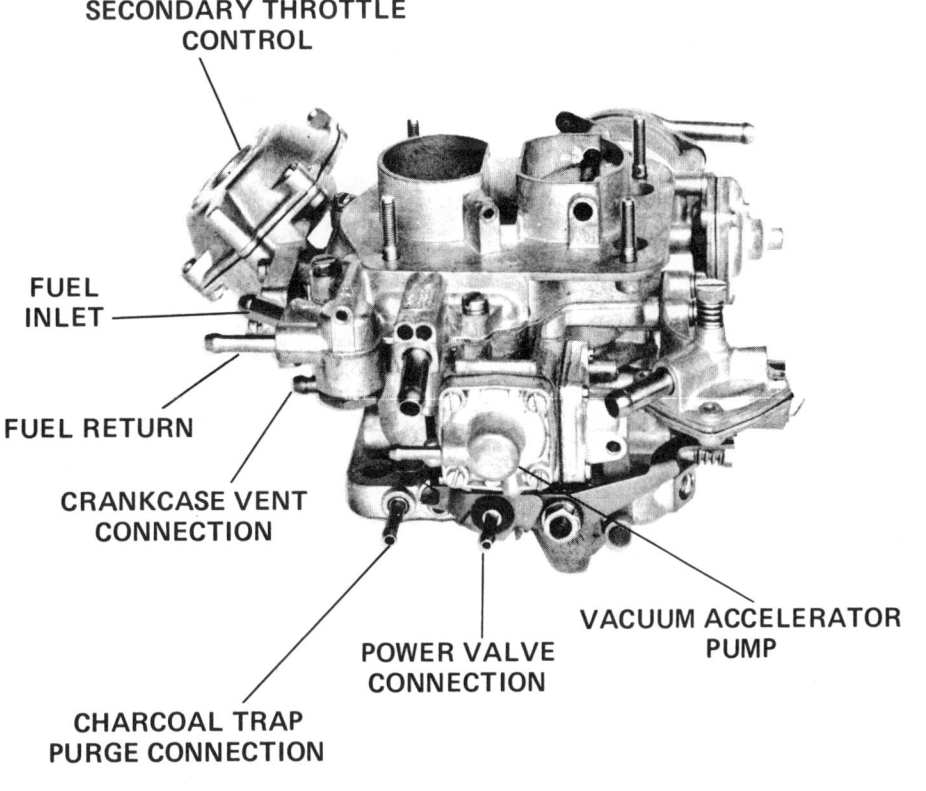

SECONDARY THROTTLE
CONTROL

FUEL
INLET

FUEL RETURN

CRANKCASE VENT
CONNECTION

VACUUM ACCELERATOR
PUMP

POWER VALVE
CONNECTION

CHARCOAL TRAP
PURGE CONNECTION

Fig. 3.7 Weber 28/30 DHTA carburettor showing vacuum accelerator pump (Sec 10)

2   If, due to major overhaul of the carburettor or as a result of fitting new parts, the fuel/air mixture requires alteration, it is preferable to carry out the adjustment using a CO exhaust gas analyser connected in accordance with the manufacturer's instructions.

3   Have the engine at normal operating temperature, then remove the plug or cap from the mixture adjusting screw. Connect a tachometer and the exhaust gas analyser to the car.

4   Turn the throttle speed screw in or out until the engine idle speed is within its specified range (see Specifications). Now adjust the mixture screw until the exhaust CO content, as indicated by the analyser, is within the specified percentage.

5   Make any fine adjustment to the throttle speed screw necessary to bring the idle speed within the specified range.

6   Where local regulations demand it, fit a new seal or blanking plug to the mixture screw.

7   Where an exhaust gas analyser is not available, a substitute adjustment method is to turn the mixture control screw in until the engine starts to run unevenly. Then unscrew it just enough to smooth the idle speed. In territories where stringent emission control legislation is in force, this latter method must be regarded as an emergency adjustment only, and should be re-checked on specialised equipment at the earliest opportunity.

11 Carburettor – removal and refitting

1   Remove the air cleaner.

2   Disconnect the accelerator control cable from the ballpin on the carburettor control swivel plate. Detach the return spring (photos).

3   Disconnect the choke control cable on all except Weber 28/30 DHTA carburettors, which have a coolant heated automatic choke. Where these carburettors are fitted, the cooling system should be partially drained and the flexible connecting hoses detached from the automatic choke housing. On other types of carburettor, only the carburettor flange adaptor is coolant heated, so the draining of the system will still apply. However, the hoses will then have to be disconnected from the lower housing.

4   Disconnect the fuel flow and return hoses from the carburettor (photo).

5   Disconnect the vacuum hose for the distributor, if one is fitted.

6   Where fitted, disconnect the electrical lead from the fuel cut-off valve.

7   On Weber 28/30 DHTA carburettors, disconnect the pipes from the carburettor for the EGR system, the power valve connection, the crankcase ventilation system and the fuel evaporative emission control system.

8   Unscrew and remove the carburettor mounting nuts and lift the carburettor from the intake manifold (photo).

9   Peel away the flange gaskets; remove the drip tray.

10   Refitting is a reversal of the removal process, but use new gaskets.

12 Carburettor – overhaul

Overhaul of a modern carburettor should not be regarded as routine and the operations should be restricted to those described for the purpose of cleaning the carburettor interior and the jets.

If wear is detected, a new or factory reconditioned unit is recommended as, in any event, small components are becoming increasingly difficult to obtain.

Always obtain a repair kit in advance of commencing the work. This will contain all the necessary gaskets and other renewable items.

1   With the carburettor removed from the engine, clean away all external dirt, using a brush and a suitable solvent (photos).

2   Detach the externally mounted diaphragm units.

3   Extract the securing screws which hold the upper body to the main body, then lift the upper body slowly so that the interconnecting link rods (on some designs of carburettor) may be disconnected by turning their anchor plates through the necessary angle to release them. On Weber 34 ICEV type carburettors, pull the link rod sleeve up against its spring (photo). Take care not to damage the float.

4   Mop or syphon out the fuel from the float bowl and remove any sediment (photo).

5   The individual jets may be removed and cleared using air pressure from a tyre pump – never probe with wire as this will ruin their calibration. Remove only one jet at a time to avoid any possibility of

refitting it in the wrong position. Always use a screwdriver or spanner of a close fitting type to avoid damage to the jets or bleed orifices.

6   When refitting a jet, tighten it securely, with a new sealing washer (if fitted). Do not overtighten it; its thread may strip out those in the alloy body of the carburettor (photo).

7   A jet of air from a tyre pump may be applied to any or all of the jets and passages which are visible, as a means of clearing the carburettor internal passages.

8   It is not usually necessary to disturb the adjustment screws or the fuel cut-off valve. The flange adaptor plate is held to the carburettor body by two screws (photos).

9   The accelerator pump diaphragm can be renewed once the pump cover is removed.

10   Flooding or heavy fuel consumption may be due to an incorrect fuel level in the float bowl, or a loose or worn fuel inlet needle valve. First remove the float pivot and detach the float. Using a socket, box or ring spanner, check the security of the needle valve seat. This must be really tight, otherwise fuel will bypass the needle valve and cause the fuel level to rise, even when the float is in the fully raised position (photo).

11   If the needle valve has been in service for a long time, it is best to renew it, also the float pivot pin, if it is grooved.

12   Once the fuel inlet valve and the float assembly have been refitted, check the float adjustment as described in the following Sections, according to carburettor type.

10.1a Carburettor mixture adjusting screw plug (arrowed)

10.1b Carburettor throttle speed adjusting screw

11.2a Accelerator cable connection to carburettor control swivel plate (arrowed)

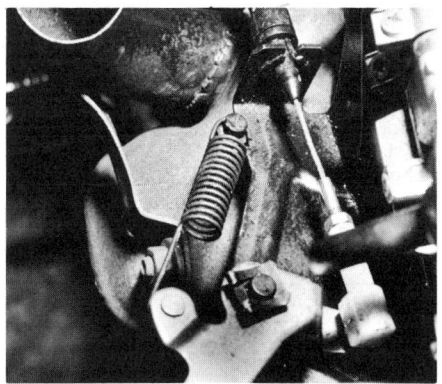

11.2b Throttle lever return spring

11.4 Carburettor fuel return hose

11.8 Removing carburettor from inlet manifold

12.1a Weber 34 ICEV carburettor viewed from accelerator pump side

12.1b Weber 34 ICEV carburettor viewed from control linkage side

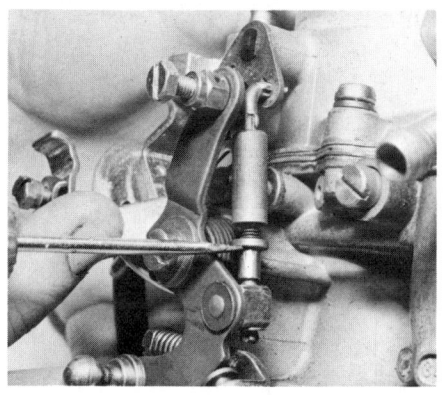

12.3 Disconnecting upper body link rod (Weber 34 ICEV type)

12.4 Weber 34 ICEV carburettor main body

12.6 Refitting carburettor jet

12.8a Removing flange adaptor plate securing screw

12.8b The flange adaptor plate removed

12.10 Upper body with float

13 Reassembly is a reversal of the dismantling process; use new gaskets and other parts from the repair kit and, as work progresses, check the other adjustments as described in the following Sections.

14 Before fitting the top cover, half fill the fuel bowl with clean fuel as an aid to rapid start-up, but keep the unit in an upright position once this is done.

15 After overhaul and the carburettor is refitted to the engine, adjust the idle as described in Section 10.

13 Carburettor (Weber 32/34 ICEV) – adjustment

Float level

1   This is done by removing the top cover, holding the cover so the float hangs down to close the needle valve.

2   Measure the distance between the surface of the cover gasket and the nearest point on the metal type float, or the furthest point of the plastic type float. If the dimension is not in accordance with Specifications (dependent upon carburettor model), bend the tab of the float arm which bears upon the fuel inlet needle valve.

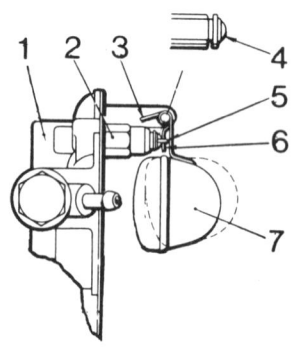 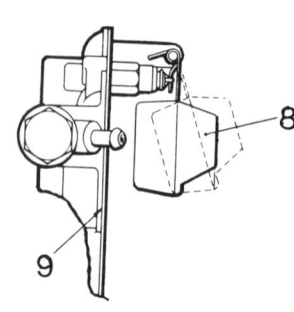

Fig. 3.8 Weber 32/34 ICEV float level setting diagram (Sec 13)

1	Carburettor top cover	6	Tang
2	Fuel inlet needle valve	7	Metal type float
3	Float stroke stop	8	Plastic type float
4	Valve ball	9	Gasket
5	Valve hook		

Choke valve plate opening (vacuum choke unloader)

3   This can only be satisfactorily checked and adjusted if an outside vacuum source and gauge are available. If they are, close the choke valve plate by moving the choke operating lever, (2) in Fig. 3.9.

4   Apply vacuum of between 300 and 400 mm Hg to the duct (7). Now measure the gap between the edge of the choke valve plate and the wall of the carburettor throat. This should be as specified in Specifications according to carburettor model. Where necessary, adjust by bending the link rod (8). See Fig. 3.9.

5   Even without the vacuum equipment, it is often possible to adjust the valve plate opening satisfactorily. If the engine tends to hesitate at cold starting, or conversely starts to 'hunt', due to overchoking, the link rod can be bent very slightly before each cold start until the conditions improve. To prevent hesitation or stalling, straighten the cranked part of the rod. To prevent 'hunting', increase the angle of the cranked part of the rod.

14 Carburettor (Solex C32/34 DISA) – adjustment

Float level

1   The operations are very similar to those described in the preceding Section, except that the carburettor cover must be inverted to allow the float arm to fully depress the needle valve. In this condition, the float arm and the surface of the twin floats nearest the cover must be parallel. If the fuel level in this type of carburettor is incorrect, (indicated by the float arm not being parallel to the carburettor cover) do not bend the float arm; fit a washer of different thickness under the fuel inlet valve seat.

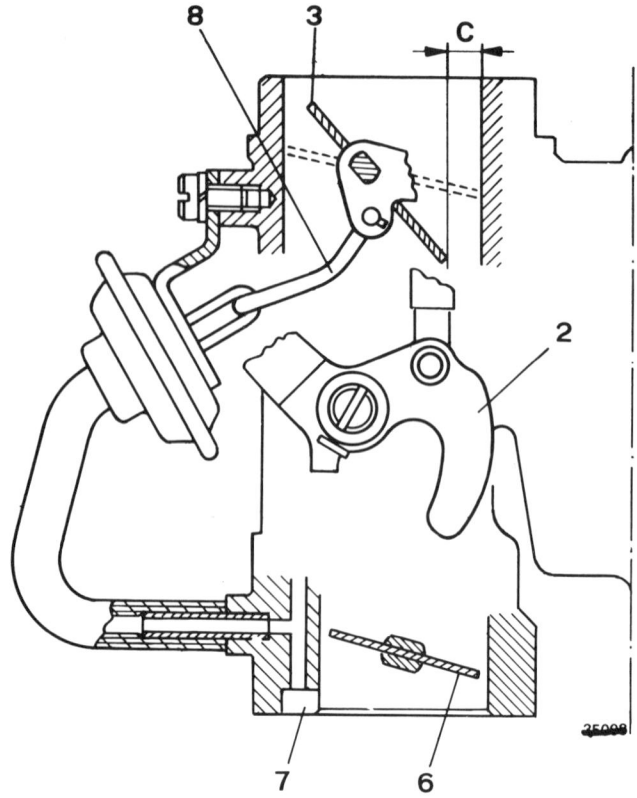

Fig. 3.9 Vacuum choke unloader diagram – Weber 32/34 ICEV (Sec 13)

2	Cam	7	Vacuum duct
3	Choke valve plate	8	Link rod
6	Throttle valve plate	C	= Choke valve plate gap

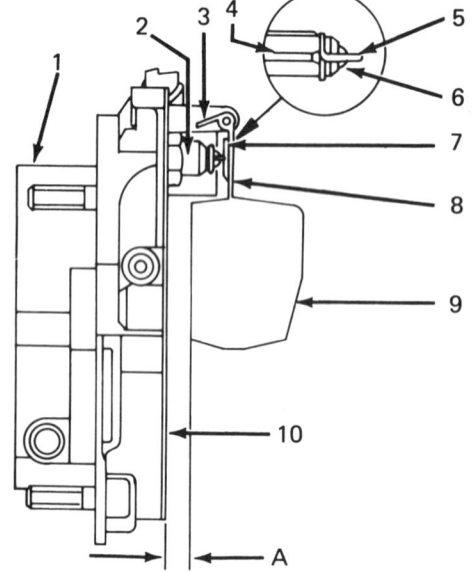

Fig. 3.10 Float level adjustment diagram – Weber 28/30 DHTA (Sec 15)

1	Top cover	6	Damper ball
2	Fuel inlet valve	7	Float tang
3	Float stroke stop	8	Float arm
4	Needle valve detail	9	Float
5	Valve hook	10	Gasket

A   (Float setting dimension) = 6.75 to 7.25 mm (0.266 to 0.285 in)

15 Carburettor (Weber 28/30 DHTA) – adjustment

Float level

1   Remove the cover assembly and hold it vertically so the float hangs downward to lightly seat the fuel inlet needle valve.

2   Measure the distance between the surface of the cover gasket and each float face. This should be between 6.75 and 7.25 mm (0.27 and 0.29 in). Make sure that the gasket-to-float distances are equal. Where adjustment is required, gently bend the float arm or tang.

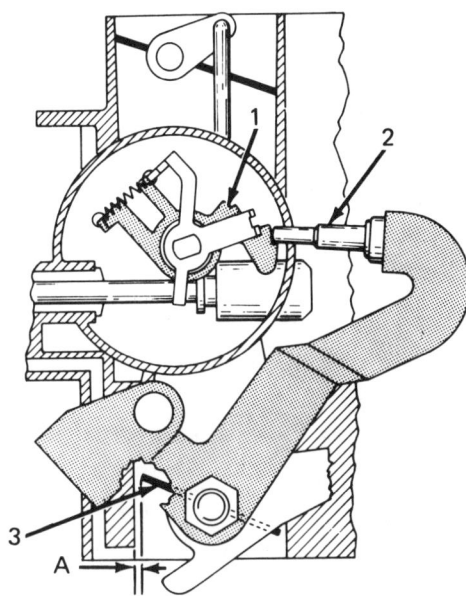

Fig. 3.11 Automatic choke adjustment – Weber 28/30 DHTA (Sec 15)

1	Fast idle cam	A = 0.85 to 0.95 mm
2	Fast idle screw	(0.033 to 0.037 in)
3	Primary throttle valve plate	

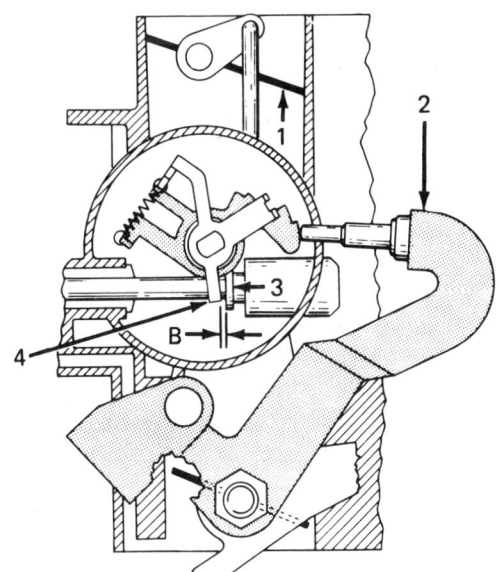

Fig. 3.12 Choke unloader adjustment diagram – Weber 28/30 DHTA (Sec 15)

1	Choke valve plate	4	Tang
2	Fast idle linkage		B = 0.3 to 1.0 mm
3	Spring bush		(0.012 to 0.039 in)

Automatic choke

3   Remove the carburettor from the engine, as previously described.

4   Extract the three equally spaced flange screws then remove the choke housing and gasket.

5   Position the fast idle screw (2) on the second step of the cam (1). See Fig. 3.11. Check the gap (A) between the edge of the primary throttle plate and the wall of the carburettor throat. The gap should be between 0.85 and 0.95 mm (0.033 and 0.037 in).Use a twist drill or wire spark plug gauge to check the gap and if adjustment is required, turn the screw (2) in or out.

Choke unloader

6   Pull the fast idle linkage fully back and close the choke valve plate with the fingers; release the linkage.

7   Measure the gap (B) between the tang (4) and the shoulder (3) of the bush. See Fig. 3.12.

8   Use a twist drill or wire spark plug gauge to measure the gap, which should be between 0.3 and 1.0 mm (0.012 and 0.039 in). To adjust the gap, bend the tang (4). See Fig. 3.12.

Fast idle cam intermediate setting

9   Position the screw (2) on the third step of the cam (3). See Fig. 3.13.

10 Check that gap C is between 2.5 and 3.0 mm (0.098 and 0.118 in). Where necessary, bend the lever (4) to achieve this dimension.

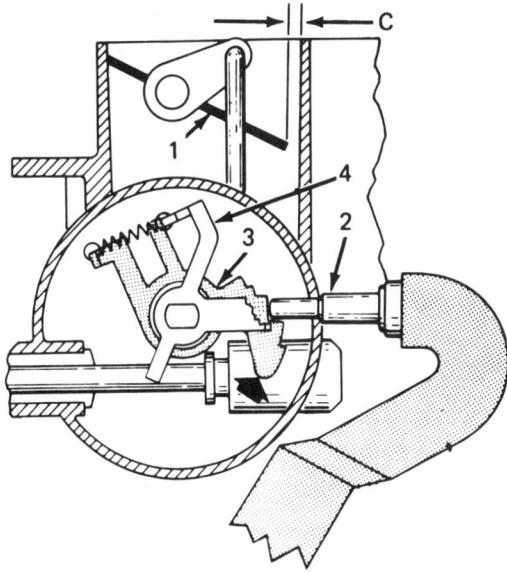

Fig. 3.13 Fast idle cam setting diagram – Weber 28/30 DHTA (Sec 15)

1	Choke valve plate	4	Lever
2	Fast idle screw		C = 2.5 to 3.0 mm
3	Fast idle cam		(0.098 to 0.118 in)

Choke unloader minimum opening

11 Position the screw on the second step of the cam (2). See Fig. 3.15.

12 A special tool (No 4460, shown in Fig. 3.14) should be obtained and fitted to the rod (7). In the absence of the special tool, the rod can be gripped with pliers, provided its jaws are insulated to prevent scoring the rod.

13 Push the rod until it makes contact with the stop screw (6), and hold it in this position.

14 Now measure the gap (D), which should be between 3.25 and 3.75 mm (0.13 and 0.15 in). Where necessary, adjust the gap by rotating the screw (6) which is accessible once the outer threaded plug (8) is extracted. See Fig. 3.15.

15 On cars equipped with an air conditioning system, a fast idle solenoid valve is fitted to the engine compartment rear bulkhead. Before removing this valve for any reason, identify the connecting hoses so that they can be reconnected correctly.

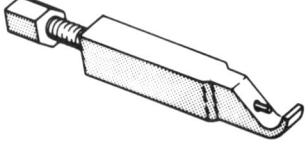

Fig. 3.14 Special tool No. 4460 (Sec 15)

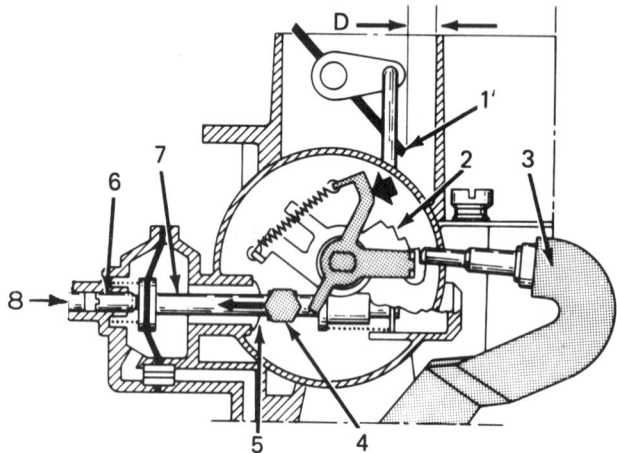

Fig. 3.15 Choke unloader minimum opening – Weber 28/30 DHTA
(Sec 15)

1   Choke valve plate
2   Fast idle cam
3   Fast idle linkage
4   Tool No 4460
5   Bush
6   Stop screw
7   Rod
8   Threaded plug
D = 3.25 to 3.75 mm
     (0.128 to 0.148 in)

Fig. 3.16 Crankcase location of the EGR valve (Sec 16)

17.2 Flame trap withdrawn from crankcase ventilation system hose

16 Emission control systems – description and maintenance

All models are equipped with a positive crankcase emission control system (see Section 17).

On cars destined for operation in North America, one or more exhaust emission control systems are fitted (see Sections 16 to 23).

On exhaust emission controlled cars, it must be appreciated that the carburettor, the distributor and the air cleaner have all been modified as a contributory means of reducing exhaust pollutants. These items must be maintained and serviced correctly; *never* tampered with to upset their original calibration or construction.

Many models are equipped with a fuel evaporative control system (see Section 22) and cars operating in California, particularly, have a catalytic converter in the exhaust system.

Maintenance consists of regularly checking the security and condition of the system hoses and electrical leads.

1   The EGR valve should be removed at the intervals specified in 'Routine Maintenance' and cleaned of all deposits with a wire brush.

2   At the specified intervals, remove the crankcase ventilation system hoses, vent body and flame trap; clean them in paraffin and keep them free from sludge or moisture.

3   Check the drivebelt tension on the air pump, if one is fitted.

4   Although the charcoal filter (used in conjunction with the fuel evaporative control system) has an unlimited life, it is recommended that it is renewed (to ensure full efficiency of the system) at the specified mileage intervals. The canister is located just below the spare wheel in the engine compartment rear bulkhead. Identify all hoses before disconnecting them. Check the condition of the fuel filler cap seal and renew it if necessary.

17 Positive crankcase ventilation system – description

This is a simple arrangement, whereby oil fumes from the sump and crankcase – and fuel vapour and exhaust gases which have passed the piston rings into the crankcase – are sucked out of the crankcase through a separator, pipeline and flame trap into the air cleaner. There, they are drawn into the intake manifold and burnt during the engine combustion cycle.

Periodically, disconnect the crankcase ventilation hose from the air cleaner and, using a pair of pliers, pull out the spirally wound wire mesh which acts as a flame trap in the event of a blow-back. Wash the flame trap in paraffin and dry it. If the inside of the hose is badly contaminated with sludge or condensation, disconnect the breather housing from the side of the crankcase and clean the interior of hose and housing (photo).

18 Exhaust gas recirculation (EGR) system – general description

This system controls the recirculation of inert exhaust gases, introduced into the intake manifold as a means of diluting the fuel/air mixture.

The result of this arrangement is that peak flame temperatures during combustion are lowered and the emission of Oxides of Nitrogen is reduced.

The EGR valve is closed during engine warm-up, being signalled from a coolant thermovalve. With the EGR valve in the closed position,

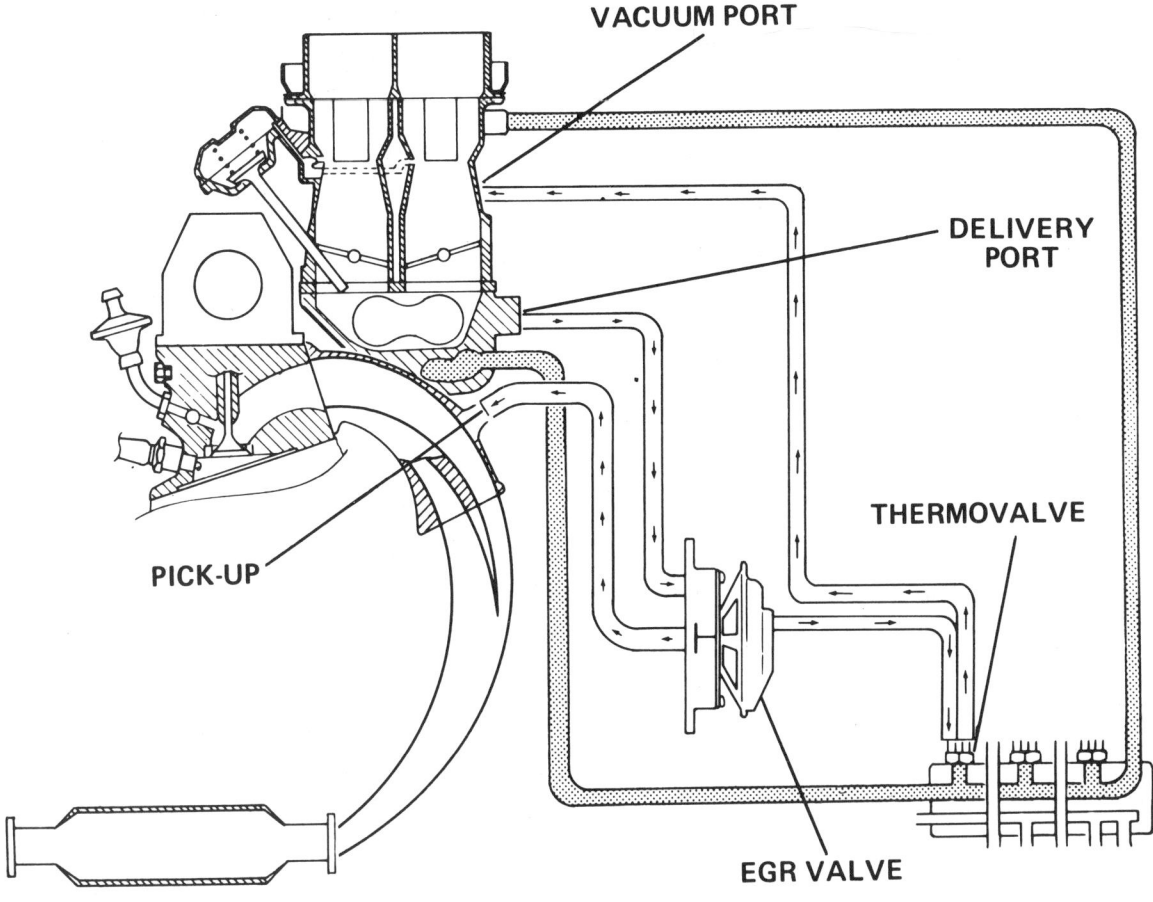

VACUUM PORT

DELIVERY PORT

THERMOVALVE

PICK-UP

EGR VALVE

Fig. 3.17 Diagrammatic layout of the EGR system (Sec 18)

Fig. 3.18 Vacuum thermovalves, EGR system (Sec 18)

recirculation of the exhaust gas does not occur and the intake mixture is not subject to dilution.

Once the engine is warm, the thermovalve opens and signals, in conjunction with exhaust gas back pressure, the EGR valve. The latter valve then opens to recirculate the exhaust gas. The vacuum pipe take-off point on the carburettor which signals engine load conditions to the EGR valve is so positioned that the recirculation of gases is at maximum volume under high engine load.

19 Air injection system (AIS) – general description

This system is fitted only to Californian versions.

It is designed to inject a controlled volume of air into the exhaust ports, to oxidise the gases and so reduce the amount of carbon monoxide hydrocarbons produced during the combustion cycle.

The system incorporates a belt-driven air pump, a non-return valve, a pressure relief valve and the necessary connecting tubes and cylinder head passages.

20 Air induction system – general description

This system is fitted to North American models except those destined for operation in California, which are equipped with an air injection system, as already described.

The differences between the air induction system and the air injection system is that in the former system, fresh air is drawn in by exhaust pulses rather than being generated by a pump.

The volume of inducted air is controlled by a reed valve mounted on the cylinder head. This acts as a high speed non-return valve, and is actuated by each exhaust pulse that passes the induction port. When the valve is open, fresh air is drawn in from the air cleaner housing through an independent filter/silencer.

The inducted air passes through a delivery passage in the cylinder head, mixing with the exhaust gas as it is expelled from the combustion chamber. Thus it ensures completion of the combustion process.

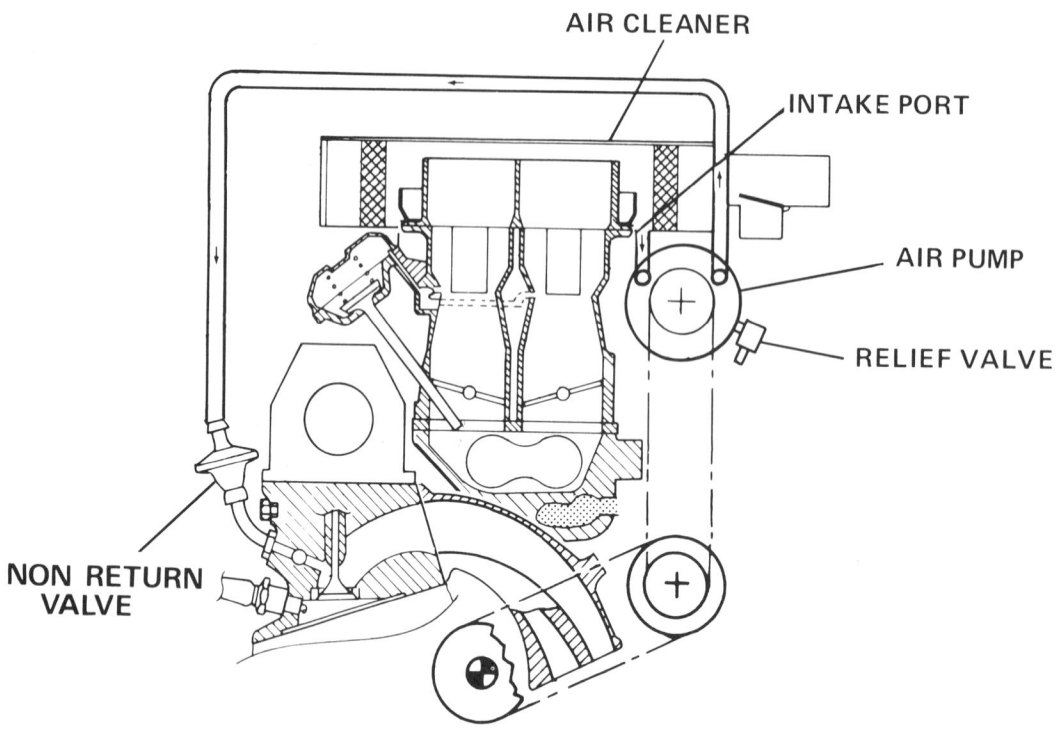

Fig. 3.19 Diagrammatic layout of the AIS system (Sec 19)

Fig. 3.20 Air pump for the AIS system (Sec 19)

Fig. 3.21 Non-return valve for the AIS system (Sec 19)

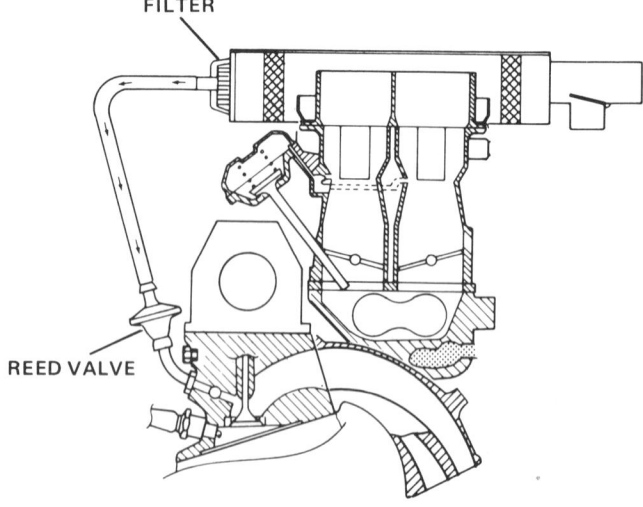

Fig. 3.22 Diagrammatic layout of the air induction system (Sec 20)

21 Air gulp system – general description

This system is fitted in conjunction with either the air injection or air induction system.

The need for this is that during deceleration, the fuel/air mixture becomes very rich and would cause backfiring in the exhaust system if not diluted during this phase.

The air gulp system provides the extra air during deceleration by means of a valve, vacuum-operated from the intake manifold.

During engine starting, the electrovalve is energised to apply

Fig. 3.23 Reed valve – air induction system (Sec 21)

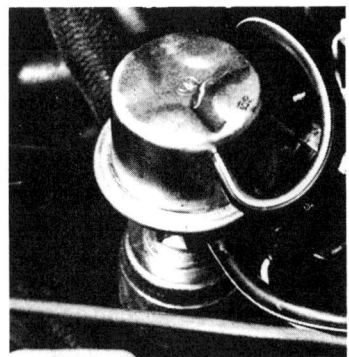

Fig. 3.25 Gulp valve on the engine compartment rear bulkhead (Sec 21)

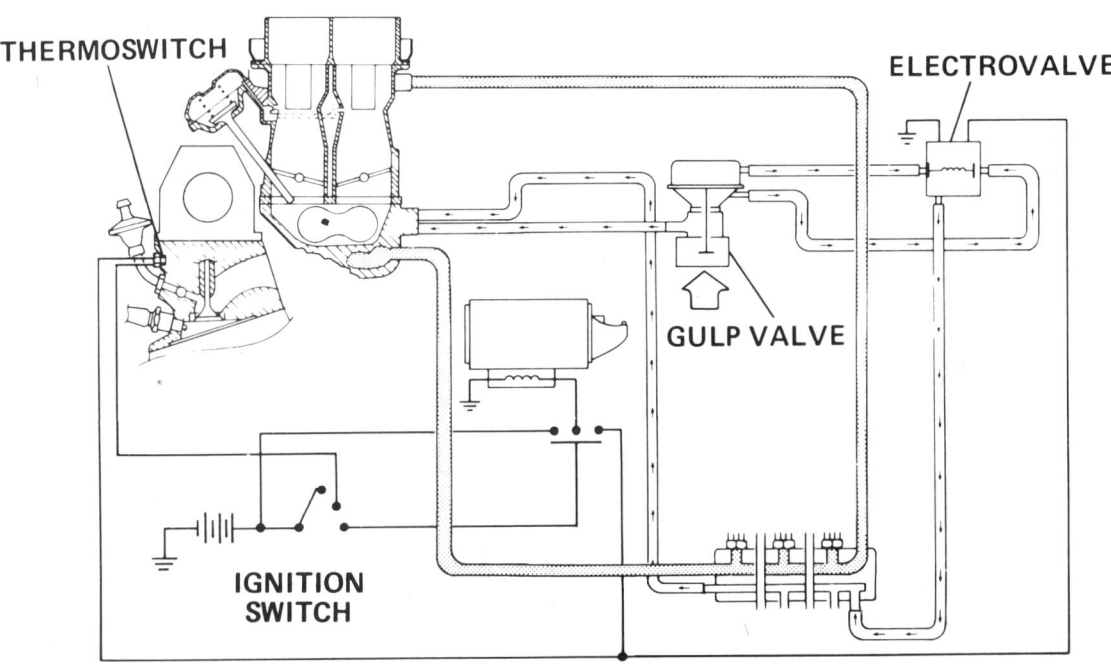

Fig. 3.24 Diagrammatic layout of the air gulp system (Sec 21)

manifold vacuum directly to the upper chamber of the gulp valve, and holds the valve shut.

During engine warm-up (when the engine is cold), a thermoswitch incorporated in the system closes to again apply manifold vacuum only to the upper chamber of the gulp valve, thus holding the valve shut. This arrangement prevents dilution of the fuel/air mixture while the automatic choke is in operation.

Once the engine is at normal operating temperature, the thermoswitch is open and the electrovalve de-energised to cause the gulp valve to open. Thus it admits fresh air to the intake manifold when the vacuum applied to the valve is high, during periods of deceleration.

22 Fuel evaporative control system – general description

The purpose of this system is to reduce the emissions of fuel vapour which occur through evaporation in the fuel tank and the carburettor bowl.

The emitted vapour is trapped in a charcoal filled canister while the car is stationary and the engine is switched off.

Once the engine is started, the carbon canister is purged by vacuum from the intake manifold. The stored vapour is drawn into the engine combustion chambers, where it is burned during the normal combustion processes.

23 Catalytic converter – general description

This device is fitted into the exhaust system of certain North American models.

The catalytic converter oxidises hydrocarbons and carbon monoxide within the exhaust system. It comprises an outer casing, filled with catalyst beads coated with palladium and platinum.

As the exhaust gases pass through the catalytic converter, chemical reactions occur producing harmless carbon dioxide and water from the noxious gases. These chemical changes occur at temperatures between 439 and 847°F (226 and 453°C).

Always use unleaded fuel in cars equipped with a catalytic converter.

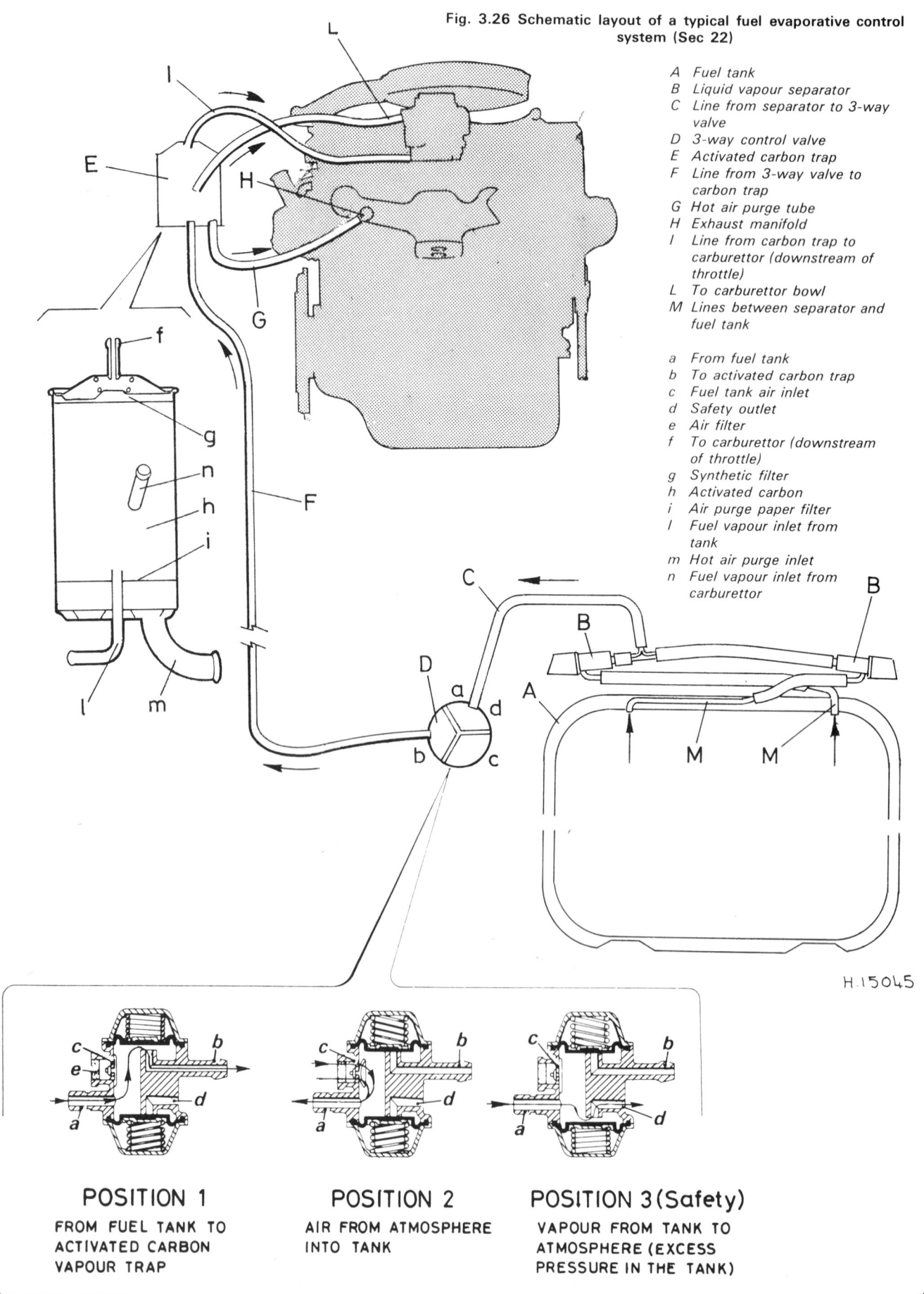

Fig. 3.26 Schematic layout of a typical fuel evaporative control system (Sec 22)

A   Fuel tank
B   Liquid vapour separator
C   Line from separator to 3-way valve
D   3-way control valve
E   Activated carbon trap
F   Line from 3-way valve to carbon trap
G   Hot air purge tube
H   Exhaust manifold
I   Line from carbon trap to carburettor (downstream of throttle)
L   To carburettor bowl
M   Lines between separator and fuel tank

a   From fuel tank
b   To activated carbon trap
c   Fuel tank air inlet
d   Safety outlet
e   Air filter
f   To carburettor (downstream of throttle)
g   Synthetic filter
h   Activated carbon
i   Air purge paper filter
l   Fuel vapour inlet from tank
m   Hot air purge inlet
n   Fuel vapour inlet from carburettor

H.15045

POSITION 1
FROM FUEL TANK TO ACTIVATED CARBON VAPOUR TRAP

POSITION 2
AIR FROM ATMOSPHERE INTO TANK

POSITION 3 (Safety)
VAPOUR FROM TANK TO ATMOSPHERE (EXCESS PRESSURE IN THE TANK)

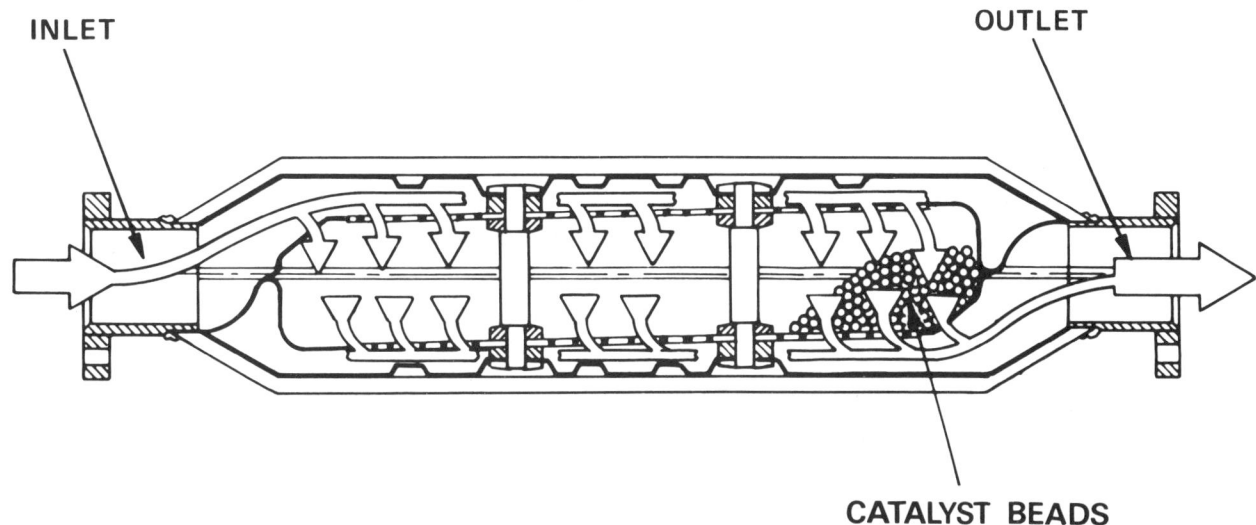

INLET   OUTLET

CATALYST BEADS

Fig. 3.27 Sectional view of a catalytic converter (Sec 23)

Excessive temperatures can be generated within the exhaust system if over-rich mixtures are used by incorrect engine tune or when decelerating for extended periods (eg when descending a long gradient).

For safety reasons, do not park the car over an area of long grass or other combustible material when the catalytic converter is hot.

24 Manifolds and exhaust system

1 The intake manifold is bolted to the rear face of the cylinder head and supports the carburettor.
2 Removal of the intake manifold (complete with carburettor) is quite straightforward once the cooling system has been partially drained and the coolant and heater hoses, vacuum pipes, choke and accelerator cables disconnected.
3 The exhaust manifold cannot be removed until the exhaust downpipe has been disconnected and the air cleaner hot air intake shroud detached.
4 Refitting is a reversal of the removal process; use new gaskets and tighten all nuts and bolts to the specified torques.
5 The exhaust system is supported on rubber suspension rings, with a figure-8 type flexible mounting at its rear end (photos).

24.5a Exhaust system suspension rings

24.5b Exhaust tailpipe flexible mounting

24.8 Exhaust system clamp

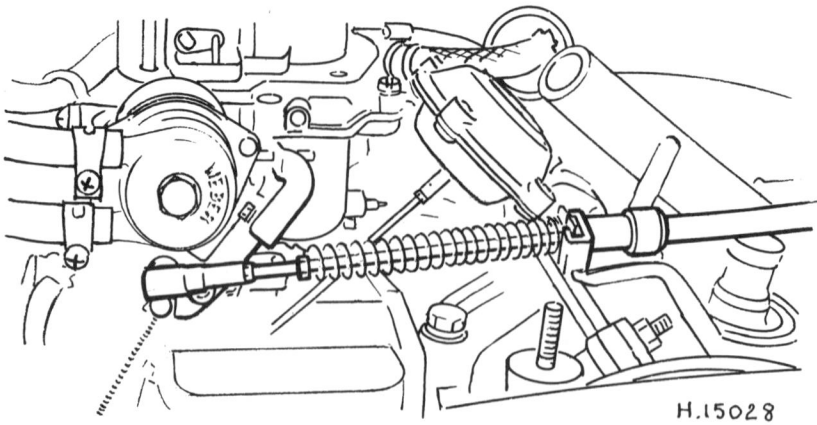

Fig. 3.28 Accelerator linkage at a Weber DHTA type carburettor (Sec 25)

25.2 Choke control lever, showing quadrant positioning ratchet

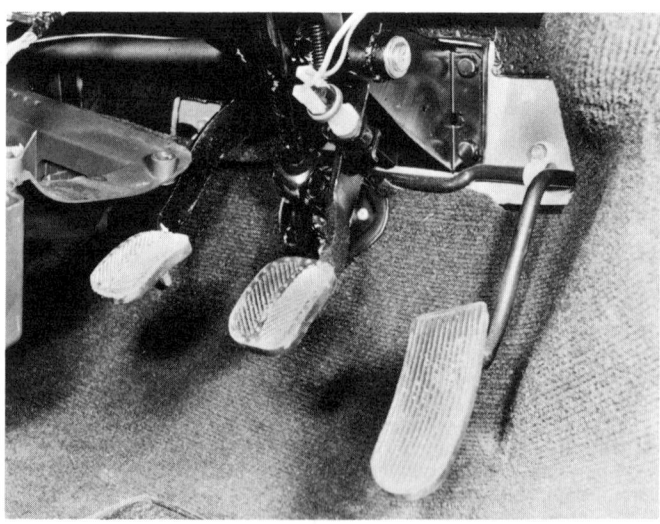

25.7 Accelerator pedal, rod and mounting

6   Do not attempt to separate the sections of the exhaust system, while in position in the car. Unbolt the pipe from the manifold and, using a screwdriver, prise off the flexible suspension rings. Provided the car is then raised on jacks, ramps or placed over an inspection pit, the complete exhaust system can be withdrawn from under the car.
7   If only one section is to be renewed, it is far easier to separate once the complete system is out of the car.
8   When refitting, grease the pipe sockets and fit the clamps loosely until the suspension rings are connected and the downpipe bolted up (using a new copper gasket). Check the attitude of the sections with regard to each other and the adjacent parts of the underbody. Fully tighten the clamps and downpipe flange nuts, remembering to bend up the lockplate tabs (photo).

25 Accelerator and choke control cables – renewal

Choke cable
1   Release the outer cable and inner cable clamp screws.
2   Working under the instrument panel, detach the lever type choke control lever by extracting its single screw (photo).

3   Carefully, note the routing of the cable, then withdraw it through the bulkhead grommets into the car interior.
4   Refitting is the reverse of the removal process, but make sure the choke lever on the carburettor is in the fully off position. Push the instrument panel choke control lever fully in, then move it out again just a fraction before tightening the cable clamp screws at the carburettor. This will ensure that, with the lever pushed fully in, the choke will be fully off without·the possibility of slight actuation due to the movement of the engine on its flexible mountings.

Accelerator cable
5   The accelerator cable is secured to the throttle lever on the carburettor by a socket and balljoint. To release the connection, slide back the split sleeve and pull the socket from the ball stud.
6   Detach the cable sleeve from the stop bracket.
7   Once the cable is unhooked from the top of the accelerator pedal rod, the cable can be withdrawn through the engine compartment rear bulkhead grommets, into the engine compartment (photo).
8   Refitting is a reversal of the removal process, but adjust the cable at the carburettor end, using the locknuts to provide full closure and opening of the throttle valve plate, relative to the fully depressed and released positions of the accelerator pedal.

26 Fault diagnosis – fuel system, carburation and emission control

Note: *Unsatisfactory engine performance and excessive fuel consumption are not necessarily the fault of the fuel system or carburettor. In fact, they more commonly occur as a result of ignition and timing faults. Even if a fault does lie in the fuel system, it will be difficult to trace unless the ignition system and valve clearances are correctly adjusted.*

Symptom	Reason/s
Difficult starting	Manual choke maladjusted or automatic choke defective Fuel tank empty or pump defective Air cleaner blocked Air leak on induction side Float chamber fuel level incorrect Vapour lock in fuel line (in hot weather or at high altitudes)
Excessive fuel consumption	Leakage from tank, pipes, pump or carburettor Blocked air cleaner Blocked hoses in fuel evaporative emission control system (if fitted) Float chamber fuel level incorrect Carburettor maladjusted or worn
Fuel starvation	Level in tank too low (especially on hills) Leak on suction side of pump (air bubbles in fuel line) Level in float chamber too low, or needle valve sticking Fuel tank breather (or fuel evaporative emission control system hoses) blocked Fuel filters blocked Fuel pump defective
Surge during deceleration (emission control models)	Throttle opener dashpot not operating correctly Fault in exhaust emission control valves
Backfiring	Air leak in exhaust system Overheating Gulp valve operating incorrectly Carburettor maladjusted or worn Valve clearance incorrect or valves burnt
Exhaust CO level too low	Idle speed too low Carburettor maladjusted or worn Engine worn
Exhaust CO level excessive	Automatic choke defective Air cleaner blocked or temperature control defective Carburettor maladjusted or worn Engine worn
Exhaust HC level excessive	Carburettor maladjusted or worn Air leak on induction side Engine worn Ignition system fault (see Chapter 4)

Chapter 4 Ignition system

For modifications, and information applicable to later models, see Supplement at end of manual

Contents

Specifications

System type

All except North American models	Battery, coil, mechanical breaker type distributor
North American models	Battery, coil, breakerless electronic type distributor
Firing order	1-3-4-2 (No 1 at timing belt end of engine)

Mechanical breaker distributor (Marelli or Ducellier)

Contact breaker gap	0.37 to 0.43 mm (0.015 to 0.017 in)
Dwell angle	52° to 58°
Static advance	5° BTDC
Centrifugal advance	25° to 29°
Vacuum advance	Not fitted
Rotor rotational direction	Clockwise
Condenser capacity	0.25 ± 0.025 µF
Coil primary resistance at 20°C	3.1 to 3.4 ohms*
Coil secondary resistance at 20°C	6500 to 12 000 ohms

* *Dependent upon make of coil*

Breakerless electronic distributor (Marelli or Bosch)

Rotor rotational direction:	
Crankcase mounted distributor	Clockwise
Camshaft carrier mounted distributor	Anti-clockwise
Timing (with stroboscope):	
Manual transmission	5° BTDC at 800 to 850 rpm
Automatic transmission	5° BTDC at 700 to 750 rpm in 'D'
Coil (Bosch system):	
Primary	1.1 to 1.7 ohms
Secondary	6000 to 10 000 ohms
Resistor	0.85 to 0.95 ohms
Distributor advance:	
Centrifugal	23° to 27° at 5500 rpm
Vacuum:	
All except California models	26° to 30° at 12 in Hg
California	16° to 18° at 12 in Hg

Spark plugs

	Standard	Resistor
Type		
Make:		
AC	42XLS	R42XLS
Bosch	W7D	WR7D
Champion	N9Y	RN9Y
Marelli	CW7LP	CW7LPR
Electrode gap	0.584 to 0.686 mm (0.023 to 0.027 in)	0.686 to 0.787 mm (0.027 to 0.031 in)

Torque wrench settings

	lbf ft	Nm
Spark plugs	27	37

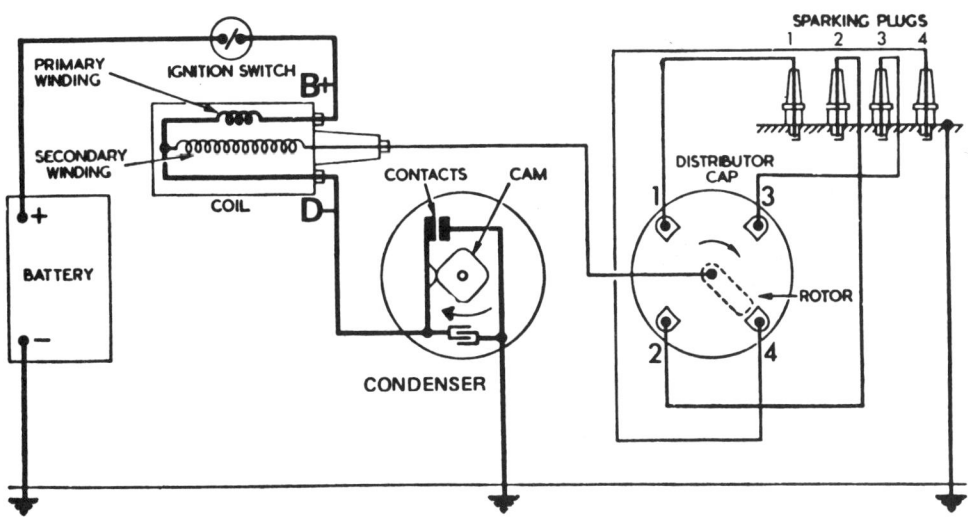

Fig. 4.1 Typical ignition circuit (mechanical contact breaker) (Sec 1)

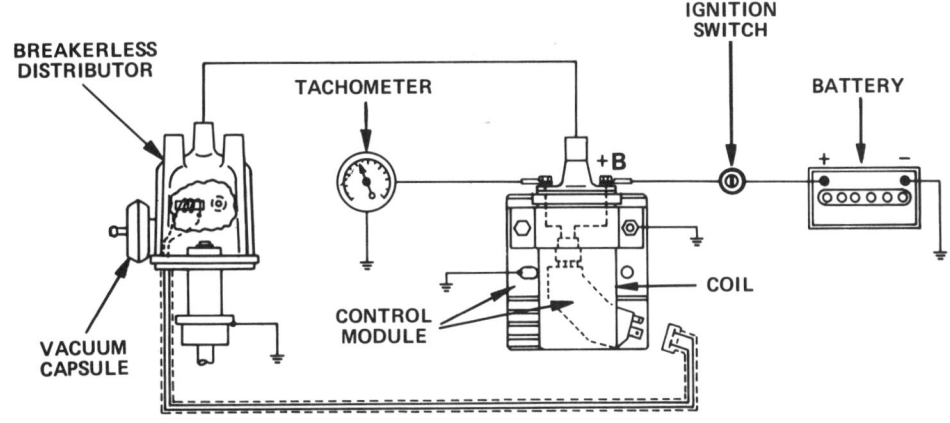

Fig. 4.2 Typical ignition circuit (breakerless system) – Marelli (Sec 1)

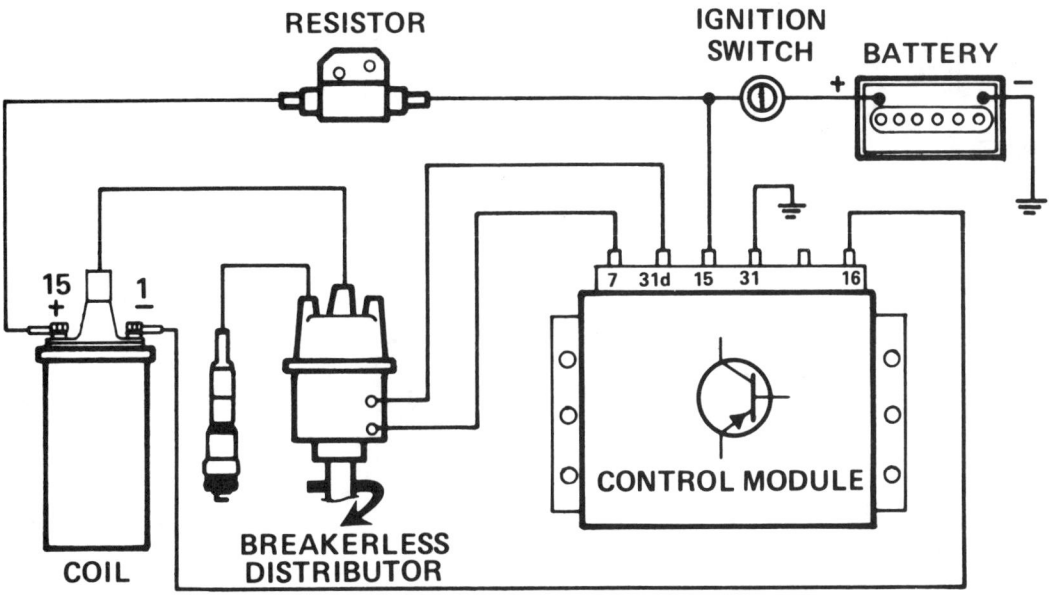

Fig. 4.3 Typical ignition circuit (breakerless system) – Bosch (Sec 1)

1 General description

The ignition system differs according to model. On versions not destined for operation in North America, a conventional mechanical contact breaker system is used on the 1301 and 1498 cc engines. On North American versions (with the 1498 cc engine), a breakerless electronic system is employed.

Mechanical contact breaker system

For the engine to run correctly, it is necessary for an electrical spark to ignite the fuel/air mixture in the combustion chamber at exactly the right moment in relation to engine speed and load. The ignition system is based on feeding low tension voltage from the battery to the coil where it is converted to high tension voltage. The high tension voltage is powerful enough to jump the spark plug gap in the cylinders under high compression pressures, providing that the system is in good condition and that all adjustments are correct.

The ignition system is divided into two circuits, the low tension (LT) circuit and the high tension (HT) circuit.

The low tension (sometimes known as the primary) circuit consists of the battery, the lead to the ignition switch, the lead from the ignition switch to the low tension or primary coil windings, and the lead from the low tension coil windings to the contact breaker points and condenser in the distributor.

The high tension circuit consists of the high tension or secondary coil windings, the heavy ignition lead from the centre of the coil to the centre of the distributor cap, the rotor arm, and the spark plug leads and spark plugs.

The system functions in the following manner: High tension voltage is generated in the coil by the interruption of the low tension circuit. The interruption is effected by the opening of the contact breaker points in this low tension circuit. High tension voltage is fed from the centre of the coil via the carbon brush in the centre of the distributor cap to the rotor arm of the distributor.

The rotor arm revolves at half engine speed inside the distributor cap, and each time it comes in line with one of the four metal segments in the cap, which are connected to the spark plug leads, the opening of the contact breaker points causes the high tension voltage to build up, jump the gap from the rotor arm to the appropriate metal segment, and so via the spark plug lead to the spark plug, where it finally jumps the spark plug gap before going to earth.

The ignition timing is advanced and retarded automatically, to ensure the spark occurs at just the right instant for the particular load at the prevailing engine speed.

The ignition advance is controlled mechanically. The mechanical governor mechanism comprises two weights, which move out from the distributor shaft as the engine speed rises, due to centrifugal force. As they move outwards, they rotate the cam relative to the distributor shaft, and so advance the spark. The weights are held in position by two springs and it is the tension of the springs which is largely responsible for correct spark advancement. A vacuum advance capsule is only fitted to certain models.

Breakerless, electronic system

The purpose of the system is as described for the mechanical breaker system in earlier paragraphs of this Section. But the method of generating the spark is different.

A Bosch or Marelli system may be fitted and comprises an ignition coil, an electronic control system and a breakerless distributor. On Bosch systems, a resistor is fitted.

The electronic system has several advantages over the conventional ignition system. These include the following:

Elimination of points adjustment and renewal
Reduction in number of moving parts
Lower current draw
Higher secondary voltage

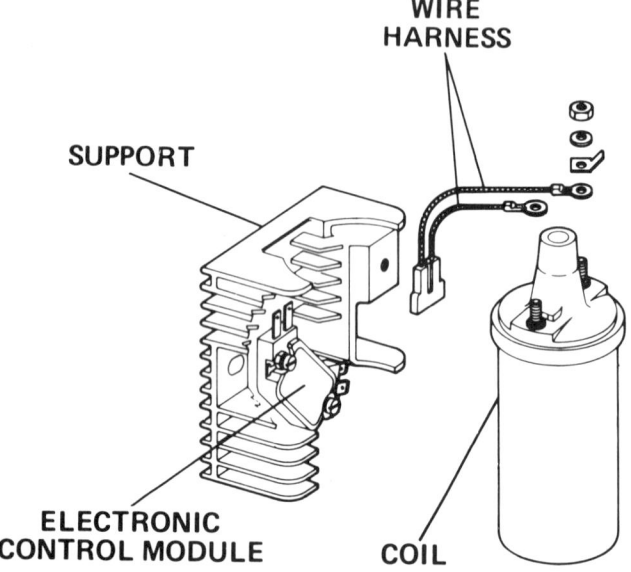

Fig. 4.4 Ignition coil and control module (breakerless system) — Bosch (Sec 1)

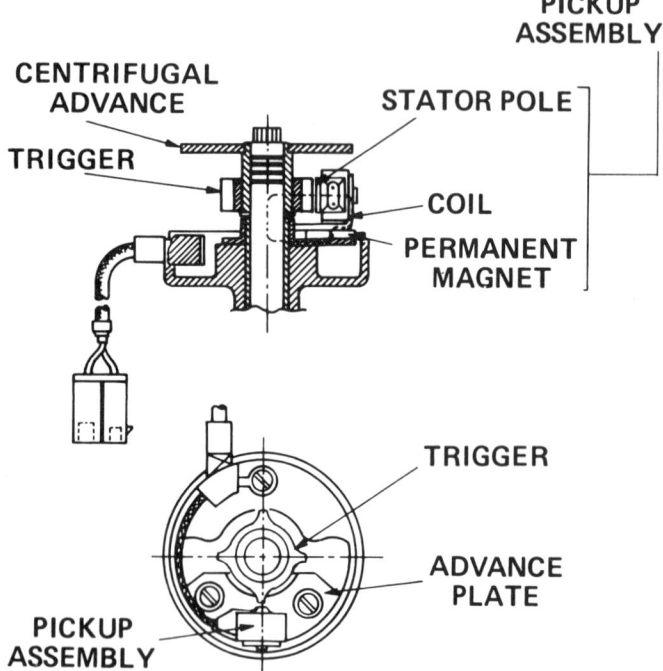

Fig. 4.5 Views of distributor assembly (breakerless type) — Bosch (Sec 1)

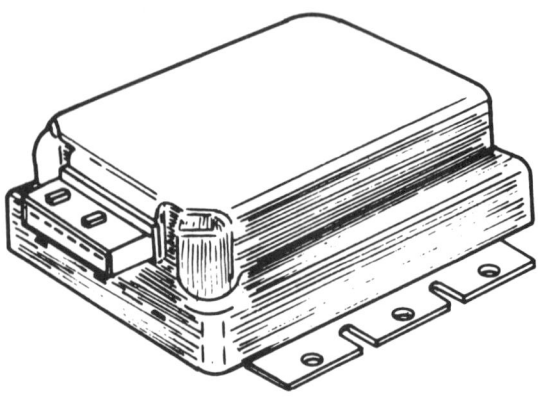

Fig. 4.6 Control module (breakerless system) — Marelli (Sec 1)

These factors improve performance and reduce the exhaust emission levels.

With electronic systems, primary voltage is applied from the battery through the ignition switch to the electronic control module, and through a resistor to the coil. The resistor acts as a heat sink.

The earth (negative) terminal of the coil is connected to the control module, which itself connects to a negative pick-up in the distributor.

Primary voltage is regulated by the control module, to supply a regulated current to the primary windings of the ignition coil. The control module is triggered by an impulse, generated within the distributor. This interrupts the coil primary circuit. Each time the primary circuit is broken, a high voltage is induced in the coil secondary windings, which is in turn distributed to the spark plugs through the conventional means of distributor cap and rotor.

A conventional, oil filled ignition coil is used. The electronic control module incorporates a current limiter to provide a constant supply to the primary circuit and so prevent damage to the coil.

The control module also monitors the impulses from the distributor pick-up assembly to provide the necessary dwell and spark duration, irrespective of engine speed.

The pick-up assembly consists of a wire wound coil, a four-pole stator and a permanent magnet. The trigger incorporates four teeth, 90° apart. As a tooth passes through the magnetic field, an electrical impulse is generated in the coil winding of the pick-up assembly and then fed to the control module, so interrupting the coil primary circuit.

A vacuum capsule is attached to the breakerless type distributor body, to provide ignition advance according to engine load. Vacuum is obtained from the carburettor bore above the throttle valve plate, and provides high vacuum during part throttle operation.

The vacuum to the distributor is controlled by a delay valve and a thermovalve. When the engine is cold, the thermovalve is closed and vacuum is applied through the delay valve, which regulates the speed of application and release of the advance mechanism. When the engine is warm, the thermovalve is open and provides instant application and release of the advance mechanism.

Mechanical contact breaker and breakerless systems

On all models (except those equipped with air conditioning), the distributor is located on the crankcase and is driven by the upper end of the oil pump driveshaft which is geared to the engine auxiliary shaft. On air conditioned models, the distributor is located on the left-hand end of the camshaft carrier and is driven from the camshaft. This alternative location is dictated by the mounting of the air conditioning condenser.

2 Mechanical contact breaker points – cleaning and adjustment

Mechanical wear of the contact breaker reduces the gap. Electrical wear builds up a 'pip' of burned metal on one of the contacts. This prevents the gap being measured for re-adjustment, and also spoils the electric circuit.

1   At the specified intervals, the points must be removed for cleaning, or renewal. They can be cleaned once; the next time, replacement points should be fitted.

2   Unclip and remove the distributor cap. Pull off the rotor arm.

3   Slide the rubber grommet on the side of the distributor body upwards, far enough for the contact breaker lead to slide out. Undo the screw holding the contact breaker to the distributor plate, and lift out both the moving and the fixed contacts (photo).

4   Clean the points by rubbing the surfaces on a fine abrasive such as an oil stone. The point surface should be shaped to a gentle convex curve. All the 'pip' burned onto one contact must be removed. It is not necessary to go on until all traces of the crater have been removed from the other. There is enough metal on the contacts to allow this to be done once. At alternative services, fit new points. Wash debris off cleaned points, and preservatives off new ones.

5   Whilst reassembling, lubricate the distributor as detailed in the next Section.

6   Now adjust the contact breaker gap. With electronic test equipment, this can be done by measuring the dwell, in accordance with the instructions of the tester. For initial adjustment, turn the engine over by putting the car in top gear, and moving it forward till the contact breaker points are open as wide as they go, with the heel of the moving contact on the top of the cam. Insert a feeler for 0.4 mm (0.015 in) between the contacts. Slacken the clamping screw so the fixed contacts can just be moved. Prise it into position so that the feeler is lightly brushed by the contacts. Carefully, tighten the screw so as not to disturb the contact. Recheck the gap, trying feelers slightly larger and smaller to see if it is right. Turn the engine over to come up on another cam, to recheck. With an old distributor, some variation must be expected from cam to cam. The gap is going to close slightly as the heel of the contact wears. So the gap must start big enough. But if the gap is too large, the dwell will not be long enough: This

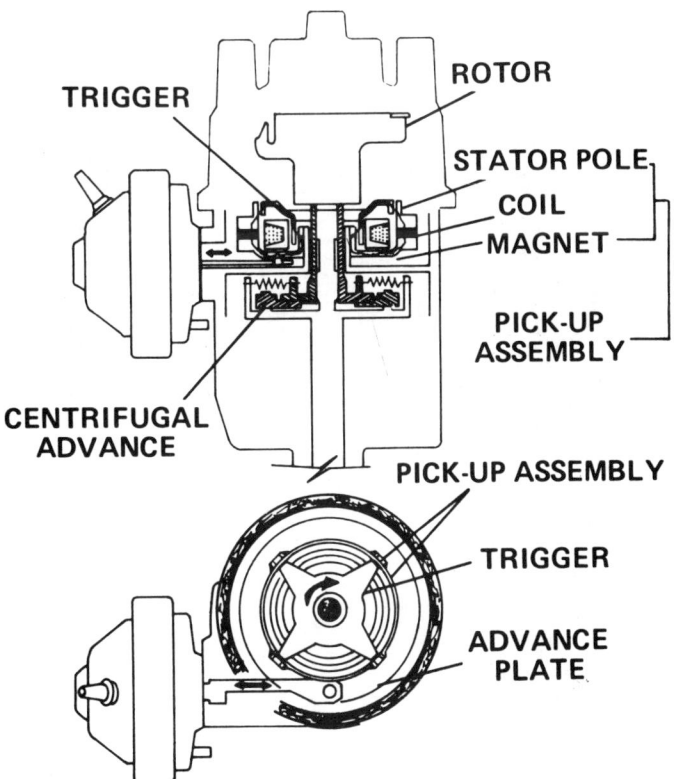

Fig. 4.7 Views of distributor assembly (breakerless type) – Marelli (Sec 1)

TRIGGER

ROTOR

STATOR POLE

COIL

MAGNET

PICK-UP ASSEMBLY

CENTRIFUGAL ADVANCE

PICK-UP ASSEMBLY

TRIGGER

ADVANCE PLATE

2.3 Contact breaker (mechanical type distributor)

means there will be insufficient time for the magnetic field to build up in the coil to give a good spark.

7 Setting the contact breaker gap with a feeler blade must be regarded as a means of ensuring that the engine will start. For optimum engine performance, the dwell angle must be checked and adjusted. *The dwell angle is the number of degrees through which the distributor cam turns between the instants of closure and opening of the contact breaker points.*

8 Connect a dwell meter in accordance with the maker's instruction. The type of meter that operates with the engine running is to be preferred; any variation in contact breaker gap, caused by wear in the distributor shaft or bushes, or the height of the distributor cam peaks, is evened out when using this.

9 The correct dwell angle is given in the Specifications at the beginning of this Chapter. If the angle is too large, increase the contact points gap. If the angle is too small, reduce the points gap. Only very slight adjustments should be made to the gap before re-checking.

10 Always check and adjust the dwell angle before timing the ignition as described in Section 4.

Wipe the rotor arm and distributor cap inside clean. Check the metal segments are not badly burned, nor have been in metal-to-metal contact due to incorrect fitting of the rotor arm. If badly worn, they will need renewal. Clean the outside of the distributor cap, and all the leads.

3.3 Oiling the distributor shaft felt pad

4.7 Timing marks, TDC arrowed

3 Mechanical type distributor – lubrication

1 At the specified service interval (whilst the contact breaker points are being cleaned), the distributor should be lubricated. This lubrication is important for the correct mechanical function of the distributor, but excess lubrication will ruin the electrical circuits, and give difficult starting.

2 Whilst the contact breaker is off, squirt some engine oil into the bottom part of the distributor, onto the centrifugal advance mechanism below the plate.

3 Wet with oil the felt pad on the top of the distributor spindle, normally covered by the rotor arm (photo).

4 Put just a drip of oil on the pivot for the moving contact.

5 Smear a little general purpose grease onto the cam, and the heel of the moving contact breaker.

4 Ignition timing (mechanical contact breaker)

As the contact breaker heel wears, the timing must be reset whenever the contact breaker points are cleaned or renewed. If this is not done, engine power and efficiency will be lowered, and the idling may be uneven or unreliable. If the timing is retarded, the idle will be smooth, but slow. If advanced, it will tend to be fast, but uneven. Variations of at least three degrees (crankshaft) are needed to make the idle appear wrong. But such variations will be showing more important loss of efficiency in fuel consumption, power, and exhaust emissions if measured with suitable equipment. If the timing has been completely lost, as opposed to needing resetting, refer first to Section 7

1 For static timing, turn the engine over by putting the car in gear and moving it forwards, until the second (5°) mark on the belt cover is opposite the notch in the crankshaft belt pulley. Do not turn the engine backwards; backlash in the distributor drive will upset the timing.

2 With the engine at this position, the points should be at the moment of opening. The ideal way to see when the points open is to wire a 12 volt bulb in series with the contact breaker points, using the wire to the coil from the switch, having taken the wire off the coil.

3 Slacken the nut on the distributor clamping plate.

Fig. 4.8 Timing marks on camshaft belt cover (Sec 4)

1	10° BTDC	3	TDC
2	5° BTDC	4	Notch in crankshaft pulley

4   Turn the distributor slightly in the direction of rotation of the cam (clockwise) to make sure the points are shut. Then carefully turn it anti-clockwise to advance the ignition, against the direction of rotation, until the points open, as shown by the light going out. If not using a light, then with the ignition on, a spark can sometimes be seen at the points, or if an ammeter is fitted, an assistant can watch this for a flicker, the ignition being on.

5   Reclamp the distributor.

6   Now recheck, by turning the engine over, forwards again, till the timing notch on the pulley is coming up to the mark again. Watch the timing light and the pulley. Turn the engine smoothly and slowly, and see where the notch was when the timing light went out. It should, of course, be opposite the 5° mark.

7   On some models, the timing scale is in the form of a small, right-angled plate, as shown in the photograph. With these models, timing marks are not embossed on the belt cover (photo). On other models, the timing marks are on the flywheel, and are visible after removing the rubber plug from the flywheel casing.

8   The timing can be set with the engine running, using a stroboscope. This method is more accurate, and such accuracy is needed to meet the American emission regulations.

9   Connect up the timing light to No. 1 cylinder plug lead in accordance with the maker's instructions. Start-up the engine. Check the idle speed is correct with a tachometer. Shine the light on the timing marks, which should have been painted white. Slacken the distributor, and move it as required to get the correct relationship of the notch on the pulley with the mark on the cover, as 'frozen' by the light. Reclamp the distributor. Speed up the engine, and check the automatic advance is working.

10   Unless the engine is idling, setting the timing by stroboscope will be inaccurate, as the automatic advance is varying the timing as the engine speeds up.

5   Breakerless (electronic) ignition – maintenance

This type of distributor is virtually maintenance free. No points adjustment, renewal or lubrication is required.

1   Occasionally, wipe the distributor cap clean and check for cracks.

2   Check the system interconnecting leads for security of connection and for the condition of the insulation.

6   Ignition timing (breakerless ignition system)

It is rare to find that the timing on this system requires adjustment; there are no contact points to wear, which could alter the timing.

1   Where it is required (perhaps after removal and refitting of the distributor), timing adjustment must be carried out using a stroboscope as described in the preceding Section 4, paragraphs 9 and 10.

2   It is important that the engine is running at the specified idling speed, according to the type of transmission fitted (see Specifications).

7   Distributor – removal and refitting

Crankcase mounted type

1   Rotate the crankshaft by means of its pulley nut, until No 1 piston is rising on its compression stroke. The best way to check this is to remove No 1 spark plug, place a finger over the hole and feel the compression being generated. Once compression is felt, keep turning the crankshaft until the notch in the pulley is in alignment with the specified BTDC timing mark.

2   Remove the distributor cap and mark the position of the contact end of the rotor in relation to the rim of the distributor body.

3   Mark the relative position of the distributor mounting flange to the crankcase.

4   Disconnect the primary lead from the distributor terminal; also disconnect the vacuum pipe, if one is fitted.

5   Unbolt the securing clamp and lift the distributor from its location (photo).

6   The driveshaft can now be extracted if necessary, by inserting the finger into the hole in the end of the shaft and withdrawing it.

7.8 Distributor driveshaft on camshaft mounted type

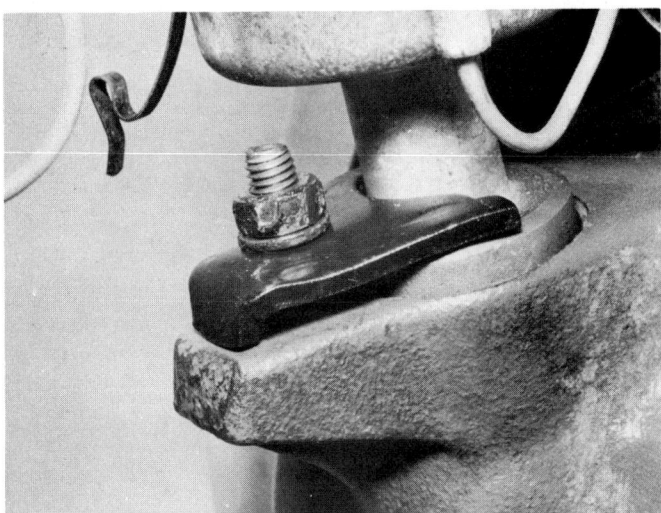

7.5 Distributor clamp plate

7.9 Distributor fitted with condenser aligned with No 2 spark plug hole

Camshaft carrier mounted type

7 The operations are very similar to those first described for the crankcase mounted type. Again, mark the position of the rotor and the distributor mounting flange to its support pedestal. The distributor is retained by three securing nuts.

8 Once withdrawn, the splined driveshaft can be withdrawn from the end of the camshaft (photo).

All types

9 Refitting presents no problem with either type of distributor as the distributor is driven by a splined shaft. Provided that the crankshaft pulley timing mark, the rotor and distributor mounting flange are set as described prior to removal, the distributor can be fitted directly into its recess. In the case of the crankcase mounted type, fitting can be achieved irrespective of the setting of the oil pump driveshaft, which is geared to the auxiliary shaft.

10 Once fitted, reconnect the leads and vacuum pipe, then check and adjust the ignition timing as described in Section 4 or 6 (according to distributor type).

11 On the camshaft carrier mounted type, use a new flange gasket if the support pedestal is removed (photo).

---

8   Distributor (mechanical breaker type) – overhaul

One of two makes of distributor may be encountered, Ducellier or Marelli. For the purpose of overhaul, there are only minor detail differences in the design of some components. Apart from the contact points, other components most likely to deteriorate with age are the cap, rotor, shaft bushes and the springs for the centrifugal weights.

1 The cap must have no flaws or cracks and the HT terminal contacts should not be severely corroded. The centre spring-loaded carbon contact is renewable. If in any doubt about the cap, buy a new one (photo).

2 The rotor deteriorates minimally, but with age the metal conductor tip may corrode. It should not be cracked or chipped and the metal conductor must not be loose. If in doubt, renew it. Always fit a new rotor if fitting a new cap.

3 To gain access to the centrifugal advance mechanism, refer to Fig. 4.11.

4 Remove the contact breaker. Take out the insulated terminal from the side of the distributor, noting how the insulators are fitted. Remove the screws that hold the plate on which the contact breaker is mounted, and lift out the plate.

5 There is no way to test the bob weight springs other than by checking the performance of the distributor on special test equipment, so if in doubt, fit new springs anyway. If the springs are loose where they loop over the posts, it is more than possible that the post grooves are worn. In this case, the various parts which include the shaft will

8.1 Carbon contact inside distributor cap

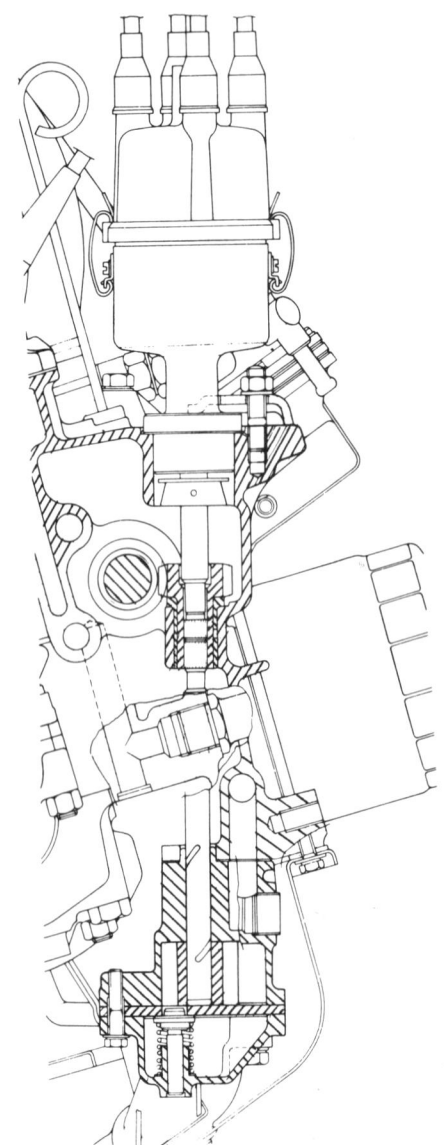

Fig. 4.9 Distributor drive arrangement on the crankcase mounted
distributor (Sec 7)

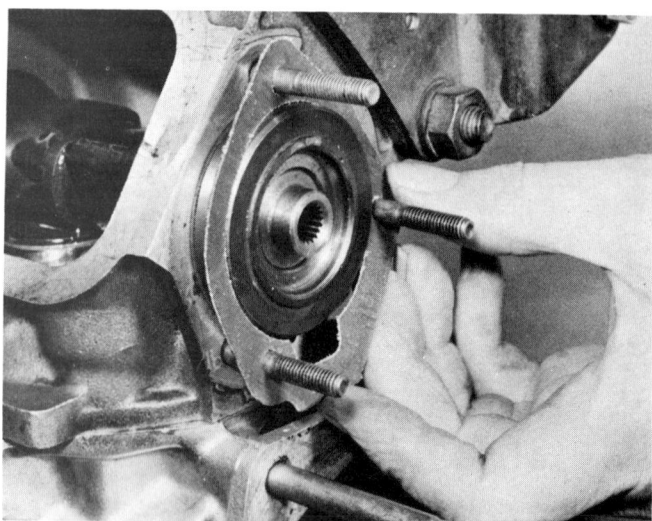

7.11 Gasket for camshaft mounted distributor

need renewal. Wear to this extent would mean that a new distributor is probably the best solution in the long run. Be sure to make an exact note of both the engine number and any serial number on the distributor when ordering.

6   The cam, with its lugs to the centrifugal advance mechanism, fits as a sleeve over the spindle. To remove it, first prise out the felt oil wick at the top. Hold the bottom of the shaft in a padded vice, and undo the screw at the top (it is a snap-ring on the Ducellier). Take off the centrifugal advance springs, being careful not to stretch them. Note how the bob weights are fitted, then pull the cam up, off the spindle. Before reassembly, put plenty of engine oil on the bearing between the cam and spindle, as not much comes from the wick.

7   If the mainshaft is slack in its bushes or the cam on the spindle, allowing sideways play, it means that the contact points gap setting can only be a compromise; the cam position relative to the cam follower on the moving point arm is not constant. It is not practical to re-bush the distributor body unless you have a friend who can bore and bush it for you. The shaft can be removed by driving out the roll pin from the retaining collar at the bottom. (The collar also acts as an oil slinger to prevent excess engine oil creeping up the shaft).

Fig. 4.10 Crankshaft carrier mounted distributor (Sec 7)

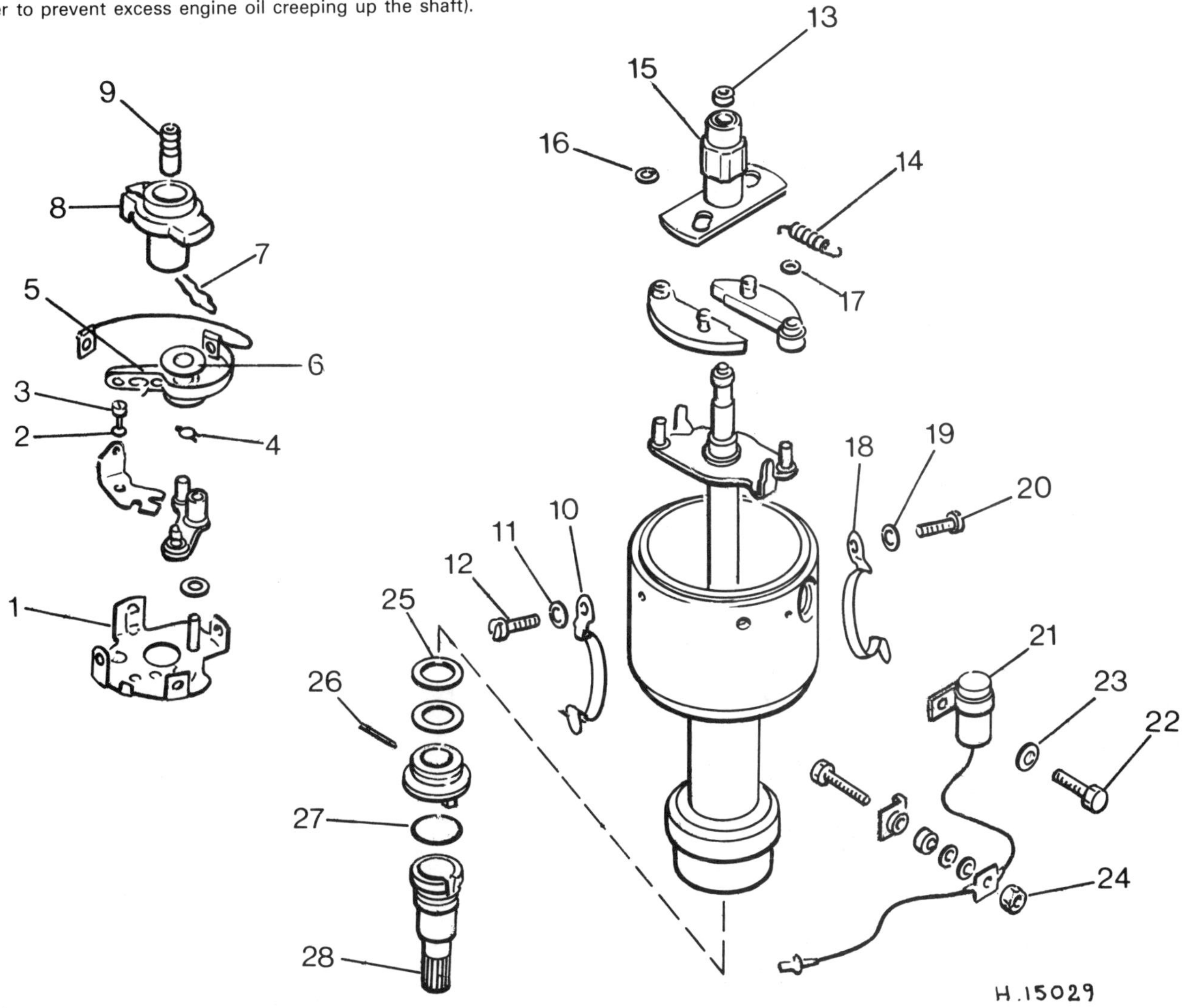

H.15029

Fig. 4.11 Exploded view of typical Ducellier distributor (Sec 8)

1	Contact breaker plate	8	Rotor	15	Cam	22	Securing screw
2	Washer	9	Carbon contact	16	Snap-ring	23	Washer
3	Screw	10	Cap clip	17	Washer	24	LT wire terminal
4	Spring clip	11	Washer	18	Cap clip	25	Washer
5	Contact breaker points	12	Screw	19	Washer	26	Roll pin
6	Washer	13	Lubricating pad	20	Screw	27	Seal
7	Spring clip	14	Centrifugal weight spring	21	Condenser (capacitor)	28	Splined shaft

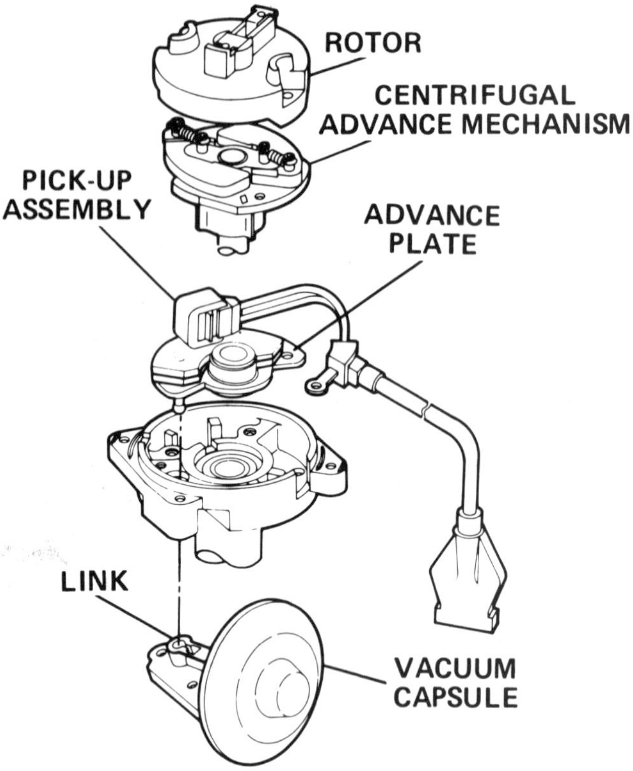

ROTOR

CENTRIFUGAL
ADVANCE MECHANISM

PICK-UP
ASSEMBLY

ADVANCE
PLATE

LINK

VACUUM
CAPSULE

Fig. 4.12 Main components of the Marelli electronic distributor
(Sec 10)

CAP

ROTOR

SHIELD

TRIGGER

PICK-UP
ASSEMBLY

VACUUM
CAPSULE

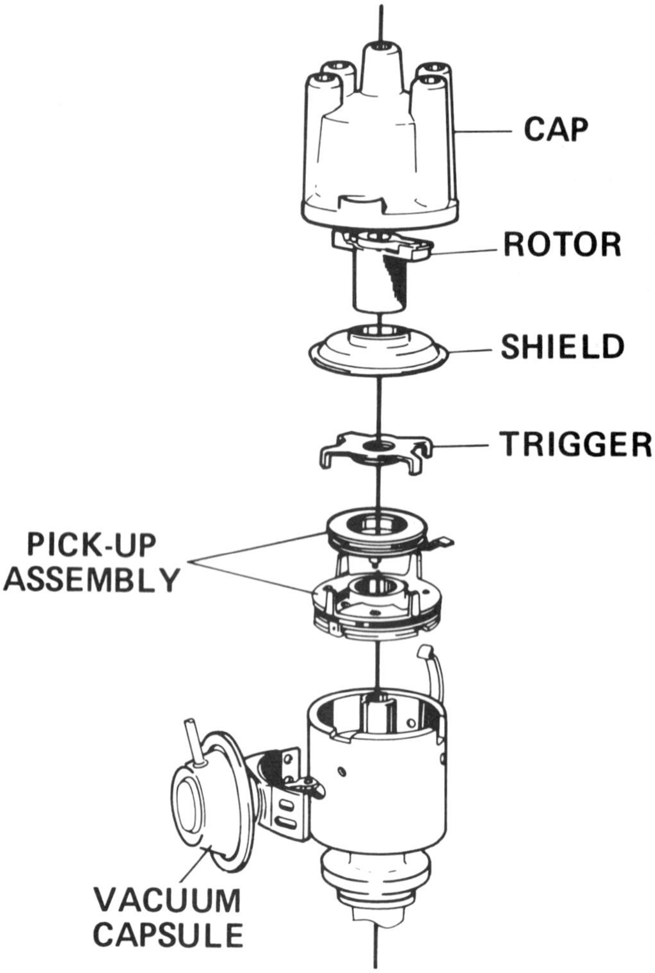

Fig. 4.13 Main components of the Bosch electronic distributor
(Sec 10)

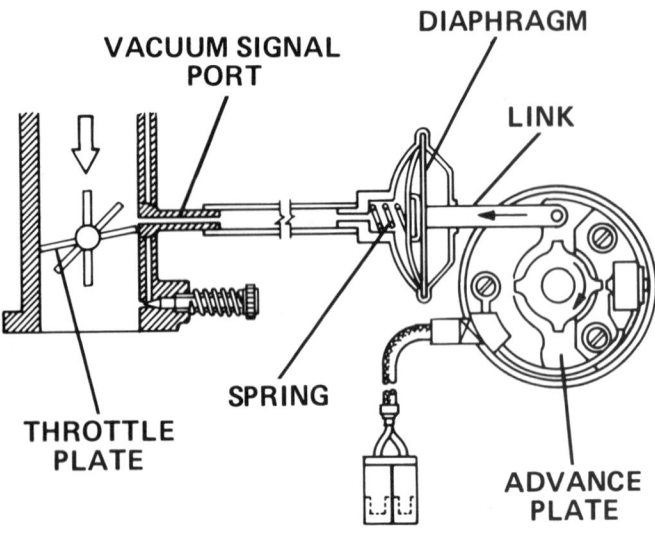

VACUUM SIGNAL
PORT

DIAPHRAGM

LINK

THROTTLE
PLATE

SPRING

ADVANCE
PLATE

Fig. 4.14 Diagrammatic view of electronic type distributor and
vacuum advance connection (Sec 10)

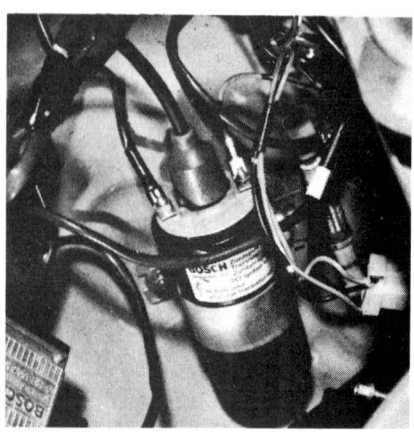

Fig. 4.15 Location of coil and resistor (Bosch electronic)
without air conditioning (Sec 13)

9 Condenser (mechanical breaker type distributor) – removal, testing and refitting

The purpose of the condenser (sometimes known as capacitor) is to ensure that when the contact breaker points open there is no sparking across them which would weaken the spark and cause rapid deterioration of the points.

The condenser is fitted in parallel with the contact breaker points. If it develops a short circuit, it will cause ignition failure as the points will be prevented from interrupting the low tension circuit.

1   If the engine becomes very difficult to start (or begins to misfire whilst running) and the breaker points show signs of excessive burning, suspect the condenser has failed with open circuit. A test can be made by separating the points by hand with the ignition switched on. If this is accompanied by a bright spark at the contact points, it is indicative that the condenser has failed.

2   Without special test equipment, the only sure way to diagnose condenser trouble is to renew a suspected unit with a new one and note if there is any improvement.

3   To remove the condenser from the distributor, take out the screw which secures it to the distributor body and slacken the insulated terminal nut enough to remove the wire connection tag.

4   When fitting the condenser, it is vital to ensure that the fixing screw is secure and the condenser tigtly held. The lead must be secure on the terminal with no chance of short circuiting.

10 Distributor (breakerless type) – overhaul

Overhaul of either the Marelli or Bosch type of distributor should not be undertaken. If wear does occur after a high mileage, a new unit should be obtained.

1   Individual components of the distributor may, however, be removed and renewed, simply by working from the cap downward and releasing the securing screws as necessary. The vacuum advance capsule is connected to the moveable mounting plate of the pick-up assembly by means of a link.

2   It is important that the air gap between the trigger and the pick-up assembly is correctly set at 0.28 to 0.48 mm (0.011 to 0.019 in).

11 Spark plugs

The correct functioning of the spark plugs is vital for the correct running and efficiency of the engine. The plugs fitted as standard are listed in the 'Specifications' at the beginning of this Chapter.

1   At the specified intervals, the plugs should be removed, examined, cleaned or if worn excessively, renewed. The condition of the spark plug will also tell much about the overall condition of the engine.

2   If the insulator nose of the spark plug is clean and white, with no deposits, this is indicative of a weak mixture, or too hot a plug. (A hot plug transfers heat away from the electrode slowly – a cold plug transfers it away quickly).

3   If the tip of the insulator nose is covered with sooty black deposits, then this is indicative that the mixture is too rich. Should the plug be black and oily, then it is likely that the engine is fairly worn, as well as the mixture being too rich.

4   If the insulator nose is covered with light tan to greyish brown deposits, then the mixture is correct and it is likely that the engine is in good condition and correctly tuned.

5   If there are any traces of long brown tapering stains on the outside of the white portion of the plug, the plug will have to be renewed, as this shows that there is a faulty joint between the plug body and the insulator, and compression is being allowed to leak away, any chips or cracks also mean that the plug should be renewed.

6   Clean around the plug seats in the cylinder head before removing the plugs, to prevent dirt getting into the cylinder. Plugs should be cleaned by a sand blasting machine, which will free them from carbon more thoroughly than cleaning by hand. The machine will also test the behaviour of the plugs under compression. Any plug that fails to spark at the recommended pressure should be renewed. It is recommended a new set of plugs is fitted, then the others can be taken later for cleaning, when more convenient. The two sets are then used concurrently; plugs can only last about 12 000 miles (20 000 km) before

their points are burned too far. So they will not require cleaning often, as renewal will be at alternate services.

7   The spark plug gap is of considerable importance, as, if it is too large or too small the size of the spark and its efficiency will be seriously impaired. The spark plug gap should be set to the gap shown in the Specifications for the best results.

8   To set it, measure the gap with a feeler gauge, and then bend open, or close, the outer plug electrode until the correct gap is achieved. The centre electrode should never be bent as this may crack the insulation and cause plug failure, if nothing worse.

9   When refitting the plug see that the washer is intact and carbon free, also that the plug seat in the cylinder head is quite clean.

10 Refit the leads from the distributor in the correct firing order, which is 1-3-4-2; No 1 cylinder being the one nearest the camshaft timing belt. The distributor cap is marked with the HT lead numbers to avoid any confusion. Simply connect the correctly numbered lead to its respective spark plug terminal

12 Distributor cap, rotor and HT leads

The distributor cap, leads, and the rotor arm distribute the high tension current to the plugs. They should all last long mileages without renewal.

If the components of the HT circuit are dirty, they will attract damp. This damp will allow the HT current to leak away. This will give difficulty in starting the engine when cold. The engine and transmission oil will be thick, so making the starter take more voltage and current, even so only cranking the engine slowly. The voltage drop due to the starter's demands means a reduced voltage in the primary circuit, and thus a corresponding fall in the secondary HT circuit. This at the very time when a strong spark is needed to fire the cold cylinder.

It is but a temporary palliative to spray the ignition leads with an aerosol damp repellent. The leads, the spark plug insulators, the outside and the inside of the distributor cap, and the rotor arm must be clean and dry.

Some plug leads are 'resistive'. They are made of cotton impregnated with carbon, to give the necessary radio interference suppression with separate suppressors. After a time, flexing makes the leads break down inside. If difficult starting persists then new leads, with normal metal core, and suppressor end fittings, could effect a cure. End fittings should not be taken off the resistive wire, as it is difficult to fit them so that a good contact is achieved.

13 Ignition coil

Coils normally run the life of a car. The most usual reason for a coil to fail is after being left with the ignition switched on but the engine not running. There is then constant current flowing, instead of the

13.1 Typical coil mounting. Note radio interference suppressor under coil mounting foot

intermittent flow when the contact breaker is opening (or pick-up assembly triggered). The coil then overheats, and the insulation is damaged (photo).

If the coil seems suspect after fault finding, the measurement of the resistance of the primary and secondary windings (using an ohmmeter) can establish its condition. If an ohmmeter is not available, it will be necessary to try a new coil.

14 Fault diagnosis – ignition system

1   With the exception of timing maladjustment or advance-retard defects, both of which will be evident as lack of performance and possibly pinking (pre-ignition) or overheating, ignition faults can be divided into two types: total failure (engine fails to start, or cuts out completely, perhaps intermittently) and partial failure (misfiring regular or otherwise, on one or more cylinder).

2   Electronic ignition, where fitted, is normally very reliable. Fault diagnosis should be confined to checking the trigger-to-pick-up gap, the continuity of leads and the security of connections, and the dryness and condition of insulation on the HT side. In particular, it is not advisable to remove HT leads when the engine is running, as the voltage present is considerably higher than that in a conventional ignition system, and there is a risk both of personal injury and of damage to the coil insulation. The checks below apply only to contact breaker ignition systems.

3   The most common cause of difficulty in starting, especially in winter, is a slow engine cranking speed combined with a poor spark at the plugs. Before commencing the checks below, ensure that the battery is fully charged, that the HT leads and distributor cap are clean and dry, that the points and plugs are in good condition and correctly gapped, and that all LT connections (including the battery terminals) are clean and tight.

Engine will not start

4   Remove a plug cap and hold the metal end of the leads about 6 mm ($\frac{1}{4}$ in) away from the block. *Hold the lead with insulating material – eg a rubber glove, a dry cloth, or insulated pliers – to avoid electric shocks.* Have an assistant crank the engine on the starter motor; a fat blue spark should be seen and heard to jump from the end of the lead to the block. If it does, this suggests that HT current is reaching the plugs, and the either the plugs themselves are defective, the timing is grossly maladjusted, or the fault is not in the ignition system. If the spark is weak or absent although the cranking speed is good, proceed with the checks below. If the cranking speed is low check the battery and starter motor.

5   Remove the HT lead which enters the centre of the distributor cap, hold the end near the block and repeat the check described above. A good spark now, if there was none at the plug lead, indicates that HT current is not being transmitted to the plug lead. Check the carbon brush and the plug lead terminals inside the distributor cap, the inside of the cap itself for dampness, cracks or tracking marks (black lines formed where insulator defects allow the passage of current), and the rotor arm for cracks or tracking. If tracking is evident on the distributor cap or rotor arm, the component must be renewed, although in an emergency it may be possible to interrupt the track by scraping or

filing. If there is no spark at the HT lead from the coil, carry on to the next check.

6   The HT lead has now been checked, with the exception of the HT lead from the coil to the distributor and the HT terminal on the coil itself. If these seem to be in order, start checking the LT system. With the distributor cap and rotor arm removed, turn the engine as necessary until the points are closed, then switch on the ignition and separate the points with an insulated screwdriver. A strong blue spark suggests condenser failure in the open circuit mode: fit a new one and the engine should run. No spark at all when the points are separated could be due to condenser failure in the short circuit mode: temporarily disconnect it and check again. If there is still no spark, either the point faces are contaminated – clean them with methylated spirit – or the fault is elsewhere in the LT system. For further checking a 12 volt test lamp or a voltmeter will be required.

7   Connect the test lamp or voltmeter between the coil contact breaker (D–) terminal and earth. Turn on the ignition and separate the points with a piece of cardboard. A reading suggests that the fault is either a broken lead between the coil and distributor or an internal fault in the coil. No reading indicates a fault further up the line, or a short circuit to earth in the distributor. Disconnect the distributor-to-coil LT lead, leaving the test lamp connected to the coil: a reading now where there was none before indicates a short circuit to earth somewhere between the lead and the fixed contact. Check the insulating washers on the moving contact pivot, the lead from the distributor LT terminal to the moving contact and the contact itself. No reading still means that further checking is required.

8   Connect the test lamp or voltmeter to the other coil LT terminal, separate the points and turn on the ignition. A reading here with none at the D– terminal confirms an internal fault in the coil, which will have to be renewed. (A reading at *both* terminals suggests an internal short circuit in the coil, or a defect in the HT winding). No reading indicates a break in supply from the battery to the coil via the ignition switch. As a 'get-you-home' measure it may be possible to connect a wire directly from the coil to the battery live (+) terminal, but check the wiring from the coil to the ignition switch and from the switch to the battery first.

Engine misfires

9   Uneven running and misfiring should first be checked by seeing that all leads, particularly HT, are dry and connected properly. See that they are not shorting to earth through broken or cracked insulation. If they are, you should be able to see and hear it. If not, then check the plugs, contact points and condenser just as you would in a case of total failure to start, A regular misfire can be isolated by removing each plug lead in turn *(not with electronic ignition)*; removing a good lead will accentuate the misfire, whilst removing the defective lead will make no difference.

10   If misfiring occurs at high speed check the points gap, which may be too small, and the plugs. Check also that the spring tension on the points is not too light thus causing them to bounce. This requires a special pull balance so if in doubt it will be cheaper to buy a new set of contacts rather than go to a garage and get them to check it. If the trouble is still not cured then the fault lies in the carburation or engine itself.

11   If misfiring or stalling occurs only at low speeds the points gap is possibly too big. If not, then the slow running adjustment on the carburettor may need attention

Measuring plug gap. A feeler gauge of the correct size (see ignition system specifications) should have a slight 'drag' when slid between the electrodes. Adjust gap if necessary

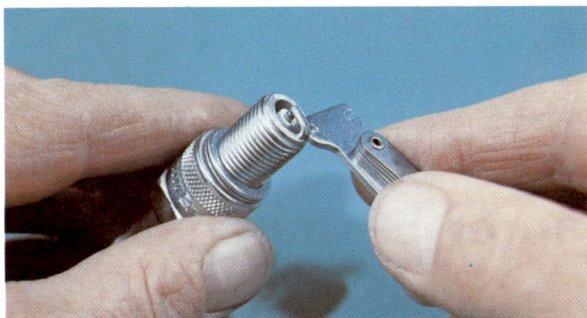

Adjusting plug gap. The plug gap is adjusted by bending the earth electrode inwards, or outwards, as necessary until the correct clearance is obtained. Note the use of the correct tool

Normal. Grey-brown deposits, lightly coated core nose. Gap increasing by around 0.001 in (0.025 mm) per 1000 miles (1600 km). Plugs ideally suited to engine, and engine in good condition

Carbon fouling. Dry, black, sooty deposits. Will cause weak spark and eventually misfire. Fault: over-rich fuel mixture. Check: carburettor mixture settings, float level and jet sizes; choke operation and cleanliness of air filter. Plugs can be re-used after cleaning

Oil fouling. Wet, oily deposits. Will cause weak spark and eventually misfire. Fault: worn bores/piston rings or valve guides; sometimes occurs (temporarily) during running-in period. Plugs can be re-used after thorough cleaning

Overheating. Electrodes have glazed appearance, core nose very white – few deposits. Fault: plug overheating. Check: plug value, ignition timing, fuel octane rating (too low) and fuel mixture (too weak). Discard plugs and cure fault immediately

Electrode damage. Electrodes burned away; core nose has burned, glazed appearance. Fault: pre-ignition. Check: as for 'Overheating' but may be more severe. Discard plugs and remedy fault before piston or valve damage occurs

Split core nose (may appear initially as a crack). Damage is self-evident, but cracks will only show after cleaning. Fault: pre-ignition or wrong gap-setting technique. Check: ignition timing, cooling system, fuel octane rating (too low) and fuel mixture (too weak). Discard plugs, rectify fault immediately

Chapter 5 Clutch

For modifications, and information applicable to later models, see Supplement at end of manual

Contents

Specifications

System .... Single dry plate, diaphragm spring with cable actuation. Ball type, grease-sealed release bearing.

Free movement .... Nil; the release bearing is in light contact with the diaphragm spring fingers

Clutch driven plate diameter
65 models .... 181.5 mm (7.15 in)
75 and North American models .... 190.0 mm (7.48 in)

Torque wrench settings

	lbf ft	Nm
Clutch-to-flywheel bolts (65 models)	12	16
Clutch-to-flywheel bolts (75 and North American models)	28	38
Release fork lockbolt	20	27
Bellhousing-to-engine bolts	33	45

1 General description

The clutch is a single dry-disc type with a diaphragm spring. The unit comprises a steel cover, dowelled and bolted to the face of the flywheel, and contains the pressure plate, pressure plate diaphragm spring and fulcrum rings.

The clutch disc is free to slide along the splined input shaft of the gearbox and is held in position between the flywheel and the pressure plate by the pressure of the pressure plate spring. Friction lining material is riveted to the clutch disc, and it has a spring-cushioned hub to absorb transmission shocks.

The release mechanism consists of an operating arm and bearing which is actuated by a cable.

2 Clutch – adjustment

1 The type of release bearing used is always in light contact with the diaphragm spring fingers. As a result of this, free play will not be felt at the clutch pedal.

2 The correct setting of the clutch pedal is obtained when the pedal pad is 30.0 mm (1.2 in) below the brake pedal pad.

3 As wear occurs to the clutch friction disc (driven plate), the clutch pedal pad will rise and reduce the differential between it and the brake pedal. When this happens, restore the correct setting by releasing the cable locknut at the release lever on the side of the clutch bellhousing, turning the adjuster nut as required. Retighten the locknut on completion (photo).

4 When the time comes that the clutch pedal can no longer be adjusted (because all the available adjustment threads on the cable end fitting have been taken up), the driven plate will have to be renewed, as described in Section 5.

5 To minimise wear in the driven plate and the release bearing, never drive with the foot resting on the clutch pedal; if stopping for

2.3 Clutch control cable adjuster

more than a few seconds with the engine running, always move the gearchange lever to neutral and release the foot from the clutch pedal.

6 If the clutch is felt to slip when accelerating hard up an incline, this may be due to wear of the friction linings, or to the driven plate being contaminated with oil or grease. In this event, the clutch must be dismantled and the components renewed as necessary, particular attention being paid to the crankshaft rear and transmission input shaft oil seals.

3 Clutch operating cable – renewal

1   Unscrew and remove the locknut and adjuster nut from the end of the clutch cable (at the release arm on the bellhousing).
2   Remove the clevis pin and disconnect the clutch cable from the top of the clutch pedal arm.
3   Withdraw the cable assembly through the engine compartment rear bulkhead grommets; remove it from the car.
4   Refit the new cable by reversing the removal operations; adjust it as described in the preceding Section.

4 Clutch pedal – removal and refitting

The clutch and brake pedals are of pendant type and pivot on a common cross-shaft.
1   Disconnect the clutch cable from the pedal arm. To do this, extract the spring retaining clip and slip the cable eye off the pedal arm pin. On

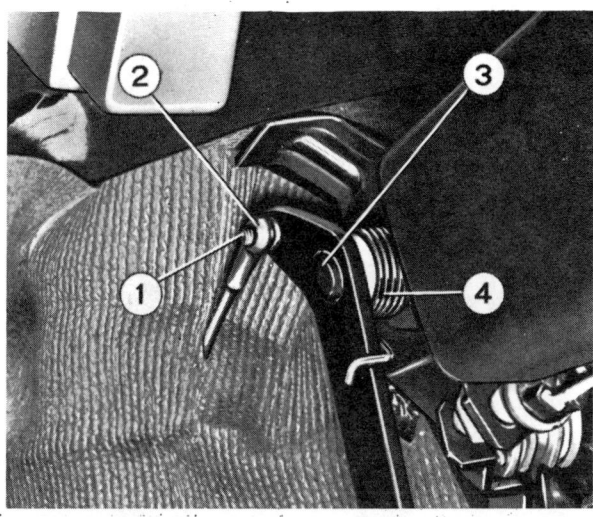

Fig. 5.1 Clutch cable attachment to pedal (Sec 4)

1	Clevis pin and clip	3	Pivot shaft
2	Cable eye	4	Pedal return spring

Fig. 5.2 Clutch and brake pedal arrangement (Sec 4)

1	Clutch pedal return spring	5	Pivot shaft spring
2	Brake pedal return spring		retaining clip
3	Brake pedal	6	Pivot shaft
4	Clutch pedal		

some models the cable end fitting is simply engaged on a hook at the top of the pedal arm.
2   Disconnect the return springs from the brake pedal arm and the clutch pedal arm.
3   Slide off the spring retaining clip from the end of the pedal cross-shaft.
4   Withdraw the clutch pedal, at the same time supporting the brake pedal assembly.
5   If required, the spacer and the brake pedal can be removed. The brake pedal-to-servo pushrod is a sliding fit, no disconnection being required.
6   Refitting is a reversal of the removal process; apply grease to the pivots, shafts and bushes.
7   Adjust the clutch cable as described in Section 2.

5 Clutch – removal, inspection and refitting

1   The clutch is accessible normally only if the transmission is removed from the car, as described in Chapter 6. Alternatively, if the engine/transmission is being removed for major overhaul, the clutch is accessible once the transmission has been separated from the engine; refer to Chapter 1.
2   Unscrew the clutch cover securing bolts evenly and progressively, until the spring pressure is relieved. Remove the bolts completely and lift the clutch cover from the flywheel. Take care to catch the driven plate, which is sandwiched between the pressure plate and the flywheel.
3   Inspect the driven plate. If the friction linings have worn down – or nearly down – to the rivet heads, it should be renewed complete. *Do not waste your time trying to rivet new linings into place; this seldom proves satisfactory.*
4   Check the clutch pressure plate/cover assembly. If the driven plate contact surfaces on the pressure plate or the flywheel are scored, grooved or tiny hair cracks are evident (caused by overheating), the flywheel should be reground or renewed and the clutch pressure plate/cover renewed. The latter are usually available as a factory reconditioned assembly. *Never dismantle the clutch assembly;* special jigs and tools are needed to reset it, even if the necessary spare parts were available.
5   To refit the clutch, locate the driven plate against the flywheel so that the projecting hub (which contains the torsion coil springs) is away from the flywheel (photo).
6   Position the clutch cover assembly on its locating dowels. Screw in the retaining bolts no more than finger tight, to allow the driven plate to slide.
7   The clutch driven plate must now be centralised. This cannot be carried out in the usual way – by using an alignment tool or old input shaft to engage in the centre of the flywheel – as the crankshaft rear mounting flange does not incorporate a bush or bearing. A piece of tubing is the best alternative to solve the problem of centralising. Obtain a piece of tubing, the outside diameter of which provides a

5.5 Fitting clutch to flywheel

5.8 Aligning clutch driven plate

5.9 Clutch driven plate correctly aligned

6.1a Clutch release bearing and fork

sliding fit in the tips of the fingers of the diaphragm spring in the clutch cover. The internal diameter of the tubing should be such that the end of the tubing will engage centrally on the chamfer of the driven plate's splined hub.

8   Hold the tool in position, so it centralises the driven plate on the flywheel. Then start to tighten the clutch cover bolts evenly and progressively, until the driven plate is just nipped between the pressure plate and the flywheel. Withdraw the tool. Note that if the cover bolts are tightened too much, the diaphragm spring fingers will grip the alignment tool and prevent its withdrawal (photo).

9   Fully tighten the clutch cover bolts. Confirmation of alignment can be made by viewing the splined hub through the circle of diaphragm spring finger tips; it should appear to be concentric (photo).

10 Before connecting the transmission to the engine, check the condition of the release components, as described in the next Section.

6   Clutch release mechanism – inspection and renewal

The clutch release bearing should be renewed at the same time as the clutch assembly is being renewed.

Renewal of the clutch release bearing is unlikely to be required at other times, unless as a result of reference to the Fault Diagnosis Section, the symptoms indicate it being necessary.

1   Extract the securing clips and withdraw the release bearing from its hub on the oil seal retainer within the clutch bellhousing (photos).

2   If the bearing is noisy or rough when turned with the fingers, or its spring finger contact area is grooved, the bearing must be renewed.

3   Examine the release lever pivot shaft bushes for wear. If they are worn, they can be extracted and new ones fitted. Even if they are in good condition, always remove the pivot shaft, after releasing its

6.1b Input shaft bearing retainer and release bearing hub

lockbolt, and apply some high melting point grease to the bushes.

4   The release bearing is grease-sealed for life. Refit by reversing the removal operations, making sure that the retaining spring clips are secure on completion and that the angled corner of the bearing backing plate is uppermost.

7   Fault diagnosis – clutch

Symptom	Reason(s)
Difficulty in engaging gear (grinding)	Clutch cable adjustment incorrect Driven plate stuck to flywheel or rusted onto input shaft splines. (Only after long disuse. It may be possible to free by starting engine with top gear engaged and pedal depressed – if not, dismantle)
Judder when taking up drive	Engine/transmission mountings loose or worn Driven plate linings contaminated or worn Pressure plate loose or defective
Clutch slip (increase in engine speed does not increase road speed)	Incorrect cable adjustment Driven plate linings worn or contaminated Pressure plate defective
Noise evident when clutch pedal depressed	Release arm pivots unlubricated Release bearing worn, loose or unlubricated Worn or damaged pressure plate

Chapter 6
Manual and automatic transmissions

For modifications, and information applicable to later models, see Supplement at end of manual

Contents

Specifications

Part A – Manual Transmission
Transmission type .... 4 or 5 forward speeds, all with synchromesh, and reverse. Integral final drive. Power transmitted to front roadwheels through open driveshafts

Application
4-speed gearbox .... 65L models
5-speed gearbox .... 65CL, 75CL and North American models

Gear ratios
1st .... 3.583 : 1
2nd .... 2.235 : 1
3rd .... 1.454 : 1
4th .... 1.042 : 1
5th .... 0.863 : 1
Reverse .... 3.714 : 1

Synchroniser type
1st/2nd .... Baulk ring and cone
3rd/4th/5th .... Porsche type

Gear backlash .... 0.1 mm (0.004 in)

Gear clearances on shafts
Reverse idler gear .... 0.08 to 0.15 mm (0.003 to 0.006 in)
Output shaft gears .... 0.04 to 0.08 mm (0.001 to 0.003 in)

Final drive
Gear type .... Helical
Ratio:
    65 models .... 3.76 : 1 (17/64)
    75 and North American models .... 3.59 : 1 (17/61)

Oil capacity (combined gearbox/final drive):
4-speed gearbox .... 5.5 Imp pints (6.6 US pints, 3.15 litres)
5-speed gearbox (65 and North American models) .... 5.7 Imp pints (6.8 US pints, 3.26 litres)
5-speed gearbox (75 models) .... 5.2 Imp pints (6.2 US pints, 2.93 litres)

Lubricant
Type/specification .... Multigrade engine oil, viscosity SAE 15W/40 to API SE (Duckhams Hypergrade)

Part B – Automatic transmission
Type ....
3-speed, fully automatic with torque converter. Final drive has separate lubrication. Power transmitted through open driveshaft to front roadwheels

Identification number .... EA 906/01 NR 11

Application ....
75CL and some North American models

Speed ratios
1st .... 2.55 : 1
2nd .... 1.45 : 1
3rd .... 1.00 : 1
Reverse .... 2.46 : 1
Final drive .... 3.56 : 1 (23/82)

Fluid capacity
Transmission/torque converter (from dry) .... 10.4 Imp pints (12.5 US pints, 5.9 litres)
Transmission/torque converter (at routine fluid change) .... 5.3 Imp pints (6.4 US pints, 3.0 litres)
Final drive .... 1.3 Imp pints (1.6 US pints, 0.75 litres)

Lubricant type/specification
Automatic transmission .... Dexron II type ATF (Duckhams D-Matic)
Final drive .... Hypoid gear oil, viscosity SAE 80W/90, to MIL-L-2105 C (Duckhams Hypoid 75W/90S)

Torque wrench settings

	lbf ft	Nm
4-speed gearbox		
Clutch bellhousing-to-engine bolts	57	78
Gearbox cover bolts	7	10
Starter motor bolts	18	25
Gearbox front cover bolts	6	8
Bellhousing-to-gearbox bolts	18	25
Mounting bracket-to-gearbox	18	25
Reverse shaft lockplate bolt	7	10
Selector fork lockbolts	13	18
Gearchange lever pivot bolt	13	18
Gearchange lever support plate bolts	7	10
Crownwheel securing bolts	50	68
Final drive housing-to-gearcase bolts	18	25
Internal selector rod spring cover bolt	18	25
5-speed gearbox		
As for 4-speed gearbox, plus the following		
Input shaft nut	87	118
Output shaft nut	87	118
Crownwheel securing bolts (65 models)	50	68
Crownwheel securing bolts (75 and North American models)	65	88
Bearing retainer bolts (75 and North American models)	7	10
Gearchange lever pivot self-locking nut	8	11
Differential side flange bolts	22	30
End cover bolts	18	25
Automatic transmission		
Driveplate-to-converter bolts	40	54
Transmission-to-engine bolts	70	95
Starter inhibitor/reversing lamp switch	24	33

PART A – MANUAL TRANSMISSION

1   General description

Your Strada may be equipped with a four or five-speed gearbox, depending upon the model. For application and specifications, refer to the Specifications Section at the beginning of this Chapter.

The shaft arrangement within the transmission is shown in Fig. 6.1; as it does not conform to the conventional in-line pattern, the upper shaft will be referred to as the input shaft and the lower one as the output shaft. The latter shaft incorporates the synchro units and the final drive pinion gear.

The synchromesh is of the spring-ring type on 1st/2nd gear and the slip-ring type on 3rd/4th gear, 5th gear synchromesh is of the Porsche type.

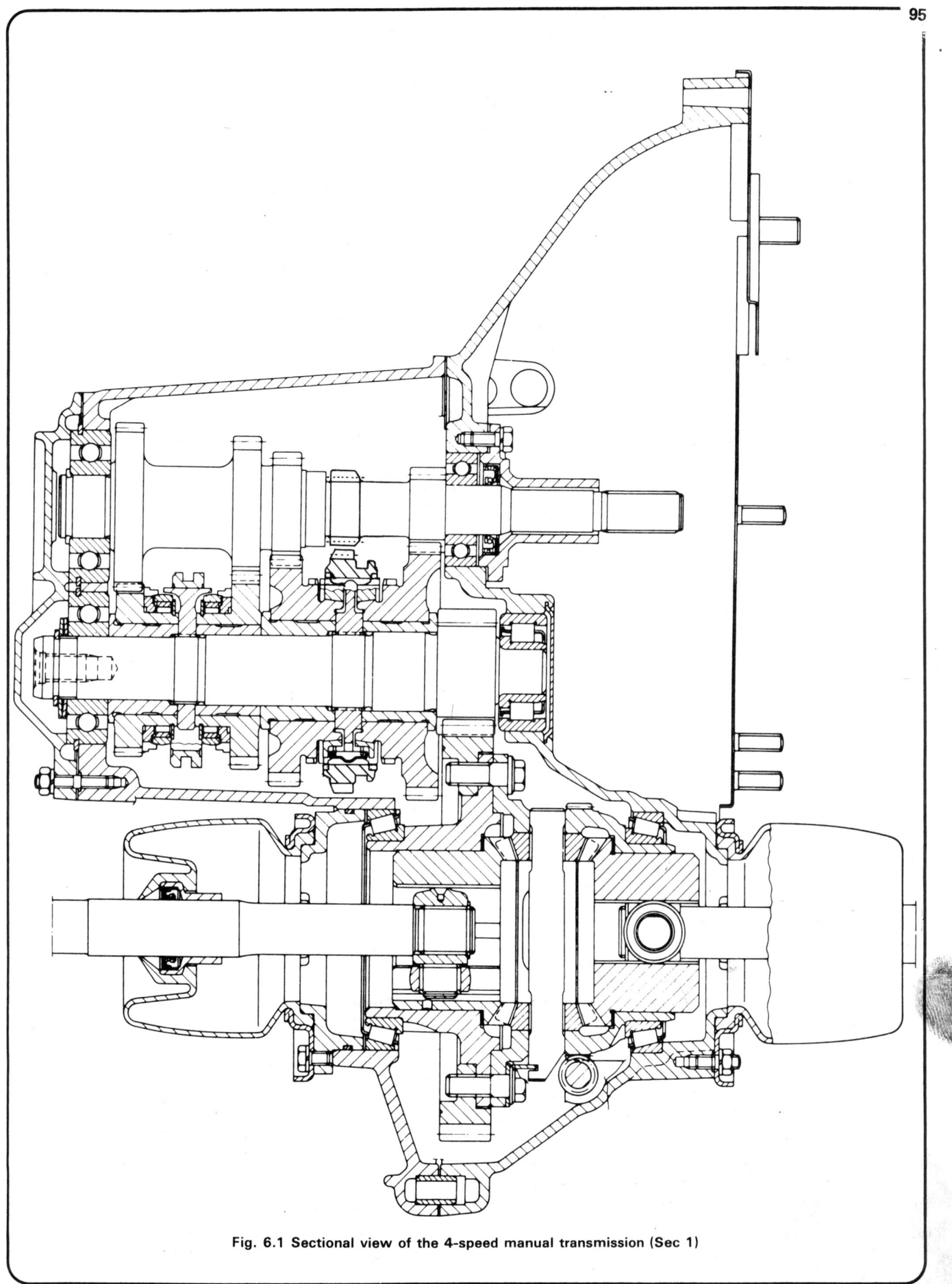

Fig. 6.1 Sectional view of the 4-speed manual transmission (Sec 1)

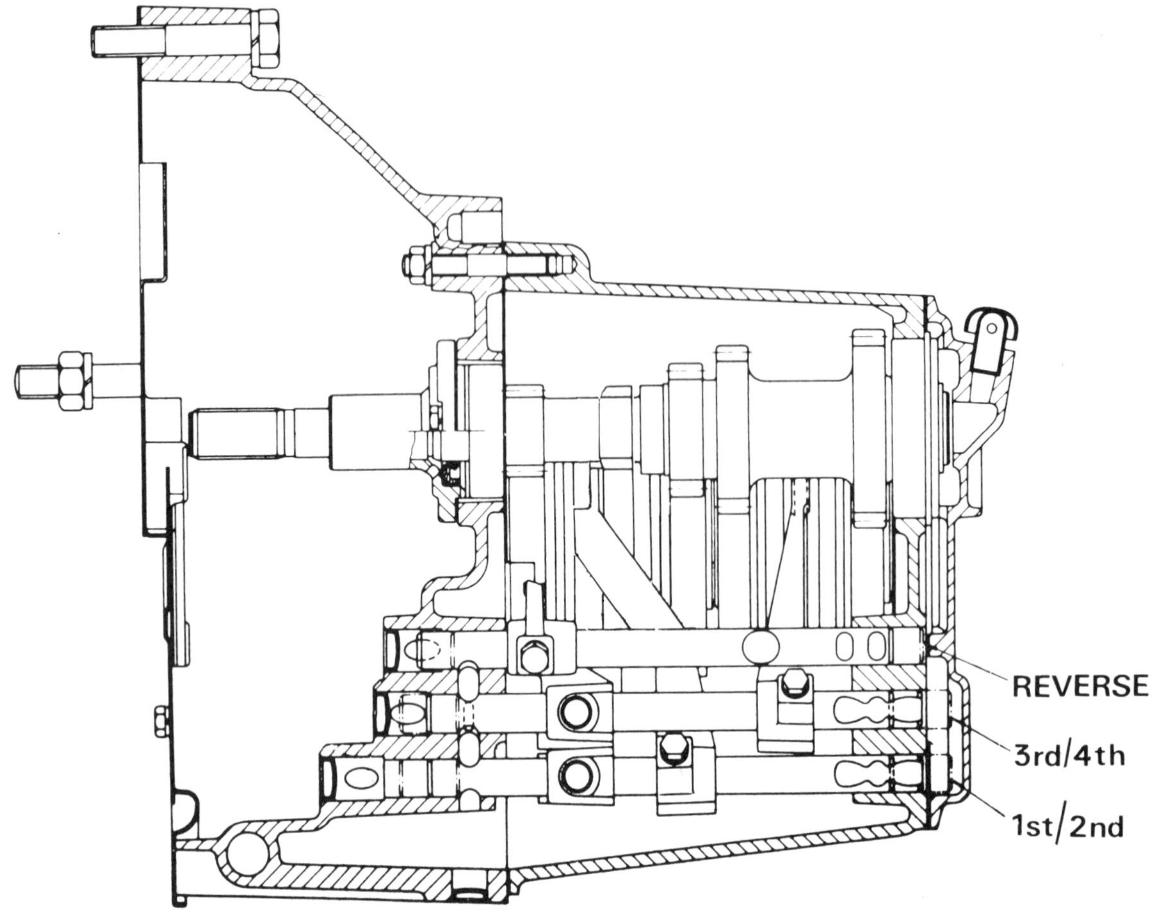

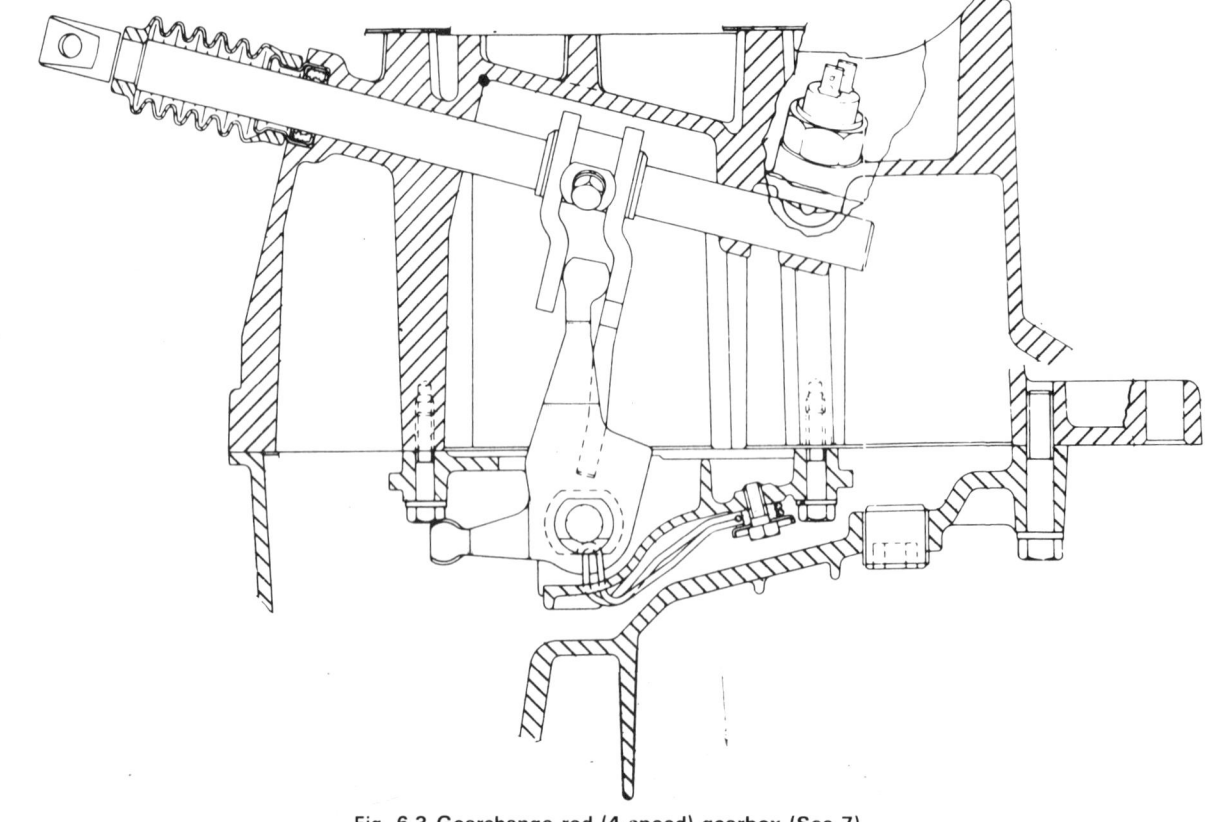

REVERSE

3rd/4th

1st/2nd

Fig. 6.2 Selector arrangement (4-speed) gearbox (Sec 1)

Fig. 6.3 Gearchange rod (4-speed) gearbox (Sec 7)

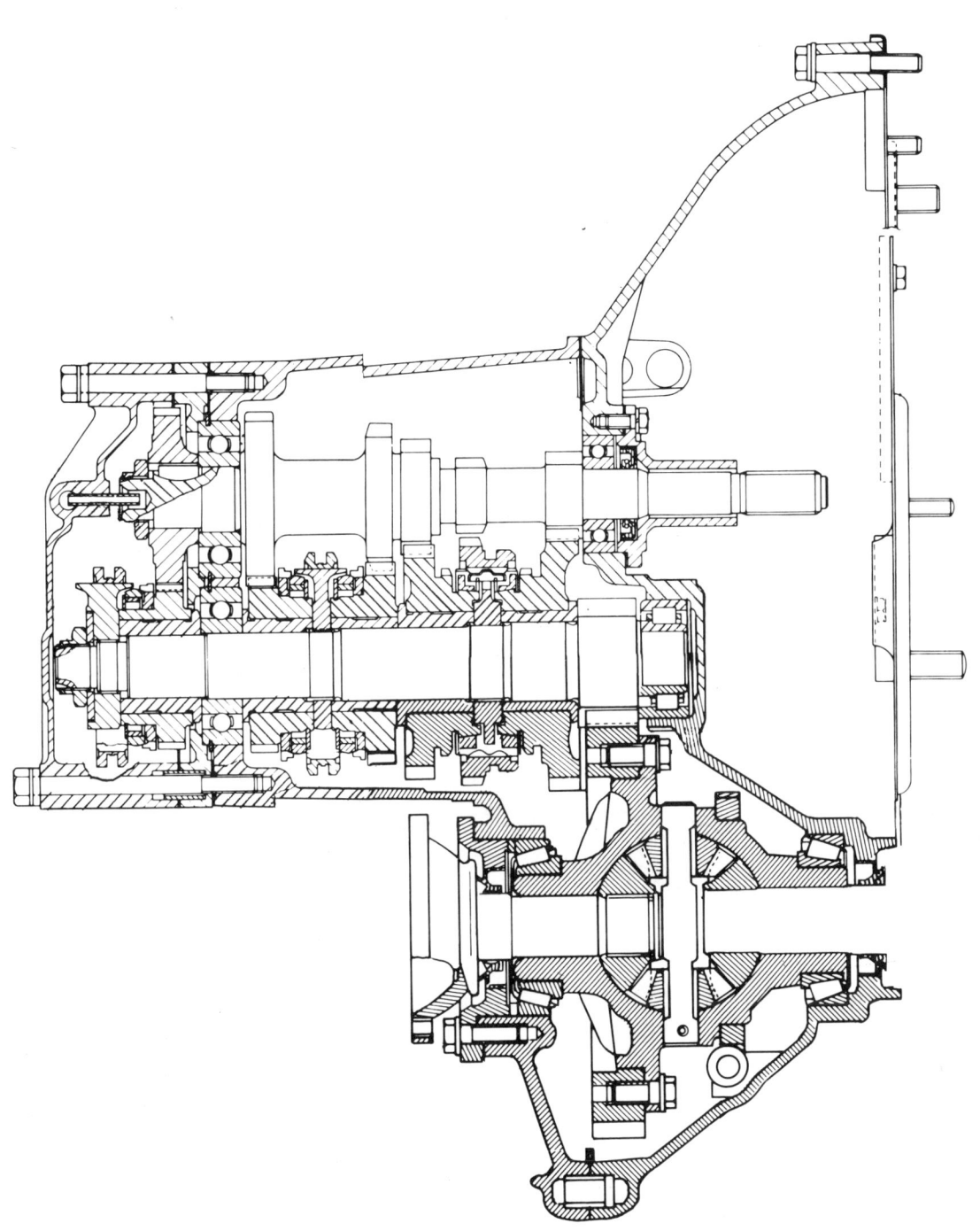

Fig. 6.4 Sectional view of the 5-speed transmission (Sec 1)

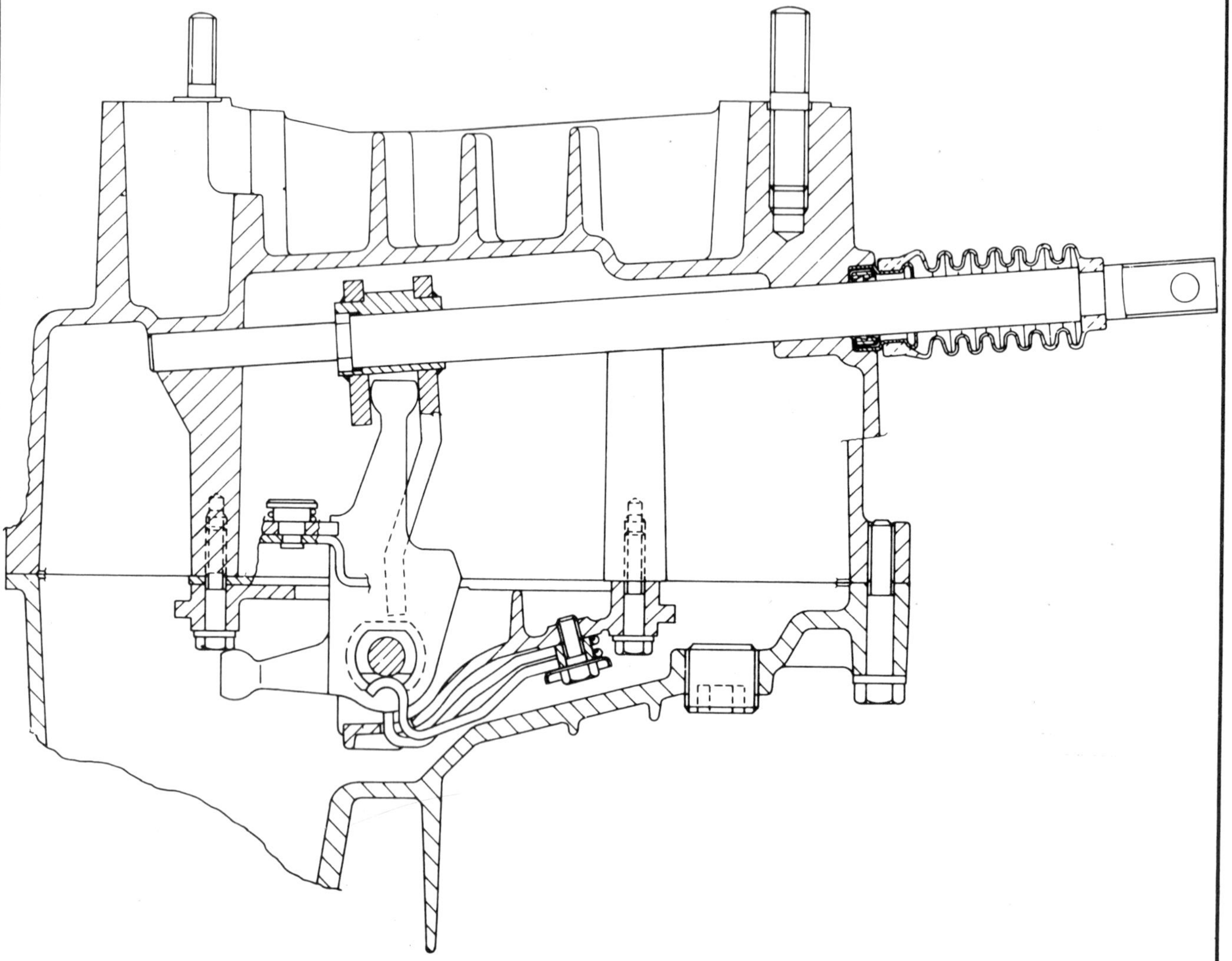

Fig. 6.5 Gearchange rod (5-speed gearbox) (Sec 1)

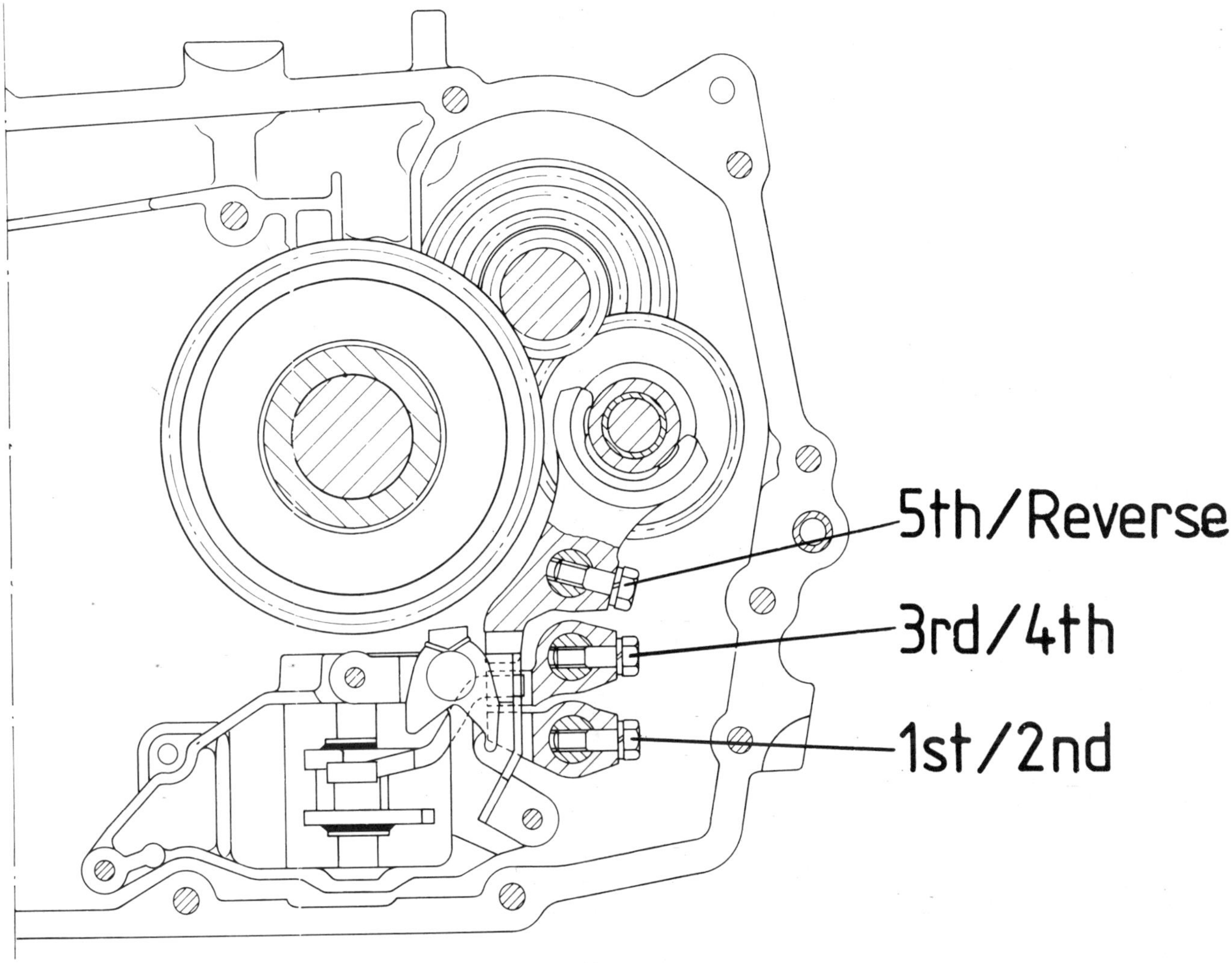

5th/Reverse

3rd/4th

1st/2nd

Fig. 6.6 Selector fork arrangement (5-speed gearbox) (Sec 1)

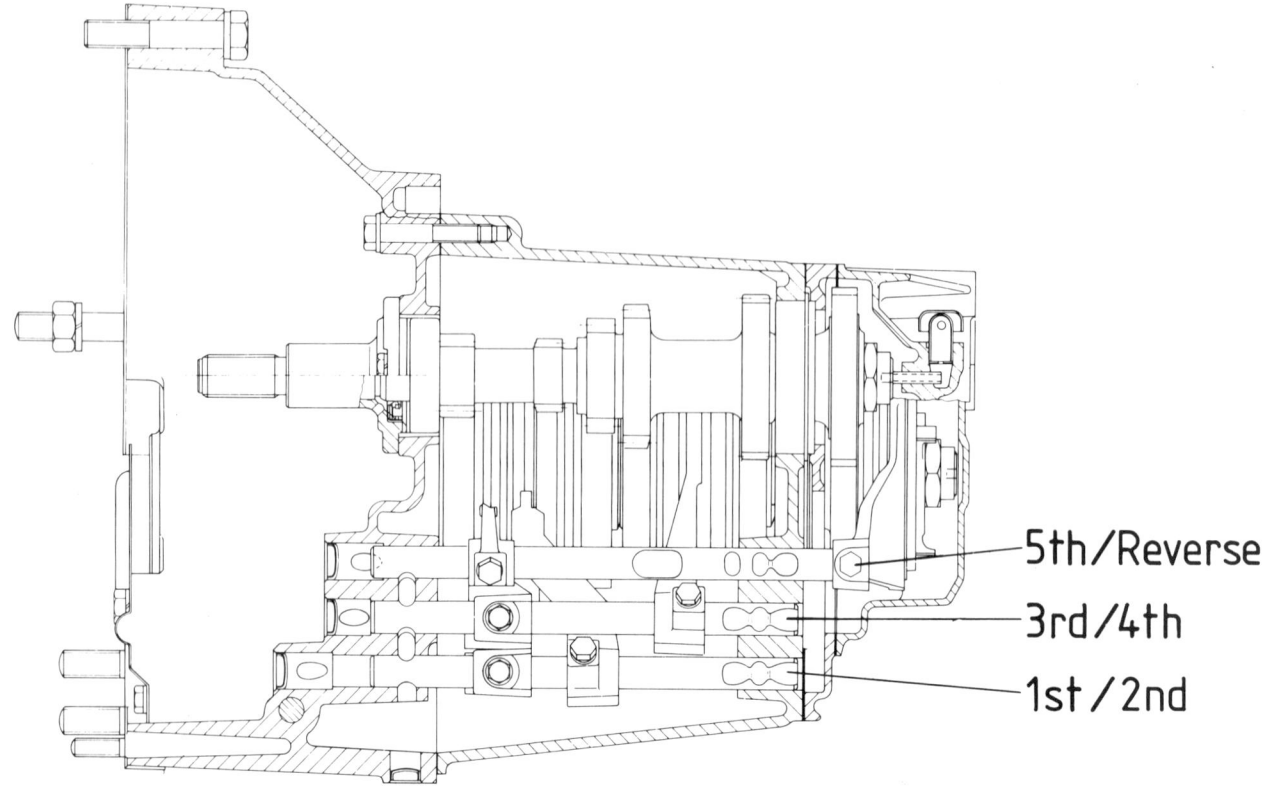

5th/Reverse

3rd/4th

1st/2nd

Fig. 6.7 Selector shaft arrangement (5-speed gearbox) (Sec 1)

The transmission can be removed from the car, leaving the engine in place. Conversely, the engine cannot be removed without the transmission. The transmission must be removed to give access to the clutch. Removal of the transmission, unlike that of the engine, does not involve use of lifting tackle, but two good jacks, and plenty of stout timber blocks will be needed. The most likely reason to remove the transmission is to cure an oil leak, or to overhaul the clutch. If the transmission itself is badly worn, its overhaul is possible without special tools. To be sure of a successful outcome, with absence of noise, the overhaul must be exceedingly thorough. The cost and the difficulty in obtaining all the parts makes the case for fitting a FIAT reconditioned unit worth considering.

Routine oil changing is not specified by FIAT, but it is recommended that the lubricant is renewed at 24 000 mile (38 000 km) intervals.

2 Transmission (65 models) – removal and refitting

The gearbox/final drive is removed from beneath the car. It will therefore be necessary to raise the front of the car on ramps or place it over an inspection pit.

1 Support the bodyframe on jacks and axle stands then remove the front roadwheels. Have an assistant apply the footbrake pedal firmly while the driveshaft-to-hub nuts are loosened. A socket and long knuckle bar will be needed for this as the nuts are very tight. Unscrew and remove both nuts.
2 Next, raise the front of the car sufficiently to enable the transmission to pass below it. Alternatively, if the car is over an inspection pit, lower the unit into the pit.
3 Disconnect the battery and remove the spare wheel from the engine compartment.
4 Disconnect the speedometer drive cable from the gearbox.
5 Disconnect the clutch operating cable from the release lever at the gearbox.
6 Disconnect the electrical leads from the reversing lamp switch on the gearbox.
7 Unbolt the front disc brake calipers and tie them up, out of the

way. This measure is taken to avoid straining the hydraulic hoses when the suspension strut lower ends are detached (see paragraphs 21 and 22).
8 Using a suitable balljoint separator, disconnect the tie-rod end balljoints from the steering arms at the base of the suspension struts.
9 Remove the shield from the left-hand side.
10 Disconnect the right-hand track control arm from its body anchorage.
11 Support the engine carefully, using a jack with a block of wood as an insulator.
12 Disconnect the earth strap from the gearbox.
13 Unscrew the bolts which hold the starter motor to the gearbox.
14 Unbolt the gear selector link by unscrewing the two bolts which hold it to the gearchange linkage joints.
15 Disconnect the centre support bracket and the flexible mounting, then remove them.
16 Unbolt and remove the flywheel guard plate.
17 Unscrew and remove the nuts which hold the radius rods to the suspension track control arms.
18 Disconnect the left-hand track control arm from its bracket on the body.
19 Support the gearbox on a jack, preferably of the trolley type, then unscrew and remove the bolts which hold the clutch housing to the engine.
20 Unbolt and remove the flexible mounting bracket from the left-hand side of the transmission. Lift the bracket away, complete with the radius rod previously released from the track control arm.
21 Remove the pinch bolts from the base of the left-hand suspension strut and tap the steering knuckle downwards, then tap or press the driveshaft out of the hub.
22 Withdraw the gearbox/final drive towards the left-hand side of the engine compartment, until the right-hand driveshaft can be disconnected from the right-hand hub after disconnecting the steering knuckle from the right-hand suspension strut.
23 Tie both driveshafts to the top of the transmission, then manoeuvre the assembly on the jack from under the front of the car.
24 Refitting is a reversal of the removal process. Make sure that, on completion, the front driveshaft nuts are tightened to the specified

Fig. 6.8 Gear selector link beneath the car (Sec 2)

1 Link   4 Selector rod
2 Locking bolts   5 Anti-vibration bracket
3 Joints

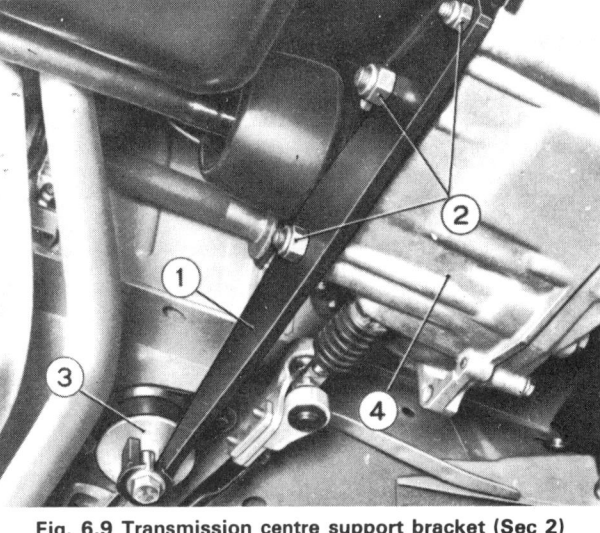

Fig. 6.9 Transmission centre support bracket (Sec 2)

1 Bracket   3 Flexible mounting
2 Mounting bolts to   4 Transmission casing
   transmission

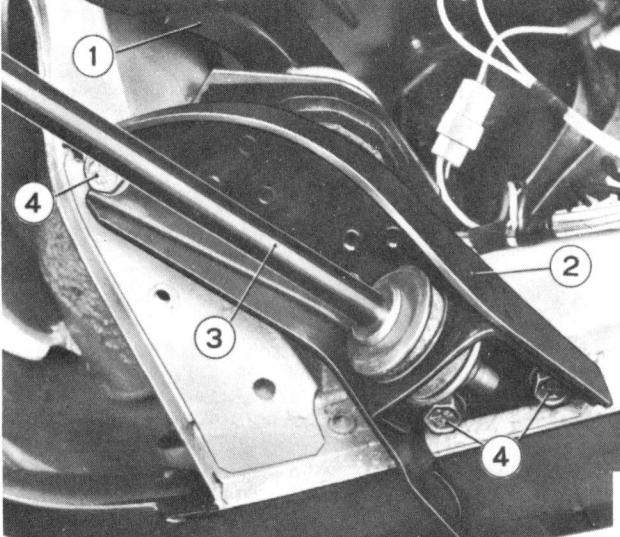

Fig. 6.10 Left-hand mounting (Sec 2)

1 Bracket   3 Suspension radius rod
2 Support   4 Bracket bolts

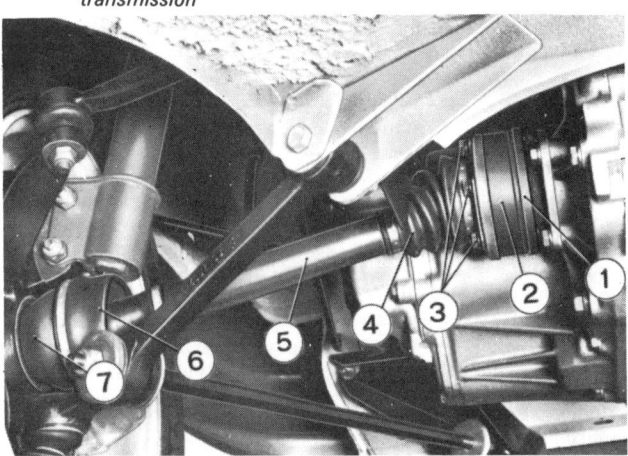

Fig. 6.11 Left-hand driveshaft (75 models) (Sec 3)

1 Flange   5 Driveshaft
2 Constant velocity balljoint   6 Dust excluding boot
3 Screws   7 Constant velocity balljoint
4 Dust excluding bellows

Fig. 6.12 Right-hand driveshaft (75 models) (Sec 3)

1 Dust excluding boot   4 Constant velocity balljoint
2 Driveshaft (inboard)   5 Driveshaft (outboard)
3 Driveshaft support

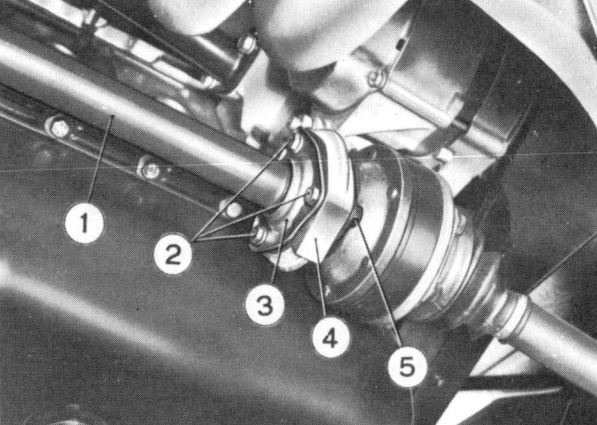

Fig. 6.13 Right-hand driveshaft support viewed from the transmission on 75 models (Sec 3)

1 Driveshaft   4 Support
2 Screws   5 Bearing retainer
3 Bearing retainer

torque and staked. Preferably, use new nuts; if they are not available, however, change them from side to side so that the original staking positions will not be used again.

3 Transmission (75 and North American models) – removal and refitting

1   The operations and their sequence are as described in the preceding Section, except in the method of disconnecting the driveshafts; they are not released from the roadwheel hubs, but are separated at their inboard flanges on the final drive housing and support (right-hand side).
2   Extract the socket-headed screws and disconnect the left-hand driveshaft, complete with constant velocity (CV) joint at the shaft inboard flange. Support the disconnected driveshaft by tying it up with wire.
3   Extract the socket screws from the CV joint flange adjacent to the right-hand driveshaft support. Disconnect the outboard right-hand driveshaft complete with CV joint from the inboard flange. Tie the shaft up, out of the way.
4   Extract the setscrews which hold the inboard section of the right-hand driveshaft to the support, then disengage the driveshaft and bearing from the support and from the final drive.
5   Remove the disconnected inboard section of the right-hand driveshaft.
6   Refitting is a reversal of the removal process, but it is recommended that the socket-headed screws for the flanges are renewed.

4 Transmission – dismantling for examination

1   Remove the driveshafts (on 65 models) as described in Chapter 7 or use two levers to prise out the left-hand flange/stub assembly from the final drive (on 75 and North American models) (photos).
2   Clean away all external dirt, also from the interior of the clutch bellhousing.
3   Place the transmission securely chocked on a clean bench.
4   Working within the clutch bellhousing, release the spring clips and withdraw the clutch release bearing.
5   Unbolt and remove the oil seal retainer from inside the clutch bellhousing.
6   Unbolt and remove the mounting bracket from the end cover on the transmission casing.
7   Unbolt the rear cover (which incorporates a breather) and remove the cover and its paper gasket (photo).
8   Stand the transmission upright on the bellhousing flange.

5-speed models
9   Release the 5th gear selector fork lockbolt and slide the fork up its selector shaft, together with the 5th gear synchro sleeve; remove the sleeve from the output shaft.
10   Grip the balljointed end of the gearchange selector rod and push or pull to select any gear.
11   Refit the 5th gear synchro sleeve to the output shaft and depress it fully to lock up 5th gear.
12   With two gears now simultaneously engaged, the input and output shaft nuts can be unscrewed, having first relieved the staking.
13   Remove the 5th gear synchro sleeve for the second time, then withdraw the 5th gear synchro hub, followed by the 5th gear from the input shaft.
14   Take off the 5th gear from the output shaft.
15   Extract the two securing screws and remove the intermediate plate and its paper gasket.

4-speed models
16   Take off the inner circlips, on the end of the input and output shafts. Note that the one on the output shaft has behind it two Belleville washers. These put a heavy load on the circlip. If it will not readily come out of its groove, the load must be taken off it as follows.
17   The Belleville washers can be compressed by screwing into the threaded end of the shaft one of the bolts that holds the transmission to the engine, using a large socket spanner to press down on the Belleville washers. Between the socket and the washer must go a semicircle of steel so the socket clears the circlip, and through the gap in it the ends of the circlip can be reached.

18   Having removed the circlips from both shafts, see if the two bearings will come off the shafts and out of the casing readily, prising with screwdrivers. If they do not, leave them on the shafts for now.

All models
19   Remove the circlips from the bearing outer races (photo).
20   Unbolt and remove the cover plate from the detent springs (photo).
21   Extract the springs, noting that two are of the same length, while the shorter one is located opposite reverse or 5th/reverse selector rod. Use a pencil magnet or tilt the gearcase to extract the detent balls (photo).
22   Unbolt the gearcase from the clutch bellhousing/final drive casing. Some of these nuts or bolts are located within the clutch bellhousing (photo).
23   Unscrew and remove the reversing lamp switch.
24   Lift the gearcase from the bellhousing/final drive half casing (photo).
25   Unbolt and remove the reverse idler shaft lockplate (photo).
26   Withdraw the reverse idler shaft and gear. Remove the reverse selector fork bolt and withdraw the fork with the gear if necessary. Do not remove the reverse or 5th/reverse selector shaft unless it is intended to renew the shafts and/or interlock plungers – see paragraph 34.
27   Remove the bolts from the 1st/2nd and 3rd/4th selector forks.
28   Lift out the meshed input and output shafts with the selector forks. Avoid withdrawing the selector shafts, unless this is to be done anyway.
29   Remove the differential/crownwheel assembly (photo). Withdraw the input and output shaft bearings, which are now visible.
30   Unbolt the gearchange rod relay housing and remove it, complete with dogs.
31   Release the lockbolt on the dog attached to the gearchange rod, and slide the rod out of the gearcase.
32   To remove the speedometer sender unit, release the union nut and unscrew it a few turns. Withdraw the sender unit (photo).
33   The nylon shaft and gear (which drive the sender unit) can be extracted if the socket headed lockscrew entered from the side of the gearcase is first unscrewed (photo).
34   The gearchange selector shafts should not be removed unless absolutely essential; the plug in the side of the gearcase may have to be prised out to retrieve and to refit the interlock plungers, although the plungers can be manipulated by careful use of a pencil magnet.
35   The gearbox components should now be dismantled and examined as described in the following Sections.

5 Inspection and renewal of components

1   Check all the components for signs of damage. All the gear teeth should be smooth and shiny, without any chips. The ball and rollers of the bearings should be unblemished.
2   The races of the final drive taper roller bearings, still in the casing, should be a smooth, even colour without any mark. Should either the rollers or the races be marked at all, the complete bearing must be renewed. In this case, the outer races must be extracted from the casing, and the rollers with the inner races pulled off the differential cage halves. The latter are strong, so it will be simple to prise them off. But the casing being soft, great care must be taken to pull the outer races out straight. FIAT have a special puller. It would be advisable to get this job done by your agent.
3   Check the clearance of the gearwheels on the output shaft against Specifications.
4   Check the synchromesh baulk rings for signs of wear. Check their fit in their respective gears. If the gears are being renewed, the synchromesh units should also be renewed. One point easy to miss in examining the gears is fracture of the small ends of the teeth that are on the outside of the synchro-ring, and are an extension of the teeth for the dog clutch to engage. If any of these are chipped, the gear must be renewed.
5   Check the casings for cracks. If there are leaks at a plug, it must be renewed. This must be tapped carefully into place, sufficient to expand it but not enough to distort it too much. If a new plug is not available, or its security is in doubt after fitting, it can be secured in place with a layer of epoxy resin, two part adhesive, round its rim. This

4.1a Differential flange/stub (75 and North American models)

4.1b Differential flange/stub retaining circlip

4.7 Unbolt the rear cover (4-speed shown)

4.19 Remove the bearing outer circlip (4-speed shown)

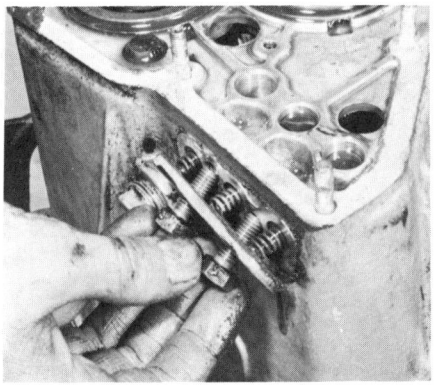
4.20 Remove the detent spring cover plate

4.21 Detent springs and balls

4.22 Remove the clutch bellhousing nuts

4.24 Lift the gearcase away

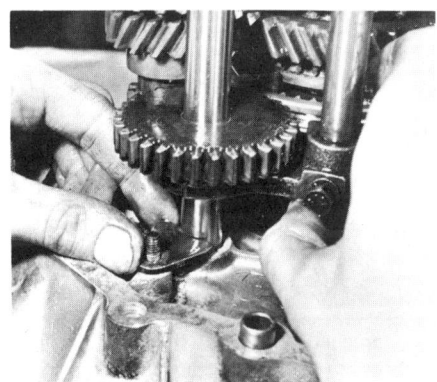
4.25 Remove the reverse idler shaft lock-plate

4.29 Lift out the final drive unit

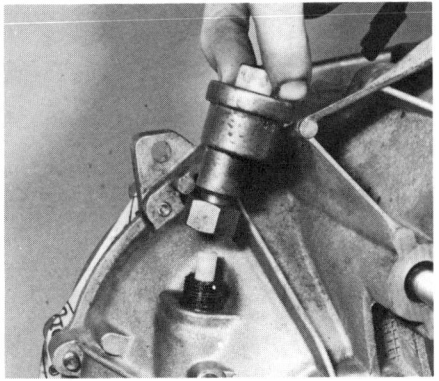
4.32 Remove the speedometer sender unit

4.33 Remove the sender unit drivegear

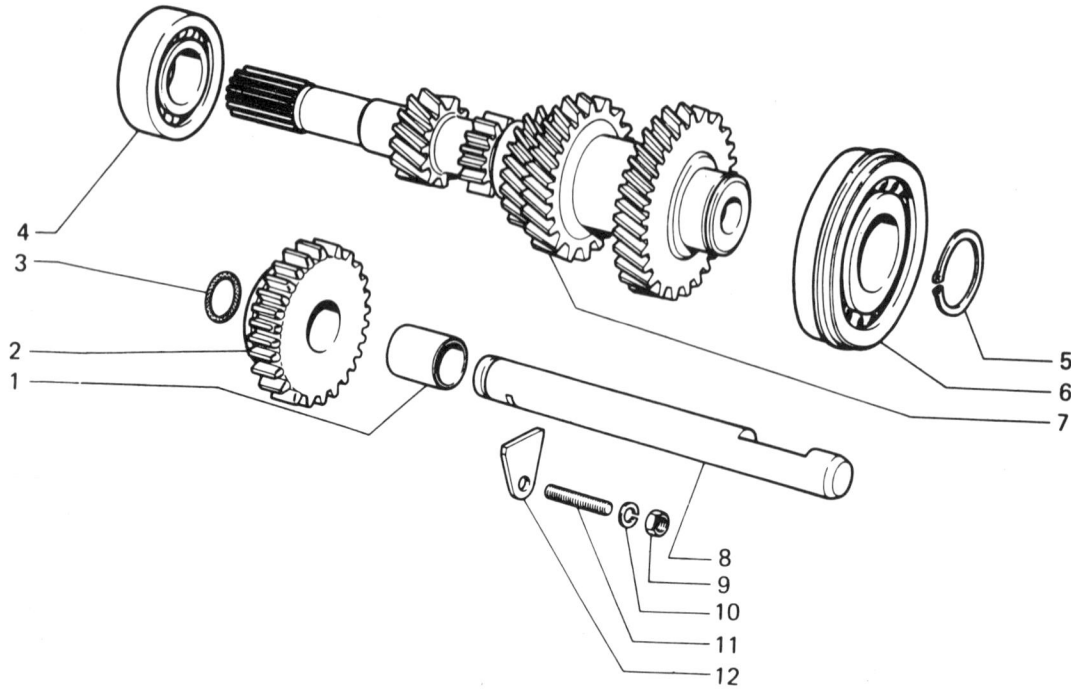

Fig. 6.14 Input and reverse gear assemblies (4-speed) (Sec 4)

1 Bush	4 Bearing	7 Input shaft/gear assembly	10 Lockwasher
2 Reverse idler gear	5 Circlip	8 Idler shaft	11 Stud
3 Oil seal	6 Bearing	9 Nut	12 Lockplate

type of adhesive requires two days to set fully at ambient temperature, but can be used in a few hours if heated in an oven.

6 Renew seals and gaskets at each dismantling.

7 Check the movement of the selector rods in their bores in the casing. They should move freely but without appreciable sideplay. Inspect the sliding surfaces of the selector forks for wear or damage.

6 Input and output shaft gears – dismantling and reassembly

Input shaft

1 Only the bearing can be renewed on the input shaft. Use a puller or press to remove and refit it (photo).

Output shaft

2 All components can be removed from the output shaft using hand pressure only, with the exception of the bearing, for which a puller will be required (photo).

3 Keep the dismantled components in the exact order and same way round as they were originally fitted.

4 A worn synchromesh unit is best renewed complete – especially if there has ben a history of noisy gearchanging – or if the synchromesh could be easily 'beaten' (photo).

5 With all parts clean, renewed (where necessary) and lightly lubricated, assemble the output shaft in the following sequence (photo).

6 Slide on the 1st speed gear bush (photo).

7 Fit the 1st speed gear (photo).

8 Fit the 1st/2nd synchro sleeve/reverse gear with baulk rings. The sleeve groove must be towards the shaft pinion gear (photo).

9 Fit the retaining circlip (photo).

10 Fit the 2nd speed gear (photo).

11 Fit the bush(es), followed by the 3rd speed gear (photo).

12 Slide on the 3rd/4th synchro sleeve (photo).

13 Fit the bush and the 4th speed gear (photo).

14 Press on the shaft bearing (photo).

4-speed models

15 Fit the two Belleville washers, their outer rims next to each other on the end of the shaft.

16 Fit the circlip. To get into its groove against the considerable pressure of the pair of washers, the latter must be compressed by a clamp. The end of the shaft is internally threaded, and the bolts fixing the transmission to the engine are the same thread. Select a socket just large enough to span the shaft but press on the circlip. The bolts are a bit long, so another socket makes a handy distance piece to use up the extra length of bolt. Screw in the bolt to push the two washers and the circlip down the shaft, watching carefully at the gap in the circlip to see when it is lined up with the groove in the shaft. Tap the circlip, which is trapped by the socket, with a small screwdriver, to push it into the groove. Release the press (photos).

5-speed models

17 Fit the washer and 5th gear bush to the end of the shaft (photo).

All models

18 The output shaft is now ready for fitting in the gearcase.

7 Differential unit – overhaul

1 The speedometer drivegear can be removed from the differential case by driving it off with a suitable drift (photo).

2 If it is wished to dismantle the differential unit, first undo the ring of bolts holding the final drive wheel to the differential, and the two halves of the differential cage together (photo).

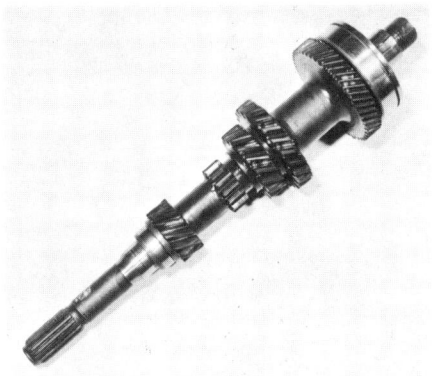

6.1 5-speed input shaft

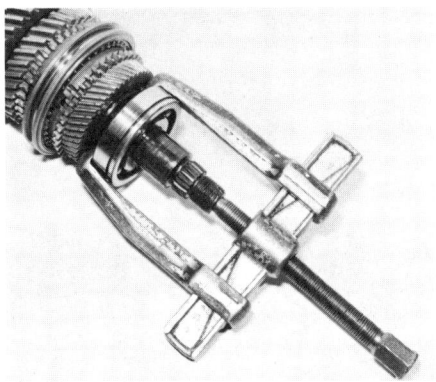

6.2 Removing the output shaft bearing

6.4a Synchro unit assembled

6.4b Fitting a synchro baulk ring

6.5 Output shaft ready for assembly of gears (5-speed shown)

6.6 Fit the 1st gear bush

6.7 Fit the 1st speed gear

6.8 Fit the 1st/2nd synchro unit. Note orientation of selector groove

6.10 Fit the 2nd speed gear

6.11 Fit the 3rd speed gear

6.12 Fit the 3rd/4th synchro unit

6.13 Fit the 4th speed gear

6.14 Locating the output shaft bearing
(5-speed shown)

6.16a Locate the Belleville washers and circlip

6.16b Use two sockets and a bolt to compress
the washers

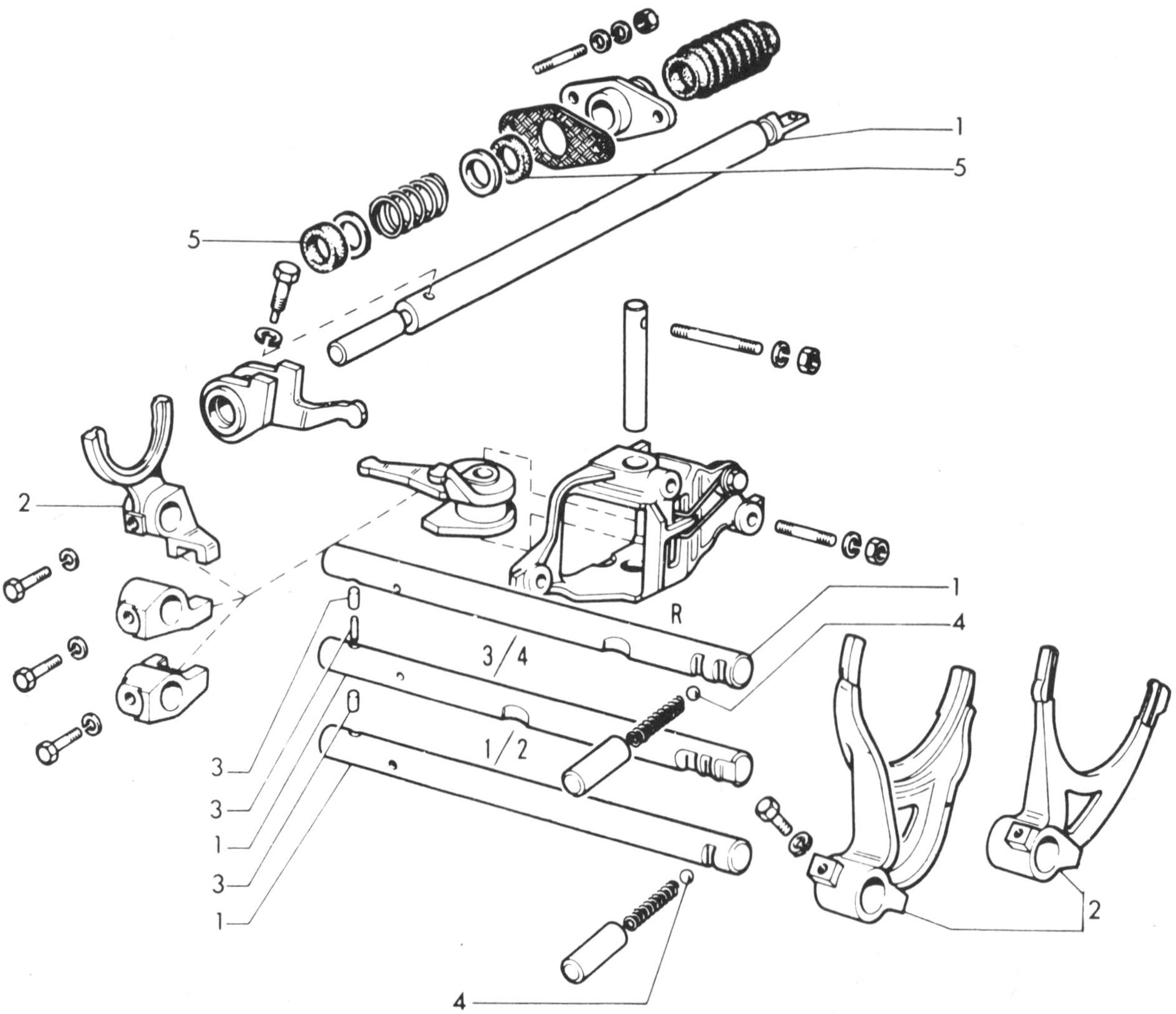

Fig. 6.15 Exploded view of the gear selector mechanism (4-speed gearbox) (Sec 4)

1 Selector rods
2 Selector forks
3 Interlock plungers

4 Detent balls (two only
   shown)
5 Seals

6.16c Locate the circlip in its groove

6.17 Fit the washer and 5th gear bush

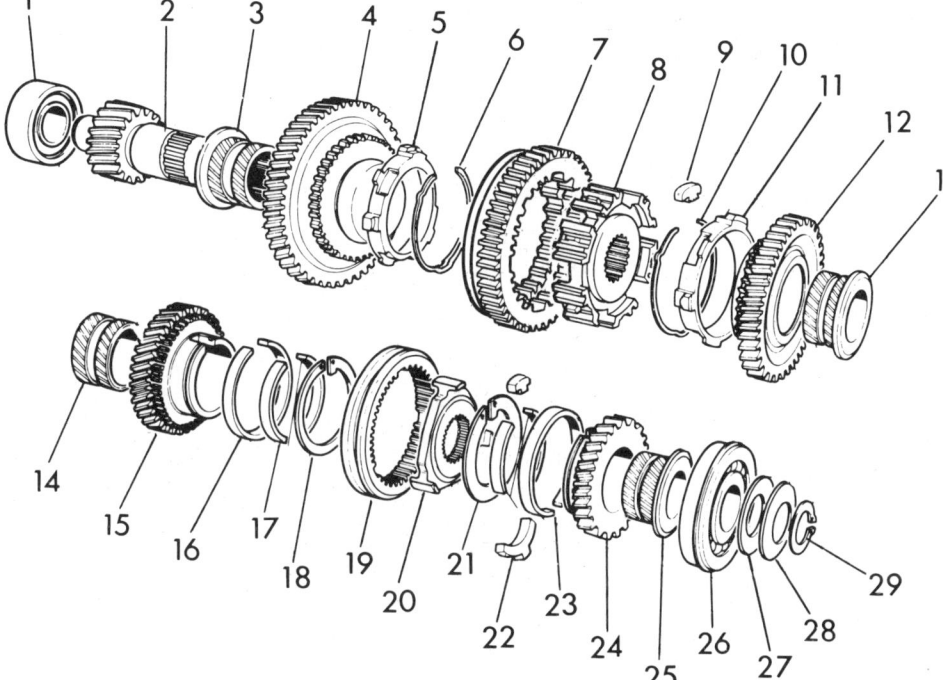

1 Bearing
2 Pinion gear to final
   drive (crownwheel)
3 Bush
4 1st speed gear
5 Synchroniser (baulk ring)
6 Spring ring
7 1st/2nd synchro sleeve
   with reverse gear
8 1st/2nd synchro hub
9 Sliding key
10 Spring ring
11 Synchroniser (baulk ring)
12 2nd speed gear
13 Bush
14 Bush
15 3rd speed gear
16 Synchroniser ring
17 Drive spring
18 Snap ring
19 3rd/4th synchro sleeve
20 3rd/4th synchro hub
21 Snap ring
22 Sliding key
23 Synchroniser ring
24 4th speed gear
25 Bush
26 Bearing
27 Belleville washer
28 Belleville washer
29 Circlip

Fig. 6.16 Exploded view of the output shaft (4-speed gearbox)
(Sec 6)

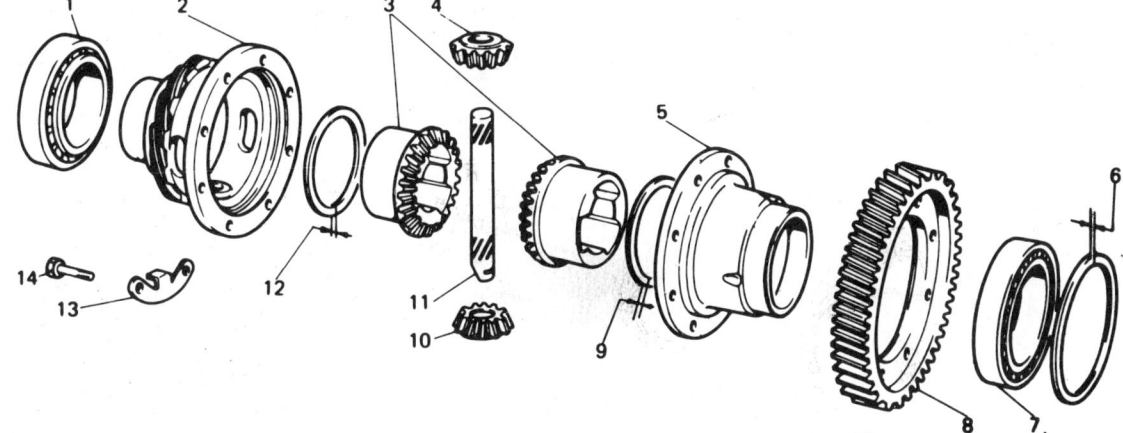

Fig. 6.17 Exploded view of the differential/final drive (Sec 7)

1 Differential case bearing	5 Differential half case	9 Thrust washer	12 Thrust washer
2 Differential half case	6 Spacer	10 Pinion bevel gear	13 Lockplate
3 Side gears	7 Differential case bearing	11 Pinion gear shaft	14 Bolt
4 Pinion gear	8 Crownwheel		

7.1 Speedometer drivegear (arrowed) on differential

7.2 Differential cage bolts

7.3 Planet gear pinion shaft lockplate

7.4 Differential dismantled

7.6 Removing a planet gear

7.7 Side gear thrust washer

3   This will also release the locking plate for the planet pinion shaft (photo).
4   Lift off the final drive wheel (photo).
5   Mark the two halves of the differential cage, with punch dots, for reassembly.
6   Prise the two halves apart. Remove the shaft and the two planet pinions (photo).
7   Take out the two bevel side gears, with their thrust washers (if fitted) from the two halves of the cage. Leave the taper roller bearings in place unless they are being renewed (photo).
8   Reassembly is the reverse of the dismantling procedure. The backlash of the side and planet gears must not exceed 0.1 mm (0.004 in). On models using thrust washers, backlash can be adjusted by fitting different thicknesses of washer. On models without thrust washers, excessive backlash means that the components must be renewed.
9   Reassembly is a reversal of the dismantling procedure. Tighten the bolts in diagonal sequence to the specified torque. If new bearings are being fitted, drive them into place carefully and evenly, applying the drift to the inner tracks. Set the preload of these bearings as described in Section 8.

8   Transmission – reassembly

1   The operations are a direct reversal of those described for dismantling in Section 4. If the selector rods were removed refit them to their holes, making sure that the interlock pin is in the centre (3rd/4th) rod with the thicker plungers between the centre and outer rods (photo). Use a pencil magnet to do this, to avoid removing the blanking plug from the gearcase. If the remote control gearchange selector shaft was removed, fit it now, together with the selector mechanism. Note the arrangement of the dogs and their inter-

connection. Check that the selector shaft oil seal is in good condition, otherwise renew it (photos).
2   Stand the mouth of the bellhousing on the bench with the selector rods pointing upwards. Place the differential/crownwheel assembly into the housing (photos).
3   Mesh the input and output shafts together so the bearings at their upper ends are level.
4   Engage the selector forks in their respective synchro sleeve grooves.
5   If the shaft bearings in the bellhousing were removed, push them into position, noting that the numbers engraved on them must be visible from the selector rod side. The input shaft bearing can only be retained in position if the retainer/oil seal is in position inside the bellhousing. If it was removed, refit it now; it will only go on in one position and so cannot be refitted incorrectly (photos).
6   With the help of an assistant, slide the meshed gear trains into position, at the same time engaging the selector forks on their rods and pushing them down until the lockbolt holes are in alignment (photo).
7   Fit and tighten the fork lockbolts for the 1st/2nd and 3rd/4th selector forks (photo).
8   Fit the reverse idler gear on its selector fork, and the idler shaft to the gear. Fit a new O-ring to the idler shaft, then insert the shaft, gear and fork, engaging the fork on the reverse or 5th/reverse selector rod (photo). Tighten the fork lockbolt.
9   Fit the reverse idler shaft lockplate (photo).
10   Locate a new gasket and lower the gearcase onto the bellhousing (photo).
11   Fit and tighten the securing nuts or bolts, noting that some of the bolts enter from within the bellhousing (photo).
12   Fit the shaft bearing outer circlips, noting that the bearings may require prising upward slightly to expose the complete width of the circlip groove. The circlip end gaps must be between the bearings, otherwise they cannot be fully engaged in their grooves (photo).

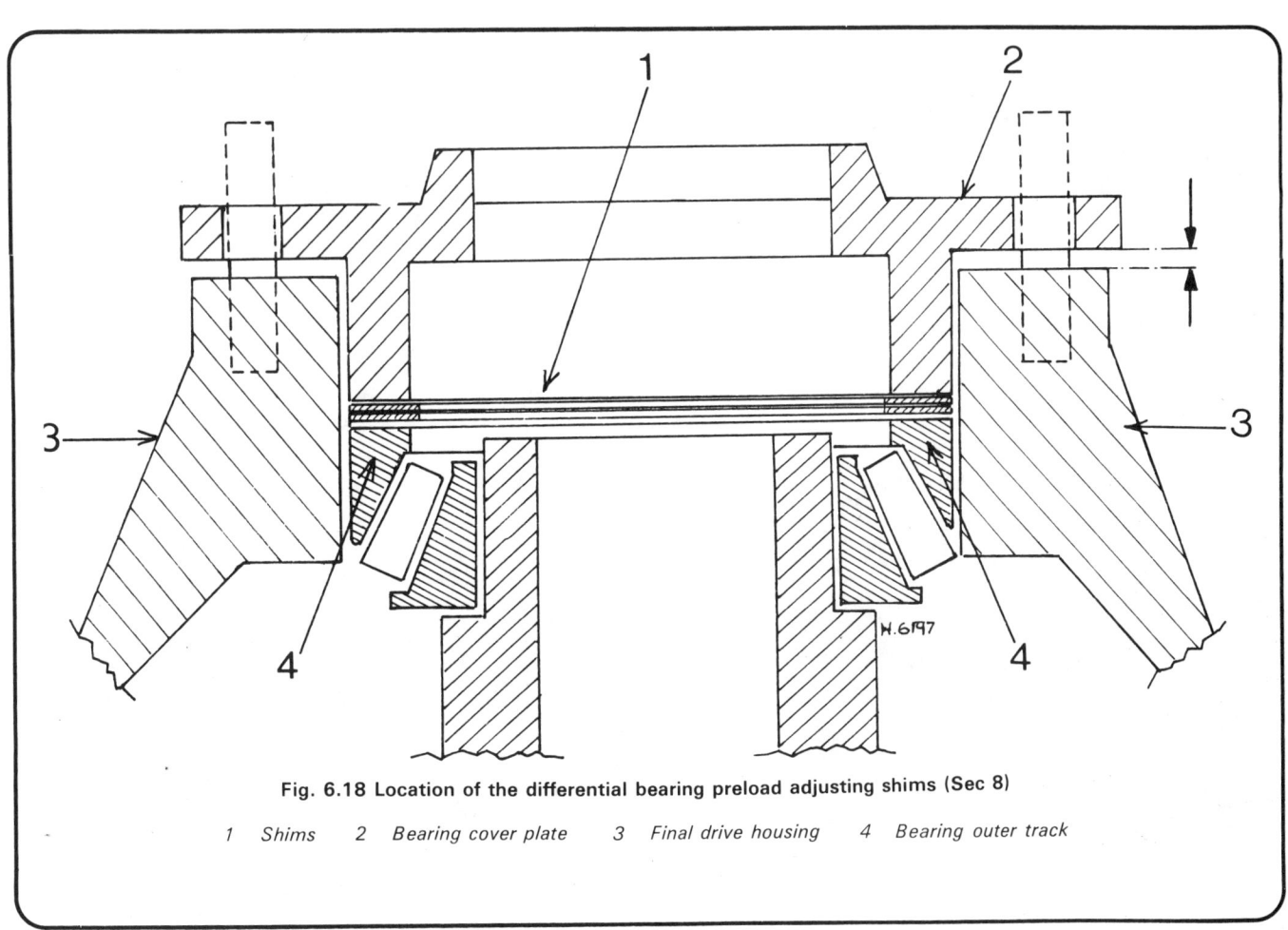

Fig. 6.18 Location of the differential bearing preload adjusting shims (Sec 8)

1   Shims   2   Bearing cover plate   3   Final drive housing   4   Bearing outer track

8.1a Thinner interlock plunger located in 3rd/4th selector rod

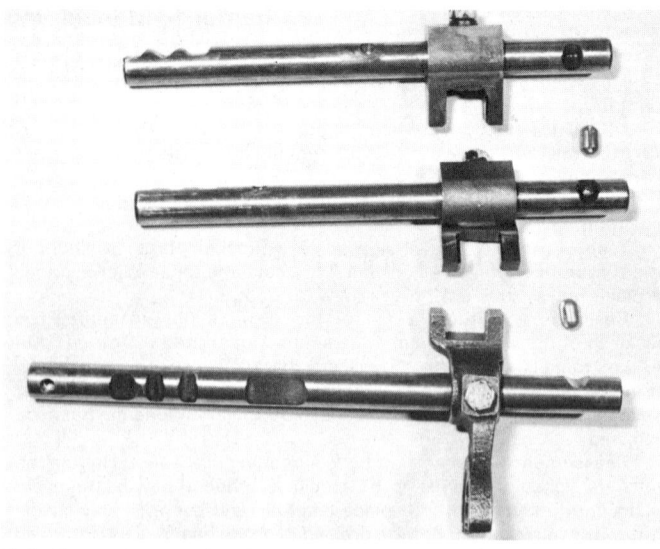

8.1b Gear selector rods – 5-speed shown. Top: 1st/2nd. Middle: 3rd/4th. Bottom: 5th/reverse

8.1c Remote control gearchange rod and dog

8.1d Gearchange selector mechanism

8.1e Gearchange selector mechanism assembled

8.1f Selector rod dogs

8.1g Remote control gearchange rod oil seal

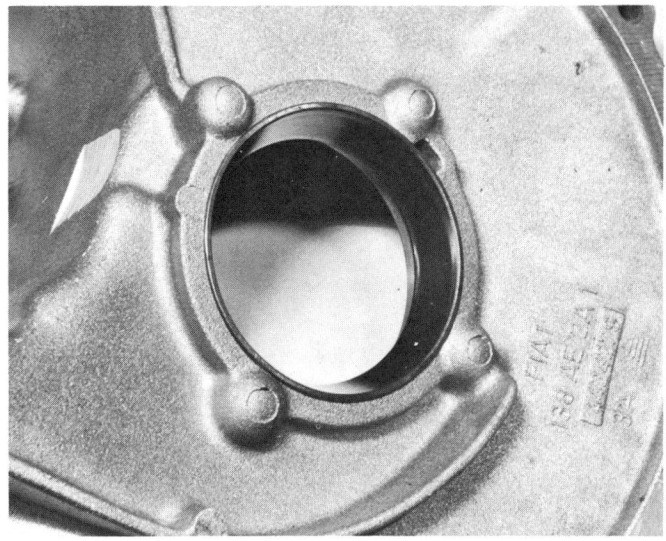

8.2a Differential bearing outer track

8.2b Differential/crownwheel installed

8.2c Selector rods located – 5-speed shown.   Left to right: 5th/reverse, 3rd/4th, 1st/2nd

8.5a Fit the input shaft bearing

8.5b Input shaft bearing inner track

8.5c Output shaft bearing

8.5d Input shaft bearing retainer and oil seal

8.5e Input shaft bearing retainer fitted to bellhousing

8.6 Gear train fitted

8.7 Fork lockbolts fitted

8.8 Fitting reverse idler shaft and gear

8.9 Fit the reverse idler shaft lockplate

8.10 Refit the gearcase

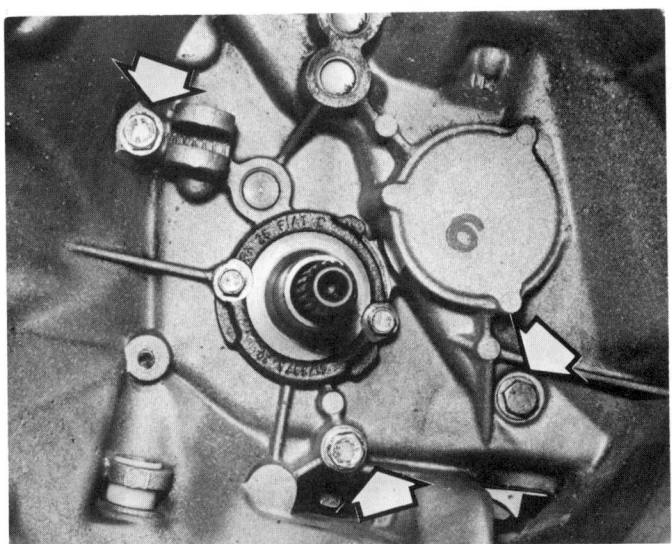

8.11 Gearcase-to-bellhousing bolts (arrowed)

8.12 Fit the outer circlips (4-speed shown)

8.14a Woodruff key on the input shaft

8.14b Fit 5th speed gear to the input shaft

8.15a Fit 5th gear speed gear to the output shaft

8.15b Fit 5th speed synchro hub to the output shaft

8.16 Fitting 5th speed synchro sleeve and selector fork

8.17 Fit the thrust washer

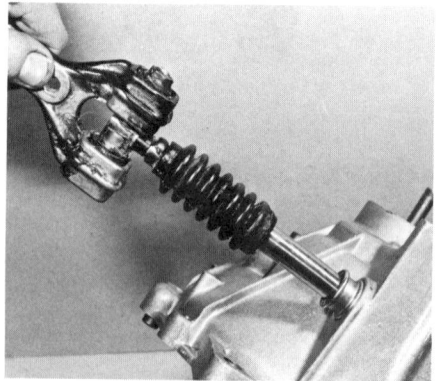

8.19 Gearchange remote control rod

8.20a Tightening a shaft nut

8.20b Staking a shaft nut

8.21 Tighten the 5th gear selector fork lockbolt

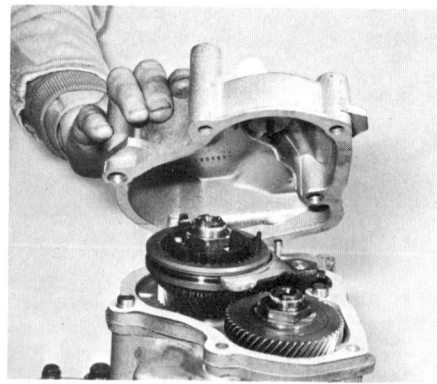

8.23 Refit the end cover (5-speed shown)

8.24 Mounting bracket and earth lead

8.25 Differential bearing adjustment shim

8.27 Measure gap between bearing cover plate and recess

8.28 Differential bearing cover oil seal

8.29 Fit the differential bearing cover

8.30a Fit the detent balls and springs.
Left to right: 5th/reverse (or reverse only),
3rd/4th, 1st/2nd

8.30b Detent spring cover plate

8.31 Fit the reversing lamp switch

8.35 Bellhousing rubber plug

5-speed models

13 Locate the intermediate plate, using a new gasket.
14 Fit the Woodruff key into its shaft groove and slide the 5th speed gear over it, onto the input shaft (photos).
15 With the 5th gear bush fitted to the output shaft (oiled liberally) slide on the 5th speed gear and synchro hub (photos).
16 Fit the 5th gear synchro sleeve with its chamfered edge away from the gear teeth (photo).
17 Tap the synchro sleeve downward so that the shift fork (not yet lockbolted) slides on its rod at the same time. Fit the shaft thrust washers (photo).
18 Insert a thin screwdriver into the lockbolt hole in the selector rod and prise it upward, so engaging 5th gear.
19 Select another gear by pushing or pulling the main gearchange operating remote control rod (photo).
20 With both shafts now prevented from rotating, screw on their nuts, tighten them to the specified torque and stake them (photos).
21 Release the 5th gear and the other gear which were selected to lock up the input and output shafts; insert and tighten the 5th gear shift fork lockbolt on its selector rod (photo).

4-speed models

22 Refit the input shaft bearing inner circlip, if it was removed. The output shaft circlip and Belleville washers should already have been fitted (Section 6).

All models

23 Refit the end cover, using a new gasket (photo).
24 Fit the end cover mounting bracket, locating the earth lead as shown (photo).
25 If the original differential bearings are being re-used, refit the original bearing adjustment shim (photo).

26 If the differential bearings have been renewed, the bearing preload must now be calculated and adjusted by means of shims. This sounds very complicated, but in fact means that when the bearing cover is bolted down, it must exert just enough pressure to give the bearings the specified preload.
27 To do this work, a suitable depth gauge will be required. First, measure the depth of the bearing cover recess. Second, measure the projection of the cover's machined section (O-ring removed). Subtract one dimension from the other and add 0.08 mm (0.003 in). This is the thickness of the shim required. Where a depth gauge is not available, shims can be inserted into the housing recess until, when the bearing cover plate is fitted (and resting under its own weight), there is a gap between the plate and the edge of the bearing recess of between 0.08 and 0.12 mm (0.003 and 0.005 in) (photo). This method is not so accurate and will require the purchase of unnecessary shims.
28 If necessary, fit a new oil seal to the differential bearing cover (photo).
29 Fit a new O-ring to the bearing cover and bolt it down, using a new paper gasket (photo).
30 Fit the detent balls and springs into their holes (remember the shorter spring for reverse or 5th/reverse) and bolt on the cover plate (photos).
31 Refit the reversing lamp switch (photo).
32 Lower the gearcase onto its base and fit the clutch release lever and bearing. Note that the cropped corner of the bearing backplate is uppermost. Fit the bearing securing clips.
33 Locate the speedometer sender unit and tighten its union nut.
34 If applicable, refit the left-hand differential output drive flange, giving it a sharp blow with the hand to overcome the resistance of its retaining snap-ring.
35 Check that the rubber plug (if fitted) is secure in its location in the bellhousing (photo).
36 Refill the transmission after it has been refitted to the car.

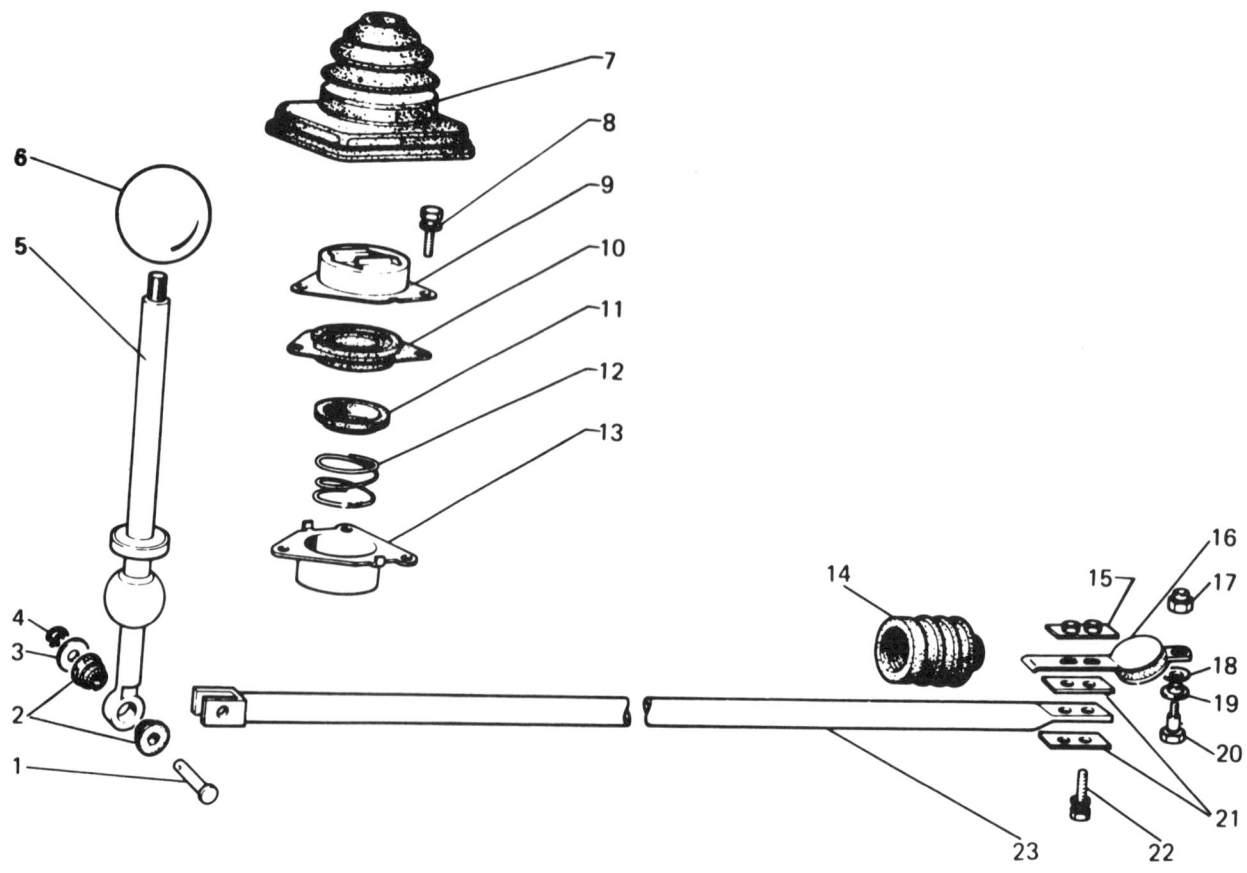

Fig. 6.19 Gearchange lever and linkage (4-speed gearbox) (Sec 9)

1	Clevis pin	13	Lower support plate
2	Flexible bush	14	Gaiter
3	Washer	15	Plate
4	Clip	16	Flexible coupling
5	Gearchange lever	17	Nut
6	Knob	18	Lockwasher
7	Gaiter	19	Bush
8	Bolt	20	Shouldered bolt
9	Upper support plate	21	Plate
10	Socket retainer	22	Bolt
11	Ball socket	23	Gear selector link
12	Coil spring		

9 Gearchange controls – dismantling and reassembly

4-speed models

1   Working inside the car, remove the dust excluding boot from the base of the gear lever.
2   Unscrew and remove the three bolts from the support plate and raise the plate so that the clip and pin (which secure the link rod to the gear lever) can be extracted. Retain the bushes and washer (photo).
3   Working under the car, remove the bolt that attaches the flexible link to the selector rod. Remove the boot and gear lever from inside the car.
4   Reassembly is a reversal of dismantling. Make sure that the flexible link is in good condition.
5   Adjust the linkage as described in Section 10.

5-speed models

6   Working inside the car, remove the centre console (photo).
7   With neutral selected, pull the dust excluding boot up the gearchange lever. Remove the three setscrews exposed at the base of the lever (photo).
8   Once the screws have been removed, rotate the plate to release it from the lugs on the lower baseplate.
9   Working under the car, remove the shields and the protective boot from under the gear lever, then unscrew and remove the pivot bolt which holds the links to the bush at the bottom of the lever.
10 Reassembly is a reversal of the dismantling process, but adjust the linkage as described in the next Section.

11 Later model cars (built in 1980) have a balljointed type connection at the base of the gearchange lever instead of the pivot bolt/clevis fork type arrangement used previously.

10 Gearchange linkage – adjustment

4-speed models

1   Place the transmission in neutral and slacken the two bolts connecting the flexible link to the link rod. The bolt holes in the flexible links are elongated to allow for adjustment.
2   Have an assistant hold the gear lever centered in the guide, with the lever vertical. Tighten the two bolts in the flexible link sandwich joint (photo).
3   Road test the car to check the engagement of each gear.

5-speed models

4   With the gear lever vertical, the transmission selector rod should be in the neutral detent, without any tendency to be under tension from one side.
5   Release the bolts, which hold the selector link to the joints on the selector rod, and have an assistant hold the gear lever vertically in the neutral mode (photo).
6   Check that the selector rod is free in the centre of its neutral detent without having any sideways tension acting upon it.
7   Tighten the locking bolts, noting the elongated slots in the selector link which allow for the necessary adjustment to be made.

9.2 Gearchange lever attachment to link (4-speed)

9.6 Remove the centre console

9.7 Gearchange lever plate exposed

10.2 Gearchange flexible linkage (4-speed)

10.5 Gearchange selector rod and link (5-speed)

**Fig. 6.20a 5-speed gearchange lever viewed from below the car
(up to 1980 models) (Sec 9)**

1   Ball and socket
2   Gearchange lever
3   Bush

4   Pivot bolt and nut
5   Gearchange selector rod
    link

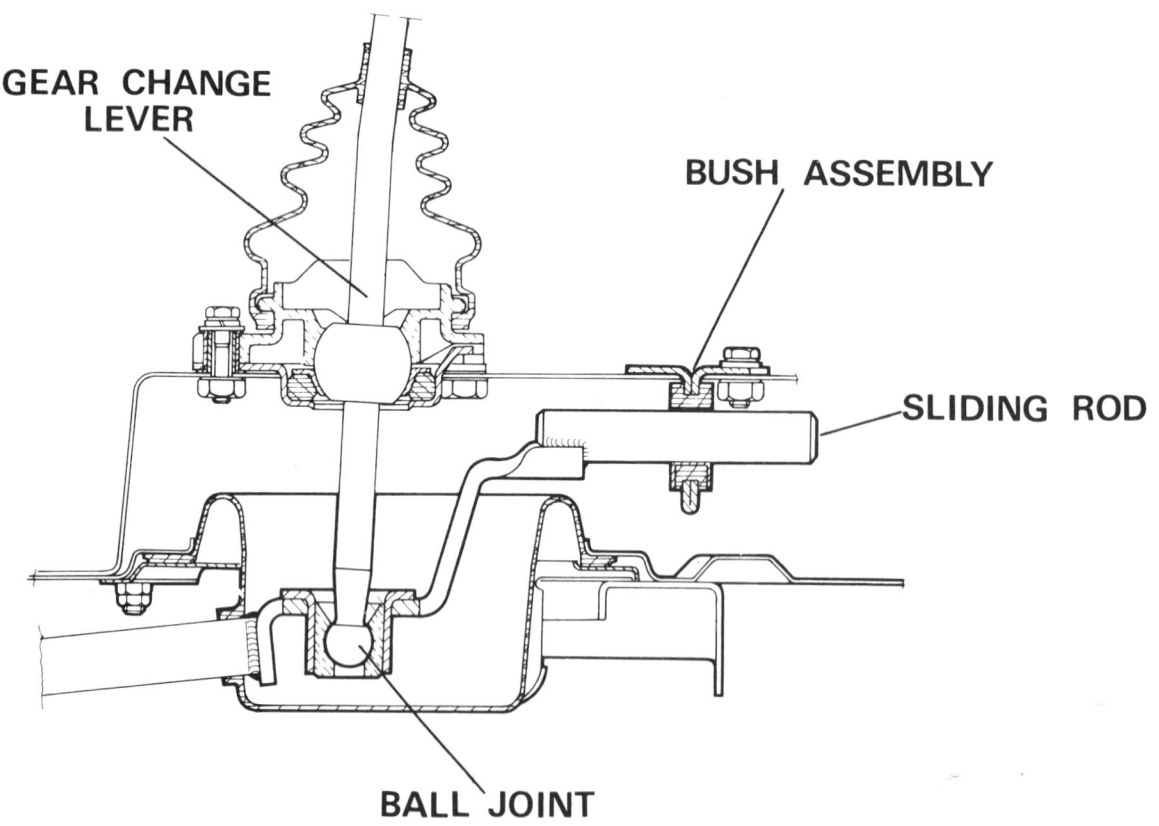

Fig. 6.20b Later type gearchange lever (1980 models on) (Sec 9)

11 Fault diagnosis – manual transmission

Note: *It is sometimes difficult to decide whether it is worthwhile removing and dismantling the gearbox for a fault which may be nothing more than a minor irritant. Gearboxes which howl, or where the synchromesh can be 'beaten' by a quick gear change, may continue to perform for a long time in this stage. A worn gearbox usually needs a complete rebuild to eliminate noise because the various gears, if re-aligned on new bearings will continue to howl when different wearing surfaces are presented to each other.*

The decision to overhaul, therefore, must be considered with regard to time and money available, relative to the degree of noise or malfunction that the driver can tolerate.

Symptom	Reason/s
Gearbox noisy in neutral	Worn input shaft bearings
	Worn output shaft bearings
Gearbox noisy in all gears	Oil level low or incorrect grade
	Worn bearings and brushes
	Excessive gear-to-shaft clearance
	Final drive incorrectly adjusted
Gearbox noisy in one particular gear	Worn or damaged gear teeth
Difficult or noisy gear selection	Worn synchro units or baulk rings
	Clutch fault (see Chapter 5)
Jumping out of gear on drive or overrun	Worn shift forks or synchro sleeve grooves
	Worn detent grooves or detent springs

PART B – AUTOMATIC TRANSMISSION

12 General description

The automatic transmission consists of a torque converter, fully automatic 3-speed gearbox, final drive gearing and a differential housed in an integral aluminium casting. The final drive lubricant is independent of the gearbox.

The torque converter is connected to the crankshaft through a flexible drive plate. The converter is a sealed unit and cannot be dismantled.

A manually operated speed selector lever and a kickdown facility for rapid downshifts when overtaking are fitted. The most important maintenance requirement is to keep the fluid at the correct level.

Due to the complexity of the automatic transmission assembly, it is essential to use special equipment for fault diagnosis and rectification. It is therefore recommended, if performance is not up to standard, or overhaul is necessary, that this work should be done by your local FIAT agent who will have the necessary equipment.

The content of the following sections is therefore confined to supplying general information and any service information that can be used by the owner.

13 Fluid level – checking

1   At the intervals specified in 'Routine Maintenance' (or earlier, if the car is subject to very arduous operating conditions), run the car on the road for at least 5 mile (8 km) until the engine and transmission are at normal operating temperatures.

2   Select P and allow the engine to idle for two or three minutes.

3   With the engine idling, withdraw the gearbox dipstick. Wipe it clean, re-insert it, then withdraw it and read off the level which should be near, but not over the max mark.

4   If necessary, top-up the level with the specified fluid through the dipstick tube. 0.7 pint (0.84 US pint, 0.4 litre) will raise the level from the MIN to the MAX mark.

5   To check the fluid level in the differential sump, jack up the car and support it on jack stands. Remove the filler plug.

6   The fluid level should be up to the bottom of the filler plug hole. If necessary, top-up with the specified fluid and refit the filler plug.

7   Remove the jack stands and lower the car. **Note**: *It is important that both levels are checked as the two sumps are completely separate.*

Fig. 6.22 Fluid filter securing screws (1) (Sec 13)

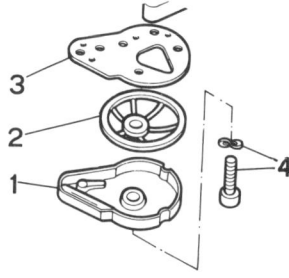

Fig. 6.23 Exploded view of the fluid filter (Sec 13)

1	Cover	3	Gasket
2	Filter mesh	4	Securing screw

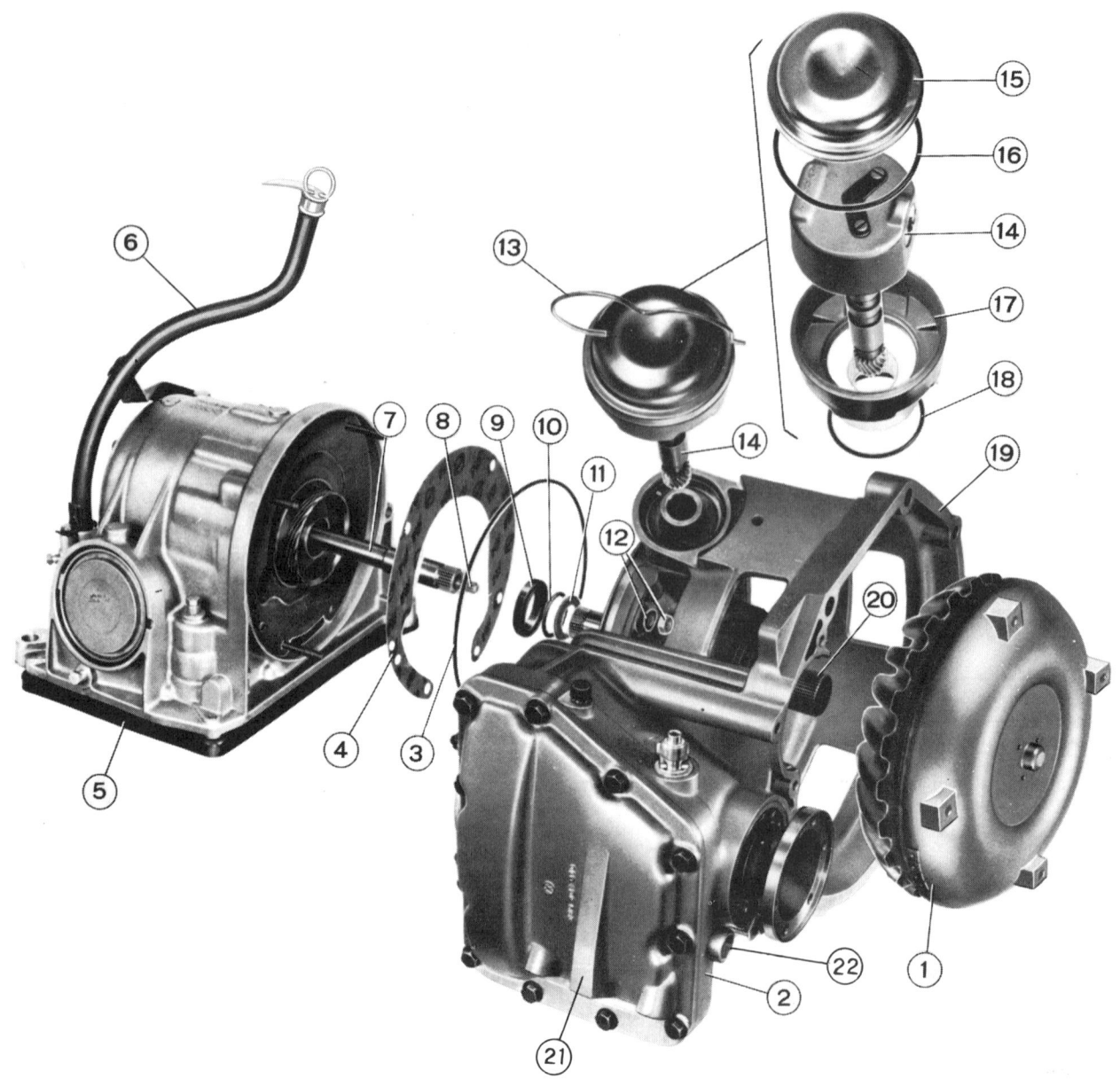

Fig. 6.21 Major assemblies of the automatic transmission (Sec 12)

1	Torque converter	8	Oil pump driveshaft	14	Centrifugal type speed	19	Torque converter
2	Final drive housing	9	Front oil seal		governor		bellhousing
3	Sealing ring	10	Pinion shaft seal	15	Governor top cover	20	Stator flange
4	Gasket	11	Thrust washer	16	Sealing ring	21	Final drive cover plate
5	Transmission casing	12	Nut and washer	17	Bottom cover	22	Final drive filler/level
6	Oil filler/dipstick tube	13	Governor retainer	18	Sealing ring		plug
7	Input shaft						

14 Fluid and filter – renewal and cleaning

1   The fluid should be drained at the intervals specified in 'Routine Maintenance', the filter inspected and renewed, if necessary, and fresh fluid used to refill the transmission to the correct level as shown on the dipstick.

2   Have the engine/transmission at normal operating temperature before draining the fluid; take care not to get scalded – the fluid will be very hot!

3   Jack up the car and support it securely on safety stands or other suitable supports.

4   Position a container with a very wide opening under the transmission sump pan, then slacken the pan securing bolts. Tap one corner of the pan to break the joint. Ease the corner of the pan down and allow to drain into the container.

5   Remove the pan securing bolts and lift it away.

6   Extract the securing screws from the filter and lift it from the valve block. Clean and dry it in suitable solvent. If the mesh is clogged with burnt resinous material (caused by overheating of the transmission fluid), renew the filter.

7   When refitting the filter, always renew the gasket.

8   Refit the sump pan (with a new gasket, if it appears to be in anything but perfect condition) and refill the transmission in the following way.

9   Select P and start the engine, letting it idle. Immediately, fill the

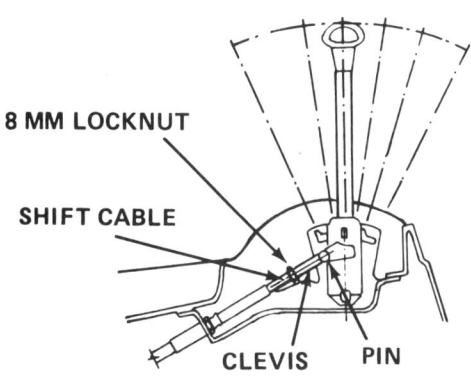

Fig. 6.24 Speed selector control lever (Sec 15)

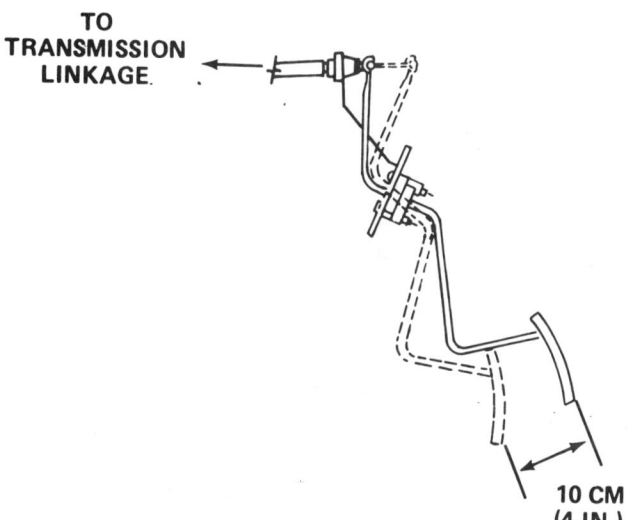

Fig. 6.25 Accelerator pedal stroke (Sec 16)

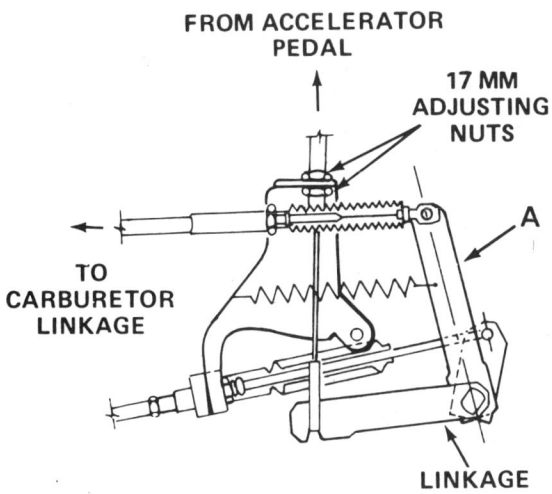

Fig. 6.26 Kickdown/accelerator cable arrangement at the transmission casing. For A see text (Sec 16)

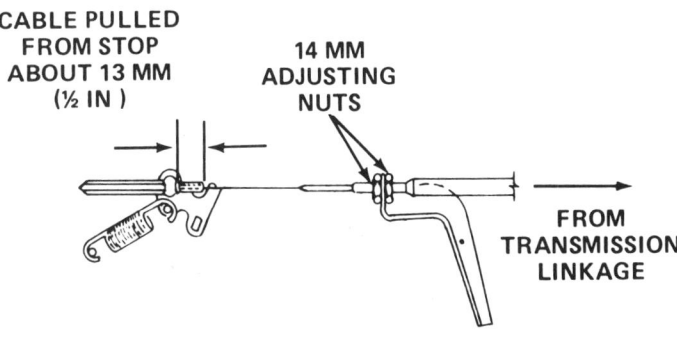

Fig. 6.27 Kickdown cable arrangement at the carburettor (Sec 16)

transmission through the filler/dipstick tube with the specified fluid until the level is between the MIN and MAX marks when the dipstick is inserted. Approximately 4.5 Imp pints (2.6 litres) of fluid will be required to do this.

10 Take the car for a test run of at least five miles, then with the car standing on a level surface with the engine idling, withdraw the dipstick, wipe it clean on a non-fluffy rag and re-insert it. If the level is below MIN, top-up to between the MIN and MAX marks. The quantity of fluid needed to raise the fluid level from the MIN to MAX mark is 0.7 Imp pints (0.4 litres).

11 If the fluid level is above the MAX mark, use a syringe with a long, flexible tube inserted into the filler tube to draw some fluid out.

12 It should be realised that the oil level on the dipstick will rise when the engine is switched off and the fluid is cold, due to some fluid draining from the torque converter. For this reason, always check the fluid level with it hot and the engine idling.

13 Renew the oil in the final drive at the same time as you renew the automatic transmission fluid. To do this will mean unbolting and removing the cover plate to let the oil drain out. The combined filler/level plug is of socket-headed type so make sure you have a suitable wrench in advance for unscrewing it.

14 Use a new gasket when refitting the cover and tighten the bolts evenly.

15 Remember to fill the final drive with the specified gear oil, *not automatic transmission fluid*.

15 Speed selector linkage – adjustment

1   Working inside the car, squeeze the selector control lever index plate and remove it to reveal the two centre console securing screws.

2   Extract these screws and remove the centre console.

3   Set the speed selector lever in PARK, release the handbrake then push and pull the car to check that the internal pawl in the transmission is fully engaged and the car cannot be rolled.

4   At the base of the selector lever, extract the clevis pin which holds the selector cable to the control lever.

5   Check that the control lever is fully is the PARK position and, after releasing the clevis locknut on the cable, adjust the clevis until the pin can be inserted through the cable and lever connecting holes in perfect alignment.

6   Lock the clevis pin then refit the centre console and the index plate.

16 Accelerator and kickdown linkage – adjustment

1   First check that there is 101.6 mm (4 in) stroke of the accelerator pedal from the fully released position to the floor mat.

2   If not, carefully bend the pedal arm to correct it.

3   Now fully depress the accelerator pedal through the kickdown detent; have an assistant check that the link A on the transmission is fully upwards. If not, release the two cable locknuts and adjust as necessary to achieve this setting (Fig. 6.26).

4   Again, fully depress the accelerator pedal through the kickdown

Fig. 6.28 Rear brake band adjusting screw (Sec 17)

1 Relay lever
2 Pivot screw
3 Rear brake band adjusting
   screw

detent. Have an assistant check that the throttle valve plate is fully open and the throttle cable pulled from its stop through a distance of approximately 13.0 mm (0.5 in). If necessary, adjust by means of the two locknuts.

17 Rear brake band – adjustment

1 This adjustment will normally only be required after a very high mileage or if an alteration in the 2/3 shift pattern indicates the need for it.

2 Release the locknut on the brake band adjusting screw. The accelerator/kickdown relay lever on the side of the transmission casing will have to be unbolted and moved to one side to gain access to the adjusting screw.

3 Tighten the adjuster screw to a torque of 10 Nm (7 lbf ft), slacken the screw and again tighten it to 5 Nm (3.5 lbf ft). The adjuster screw is of the hexagon, socket-headed type and in the absence of a suitably calibrated torque wrench, a spring balance can be attached to an Allen key and this used to set the torque; remember, however, to attach the balance to the correct point on the Allen key, 1 inch or 12 inches from

Fig. 6.29 Automatic transmission, viewed from underneath (Sec 17)

1 Driveshaft
2 Anti-roll bar
3 Centre crossmember support
4 Transmission fluid sump pan

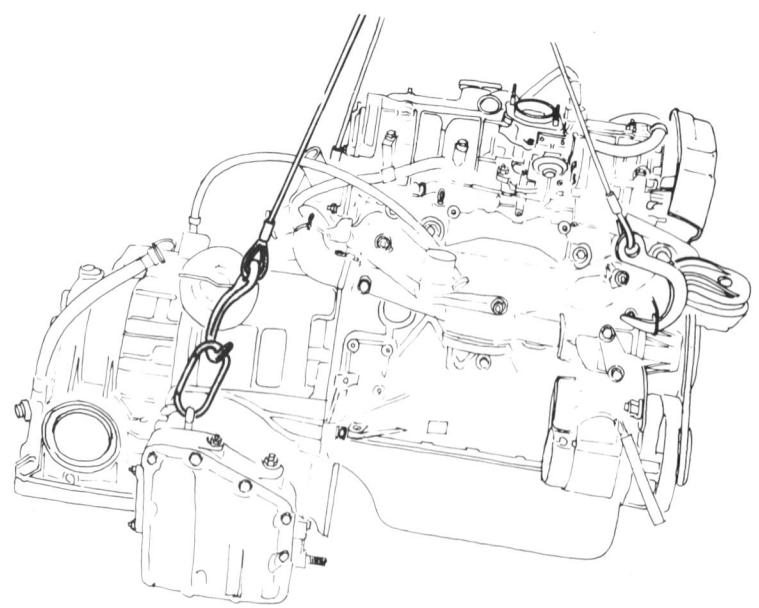

Fig. 6.30 Lifting hook attachment points for removal of the
engine/automatic transmission (Sec 18)

the centre of the screw recess dependent upon whether lbf in or lbf ft are the units being used.

4   Once the screw is correctly torqued, tighten the locknut without moving the screw.

18   Automatic transmission – removal and refitting

1   The engine/transmission should be removed as a combined assembly from beneath the car and the transmission separated once removed.

2   Position the car over an inspection pit or raise the front sufficiently high for the engine/transmission to pass under the front end during removal.

3   Unbolt and remove the transmission sump pan and drain the fluid into a container.

4   Unbolt and remove the bonnet lid and, with the help of an assistant, store it in a safe place where it will not be scratched.

5   Disconnect the lead from the battery negative terminal.

6   Drain the cooling system (see Chapter 2).

7   Disconnect the radiator coolant hoses from the engine.

8   Disconnect the heater hoses from the heater within the engine compartment.

9   Remove the air cleaner.

10   Disconnect the choke operating linkage or hoses.

11   Disconnect the fuel pipes from the fuel pump.

12   Disconnect the vacuum hose which runs from the intake manifold to the brake servo unit.

13   Disconnect the HT leads from the spark plugs and remove the distributor cap.

14   Disconnect the LT lead from the distributor.

15   Disconnect the leads from the coolant temperature and oil pressure sender units.

16   Disconnect the leads from the starter motor.

17   Disconnect the speedometer lead from the final drive sender unit.

18   Disconnect the leads from the alternator.

19   Unscrew and remove the nuts from the engine mountings.

20   Attach a suitable hoist or lifting gear to the engine/transmission and take its weight.

21   Working under the car, remove the anti-roll bar.

22   Unbolt and disconnect the driveshafts from their inboard flanges.

Tie the disconnected shafts up out of the way.

23   Unbolt and remove the central supporting crossmember from under the engine/transmission.

24   Remove the shields and disconnect the exhaust downpipes, then remove the exhaust system by slipping off the rubber rings.

25   Disconnect the earth strap from the transmission casing.

26   On the side of the transmission casing, disconnect the speed selector linkage, the accelerator cable/kickdown cable assembly.

27   Carefully lower the engine/transmission until it is either resting on the floor or in the inspection pit. The car can then be moved or lifted rearwards, or conversely – if the engine/transmission is lowered onto a trolley – the complete assembly can be withdrawn, leaving the car in its original position.

28   Remove the starter motor, then, working throught the starter motor aperture, unscrew and remove the screws which hold the torque converter to the driveplate on the end of the crankshaft. There is no need to mark their relative positions as the torque converter is carefully balanced during production and can be refitted in any position.

29   To bring each of the torque converter bolts into view, turn the crankshaft by applying a spanner to the crankshaft pulley securing nut.

30   Once the transmission-to-engine bolts have been withdrawn, pull the transmission from the engine just enough to be able to prise the torque converter towards the gear casing. Use a piece of wood as a lever. Keep the torque converter in full engagement with the drive tangs of the fluid pump of the transmission until the transmission is removed from the car. Then make up a clamp to retain the torque converter while the transmission is out of the car. If the torque converter is allowed to fall out of the converter bellhousing, the fluid seal will be damaged, also the torque converter; there will be considerable spillage of fluid.

31   Refitting is a reversal of the removal process; fill the transmission and the cooling system.

19   Fault diagnosis – automatic transmission

The majority of faults which occur in an automatic transmission are due to lack of fluid or to a clogged fluid filter. Correct adjustment of the speed selector linkage and kickdown mechanism is also essential. Other than these items, the diagnosis of a fault should be carried out with the transmission still in the car – definitely a job for your dealer due to the need for special gauges and equipment.

Fig. 6.31 Kickdown/accelerator linkage at carburettor (Sec 18)

1	*Throttle cable return*	*3*	*Air cleaner*
	spring	*4*	*Throttle cable*
2	*Choke cable*		

Fig. 6.32 Engine/automatic transmission removed from beneath the car (Sec 18)

Chapter 7 Driveshafts

For modifications, and information applicable to later models, see Supplement at end of manual

Contents

Specifications

Type

65 models	Open tubular with constant velocity (CV) joint at outboard end and Tripode joint at inboard end
75 and North American models	Open tubular with constant velocity (CV) joint at outboard and inboard ends. Right-hand shaft in two sections, centre support bearing

Lubricant type/specification

Tripode joint	Lubricated by gearbox/final drive oil
CV joint	Multi-purpose lithium-based grease with molybdenum disulphide, to NLGI No 2 (Duckhams LBM 10)
Lubricant capacity (each CV joint)	125 cc

Torque wrench settings

	lbf ft	Nm
Driveshaft-to-hub nut	160	218
Radius rod nut	50	68
Track control arm pivot nuts	30	40
Tie-rod end balljoint nut	36	49
Boot retainer screws	6	8
Driveshaft flange screws	22	30

1 General description

Power from the final drive is transmitted to the front roadwheels through open tubular shafts.

The shaft incorporates joints at each end but their design differs between the 65 and the 75 or North American models. Left and right-hand shafts are of unequal length.

65 models

At the inner ends of the shafts are universal joints of the Tripode type. These allow for axial movement as well as wheel movement on the suspension.

At the outer ends are constant velocity (CV) joints. These allow for the movement of the wheels on the suspension and the swivelling of the steering.

The main part of the shaft fits into the joints at both ends by splines, held by circlips. Rubber boots keep the lubricant in, and the road dirt out.

The Tripode joints are located in the bevel side gears of the differential, and are lubricated by the transmission oil. The constant velocity joints are packed for life with molybdenum disulphide grease.

Provided the rubber boots are in good condition and keep out the dirt, the constant velocity joints last well, though on cars used in towns or hills, with a high proportion of driving hard in low gears, they are unlikely to last as long as the rest of the transmission. The Tripode joints should last the life of the transmission.

75 and North American models

The left-hand driveshaft has a constant velocity joint at each end and the inboard end is connected to the differential by means of flanges held together by socket-headed screws.

The right-hand driveshaft also has a constant velocity joint at each end, but the inboard joint is bolted to a crankcase mounted support/bearing assembly. An inner fixed extension shaft then connects the final drive to the driveshaft inboard flange.

2 Driveshafts – maintenance and inspection

1 Maintenance is virtually unnecessary except to check occasionally the security of the flange connecting screws.

2 Inspection is the more important task, and this must be carried out frequently. First, check the flexible boots for splits or cuts. Immediately any defect is observed, the boot must be removed, the lubricant renewed and a new boot fitted (see Section 3).

3 Wear in the constant velocity (CV) joints is usually indicated by a clicking noise. Wear in the shaft-to-hub splines and in the inboard Tripode joints (65 models) is unlikely to occur unless the hub nut has been loose or the joint boot split and has been allowed to operate in this condition over an extended period.

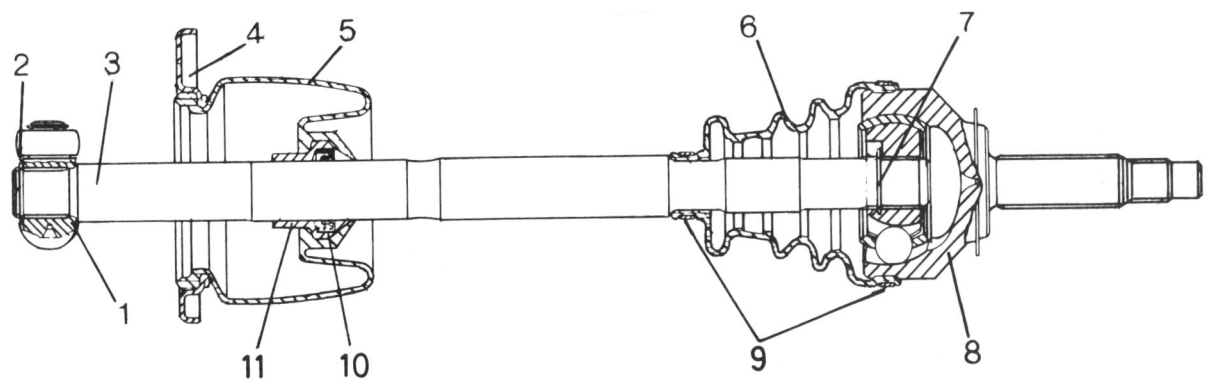

Fig. 7.1 Typical driveshaft assembly (65 models) (Sec 1)

1	Inboard Tripode type joint	4	Boot retaining flange	7	Snap-ring
2	Circlip	5	Boot	8	Constant velocity (CV) joint
3	Driveshaft	6	Boot	9	Boot clamping rings
				10	Integral oil seal
				11	Oil seal retainer

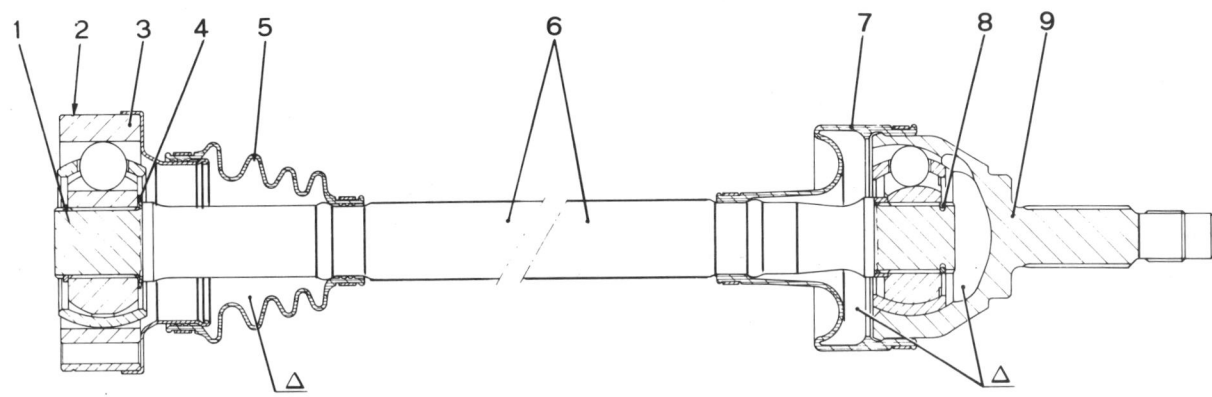

Fig. 7.2 Left-hand driveshaft assembly (75 models) (Sec 1)

1	Circlip	5	Flexible boot	8	Circlip
2	Reference groove (nearest final drive output flange)	6	Driveshaft	9	Constant velocity joint (outboard end)
3	Constant velocity joint (inboard, final drive end)	7	Flexible boot	△	Lubricant
4	Spring washer				

1.0a Driveshaft CV joint support and alternator mounting (75 and North American models)

1.0b Right-hand driveshaft connection to support (75 and North American models)

3   Driveshaft flexible boot – renewal

1   Although it is possible to renew the outer joint boot (65 models) and the inboard boot (75 and North American models) without having to remove the driveshaft, there is little to be gained. And with 65 models, the inboard joint is almost certainly bound to fall out of the final drive.
2   The simplest way, therefore, is to remove the driveshaft, release the boot clip, extract the joint securing circlip and remove the joint – all as described in Sections 6 or 7.
3   Make good any loss of lubricant and fit the new boot. Refit the driveshaft by reversing the removal operations.

4   Driveshaft (65 models) – removal and refitting

1   Place the car over an inspection pit or run the front wheels up on ramps.
2   Support the body underframe on jacks and axle stands then remove the front roadwheel.
3   Have an assistant apply the footbrake firmly while the driveshaft-to-hub nut is loosened. A socket and long knuckle bar will be needed for this; the nut is very tight. Unscrew and remove the nut.
4   Unbolt the brake caliper on the side from which the driveshaft is being removed and tie it up out of the way. This is to avoid straining the hydraulic flexible hose when the steering knuckle is disconnected from the lower end of the strut.
5   Using a suitable balljoint separator, disconnect the tie-rod and balljoint from the steering arm at the base of the suspension strut.
6   If the left-hand driveshaft is being removed, withdraw the engine shield.
7   Disconnect the track control arm from its body anchorage.
8   Unscrew and remove the nut which holds the radius rod to the track control arm.
9   Remove the pinch bolts from the base of the suspension strut, tap the steering knuckle down, then press or tap the driveshaft out of the hub. If the end of the shaft has to be tapped, temporarily refit the nut by screwing it on a few turns to protect the threads. Use a plastic faced hammer.
10   Support the driveshaft and unbolt the inboard boot retaining flange. Withdraw the shaft from the differential/final drive.
11   Refitting is the reversal of the removal process, but pack the outboard joint adequately with molybdenum disulphide grease before fitting the boots, if they have been removed.
12   Tighten the driveshaft/hub nut to the specified torque and stake the nut into the shaft notch. Preferably use a new nut; alternatively, change the nuts from side to side to avoid the original staking positions being used again.
13   Check the transmission oil level and top up if necessary.

5   Driveshaft (75 and North American models) – removal and refitting

1   Place the car over an inspection pit or run the front end up onto ramps to provide adequate working clearance.
2   Remove the front driveshaft shields, where these are fitted.

Left-hand driveshaft
3   Unscrew and remove the socket-headed screws which hold the inboard driveshaft flange to the differential/final drive output flange. Lower the driveshaft and support it (photo).

Right-hand driveshaft
4   Unscrew and remove the socket-headed screws which hold the inboard driveshaft flange to the constant velocity joint at the bearing support bracket. Lower the driveshaft and support it.

Left or right-hand driveshaft
5   Support the bodyframe and remove the roadwheel.
6   Have an assistant apply the footbrake firmly and then, using a socket and long knuckle bar, unscrew and remove the driveshaft-to-hub nut. The nut is likely to be very tight. Remove the washer (photos).
7   Press the splined end of the driveshaft out of the hub. If it is tight,

5.3 Disconnecting inboard end of left-hand driveshaft (75 and North American models)

5.6A Removing driveshaft/hub nut

5.6B Driveshaft/hub nut thrust washer

temporarily screw the nut on a few turns and tap the shaft out with a plastic faced hammer.

Right-hand driveshaft (inboard section)

8   If the fixed section of the right-hand driveshaft must be removed, extract the setscrews which hold it to the bearing support. Disengage the driveshaft and bearing from the support, then pull the assembly out of the final drive.

9   Refitting of left and right-hand driveshafts is a reversal of the removal process. Tighten nuts and bolts to the specified torque, using new socket-headed screws. **Note:** *Use new nuts at the driveshaft-to-hub attachment, to overcome staking the nut in its original position. If both driveshafts are removed at the same time, change the nuts from side to side to present a new staking point.*

---

6   Driveshaft joints (65 models) – overhaul

Outboard (constant velocity) joints

1   Refer to Section 7, paragraphs 1 to 5.

Inboard (Tripode) joints

2   Push back the dust excluding boot to expose the spider.

3   Extract the circlip, then withdraw the roller and needle bearing assembly from the shaft (photo).

4   A new joint is supplied complete, individual parts are not available.

5   Always fit a new circlip to secure the spider.

6   If the inboard dust-excluding boot must be renewed, the outboard joint must be detached from the shaft as described in Section 7.

7   Use plenty of oil or grease on the shaft when sliding the boots on or off and take care not to damage the integral oil seal in the inboard boot. The lips of this seal should be filled with joint grease.

---

7   Driveshaft joints (75 and North American models) – overhaul

Before dismantling a constant velocity joint, check that spares are available. Unless the purpose of dismantling is solely to renew the lubricant, it will probably be necessary to renew the joint complete.

Outboard joints

1   Remove the securing clips and push back the dust-excluding boot.

2   Press or drive the joint off the hub end of the shaft. The joint

retaining circlip will be compressed into its groove, allowing joint removal. Protect the end of the shaft.

3   Dismantling and reassembly of the outboard joints is similar to the procedure for the inboard joints given later in this Section.

4   If a joint is to be renewed, note that shafts and joints are matched in production. Matching class is denoted by a blue or red paint mark on the shaft, and a blue, red or white mark on the joint. A blue coded joint may only be fitted to a blue coded shaft, and similarly for red coded items. White coded joints are 'universal' and will fit either shaft; presumably these are supplied as spares, since the parts list does not offer a choice of grade.

5   Refit in the reverse order of removal. Remember to renew the rubber boots, if necessary, before refitting the joint.

Inboard joints

6   The joint can be withdrawn from the shaft after peeling back the rubber boot and extracting the retaining circlip (photos).

6.3 Inboard 'Tripode' joint (65 models)

7.6A Inboard CV joint circlip

7.6B Removing inboard CV joint from driveshaft

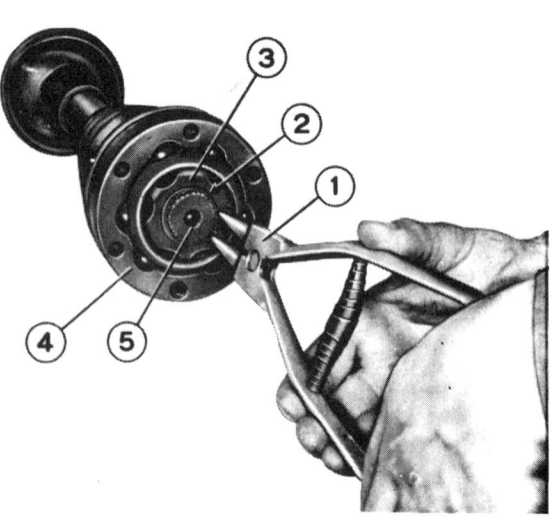

Fig. 7.3 Extracting circlip from CV joint (Sec 7)

1   Circlip pliers   4   Socket
2   Circlip   5   Splined driveshaft
3   Ball centre track

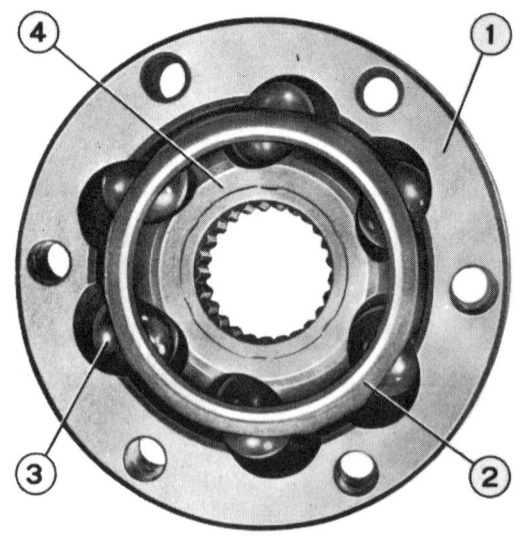

Fig. 7.4 End view of CV joint (Sec 7)

1   Socket   2   Ball cage   3   Ball   4   Ball centre track

7   If it is wished to dismantle the joint, clean away the grease and tap the joint from its backplate (photo).

8   Turn the ball/cage assembly through 90°, mark its relative position to the outer track and withdraw it (photo).

9   The balls are a light snap fit in the cage. Once they are removed, the inner and outer cage members can be separated; again, mark the side of the cages in relation to the outer track (photos).

10 When reassembling, pack the joint with special Fiat Tutela MRM2 lubricant; if this is not available, use molybdenum disulphide grease.

11 The reference groove on the outer track must be assembled so that it is towards the final drive when refitted (photos).

12 Fit the rubber boot, pack plenty of lubricant into it and secure the joint with a new circlip.

13 The bearing within the support at the junction of the fixed and moveable sections of the right-hand shaft can be renewed after removing the bearing retainer plate bolts, the circlip and pressing the shaft out of the bearing (photo).

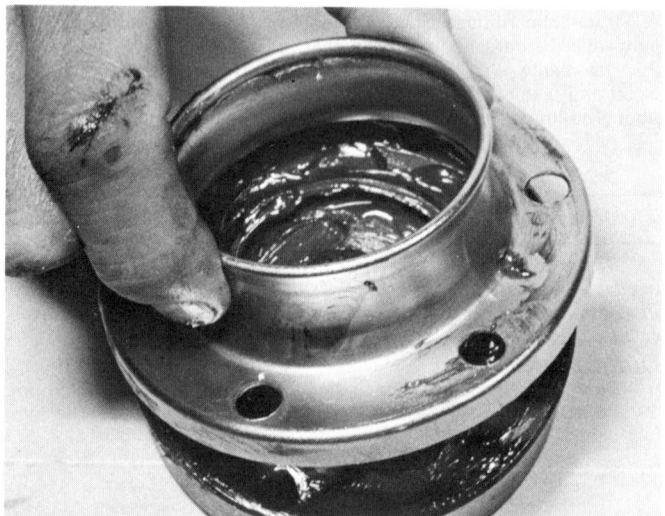

7.7 Separating CV joint from backplate

7.8 Removing CV joint ballcage from outer track

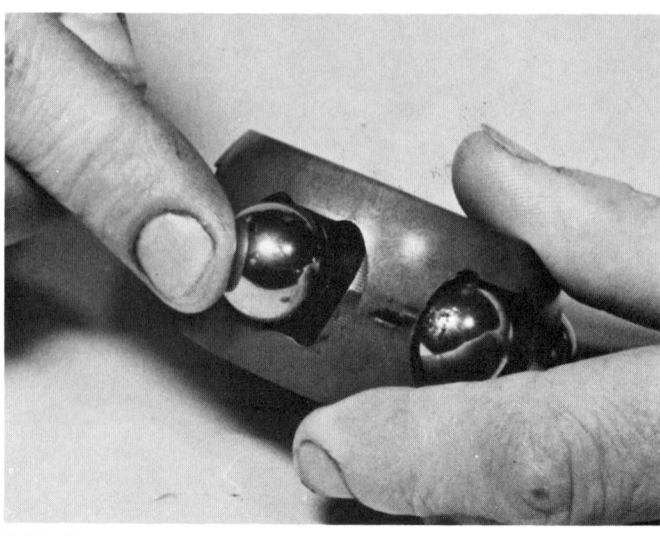

7.9A CV joint balls and cage

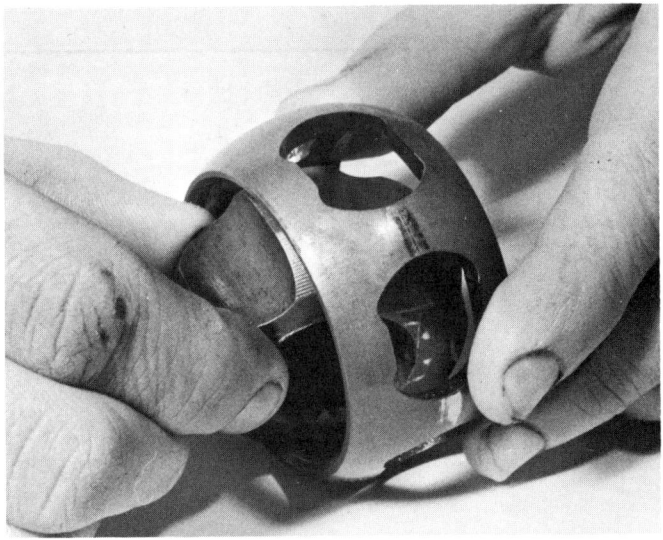

7.9B Separating inner and outer cage members

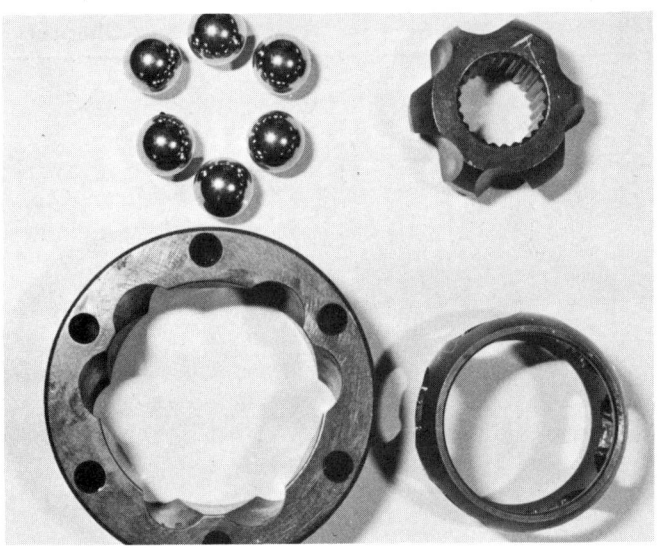

7.9C Components of a CV joint

7.11A Reference groove on CV joint outer track

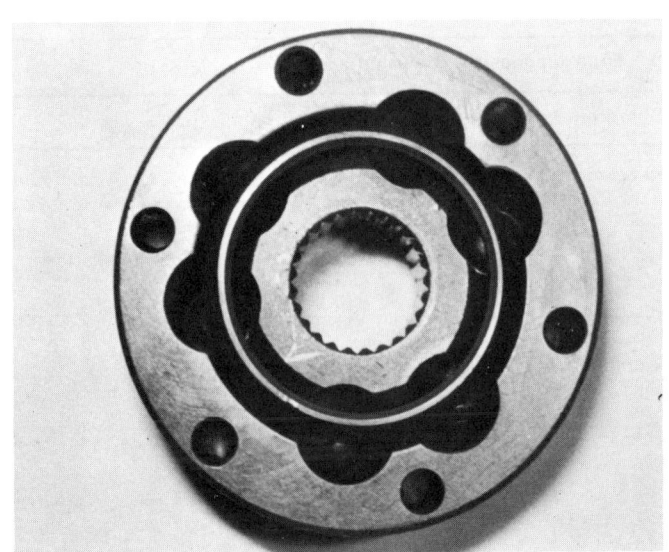

7.11B Assembled CV joint

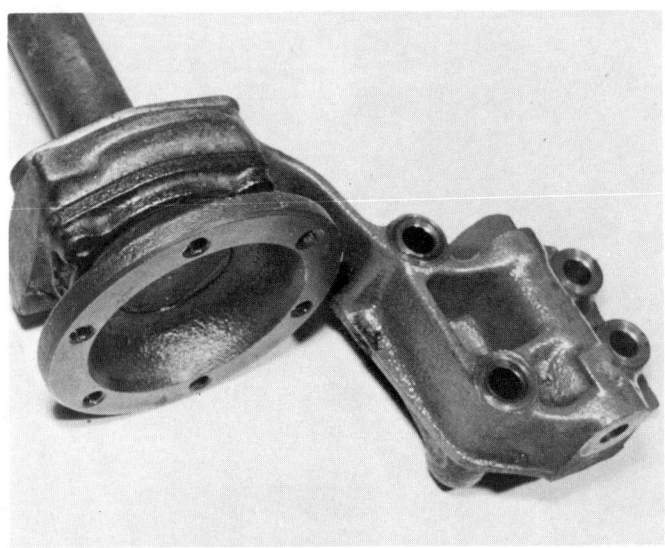

7.13 Right-hand driveshaft support (75 and North American models)

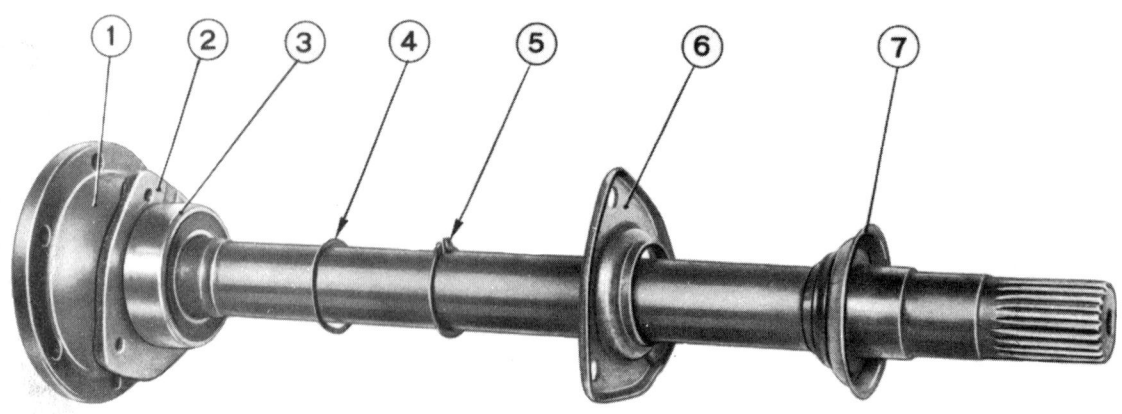

Fig. 7.5 Right-hand fixed driveshaft assembly (75 models) (Sec 7)

1   Driveshaft flange to centre CV joint   3   Ball bearing   5   Circlip   7   Boot to final drive
2   Bearing retainer plate   4   Spring washer   6   Bearing retainer to support

---

8   Fault diagnosis – driveshafts

Symptom	Reason(s)
Knock or clunk when taking up drive	Loose driveshaft-to-hub nut
	Loose driveshaft flange bolts
	Worn final drive-to-shaft splines
	Worn shaft-to-hub splines
	Worn CV or Tripode joint (65 models)
Clicking or knocking, especially when cornering	Worn or damaged CV joint
Vibration (check wheel balance first)	Bent driveshaft
	Worn driveshaft/hub bearings
	Worn CV joint
	Loose hub mountings

Chapter 8 Braking system

For modifications, and information applicable to later models, see Supplement at end of manual

Contents

Specifications

System type	Hydraulic, dual line with servo assistance. Disc front, drum rear, pressure differential valve. Handbrake mechanical to rear wheels.

Discs
Diameter	227 mm (8.940 in)
Thickness:	
New	10.7 mm (0.421 in)
Minimum after regrind	9.35 mm (0.368 in)
Maximum run-out	0.025 mm (0.001 in)
Friction material minimum thickness	1.5 mm (0.06 in)
Caliper type	Single cylinder, sliding

Drums
Diameter	185.24 to 185.52 mm (7.293 to 7.304 in)
Diameter (minimum after regrind)	186.33 mm (7.336 in)
Friction materal minimum thickness	1.5 mm (0.06 in)

Brake fluid type/specification	Hydraulic fluid to FMVSS 116 DOT 3 (Duckhams Universal Brake and Clutch Fluid)

Torque wrench settings
	lbf ft	Nm
Rear wheel cylinder bolts	7	10
Flexible hose to caliper	20	27
Caliper mounting bolts	35	48
Pipeline union to rear wheel cylinder	14	19
Pressure regulator valve mounting bolt	18	25
Master cylinder mounting nuts	18	25
Servo mounting nuts	18	25
Rear brake backplate bolts	18	25

1 General description

The braking system is hydraulically operated, with vacuum servo assistance.

The front brakes are of disc type, with single cylinder sliding calipers with self-adjusting rear drums.

A pressure differential valve is located at the rear of the car to provide a control on the pressure applied to front and rear brake circuits, according to load and deceleration. This avoids the possibility of rear wheel lock-up during heavy brake applications and if lightly loaded.

The handbrake operates through a cable to the rear brakes.

2 Maintenance and inspection

1   Regularly, check the level of fluid in the brake master cylinder reservoir. Although a low level warning lamp is fitted, this doubles for the handbrake ON warning lamp; confusion may be caused, unless the lamp comes on during normal motoring and then this is most likely to be caused by a leak in the system occurring suddenly. There is no substitute for a visual check of the fluid level at weekly intervals. There is no need to remove the fluid reservoir cap to check the level as the reservoir casing is translucent. The warning lamp can be checked periodically if the ignition key is turned to MAR and the cap depressed with the finger. The warning lamp should come on.

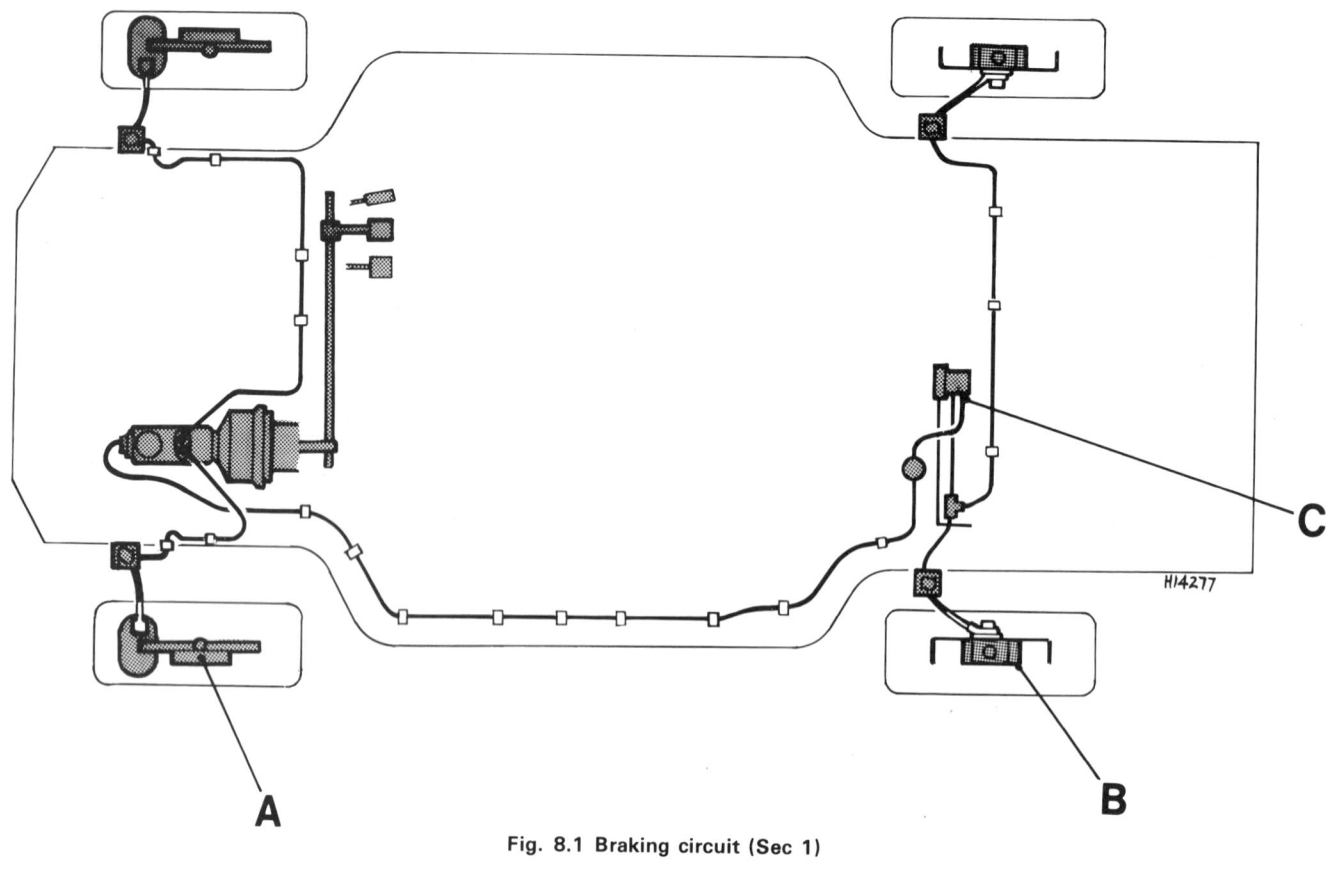

Fig. 8.1 Braking circuit (Sec 1)

A   Disc brakes   C   Pressure regulator
B   Drum brakes

2   Use only specified fluid for topping-up or refilling the brake hydraulic system. The use of anything else will deform or destroy the system seals.

3   At the intervals specified in 'Routine Maintenance', check all hydraulic pipes for damage or corrosion, the flexible hoses for chafing or perishing and for leaks at the unions and hydraulic assemblies. Renew the seals as necessary.

4   At the specified intervals, check the wear of the disc pad and rear brake shoe friction linings, as described in the following Sections.

3   Disc pads – inspection and renewal

1   Jack up the front of the car and remove the roadwheels.

2   Inspect the thickness of the friction material on each pad. If it is 1.6 mm (0.06 in) or less, the pads must be renewed.

3   To remove the pads, extract the spring clips and slide out the locking blocks (photo).

4   Lift the cylinder body from the disc and withdraw the pads, one from each side of the disc. Remove the anti-rattle springs (photo).

5   Brush away any dust and dirt from the caliper, taking care not to inhale the dust – this contains asbestos and is thus potentially injurious to health.

6   As the new pads are thicker than the old ones, the caliper piston must be depressed into its cylinder to accommodate them. This will cause the fluid level to rise in the reservoir. Anticipate this by syphoning some out beforehand, but take care not to let it drip onto the paintwork – it acts as an effective paint stripper!

7   Refit the anti-rattle springs, the pads (friction lining-to-disc), the cylinder body, the locking blocks and the retaining clips.

8   Refit the roadwheel and apply the footbrake hard, several times, to bring the pads into contact with the brake disc.

9   Renew the pads on the opposite brake. The pads should always be renewed in axle sets.

10 Top up the fluid reservoir.

4   Rear brake shoes – inspection and renewal

1   Jack up the rear of the car and remove the roadwheels.

2   Fully release the handbrake.

3   Unscrew and remove the drum securing bolts. One of these is a long locating spigot for the roadwheel (photo).

4   Pull off the drum. If it is tight, clean off the rust at its joint with the hub flange, and apply a little penetrating fluid. Two bolts may be screwed into the drum securing bolt holes if necessary and the drum thus eased off the hub. The securing bolt holes are tapped for this purpose (photo).

5   Brush away all the dust and dirt from the shoes and operating mechanism, taking care not to inhale it.

6   The friction linings fitted as original equipment are of the bonded type and the rivet heads normally used as a guide to wear are not, of course, fitted. However, if the thickness of the friction linings is down to 1.6 mm (0.06 in) or less, the shoes must be renewed. Always purchase new or factory relined brake shoes.

7   Before removing the brake shoes, note the way in which the shoes are positioned, with respect to leading and trailing ends (the end of the shoe not covered by lining material). Note also into which holes in the shoe web the return springs are connected. Sketch the shoes or mark the holes on the new shoes with quick drying paint if you are doubtful about remembering.

8   Undo the steady springs by depressing and rotating their caps a quarter turn to disengage the slot from the pin (photo).

9   Pull a shoe (if a right-handed person, the right shoe) out from its

3.3A Disc caliper locking block spring pin

3.3B Sliding out caliper locking block

3.4A Removing caliper cylinder assembly

3.4B Removing disc pad

3.4C Location of disc pad anti-rattle spring

4.3 Brake drum securing bolts

4.4 Removing brake drum. Note tapped securing bolt holes

4.7 Rear brake assembly

4.8 Removing brake shoe steady spring

4.10a Brake shoe upper return spring

4.10b Brake shoe lower return spring

seat on the wheel cylinder, and pivot at the bottom, and work it up the post of the self-adjuster. Note the cut-outs in the hub flange which provide space for removal of the self-adjusters.

10 Once off the self-adjuster post, the pull-off spring tension is eased, as the shoe can move towards the other, so the springs can be unhooked (photos).

11 Take off the other shoes.

12 The self-adjusters must now be transferred to the new shoes. To undo them, the spring must be compressed to allow the circlip to be undone. The spring is strong. If possible, get the FIAT agents to make the transfer, if buying the new shoes from them. Otherwise a clamp must be organised. A vice, a carpenter's G-clamp, or a valve spring compressor are all possibilities. Small spacers will be required between the clamp and the adjuster washer to avoid trapping the circlip.

13 After high mileages, the self-adjusters need renewal. The washers wear, the hole in the bush also gets bigger, so the adjustment provided is not close enough.

14 If the hydraulic cylinder needs overhaul, now is the time with the shoes out of the way, especially if there is evidence of fluid leakage.

15 When reassembling the new shoes with the adjusters, and the shoes to the brakes, put a slight smear of grease on all the working surfaces for the adjusters, the bottom shoe pivot, and the steady springs, but not where the shoe sits on the hydraulic cylinder piston.

16 Fit the first shoe (the left one if right-handed) into place with the springs fitted. Hook the second shoe onto the springs, and then pull it

across until the self-adjuster can be fitted over its post. Then wriggle the shoe down into position, and work the ends of the shoe into place. Make sure the handbrake linkage is in place.

17 Hold the steady pins in position from the rear of the backplate. Fit the small coil springs and the retaining cap, again using pliers to grip the cap and to depress and turn it to engage the pin.

18 Before refitting the drum, clean it out and examine it for grooves or scoring (refer to Section 8).

19 Using a soft-faced mallet, tap the shoes in towards the centre of the hub. They will move against the pressure of the self-adjuster coil springs and permit the brake drum to be fitted. This should now be done and the bolts screwed in.

20 Refit the roadwheel and apply the footbrake two or three times, to position the shoes close to the drum.

21 Renew the shoes on the opposite brake in a similar way.

22 The handbrake should be automatically adjusted by the action of the shoe adjuster. If the handbrake control lever has excessive travel, refer to Section 13 for separate adjusting instructions.

5 Caliper – removal, overhaul and refitting

Note: *Purchase a repair kit in advance of overhaul.*

1 Jack up the front roadwheel and remove it.

2 Brush away all dirt from the caliper assembly and the flexible pipe, particularly the fixing bracket and union at the car end of the flexible pipe.

3 Have ready a container suitable to catch the brake fluid, and sheets of clean newspaper on which to put parts.

4 Take out the spring clips and locking blocks, and take the caliper off the support bracket.

5 Disconnect the hydraulic flexible pipe at the under wing support bracket and cap both pipe ends. It may help to prevent loss of fluid if the vent in the reservoir cap is sealed with adhesive tape, to create a vacuum.

6 Remove the caliper to the bench or other work surface, and clean it thoroughly with hydraulic fluid or methylated spirit.

7 Depress the piston until the dust excluding boot can be removed.

8 Now apply air pressure to the flexible hose and eject the piston. Quite a low pressure is required for this, such as can be generated with a hand or foot operated pump.

9 Pick out the piston seal from its groove in the cylinder. Use a sharp probe, but take care to avoid scratching the cylinder bore.

10 Examine the surface of the piston and cylinder bore. If either is scored or shows metal-to-metal rubbed areas, the complete assembly should be renewed.

11 If the components are in good condition, discard the oil seals, clean the piston and cylinder and fit the new seal for the piston. This is included in the repair kit. Use the fingers only to manipulate it into its groove.

12 Lubricate the piston with clean hydraulic fluid and insert it partially into the cylinder.

13 Fit the new dust excluding boot to its projecting end, push the piston fully into the cylinder and engage the dust excluder with the rim of the cylinder.

14 Refit the caliper, reconnect the flexible hose, then bleed the front hydraulic circuit (refer to Section 12).

6 Rear wheel cylinder – removal, overhaul and refitting

Note: *Purchase a repair kit in advance of overhaul.*

1 If fluid seepage is observed from the ends of the rear wheel cylinder when the brake drum has been removed, the seals are leaking and immediate action must be taken.

2 Although the cylinder can be dismantled without taking it from the backplate, this is not recommended due to the possibility of under wing dirt and mud dropping onto the components as work proceeds.

3 Remove the brake shoes, as described in Section 4.

4 Disconnect the hydraulic line from the wheel cylinder and cap the open end of the pipe. It may help to reduce the loss of fluid if the vent hole in the reservoir cap is taped over to create a vacuum.

5 Unscrew and remove the setscrews which hold the cylinder to the backplate and withdraw the cylinder. Prise off the rubber dust excluding boots.

6 Apply gentle air pressure from a hand or foot operated pump to

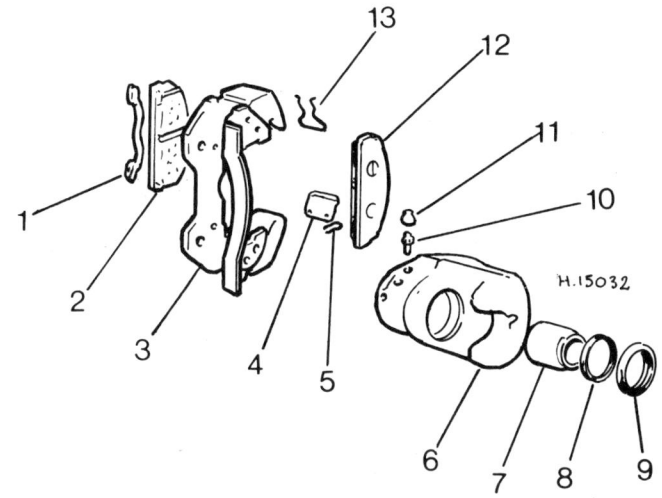

Fig. 8.2 Exploded view of a front caliper (Sec 5)

1	*Pad anti-rattle spring*	*7*	*Piston*
2	*Lining pad*	*8*	*Seal*
3	*Support bracket*	*9*	*Dirt excluder*
4	*Locking block*	*10*	*Bleed nipple*
5	*Spring clip for locking block*	*11*	*Bleeder dust cap*
6	*Caliper body*	*12*	*Pad*
		13	*Spring clip for caliper*

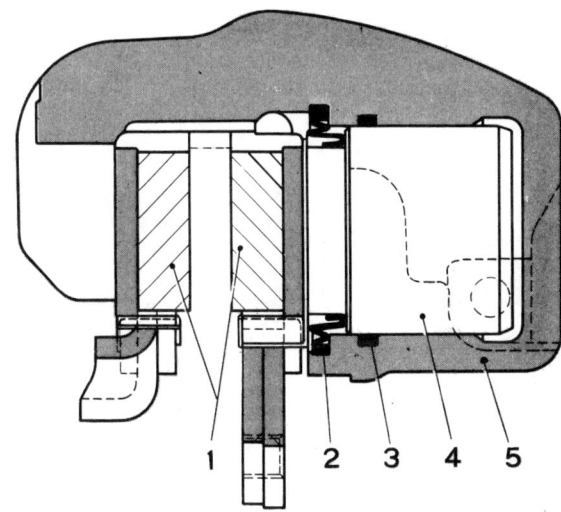

Fig. 8.3 Sectional view of a front brake caliper (Sec 5)

1	*Pads*	*4*	*Piston*
2	*Dust excluder*	*5*	*Caliper body*
3	*Piston seal*		

eject the pistons and spring.

7 Inspect the piston and cylinder bore surfaces for scoring or evidence of metal-to-metal rubbing areas. If these are found, discard the assembly and purchase a new one.

8 If the components are in good condition, note which way round the lips are fitted, then discard the seals and boots and wash the pistons and cylinder bore in clean hydraulic fluid or methylated spirit.

9 Manipulate the new seals into position, using the fingers only for this job.

10 Dip the pistons in clean hydraulic fluid and insert them with the coil spring and washers into the cylinder.

11 Fit the new dust excluding boots.

12 Refit the wheel cylinder to the backplate, reconnect the hydraulic pipe, then refit the shoes, the drum and the roadwheel.

13 Bleed the rear hydraulic circuit as described in Section 12.

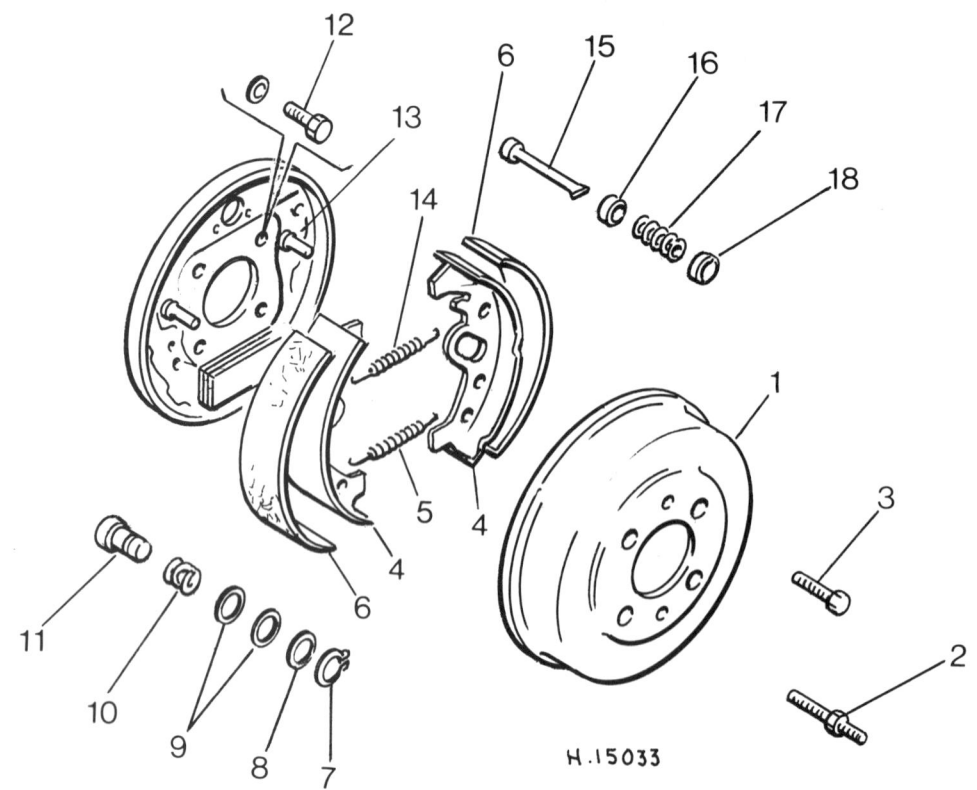

H.15033

Fig. 8.4 Rear brake components (Sec 6)

1	Drum	6	Linings	10	Self adjuster spring	15	Steady pin
2	Long headed bolt	7	Circlip	11	Bush	16	Inner cup
3	Drum bolt	8	Washer	12	Backplate fixing bolts	17	Steady spring
4	Brake shoes	9	Self adjuster friction	13	Backplate	18	Spring retainer
5	Lower pull-off spring		washers	14	Top pull-off spring		

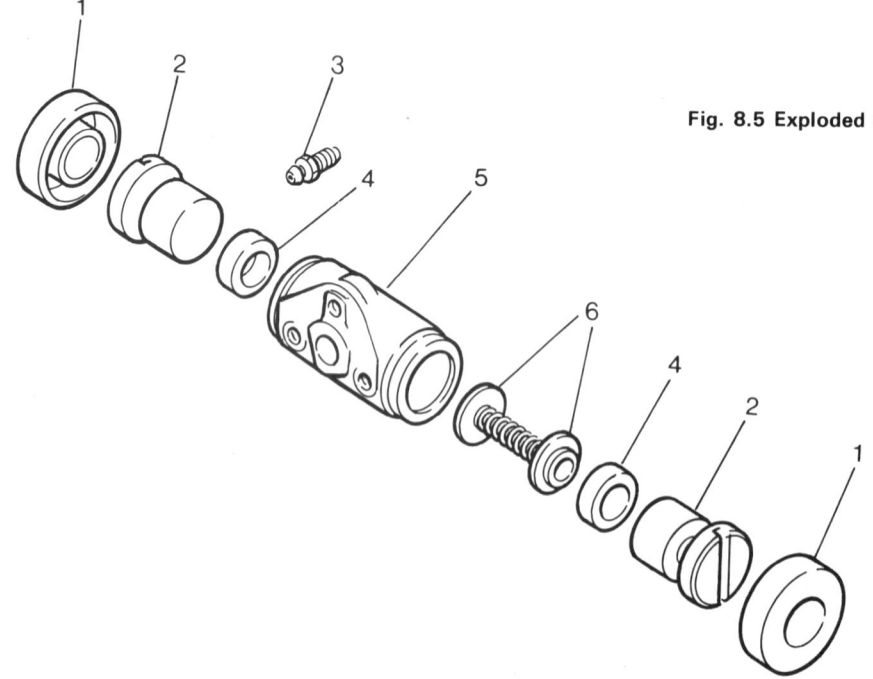

Fig. 8.5 Exploded view of a rear wheel cylinder (Sec 6)

1　Dust excluding boots
2　Pistons
3　Bleed nipple
4　Seals
5　Cylinder body
6　Spring and washers

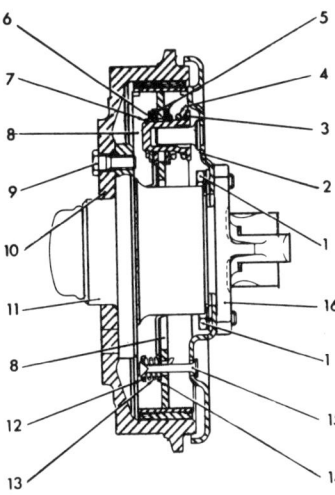

Fig. 8.6 Sectional view of a rear brake (Sec 6)

1	Backplate bolts	9	Drum securing bolt
2	Backplate	10	Drum
3	Self adjuster bush	11	Hub
4	Spring	12	Steady spring cap
5	Friction washers	13	Steady spring
6	Washer	14	Inner cup of steady spring
7	Circlip	15	Pin
8	Shoe with lining	16	Axle flange

9.1 Brake master cylinder/vacuum servo

9.3 Removing brake fluid reservoir cap and float

7 Front disc – inspection and renovation or renewal

1   Whenever the front disc pads are being checked for wear, take the opportunity to inspect the discs for deep scoring or grooving. After a high mileage, the disc may become reduced in thickness away from the extreme outer edge of the disc. If this wear is rapid, it is possible that the friction pads are of too hard a type.

2   If the disc has evidence of many tiny cracks, these may be caused by overheating due to a seized caliper piston in the 'applied' position.

3   The foregoing conditions may be corrected by regrinding the disc provided that the the thickness of the disc is not reduced below that specified by such action. Alternatively, fit a new disc.

4   To remove a disc, take off the caliper and pads as described in Section 3. Tie the caliper up, out of the way.

5   Knock back the tabs of the lockplates and unbolt the caliper support bracket from the steering knuckle.

6   Unscrew and remove the two bolts which hold the disc assembly to the hub. One of these bolts is for wheel locating purposes.

7   Pull the disc from the hub. If it is very tight and reasonable tapping will not dislodge it, use an extractor (FIAT tools A47210/371, A47211/755 or A40005/004).

8   Refitting is a reversal of the removal process. If the disc has excessive run-out, repositioning it in relation to the hub may bring it within tolerance by cancelling out the run-out characteristics in the hub and disc, once the most suitable fitted position has been found.

8 Rear drum – inspection and renovation or renewal

1   Whenever the rear brake linings are being checked for wear, take the opportunity to inspect the internal surfaces of the brake drums.

2   If the drums are grooved or deeply scored, they may be reground, provided that their new internal diameter will not then exceed the specified dimension. If it will, or the drum is cracked, it must be renewed.

3   Removal and refitting of a brake drum is described in Section 4.

9 Master cylinder – removal, overhaul and refitting

1   The master cylinder is mounted on the front face of the brake vacuum servo unit (photo).

2   Cover the front wings with polythene sheeting or similar material, in case hydraulic fluid spills onto the paintwork of the car during removal of the cylinder.

3   Detach the leads from the terminals on the reservoir cap, then unscrew and remove the cap and float (photo).

4   Unscrew the pipe unions and prise the pipes carefully away from the master cylinder. Cap the open ends of the pipes and catch any fluid leaking from the master cylinder in a suitable container.

5   Unscrew the mounting nuts and withdraw the master cylinder from the servo unit.

6   Clean away all external dirt and tip out the fluid from the reservoir and cylinder body.

7   The fluid reservoirs need not be removed from the master cylinder but if they are, renew the rubber sealing collars when refitting.

8   Grip the master cylinder in a vice, then unscrew and remove the end plug. Catch the coil spring.

9   Using a thin rod, apply pressure to the end of the primary piston then unscrew and remove the two stop bolts and sealing washers.

10   The internal piston assemblies with seals and springs can now be

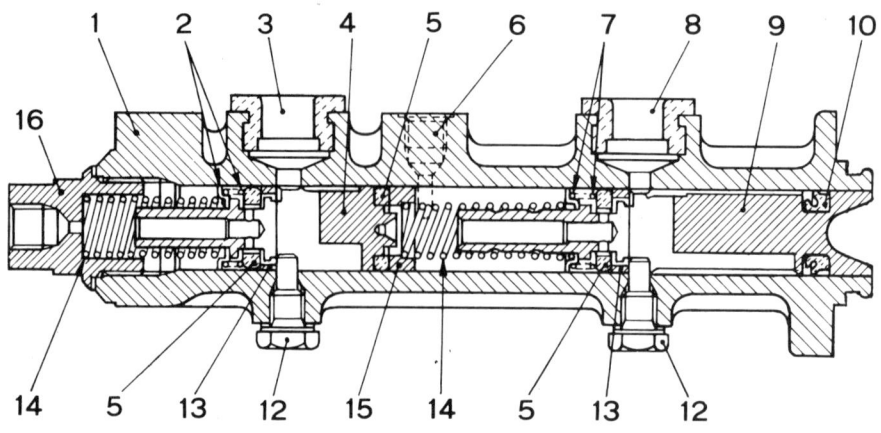

Fig. 8.7 Sectional view of the master cylinder (Sec 9)

1	Cylinder body	5	Seal
2	Spring and cup	6	Fluid outlet to front brakes
3	Inlet from reservoir	7	Spring and cup
4	Secondary piston	8	Inlet from reservoir
9	Primary piston	14	Springs
10	Seal	15	Seal
12	Stop bolts	16	End plug and fluid outlet to rear brakes
13	Spacer		

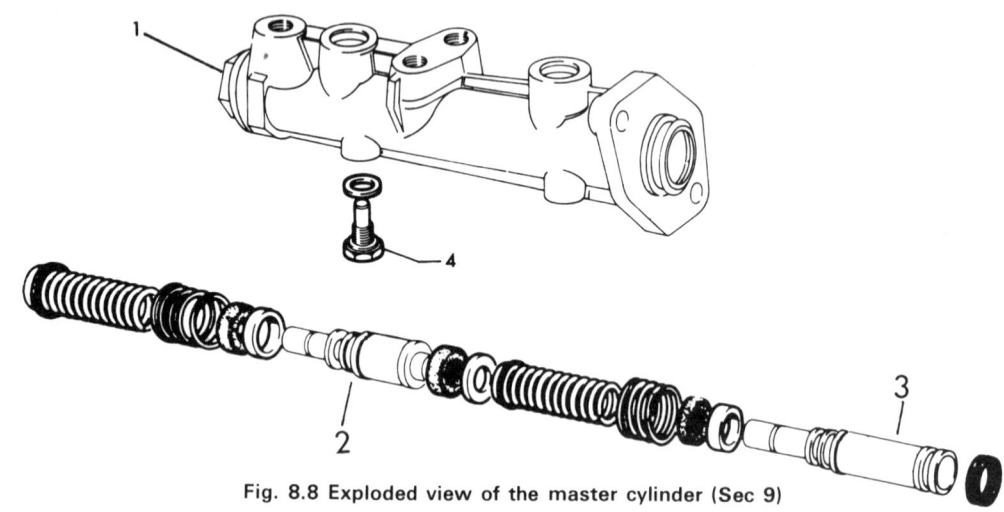

Fig. 8.8 Exploded view of the master cylinder (Sec 9)

1	Cylinder body	3	Primary piston
2	Secondary piston	4	Stop bolt

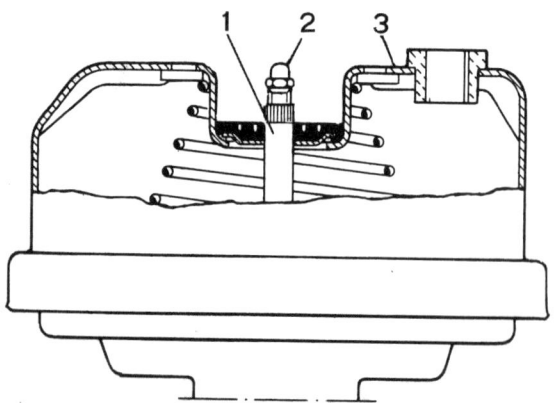

Fig. 8.10 Cutaway view of vacuum servo unit (Sec 9)

1	Pushrod	3	Front shell
2	Adjuster screw		

pushed out of the cylinder body. Keep all the components in their originally fitted sequence and note in which direction the seal lips are located.

11 Inspect the surfaces of the piston and cylinder bore. If scoring or metal-to-metal rubbing areas are evident, renew the master cylinder complete.

12 If the components are in good condition, discard the old seals and manipulate the new ones into position, using the fingers only.

13 Refit by reversing the removal operations; apply pressure to the piston ends so that that stop bolts can be fitted, then tighten the end plug. Make sure that the grooves in the pistons engage in the stop bolts.

14 Before refitting the master cylinder to the servo, measure the projection of the servo piston pushrod. When the master cylinder is fitted, there must be a clearance (see A in Fig. 8.9) between the end of the pushrod and the primary piston end face of between 0.825 and 1.025 mm (0.03 and 0.04 in). A depth gauge will be required for these measurements, the reference point being the mating surfaces of the master cylinder and the vacuum servo.

15 Alter the adjusting screw on the servo as necessary and lock it by applying locking compound to the threads on completion.

16 Bolt the master cylinder to the vacuum servo; reconnect the fluid pipelines and reservoir cap leads.

17 Bleed the complete hydraulic system, as described in Section 12.

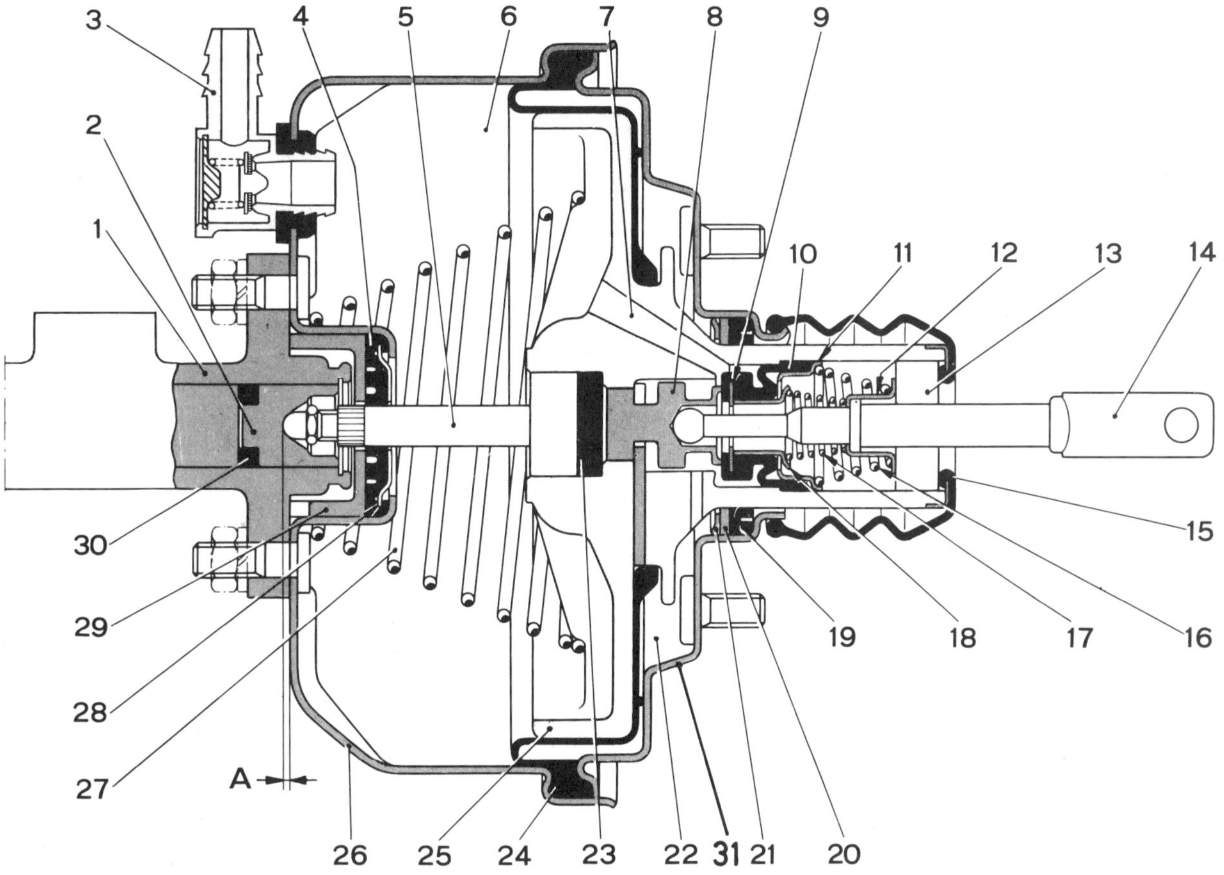

Fig. 8.9 Sectional view of vacuum servo unit (Sec 9)

1	Master cylinder	8	Plunger	16	Return spring	24	Diaphragm
2	Master cylinder primary	9	Seal centraliser	17	Valve spring	25	Vacuum piston
	piston	10	Valve	18	Valve cup	26	Front shell
3	Non-return valve	11	Spring cup	19	Rear seal	27	Return spring
4	Front seal	12	Spring cup	20	Seal	28	Cup
5	Push rod	13	Filter	21	Cup	29	Guide bush
6	Front chamber	14	Pushrod	22	Rear chamber	30	Seal
7	Vacuum port	15	Dust excluding boot	23	Backing plate	31	Rear shell

A = Projection of pushrod above vacuum cylinder face

10 Pressure differential regulator – adjustment, removal and refitting

It is important that the brakes do not lock the rear wheels when the brakes are used hard. Sliding tyres do not give such good grip, so the braking distance will be longer. Worse still, if it is the back wheels that lock, the car is unstable, and control may be lost. The braking that can be applied to the rear wheels without them locking depends upon the weight upon them. So a regulator is fitted coupled to the rear suspension, and this limits the hydraulic pressure passed to the rear brakes when the rear of the car is high, either due to being unladen, or if pitching forward under heavy braking.

1   The regulator is operated from a rod attached to the rear left-hand suspension arm (photo).

2   Under normal driving, failure or incorrect adjustment of the regulator is difficult to detect. First test the rear brakes by applying the handbrake at about 15 mph, and check it can lock the rear wheels. This proves the brake shoes are in order.

3   Now test the brakes from about 20 mph on a dry smooth level road. It should be possible to lock the front wheels. Wheel locking is shown by the noise, smoke, and by leaving black tyre marks. If under these conditions the rear brakes lock, particularly if the lock before the front, under less hard pedal pressure, it is indicated that the pressure

10.1 Pressure differential regulator

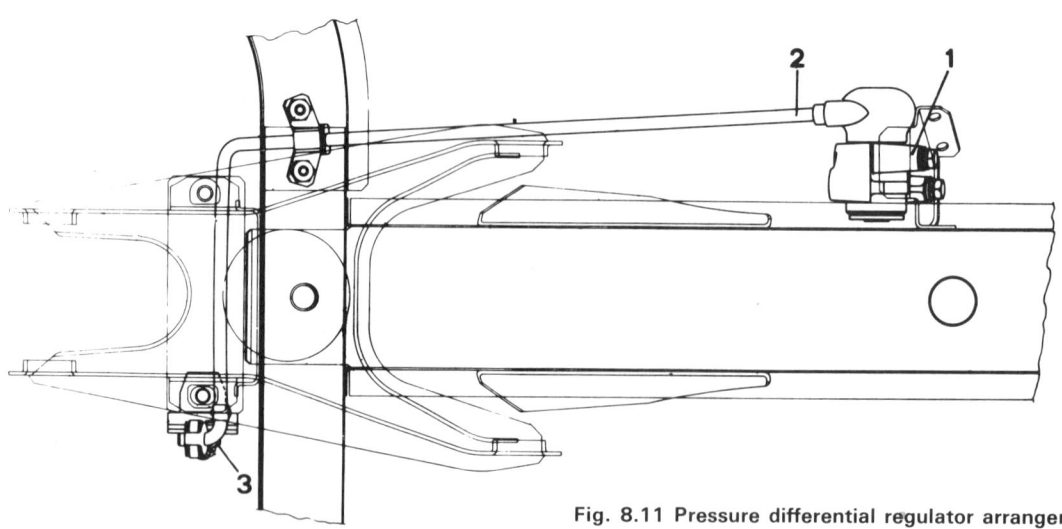

Fig. 8.11 Pressure differential regulator arrangement (Sec 10)

1	Pressure regulator	3	Tie-rod
2	Torsion bar		

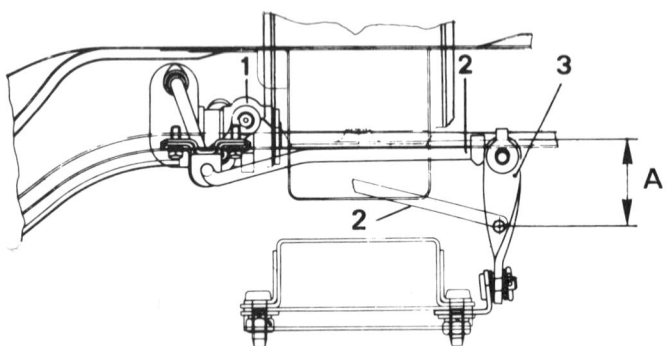

Fig. 8.12 Pressure regulator adjustment diagram (Sec 10)

1	Pressure regulator	3	Tie-rod
2	Torsion bar		

A = Distance between bump rubber mounting face and centre of torsion bar pulled downward 49.0 to 59.0 mm (1.9 to 2.3 in)

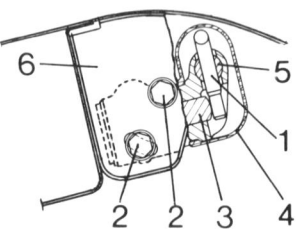

Fig. 8.13 Pressure regulator mounting details (Sec 10)

1	Torsion bar	4	Dust excluding boot
2	Mounting screws	5	Pin
3	Piston	6	Mounting bracket

is not being limited.

4   Now stop from about 50 mph hard, but not as hard as possible. Get out of the car and feel the temperature of the rear brake drums. They should be very hot. If not, the regulator is keeping all pressure off them.

5   Have the car on level ground, unladen but with a full fuel tank.

6   Refer to Fig. 8.12 and disconnect the torsion bar (2) from the tie-rod (3).

7   Release the regulator mounting screws.

8   Pull the disconnected end of the torsion bar downward until the distance (A) between it and the mounting surface of the suspension bump rubber is between 49.0 and 59.0 mm (1.9 and 2.3 in). See Fig. 8.12.

9   Hold the rod in this position and pivot the regulator on its mounting screws until the piston (8) just contacts the opposite end of the torsion bar.

10 Tighten the regulator mounting screws.

11 Reconnect the torsion bar to the tie-rod.

12 If the regulator leaks or cannot be adjusted satisfactorily, renew it complete. To do this, disconnect the pipelines from it, unbolt it and disconnect the tie-rod from the suspension.

13 Refit the new unit, bleed the hydraulic rear circuit (see Section 12) and adjust the regulator as described earlier in this Section.

11 Hydraulic rigid pipes and flexible hoses – renewal

Flexible hoses

1   Periodically, all brake pipes, pipe connections and unions should be completely and carefully examined.

2   First examine for signs of leakage where the pipe unions occur. Then examine the flexible hoses for signs of chafing and fraying and, of course, leakage. This is only a preliminary part of the flexible hose inspection, as exterior condition does not necessarily indicate the interior condition, which will be considered later.

3   Flexible hoses are always mounted at both ends in a rigid bracket attached to the body or a sub-assembly. To remove them, it is necessary first of all to unscrew the pipe unions of the rigid pipes which go into them. The hose ends can then be unclipped from the brackets. The mounting brackets, particularly on the body frame, are not very heavy gauge and care must be taken not to wrench them off (photo).

11.3 Typical flexible/rigid pipeline connection and bracket

12.9 Typical automatic brake bleeder

4   With the flexible hose removed, examine the internal bore. If it is blown through first, it should be possible to see through it. Any specks of rubber which come out, or signs of restriction in the bore, mean that the inner lining is breaking up and the pipe must be renewed.

5   When refitting the flexible pipes, check they cannot be under tension, or rub, when the wheels are at the full range of suspension or steering movement.

6   Bleed the system (see Section 12) on completion.

Rigid pipes

7   Inspect the condition of the braking system rigid pipelines at frequent intervals. They must be cleaned off and examined for any signs of dents (or other percussive damage) and rust and corrosion. Rust and corrosion should be scraped off and, if the depth of pitting in the pipes is significant, they will need renewal. This is particularly likely in those areas underneath the car body and along the rear axle where the pipes are exposed to the full force of road and weather conditions.

8   Rigid pipe removal is usually straightforward. The unions at each end are undone, the pipe and union pulled out, and the centre sections of the pipe removed from the body clips where necessary. Underneath the car, exposed unions can sometimes be very tight. As one can use only an open-ended spanner and the unions are not large, burring of the flats is not uncommon when attempting to undo them. For this reason, a self-locking grip wrench (Mole) is often the only way to remove a stubborn union.

9   Rigid pipes which need renewal can usually be purchased at any garage where they have the pipe, unions and special tools to make them up. All they need to know is the total length of the pipe, the type of flare used at each end with the union, and the length and thread of the union. FIAT is metric, remember.

10   Fitting your new pipes is a straightforward reversal of the removal procedure. If the rigid pipes have been made up, it is best to get all the sets (blends) in them before trying to fit them. Also, if there are any acute bends, ask your supplier to put these in for you on a tube bender. Otherwise, you may kink the pipe and thereby restrict the bore area and fluid flow.

11   Bleed the system (see Section 12) on completion.

12 Hydraulic system – bleeding

This is not a routine service operation and will 'normally' only be required if the system has been 'broken' – to renew a component.

At the specified intervals, bleeding is carried out to renew the hydraulic fluid; after a period of time, this tends to become contaminated with water vapour picked up from the atmosphere.

If the brake pedal feels spongy – or if when depressed repeatedly its travel (stroke) decreases to provide more effective braking, air is then probably present in the system and must be bled out.

1   To bleed the brakes, first destroy the vacuum in the servo by repeated applications of the footbrake pedal.

2   Check that the master cylinder fluid reservoir is full, then connect a bleed tube to the first bleed nipple. If a component in the front circuit has been removed and renewed, only that hydraulic circuit need be bled. Similarly, if a component in the rear circuit has been removed or renewed, bleed only that circuit. If the master cylinder has been disturbed (or the need is for a renewal of the system fluid), the complete system must be bled.

3   Pour some hydraulic fluid into a jar and immerse the open end of the bleed tube in the fluid.

4   Unscrew the bleed nipple half a turn. To avoid burring the nipple, it is recommended that a small ring spanner is slid up the bleed tube before it is inserted in the jar. The use of an open-ended spanner may damage the flats on the nipple.

5   Have an assistant apply full strokes of the pedal, alternating sharp applications with slow ones. As soon as the air bubbles cease emerging from the open end of the bleed tube under the fluid, have the pedal held in the fully depressed position while the bleed screw is tightened. Do not overtighten a bleed screw. Always allow the brake pedal to return unassisted during pumping for bleeding operations.

6   Top-up the fluid reservoir and repeat the operations on the next bleed screw. If the complete system is being bled, start at the wheel cylinder furthest from the master cylinder.

7   Note that the rear compartment of the fluid reservoir supplies the front circuit.

8   Keep the fluid reservoir topped-up at all times with clean fluid. Discard fluid bled from the system; or only use it for bleed jar purposes.

9   Good results are often achieved using one of the proprietary pressure bleed kits available (photo). These pressurise the master cylinder fluid reservoir from the spare wheel tyre. With this arrangement, the necessity for pumping the pedal is eliminated. An assistant is not required if an automatic brake bleeder is used; this incorporates a one-way valve.

13 Handbrake – adjustment

Adjustment is normally automatic, by the movement of the rear brake shoes on their automatic adjusters.

However, due to cable stretch, supplementary adjustment is occasionally required at the control lever adjuster nut. The need for this adjustment is usually indicated by excessive movement of the control lever when fully applied.

1   Jack up the rear of the car and apply the handbrake control lever over three or four notches. The rear wheels should be locked. If they are not, turn the adjuster nut as necessary to achieve the correct setting of the cable (photo).

2   If correct adjustment cannot be obtained, the cable is stretched and must be renewed as described in the next Section.

14 Handbrake cable – renewal

1   Chock the roadwheels and fully release the handbrake control lever.
2   The primary (front) cables can be removed by unbolting the lever from under the floor pan, then disconnecting the cable pulley and trunnion.
3   To remove the secondary (rear) cable, pull out the spring clip and detach the equaliser pulley (photo).
4   Disconnect the two cable eyes from the actuating levers at each brake backplate (photo).
5   Disconnect the cable clips from the body and suspension struts.
6   Draw the loop of the cable towards the front of the car, drawing both cable ends out of the support plate.
7   Refitting is a reversal of the removal process, but slacken the adjuster nut right off before the primary cable is fitted.
8   Adjust the cable as described in Section 13 when the work is completed.

15 Vacuum servo unit – description

A vacuum servo unit is fitted into the brake hydraulic circuit in series with the master cylinder, to provide assistance to the driver when the brake pedal is depressed. This reduces the effort required by the driver to operate the brakes under all braking conditions.

The unit operates by vacuum obtained from the induction manifold and comprises basically a booster diaphragm and non-return valve. The servo unit and hydraulic master cylinder are connected together so that the servo unit piston rod acts as the master cylinder pushrod. The driver's braking effort is transmitted through another pushrod to the servo unit piston and its built-in control system. The servo unit piston does not fit tightly into the cylinder, but has a strong diaphragm to keep its edges in constant contact with the cylinder wall, so assuring an air tight seal between the two parts. The forward chamber is held under vacuum conditions created in the inlet manifold of the engine and, during periods when the brake pedal is not in use, the controls open a passage to the rear chamber so placing it under vacuum conditions as well. When the brake pedal is depressed, the vacuum

13.1 Handbrake adjuster (arrowed)

14.3 Handbrake cable equaliser pulley

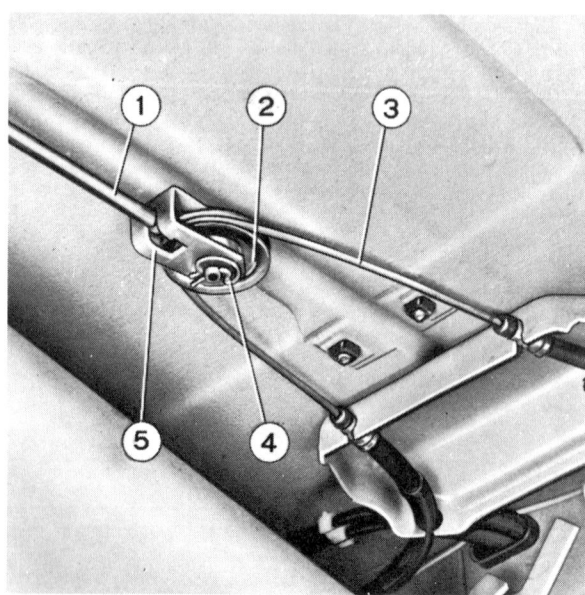

Fig. 8.15 Handbrake equaliser pulley details (Sec 14)

1   Primary (front) cable   4   Clip
2   Pulley   5   Clevis fork
3   Secondary (rear cable)

14.4 Handbrake cable attachment to shoe actuating levers

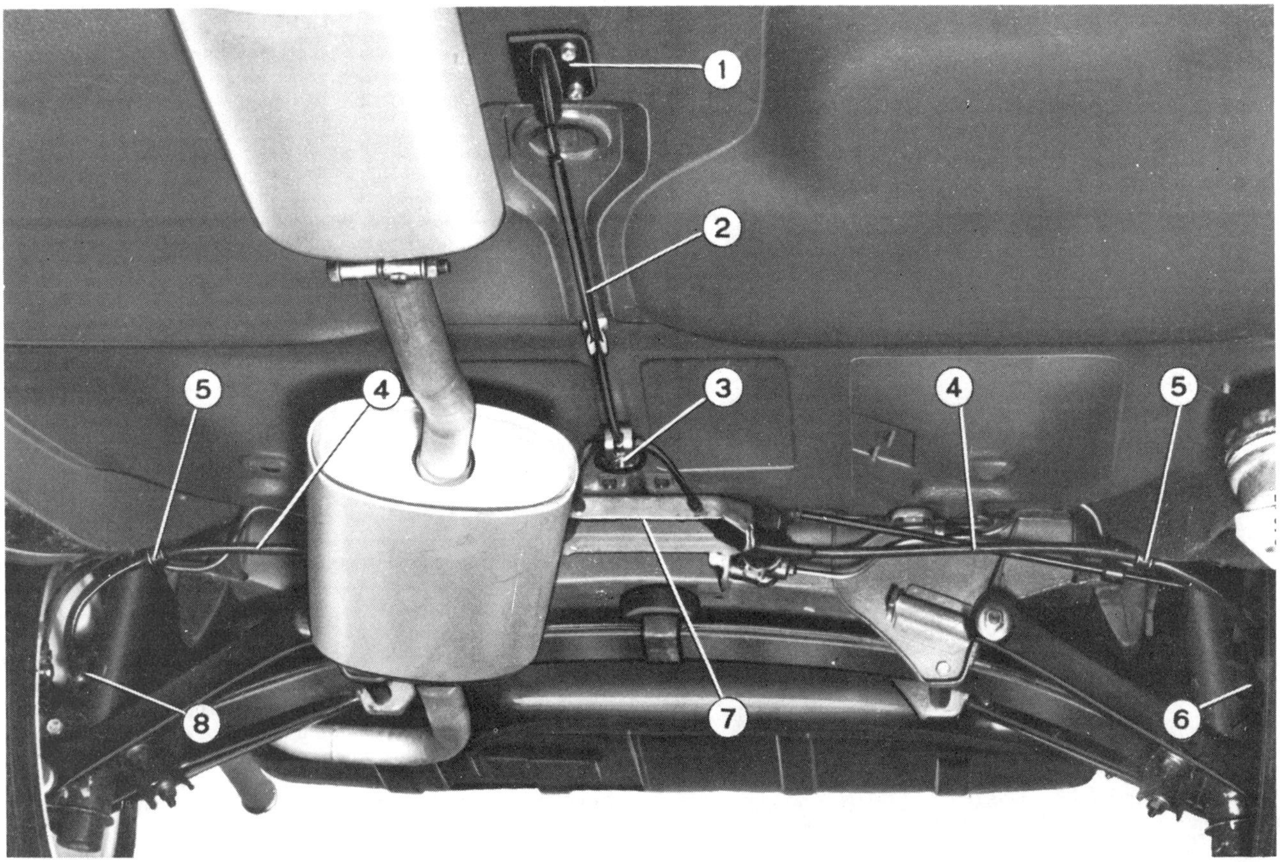

Fig. 8.14 Handbrake cable and linkage (Sec 14)

1   Control lever support
2   Primary (front) cable
3   Equaliser pulley
4   Secondary (rear) cable
5   Cable clips
6   Cable attachment to left

   rear suspension strut
7   Support bracket
8   Cable attachment to right
   rear suspension strut

passage to the rear chamber is cut off and the chamber opened to atmospheric pressure. The consequent rush of air pushes the servo piston forward in the vacuum chamber and operates the main pushrod to the master cylinder.

The controls are designed so that assistance is given under all conditions and, when the brakes are not required, vacuum in the rear chamber is established when the brake pedal is released. All air from the atmosphere entering the rear chamber is passed through a small air filter.

Under normal operating conditions, the vacuum servo unit is very reliable and does not require overhaul except at very high mileages. In this case, it is far better to obtain a service exchange unit, rather than repair the original unit.

It is emphasised that the servo unit assists in reducing the braking effort required at the foot pedal and in the event of its failure, the hydraulic braking system is in no way affected except that the need for higher pressures will be noticed.

---

16 Vacuum servo unit – servicing and testing

---

1   Regularly, check that the vacuum hose which runs between the servo unit and the inlet manifold is in good condition and is a tight fit at both ends (photo).
2   At the specified intervals, renew the air filter which is located around the brake pedal push rod. Access to this is obtained by disconnecting the pushrod from the cross-shaft or pedal arm, withdrawing the pushrod, dust excluding boot and end cap.
3   If the new filter is cut diagonally from its centre hole, future renewal can be carried out without the need for disconnection of the pushrod.

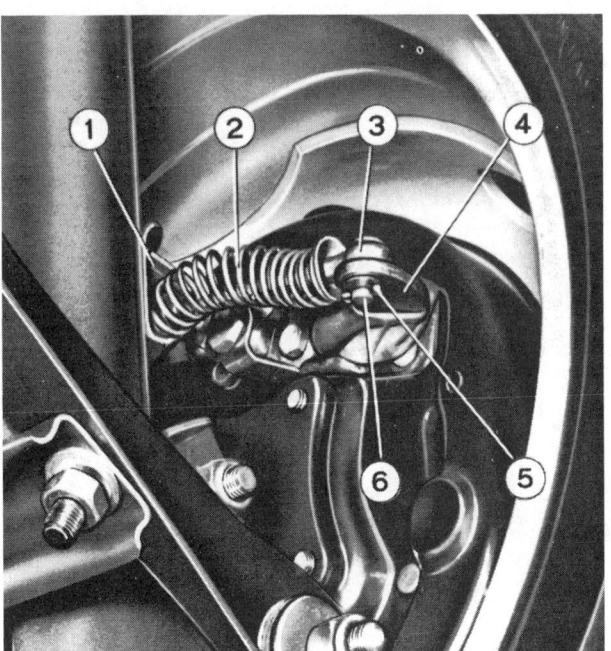

Fig. 8.16 Handbrake cable attachment to brake actuating lever (Sec 14)

1   Attachment to suspension
   strut
2   Coil spring
3   Cable eye
4   Brake actuating lever
5   Split pin
6   Clevis pin

16.1 Brake servo vacuum hose attachment to inlet manifold

4   If the efficiency of the servo unit is suspect, it can be checked out in the following way.
5   Run the engine, then switch off the ignition. Depress the footbrake pedal; the distinctive in-rush of air into the servo should be clearly heard. It should be possible to repeat this operation several times before the vacuum in the system is exhausted.
6   Start the engine and have an assistant apply the footbrake pedal and hold it down. Disconnect the vacuum hose from the servo. There should not be any in-rush of air into the servo through the connecting stub. If there is, the servo diaphragm is probably faulty. During this test, expect the engine to idle roughly, unless the open end of the hose to the inlet manifold is plugged. Reconnect the hose.
7   With the engine off, depress the brake pedal fully. Start the engine with the brake pedal still depressed; the pedal should be felt to go down fractionally.
8   If the results of these tests are not satisfactory, remove the unit and fit a new one as described in the next Section. *Do not attempt to repair the servo yourself.*

17 Vacuum servo unit – removal and refitting

1   Syphon as much fluid as possible out of the master cylinder reservoir.
2   Disconnect electrical leads from the terminals in the reservoir cap then uncouple the rigid pipelines from the master cylinder body. Be prepared to catch leaking fluid and plug the open ends of the pipelines.
3   The master cylinder can be unbolted now from the servo unit, or detached later when the complete assembly is withdrawn.
4   Working inside the car, disconnect the servo pushrod from the pedal or cross-shaft, then remove the servo mounting nuts.
5   Withdraw the servo assembly into the engine compartment, then remove it to the bench. If the master cylinder is still attached, cover the wings with protective sheeting, in case brake fluid is spilled during removal.
6   Refitting is a reversal of the removal process, but adjust the pushrod clearance as described in Section 9. On completion of refitting, bleed the complete hydraulic system as described in Section 12. **Note**: *Where the help of an assistant is available, the servo pushrod need not be disconnected from the pedal or cross-shaft. The rod is a sliding fit in the servo and the servo can be simply pulled off the rod. Refitting without having disconnected the rod from the pedal or cross-shaft is problematic, unless the help of an assistant is available.*

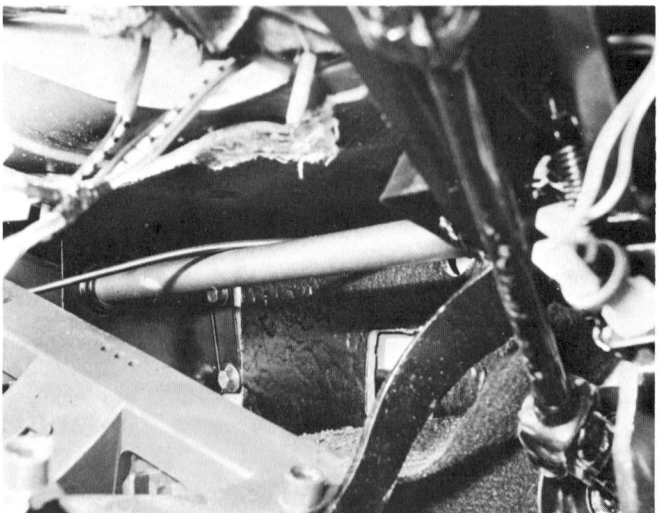

18.3 Brake pedal cross-shaft (right-hand drive models)

18 Brake pedal – removal and refitting

1   Removal of the brake pedal is described in conjunction with that for the clutch pedal in Chapter 5, Section 4.
2   The servo unit and the master cylinder are mounted on the rear left-hand side of the engine compartment, irrespective of whether the car is left-hand or right-hand drive.
3   On right-hand drive cars, the connection of the brake pedal to the servo unit is accomplished by means of a cross-shaft running inside the car, below the facia panel (photo).

19 Brake stop lamp switch

1   The switch is mounted on a small bracket above the brake pedal arm (photo).
2   With the ignition on, the stop lamps should illuminate when the pedal pad has been depressed by 3.2 mm (0.125 in).
3   Adjust the switch position, if necessary, by releasing the switch locknuts.

19.1 Brake stop lamp switch

20 Fault diagnosis – braking system

Symptom	Reason(s)
Excessive pedal travel	Pads or shoes excessively worn Incorrect pedal or servo pushrod adjustment Automatic adjusters faulty Seized wheel cylinder or caliper piston Master cylinder seals worn
Pedal feels spongy or soggy	Air in hydraulic system Low fluid level Loose connections Flexible hose perished Defective wheel cylinder or caliper seal
Pedal feels springy	New pads or linings not bedded-in Master cylinder mounting loose
Excessive effort required to stop car	Worn or contaminated linings or pads Incorrect grade of lining or pad material Servo vacuum hose leaking or disconnected Faulty servo or non-return valve Seized caliper or wheel cylinger piston Rear shoes fitted incorrectly with regard to leading and trailing ends One circuit defective on dual circuit hydraulic system
Brakes pull to one side	Friction linings contaminated on one side of car Seized hydraulic piston on one side of car Different types of linings fitted on different sides of car, or new linings on one side only Seized automatic adjuster on one side of car
Pedal vibrates when brakes applied	Discs or drums distorted Friction linings excessively worn Loose backplate or caliper mounting bolts Wear in steering or suspension components
Brakes drag	Handbrake linkage overadjusted or seized Seized caliper or wheel cylinder piston
Brakes squeal	Drums or discs rusty or damp (temporary fault – no action necessary) Dust or grit in brake drums Linings excessively worn

Chapter 9 Electrical system

For modifications, and information applicable to later models, see Supplement at end of manual

Contents

Specifications

System type .... 12V, alternator, battery, pre-engaged starter

Battery .... 45Ah at 20hr discharge rate

Alternator
Make .... Bosch or Marelli
Continuous rating 45A
Maximum output 50A
Voltage regulator .... Integral electronic
Regulating voltage .... 13.9 to 14.5 V at 2000 (engine) rpm

Starter motor (pre-engaged)
Make .... Marelli or Femsa
Output .... 0.8 or 0.9 kW

Fuses (except North American models)

Number	Circuits protected	Rating (A)
1	Reversing lamp, heated rear window relay, stop lamps, direction indicators, warning lamps for direction indicators, fuel reserve, coolant temperature, low brake fluid. Fuel gauge, heater fan and resistor, clock, automatic transmission indicator lamp	8
2	Windscreen wiper, washer (also rear screen, if fitted)	8
3	Right-hand front parking and left-hand tail lamps	8
4	Left-hand front parking, right-hand tail lamps. Rear number plate and instrument panel lamps. Cigar lighter illumination, clock illumination, parking lamp warning lamp	8
5	Left-hand headlamp dipped beam, rear fog lamp and warning light	8
6	Right-hand headlamp dipped beam	8
7	Left-hand headlamp main beam and warning light	8
8	Right-hand headlamp main beam	8
9	Horn and relay, radiator electric fan	16
10	Clock, cigar lighter, courtesy lamps	8
11	Hazard warning system, heated rear window	16

In-line fuses
Radio 2.5A

Relays (except North American models)
Horn
Heated rear window
Starter (automatic transmission)

Fuses (North American models)
As for other models described previously but add the following

Number 1 .... Gulp valve electrovalve, seat belt warning and indicator, tachometer, instrument panel lamp rheostat

Number 10 .... Buzzer (seat belt warning and anti-theft system)

Relays (North American models)
Horn
Heated rear window
Starter (automatic transmission)
Air conditioning system (three)
Seat belt warning system
Radiator cooling fan

Bulbs

Lamp	Wattage
Headlamp	40/45
Front parking	5
Direction indicator	21
Side marker/direction indicator repeater	4 (complete lamp)
Tail	5
Stop	21
Reversing	21
Fog	21
Direction indicator	21
Rear number plate	5
Courtesy	5
Cigar lighter	4
Warning, indicator and panel illumination bulbs except ignition warning and automatic transmission selector plate	1.2
Ignition warning	3
Automatic transmission selector plate	3

Torque wrench settings

	lbf ft	Nm
Alternator mounting bolts	36	49
Starter motor mounting bolts	19	25

1 General description

The electrical system is of the conventional 12 volt type and employs a belt driven alternator for charging the battery.

The electrical equipment is adequate but not elaborate; the system is fused and includes two separate relays for the horn and heated rear window.

On cars destined for operation in North America, certain additional circuits are fitted to operate the emission control systems, air conditioning (where fitted), seat belt and anti-theft warning devices.

2 Battery – maintenance

1 A modern battery charged by an alternator will probably only require topping-up with water every six months, but this fact should not stop you checking the electrolyte level in the unit every week, as this is really the only indication that the battery is not being overcharged.

2 The level of the electrolyte should be just above the top edges of the plates visible when the filler/vent plugs are unscrewed and removed.

3 Some types of battery have a translucent casing marked with the electrolyte level. Other types have a lid which, when removed, exposes a trough. Water should be poured into the trough until it begins to collect in the bottom. Refit the lid and the level is automatically adjusted in each cell.

4 Periodically, check the security of the leads to the battery terminals. Clean away any corrosion and smear the terminals and posts with petroleum jelly; *never use grease for this job.*

5 Keep the top of the battery dry and mop up any spilled water with a rag or paper towel.

6 Ordinary tap water should not be used for topping-up a battery. Obtain some distilled or purified water from the chemists or use melted ice from the freezer compartment of your refrigerator which has built up as a result of condensation.

3 Battery – faults and corrosion

1 The most likely fault which will occur in a battery is a low state of charge.

2 If this has been caused by leaving the lights on overnight, the car should be started by pushing it or by attaching booster cables to the battery (see Section 6). After a few miles running, the alternator will have re-charged it.

3 If the battery is found to be in a low state of charge (or discharges after normal road use without excessive use of electrical equipment) then provided the alternator is working correctly (with the drivebelt properly tensioned), the battery must be suspected.

4 Use a hydrometer to check the specific gravity of each battery cell. Refer to the following table for specific gravity levels at various electrolyte temperature levels. Any variation in specific gravity in excess of 0.025 between the cells will probably be due to general old age, causing buckling of the plates or the electrolyte having been spilled at some time and the electrolyte from one cell having been replaced with water only.

Specific gravity – battery fully charged

1.268 at 100°F or 38°C electrolyte temperature
1.272 at 90°F or 32°C electrolyte temperature
1.276 at 80°F or 27°C electrolyte temperature
1.280 at 70°F or 21°C electrolyte temperature
1.284 at 60°F or 16°C electrolyte temperature
1.288 at 50°F or 10°C electrolyte temperature
1.292 at 40°F or 4°C electrolyte temperature
1.296 at 30°F or -1.5°C electrolyte temperature

Specific gravity – battery fully discharged

1.098 at 100°F or 38°C electrolyte temperature
1.102 at 90°F or 32°C electrolyte temperature
1.106 at 80°F or 27°C electrolyte temperature

1.110 at 70°F or 21°C electrolyte temperature
1.114 at 60°F or 16°C electrolyte temperature
1.118 at 50°F or 10°C electrolyte temperature
1.122 at 40°F or 4°C electrolyte temperature
1.126 at 30°F or -1.5°C electrolyte temperature

5   If general deterioration is suspected, have the battery tested by your dealer before purchasing a new one.
6   If the electrolyte is at fault, have the battery drained and refilled by your dealer. Do not become involved in trying to mix your own electrolyte – battery acid is dangerous and is not the sort of thing to have lying about at home.
7   Corrosion of the insulation of the battery leads or the battery clamps and support tray is often caused by careless topping-up, a cracked casing due to impact from a tool or jarring onto the floor during removal. It is sometimes the result of excessive overcharging, with too high a level of electrolyte in the cells.
8   Where corrosion is evident as white fluffy deposits, remove the battery (see next Section) and neutralise the corrosion with household ammonia. When the parts are rinsed and dry, paint over them with underseal or similar anti-corrosive paint.

4   Battery – removal and refitting

1   Open the bonnet. The battery is located on a platform at the front left-hand side of the engine compartment.
2   Disconnect the negative lead, then the positive lead, in that order, from the battery terminals.
3   Unscrew the battery clamp plate from the bottom of the front face of the battery case. The clamp bolt also retains a plastic heat insulating shield (photo).
4   Remove the shield and the battery.
5   Refit the battery by reversing the removal operations.

5   Alternator – description

The alternator may be of Bosch or Marelli construction and has an integral voltage regulator.
The alternator generates current at much lower revolutions than a dynamo; the battery does not therefore discharge, even under idling or slow motoring conditions.
The alternator develops its current in the stationary windings, the rotor carrying this field. The brushes therefore carry only a small current, so they last a long time, and only simple slip rings are needed instead of a commutator.
The AC voltage is rectified by a bank of diodes. These also prevent battery discharge through the alternator.

6   Alternator – maintenance and precautions

To avoid damage to the alternator, the following precautions should be observed.
1   Disconnect the leads from the battery before connecting a mains charger to the battery terminals.
2   Never stop the engine by pulling off one of the battery leads.
3   Disconnect the battery if electric welding is to be carried out on the vehicle.
4   If using booster cables from another battery to start the car, make sure that they are connected positive to positive and negative to negative.
5   Maintenance consists of keeping the outside of the alternator clean, the electrical connections secure and the drivebelt correctly tensioned.

7   Alternator – testing

1   Before suspecting a fault in the alternator, make sure that its electrical connections are secure and that the drivebelt is correctly tensioned. Also make sure that the battery is in good condition.
2   Start the engine and allow it to idle. Connect a voltmeter (range 0 to 20 volts dc) across the battery terminals. The voltmeter should read between 12 and 13 volts.

4.3 Battery

3   Increase the engine speed to approximately 2500 rpm: the voltmeter reading should increase to between 13 and 14 volts. No increase, or an increase to 15 volts or more, suggests that the alternator or voltage regulator is faulty.
4   Further testing should be left to an electrical expert. The home mechanic with an interest in electrical systems will find further test procedures in the Automobile Electrical Manual, available from the publishers of this book.

8   Alternator – removal and refitting

1   Disconnect the leads from the terminals on rear face of the alternator.
2   Release the alternator adjuster link and pivot mounting bolts, swing the alternator in (towards the engine) and slip the drivebelt from the pulley.
3   Remove the previously slackened bolts, then remove the alternator.
4   Refitting is a reversal of the removal process; take care to tension the drivebelt as described in Section 6.

9   Alternator – overhaul

The alternator normally has a very long and trouble-free life. When a fault does develop (or after a high mileage, when wear in the bearings is evident), complete renewal with a new or factory rebuilt unit is recommended.
Where the necessary parts are available, overhaul can be carried out in the following way (both makes of alternator are similar but only the Bosch is described in detail here).
1   The regulator is fitted into the alternator housing. Remove a small screw and it may be removed.
2   Inside it will be seen the two slip-ring brushes. These must be free in the guides and at least 5 mm (0.2 in) long. The new length is 10 mm (0.4 in). The brushes may be renewed by unsoldering the leads from the regulator, fitting new brushes and resoldering the leads.
3   Undo the pulley nut and remove the pulley, the spacer ring, the large washer and the fan. Note which way the fan fits to make assembly easier. There is an arrow showing the direction of rotation.
4   Remove the bracket from the housing which held the wiring plug and if not already removed, take away the regulator.
5   Undo the housing bolts and separate the components. The rotor will stay in the endplate and the housing bearing will stay on the shaft. Have a good look at the various components. Clean off all the dust using a soft brush, then wipe them clean.
6   Any smell of burnt carbon or signs of over-heating must be investigated. Check the slip-rings for burning, scoring and ovality. You

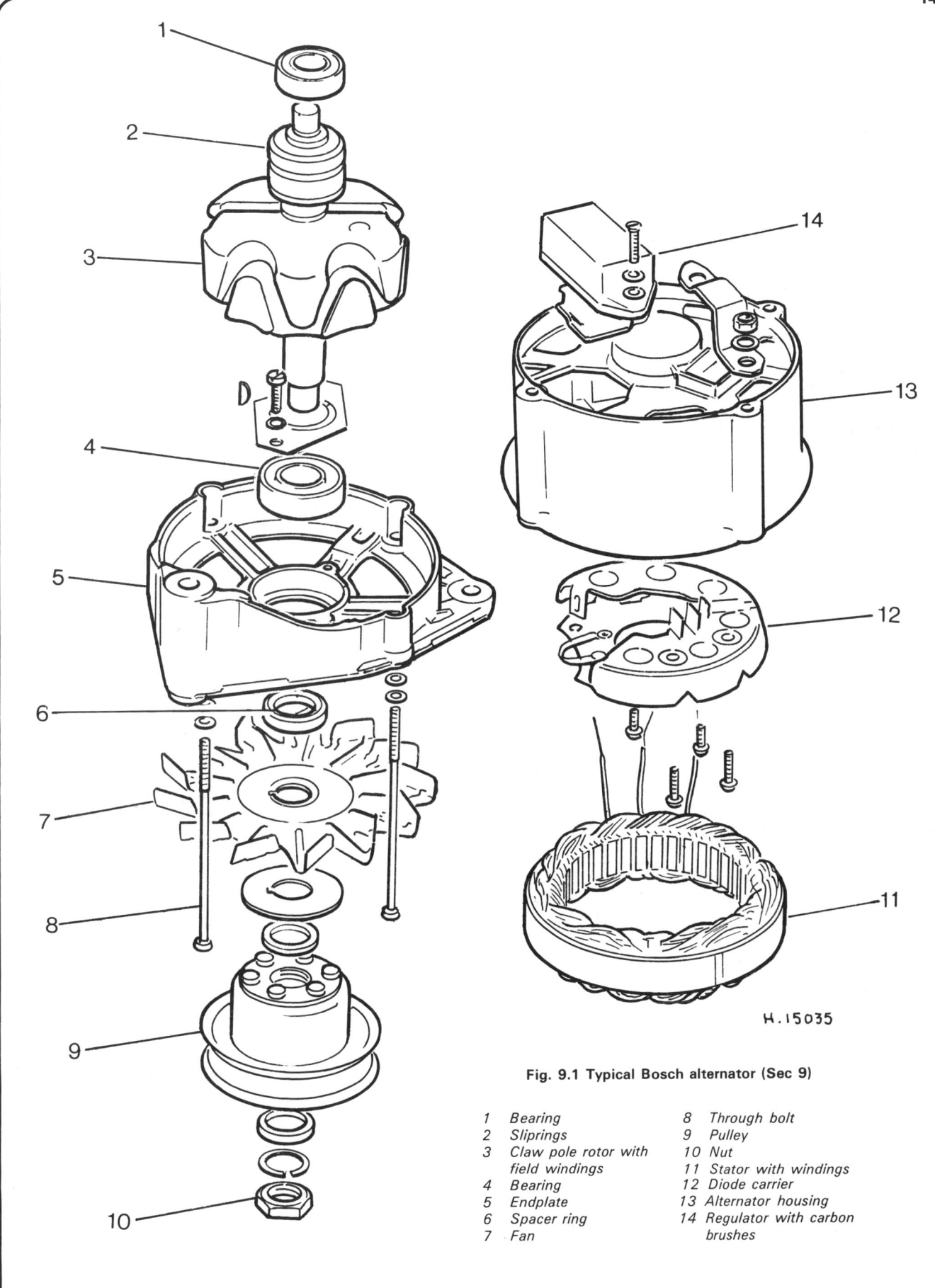

H.15035

Fig. 9.1 Typical Bosch alternator (Sec 9)

1	Bearing	8	Through bolt
2	Sliprings	9	Pulley
3	Claw pole rotor with field windings	10	Nut
4	Bearing	11	Stator with windings
5	Endplate	12	Diode carrier
6	Spacer ring	13	Alternator housing
7	Fan	14	Regulator with carbon brushes

will have had reason to check the bearings before dismantling, but have a further look now. At this point you must make up your mind whether to do the repair job yourself, or whether to take the alternator to a specialist. If you have the tools and the skill, it is possible to renew the bearings, renew the diode carrier complete, clean up the slip-rings and to fit a new rotor or stator. It is not possible to repair the winding, renew individual diodes, renew the slip-rings or repair the fan.

7   Deal with the rotor first. The rotor may be removed from the endplate by using a mandrel press. Then take the screws out of the cover over the endplate bearing and press the bearing out of the frame. The slip-ring end bearing may be pulled off using an extractor on the inner race. If you pull on the outer race the bearing will be scraped. Replace the bearings with new ones if necessary.

8   The slip-rings may be cleaned up by the use of fine glasspaper.

9   Test the rotor electrically. Check the insulation resistance between the slip rings and the shaft. This must be infinity. If it is not, there is a short circuit and the armature must be renewed. Get an auto-electrical specialist to confirm your findings first. Check the resistance of the winding. Measure this between slip rings. It should be about 4 ohms. If there is an open circuit or high resistance, then again the rotor must be renewed.

10   The stator and the diode carrier are connected by wires. Make a simple circuit diagram so that you know which wire goes to which diode then unsolder the connections. This is a delicate business as excess heat will destroy the diode and possibly the winding. Grip the wire as close as possible to the soldered joint with a pair of long nosed pliers and use as small a soldering iron as possible.

11   The stator winding may now be checked. First check that the insulation is sound. The resistance between the leads and the frames must be infinity. Next measure the resistance of the winding. It should be of the order of 1.3 ohms between leads. A zero reading means a short circuit, and of course a high or infinity reading, an open circuit.

12   The diode carrier may now be checked. Each diode should be checked in turn. Use a test lamp or an ohmmeter. Current must flow only one way; ie the resistance measured one way must be high and the other way (reverse the leads), low. Keep the current down to 0.8 amps and do not allow the diode to heat up. If the resistance both ways is a high one, then the diode is open circuited; a low one, short circuited. If only one diode is defective, the whole assembly (diode plate) must be renewed.

13   Reconnect the stator winding to the diode circuit, again be careful not to overheat the diode, and reassemble the stator and diode carrier to the housing.

14   A new diode carrier, or a new stator may be fitted, but be careful to get the correct parts.

15   Assembly is the reverse of dismantling. Be careful to assemble the various washers correctly.

10 Starter motor – description and in-car testing

1   The starter motor may be one of three different makes, all of which are of pre-engaged type.

2   This type of starter motor incorporates a solenoid mounted on top of the starter motor body. When the ignition switch is operated, the solenoid moves the starter drive pinion, through the medium of the shift lever, into engagement with the flywheel (or driveplate) starter ring gear. As the solenoid reaches the end of its stroke, and with the pinion by now partially engaged with the flywheel ring gear, the main fixed and moving contacts close and engage the starter motor to rotate the engine.

3   This pre-engagement of the starter drive does much to reduce the wear on the flywheel ring gear associated with inertia type starter motors.

4   If the starter fails, some fault-finding can be done with it still on the car. Check the ignition warning light comes on, and does not go out when the starter is switched on. If it goes out, the fault is probably in the battery. If it stays bright, get an assistant to work the switch, whilst listening to the starter. Listen to find out if the solenoid clicks into position. If it does not, pull the red solenoid wire, and check it with a test bulb. If the wire is live when the key is turned, but the solenoid does not move, take off the starter and remove it to the bench for overhaul.

11 Starter motor – removal and refitting

1   Disconnect the earth lead from the negative terminal of the battery.

2   Disconnect the lead from the starter solenoid and the heavy cable from the battery (photo).

3   Remove the mounting bolts and lift out the starter (photo).

4   Refitting is the reverse of the removal sequence. Make sure the electrical connections are secure.

12 Starter motor – overhaul

1   Having removed the starter from the engine, first clean the outside.

2   If the starter has been removed because it will not work, before stripping it, test to see where the defect is, and decide whether to try repairing it, or if it is better to obtain a replacement. Connect a lead from the battery negative terminal to the starter body, using one of the bolts that held it to the engine. Connect the positive battery terminal to the little solenoid terminal. The solenoid should slide the starter's gear along the shaft, but the starter will not turn because there is no power to the motor terminal. Now connect battery power to that terminal. With the solenoid live, the starter should turn after the gear has slid into engagement. If it does not try the wire direct to the motor's lead on the solenoid terminal nearer the motor main body, on which is the lead into the motor. If the motor now turns it shows that the switch part of the solenoid is faulty.

3   The starter should be dismantled for cleaning and renewing of the brushes whenever its performance deteriorates.

4   Take off the nut on the solenoid, and disconnect the cable from the solenoid to the motor, the field connection.

5   Remove the nuts and washers on the long studs holding the solenoid to the end frame. Lift off the solenoid, unhooking it from the shift lever.

6   Slacken and slide off the dust cover on the end of the yoke, to uncover the brushes.

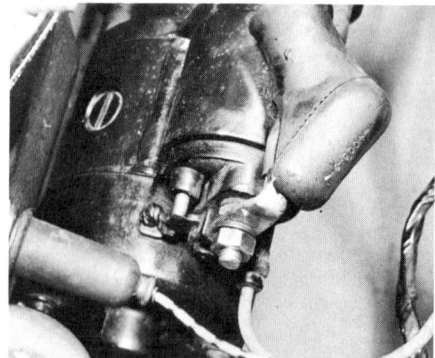
11.2 Starter solenoid terminals

11.3 Removing starter motor

12.13 Starter drivegear

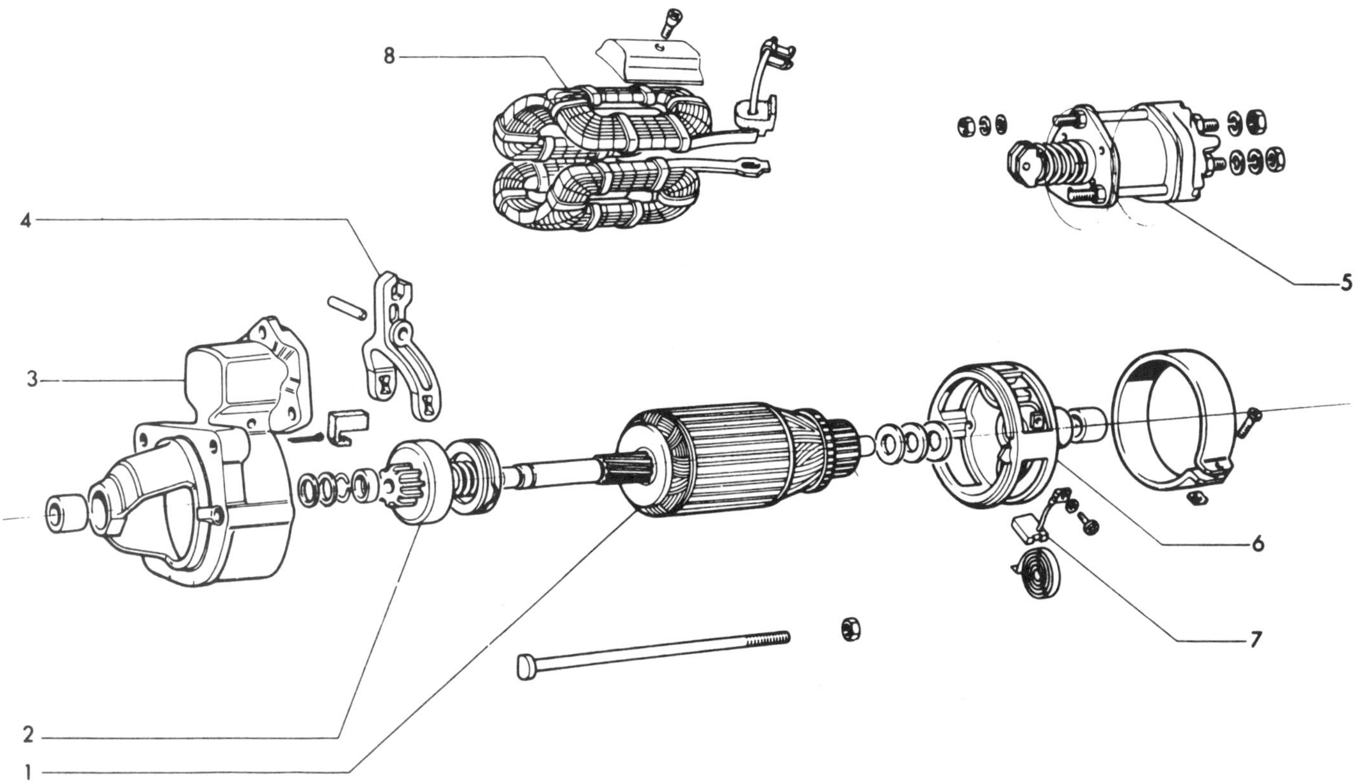

Fig. 9.2 Exploded view of typical starter motor (Sec 12)

1 Armature	3 Drive end bracket	5 Solenoid	7 Brush
2 Drive pinion/clutch	4 Shift lever	6 Brush endplate	8 Field windings

7   Disconnect the wire from the field winding to its brush.

8   Hook up the brush springs on the sides of the brush holders, so the load is taken off them.

9   Undo the nuts on the long through bolts holding the whole motor together.

10 Take off the brush-end endplate, and retrieve the one fibre and two steel washers from the end of the armature shaft.

11 Tip the motor pinion end down, and lift the yoke off the armature and pinion end frame.

12 Take out its split pin, and remove the pivot pin for the shift lever, from the 'waist' of the pinion housing.

13 Take the pinion housing off the assembly of armature, pinion and gear lever (photo).

14 Clean all the parts by wiping. Do not immerse in cleaning liquid, especially the freewheel and the armature bushes in the end frames, as the liquid will get into the freewheel race and the pores of the bushes.

15 Check the condition of the commutator. If it is dirty and blackened, clean it with a rag, dampened with petrol. If the commutator is in good condition, the surface will be smooth and free from pitting or burnt areas, and the insulated segments clearly defined.

16 Scrape the dirt out of the undercut gaps of insulator between the metal segments with a narrow screwdriver. If the metal segments have worn level with the insulators, undercut the insulators to a depth of 0.5 to 0.7 mm (0.012 to 0.027 in) below the surface of the metal segments using a 1.0 mm (0.039 in) thick hacksaw blade.

17 If, after the commutator has been cleaned, pitted and burnt spots are still present, wrap a strip of fine glass paper round the commutator. Rub the patches off while turning the armature so that the rubbing is spread evenly all over. Finally, polish the commutator with metal polish, then clean out the gaps.

18 Clean every part thoroughly when finished and ensure that no rough edges are left as any roughness will cause excessive brush wear.

19 Before reassembly, lubricate the splines of the freewheel with general purpose grease. Use a thin oil on the spiral splines. Use engine oil for the armature bushes, allowing it time to soak in before assembly.

20 Fit the brushes in their guides, but clip them back so that they will clear the commutator by putting the springs on their side. The springs can be hooked into place after the brush endplate has been fitted.

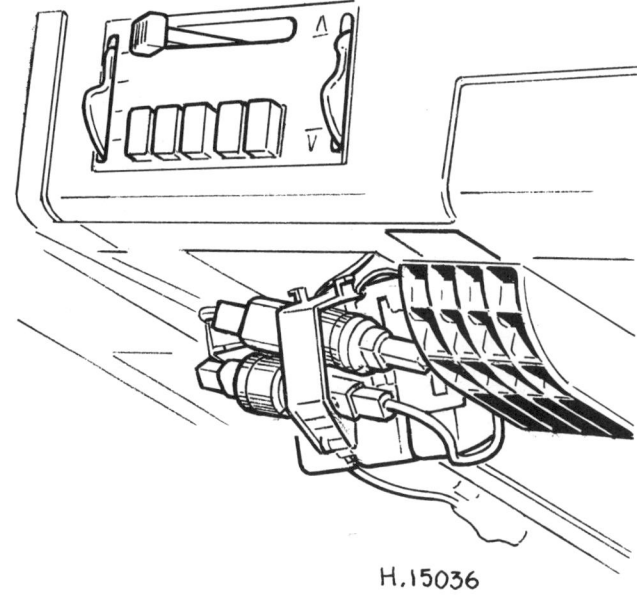

H.15036

Fig. 9.3 Air conditioner fuse unit (Sec 13)

13 Fuses and relays

Fuses

1   The fuse block is located under the left-hand end of the facia panel (photos).
2   The fuses are of cartridge type, 8A or 16A rating, and protect the circuits as listed in the Specifications section at the beginning of this Chapter.
3   The cover for the fuses is of snap-on type; spare fuses are carried in the assembly and three spare positions are available for additional accessory circuits, where necessary.
4   On cars with air conditioning, an additional fuse unit is located adjacent to the main one, the cover being retained by screws.
5   Where a radio or other in-car entertainment unit is fitted, an in-line fuse is located in the power line.

Relays

6   All models are fitted with a horn relay and heated rear window relay, located at the fuse block under the facia panel.
7   On cars equipped with air conditioning, three relays are mounted on the underside of the air conditioner control panel. These relays control the operation of the condenser and evaporator and the condenser cooling fan.
8   On models equipped with automatic transmission, a starter relay is located on the fuse block.
9   On North American versions, additional relays for the seat belt warning system and radiator cooling fan are located on a panel underneath the fuse box.
10 A relay can usually be heard to operate. If it cannot, and the fuse and accessory or component has been checked out (the latter with an independent power supply), then the relay is at fault and must be renewed, no repair being possible.

14 Flasher unit

1   The direction indicator and hazard warning unit is essentially another relay, and is located behind the facia panel against the left-hand side of the glove compartment liner.
2   The flasher unit can be seen through an opening in the liner; it is held in a support clip which is itself clipped into the facia panel (photos).
3   If the flasher lamps start to operate rapidly, as indicated by the indicator lamps on the instrument panel, this condition is probably caused by a blown bulb or poor earthing of the bulb holder.
4   Complete or partial failure of the system may be due to a blown fuse, insecure wiring or connections. If these are satisfactory, the fault must lie in the flasher unit which should be renewed with one of a similar type.

15 Bulbs – renewal

1   Whenever a bulb is suspected of having failed (unless its filament can be clearly seen to be broken), test it in an alternative lamp holder.
2   Corrosion within the bulb holder may also prevent a bulb from illuminating.
3   Always renew a bulb with one of similar type and wattage.

Headlamp

4   Open the bonnet, disconnect the electrical plug from the rear of the headlamp and peel away the rubber dust excluding boot (photo).
5   Release the spring retainer from the bulb holder and withdraw the bulb/holder (photos).
6   Reassembly is a reversal of the dismantling process, but make sure that the 'pip' on the holder flange engages in the slot in the lamp body.
7   Take care not to exert too much pressure on the back of the headlamp during bulb renewal; the lamp unit could be pushed off its mounting screws and fall to the floor (photo).

Parking, direction indicator and rear lamps

8   All these lamps have lenses secured by external screws.
9   The bulbs are of bayonet fitting type and are accessible after removal of the lens (photos).

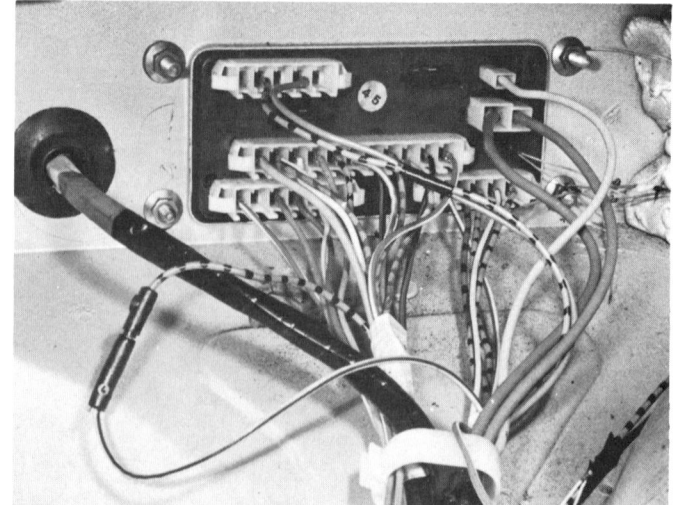
13.1A Engine compartment bulkhead cable entry

13.1B Fuse block

14.2A Flasher unit clip (arrowed)

14.2B Flasher unit removed

15.4 Headlamp connecting plug

15.5A Headlamp bulb holder spring retainer

15.5B Removing headlamp bulb

15.7 Withdrawing headlamp unit

15.9A Front parking/direction indicator lamp

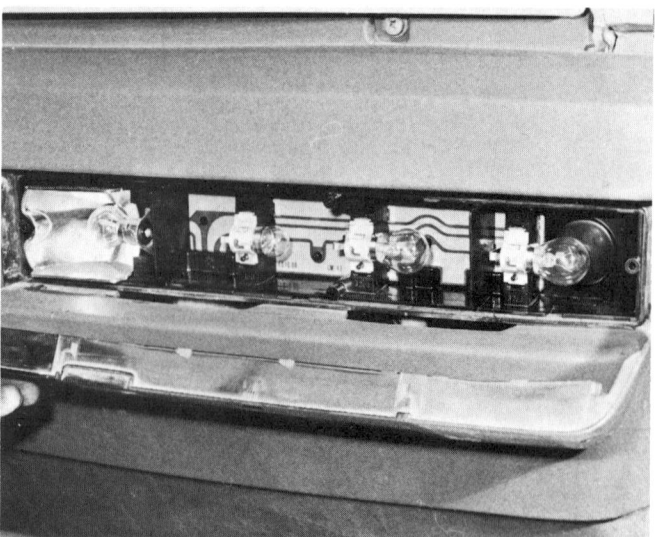

15.9B Rear lamp cluster

15.11 Side marker (repeater) lamp

15.12 Rear number plate lamp

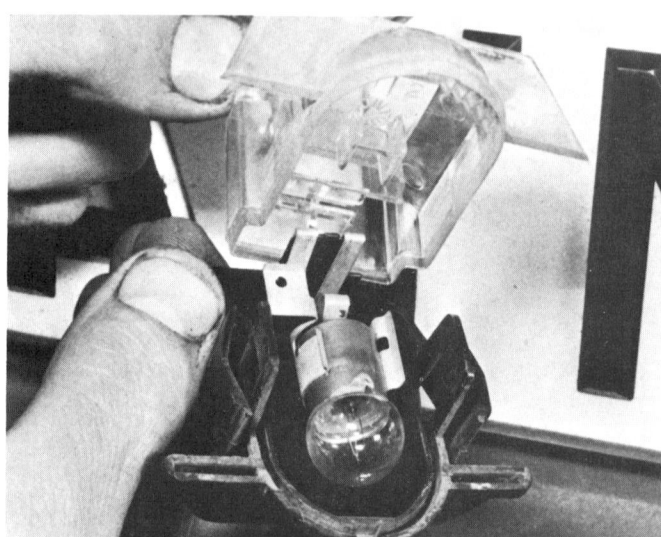

15.13 Rear number plate lamp lens and bulb

15.14A Front interior lamp

15.14B Rear interior lamp

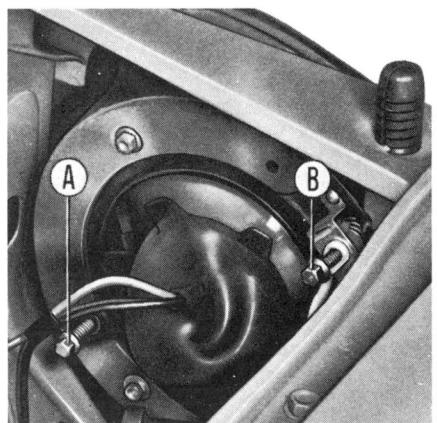

Fig. 9.4 Headlamp beam alignment screws (Sec 16)

A   Horizontal   B   Vertical

H.15037

Fig. 9.5 Ignition key positions (Sec 17)

ST   Ignition off, key withdrawn
MAR   Ignition on
AVV   Start

Side repeater lamp

10 The lamp/bulb assembly is disposable and a complete unit must be fitted if the bulb blows.
11 Depress the retaining tang under the front wing and withdraw the lamp. Pull the lamp from the connector plug (photo).

Rear number plate lamp

12 Access to the bulb is obtained by prising the lamp holder from the bumper, using a screwdriver (photo).
13 Separate the lens from the bulb/holder (photo).

Interior lamps

14 Prise the lamps carefully from their apertures, disconnect the electrical leads and renew the bulb (photos).

Instrument panel warning and indicator lamps

15 Access to these wedge-base bulbs is obtained after withdrawal of the instrument panels, as described in Section 25.

16 Headlamp – alignment

It is strongly recommended that alignment of the headlamps is carried out by your dealer on optical beam setting equipment
In an emergency, however, the headlamp beams can be adjusted using the screws located at the rear of the lamp within the engine compartment.

17 Steering column switches and lock

To remove the combination switches (headlamp dip, direction indicator and windscreen wash/wipe), carry out the following operations.
1   Disconnect the battery and check that the steering wheel and front roadwheels are in the straight-ahead position.
2   Prise out the horn button from the centre of the steering wheel.
3   Extract the two horn contact coil springs now exposed.
4   Unscrew and remove the steering wheel retaining nut, and pull off the steering wheel. If it is stuck, tap the rim of the wheel upwards with the palms of the hands.
5   Extract the screws which hold the upper and lower halves of the steering column shrouds together and remove the shrouds.
6   The switches can now be removed, once the multi-connectors are separated. Note the position of the direction indicator cancelling cam.
7   The steering column lock with ignition switch can be unbolted from the steering column and removed after withdrawal of the two bolts which hold the halves of the lock together (photo).
8   Refitting is a reversal of the removal process. Do not fully tighten the lockbolts until the action of the key in the lock cylinder has been

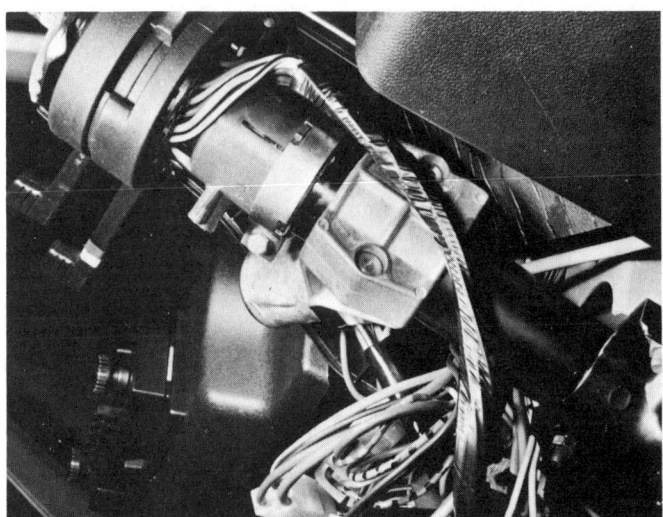

17.7 Steering column lock

18.3 Courtesy lamp switch

checked. To do this, wait until after the steering wheel has been refitted and the column shaft can be turned. Do not fit the column lower shroud until after the lock has been proved satisfactory; the lock securing bolts may need releasing slightly for the position of the lock to be adjusted to provide smoother operation when the ignition key is turned.

9   Refit the steering wheel so the spokes are in the lower half of the wheel and at equal angles with the front roadwheels in the straight-ahead attitude.

10   The ignition key positions are shown in the diagram. If the engine fails to start the first time, always return the key to the ST position before actuating the starter again.

18 Panel switches – removal and refitting

1   The panel switches are not repairable, but when pushed out of their panel locations after depressing their locating tags, detach the leads from the switch terminals, identifying each wire for correct re-connection.

2   Remember that, contrary to universal coding practice, the switches are ON when the green section of the switch rocker is visible.

3   The door pillar courtesy lamp switches are retained by a single screw (photo).

19 Horns

1   The dual horns are located just below the radiator top crossmember and to the rear of the radiator grille (photo).

2   Adjustment is not normally required to a horn, but if the horn note does alter over a period of time, the trimmer screw can be turned fractionally in either direction after releasing the screw locknut.

20 Windscreen wiper blades and arms – removal and refitting

1   To remove a windscreen wiper blade, pull the wiper arm from the glass until it locks.

2   Depress the socket of the wiper blade until the 'pip' on the arm can be seen to drop out of the hole in the socket, then simply pull the blade from the arm (photo).

3   To refit the blade, push it onto the end of the wiper arm until the 'pip' snaps into the hole in the blade socket.

4   To remove a wiper arm/blade assembly, first apply masking tape along the upper edge of the wiper blade onto the windscreen glass, as a guide to wiper arm alignment when refitting.

5   Pull the wiper arm away from the screen until it locks. Depress the spring retainer (which locks the arm to its spindle) and pull the arm

19.1 Horn arrangement

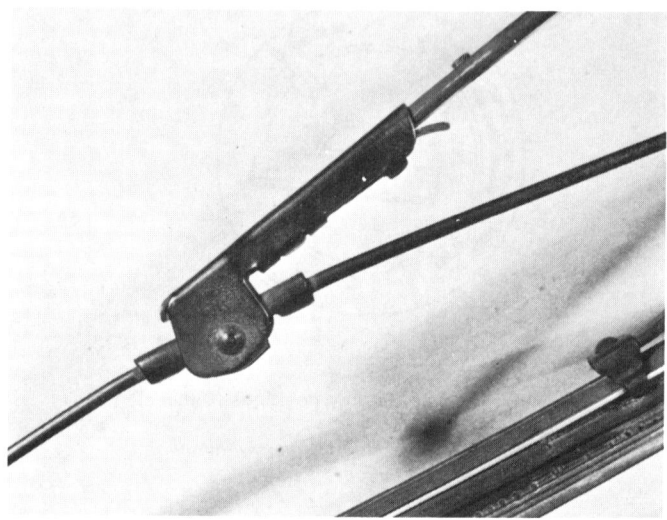
20.2 Wiper blade attachment

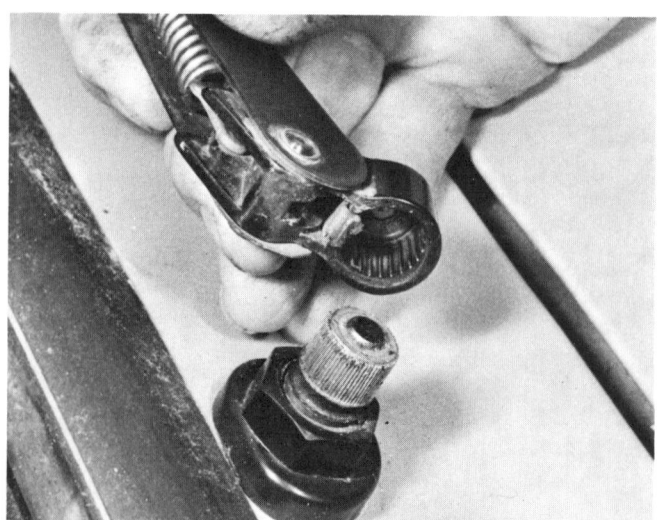
20.5 Wiper arm attachment

21.1 Windscreen wiper motor and linkage

22.2 Rear screen wiper motor

23.5 Rear screen washer reservoir and pump

23.6 Typical headlamp washer pump

from the spindle. If it is tight, lever the arm off gently with a screwdriver inserted between the rim of the splined section of the arm and the spindle collar (photo).
6   Refitting the arm is a reversal of the removal process but do not push it fully home on its splines until the alignment of the blade has been checked against the windscreen glass.

21 Windscreen wiper motor and linkage – removal and refitting

1   The wiper motor and linkage is located under the scuttle at the rear of the engine compartment, on the left or right-hand side according to which side the steering is fitted (photo).
2   To remove the complete motor/linkage assembly, first take off the wiper arms and blades as described in the preceding Section.
3   Unscrew and remove the nut which attaches the spindle operating link to the motor drive shaft.
4   Disconnect the leads from the motor.
5   Unbolt the wiper motor from its mounting bracket. Lower the motor and remove it.
6   If the spindle securing nuts are now removed, the linkage can be lowered and withdrawn from beneath the scuttle.
7   Refitting is a reversal of the removal process.

22 Rear screen wiper and linkage – removal and refitting

1   The rear screen wiper arm and blade are removed in exactly the same way as for the windscreen (see Section 20).
2   To remove the motor and drive spindle, first remove the spindle nut from outside the hatchback lid, then raise the lid and unbolt the motor. Withdraw it until the electrical leads can be disconnected (photo).

23 Washer fluid reservoirs and pumps

Windscreen washer
1   The location of the windscreen washer fluid reservoir (with incorporated electric pump) varies according to model.
2   On 65 models, the assembly is located in the right-hand rear cover of the engine compartment.
3   On 75 and North American models without air conditioning, the

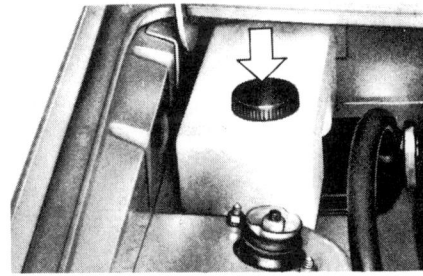

Fig. 9.6 Washer fluid location (65 models) (Sec 23)

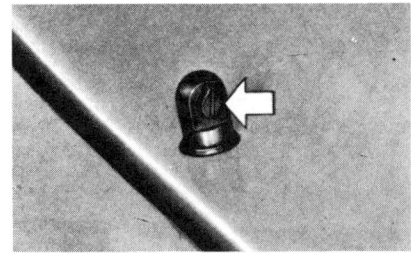

Fig. 9.7 Washer jet (Sec 23)

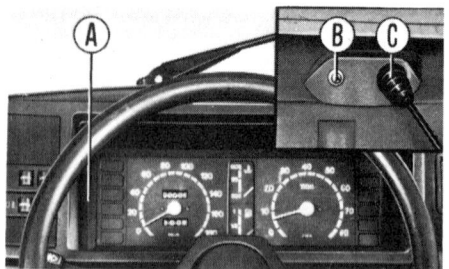

Fig. 9.8 Instrument panel (LHD models) (Sec 24)

A   Panel
B   Panel securing screw on engine compartment bulkhead
C   Speedometer cable grommet

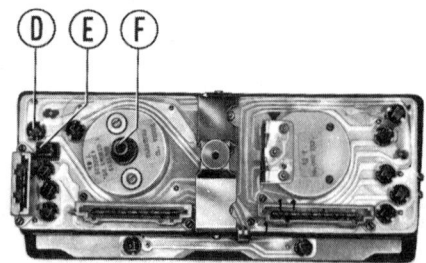

Fig. 9.9 Reverse side of LHD type instrument panel (Sec 24)

D   Indicator bulb holder (parking lamp)
E   Indicator bulb holder (ignition warning lamp)
F   Speedo cable connection

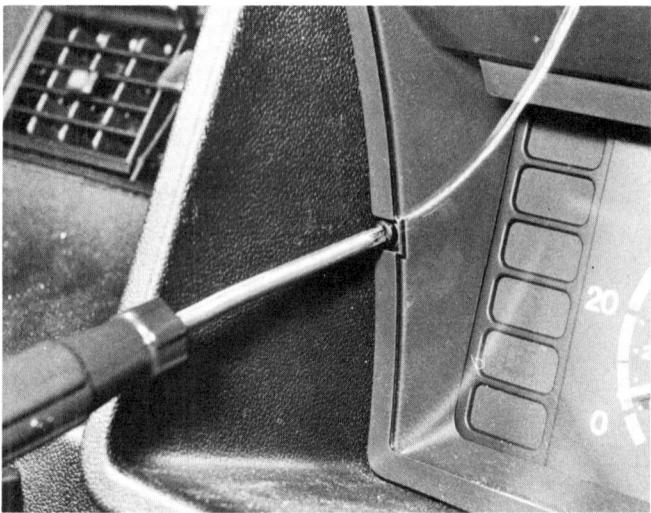

25.2 Instrument panel securing screw

Fig. 9.10 Repairing a heated rear screen element (Sec 26)

reservoir and pump are located next to the radiator, adjacent to its right-hand side.

4   On models with air conditioning, the reservoir and pump are located in the same position as on 65 models.

Rear window washer

5   The fluid reservoir and pump are located at the left-hand side of the luggage compartment (photo).

Headlamp washer

6   On cars fitted with this device, jets only are used to clean the headlamp glasses; the fluid reservoir and pump are located at the front left-hand corner of the engine compartment (photo).

Jets

7   These are adjustable with a screwdriver for vertical alteration of the jet pattern. For horizontal adjustment, twist the jet holder.

24 Speedometer cable – renewal

1   On LHD models, the speedometer is driven by a conventional inner and outer cable assembly. On RHD models, the speedometer is driven from an electronic transmitter unit through electric leads.

2   To renew a cable on LHD models, disconnect the cable from the transmission.

3   Refer to Fig. 9.8. Working within the engine compartment at the rear bulkhead, extract the screw (B) adjacent to the speedometer cable grommet (C). Slide the grommet and support plate down the speedometer cable.

4   The cable can now be disconnected from the speedometer head.

5   Withdraw the cable from the bulkhead.

6   Fitting the rear cable is a reversal of the removal process.

7   On some models, the routing of the speedometer cable differs from that just described and with this type of fitting, the instrument panel is retained by screws accessible from within the car. Withdraw the panel just far enough to be able to release the cable from the rear of the speedometer head.

8   On models with an electronic speedometer, note that the instrument is easily damaged by voltage surges. Such surges may arise from outside the vehicle (eg boost charging the battery). Observe the precautions given in Section 6 to avoid damage.

9   The sender unit used with the electronic speedometer can be seen in photo 4.32, Chapter 6. If a fault develops in either the sender or the speedometer head, make sure first that the wiring between the two units is satisfactory. If this is in order, consult your Fiat dealer to obtain a new or overhauled unit.

25 Instrument panel – removal and refitting

1   With early, cable driven speedometers, the instrument panel is free for removal once the operations described in paragraphs 3 and 4 of Section 24 have been carried out.

2   On later models, with a speedometer cable routed through the left-hand joint of the wing valance and the engine compartment rear bulkhead – or with an electronic type transmitter unit – extract the instrument panel fixing screws inside the car.

3   Withdraw the panel far enough to be able to disconnect the drive cable from the rear of the speedometer head, or to disconnect the

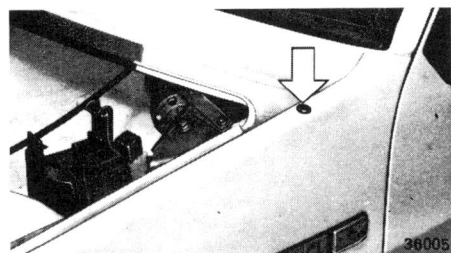

Fig. 9.11 Aerial mounting point on left-hand front wing (Sec 29)

Fig. 9.12 Radio installation (Sec 29)

C Power supply lead

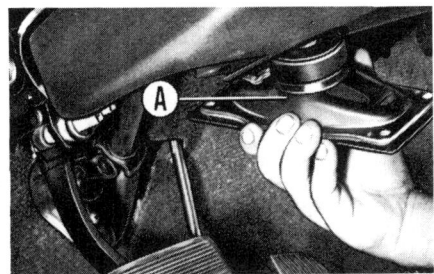

Fig. 9.13 Fitting a single loudspeaker (A) (Sec 29)

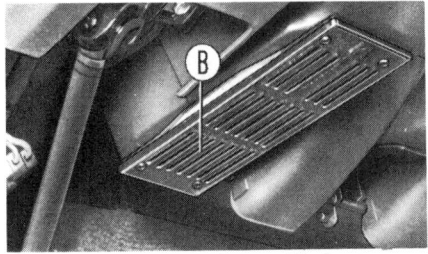

Fig. 9.14 Single loudspeaker grille (B) (Sec 29)

electrical leads, according to type of speedometer fitted.

4 Complete withdrawal of the instrument panel can only be achieved if the panel is tilted and lifted upwards in order to disconnect the wiring multi-pin connectors.

5 Refitting is a reversal of the removal process.

26 Heated rear window – precautions and repair

1 To prevent damage to the elements of the heated rear window, observe the following precautions:

(a) *Clean the interior surface of the glass with a damp cloth or chamois leather, rubbing in the direction that the elements run*

(b) *Avoid scratching the elements with rings on the fingers or contact with articles in the luggage compartment*

(c) *Do not stick adhesive labels over the elements*

2 Should the element be broken, it can be repaired using a conductive silver paint, without the need to remove the glass from the window.

3 The paint is available from many sources and should be applied with a soft brush to a really clean surface. Use two strips of masking tape as a guide to the thickness of the element to be repaired.

4 Allow the new paint to dry thoroughly before switching the heater on.

27 Seat belt warning system

On models destined for operation in North America, a seat belt warning system is fitted.

1 Any attempt to start the car without it being in neutral or having the front seat belts fastened (if occupied) will only result in the illumination of a warning lamp and the actuation of a warning buzzer.

2 Any fault in the system may be due to a blown fuse or poor electrical connections. If these are satisfactory, the weight sensitive seat switches or belt anchorage clip switches may be at fault.

3 With this system, the car engine may be started for tuning or repair purposes without having the seat belts connected, by reaching in through an open window to turn the ignition key.

28 Anti-theft warning system

This system is fitted to models destined for operation in North America.

If an attempt is made to open the car door from inside the car,

without having first withdrawn the ignition key, a warning buzzer will sound.

This will prevent the car being left with the ignition key still in the lock.

The buzzer used in this system is the same one used for the seat belt warning system.

29 Accessories – fitting

Radio

On models not equipped with a radio or cassette player as standard equipment, a suitable set may be fitted in the following way.

1 Prise out the blanking panel from the facia panel.

2 The next step is to fit the aerial. The most satisfactory position is on the roof, centred over the windscreen. If this location is adopted, the aerial lead will have to be fed along behind the sun visors and down one of the windscreen pillars. Removal of the interior mirror will be necessary in order to drill the mounting hole and feed the cable.

3 If the aerial is to be mounted on either front wing, it should be located on the upper surface at a point about 50 mm (2 in) ahead of the windscreen pillar. Plugs are factory fitted on some models to blank off holes already drilled.

4 To drill the mounting hole for the aerial, a tank cutter (or similar device) will save a lot of time and energy rather than having to open out a small hole by filing. Take steps to trap metal filings and remove the paint as necessary to provide a sound earth contact for the aerial mounting base. Smear petroleum jelly over the bare metal before fitting the aerial, to prevent rusting.

5 Once the aerial is fitted, pass the lead behind the instrument panel so that it emerges from the radio aperture in the facia panel. With a wing mounted aerial, pass the lead through the grommet provided in the engine compartment rear bulkhead. If necessary, withdraw the instrument panel (see Section 25) for better access to route the lead to the radio aperture.

6 Power supply (red/white) and door mounted loudspeaker leads are factory fitted and located behind the radio blanking panel.

7 Connect the power supply lead to the radio and the newly fitted aerial lead, followed by the right-hand loudspeaker leads (black/mauve and black/pink). Connect the left-hand loudspeaker leads (black/red and black/white).

8 Make sure that the power supply lead has a 2.5 A fuse inside the in-line fuse holder, then push the radio into position and secure it. Make sure the fixing screws provide a good earth contact between the radio casing and the body.

9 Prise out the speaker grilles from the doors, connect the speaker

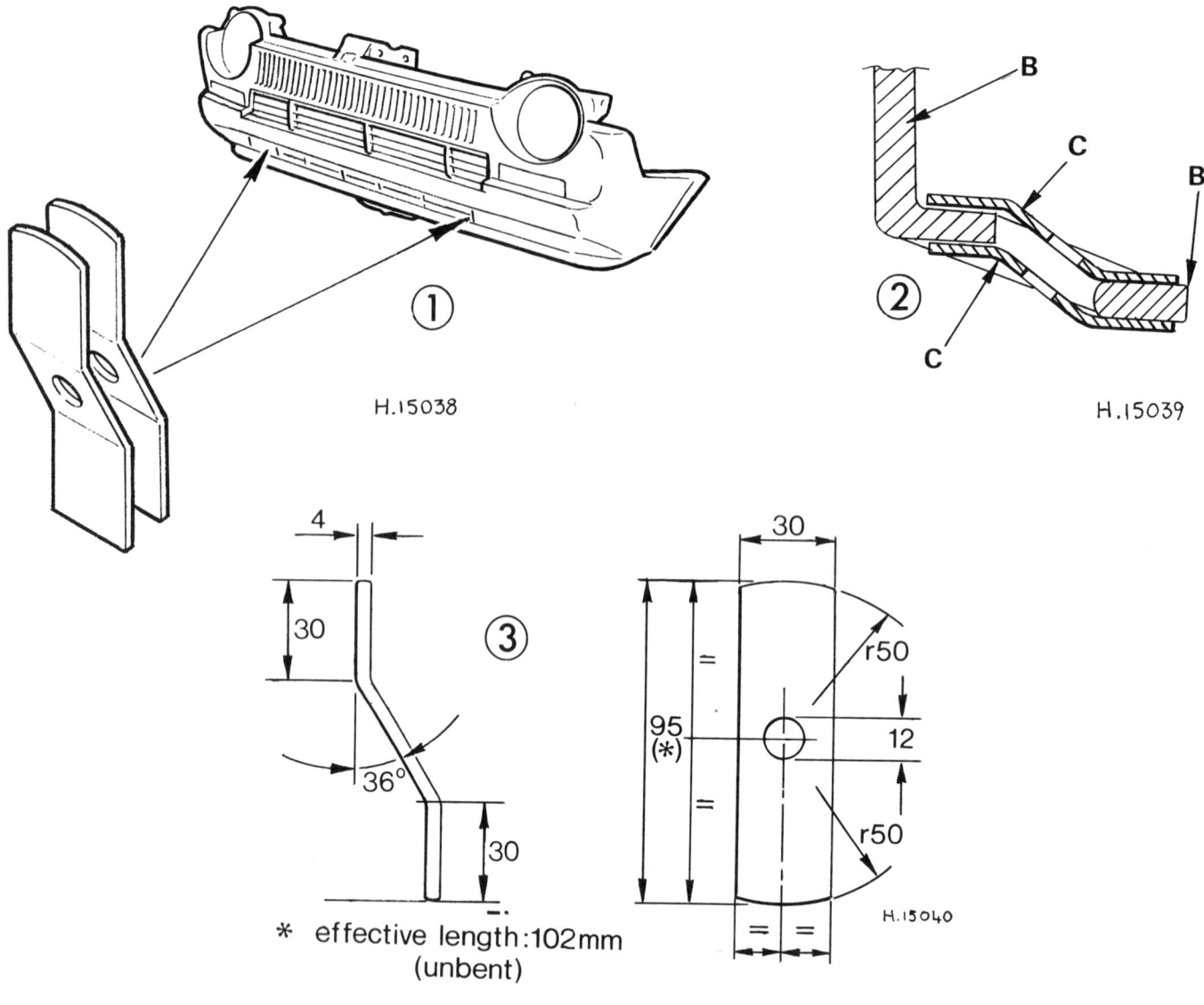

Fig. 9.15 Diagram for fabrication of auxiliary lamp bracket
(Sec 29)

1   Brackets and location
2   Sectional view of brackets
    b   Front plastic panel of car
    c   Brackets
3   Bracket dimensions (in mm) – two per lamp required, clamped
    in position by tightening lamp bolt

leads to the loudspeaker terminals, secure the speakers and refit the grilles.

10 If a radio is being fitted for which there is only a single loudspeaker, provision is made for this under the left-hand side of the facia panel. With this fitting, ignore the factory fitted speaker leads and connect the new leads supplied between the speaker and the radio set.

11 Once the radio is fitted, trim the aerial in accordance with the manufacturer's instructions.

12 With the engine running, it is possible that interference may be picked up, in which case suppressors will have to be fitted. The suppressors needed to eliminate interference will include the following. If they are fitted in the sequence listed, they may not all be required, as the problem may be overcome using some or all ignition suppressors only.

(a) Coil centre head to distributor (use a 10 000 to 15 000 ohm suppressor
(b) Coil positive (+) to earth (use a 1.0 mf capacitor under the coil mounting bolt)

(c) Spark plug suppressor caps
(d) Alternator large terminal (30 or B+) to earth (use a 1.0 to 3.0 mf capacitor)

Auxiliary lamps

13 The front plastic shield should not be drilled for mounting auxiliary lamps.

14 Clamp brackets should be made up to the dimensions shown in Fig. 9.15, which will provide a secure mounting yet leave the front panel undamaged.

15 Power for the lamps may be taken from another terminal such as the brake stop lamp switch, using a 'piggy back' connector. Fuse the new circuit with an in-line fuse holder or use one of the spare positions in the main fuse block if the necessary additional fuse holding clip assembly can be obtained from your FIAT dealer.

16 Make sure you use cable of sufficient thickness when connecting accessories which have a high consumption (amperage) such as fog and spot lamps.

Wiring diagram key for Strada CL

1 Front direction indicators (21 W, spherical)
2 Repeater lamps (4 W, tubular)
3 Side lamps (5 W, spherical)
4 Headlamp main and dipped beams (45/40 W, spherical)
5 Ignition coil
6 Ignition distributor
7 Oil pressure w/l transmitter
8 Engine coolant temperature transmitter
9 Starter motor
10 Radiator fan switch
11 Radiator fan motor
12 Horns
13 Battery
14 Preset cable – horn (L version)
15 Spark plugs
16 Windscreen water pump
17 Alternator
18 Heater fan ballast resistor
19 Reversing lamp switch
20 Low brake fluid level w/l transmitter
21 Centralised connection unit as viewed from engine
   compartment
22 Standard wiring identification numbers
23 Heated rear screen relay
24 Preset connection – starter inhibitor switch (automatic
   gearbox)
25 Horn relay
26 Screen wiper motor
27 Windscreen wiper interrupter
28 Direction indicator flasher
29 Centralised connection unit as viewed from engine
   compartment
30 Centralised connection unit as viewed from passenger
   compartment
31 Modular cable identification letters
32 Fuses
33 Centralised connection unit as viewed from passenger
   compartment
34 Headlamp w/l (1.2 W, w/b)
35 Side lamp w/l (1.2 W, w/b)
36 Rear fog lamp w/l (1.2 W, w/b)
37 Instrument panel lights (1.2 W, w/b)
38 Panel connectors
39 Engine coolant temperature gauge
40 Preset connection – quartz crystal clock

41 Direction indicator w/l (1.2 W. w/b)
42 Hazard w/l (1.2 W w/b)
43 Lighting/panel light switch
44 Rear fog lamp switch
45 Oil pressure w/l (1.2 W, w/b)
46 Ignition w/l (3 W, w/b)
47 Heated rear screen w/l (1.2 W, w/b)
48 Preset connection – hazard warning switch (where
   mandatory)
49 Warning light housing
50 Ignition switch
51 Fuel gauge
52 Quartz crystal clock
53 Handbrake 'on'/low brake fluid level w/l (1.2 W, w/b)
54 Fuel w/l (1.2 W, w/b)
55 Warning light housing
56 Preset connection – radio fuse
57 Preset connection – radio
58 Preset connection – rear screen wiper switch
59 Preset cable – digital clock earth
60 Heated rear screen switch
61 Preset cables – switches illumination light guide cable lamp
62 Heater fan switch – 4-position
63 Heater ideogram lamp (1.2 W, w/b)
64 Heater control lamps (1.2 W, w/b)
65 Cigar lighter/light (4 W, tubular)
66 Direction indicator switch
67 Headlamp switch
68 Windscreen wiper/washer switch
69 Horn control
70 Door switches
71 Preset connection – loudspeakers
72 Heater fan
73 Handbrake 'on' signal switch
74 Front courtesy light/switch (5 W, festoon)
75 Stop lamp switch
76 Rear courtesy lights/switches (4 W, festoon)
77 Fuel gauge transmitter
78 Heated rear screen (if fitted)
79 Rear direction indicators (21 W, spherical)
80 Stop lamps (21 W, spherical)
81 Rear lamps (5 W, spherical)
82 Reversing lamp (21 W, spherical)
83 Number plate lamp (21 W, spherical)
84 Rear fog lamp (21 W, spherical)

w/l = warning light
w/b = wedge-base

Key to cable colours

A = light blue
B = white
C = amber
G = yellow

H = grey
L = blue
M = brown
N = black

R = red
S = pink
V = green
Z = mauve

For later models see Chapter 13

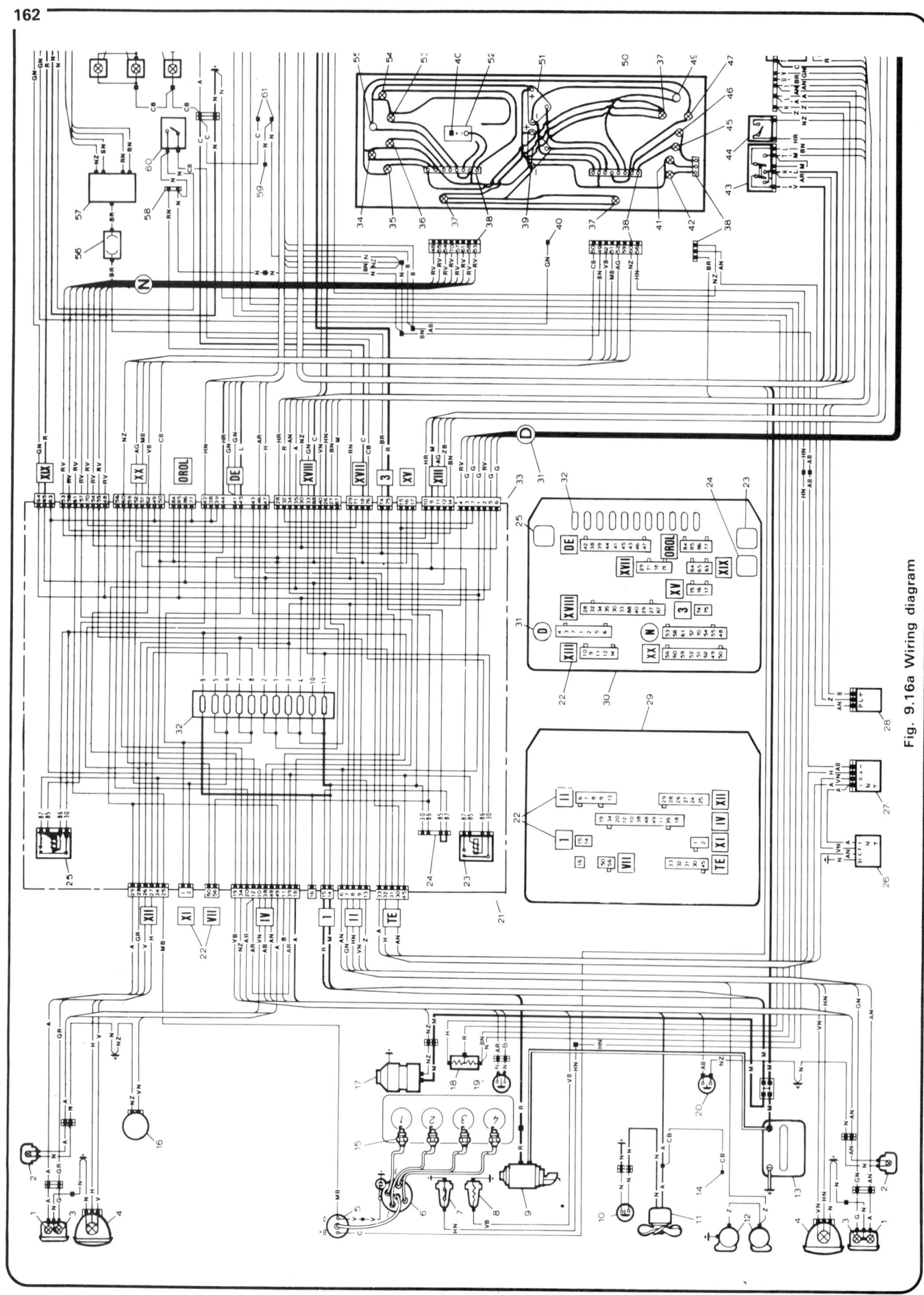

Fig. 9.16a Wiring diagram

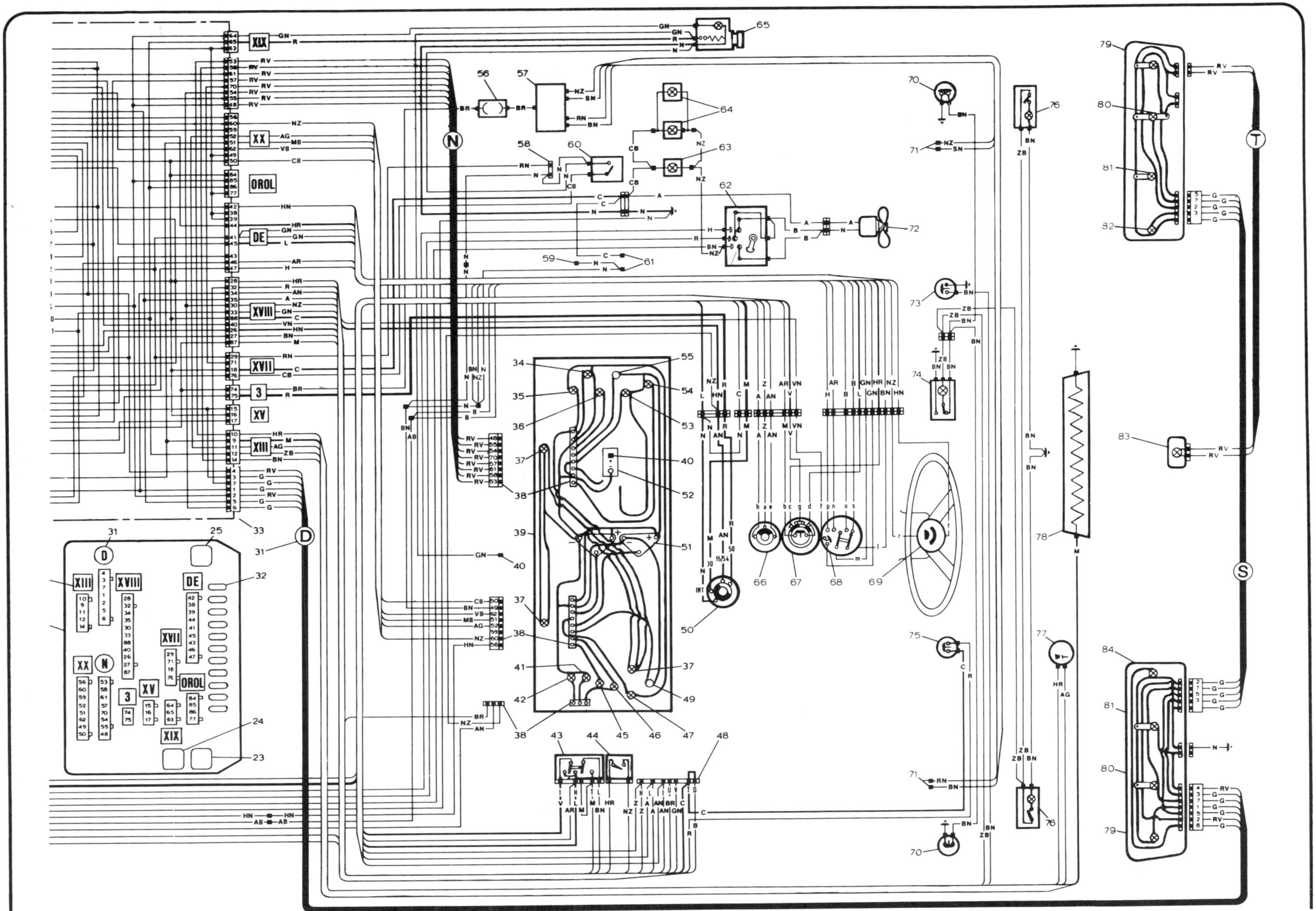

Fig. 9.16b Wiring diagram (continued)

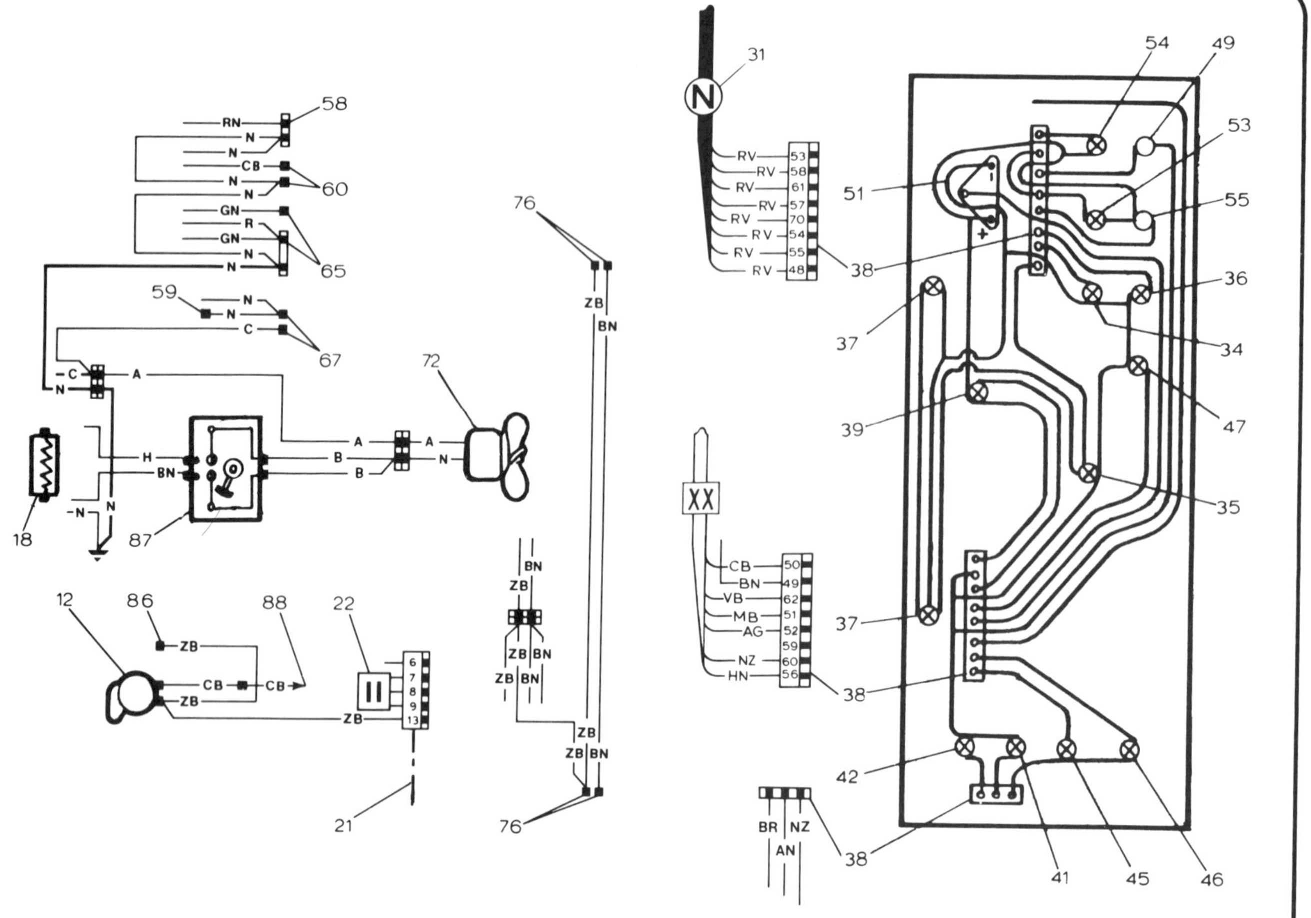

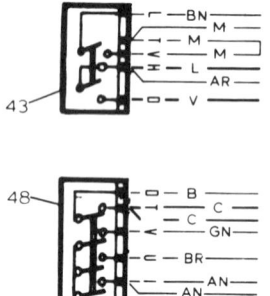

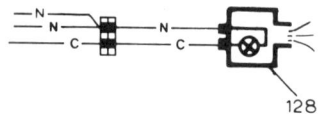

Central European Version

Variants with respect to CL Version

43 Lighting/panel light switch
48 Hazard warning switch (Where mandatory)

Additional Wiring - Illuminated Switches
128 Light guide cable lamp

Variants with respect to CL versions

12 Horns
18 Heater fan ballast resistor
21 Centralised connection unit as viewed from engine compartment
22 Standard wiring identification numbers
34 Headlamp w/l (1,2 W, w/b)
35 Side lamp w/l (1,2 W, w/b)
36 Rear fog lamp w/l (1,2 W, w/b)
37 Instrument panel lights (1,2 W. w/b)
38 Panel connectors
39 Engine coolant temperature w/l (1,2 W, w/b)
41 Direction indicator w/l (1,2 W, w/b)
42 Hazard w/l (1,2 W, w/b)
45 Oil pressure w/l (1,2 W, w/b)
46 Ignition w/l (3 W, w/b)
47 Heated rear screen w/l (1,2 W, w/b)
49 Warning light housing
51 Fuel gauge
53 Handbrake ON/low brake fluid level w/l (1,2 W, w/b)
54 Fuel w/l (1,2 W, w/b)
55 Warning light housing
58 Preset connection - Rear screen wiper switch
59 Preset cable - digital clock earth
60 Preset connection - Heated rear screen switch
61 Preset cables - Switches illumination light guide cable lamps
65 Preset cables: Cigar lighter
72 Heater fan
76 Preset cables: Rear interio lights
86 Preset cable for a second horn
87 Heater fan switch, two-position
88 To radiator fan terminal

Fig. 9.16c Wiring diagram (continued)

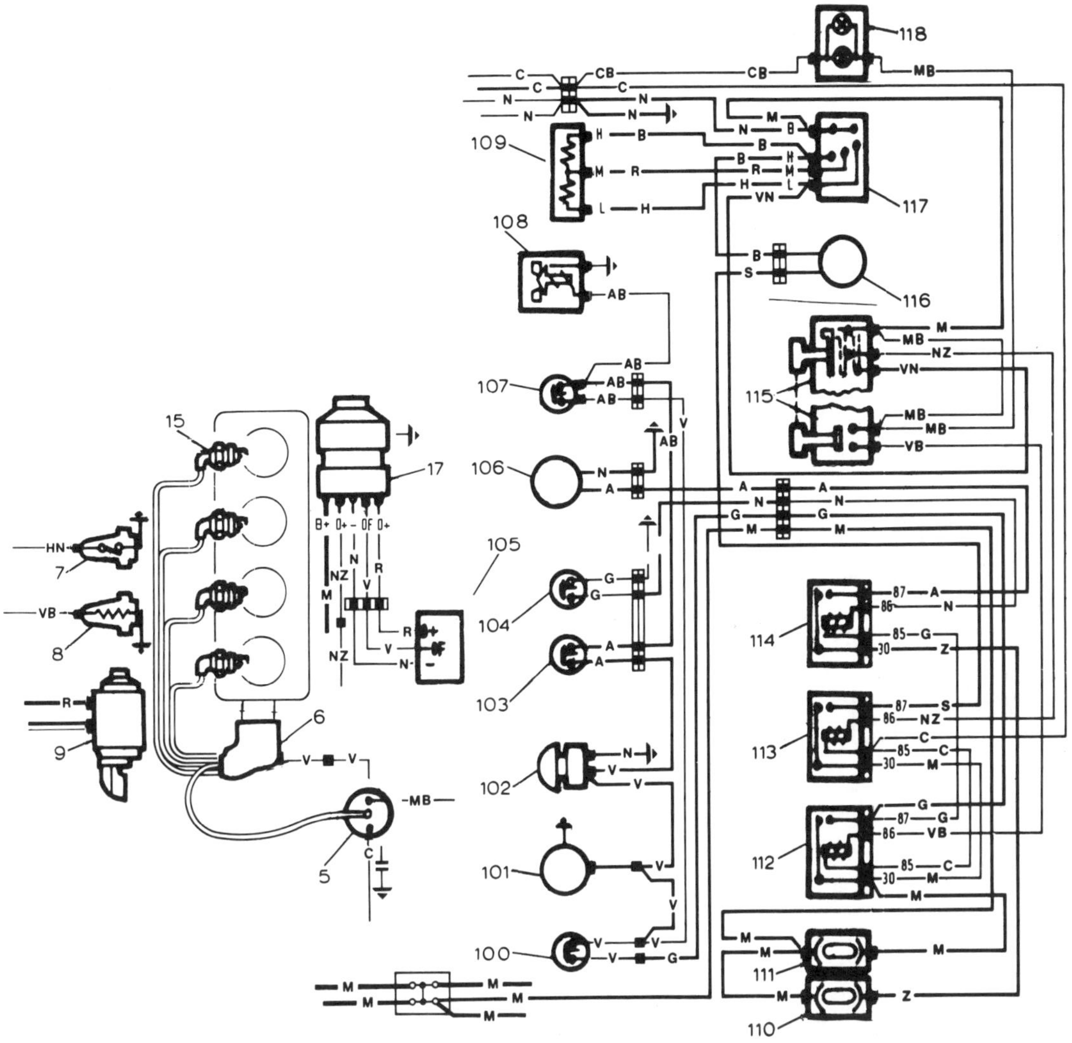

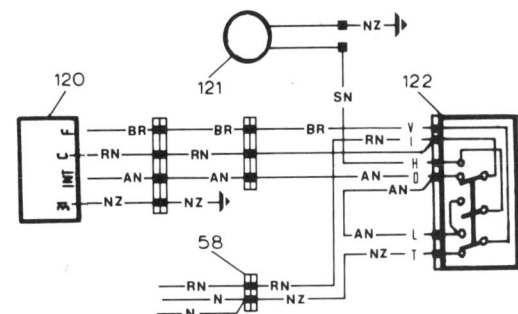

Additional Wiring - Air Conditioner

  5 Ignition coil
  6 Ignition distributor
  7 Oil pressure w/l transmitter
  8 Engine coolant temperature transmitter
  9 Starter motor
 15 Spark plugs
 17 Alternator
100 Cut-out switch
101 Compressor
102 Fast idle solenoid valve
103 Safety switch
104 Condenser cooling fan motor thermoswitch
105 Voltage regulator
106 Condenser cooling fan motor
107 Anti-frost valve thermoswitch
108 Anti-frost valve
109 Evaporator and heater motor speed selector resistor
110 Condenser motor fuse
111 Compressor fuse
112 Condenser relay
113 Evaporator relay
114 Condenser cooling fan relay
115 Conditioner control board
116 Evaporator fan motor
117 Evaporator and heater motor speed selector switch
118 Conditioner controls illumination lights (1,2 W, w/b)

Additional Wiring - Rear Screen Wiper

 58 Rear screen wiper connector
120 Screen wiper motor
121 Screen washer pump
122 Screen wiper motor switch

Fig. 9.16d Wiring diagram (continued)

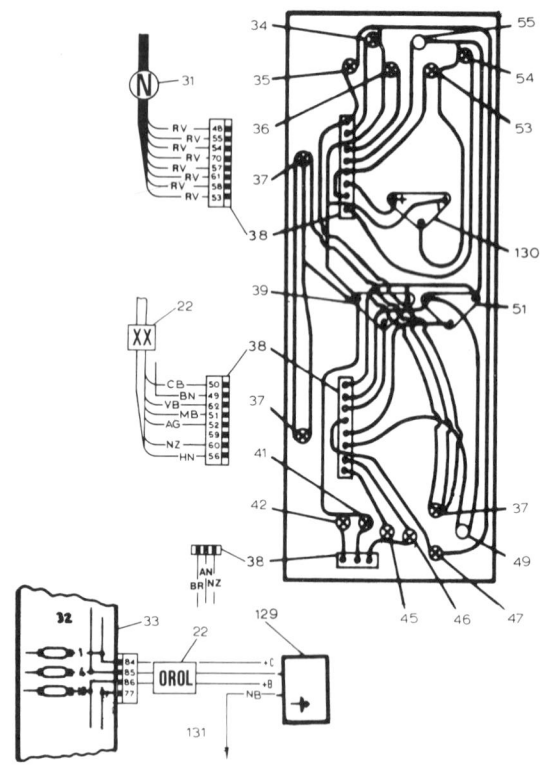

Additional Wiring - Tachometer and Digital Clock (CL versions)

22 Standard wiring identification numbers
31 Modular cable identification letters
32 Fuses
33 Centralised connection unit as viewed form passenger's compartment
34 Headlamp w/l (1,2 W, w/b)
35 Side lamp w/l (1,2 W, w/b)
36 Rear fog lamp w/l (1,2 W, w/b)
37 Instrument panel lights (1,2 W, w/b)
38 Panel connectors
39 Engine coolant temperature gauge
41 Direction indicator w/l (1,2 W, w/b)
42 Hazard w/l (1,2 W, w/b)
45 Oil pressure w/l (1,2 W, w/b)
46 Ignition w/l (1,2 W, w/b)
47 Heated rear screen w/l (1,2 W, w/b)
49 Warning light housing
51 Fuel gauge
53 Handbrake ON/low brake fluid level w/l (1,2 W, w/b)
55 Warning light housing
129 Digital clock
130 Electronic tachometer
131 To terminal 59
w/b = wedge-base

Additional Wiring - Automatic Gearbox (CL versions)

22 Standard wiring identification numbers
24 Starter relay
33 Centralised connection unit as viewed from passenger's compartment
126 Selector lever indicator light (3 W, w/b)
127 Starter/reverse inhibitor switch

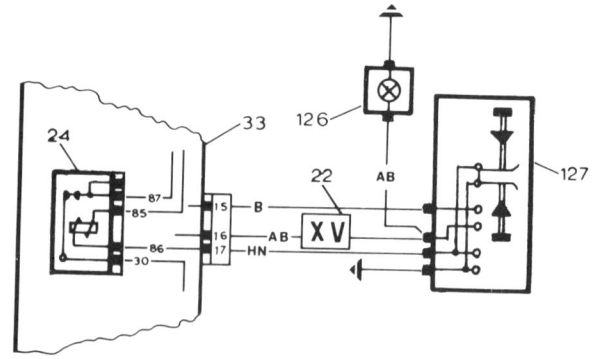

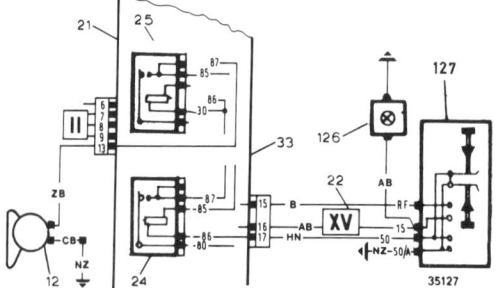

Additional Wiring - Automatic Gearbox (L versions)

12 Horn
21 Centralised connection unit as viewed from engine compartment
22 Standard wiring identification numbers
24 Starter relay
25 Horn relay
33 Centralised connection unit as viewed from passenger's compartment
126 Selector lever indicator light (3 W, w/b)
127 Starter/reverse inhibitor switch

Fig. 9.16e Wiring diagram (continued)

30 Fault diagnosis – electrical system

Note: *Electrical faults not dealt with below can usually be attributed to defects in current supply (blown fuse or defective relay, loose connections or broken wires) or earth return (loose or corroded mountings).*

Symptom	Reason/s
Starter motor fails to turn engine	Battery discharged Battery defective internally Battery terminal leads or earth strap loose or corroded Engine earth strap broken or insecure Loose or broken connections in starter motor circuit Starter motor switch or solenoid faulty Starter motor brushes worn, sticking, or brush wires loose Commutator dirty, worn, or burnt – insulators require undercutting Starter motor armature faulty Field coils earthed
Starter motor turns engine very slowly	Battery in discharged condition Starter motor brushes worn, sticking, or brush wires loose Loose wires in starter motor circuit Starter motor armature faulty
Starter motor operates without turning engine	Starter motor pinion sticking Pinion or flywheel gear teeth worn or broken
Starter motor noisy or excessively rough in engagement	Pinion or flywheel gear teeth worn or broken Starter motor retaining bolts loose
Battery will not hold charge	Electrolyte level too low Battery defective internally Electrolyte too weak (after spillage or leakage) Alternator drivebelt slipping Loose connections or broken wires in charging circuit Short circuit causing battery drain Alternator faulty
Ignition light fails to go out when engine running	Alternator drivebelt slipping or broken Fault in charging circuit Fault in alternator
Ignition light fails to come on with ignition on and engine stopped	Ignition light bulb blown Fault in bulb holder, printed circuit or wiring Alternator faulty
Fuel or temperature gauges give no reading	Wiring to gauges disconnected Fuel gauge tank unit faulty Temperature gauge transmitter faulty Wiring from transmitters to gauges broken or disconnected Gauges faulty Fuse blown
Fuel or temperature gauges give maximum readings all the time	Fuel gauge tank unit faulty Wiring from fuel gauge to tank unit earthed Wiring from temperature gauge to transmitter earthed Gauges faulty Temperature gauge transmitter faulty
Instrument readings increase with engine speed	Voltage stabilizer faulty
Lights do not come on	Light bulb filament burnt out Fuse blown Battery discharged Excessive corrosion on bulbs or bulb holders Wiring loose, disconnected or broken Light switch faulty
Light(s) very dim	Bulb or bulb holder not making good earth connection Incorrect bulb fitted Lamp glasses dirty Reflector tarnished or dirty Corroded or poor electrical connections
Wiper motor fails to work	Fuse blown Wiring loose, disconnected, or broken

Sympton	Reason/s
	Switch faulty
	Brushes worn
	Armature faulty
	Field coils faulty
Wiper motor works very slowly	Commutator dirty or burnt
	Armature faulty
	Brushes worn
	Armature bearings dry or misaligned
	Drive to wheelboxes bent or unlubricated
	Wheelboxes binding or damaged
Wiper motor works but blades remain static	Wheelboxes damaged or worn
	Wiper motor gearbox parts badly worn
	Wiper arms loose on spindles

Chapter 10 Steering

For modifications, and information applicable to later models, see Supplement at end of manual

Contents

Specifications

System type .... Rack and pinion with universally jointed column/shaft assembly

Steering wheel lock to lock .... 3.5 turns

Turning circle .... 10.3 m (33.8 ft)

Steering geometry
Steering angles of roadwheels on turns:
    Inner wheel .... 34° to 37°
    Outer wheel .... 31° 45'
Front wheel toe-out (unladen) .... 2.5 to 4.5 mm (0.10 to 0.18 in)
Castor (unladen) .... 1° 30' to 2° 40' positive
Camber (unladen) .... 1° 10' to 2° 10' positive
Front track:
    65 and North American models .... 1400 mm (55.12 in)
    75 models .... 1410 mm (55.51 in)

Lubricant capacity
Earlier models (oil) .... 0.25 Imp pints (0.31 US pints, 0.14 litres)
Later models (grease) .... 140 cc (0.14 litres)

Lubricant type/specification
Earlier models .... Hypoid gear oil, viscosity SAE 80W/90, to MIL-L-2105 C (Duckhams Hypoid 75W/90S)
Later models .... Lithium-based grease with molybdenum disulphide (FIAT K854)

Torque wrench settings

	lbf ft	Nm
Steering wheel nut	36	49
Steering column coupling pinch bolts	20	27
Steering gear mounting bolts	18	25
Tie-rod balljoint taper pin nut	25	34
Tie-rod end locknut	36	49
Column pressed steel mounting bracket bolts	6	8
Roadwheel bolt	63	86
Pinion bearing plate bolt	22	30
Rack damper cover plate bolt	22	30

1 General description

The steering gear is of rack and pinion type. The rack and pinion housing is bolted to the lower front face of the engine compartment rear bulkhead.

The steering column incorporates two universal joints to provide the most suitable steering wheel position and to ensure that, in the event of a front end collision, the steering column shaft will deflect sideways and not transmit end thrust to the steering wheel.

2 Steering gear – maintenance and inspection

1 At the intervals specified in 'Routine Maintenance', inspect the gaiters on the rack and pinion housing for splits and leakage of the lubricant. If evident, renew the gaiters and replenish the lubricant as described in Section 4.

2 Check the free movement (lost motion) at the steering wheel. If this is any more than fractional, the rack and pinion housing will have to be removed for adjustment or renewal (refer to Section 9) or the tie-

rod ends renewed (see Section 3).

3   The tie-rod ends can be checked for wear by having an assistant turn the steering wheel in each direction (without applying sufficient force to move the roadwheels) while the movement of each tie-rod balljoint is observed, relative to the steering arms (these are attached to the base of the suspension struts).

3   Tie-rod end balljoints – renewal

1   Wear the tie-rod end balljoints can only be overcome by renewal, no adjustment being possible. The balljoints are grease-sealed and require no attention during their life, except to check their dust excluding boots for splits at the specified inspection intervals.

2   Jack up the front of the car and remove the roadwheel from the side on which the balljoint is to be renewed.

3   Unscrew the tie-rod balljoint taper pin nut and, using a suitable extractor, separate the tie-rod balljoint from the eye of the steering arm.

4   Release the locknut on the tie-rod, unscrewing it only just enough to be able to unscrew the tie-rod end from the tie-rod.

5   With the tie-rod end removed, wire brush the threads on the tie-rod without disturbing the position of the locknut; apply grease to the threads and screw on the new tie-rod end until the locknut can be tightened by turning it through the same amount of rotation it was given when unscrewed.

6   Reconnect the balljoint taper pin to the eye of the steering arm and tighten the retaining nut to the specified torque. *Never grease the taper pin or eye;* the pin will otherwise turn when the nut is tightened. If a taper pin is inclined to rotate when a nut is being tightened, apply pressure to the socket of the joint to force the taper pin into closer contact with the tapered hole in the eye. If a taper pin is pointing downward, a strong lever can be used to apply the extra pressure. Where the taper pin of a balljoint points upward, a jack placed under the joint socket will produce the desired result.

7   Although the careful fitting of the new tie-rod end will have approximately maintained the original front wheel alignment of the car, manufacturing differences alone of the new component make it essential to check the setting, as described in Section 10, and to adjust if necessary.

4   Rack and pinion housing – oil leak rectification

1   If lubricant is found to be leaking from the gaiters (at the ends of the housing), first check that the gaiter clips are secure.

2   If the lubricant is leaking from the gaiter through a split, the gaiter can be removed in the following way, without the necessity of withdrawing the gear from the car.

3   Remove the tie-rod end from the side concerned, as described in the preceding Section.

4   Release the gaiter clips; draw the gaiter from the rack housing and off the tie-rod (photo).

5   If the gaiter has only just split, road dirt is unlikely to have entered and lubricant can be wiped away. If it is severely grit contaminated, the steering gear should be completely removed, the original lubricant flushed out and new lubricant pumped in.

6   If the gear does not have to be removed from the car, slide the new gaiter into position and secure it with the inboard clip.

7   If, on inspection, the lubricant used was found to be oil, place the nozzle of an oil can under the smaller diameter gaiter neck and pump in specified lubricant until the bellows of the gaiter can be felt to be about half filled. Remove the oil can and secure the outboard clip.

8   On later models, the steering gear lubricant was changed to grease, as a means of reducing the possibility of oil seal leakage. When recharging the gaiter with this type of lubricant, give full steering lock to the side being replenished so that the extended section of the rack will take the grease into the housing as it returns.

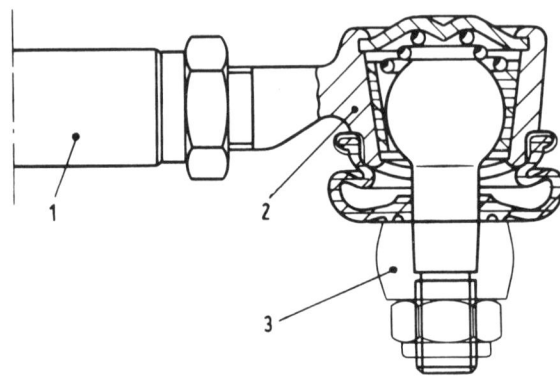

Fig. 10.1 Sectional view of typical balljoint (Sec 3)

1   Track rod   3   Steering arm
2   Balljoint socket

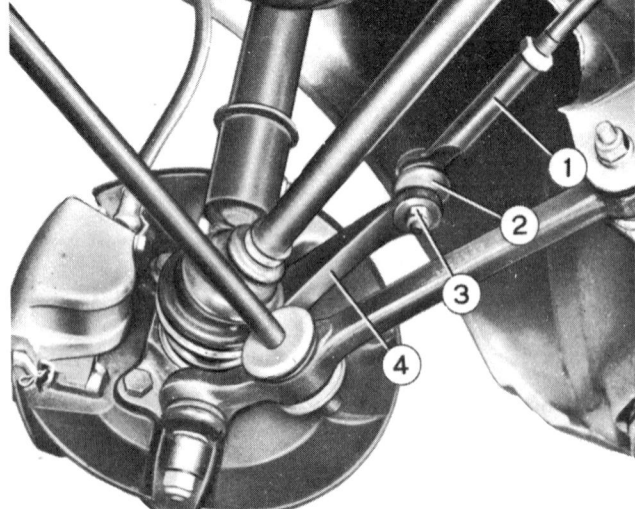

Fig. 10.2 Tie-rod attachment to steering arm (Sec 3)

1   Tie-rod end   3   Taper pin retaining
2   Dust excluding boot   nut
                                  4   Steering arm

4.4 Pinion end of steering rack housing

9 If the pinion oil seal is leaking, it can only be renewed if the steering gear is removed (see Section 8) and dismantled (see Section 9).

10 Reconnect the tie-rod end to the tie-rod and the eye of the steering arm. Provided the locknut is tightened by only rotating it through the same distance by which it was loosened, the front wheel alignment (tracking) should not have been unduly disturbed. Even so, check the alignment as described in Section 10.

5 Steering wheel – removal and refitting

1 Disconnect the battery negative lead.
2 Set the steering wheel and the front roadwheels in the straight-ahead attitude.
3 Prise out the horn button from the centre of the steering wheel.
4 Extract the two coil (horn contact) springs now exposed (photo).
5 Unscrew and remove the steering wheel securing nut, then pull the wheel from the column shaft. If it is tight on its splines, tap it upward at the wheel rim, using the palms of the hands.

6 Refitting is a reversal of the removal process; make sure that the spokes of the wheel are in the lower part of the wheel.
7 Tighten the securing nut to the specified torque.

6 Steering column – removal and refitting

1 Remove the steering wheel, as described in the preceding Section.
2 Remove the securing screws then withdraw the upper and lower sections of the steering column shroud (photo).
3 Disconnect the wiring harness connector plugs at the sides of the steering column.
4 Unbolt the steering column pressed steel bracket and lower the column down to rest on the front seat (photo).
5 Working between the accelerator and brake pedals, extract the pinch bolt and pull the coupling from the splines of the pinion shaft of the steering gear. If the coupling is tight, open its jaws slightly with a screwdriver.

Fig. 10.3 Using a puller to separate a balljoint from a steering arm (Sec 3)

| 1 | Tie-rod end | 3 | Steering arm |
| 2 | Puller | | |

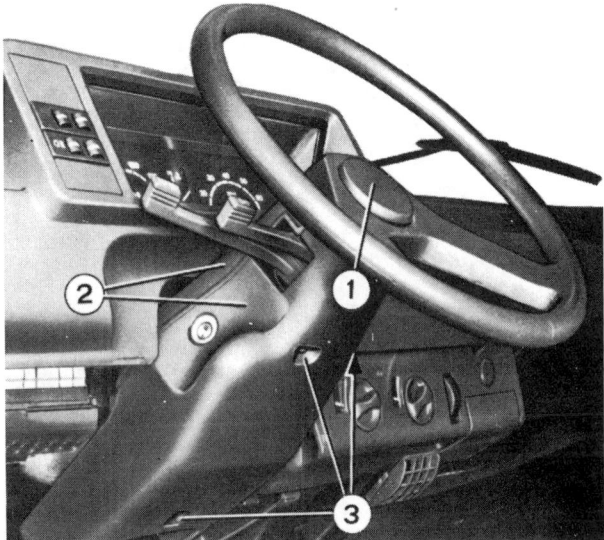

Fig. 10.4 Steering wheel detail (LHD shown) (Sec 5)

| 1 | Horn button | 3 | Shroud retaining screws |
| 2 | Column shrouds | | |

5.4 Horn button and contact springs

Fig. 10.5 Steering wheel attachment (LHD shown) (Sec 5)

| 1 | Securing nut | 3 | Steering wheel |
| 2 | Column shaft | 4 | Horn contact springs |

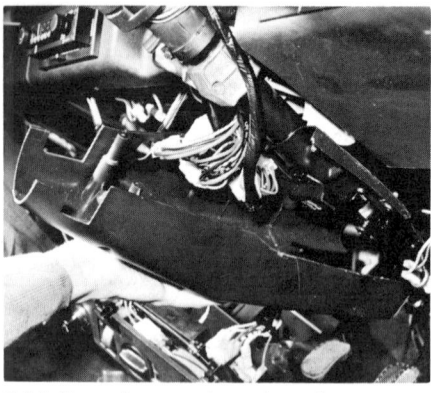
6.2A Removing steering column lower shroud

6.2B Removing steering column upper shroud

6.4 Steering column mounting bracket

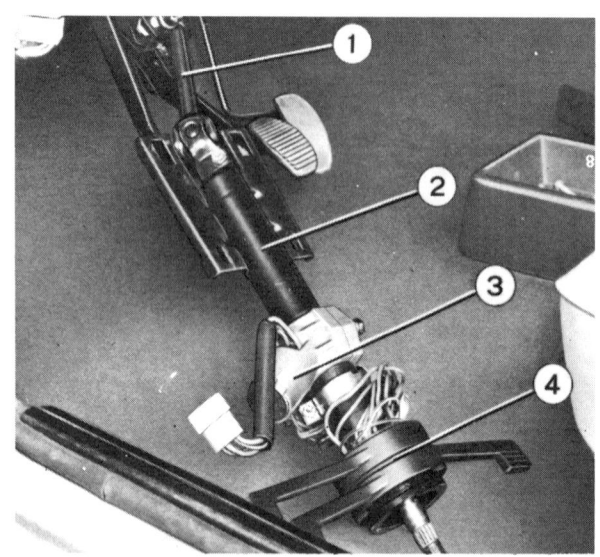

Fig. 10.6 Upper section of steering column lowered from facia panel (LHD shown) (Sec 6)

1   Lower universally jointed shaft
2   Column tube and upper bracket
3   Ignition switch/steering lock
4   Combination switches

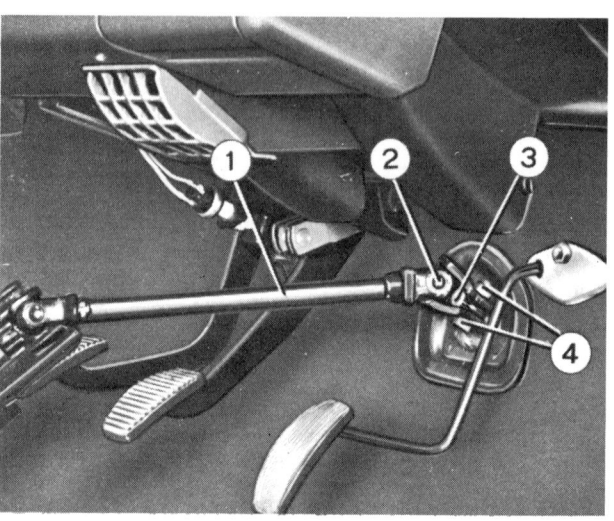

Fig. 10.7 Steering column shaft (LHD shown) (Sec 6)

1   Universally jointed shaft
2   Lower universal joint
3   Steering gear splined pinion shaft
4   Coupling pinch bolt

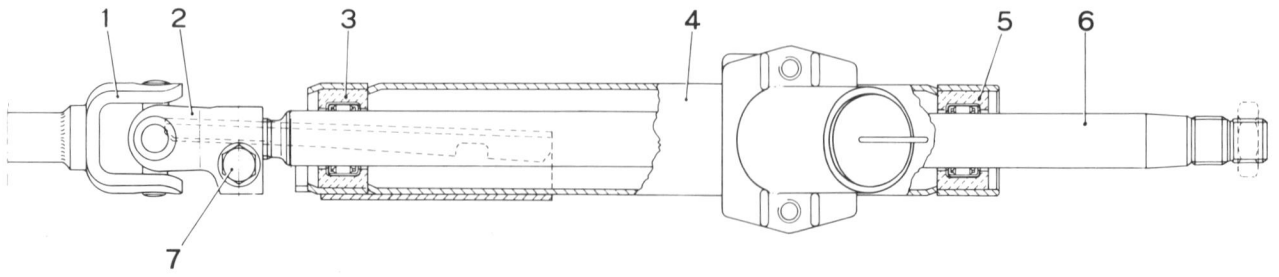

Fig. 10.8 Cutaway view of steering column (Sec 7)

1   Universal joint yoke   3   Lower bearing   5   Upper bearing   7   Pinch bolt
2   Coupling   4   Column tube   6   Steering shaft

6   Withdraw the column assembly from the car.

7   Refitting is a reversal of the removal process, but make sure that the front roadwheels have not been moved from their straight-ahead position.

8   Refit the upper mounting bracket after the bottom end of the column has been reconnected; try to position the bracket so that the retaining bolts and washers are tightened into their original, scored marks on the bracket. This will ensure that the universally jointed section of the column shaft maintains its originally fitted attitude. **Note**: *Do not tighten beyond the specified torque.*

7   Steering column – overhaul

1   With the column/shaft removed from the car, as described in the preceding Section, first withdraw the combination switches as described in Chapter 9, Section 17.

2   If the reason for overhaul is to renew the column bearings, insert the ignition key and turn it to release the steering column lock.

3   The bearing retaining staking at the ends of the column tube will have to be relieved and the shaft then pushed backwards and forwards to eject the bearings.

4   To remove the lower bearings, the coupling pinch bolt will have to be extracted and the universally jointed section of the shaft disconnected.

5   Apply grease to the bearings; tap them into position (until they seat against the crimped stops in the column tube), then stake over the ends of the tube.

Fig. 10.9 Steering gear location (LHD shown) (Sec 8)

1   *Mounting bolts*   3   *Pinion shaft*
2   *Rack and pinion housing* 4   *Mounting brackets*

6   Reassembly and refitting are reversals of the removal and dismantling sequences. Note that the splined couplings must be correctly located on their shafts before the pinch bolt can be passed through the groove in the shaft. Never hammer the bolt to drive it through – readjust the coupling position by sliding it slightly up or down the shaft.

8   Steering gear – removal and refitting

1   Raise the front of the car and support it securely.

2   Remove the roadwheels.

3   Unscrew the nut which holds each tie-rod end balljoint to the eye of the steering arm.

4   Working within the car, centralise the steering wheel so that the roadwheels, if fitted, would be in the straight-ahead position. Mark the relationship of the column lower coupling to the splined pinion, then unscrew and remove the coupling pinch bolt.

5   Working within the engine compartment, unbolt and remove the rubber insulated clamps which hold the steering gear to the rear bulkhead.

6   Support the steering gear and withdraw it first downward from the bulkhead (to draw the splined pinion from the column coupling), then remove it sideways from under one of the wheel arches.

7   Refitting is a reversal of the removal process; be sure to align the pinion shaft and column coupling marks, otherwise the position of the steering wheel in the straight-ahead attitude will be altered.

9   Steering gear – overhaul and adjustment

1   If anything more than renewal of the pinion shaft oil seal or gaiters (see Section 4) or adjustment of the gear is required, a new, complete assembly will have to be purchased; individual components are not supplied.

2   With the steering gear removed, clean away external dirt then grip the pinion housing flats in the jaws of a vice fitted with soft metal protectors.

Pinion – oil seal renewal and bearing adjustment

3   Unscrew and remove the bolts, then take off the pinion bearing plate from the housing.

4   Drive the old seal from the plate and press a new one squarely into position.

5   It is possible that the original shims are still providing the correct adjustment, but it is recommended that the following check is carried out.

6   Fit the bearing plate without a gasket and having screwed in the retaining bolts only finger tight.

7   Using feeler blades, measure the gap (which we will call measurement B) between the plate and the housing.

8   Measure the thickness (which we will call measurement A) of a new gasket using a micrometer or similar thickness gauge.

9   Subtract the thickness (A) of the gasket from the plate-to-housing gap (B). Shims should now be fitted thicker in total by between 0.025 and 0.13 mm (0.001 and 0.005 in) than the calculated result (B minus

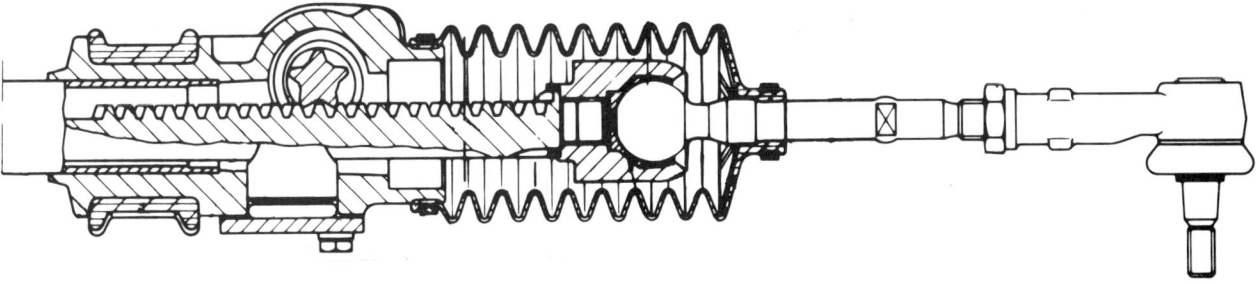

Fig. 10.10 Cutaway view of pinion end of steering gear (Sec 9)

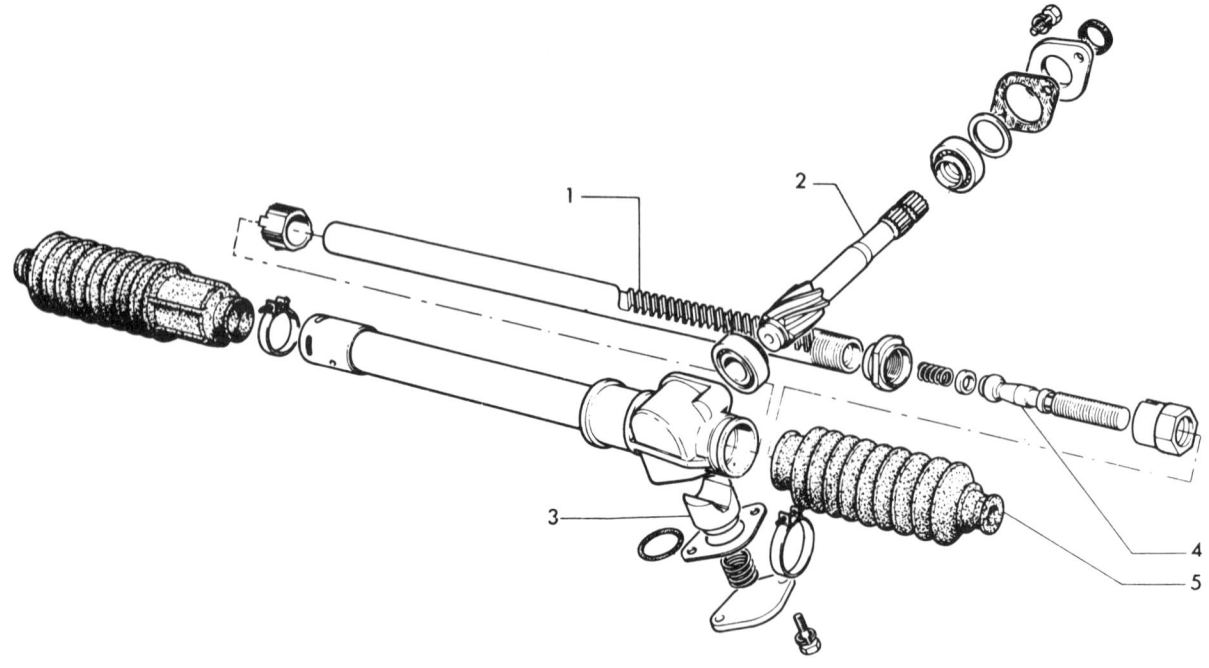

Fig. 10.11 Exploded view of the steering gear (LHD shown) (Sec 9)

1	Rack	3	Rack damper	5	Gaiter
2	Pinion shaft	4	Tie-rod ball-pin		

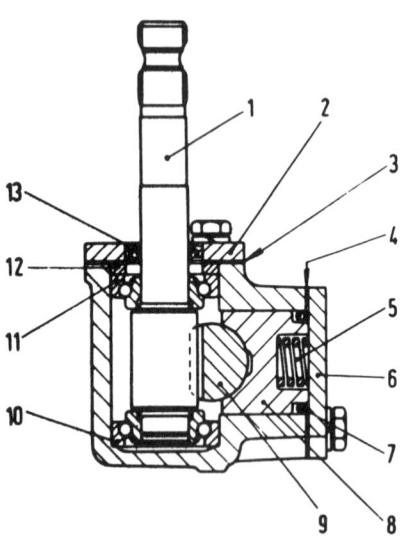

Fig. 10.12 Sectional view of pinion/damper housing (Sec 9)

1	Pinion shaft	8	Slipper
2	Cover plate	9	Rack
3	Gasket	10	Pinion lower bearing
4	Rack damper adjusting	11	Pinion upper bearing
	shims	12	Pinion bearing adjusting
5	Spring		shims
6	Damper cover plate	13	Oil seal
7	Seal		

A). Shims are available in thicknesses of 0.12, 0.20, 0.25 and 0.50 mm (0.005, 0.008, 0.010 and 0.020 in).

10 Fit the shims, the gasket, bearing plate and bolts. If the adjustment is correct, the pinion should turn smoothly, without stiffness or endfloat.

Rack damper – adjustment

11 The slipper in the rack housing presses the rack into mesh with the pinion. This cuts out any backlash between the gears. Also, due to its pressure, it introduces some stiffness into the rack, which cuts out excessive reaction from the road to the steering wheel.

12 In due course, wear reduces the pressures exerted by the slipper. The pressure is controlled by the cover plate and a spring.

13 The need for resetting of the slipper if the car has run a long mileage, but the rack is not being dismantled, is not easy to detect. On bumpy roads, the shock induced through the steering will give a feeling of play, and sometimes faint clonking can be heard. In extreme cases, free play in the steering may be felt, though this is rare. If the steering is compared with that of a new rack on another car, the lack of friction damping is quite apparent in the ease of movement of the steering wheel of the worn one.

14 Centralise the steering rack.

15 Take the cover plate off the damping slipper, remove the spring and shims, and refit it. Refit the bolts, but only tighten them enough to hold the slipper firmly against the rack.

16 Turn the pinion through 180° either way to settle the rack.

17 Measure the gap between the cover plate and the rack housing.

18 Select shims to a thickness of 0.5 to 0.13 mm (0.02 to 0.005 in) more than the measured gap. (Shims are available in 0.10 and 0.15 mm (0.004 and 0.006 in) thicknesses).

19 Remove the cover plate again, and refit the spring.

20 Smear each shim with soft setting gasket compound, and fit them and the cover plate.

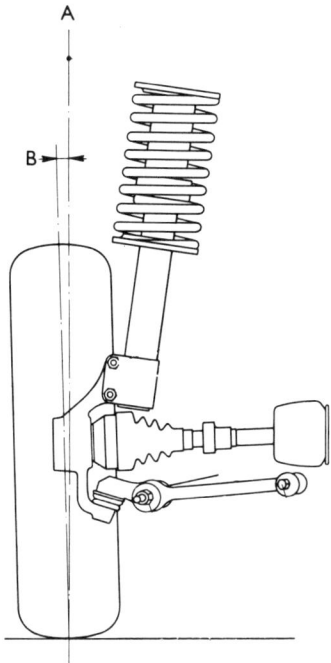

Fig. 10.13 Camber angle diagram (Sec 10)

A   Vertical   B   Camber angle (positive)

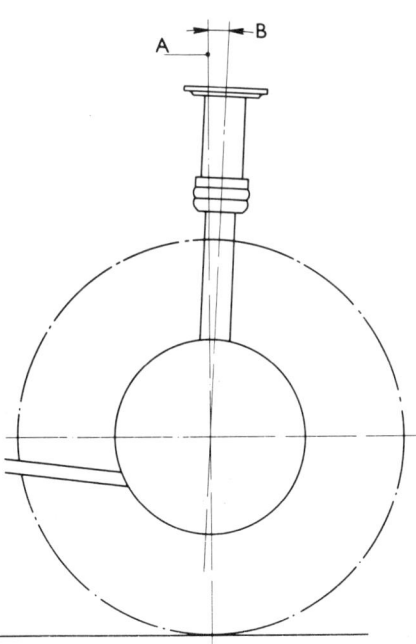

Fig. 10.14 Castor angle diagram (Sec 10)

A   Vertical   B   Castor angle (positive)

Lubricant

21 After any disturbance of the pinion bearing plate or rack damper assembly, lubricant which may have ben lost should be replenished (making sure that the rack housing is not over-filled).

22 On earlier models, the lubricant used is oil; on later versions, grease. It is recommended that at the time of overhaul or adjustment, if oil is being used, the opportunity is taken to drain the lubricant and refill with specified grease.

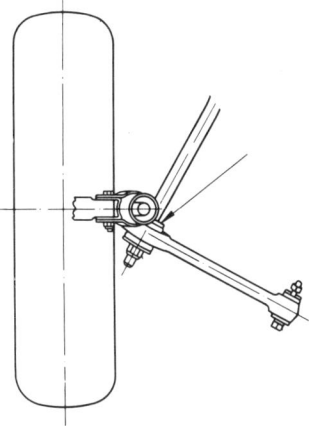

Fig. 10.15 Location of castor adjusting shims (Sec 10)

23 Lubricant is best drained or injected into the rack housing after removal of the rack damper components.
24 Do not exceed the specified quantity of 140 cc (0.14 litres).

10 Front wheel alignment and steering angles

1   Accurate front wheel alignment is essential for good steering and slow tyre wear. Before considering the steering angle check that the tyres are correctly inflated, that the front wheels are not buckled, the hub bearings are not worn or incorrectly adjusted and that the steering linkage is in good order, without slackness or wear at the joints or suspension bushes.
2   Wheel alignment consists of four factors:
Camber is the angle at which the front wheels are set from the vertical, when viewed from the front of the car. Positive camber is the amount (in degrees) that the wheels are tilted outwards at the top from the vertical. The camber angle is set in production and is not adjustable. It can alter, however, if the inboard bushes on the track control arm become grossly worn or are damaged as a result of collision damage to the front end of the car.
Castor is the angle between the steering axis and a vertical line, when viewed from each side of the car. The angle is adjustable by varying the number of shims fitted to the radius rod (or to the anti-roll bar models with automatic transmission). Due to the need for special equipment, measuring the castor angle is not within the scope of the home mechanic.
Steering axis inclination is the angle, when viewed from the front of the car, between the vertical and an imaginary line drawn between the upper and lower suspension leg pivots.
Toe-out is the amount by which the distance between the inner rims at the front of the roadwheels (measured at hub height) is more than the diametrically opposite distance measured between the inner rims at the rear of the roadwheels.
3   Front wheel alignment checks (toe-out on the Strada) are best carried out with modern setting equipment, but a reasonably accurate alternative and adjustment procedure is as follows:
4   Place the car on level ground with the wheels in the straight-ahead position.
5   Obtain or make a tracking gauge. One may be easily made from tubing, cranked to clear the sump and bellhousing, having an adjustable nut and setscrew at one end.
6   With the gauge, measure the distance between the two inner rims of the front roadwheels, at hub height and at the rear of the wheels.
7   Push the vehicle so that the roadwheel turns through half a turn (180°). Measure the distance between the two inner rims at hub height at the front of the wheel. This last measurement should be more than the first by the specified toe-out (see Specifications Section).
8   Where the toe-out is found to be incorrect, slacken the locknuts on each outer tie-rod and rotate each tie-rod an equal amount until the correct toe-out is obtained.

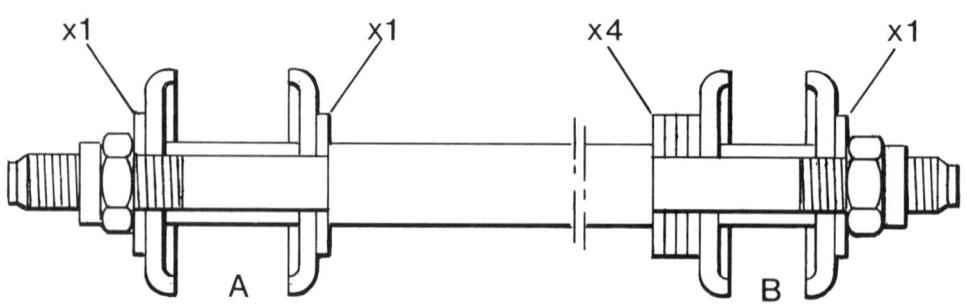

Fig. 10.16 Location of castor adjusting shims on later 65 models.
Numbers indicate maximum shims (Sec 10)

A   Track control arm side
B   Body bracket side

H.15041

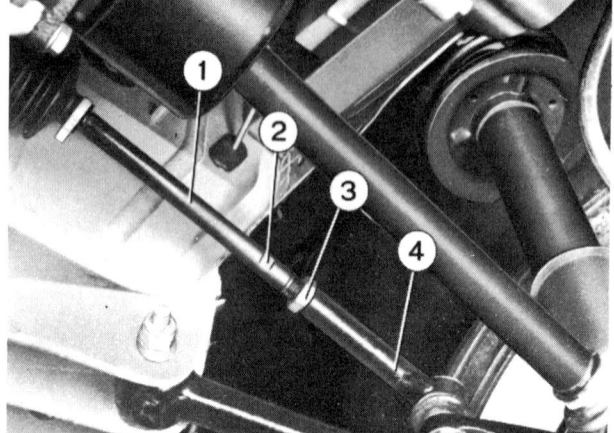

Fig. 10.17 Tie-rod, showing flats for open-ended spanner (Sec 10)

1	Tie-rod	3	Locknut
2	Flat	4	Tie-rod end

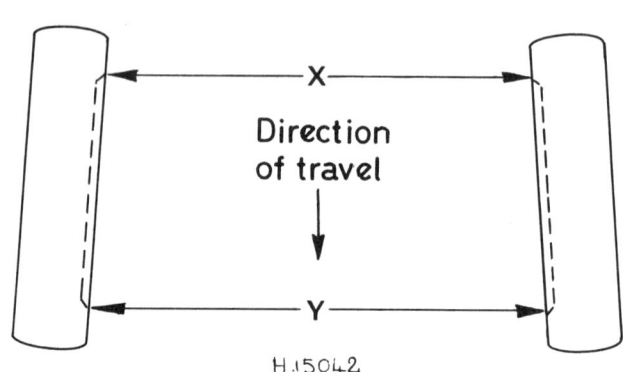

Fig. 10.18 Front wheel alignment diagram (Sec 10)

X   Rear dimension
Y   Front dimension
X minus Y = Toe-out

9   Tighten the locknuts, at the same time holding the tie-rod stationary using an open-ended spanner on the flats provided.

10   It is important to keep the length of the tie-rods equal, otherwise the position of the steering wheel spokes will alter and the angle of the roadwheels will be incorrect on turns – this will cause scrubbing of the tyre treads. If new tie-rod ends have been fitted (or the tie-rods have been incorrectly set by a previous owner), start the checking and

adjustment operation after the tie-rods have been set to equal lengths. Measure between the balljoint centres and the edge of the flat on the tie-rod.

11   When adjustment is correct, check that rotation of the tie-rod has not caused the steering gear housing gaiter to twist.

12   Refer to Chapter 11 for details of rear wheel alignment and suspension angles.

11 Fault diagnosis – steering

Note: *Before diagnosing steering faults, be sure that trouble is not due to incorrect or uneven tyre pressures, inappropriate tyre combinations, or braking system or suspension defects*

Symptom	Reason/s
Car pulls to one side	Incorrect steering geometry Collision damage
Car wanders when driven straight-ahead	Play in steering gear Wear in steering balljoints
Heavy or stiff steering	Lack of lubricant in steering gear or balljoints Incorrect steering geometry Collision damage
Play at steering wheel	Wear in steering rack or balljoints Loose steering shaft coupling pinch-bolt or worn splines Worn steering column/shaft universal joints
Vibration at steering wheel	Roadwheels out of balance or loose Tyre damage Loose driveshaft-to-hub nuts
Rattles from steering when traversing rough surfaces	Steering damper defective or in need of adjustment Loose steering column mounting bolts Loose steering column/shaft coupling pinch-bolts Loose steering rack housing mounting bolts Worn steering column bearings
Excessive or uneven tyre wear	Incorrect steering geometry Worn steering components Collision damage

Chapter 11 Suspension

For modifications, and information applicable to later models, see Supplement at end of manual

Contents

Specifications

Front suspension

Type	Independent, MacPherson strut. Anti-roll bar fitted to models with automatic transmission.
Castor, camber and toe-in	Refer to Specifications in Chapter 10
Coil spring grading	Yellow or green. Always fit as colour matched pairs

Rear suspension

Type	Independent, hydraulic strut with transverse leaf spring and lower wishbone arm.
Camber (unladen)	+0°30' to +1°30'
Toe-in	0 to 4.0 mm (0 to 0.16 in)

Roadwheels

Type	Pressed steel, bolt on
Size:	
All except North American models	4.5J x 13
North American models	4.5B x 13

Tyres

Type	Radial ply, tubeless
Size:	
L and North American models	145SR–13
CL models	165/70 SR–13

Tyre pressures, cold, in bar (lbf/in^2):	Front	Rear
UK models, normal load	1.9 (28)	1.8 (26)
UK models, full load	1.9 (28)	2.1 (30)
North American models, all conditions	2.2 (32)	2.2 (32)

Torque wrench settings

Front suspension	lbf ft	Nm
Hub nut	160	216
Track control arm pivot nut	30	40
Radius rod-to-track control arm nut	50	68
Track control arm balljoint nut	40	54
Strut-to-steering knuckle pinch bolt	43	58
Strut upper mounting nut	25	34
Strut piston nut	22	30
Radius rod-to-body bracket	36	49

Rear suspension		
Hub nut	160	216
Leaf spring rubber buffer anchor plate nut	22	30
Wishbone-to-hub nut	57	78

Wishbone inner pivot-to-body nut	36	49
Wishbone inner pivot nuts	30	40
Leaf spring guide pin nut	24	33
Strut-to-hub carrier nut	43	58
Strut upper mounting nut	18	24

Roadwheels

Roadwheel bolts	63	86

1 General description and inspection

Both the front and rear suspension systems are of independent type.

The front suspension comprises MacPherson type struts, hydraulically damped with coil springs. The steering knuckle is bolted to the base of the strut, and located by a track control arm and a radius rod on all but automatic transmission models – here an anti-roll bar is used instead of radius rods.

The rear suspension also comprises hydraulic type struts combined with a transversely mounted leaf spring (photo). The base of the rear suspension strut is located by a wishbone which also provides an anchorage for the leaf spring.

The roadwheels are of pressed steel construction and radial ply tyres are fitted.

Inspection

At the intervals specified in 'Routine Maintenance', carry out the following work.

1   Check each suspension strut for leaking hydraulic fluid. Check their damping efficiency by bouncing the car up and down. If the car continues to oscillate for two or three seconds after this, the struts have failed and a more detailed investigation will have to be undertaken of each individual strut (refer to the next Section).

2   With the car parked on level ground, check that it sits level from left to right, and does not appear to be drooping at one end, particularly down at the back.

3   Examine all the rubber bushes of the suspension arms and rear spring mountings. The rubber should be firm, not softened by oil or cracked by weathering. The pin pivoted in the bush should be held central, and not able to make metal-to-metal contact.

4   Check the outside of the springs. If rusting, they should be sprayed with oil.

5   Check the transverse rear leaf spring for cracks at the edges of the leaves.

6   Check the tightness of all nuts, particularly those holding the front suspension strut to the steering knuckle.

7   Grip the top of each wheel, in turn, and rock vigorously. Any looseness in the bearings, or the suspension can be felt, or failed rubber bushes giving metal-to-metal contact heard.

8   Check the front wheel alignment (see Chapter 10) and the rear wheel alignment, (see Section 10 of this Chapter) at the intervals specified in 'Routine Maintenance'.

2 Front suspension strut – removal and refitting

1   Jack up the front of the car and remove the roadwheel.

2   Compress the coil spring on the strut, using the adjustable clamps readily available at most motor accessory stores.

3   Support the base of the steering knuckle on a second jack, then unbolt the mounting nuts which hold the top of the suspension strut to the wing valance under the bonnet.

4   Unscrew and remove the two pinch bolts which secure the steering knuckle to the base of the strut. Push the strut inward and draw it out from under the wing.

5   If the strut is to be dismantled, unscrew and remove the centre nut from the top of the piston rod. Take off the upper mounting components.

6   Carefully, unscrew the coil spring clamps until the tension on the spring is released. Then take off the spring.

7   If the suspension leg is leaking hydraulic fluid or if, by pushing and pulling the piston rod, the damping resistance is found to be weak or jerky, the leg will have to be replaced by a new assembly. It may be

1.0 One side of rear suspension

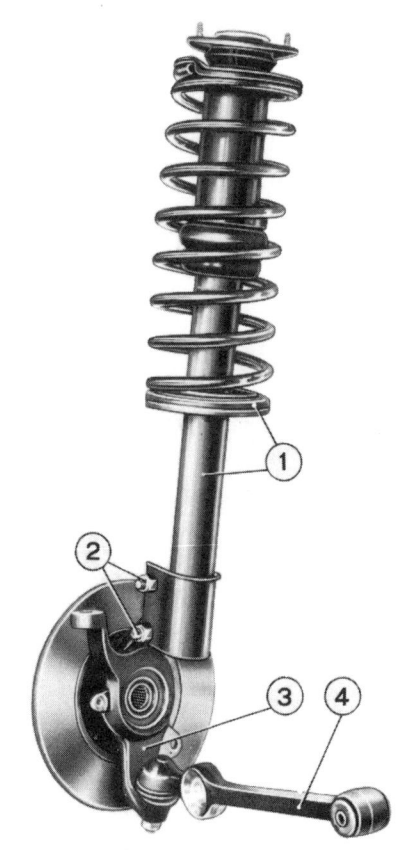

Fig. 11.1 Typical front suspension strut (Sec 2)

1	*Strut assembly*	*3* *Steering knuckle*
2	*Pinch bolts*	*4* *Track control arm*

Fig. 11.2 Suspension strut upper mounting (Sec 2)

possible to obtain a rebuilt unit or a cartridge insert, to be fitted by following the particular manufacturer's instructions.

8 The original coil spring can be refitted unless this too has weakened or is broken. In this case, unless a spring with the same colour marking as the original can be obtained, both front springs will have to be renewed with a colour matched pair.

9 Reassembly and refitting of the strut to the car is a reversal of the dismantling and removal sequences respectively; pack the upper thrust bearing with grease.

3   Front track control arm – removal and refitting

65 models

1 Raise the front of the car and support it securely on axle stands.

2 Remove the roadwheel.

3 Have an assistant apply the footbrake fully whilst you unscrew and remove the driveshaft-to-hub nut.

4 Unbolt the caliper and tie it up, out of the way.

5 Using a suitable balljoint separator, disconnect the tie-rod end from the eye of the steering arm.

6 Unbolt the radius rod from the body attachment bracket.

7 Unscrew and remove the pinch bolts which hold the steering knuckle to the base of the suspension strut. Lower the steering knuckle from the strut.

8 Unscrew and remove the pivot bolt from the inboard end of the track control arm.

9 Without disconnecting the inboard end of the driveshaft, press or tap the driveshaft from the hub as the latter is pulled outwards.

10 Detach the radius rod from the track control arm, noting carefully the number and location of the castor setting shims.

11 Remove the nut which retains the track control arm balljoint to the steering knuckle and, using a suitable extractor, separate the balljoint from the steering knuckle.

75 and North American models

12 Raise the front of the car and remove the roadwheel.

13 Disconnect the driveshaft at its inboard flange and then, with an assistant fully applying the footbrake, unscrew and remove the driveshaft-to-hub nut.

14 Tap or press the driveshaft from the hub.

15 On cars with manual transmission, unbolt the radius rod bracket from the bodyframe.

16 On cars with automatic transmission (which have an anti-roll bar instead of radius rods), unbolt the clamps from the body.

17 Unscrew and remove the nut which holds the end of the radius rod or anti-roll bar to the track control arm. Note carefully the location and number of castor setting shims, then pull the rod or bar from the track control arm.

2.8 Front coil spring correctly located in lower seat

4.1 Radius rod body attachment bracket

18 Unscrew the nut which retains the track control arm balljoint to the steering knuckle and, using a suitable extractor, separate the balljoint from the steering knuckle.

19 Unscrew the pivot bolt from the inboard end of the track control arm and remove the arm from the car.

All models

20 If the balljoint or bushes are worn, renew the control arm as an assembly.

21 Refitting the track control arm is a reversal of the removal process, according to model and transmission. Tighten all nuts and bolts to the specified torque. Use a new driveshaft-to-hub nut.

---

4 Front suspension radius rod – removal and refitting

1 To remove a radius rod from all models equipped with manual transmission, unbolt the radius rod from the body attachment bracket (photo).

2 Note the location and number of the castor setting shims at the front end of the rod, then unscrew the nut and withdraw the rod from the track control arm (photo).

3 Refer to Chapter 10, Section 10, for further details of steering angles and adjustment.

4 Refitting is a reversal of the removal process.

---

5 Front anti-roll bar – removal and refitting

1 To remove the anti-roll bar (fitted only to models having automatic transmission), note the location and number of shims fitted at the ends of the car where it connects with the track control arm, then unscrew and remove the nuts from the ends of the bar.

2 Unbolt the clamps and rubber insulators which hold the anti-roll bar to the body and pull the bar from the track control arms.

3 Refitting is a reversal of the removal process; tighten all bolts to the specified torque when the weight of the car is on its roadwheels.

---

6 Front hub/steering knuckle – removal, overhaul and refitting

65 models

1 Remove the hub/knuckle as described in Section 3, paragraphs 1 to 11.

2 Unbolt and remove the brake disc.

75 and North American models

3 Raise the front of the car and remove the roadwheel.

4 Remove the driveshaft as described in Section 3, paragraphs 13 and 14.

5 Carry out the operations then described in Section 3, paragraphs 15 to 18.

6 Using a balljoint extractor, disconnect the tie-rod end from the steering arm on the steering knuckle.

7 Remove the pinch bolts at the base of the suspension strut, tap the steering knuckle downward and remove it complete with hub and disc.

8 Unbolt and remove the brake disc.

All models

9 Normally the front wheels should be silent, have neglible rim-rock, and turn smoothly. Incipient failure of the bearings will show by any of these signs. The bearings are sealed for life. They are a press fit in the hub, and need such force to extract them that this should only be done to replace them, as they will be overloaded by the stress.

10 Now the hub must be pressed out of the bearings. It is a tight fit, and may have rusted in. A good soak in penetrating oil will help. The steering knuckle must be well supported whilst the hub is pressed from the inside. The press mandrel must only rest on the hub, not the bearing inner race. Again, the help of a FIAT agent is recommended, as they have the special press tools.

11 Once the hub is out, the bearing ring nut on the outside can be reached. This is screwed in, and should have been staked in position with a punch. The staking should be cut away, and the ring nut unscrewed.

4.2 Outboard end of front suspension track control arm

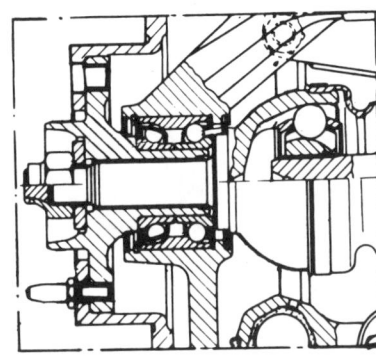

Fig. 11.3 Part sectional view of steering knuckle (Sec 6)

12 A press will be needed to remove the bearings from the steering knuckle and once subjected to the force of a press they will be destroyed and cannot be used again.

13 Clean away all rust from the bearing recess and press in the new bearings.

14 Use a new ring nut and, when fully tightened, stake it in position.

15 Press the hub into the steering knuckle.

16 Refit the steering knuckle, suspension and driveshaft components, according to model, by reversing the removal operations.

---

7 Rear leaf spring – removal and refitting

1 Raise the rear of the car and support it securely on axle stands (or blocks placed under the sill jacking points) so that the roadwheels hang free.

2 Remove the roadwheels.

3 Disconnect the torsion bar of the brake pressure regulating valve from its connecting link to the suspension wishbone (refer to Chapter 8).

4 Place a hydraulic jack under the outer end of the spring and raise the jack just enough to relieve the tension in the spring. Take care to prevent the jack slipping along the spring leaf; tilt the jack and place a rubber disc between the jack and the spring to provide some measure of resistance against slipping.

5 Unscrew the nuts and remove the anchor plate with rubber buffer from the underside of the wishbone.

6 Carefully, lower the jack and place it under the opposite end of the leaf spring; remove the anchor plate with rubber buffer from that end.

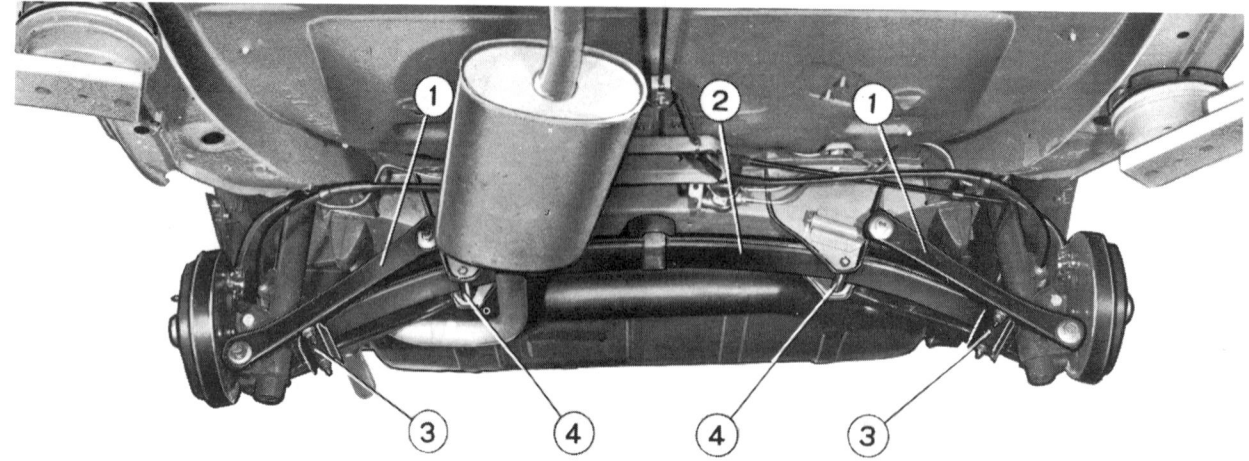

Fig. 11.4 Rear leaf spring and attachment points (Sec 7)

1	Wishbone arm	3	Rubber buffer and anchor plate
2	Leaf spring	4	Guide pin

8.2 Rear hub dust cap

7   Remove the spring guide pin from the side under which the jack is positioned then, very carefully, lower the jack.
8   Jack up the end of the spring which was first released and remove the guide pin. Again, lower the jack gradually until the tension is completely off the spring, then lift the spring from the car.
9   Refit the spring by reversing the removal operations.

8 Rear hub – removal, overhaul and refitting

1   Jack up the rear of the car and remove the roadwheel.
2   Tap off the hub dust cap (photo).
3   With a long knuckle bar and a socket, unscrew and remove the hub nut.
4   Remove the brake drum.
5   A slide hammer must now be bolted to the hub flange to remove the hub.
6   The hub and bearing are only supplied as a complete assembly.
7   Tap the hub/bearing onto the stub axle, applying pressure only to the bearing inner track.
8   Fit a new hub nut and tighten it to the specified torque. Fit the brake drum and the dust cap. If a suitably calibrated torque wrench is not available to tighten the hub nut, use a knuckle bar of 457 mm (18

in) in length with a socket attached. If full hand pressure is given, the nut will be tightened to a torque very near that specified.

9 Rear suspension – removal, dismantling and refitting

1   If attention is required to the hydraulic suspension strut or to the suspension wishbone, it is recommended that that particular side of the suspension be removed complete and dismantled on the bench.
2   Raise the rear of the car and support it securely on axle stands, placed under the sill jacking points.
3   Remove the roadwheel.
4   Disconnect the handbrake cable from the lever on the backplate, by extracting the split pin and the clevis pin.
5   Disconnect the torsion bar from the link which, in turn, actuates the brake pressure regulator valve.
6   Disconnect the brake hydraulic line and plug the open lines. The disconnection is best carried out at the T-union near to the pressure regulating valve. Release any clips which retain the pipeline to the body floor pan.
7   Place a jack under the base of the suspension strut and raise it slightly.
8   Working within the luggage compartment, pull off the covering cap and release the upper mounting of the suspension strut (photo).
9   Still keeping the jack in position under the strut, raise the end of the leaf spring with a second jack, until the tension is relieved and the anchor plate and rubber buffer can be removed.
10 Lower the spring jack slowly and remove it.
11 The inboard ends of the suspension wishbone can now be unbolted from the bodyframe brackets; note carefully the exact location and number of shims fitted behind the wishbone pivot shaft – these control both the camber angle and the toe-in of the rear wheels (photo).
12 With the suspension free, withdraw it from under the wheel arch.
13 Clean away external dirt and dismantle as necessary. To remove the strut, extract the pinch bolts which secure it to the hub carrier, and unscrew the nuts from the wishbone pivots.
14 If the strut shows signs of fluid leakage, or when its piston rod is moved in or out no resistance is felt or the movement is jerky, then the strut should be renewed or it may be possible to fit a new insert by carefully following the manufacturer's instructions.
15 Worn bushes in the wishbone arms can be removed and new ones fitted, using a press or by making up a tool with a bolt, nut washers and suitable diameter tubular distance pieces.
16 Reassembly and refitting are reversals of the dismantling and, removal procedures respectively.
17 Bleed the rear brake circuit on completion.
18 Fully tighten all bolts to the specified torque, but only after the weight of the car has been lowered onto its roadwheels.
19 Provided no new major components have been fitted during the

9.8 Rear suspension strut upper mounting

9.11 Inboard end of rear suspension wishbone

Fig. 11.5 Rear suspension wishbone pivot nuts (Sec 9)

1   Inboard pivot   2   Outboard pivot

overhaul, and the original shims have been refitted at the wishbone inner pivots, the camber and toe-in should not have altered. It is, however, recommended that the rear wheel camber angle and wheel alignment is checked as soon as possible, as described in the next Section.

10 Rear wheel alignment

It is important, in the interests of slow tyre wear and optimum roadholding qualities, that the rear wheel alignment is correct. This does not normally require adjustment, unless the suspension has been dismantled and new components fitted.

1   By fitting shims of equal thickness between the wishbone inner pivot mountings and the bracket on the bodyframe, the camber angle is adjusted. If the thickness of the shims between the wishbone front and rear mounting points is then adjusted, the wheel alignment can be altered to provide the specified toe-in.

2   To set these angles really accurately, special gauges and equipment are required – the work should therefore be left to your dealer. In an emergency, the use of a tracking gauge, as described for front wheel alignment, can provide a reasonably accurate setting. But as

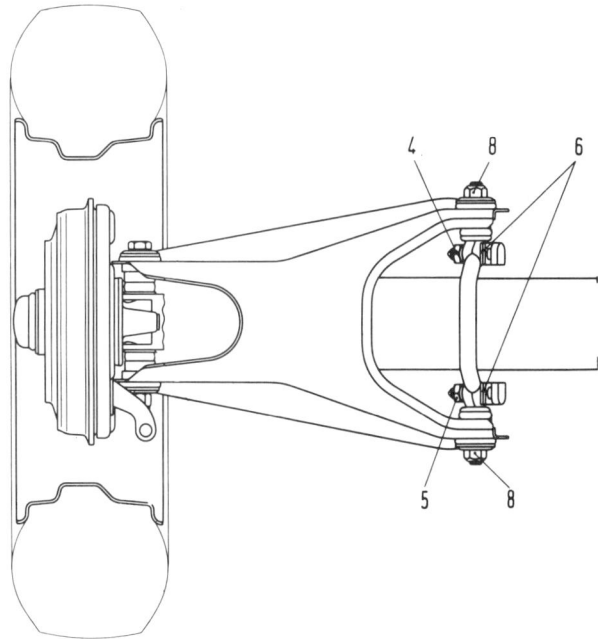

Fig. 11.6 Location of rear wheel alignment shims (Sec 10)

4   Pivot securing bolts to bodyframe
5   Pivot securing bolts to bodyframe
6   Shims
8   Wishbone pivot nuts

any alteration may upset the camber angle, it is not really a job for the home mechanic. The camber angle must always be set before the toe-in is altered.

11 Roadwheels and tyres

1   The roadwheels are of pressed steel type, using bolts to retain them to the hub flanges. No hub caps are fitted.

2   Periodically, remove the wheels, clean the inside and outside, and make good any rusty patches.

3   Keep the wheel retaining bolts lightly greased and tighten them fully after fitting the wheel.

4   Keep the tyres inflated to specified pressure and inspect the treads and sidewalls regularly for cuts, blisters or damage.

5   If the wheels and tyres have been balanced on the car, they should not be moved from their original positions, nor their location on the hub be altered; paint one bolt hole on the wheel, and the matching one on the hub flange, before removing the wheel or the original balance will be lost at time of refitting.

6   If the wheels have been balanced off the car, they may be moved to even out the tread wear. With the radial tyres fitted as original equipment, however, only move them from front to rear and rear to front on the same side of the car. *Do not change them from side to side.*

7   If the spare wheel is introduced into the tyre rotational scheme, mark it as to which side it is fitted and from which side the 'new' spare came from. Keep the wheels to that side of the car in future movements.

8   It is recommended that the wheel is re-balanced after a puncture is repaired and at halfway through the life of the tyre (perhaps 15 000 miles (24 000 km) approximately) when loss of tread rubber due to wear may have altered the original balance.

9   Tyre tread wear characteristics are illustrated. Apart from those shown, if parts of the tread are scooped out or flattened, this may be caused by out of balance wheels or repeated heavy brake applications, causing the wheels to lock.

10 Bulges or blisters on the tyre sidewalls may be caused by striking kerbs or mounting the kerb at anything more than a walking pace.

11 Scrubbing the tyres can occur where the roadwheel steering angles are incorrect on steering lock. This may be due to the lengths of the tie-rods being unequal.

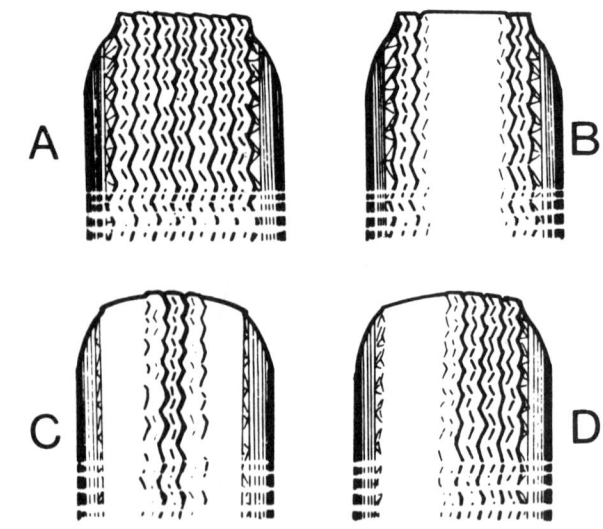

Fig. 11.7 Tyre tread wear patterns and causes (Sec 11)

A   'Feathering' due to incorrect toe-in
B   Over inflation
C   Under inflation
D   Wear due to incorrect camber, worn wheel bearings and fast cornering

12 Fault diagnosis – suspension

Note: *Before diagnosing suspension defects, be sure that trouble is not due to incorrect or uneven tyre pressures, or inappropriate tyre combinations*

Symptom	Reason/s
Car pulls to one side	Worn or weak shock absorbers or struts on one side
Excessive roll on corners	Weak shock absorbers or struts Transverse leaf spring weak or cracked
Car wanders or skips on rough surfaces	Defective shock absorbers or struts
Vibration and wheel wobble	Loose or defective shock absorbers or struts
Excessive or uneven tyre wear	Worn suspension components

Chapter 12 Bodywork

For modifications, and information applicable to later models, see Supplement at end of manual

Contents

1 General description

The body is of all steel construction, without a separate chassis frame.

All models are of hatchback design and are available in three or five door versions. Equipment on standard versions is adequate, while upmarket models have a number of additional items, including the following:

Front seat head restraints
Fitted carpets
Split rear seats

In the interest of economy of repair, the front wings are of bolt-on type, also the front and rear plastic panels are detachable.

2 Maintenance – bodywork and underframe

1 The general condition of a car's bodywork is the thing that significantly affects it value. Maintenance is easy but needs to be regular. Neglect, particularly after minor damage, can lead quickly to further deterioration and costly repair bills. It is important also to keep watch on those parts of the car not immediately visible, for instance the underside, inside all the wheel arches and the lower part of the engine compartment.

2 The basic maintenance routine for the bodywork is washing – preferably with a lot of water, from a hose. This will remove all the loose solids which may have stuck to the car. It is important to flush these off in such a way as to prevent grit from scratching the finish. The wheel arches and underframe need washing in the same way to remove any accumulated mud which will retain moisture and tend to encourage rust. Paradoxically enough, the best time to clean the underframe and wheel arches is in wet weather when the mud is thoroughly wet and soft. In very wet weather the underframe is usually cleaned of large accumulations automatically and this is a good time for inspection.

3 Periodically, it is a good idea to have the whole of the underframe of the car steam cleaned, engine compartment included, so that a thorough inspection can be carried out to see what minor repairs and renovations are necessary. Steam cleaning is available at many garages and is necessary for removal of the accumulation of oily grime which sometimes is allowed to become thick in certain areas. If steam cleaning facilities are not available, there are one or two excellent grease solvents available which can be brush applied. The dirt can then be simply hosed off.

4 After washing paintwork, wipe off with a chamois leather to give an unspotted clear finish. A coat of clear protective wax polish will give added protection against chemical pollutants in the air. If the paintwork sheen has dulled or oxidised, use a cleaner/polisher combination to restore the brilliance of the shine. This requires a little effort, but such dulling is usually caused because regular washing has been neglected. Always check that the door and ventilator opening drain holes and pipes are completely clear so that water can be drained out. Bright work should be treated in the same way as paintwork. Windscreens and windows can be kept clear of the smeary film which often appears, by adding a little ammonia to the water. If they are scratched, a good rub with a proprietary metal polish will often clear them. Never use any form of wax or other body or chromium polish on glass.

3 Maintenance – upholstery and carpets

1 Mats and carpets should be brushed or vacuum cleaned regularly to keep them free of grit. If they are badly stained remove them from the car for scrubbing or sponging and make quite sure they are dry before refitting. Seats and interior trim panels can be kept clean by a wipe over with a damp cloth. If they do become stained (which can be more apparent on light coloured upholstery) use a little liquid detergent and a soft nail brush to scour the grime out of the grain of the material. Do not forget to keep the head lining clean in the same way as the upholstery. When using liquid cleaners inside the car do not over-wet the surfaces being cleaned. Excessive damp could get into the seams and padded interior causing stains, offensive odours or even rot. If the inside of the car gets wet accidentally it is worthwhile taking some trouble to dry it out properly, particularly where carpets are involved. *Do not leave oil or electric heaters inside the car for this purpose.*

4 Minor body damage – repair

The photographic sequences on pages 190 and 191 illustrate the operations detailed in the following sub-sections.

Repair of minor scratches in the car's bodywork

If the scratch is very superficial, and does not penetrate to the metal of the bodywork, repair is very simple. Lightly rub the area of the scratch with a paintwork renovator, or a very fine cutting paste, to remove loose paint from the scratch and to clear the surrounding bodywork of wax polish. Rinse the area with clean water.

Apply touch-up paint to the scratch using a thin paint brush; continue to apply thin layers of paint until the surface of the paint in the scratch is level with the surrounding paintwork. Allow the new paint at least two weeks to harden: then blend it into the surrounding paintwork by rubbing the paintwork, in the scratch area, with a paintwork renovator or a very fine cutting paste. Finally, apply wax polish.

Where the scratch has penetrated right through to the metal of the bodywork, causing the metal to rust, a different repair technique is required. Remove any loose rust from the bottom of the scratch with a penknife, then apply rust inhibiting paint to prevent the formation of rust in the future. Using a rubber or nylon applicator fill the scratch with bodystopper paste. If required, this paste can be mixed with cellulose thinners to provide a very thin paste which is ideal for filling narrow scratches. Before the stopper-paste in the scratch hardens, wrap a piece of smooth cotton rag around the top of a finger. Dip the finger in cellulose thinners and then quickly sweep it across the surface of the stopper-paste in the scratch; this will ensure that the surface of the stopper-paste is slightly hollowed. The scratch can now be painted over as described earlier in this Section.

Repair of dents in the car's bodywork

When deep denting of the vehicle's bodywork has taken place, the first task is to pull the dent out, until the affected bodywork almost attains its original shape. There is little point in trying to restore the original shape completely, as the metal in the damaged area will have stretched on impact and cannot be reshaped fully to its original contour. It is better to bring the level of the dent up to a point which is about $\frac{1}{8}$ in (3 mm) below the level of the surrounding bodywork. In cases where the dent is very shallow anyway, it is not worth trying to pull it out at all. If the underside of the dent is accessible, it can be hammered out gently from behind, using a mallet with a wooden or plastic head. Whilst doing this, hold a suitable block of wood firmly against the outside of the panel to absorb the impact from the hammer blows and thus prevent a large area of the bodywork from being 'belled-out'.

Should the dent be in a section of the bodywork which has double skin or some other factor making it inaccessible from behind, a different technique is called for. Drill several small holes through the metal inside the area – particularly in the deeper section. Then screw long self-tapping screws into the holes just sufficiently for them to gain a good purchase in the metal. Now the dent can be pulled out by pulling on the protruding heads of the screws with a pair of pliers.

The next stage of the repair is the removal of the paint from the damaged area, and from an inch or so of the surrounding 'sound' bodywork. This is accomplished most easily by using a wire brush or abrasive pad on a power drill, although it can be done just as effectively by hand using sheets of abrasive paper. To complete the preparation for filling, score the surface of the bare metal with a screwdriver or the tang of a file, or alternatively, drill small holes in the affected area. This will provide a really good 'key' for the filler paste.

To complete the repair see the Section on filling and re-spraying.

Repair of rust holes or gashes in the car's bodywork

Remove all paint from the affected area and from an inch or so of the surrounding 'sound' bodywork, using an abrasive pad or a wire brush on a power drill. If these are not available a few sheets of abrasive paper will do the job just as effectively. With the paint removed you will be able to gauge the severity of the corrosion and therefore decide whether to renew the whole panel (if this is possible) or to repair the affected area. New body panels are not as expensive as most people think and it is often quicker and more satisfactory to fit a new panel than to attempt to repair large areas of corrosion.

Remove all fittings from the affected area except those which will act as a guide to the original shape of the damaged bodywork (eg headlamp shells etc). Then, using tin snips or a hacksaw blade, remove all loose metal and any other metal badly affected by corrosion. Hammer the edges of the hole inwards in order to create a slight depression for the filler paste.

Wire brush the affected area to remove the powdery rust from the surface of the remaining metal. Paint the affected area with rust inhibiting paint; if the back of the rusted area is accessible treat this also.

Before filling can take place it will be necessary to block the hole in some way. This can be achieved by the use of zinc gauze or aluminium tape.

Zinc gauze is probably the best material to use for a large hole. Cut a piece to the approximate size and shape of the hole to be filled, then position it in the hole so that its edges are below the level of the surrounding bodywork. It can be retained in position by several blobs of filler paste around its periphery.

Aluminium tape should be used for small or very narrow holes. Pull a piece off the roll and trim it to the approximate size and shape required, then pull off the backing paper (if used) and stick the tape over the hole; it can be overlapped if the thickness of one piece is insufficient. Burnish down the edges of the tape with the handle of a screwdriver or similar, to ensure that the tape is securely attached to the metal underneath.

Bodywork repairs – filling and re-spraying

Before using this Section, see the Sections on dent, deep scratch, rust holes and gash repairs.

Many types of bodyfiller are available, but generally speaking those proprietary kits which contain a tin of filler paste and a tube of resin hardener are best for this type of repair. A wide, flexible plastic or nylon applicator will be found invaluable for imparting a smooth and well contoured finish to the surface of the filler.

Mix up a little filler on a clean piece of card or board – measure the hardener carefully (follow the maker's instructions on the pack) otherwise the filler will set too rapidly or too slowly.

Using the applicator apply the filler paste to the prepared area; draw the applicator across the surface of the filler to achieve the correct contour and to level the filler surface. As soon as a contour that approximates the correct one is achieved, stop working the paste – if you carry on too long the paste will become sticky and begin to 'pick up' on the applicator. Continue to add thin layers of filler paste at twenty-minute intervals until the level of the filler is just proud of the surrounding bodywork.

Once the filler has hardened, excess can be removed using a metal plane or file. From then on, progressively finer grades of sandpaper should be used, starting with a 40 grade production paper and finishing with 400 grade wet-and-dry paper. Always wrap the abrasive paper around a flat rubber, cork, or wooden block – otherwise the surface of the filler will not be completely flat. During the smoothing of the filler surface the wet-and-dry paper should be periodically rinsed in water. This will ensure that a very smooth finish is imparted to the filler at the final stage.

At this stage the dent should be surrounded by a ring of bare metal, which in turn should be encircled by the finely 'feathered' edge of the good paintwork. Rinse the repair area with clean water, until all of the dust produced by the rubbing-down operation has gone.

Spray the whole repair area with a light coat of primer – this will show up any imperfections in the surface of the filler. Repair these imperfections with fresh filler paste or bodystopper, and once more smooth the surface with abrasive paper. If bodystopper is used, it can be mixed with cellulose thinners to form a really thin paste which is ideal for filling small holes. Repeat this spray and repair procedure until you are satisfied that the surface of the filler, and the feathered edge of the paintwork are perfect. Clean the repair area with clean water and allow to dry fully.

The repair area is now ready for final spraying. Paint spraying must be carried out in warm, dry, windless and dust free atmosphere. This condition can be created artificially if you have access to a large indoor working area, but if you are forced to work in the open, you will have to pick your day very carefully. If you are working indoors, dousing the floor in the work area with water will help to settle the dust which would otherwise be in the atmosphere. If the repair area is confined to one body panel, mask off the surrounding panels; this will help to minimise the effects of a slight mis-match in paint colours. Bodywork fittings (eg chrome strips, door handles etc) will also need to be masked off. Use genuine masking tape and several thicknesses of newspaper for the masking operations.

Before commencing to spray, agitate the aerosol can thoroughly, then spray a test area (an old tin, or similar) until the technique is mastered. Cover the repair area with a thick coat of primer; the thickness should be built up using several thin layers of paint rather than one thick one. Using 400 grade wet-and-dry paper, rub down the surface of the primer until it is really smooth. While doing this, the work area should be thoroughly doused with water, and the wet-and-dry paper periodically rinsed in water. Allow to dry before spraying on more paint.

Spray on the top coat, again building up the thickness by using several thin layers of paint. Start spraying in the centre of the repair area and then, using a circular motion, work outwards until the whole repair area and about 2 inches of the surrounding original paintwork is covered. Remove all masking material 10 to 15 minutes after spraying on the final coat of paint.

Allow the new paint at least two weeks to harden, then, using a paintwork renovator or a very fine cutting paste, blend the edges of the paint into the existing paintwork. Finally, apply wax polish.

5 Major body damage – repair

Where extensive damage has occurred, or large areas need renewal due to neglect, new panels will have to be welded in or – in the case of the front wings and front and rear plastic panels – bolted on. Any welding operation is best left to professionals. If the damage is due to impact, it will also be necessary to completely check the alignment of the bodyshell structure. Due to the principle of construction, the strength and shape of the whole can be affected by damage to a part. In such instances, the services of a FIAT agent with specialist checking jigs are essential. If a body is left misaligned, it is first of all dangerous as the car will not handle properly, and secondly, uneven stresses will be imposed on the steering, engine and transmission, causing abnormal wear or complete failure. Tyre wear may also be excessive.

6 Maintenance – hinges and locks

1   Oil the hinges of the bonnet, boot and doors with a drop or two of light oil periodically. A good time is after the car has been washed.
2   Oil the bonnet, release the catch pivot pin and the safety catch pivot pin periodically.
3   Do not over lubricate door latches and strikers. Normally, a little oil on the rotary cam spindle alone is sufficient.

7 Doors – tracing rattles and their rectification

1   Check first that the door is not loose at the hinges and that the latch is holding the door firmly in position. Check also that the door lines up with the aperture in the body.
2   If the hinges are loose, or the door is out of alignment, it will be necessary to reset the hinge positions, as described in Section 11.
3   If the latch is holding the door properly, it should hold the door tightly when fully latched and the door should line up with the body. If it is out of alignment, it needs adjustment as described. If loose, some part of the lock mechanism must be worn out and requires renewal.
4   Other rattles from the door would be caused by wear or looseness in the window winder, the glass channels and sill strips or the door buttons and interior latch release mechanism.

8 Front panel – removal and refitting

1   The front panel is a plastic moulding and incorporates the radiator air intake grille and the front bumper (except North American models; see Section 13).
2   Open the bonnet and disconnect the electrical leads from the front lamps.
3   Working under the front wings, unscrew and remove the bolts which connect the joint ends of the front wing and the front panel.
4   Now move to the front of the car; unscrew and remove the screws from the front face of the panel.
5   Lift the panel from the car.
6   The headlamp retaining bolts are accessible from the inner face of the front panel.
7   Refitting is a reversal of the removal process. It is recommended

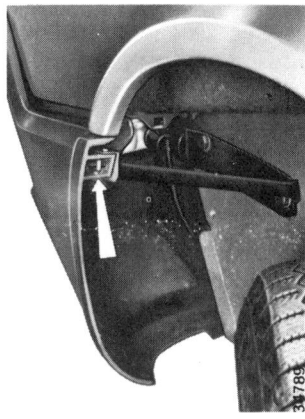

Fig. 12.1 Front panel under wing bolts (Sec 8)

Fig. 12.2 Front panel securing screws (Sec 8)

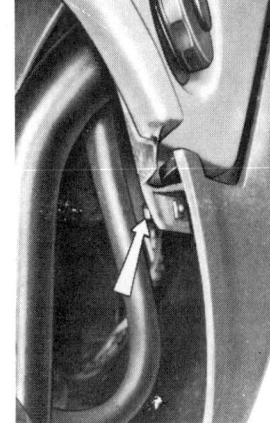

Fig. 12.3 Rear panel under wing bolts (Sec 9)

that the underwing securing bolts are kept smeared with heavy grease to prevent corrosion.

9 Rear panel – removal and refitting

1   The rear panel is a plastic moulding which serves as the rear bumper and incorporates the rear lamp clusters (refer to Section 13 for North American cars' bumpers).
2   Working under the rear wings, unscrew and remove the bolts which connect the rear panels to the body.
3   Now move the rear of the car and unscrew the panel retaining screws.
4   Gently, pull the rear panel from the car until the rear lamp electrical plugs can be disconnected.
5   To remove the lamps from the panel, first detach the lenses and then pull the lamp bodies from the inner surface of the panel.
6   Refitting is a reversal of the removal process. It is recommended that the under wing securing bolts are kept smeared with heavy grease to prevent corrosion.

10 Front wing – removal and refitting

1   Open the bonnet.
2   Squeeze the retaining tang and withdraw the side marker (re-

peater) lamp from the wing, then disconnect its electrical leads.
3   Remove the front panel, as described in Section 8. If the wings are fitted with protective liners, remove them from under the wing by extracting the securing screws (photo).
4   Unscrew the bolts from the channel at the top of the wing; also the bolt (2) from the front of the wheel arch, shown in Fig. 12.6.
5   Working inside the car, detach the trim panel from behind the front door pillar, then unscrew and remove the bolt which is positioned about halfway up the pillar between the floor and the windscreen (it holds the rear edge of the wing to the pillar).
6   Open the door fully and extract the screw from the upper corner of the front wing.
7   Extract the screw from the sill, just forward of the leading edge of the front door.
8   Run a knife round the mating faces of the wing and the body to break the adhesion of the mastic; lift the wing from the car.
9   Before fitting the new wing, scrape off the old mastic and apply a bead of fresh material to the wing-to-body mating surface on the body.

10.3 Retaining bolt for underwing plastic panel

Fig. 12.4 Rear panel securing screws (Sec 9)

Fig. 12.5 Rear panel removed (Sec 9)

1   *Mounting brackets*
2   *Rear lamp connecting plugs*

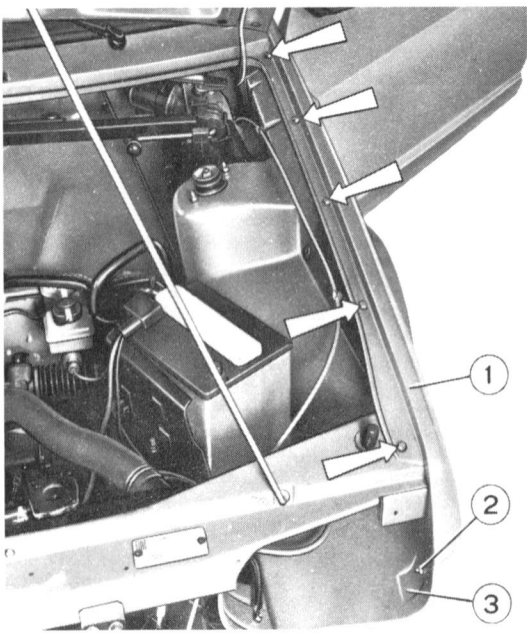

Fig. 12.6 Front wing upper and front mounting bolts (Sec 10)

1   *Wing panel*   3   *Wing valance*
2   *Front bolt*

10 Once fitted, apply an underbody protective coating to the under-surface of the wing, then refinish the wing upper surface to match the original body colour.

11 Bonnet – removal, refitting and adjustment

1 Open the bonnet and support it on its strut (photo).
2 Mark the position of the hinge bolts to the hinges and the hinges to the bonnet, then release the bolts (photo).
3 With at least one assistant supporting the weight of the bonnet, fold away the strut, remove the hinge bolts and lift the bonnet from the car.
4 When refitting, the hinge bolt holes are elongated to provide adjustment in a fore and aft direction. If the bonnet must be adjusted sideways to centralise it within the inboard edges of the wings, the hinge arms should be carefully bent.
5 Adjust the bonnet lock to provide smooth, positive closure; also adjust the front bump rubbers, to prevent any tendency to rattle when the car is operational (photos).

11.1 Strut locating hole in bonnet lid

11.2 Bonnet hinge

11.5A Bonnet lock

11.5B Bonnet safety catch

Fig. 12.7 Front wing bolt to pillar (Sec 10)

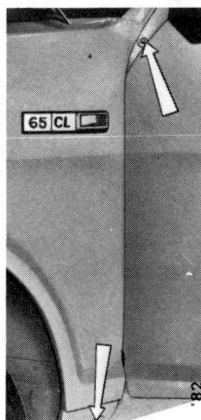

Fig. 12.8 Front wing upper and sill bolts (Sec 10)

This sequence of photographs deals with the repair of the dent and paintwork damage shown in this photo. The procedure will be similar for the repair of a hole. It should be noted that the procedures given here are simplified – more explicit instructions will be found in the text

In the case of a dent the first job – after removing surrounding trim – is to hammer out the dent where access is possible. This will minimise filling. Here, the large dent having been hammered out, the damaged area is being made slightly concave

Now all paint must be removed from the damaged area, by rubbing with coarse abrasive paper. Alternatively, a wire brush or abrasive pad can be used in a power drill. Where the repair area meets good paintwork, the edge of the paintwork should be 'feathered', using a finer grade of abrasive paper

In the case of a hole caused by rusting, all damaged sheet-metal should be cut away before proceeding to this stage. Here, the damaged area is being treated with rust remover and inhibitor before being filled

Mix the body filler according to its manufacturer's instructions. In the case of corrosion damage, it will be necessary to block off any large holes before filling – this can be done with aluminium or plastic mesh, or aluminium tape. Make sure the area is absolutely clean before ...

... applying the filler. Filler should be applied with a flexible applicator, as shown, for best results; the wooden spatula being used for confined areas. Apply thin layers of filler at 20-minute intervals, until the surface of the filler is slightly proud of the surrounding bodywork

Initial shaping can be done with a Surform plane or Dreadnought file. Then, using progressively finer grades of wet-and-dry paper, wrapped around a sanding block, and copious amounts of clean water, rub down the filler until really smooth and flat. Again, feather the edges of adjoining paintwork

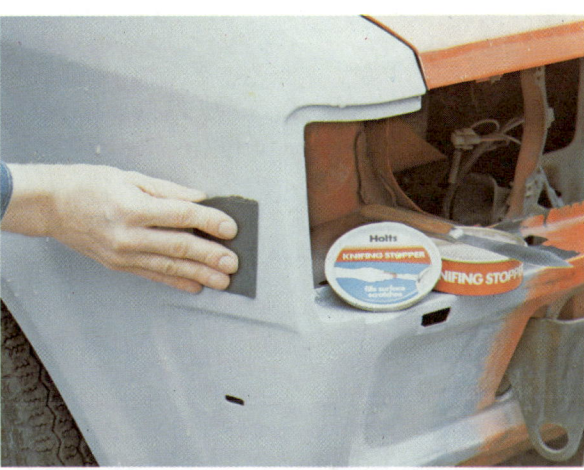

Again, using plenty of water, rub down the primer with a fine grade wet-and-dry paper (400 grade is probably best) until it is really smooth and well blended into the surrounding paintwork. Any remaining imperfections can now be filled by carefully applied knifing stopper paste

The top coat can now be applied. When working out of doors, pick a dry, warm and wind-free day. Ensure surrounding areas are protected from over-spray. Agitate the aerosol thoroughly, then spray the centre of the repair area, working outwards with a circular motion. Apply the paint as several thin coats

The whole repair area can now be sprayed or brush-painted with primer. If spraying, ensure adjoining areas are protected from over-spray. Note that at least one inch of the surrounding sound paintwork should be coated with primer. Primer has a 'thick' consistency, so will find small imperfections

When the stopper has hardened, rub down the repair area again before applying the final coat of primer. Before rubbing down this last coat of primer, ensure the repair area is blemish-free — use more stopper if necessary. To ensure that the surface of the primer is really smooth use some finishing compound

After a period of about two weeks, which the paint needs to harden fully, the surface of the repaired area can be 'cut' with a mild cutting compound prior to wax polishing. When carrying out bodywork repairs, remember that the quality of the finished job is proportional to the time and effort expended

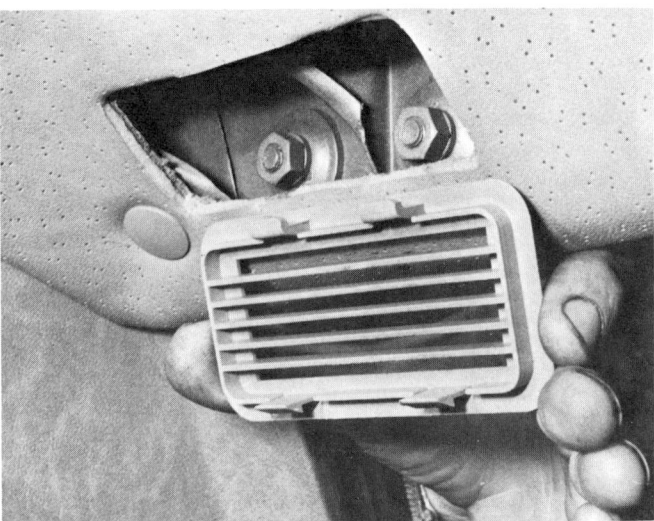

12.3 Stale air extractor grille removed to show tailgate hinge nuts

12 Tailgate – removal and refitting

1   Open the tailgate and disconnect the leads from the heated rear window.
2   Disconnect the support from the tailgate, by unscrewing its upper nut while an assistant holds the tailgate in the fully open position.
3   Prise out the air extractor grilles from inside the car to expose the hinge securing nuts (photo).
4   Unscrew and remove the nuts, then lift the tailgate from the car.
5   Refitting is a reversal of the removal process, but do not fully tighten the hinge nuts until the tailgate has been adjusted – this should provide an even gap all round its edge.
6   The lock mechanism should be adjusted within the limits of its elongated bolt holes, to provide smooth positive closure.

13 Bumpers (North American models) – description

1   On these models, the front and rear bumpers are of impact absorbing type, and incorporate a polished alloy member.
2   The front bumper bar incorporates direction indicator and running lamps.
3   The bumper assemblies are bolted into position and the front and rear panels (see Sections 8 and 9) are modified to accept them.

14 Sliding roof – removal and refitting

1   Open the sliding roof fully, remove the small screw from the stainless steel rail, then withdraw the rail.
2   Pull the sliding roof towards the front of the car until the slides are in alignment with the apertures. Lift the roof from the aperture.
3   The roof lining tensioner is removed in a similar way to that just described for the sliding roof panel.

15 Facia panel – removal and refitting

1   Disconnect the battery.
2   Refer to Chapter 9, Section 25 and remove the instrument panel.
3   Refer to Chapter 10, Section 5 and remove the steering wheel.
4   Remove the panel switches and disconnect the clock.
5   Working within the engine compartment, remove the three nuts, arrowed in Fig. 12.11, from the rear bulkhead.
6   Working within the car, remove the screw from each end of the facia panel.
7   Draw the facia panel towards you, while sitting in one of the front seats. Then press it out sideways from the interior of the car.
8   Refitting is a reversal of the removal process.

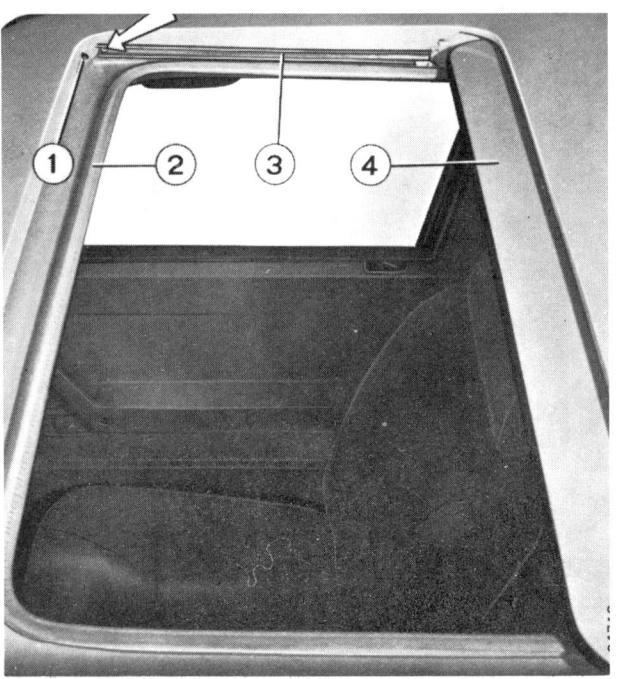

Fig. 12.9 Sliding roof details (Sec 14)

| 1 Drain hole | 3 Rail |
| 2 Weatherstrip | 4 Sliding panel |

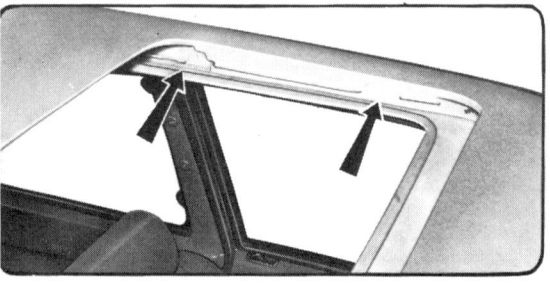

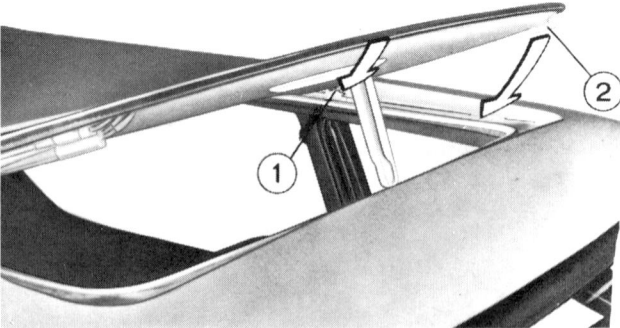

Fig. 12.10 Sliding roof slides and apertures (Sec 14)

16 Door – removal and refitting

1   Open the door and disconnect the door check by pressing the spring arms together.
2   Open the door fully and mark the position of the hinges in relation to the door edge.
3   Support the door on jacks or blocks covered with rags to prevent damage to the paintwork.
4   Unscrew and remove the bolts which hold the hinges to the door, then lift the door away.
5   Refit the door by reversing the removal operations, but do not fully tighten the bolts until the door alignment has been checked. To do this,

Fig. 12.11 Facia panel mounting nuts (Sec 15)

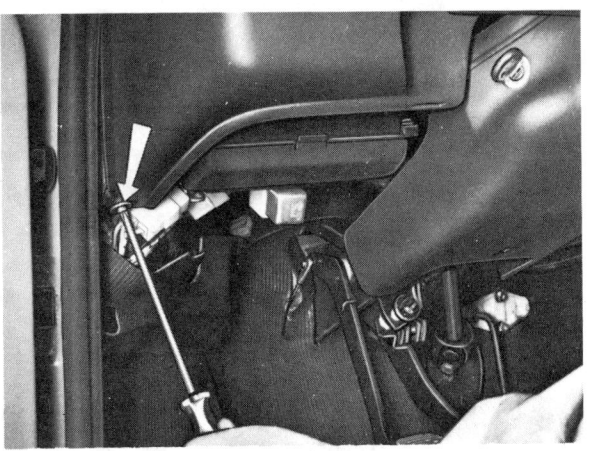

Fig. 12.12 Facia panel mounting screw inside car (LHD shown) (Sec 15)

Fig. 12.13 Withdrawing facia panel (LHD shown) (Sec 15)

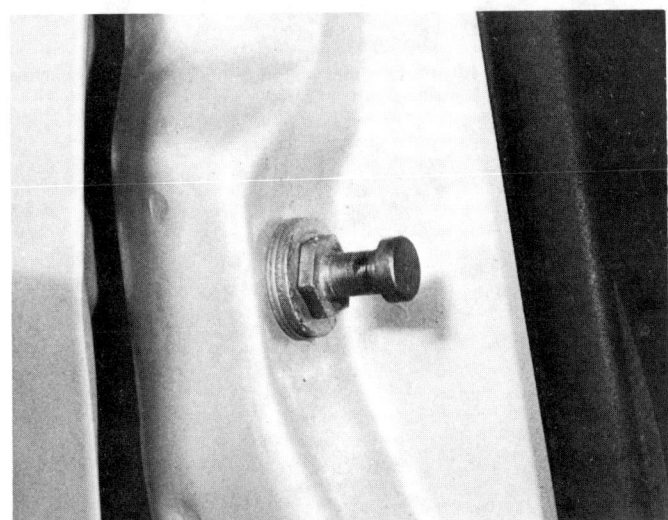

16.7 Door lock striker

gently close the door, removing the striker, should it interfere with the door closing.

6   There should be an even gap all round the door edge. The door can be moved up and down and towards the front or rear of the car to achieve this.

7   If the door exterior panel is not flush, when closed, with the wing or body panels adjacent to it, shims can be removed or added at the back of the hinges to correct the misalignment (photo).

8   Position the striker so that it passes just beneath the tip of the upper jaw of the latch as the door closes. Tighten the striker with a ring spanner (photo).

17 Door – dismantling and reassembly

1   Open the door, wind the window fully up and note the setting of the window regulator handle.

2   Make up a length of wire with a small hook at its end; pass it between the handle and its mounting boss, engaging the hook with the handle retaining clip.

3   Give the wire a sharp jerk to release the clip.

4   Pull the handle from the splined spindle of the regulator.

5   Extract the two screws from the armrest (photo).

6   Remove the trim from the door interior handle by pressing it inward slightly and sliding it rearward, to release its retaining lugs (photo).

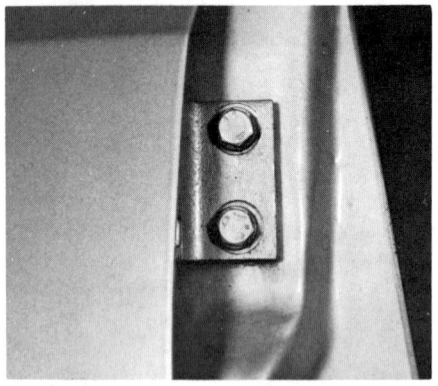
16.8 Door hinge-to-body pillar bolts

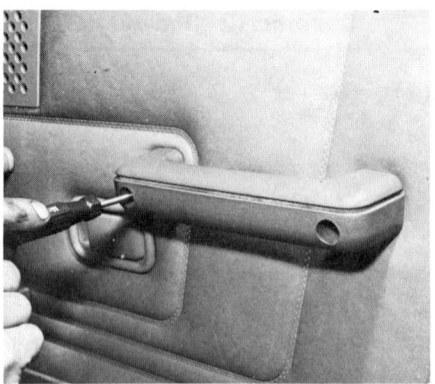
17.5 Removing an armrest screw

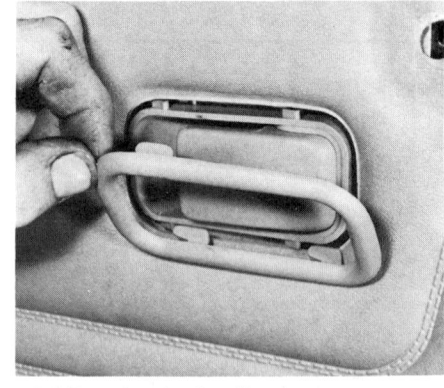
17.6 Door interior handle trim

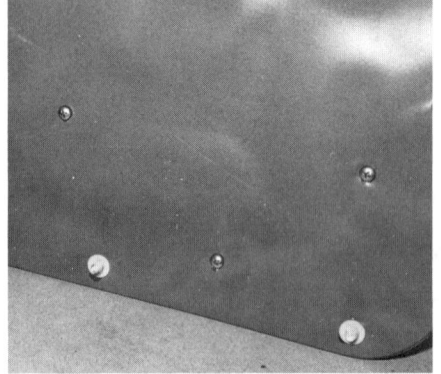
17.8 Door trim panel securing clips. Screws retain door trim panel tidy compartment

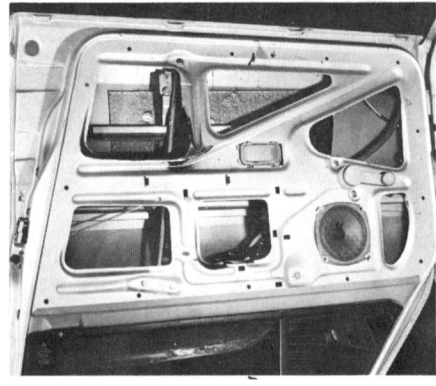
17.9 Door cavity exposed

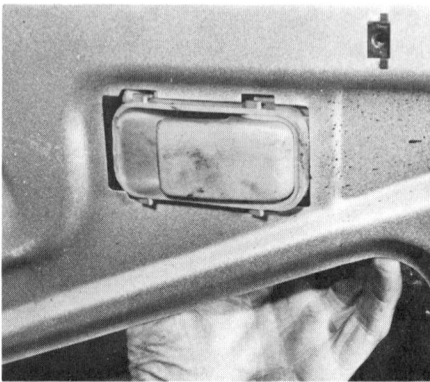
17.10A Releasing door lock remote control handle

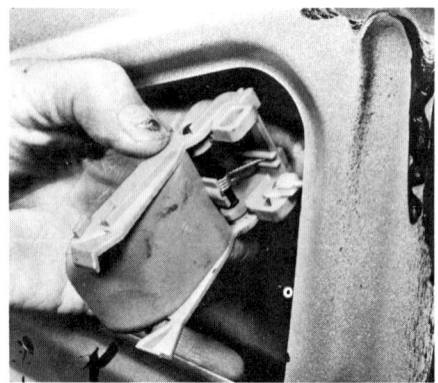
17.10B Removing door lock remote control handle from door cavity

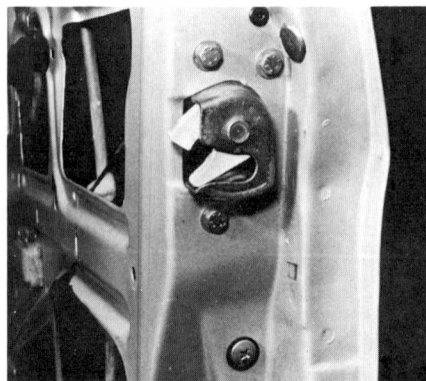
17.11 Door lock/latch

17.12 Door exterior handle retaining screw (arrowed)

17.15 Door glass carrier bolts

17.21A Window regulator handle retaining spring

17.21B Fitting the window regulator handle

7 If loudspeakers are located in the doors, prise out the speaker grille, then extract the speaker securing screws. Withdraw the speaker until the connecting leads can be detached.

8 Slide a broad blade between the bottom edge of the door interior trim panel and the door, to release one or two of the securing clips. The fingers can now be used to release the remaining clips all round the edge of the door (photo).

9 With the door cavity now exposed, dismantling can be carried out as necessary (photo).

10 The lock handle can be slid slightly to one side to align the tangs with the cut-outs, depressed inwards then lowered and the remote control rod disconnected (photos).

11 The door lock can be removed, after having extracted the securing screws from the edge of the door (photo).

12 The door exterior handle securing screws are accessible through the hole directly above the door latch and to the left of the hole, immediately inside the door cavity (photo).

13 To remove the main glass from the door, temporarily fit the winder handle and lower the glass fully.

14 Prise out the weatherstrip from the upper edge of the door panel.

15 Unscrew and remove the glass carrier bolts (photo).

16 Withdraw the glass carrier.

17 Withdraw the glass upwards out of the door and towards the outside of the car, rotating its leading edge also in an upward direction.

18 Remove the regulator screws and withdraw the regulator.

19 Where the quarter-light must be removed, this can be done independently of the main glass. First, wind the window fully down then extract the screws which hold the top and bottom of the sliding glass channel (the channel nearest the front of the car on front door of all models and the rearmost channel on rear doors of four-door cars).

20 The quarter-light, complete with weatherstrip, can now be removed.

21 Reassembly is a reversal of the dismantling process. To fit the window regulator handle, locate the spring and then give the handle a sharp blow with the hand to drive it onto the splines of the regulator spindle (photos).

18 Windscreen glass – removal and refitting

The windscreen glass is of the laminated type and even if cracked, can be removed in one piece.

It is strongly recommended that you leave windscreen renewal to the experts. Laminated screens will not stand the amount of stress

Fig. 12.14 Removing door glass weatherstrip (Sec 17)

1 Weatherstrip   3 Support
2 Weatherstrip

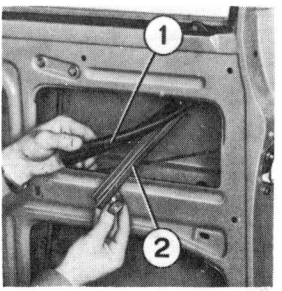

Fig. 12.16 Withdrawing door glass weatherstrip (1) and glass runner (2) (Sec 17)

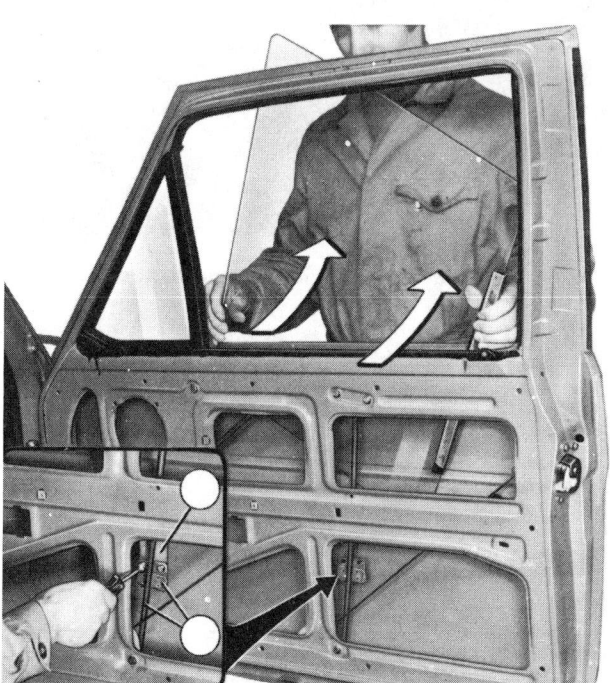

Fig. 12.15 Removing door glass (Sec 17)

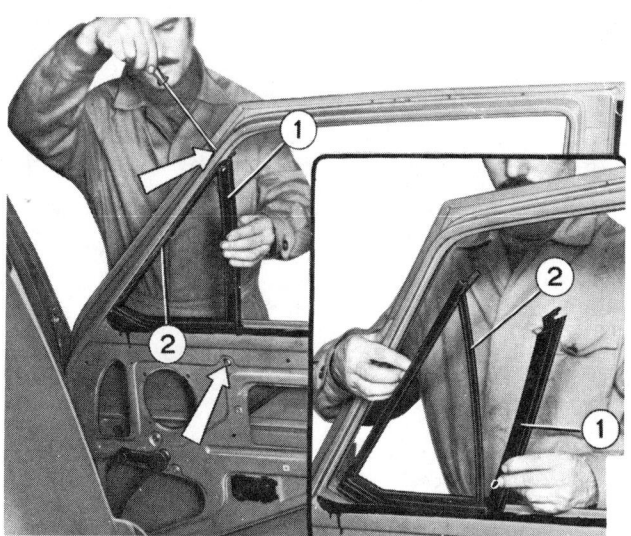

Fig. 12.17 Removing a fixed quarter-light (Sec 17)

1 Runner for sliding glass
2 Weatherstrips

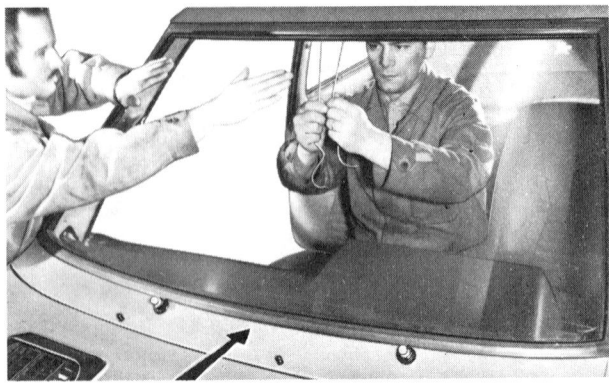

Fig. 12.18 Fitting the windscreen (Sec 18)

Starting point (arrowed)

toughened glass will tolerate during fitting. For those who are prepared to do the work themselves, however, carry out the following sequence of operations.

1   Remove the wiper arms and blades.
2   Unfortunately, the lower rubber surround of the screen is obstructed by the facia panel and this will have to be partially withdrawn, as described in Section 15 of this Chapter.
3   Sitting in the front seats, apply pressure with the feet (suitably protected with soft shoes or slippers) to the top corners of the glass and push the glass and rubber surround off the body flange. Have an assistant ready to catch the glass.
4   Make sure that the rubber surround and the body flange are clean and free from old sealant. If the rubber has hardened or otherwise deteriorated, renew it.
5   Fit the rubber surround to the glass, smear petroleum jelly lightly into the body flange groove of the rubber surround, then insert a length of nylon or terylene cord into the groove so that the ends of the cord overlap at the centre of the bottom of the screen.
6   Engage the bottom edge of the rubber with the body flange and, with an assistant applying gentle pressure to the glass, withdraw the two ends of the cord simultaneously to engage the lip of the rubber with the body flange. Apply the pressure from outside the glass so that it follows the two places where the cord is being drawn out.
7   Refit the facia panel and the wiper arms.
8   Renewal of the rear screen is similar to the procedure just described, but it is of toughened glass. When shattered, therefore, make sure that all the glass fragments are removed from the rubber surround before using it again.

19 Front seat – removal and refitting

1   Using an Allen key, extract the socket-headed screws which hold the seat slide channels to the floor.
2   On cars which have tipping front seats, unscrew and remove the bolts which hold the seat anchor clips to the floor.
3   Remove the seat.
4   On North American vehicles, disconnect the seat belt buzzer switch leads as necessary.
5   Refitting is a reversal of the removal process. It is recommended that the screw threads are coated with thick grease to prevent them rusting from underneath the car and making removal difficult at a future date.

20 Rear seat – removal and refitting

1   To remove a rear seat (single bench *or* split), extract the hinge screws from below the front edge of the seat cushion.
2   Remove the cushion, then remove the screws from the seat back lower pivots. Lift the seat back from the car, having first released the latches.
3   Refitting is a reversal of the removal process.

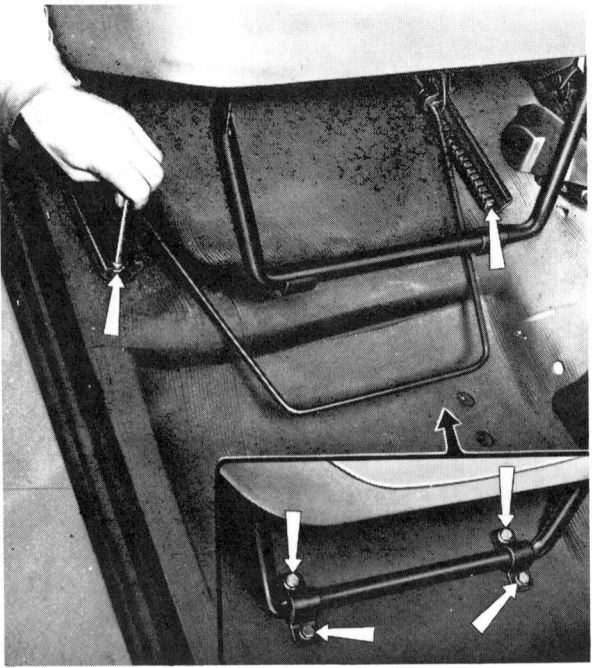

Fig. 12.19 Front seat securing screws (Sec 19)

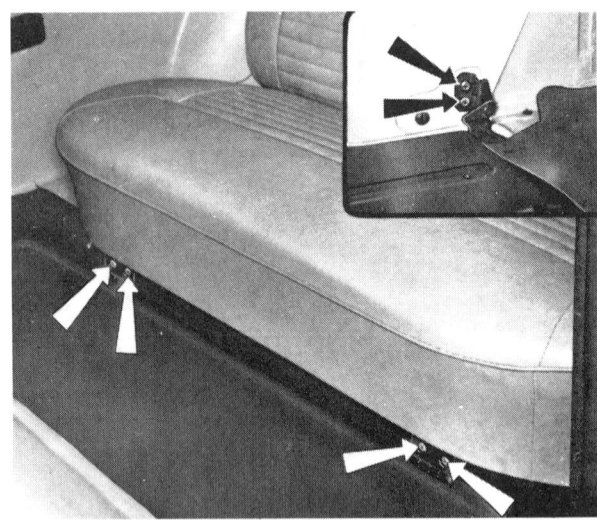

Fig. 12.20 Rear seat attachment points (Sec 20)

21 Rear interior trim panel – removal and refitting

1   The rear trim panel is fitted to three-door models.
2   Pull the rear seat cushion forward.
3   Remove the seat back.
4   Peel the lip of the glass weatherstrip upward to release the top edge of the plastic trim panel from it, by pulling it towards you.
5   Release the plastic retaining clips and remove the panel.
6   Refitting is a reversal of the removal process.

22 Rear shelf – removal and refitting

1   Remove the rear trim panel, as described in the preceding Section.
2   Extract the screws and remove the shelf supports.

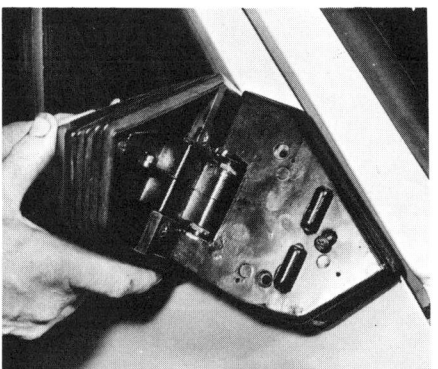

23.2 Exterior rear view mirror hinged back and showing mounting screws

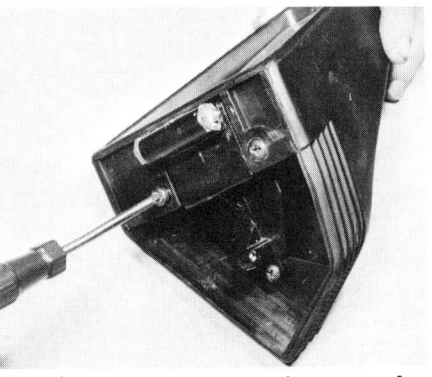

23.5a Removing mirror securing screws from mirror casing

23.5b Sliding out the mirror

23.5c Mirror with spring-loaded balljoint withdrawn from casing

Fig. 12.21 Rear interior trim panel (Sec 21)

Retainers arrowed

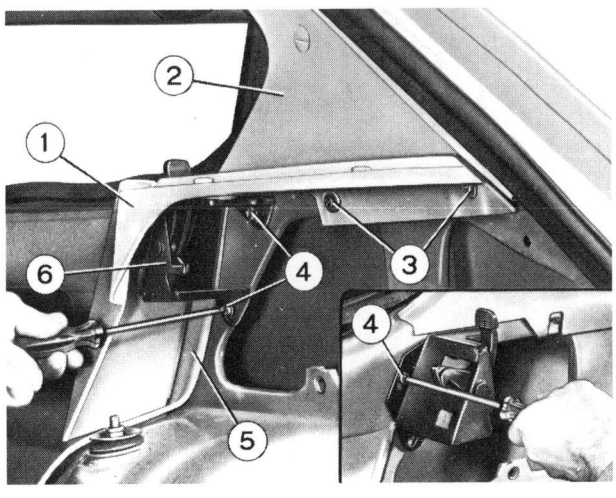

Fig. 12.22 Rear shelf support bracket (Set 22)

1 Support bracket	4 Seat back latch
2 Rear quarter trim panel	5 Liner
3 Screws	6 Seat back latch

3 Manoeuvre the shelf from the car.
4 The release mechanism for the seat back can be removed, if required, by extracting its securing screws.
5 Refitting is a reversal of the removal process. Adjust the seat back latches by moving them within the limits of their elongated holes, the screws only partially tightened.

23 Exterior rear view mirror

1 Normal adjustment is simply carried out by moving the mirror glass within the casing.
2 If the outboard edge of the mirror casing is given a sharp blow towards the rear of the car, a spring/loaded ball socket is disconnected and the mirror assembly pivots rearward (photo).
3 The mirror can be removed from the car by striking it as just described, to cause it to pivot. Then pull the assembly sharply from its second pair of ball sockets.
4 The baseplate is secured to the door by screws.
5 The mirror glass can be withdrawn from the casing, once the two retaining screws have been removed (photos).
6 Refitting is a reversal of the removal process. If any difficulty is encountered in engaging the spring-loaded balls in their sockets, slide a knife blade between the two adjacent components, to compress the ball as they are brought into their locked position.

Fiat Strada 105 TC

Fiat Strada Abarth 130 TC

Fiat Strada 85 Super

Fiat Strada 60 Comfort ES

Chapter 13 Supplement:
Revisions and information on later models

Contents

1 Introduction

This Supplement contains information which is additional to, or a revision of, material in the first twelve Chapters of this manual. Although much of the information in this Supplement relates to Strada II models (introduced in May 1983), twin cam (TC) models, and 1985 'face-lifted' versions, some details apply to all models from the start of production.

Unless otherwise stated, reference to 'early' models means cars produced or sold before the introduction of the Strada II.

The Sections in the Supplement follow the same order as the Chapters to which they relate. The Specifications are all grouped together for convenience, but they follow Chapter order.

It is recommended that before any particular operation is undertaken, reference be made to the appropriate Section(s) of the Supplement. In this way any changes to procedures or components can be noted before referring to the main Chapters.

Project vehicle

The vehicle used in the preparation of this Supplement, and appearing in many of the photographic sequences was a Fiat Strada 85 Super.

2 Specifications

The specifications below are a revision of, or additional to, those at the beginning of the preceding Chapters

Engine – early models
Crankshaft and bearings
Main bearing running clearance – US models .... 0.050 to 0.095 mm (0.0020 to 0.0037 in)

Valve clearances
For valve timing check only:
Inlet .... 0.60 mm (0.024 in)
Exhaust .... 0.65 mm (0.026 in)

Valve springs
Length under load:
Inner, 14.9 kg (32.9 lb) .... 31 mm (1.22 in)
Outer, 38.9 kg (85.8 lb) .... 36 mm (1.42 in)
Minimum acceptable load for above dimensions:
Inner .... 13.5 kg (29.8 lb)
Outer .... 36.0 kg (79.4 lb)

Lubrication system
Oil pump tolerances – US models:
Gear endfloat .... 0.020 to 0.105 mm (0.0008 to 0.0041 in)
Gear-to-body clearance .... 0.110 to 0.180 mm (0.0043 to 0.0071 in)

Torque wrench settings – US models

	lbf ft	Nm
Air pump-to-support bolt	21	29
Air pump-to-cylinder head extension bolt	21	29
Coolant pump-to-crankcase bolts	21	29
Gulp valve electrovalve thermoswitch	36	49
Coolant temperature sender	36	49
Oil pressure sender	24	32

Engine – Strada II (May 1983 to 1985) except TC
For specifications not given here, refer to Chapter 1
General
Maker's designation:	
1100	138 B.000
1100 ES	138 B1.000
1300 and 1300 S	138 B2.000
1500 and 1500 S	138 B3.000 (automatic)
Bore – 1100 and 1100 ES	80 mm (3.150 in) nomimal
Stroke:	
1100 amd 1100 ES	55.5 mm (2.185 in)
1299 – see Section 7, paragraph 19	55.4 mm (2.181 in)
Displacement:	
1100 and 1100 ES	1116 cc (68.1 cu in)
1300 – see Section 7, paragraph 19	1299 cc (79.2 cu in) or 1301 cc (79.4 cu in)
Compression ratio:	
1100	9.2:1
1100 ES	9.6:1
1500 and 1500 S	9.2:1
Maximum power (DIN):	
1100 and 1100 ES	40.5 kW (54.3 bhp, 55.1 CV) @ 5600 rpm
1300 and 1300 S	50.0 kW (67.1 bhp, 68.0 CV) @ 5700 rpm
1500 and 1500 S	60.3 kW (80.9 bhp, 82.0 CV) @ 5600 rpm
Maximum torque (DIN):	
1100	8.7 kgf m (62.9 lbf ft) @ 2900 rpm
1100 ES	9.0 kgf m (65.1 lbf ft) @ 2900 rpm
1300 and 1300 ES	10.2 kgf m (73.8 lbf ft) @ 2900 rpm
1500 and 1500 S	12.2 kgf m (88.2 lbf ft) @ 3000 rpm

Crankcase and cylinder block
Cylinder bores (standard) – 1100 and 1100 ES	80.000 to 80.050 mm (3.1496 to 3.1516 in) in steps of 0.010 mm (0.0004 in)

Pistons and rings
Standard diameters – 1100 and 1100 ES:	
Grade A	79.940 to 79.950 mm (3.1472 to 3.1476 in)
Grade C	79.960 to 79.970 mm (3.1480 to 3.1484 in)
Grade E	79.980 to 79.990 mm (3.1488 to 3.1492 in)
Clearance in bore – 1100 and 1100 ES	0.05 to 0.07 mm (0.0020 to 0.0028 in)
Weight variation between pistons (all models)	5g (0.175 oz) max
Gudgeon pin bore – 1100 and 1100 ES:	
Grade 1	21.984 to 21.988 mm (0.8655 to 0.8657 in)
Grade 2	21.988 to 21.992 mm (0.8567 to 0.8658 in)
Grade 3	21.992 to 21.996 mm (0.8658 to 0.8660 in)
Gudgeon pin diameter – 1100 and 1100 ES:	
Grade 1	21.970 to 21.974 mm (0.8650 to 0.8651 in)
Grade 2	21.974 to 21.978 mm (0.8651 to 0.8653 in)
Grade 3	21.978 to 21.982 mm (0.8653 to 0.8654 in)
Oversize	+ 0.2 mm (0.0079 in)
Gudgeon pin clearance in piston – 1100 and 1100 ES	0.010 to 0.018 mm (0.004 to 0.007 in)
Piston ring grooves vertical dimension – 1100 and 1100 ES:	
Top	1.535 to 1.555 mm (0.0604 to 0.0612 in)
Intermediate	2.015 to 2.035 mm (0.0793 to 0.0801 in)
Bottom	3.957 to 3.977 mm (0.1558 to 0.1566 in)
Piston ring vertical clearance in groove – 1100 and 1100 ES:	
Top	0.045 to 0.077 mm (0.0018 to 0.0030 in)
Intermediate	0.025 to 0.057 mm (0.0010 to 0.0022 in)
Bottom	0.020 to 0.052 mm (0.0008 to 0.0021 in)
Ring end gap in bore – 1100 and 1100 ES:	
Top	0.30 to 0.45 mm (0.0118 to 0.0177 in)
Intermediate	0.20 to 0.35 mm (0.0079 to 0.0138 in)
Bottom	0.20 to 0.35 mm (0.0079 to 0.0138 in)

Connecting rods – 1100 and 1100 ES
Gudgeon pin bore	21.940 to 21.960 mm (0.8638 to 0.8646 in)
Gudgeon pin interference in bore	0.010 to 0.042 mm (0.0004 to 0.0017 in)

Crankshaft and bearings
Main bearing journal diameter – 1100 and 1100 ES	50.785 to 50.805 mm (1.9994 to 2.0002 in)
Crankpin diameter – 1100 and 1100 ES	45.498 to 45.518 mm (1.7913 to 1.7920 in)
Main bearing shell thickness (standard) – 1100 and 1100 ES	1.825 to 1.831 mm (0.0719 to 0.0721 in)
Main bearing running clearance – 1100 and 1100 ES	0.040 to 0.085 mm (0.0016 to 0.0034 in)

Big-end bearing shell thickness (standard):
    1100, 1100 ES, 1300 and 1300 S .... 1.531 to 1.538 mm (0.0603 to 0.0606 in)
    1500 and 1500 S .... 1.535 to 1.541 mm (0.0604 to 0.0607 in)

Cylinder head

Valve guide oversizes available .... +0.05, 0.10 and 0.25 mm (0.0020, 0.0039 and 0.0098 in)

Valves

Exhaust valve head diameter:
    1100, 1100 ES, 1300 and 1300 S .... 30.85 to 31.45 mm (1.2146 to 1.2382 in)
    1500 and 1500 S .... 32.85 to 33.45 mm (1.2933 to 1.3169 in)

Valve springs

Length under load – inner:
    14.9 ± 0.5 kg (32.9 ± 1.1 lb) .... 31.0 mm (1.221 in)
    28.1 ± 1.2 kg (62.0 ± 2.7 lb) .... 21.5 mm (0.847 in)
Length under load – outer:
    38.9 ± 1.5 kg (85.8 ± 3.3 lb) .... 36.0 mm (1.417 in)
    59.5 ± 2.5 kg (131.2 ± 5.5 lb) .... 26.5 mm (1.043 in)

Camshaft

Cam lift (inlet and exhaust) .... 8.8 mm (0.3465 in)

Valve clearances

Running clearances (cold):
    Inlet .... 0.40 mm (0.016 in)
    Exhaust .... 0.50 mm (0.020 in)
For valve timing check only .... 0.80 mm (0.032 in) inlet and exhaust
Range of adjustment shims .... 3.25 to 4.70 mm (0.1280 to 0.1850 in) in steps of 0.05 mm (0.0020 in)

Valve timing

	1100 ES	1100, 1300 & 1300 S	1500 & 1500 S
Inlet opens	9° BTDC	7° BTDC	6° BTDC
Inlet closes	31° ABDC	35° ABDC	46° ABDC
Exhaust opens	39° BBDC	37° BBDC	47° BBDC
Exhaust closes	1° ATDC	5° ATDC	7° ATDC

Lubrication system

Oil pump tolerances:
    Gear-to-body clearance .... 0.110 to 0.180 mm (0.0043 to 0.0071 in)
    Gear endfloat .... 0.020 to 0.105 mm (0.0008 to 0.0041 in)
    Driven gear play on shaft .... 0.010 to 0.050 mm (0.0004 to 0.0020 in)
    Driving gear shaft play .... 0.016 to 0.055 mm (0.0006 to 0.0022 in)
    Backlash between gears .... 0.31 mm (0.0122 in)
Oil pressure at 100°C (212°F) (engine running) .... 3.5 to 5.0 kgf/cm² (50 to 71 lbf/in²)
Oil pressure relief valve spring length under load:
    4.6 ± 0.15 kg (10.1 ± 0.3 lb) .... 22.5 mm (0.8858 in)
    5.0 ± 0.15 kg (11.0 ± 0.3 lb) .... 21.0 mm (0.8268 in)
Oil capacity:
    From dry .... 4.4 litres (7.8 pints) approx
    Drain and refill (including filter change) .... 4.1 litres (7.2 pints) approx

Engine – Strada II (1985 on) except TC

For specifications not given here, refer to those for earlier Strada II models

General

Maker's designation:
    1100 .... 146 A4.000
    1100 ES 138 C1.000
    1300 .... 149 A7.003
    1500 manual 149 A5.000
    1500 automatic 138 B.3000
Compression ratio:
    1300 and 1500 .... 9.5:1
Maximum power (EEC):
    1100 .... 43 kW (58.5 bhp) at 5700 rpm
    1100 ES .... 40 kW (55 bhp) at 5600 rpm
    1300 .... 48 kW (65 bhp) at 5600 rpm
    1500 manual .... 58 kW (79 bhp) at 5500 rpm
    1500 automatic .... 60 kW (82 bhp) at 5600 rpm
Maximum torque (EEC):
    1100 .... 87 Nm (64 lbf ft) at 3000 rpm

1100 ES .... 88 Nm (65 lbf ft) at 2900 rpm
1300 .... 100 Nm (74 lbf ft) at 3000 rpm
1500 manual .... 122 Nm (90 lbf ft) at 2900 rpm
1500 automatic .... 119.7 Nm (88 lbf ft) at 3000 rpm

Crankshaft and bearings

	1100 and 1300	**1500**
Main bearing journal diameter	50.790 to 50.810 mm (1.9996 to 2.0004 in)	50.780 to 50.800 mm (1.9992 to 2.0000 in)
Crankpin diameter	45.503 to 45.523 mm (1.7915 to 1.7922 in)	45.503 to 45.513 mm (1.7915 to 1.7918 in)
Main bearing running clearance	0.035 to 0.080 mm (0.0014 to 0.0031 in)	0.027 to 0.062 mm (0.0011 to 0.0024 in)
Big-end bearing undersizes	0.254 to 0.508 mm (0.0010 to 0.0200 in)	
Big-end running clearance	0.031 to 0.081 mm (0.0012 to 0.0032 in)	0.025 to 0.063 mm (0.0010 to 0.0025 in)

Valves

Head diameter:	**1100 and 1300**	**1500**
Inlet	35.85 to 36.15 mm (1.4114 to 1.4232 in)	35.85 to 36.15 mm (1.4114 to 1.4232 in)
Exhaust	30.85 to 31.45 mm (1.2146 to 1.2382 in)	32.85 to 33.45 mm (1.2933 to 1.3169 in)

Valve timing

1300:
    Inlet opens .... 9° BTDC
    Inlet closes .... 31° ABDC
    Exhaust opens .... 39° BBDC
    Exhaust closes .... 1° ATDC
1500 manual:
    Inlet opens .... 7° BTDC
    Inlet closes .... 35° ABDC
    Exhaust opens .... 37° BBDC
    Exhaust closes .... 5° ATDC
1500 automatic:
    Inlet opens .... 6° BTDC
    Inlet closes .... 46° ABDC
    Exhaust opens .... 47° BBDC
    Exhaust closes .... 7° ATDC

Torque wrench settings

	lbf ft	Nm
Crankcase breather bolt	17	23
Cylinder head bolts (see text):		
Stage 1	15	20
Stage 2	30	40
Tighten a further 180° in two stages		
Oil pressure switch	24	32
Coolant temperature sender	36	49

Engine – 105 TC

General

Type .... Four-cylinder, four-stroke, twin overhead camshafts
Maker's designation 138 AR.000
Bore .... 84 mm (3.307 in) nominal
Stroke .... 71.5 mm (2.815 in)
Displacement .... 1585 cc (96.7 cu in)
Compression ratio .... 9.3 : 1
Firing order .... 1 – 3 – 4 – 2 (No 1 at timing belt end)
Maximum power (DIN) .... 77.2 kW (104 bhp, 105 CV) @ 6100 rpm
Maximum torque (DIN) .... 13.6 kgf m (98.4 lbf ft) @ 4000 rpm

Crankcase and cylinder block

Main bearing bores .... 56.717 to 56.730 mm (2.233 to 2.234 in)
Auxiliary shaft bearing bores:
    Front .... 51.120 to 51.150 mm (2.013 to 2.014 in)
    Rear .... 42.030 to 42.060 mm (1.655 to 1.656 in)
Cylinder bores .... 84.000 to 84.050 mm (3.3071 to 3.3091 in) in graded steps of 0.010 mm (0.0004 in)

Pistons and rings

Diameter (standard):
    Grade A .... 83.930 to 83.940 mm (3.3043 to 3.3047 in)
    Grade C .... 83.950 to 83.960 mm (3.3051 to 3.3055 in)
    Grade E .... 83.970 to 83.980 mm (3.3059 to 3.3063 in)
Clearance in bore .... 0.06 to 0.08 mm (0.0024 to 0.0032 in)

Oversizes available .... + 0.2, 0.4 and 0.6 mm (0.008, 0.016 and 0.024 in)
Weight variation between pistons .... 5g (0.175 oz) max
Gudgeon pin bore:
    Grade 1 .... 21.996 to 21.999 mm (0.8660 to 0.8661 in)
    Grade 2 .... 21.999 to 22.002 mm (0.8661 to 0.8662 in)
Gudgeon pin diameter:
    Grade 1 .... 21.991 to 21.994 mm (0.8658 to 0.8659 in)
    Grade 2 .... 21.994 to 21.997 mm (0.8659 to 0.8660 in)
    Oversize .... + 0.2 mm (0.008 in)
Gudgeon pin clearance in piston .... 0.002 to 0.008 mm (0.00008 to 0.00032 in)
Piston ring grooves – vertical dimension:
    Top .... 1.535 to 1.555 mm (0.0604 to 0.612 in)
    Intermediate .... 2.030 to 2.050 mm (0.0799 to 0.0807 in)
    Bottom .... 3.967 to 3.987 mm (1.1562 to 0.1570 in)
Piston ring thickness:
    Top .... 1.478 to 1.490 mm (0.0582 to 0.0587 in)
    Intermediate .... 1.978 to 1.990 mm (0.0779 to 0.0784 in)
    Bottom .... 3.925 to 3.937 mm (0.1545 to 0.1550 in)
Piston ring vertical clearance in groove:
    Top .... 0.045 to 0.077 mm (0.0018 to 0.0030 in)
    Intermediate .... 0.040 to 0.072 mm (0.0016 to 0.0028 in)
    Bottom .... 0.030 to 0.062 mm (0.0012 to 0.0024 in)
Ring end gap in bore:
    Top .... 0.30 to 0.45 mm (0.0118 to 0.0177 in)
    Intermediate .... 0.30 to 0.45 mm (0.0118 to 0.0177 in)
    Bottom .... 0.25 to 0.40 mm (0.0098 to 0.0158 in)

Connecting rods

Big-end bearing bore .... 51.330 to 51.346 (2.0209 to 2.0215 in)
Small-end bush bore .... 23.939 to 23.972 mm (0.9425 to 0.9438 in)
Small-end bush outside diameter .... 24.016 to 24.041 mm (0.9455 to 0.9465 in)
Small-end bush inside diameter:
    Grade 1 .... 22.004 to 22.007 mm (0.8663 to 0.8664 in)
    Grade 2 .... 22.007 to 22.010 mm (0.8664 to 0.8665 in)
Gudgeon pin clearance in bush .... 0.010 to 0.016 mm (0.0004 to 0.0006 in)
Bush intermediate in connecting rod .... 0.044 to 0.102 mm (0.0017 to 0.0040 in)

Crankshaft and bearings

Main bearing journal diameter .... 52.985 to 53.005 mm (2.0860 to 2.0868 in)
Crankpin diameter .... 48.224 to 48.244 mm (1.8986 to 1.8994 in)
Crankpin length .... 27.975 to 28.025 mm (1.1014 to 1.1033 in)
Main bearing shell thickness (standard) .... 1.834 to 1.840 mm (0.0722 to 0.0724 in)
Main bearing undersizes .... 0.254, 0.508, 0.762 and 1.016 mm (0.010, 0.020, 0.030 and 0.040 in)
Main bearing running clearance .... 0.032 to 0.077 mm (0.0013 to 0.0030 in)
Big-end bearing shell thickness (standard) .... 1.524 to 1.528 mm (0.0600 to 0.0602 in)
Big-end bearing undersizes .... As for main bearings
Big-end bearing running clearance .... 0.030 to 0.074 mm (0.0012 to 0.0029 in)
Thrust washer thickness (standard) .... 2.310 to 2.360 mm (0.0910 to 0.0929 in)
Thrust washer oversize .... + 0.127 mm (0.0050 in)
Crankshaft endfloat .... 0.055 to 0.305 mm (0.0022 to 0.0120 mm)

Cylinder head

Valve guide bore in head .... 13.950 to 13.977 mm (0.5492 to 0.5503 in)
Valve guide outside diameter:
    Standard .... 14.040 to 14.058 mm (0.5528 to 0.5535 in)
    Oversizes available .... + 0.05, 0.10 and 0.25 mm (0.002, 0.004 and 0.010 in)
Valve guide interference in head .... 0.063 to 0.108 mm (0.0025 to 0.0043 in)
Valve guide internal diameter .... 8.022 to 8.040 mm (0.3158 to 0.3165 in)
Valve seat angle .... 45° ± 5'
Valve seat width .... 2 mm (0.08 in) approx

Valves

Head diameter:
    Inlet .... 43.2 to 43.7 mm (1.700 to 1.720 in)
    Exhaust .... 35.8 to 36.8 mm (1.410 to 1.449 in)
Stem diameter .... 7.974 to 7.992 mm (0.3139 to 0.3147 in)
Valve clearance in guide .... 0.030 to 0.066 mm (0.0012 to 0.0026 in)

Valve springs

Length under load – inner:
    14.9 ± 0.5 kg (32.8 ± 1.1 lb) .... 31.0 mm (1.221 in)
    28.1 ± 1.2 kg (62.0 ± 2.7 lb) .... 21.5 mm (0.847 in)

Length under load – outer:
    38.9 ± 1.5 kg (85.8 ± 3.3 lb) .... 36.0 mm (1.417 in)
    59.5 ± 2.5 kg (131.2 ± 5.5 lb) .... 26.5 mm (1.043 in)

Camshafts, camshaft carriers and tappets

Camshaft bearing journal diameters:
    Front .... 29.944 to 29.960 mm (1.1789 to 1.1795 in)
    Centre .... 45.755 to 45.771 mm (1.8014 to 1.8020 in)
    Rear .... 46.155 to 46.171 mm (1.8171 to 1.8178 in)
Cam lift (inlet and exhaust) .... 9.564 mm (0.3765 in)
Camshaft bearing bores in carrier:
    Front .... 30.009 to 30.034 mm (1.1815 to 1.1824 in)
    Centre .... 45.800 to 45.825 mm (1.8032 to 1.8041 in)
    Rear .... 46.200 to 46.225 mm (1.8189 to 1.8199 in)
Camshaft bearing running clearance:
    Front .... 0.049 to 0.090 mm (0.0019 to 0.0035 in)
    Centre and rear .... 0.029 to 0.070 mm (0.0011 to 0.0028 in)
Tappet diameter .... 36.975 to 36.995 mm (1.4557 to 1.4565 in)
Tappet bore in housing .... 37.000 to 37.025 mm (1.4567 to 1.4577 in)
Tappet clearance in housing .... 0.005 to 0.050 mm (0.0002 to 0.0020 in)

Valve clearances

Running clearance (cold):
    Inlet .... 0.45 mm (0.018 in)
    Exhaust .... 0.50 mm (0.020 in)
For valve timing check only .... 0.80 mm (0.032 in) inlet and exhaust
Method of adjustment .... Selective shims
Range of shim sizes .... 3.25 to 4.70 mm (0.1280 to 0.1850 in) in steps of 0.05 mm (0.0020 in)

Valve timing

	Pre-May '83	May '83 on
Inlet opens	5° BTDC	10° BTDC
Inlet closes	53° ABDC	48° ABDC
Exhaust opens	53° BBDC	53° BBDC
Exhaust closes	5° ATDC	5° ATDC

Auxiliary shaft

Bearing bush internal diameter:
    Front .... 48.084 to 48.104 mm (1.8931 to 1.8939 in)
    Rear .... 39.000 to 39.020 mm (1.5354 to 1.5362 in)
Bearing bush fit in block .... Interference fit
Bearing journal diameter:
    Front .... 48.013 to 48.038 mm (1.8903 to 1.8913 in)
    Rear .... 38.929 to 38.954 mm (1.5326 to 1.5336 in)
Bearing running clearance .... 0.046 to 0.091 mm (0.0018 to 0.0036 in)

Lubrication system

Oil pump tolerances:
    Gear-to-body clearance .... 0.110 to 0.180 mm (0.0043 to 0.0071 in)
    Gear endfloat .... 0.031 to 0.116 mm (0.0012 to 0.0046 in)
    Driven gear play on shaft .... 0.017 to 0.057 mm (0.0007 to 0.0022 in)
    Driving gear shaft play .... 0.016 to 0.055 mm (0.0006 to 0.0021 in)
    Backlash between gears .... 0.15 mm (0.0059 in)
Oil pressure at 100°C (212°F) .... 3.5 to 5.0 kgf/cm² (50 to 71 lbf/in²)
Oil pressure relief valve spring length under load:
    4.6 ± 0.15 kg (10.1 ± 0.3 lb) .... 22.5 mm (0.8858 in)
    5.0 ± 0.15 kg (11.0 ± 0.3 lb) .... 21.0 mm (0.8268 in)
Oil capacity – pre-May '83 models:
    From dry .... 5.5 litres (9.7 pints) approx
    Drain and refill (including filter change) .... 4.8 litres (8.5 pints) approx
Oil capacity – later models:
    From dry .... 5.3 litres (9.3 pints)
    Drain and refill (including filter change) .... 4.6 litres (8.1 pints)

Torque wrench settings

	lbf ft	Nm
Main bearing cap bolts:		
Front (M10)	59	80
Others (M12)	83	113
Crankcase breather bolt	17	23
Cylinder head bolts (see text):		
Models up to engine No 1 364 207:		
Stage 1	18	25
Stage 2	41	55
Stage 3	63	85
Later models:		
Stage 1	15	20

Torque wrench settings (continued)

	lbf ft	Nm
Stage 2	30	40
Tighten a further 180° on two stages		
Additional cylinder head bolts (1500 cc engine)	22	30
Camshaft carrier bolts	16	22
Manifold nuts and bolts	18	25
Big-end nuts	38	51
Flywheel-to-crankshaft bolts	61	83
Camshaft sprocket bolts	87	118
Timing belt tensioner nut	33	44
Oil pump securing bolts	15	20
Crankshaft pulley nut	145	196
Crankshaft pulley bolt (left-hand thread)	133	180
Oil filter housing bolts	36	49
Alternator-to-crankcase nut	51	69
Alternator-to-upper bracket nut	32	43
Alternator upper bracket-to-crankcase bolt:		
Plain bolts	38	52
Olive green bolts	52	71
Alternator upper bracket-to-camshaft carrier brackets	11	15
Driveshaft support mounting bolt	18	25
Driveshaft support mounting nut	41	56
Oil pressure switch	24	32
Coolant temperature sender	36	49
Oil pressure gauge sender	27	37
Oil temperature gauge sender	36	49
Spark plugs	27	37

Engine – 130 TC

Specifications as for 105 TC except as given below

General

Maker's designation	138 AR2.000
Stroke	90 mm (3.543 in)
Displacement	1995 cc (121.7 cu in)
Compression ratio	9.45 : 1
Maximum power (DIN)	95.6 kW (128 bhp, 130 CV) @ 5900 rpm
Maximum torque (DIN)	18 kgf m (130 lbf ft) @ 3600 rpm

Pistons and rings

Diameter (standard):	
Grade A	83.940 to 83.950 mm (3.3047 to 3.3051 in)
Grade C	83.960 to 83.970 mm (3.3055 to 3.3059 in)
Grade E	83.980 to 83.990 mm (3.3063 to 3.3067 in)
Oversize available	+ 0.4 mm (0.016 in)
Piston clearance in bore	0.05 to 0.07 mm (0.0020 to 0.0028 in)
Piston ring thickness:	
Intermediate	1.980 to 2.000 mm (0.0780 to 0.0787 in)
Bottom	3.922 to 3.937 mm (0.1544 to 0.1550 in)
Piston ring vertical clearance in grooves:	
Intermediate	0.030 to 0.062 mm (0.0012 to 0.0024 in)
Ring end gap in bore:	
Top	0.25 to 0.50 mm (0.0098 to 0.0197 in)

Connecting rods

Big-end bearing bore	53.897 to 53.913 mm (2.1219 to 2.1226 in)

Crankshaft and bearings

Main bearing journal diameter:	
Grade 1	52.995 to 53.005 mm (2.0864 to 2.0868 in)
Grade 2	52.985 to 53.995 mm (2.0860 to 2.0864 in)
Crankpin diameter:	
Grade A	50.797 to 50.807 mm (1.9999 to 2.0003 in)
Grade B	50.787 to 50.797 mm (1.9995 to 1.9999 in)
Main bearing shell thickness:	
Grade 1	1.834 to 1.840 mm (0.0722 to 0.0724 in)
Grade 2	1.839 to 1.845 mm (0.0724 to 0.0726 in)
Main bearing running clearance	0.031 to 0.067 mm (0.0012 to 0.0026 in)
Big-end bearing shell thickness:	
Grade A	1.527 to 1.533 mm (0.0601 to 0.0604 in)
Grade B	1.532 to 1.538 mm (0.0603 to 0.0606 in)
Big-end bearing running clearance	0.024 to 0.062 mm (0.0010 to 0.0024 in)

Camshafts

Cam lift (inlet and exhaust)	10.033 mm (0.3950 in)

Valve timing
Inlet opens .... 7° BTDC
Inlet closes .... 52° ABDC
Exhaust opens .... 51° BBDC
Exhaust closes .... 8° ATDC

Lubrication system
Oil pressure relief valve spring length under load:
   5.95 to 6.45 kg (13.1 to 14.2 lb) .... 22.5 mm (0.89 in)
Oil capacity – from dry:
   Steel sump .... 5.7 litres (10.0 pints) approx
   Aluminium sump .... 5.3 litres (9.3 pints) approx
Drain and refill (including filter change):
   Steel sump .... 4.8 litres (8.5 pints) approx
   Aluminium sump .... 4.4 litres (7.8 pints) approx

Torque wrench settings

	lbf ft	Nm
Big-end nuts	55	74
Flywheel-to-crankshaft bolts	105	142
Engine support bracket bolts:		
To cylinder head (M12)	66	90
Mounting support (M8)	20	27
Oil cooler-to-front crossmember nut	18	25
Oil cooler take-off flange hollow bolt	27	36

Cooling system – Strada II and all TC

Thermostat
Opening temperature:
   All except 130 TC .... 83° to 87°C (181° to 189°F)
   130 TC .... 77° to 81°C (171° to 178°F)
Fully open (all models) .... 95°C (203°F)

Radiator cap pressure rating
Except TC .... 1 kgf/cm² (14 lbf/in²)
105 and 130 TC .... 0.8 kgf/cm² (11 lbf/in²)

Coolant pump
Clearance between blades and casing:
   Except TC .... 0.8 to 1.3 mm (0.032 to 0.051 in)
   105 and 130 TC .... 1.0 mm (0.039 in)

Coolant capacity
1100:
   Up to 1985 .... 7.0 litres (12.3 pints) approx
   From 1985 .... 6.7 litres (11.8 pints) approx
1300:
   Up to 1985 .... 7.0 litres (12.3 pints) approx
   From 1985 .... 6.9 litres (12.1 pints) approx
1500 .... 7.0 litres (12.3 pints) approx
105 and 130 TC .... 7.5 litres (13.2 pints) approx

Fuel system – early models

Carburettor – Super 85
Type .... Weber 34 DMTR 53/250 or Solex 34 CIC/2

Calibration – Weber 34 DMTR 53/250:	Primary	Secondary
Venturi	23 mm	26 mm
Auxiliary venturi	4 mm	4 mm
Main jet	1.20 mm	1.35 mm
Air correction jet	1.75 mm	2.20 mm
Emulsion tube	F30	F38
Idle fuel jet	0.47 mm	0.50 mm
Idle air jet	1.55 mm	0.70 mm
Accelerator pump jet	0.40 mm	–
Accelerator pump outlet	0.40 mm	–
Superfeed fuel jet	–	0.70 mm
Superfeed mixture jet	–	2.00 mm
Needle valve	1.75 mm	–
Idle adjustment hole	1.25 mm	–
Accelerator pump delivery	8.5 cc per 10 strokes	
Float level	7 mm	

Calibration – Solex 34 CIC/2	Primary	Secondary
Venturi	23 mm	27 mm
Auxiliary venturi	4 mm	4 mm

Main jet	1.15 mm	1.32 mm
Air correction jet	1.90 mm	1.50 mm
Emulsion tube	86	87
Idle fuel jet	0.45 mm	0.45 mm
Idle air jet	1.30 mm	1.00 mm
Accelerator pump jet	0.50 mm	–
Accelerator pump outlet	0.45 mm	–
Needle valve	1.60 mm	–
Anti-syphon device	1.50 mm	–
Idle adjustment hole	1.70 mm	–
Float level	4 to 5 mm	
Throttle valve opening for fast idle	1.0 mm	–
Choke valve opening by vacuum unloader	5.0 mm	

Fuel system – Strada II and all TC

Fuel pump
Type:
All except 130 TC	Mechanical, driven from auxiliary shaft
130 TC	Electric

Flow rate capacity:
Except TC	75 litres (132 pints) per hour
105 TC	100 litres (176 pints) per hour
130 TC	150 litres (264 pints) per hour

Fuel pressure:
Except TC	0.18 kgf/cm² (2.6 lbf/in²) @ 4000 engine rpm
105 TC	0.25 to 0.30 kgf/cm² (3.6 to 4.3 lbf/in²) @ 4000 engine rpm
130 TC	0.15 to 0.41 kgf/cm² (2.1 to 5.8 lbf/in²) @ 12 volts
Pressure regulation (mechanical pump)	By gasket thickness (see text)

Fuel tank capacity

	55.0 litres (12.1 gallons)

Carburettor application
1100 (up to 1985)	Weber 32 ICEV 51/250 or Solex C 32 DISA/12
1100 (1985 on)	Weber 30/32 DMTE 8/250 or Solex 30/32 CIC 9
1100 ES (up to 1985)	Weber 30 DMTE/250 or Solex C 30 CIC/1
1100 ES (1985 on)	Weber 30 DMTE 7/250
1300 and 1300 S	Weber 30/32 DMTR 90/250, -/150 (with air conditioning) or -/450 (automatic), or Solex C 30/32 CIC/1
1500 and 1500 S (up to 1985)	Weber 32/34 DMTR 81/250, -/150 (with air conditioning), -/450 (automatic) or -/350 (automatic with air conditioning), or Solex C 32/34 CIC/1
1500 S (1985 on)	Weber 32/34 TLDE/150
105 TC (up to April 1983)	Weber 34 DAT 11/251
105 TC (May 1983 on)	Weber 32/34 DMTR 82/250
130 TC	Twin Solex C 40 ADDHE 27 or Weber 40 DCOE

Carburettor calibration
Weber 32 ICEV 51/250:
Venturi	22 mm
Auxiliary venturi	3.5 mm
Main jet	1.15 mm
Air bleed jet	1.90 mm
Emulsion tube	F74
Idle fuel jet	0.47 mm
Idle air jet	1.55 mm
Accelerator pump jet	0.40 mm
Accelerator pump outlet	0.45 mm
Superfeed fuel jet	0.90 mm
Superfeed mixture jet	2.50 mm
Needle valve	1.50 mm
Anti-syphon device	1.00 mm
Idle mixture adjustment hole	1.50 mm
Accelerator pump delivery	3.2 to 5.2 cc per 10 strokes
Float level	10.75 ± 0.25 mm
Throttle valve opening for fast idle	0.85 to 0.90 mm
Choke valve opening by vacuum unloader	4 ± 0.25 mm

Solex C 32 DISA/12:
Venturi	22 mm
Auxiliary venturi	3.4 mm
Main jet	1.22 mm
Air bleed jet	2.00 mm
Emulsion tube	86
Idle fuel jet	0.57 mm
Idle air jet	1.40 mm

Accelerator pump jet	0.45 mm	
Accelerator pump outlet	0.50 mm	
Superfeed fuel jet	1.15 mm	
Superfeed mixture jet	2.00 mm	
Needle valve	1.60 mm	
Anti-syphon device	1.60 mm	
Idle mixture adjustment hole	1.70 mm	
Accelerator pump delivery	3.5 ± 0.5 cc per 10 strokes	
Float level	2.5 ± 0.5 mm	
Throttle valve opening for fast idle	0.95 ± 0.05 mm	
Choke valve opening by vacuum unloader	5 ± 0.25 mm	

Weber 30 DMTE/250:	Primary	Secondary
Venturi	18 mm	20 mm
Auxiliary venturi	3 mm	4.5 mm
Main jet	0.80 mm	0.87 mm
Air bleed jet	1.70 mm	1.50 mm
Emulsion tube	F27	F27
Idle fuel jet	0.45 mm	0.45 mm
Idle air jet	1.10 mm	0.90 mm
Accelerator pump jet	0.40 mm	–
Accelerator pump outlet	0.40 mm	–
Superfeed fuel jet	–	0.75 mm
Superfeed mixture jet	–	2.00 mm
Needle valve	1.50 mm	
Anti-syphon device	1.00 mm	
Idle mixture adjustment hole	1.50 mm	–
Accelerator pump delivery	8.5 to 12.5 cc per 10 strokes	
Float level	7 ± 0.25 mm	
Throttle valve opening for fast idle	0.9 to 1.0 mm	–
Choke valve opening (mechanical unloading)	7.0 to 7.5 mm	
Choke valve opening by vacuum unloader	4.5 to 5.0 mm	

Solex C 30 CIC/1:	Primary	Secondary
Venturi	18 mm	20 mm
Auxiliary venturi	3.2 mm	3.2 mm
Main jet	1.07 mm	1.07 mm
Air bleed jet	2.20 mm	1.60 mm
Emulsion tube	95	87
Idle fuel jet	0.47 mm	0.52 mm
Idle air jet	1.20 mm	1.60 mm
Accelerator pump jet	0.50 mm	–
Accelerator pump outlet	0.45 mm	–
Needle valve	1.60 mm	
Anti-syphon device	1.80 mm	–
Idle mixture adjustment hole	1.20 mm	–
Accelerator pump delivery	8.5 ± 1 cc per 10 strokes	
Float level	7 ± 0.5 mm	
Throttle valve opening for fast idle	0.9 to 1.0 mm	–
Choke valve opening by vacuum unloader	5.0 ± 0.25 mm	

Weber 30/32 DMTR series:	Primary	Secondary
Venturi	19 mm	23 mm
Auxiliary venturi	3.5 mm	5.0 mm
Main jet	0.87 mm	0.95 mm
Air bleed jet	1.85 mm	1.75 mm
Emulsion tube	F43	F38
Idle fuel jet	0.50 mm	0.50 mm
Idle air jet	1.10 mm	0.70 mm
Accelerator pump jet	0.45 mm	–
Accelerator pump outlet	0.40 mm	–
Superfeed fuel jet	–	0.80 mm
Superfeed mixture jet	–	2.00 mm
Needle valve	1.50 mm	
Anti-syphon device	1.00 mm	–
Idle mixture adjustment hole	1.50 mm	–
Accelerator pump delivery	8.5 to 12.5 cc per 10 strokes	
Float level	7 ± 0.25 mm	
Throttle valve opening for fast idle (choke out):		
Without air conditioning	0.90 to 0.95 mm	–
With air conditioning	0.95 to 1.00 mm	–
Choke valve opening (mechanical unloading)	7.0 to 7.5 mm	
Choke valve opening by vacuum unloader	4.0 ± 0.25 mm	
Throttle valve partial opening	6.70 ± 0.25 mm	
Throttle valve full opening	14.0 ± 0.5 mm	15.0 ± 0.5 mm

Solex C30/32 CIC/1:

	Primary	Secondary
Venturi	19 mm	23 mm
Auxiliary venturi	3.2 mm	4.0 mm
Main jet	1.15 mm	1.27 mm
Air bleed jet	2.30 mm	2.00 mm
Emulsion tube	95	95
Idle fuel jet	0.50 mm	0.50 mm
Idle air jet	1.20 mm	1.60 mm
Accelerator pump jet	0.50 mm	–
Accelerator pump outlet	0.45 mm	–
Needle valve	1.60 mm	
Anti-syphon device	1.80 mm	–
Idle mixture adjustment hole	1.60 mm	–
Accelerator pump delivery	8.5 ± 1 cc per 10 strokes	
Float level	7.0 ± 0.5 mm	
Throttle valve opening for fast idle	0.90 to 1.00 mm	–
Choke valve opening by vacuum unloader	5.00 ± 0.25 mm	

Weber 32/34 DMTR series except suffix 82/250:

	Primary	Secondary
Venturi	22 mm	24 mm
Auxiliary venturi	3.5 mm	5.0 mm
Main jet	1.00 mm	1.05 mm
Air bleed jet	1.90 mm	1.70 mm
Emulsion tube	F22	F38
Idle fuel jet	0.50 mm	0.70 mm
Idle air jet	1.40 mm	0.70 mm
Accelerator pump jet	0.55 mm	–
Accelerator pump outlet	0.40 mm	–
Superfeed fuel jet	–	0.7 mm
Superfeed mixture jet	–	2.00 mm
Needle valve	1.75 mm	
Anti-syphon device	1.00 mm	–
Idle mixture adjustment hole	1.70 mm	–
Accelerator pump delivery	8.5 to 12.5 cc per 10 strokes	
Float level	7.0 ± 0.25 mm	
Throttle valve opening for fast idle	1.0 to 1.05 mm	–
Choke valve opening by vacuum unloader	6.00 ± 0.25 mm	
Throttle valve partial opening	7.20 ± 0.25 mm	–
Throttle valve full opening	15.0 ± 0.5 mm	16.0 ± 0.5 mm

Solex C32/34 CIC/1:

	Primary	Secondary
Venturi	22 mm	24 mm
Auxiliary venturi	3.2 mm	4.0 mm
Main jet	1.35 mm	1.45 mm
Air bleed jet	2.30 mm	2.00 mm
Emulsion tube	95	95
Idle fuel jet	0.55 mm	0.50 mm
Idle air jet	1.20 mm	1.60 mm
Accelerator pump jet	0.50 mm	–
Accelerator pump outlet	0.45 mm	–
Needle valve	1.60 mm	
Anti-syphon device	1.80 mm	–
Idle mixture adjustment hole	1.60 mm	–
Accelerator pump delivery	8.5 ± 1 cc per 10 strokes	
Float level	7.0 ± 0.5 mm	
Throttle valve opening for fast idle	0.90 to 1.00 mm	–
Choke valve opening by vacuum unloader	5.00 ± 0.25 mm	

Weber 34 DAT 11/251:

	Primary	Secondary
Venturi	23 mm	27 mm
Auxiliary venturi	4 mm	4 mm
Main jet	1.07 mm	1.15 mm
Air bleed jet	1.70 mm	1.80 mm
Emulsion tube	F27	F38
Idle fuel jet	0.50 mm	0.50 mm
Idle air jet	1.10 mm	1.30 mm
Accelerator pump jet	0.50 mm	–
Accelerator pump outlet	0.40 mm	–
Superfeed fuel jet	–	0.80 mm
Superfeed mixture jet	–	2.00 mm
Needle valve	1.75 mm	
Anti-syphon device	1.20 mm	–
Idle mixture adjustment hole	1.20 mm	–
Accelerator pump delivery	10 to 15 cc per 10 strokes	
Float level	7.0 ± 0.25 mm	
Throttle valve opening for fast idle	0.9 to 1.0 mm	–

Weber 32/34 DMTR 82/250:	Primary	Secondary
Venturi	22 mm	24 mm
Auxiliary venturi	4.0 mm	4.5 mm
Main jet	1.02 mm	1.20 mm
Air bleed jet	1.60 mm	2.05 mm
Emulsion tube	F27	F27
Idle fuel jet	0.50 mm	0.50 mm
Idle air jet	1.10 mm	1.30 mm
Accelerator pump jet	0.50 mm	–
Accelerator pump outlet	0.40 mm	–
Superfeed fuel jet	–	1.10 mm
Superfeed mixture jet	–	2.00 mm
Needle valve	1.75 mm	
Anti-syphon device	1.00 mm	
Idle mixture adjustment hole	1.50 mm	–
Accelerator pump delivery	8.5 to 12.5 cc per 10 strokes	
Float level	7.0 ± 0.25 mm	
Throttle valve opening for fast idle	1.00 to 1.05 mm	–
Choke valve opening by vacuum unloader	4.50 ± 0.25 mm	
Throttle valve partial opening	7.20 ± 0.25 mm	–
Throttle valve full opening	15.0 ± 0.5 mm	16.0 ± 0.5 mm

Solex C 40 ADDHE 27:	Primary	Secondary
Venturi	32 mm	32 mm
Auxiliary venturi	4.8 mm	4.8 mm
Main jet	1.45 mm	1.45 mm
Air bleed jet	1.90 mm	1.90 mm
Emulsion tube	AO4	AO4
Idle fuel jet	0.54 mm	0.54 mm
Idle air jet	1.80 mm	1.80 mm
Accelerator pump jet	0.45 mm	0.45 mm
Idle mixture adjustment hole	1.40 mm	1.40 mm
Accelerator pump delivery	6 to 10 cc per 10 strokes	
Float level	4.0 ± 0.5 mm	

Weber 32/34 TLDE/150:	Primary	Secondary
Venturi	21	24
Auxiliary venturi	300	300
Main jet	112 ± 6	140 ± 3
Air correction jet	160 $^{+\ 0}_{-\ 10}$	160 ± 5
Emulsion tube	F74	F25
Power jet	60	–
High speed fuel bleed	–	70 ± 5
High speed air bleed	–	200
Idle jet	47 ± 3	40 ± 3
Idle air bush	140 ± 5	100 ± 5
Needle valve	175	
Pump jet	40	
Pump bleed	40	
Float height	30 ± 0.25 mm	
Principle throttle valve opening	7.2 ± 0.25 mm	
Throttle valve opening for fast idle	0.95 ± 0.05 mm	
Choke valve opening by pneumatic pulldown	4.5 ± 0.25 mm	

Weber 40 DCOE 145/146:	Primary	Secondary
Venturi diameter	32.0 mm	32.0 mm
Main jet	138	145
Air correction jet	175	190
Emulsion tube	F41	F41
Idle jet	58	54
Idle air bleed	–	180
Accelerator pump jet	35	45
Accelerator pump delivery	3.5 cc per 10 strokes	
Fuel inlet needle valve	1.50 mm	
Float setting	6.75 to 7.25 mm	

Idle adjustment data

Idle speed:	
1100 ES	750 ± 50 rpm
All other models	850 ± 50 rpm
CO emission at idle:	
1100, 1300 and 1500:	
Up to 1985	1.0 to 2.5%
From 1985	0.5 to 1.5%
105 and 130 TC	1.0 to 2.5%

Ignition system
General
System type:
1300 models (from 1985) and 105 TC (up to April 1983) .... Electronic breakerless (impulse generator and inductive discharge types)

1500 models (from 1985), 105 TC (from April 1983),
130 TC and 1100 ES .... Digiplex electronically-controlled

Distributor (conventional system)
Make and type .... Ducellier 525537 A, Ducellier 525342 A or Marelli S 178 HX
Contact breaker gap .... 0.37 to 0.43 mm (0.015 to 0.017 in)
Dwell angle .... 55° ± 3°

Distributor (impulse generator system)
Make and type .... Marelli SE 100 CX
Rotor-to-stator gap .... 0.30 to 0.40 mm (0.012 to 0.016 in)

Distributor (inductive discharge system)
Make and type .... Marelli SM 800 AX, SM 801 AX or Bosch 0.237.001.002
Rotor-to stator gap:
Marelli .... 0.3 to 0.4 mm (0.012 to 0.016 in)
Bosch .... Not applicable

Distributor (Digiplex system)
Make and type .... Marelli DT 402 BX
Rotor arm resistance .... 1000 ohms approx
Control unit type:
1100 ES (up to 1985) .... Marelli MED 404 A
1100 ES (from 1985) .... Marelli MED 414 A
1500 .... Marelli MED 416 A
105 TC .... Marelli MED 406 A
130 TC .... Marelli MED 408 A

Ignition coil
Make and type:
Conventional system .... Marelli BE 200 B, Bosch 0.221, 119, 048, Klitz OEM G 52 S or Iskra ATA 0115
Impulse generator system .... Marelli BAE 506 A
Inductive discharge system .... Marelli BAE 207 A, or Bosch 0.221, 122, 012
Digiplex system .... Marelli BAE 209 B

Winding resistance:	Primary (ohms)	Secondary (kilohms)
Marelli BE 200 B	3.0 to 3.3	8.5 to 10.5
Bosch 0.221, 119, 048	2.6 to 3.1	8.5 to 12.0
Klitz OEM G 52 S	2.82 ± 0.14	7.10 ± 0.36
Iskra ATA 0115	3.30 ± 0.13	7.50 ± 0.75
Marelli BAE 506 A	0.76 to 0.92	3.33 to 4.07
Marelli BAE 207 A	0.75 to 0.81	9.5 to 11.5
Bosch 0.221, 122, 012	1.2 to 1.6	6.0 to 10.0
Marelli BAE 209 B	0.310 to 0.378	3.33 to 4.07

Ignition sensors (Digiplex system)
Make and type:
RPM (flywheel) sensor .... Marelli SEN 8 E
TDC (pulley) sensor .... Marelli SEN 8 D
Gap between sensor and teeth:
RPM .... 0.25 to 1.30 mm (0.010 to 0.051 in)
TDC .... 0.4 to 1.0 mm (0.016 to 0.039 in)
Resistance .... 612 to 748 ohms

Spark plugs*
Make and type:
1100, 1100 ES, 1300 S .... Champion RN9YC, Bosch WR7DC, Marelli F7LCR, Fiat V4LSR, or equivalent
1500 and 1500 S .... Champion RN7YC, Bosch WR6DC, Marelli F7LCR, Marelli F8LCR, Fiat V4JR, or equivalent
105 TC (all models) .... As for 1100/1300 models above
130 TC .... Champion RN7YC, Bosch WR6DC, or equivalent
Electrode gap (all models) .... 0.7 to 0.8 mm (0.028 to 0.032 in)
Consult owner's handbook or a Fiat dealer for latest recommendations

Ignition timing

Conventional and impulse generator systems	10° BTDC static or idle
Inductive discharge system	10 to 12° BTDC nominal (not adjustable)
Digiplex system	10 to 12° BTDC nominal (not adjustable)

Clutch

Adjustment (Strada II and all TC)

Pedal position	8 to 12 mm (to 0.32 to 0.47 in) higher than brake pedal

Driven plate diameter

Strada II:

1100 and 1300	181.5 mm (7.15 in)
1500	190 mm (7.48 in)
105 TC (all models) and 130 TC	200 mm (7.87 in)

Torque wrench settings

	lbf ft	Nm
Pressure plate-to-flywheel bolts:		
105 TC and 130 TC	28	38
Other models	Not specified	
Clutch release fork lockbolt:		
105 TC and 130 TC	19	26
Other models	Not specified	

Manual transmission

Gear ratios

Strada II (except all TC and 1100 and 1300 models from 1985):

1st	4.090 : 1
2nd	2.235 : 1
3rd	1.461 : 1
4th	1.034 : 1
5th (when fitted – 1100)	0.863 : 1 (1100) or 0.827 : (1300/1500)
Reverse	3.714 : 1

105 TC (all models)

1st	3.583 : 1
2nd	2.235 : 1
3rd	1.550 : 1
4th	1.163 : 1
5th	0.959 : 1
Reverse	3.714 : 1

130 TC:

1st	3.583 : 1
2nd	2.235 : 1
3rd	1.542 : 1
4th	1.154 : 1
5th	0.967 : 1
Reverse	3.667 : 1

1100 (1985 on):

1st	4.091 : 1
2nd	2.235 : 1
3rd	1.469 : 1
4th	1.043 : 1
5th	0.863 : 1
Reverse	3.717 : 1

1300 and 1500 (1985 on):

1st	4.091 : 1
2nd	2.235 : 1
3rd	1.469 : 1
4th	1.043 : 1
5th	0.827 : 1
Reverse	3.717 : 1

Final drive ratio

Strada II (except TC):

1100 and 1300	3.765 : 1
1500	3.588 : 1
105 TC:	
Up to April 1983	3.765 : 1
April 1983 on	3.588 : 1
130 TC	3.400 : 1

Lubrication

Lubricant capacity:

4-speed	3.0 litres (5.3 pints) approx
5-speed	3.3 litres (5.8 pints) approx

Automatic transmission (from 1985)
Speed ratios
1st	2.714 : 1
2nd	1.500 : 1
3rd	1.100 : 1
Reverse	2.430 : 1
Final drive	3.409 : 1

Driveshafts
Type
75 models from 1981, and all Strada II except automatic and TC	One-piece, CV joints at outboard ends, Tripode joints at inboard ends
Automatic, 105 TC and 130 TC:	
Left-hand	One-piece, CV joints at both ends.
Right-hand	Two-piece with centre support bearing, CV joints at both ends of outer section

Braking system – Strada II and all TC
Brake discs
Diameter:
All except TC	227 mm (8.94 in)
105 TC up to April '83	251 mm (9.88 in)
105 TC from May '83	257 mm (10.12 in)
130 TC	243 mm (9.57 in)

Thickness, new:
All except TC	10.7 to 10.9 mm (0.42 to 0.43 in)
105 TC up to April '83	10.9 to 11.1 mm (0.43 to 0.44 in)
105 TC from May '83	11.9 to 12.1 mm (0.47 to 0.48 in)
130 TC	19.9 to 20.1 mm (0.78 to 0.79 in)

Thickness, refinishing limit:
All except TC	9.7 mm (0.38 in)
105 TC up to April '83	9.5 mm (0.37 in)
105 TC from May '83	11.3 mm (0.45 in)
130 TC	19.0 mm (0.75 in)

Thickness wear limit:
All except TC	9.0 mm (0.35 in)
105 TC up to April '83	9.0 mm (0.35 in)
105 TC from May '83	10.8 mm (0.43 in)
130 TC	18.5 mm (0.73 in)

Brake drums
Internal diameter – refinishing limit:
105 TC up to April '83	186.83 mm (7.356 in)
All other models	186.33 mm (7.336 in)

Internal diameter – wear limit
105 TC up to April '83	187.00 mm (7.362 in)
All other models	186.83 mm (7.356 in)

Brake servo
Pushrod free play:
130 TC	0.3 to 0.5 mm (0.012 to 0.020 in)
All other models	0.825 to 1.025 mm (0.033 to 0.040 in)

Hydraulic system
Rear wheel cylinder diameter:
105 TC up to April '83	17.46 mm ($^{11}/_{16}$ in)
105 TC from May '83 and 130 TC	19.05 mm ($^3/_4$ in)
Other models (initial production)	17.46 mm ($^{11}/_{16}$ in)
Other models (with yellow mark on backplate)	19.05 mm ($^3/_4$ in)

Pressure differential regulator calibration load (see text) – except TC:
Unmarked spring, $^{11}/_{16}$ in cylinders	6.0 kg (13.2 lb)
Unmarked spring, $^3/_4$ in cylinders	3.0 kg (6.6 lb)
Yellow marked spring, $^{11}/_{16}$ in cylinders	9.0 kg (19.9 lb)
Yellow marked spring, $^3/_4$ in cylinders	4.5 kg (9.9 lb)

Pressure differential regulator calibration load – TC from May 1983:
105 TC	2.5 kg (5.5 lb)
130 TC	6.5 kg (14.3 lb)

Torque wrench setting
	lbf ft	Nm
Caliper securing bolts (105 TC from May 1983)	65	88

Electrical system – early models
Fuses – Super 85
Fuse No	Rating (A)	Circuit(s) protected
1	8	Instruments and instrument illumination, ignition switch, reversing light, direction indicators, stop-lights, heater blower relay, power window relay, braking system warning lights, coolant level warning

Fuse No	Rating (A)	Circuit(s) protected
		light, automatic transmission selector illumination
2	8	Windscreen and rear window wipers and washers
3	8	RH side and tail lights
4	8	LH side and tail lights, luggage area light, number plate light, clock illumination, sidelight pilot light, cigarette lighter illumination
5	8	LH dipped beam, rear foglight
6	8	RH dipped beam
7	8	LH main beam, main beam pilot light
8	8	RH main beam
9	16	Radiator fan motor, horns and horn relay
10	8	Clock, cigarette lighter, interior light, ignition key illumination
11	16	Hazard warning flasher, heated rear window
12	8	Headlamp washers (when fitted)
13	16	Power window motors (when fitted)
14	8	Heater blower motor, glovebox light, heater control and switch illumination

Electrical system – Strada II and all TC

Battery

Capacity (at 20-hour rate):	
105 TC up to April '83	48 Ah
105 TC (later models)	45 Ah
130 TC	45 Ah
Other models – 1100	30 Ah
Other models – 1300/1500	40 Ah

Alternator

Make	Marelli, Bosch or Mitsubishi
Maximum output	55A, 65A or 70A according to model
Regulated voltage	14.0 to 14.3 volts at 20°C (68°F)

Starter motor

Make	Bosch, Ducellier, Femsa or Marelli
Output	0.8 to 1.1 kW according to model
Armature shaft endfloat	0.15 to 0.45 mm (0.006 to 0.018 in)

Fuses – early 105 TC

As for early Super 85

Fuses – Strada II, including TC

Fuse No*	Rating (A)	Circuit(s) protected
1	10	Instruments, warning lights, stop-lights, reversing lights, digital clock (ignition-controlled feed)
2	20	Wipers and washers
3	7.5	LH sidelight, RH tail light, RH number plate light, cigarette lighter light
4	7.5	RH sidelight, LH tail light, LH number plate light, clock and instrument panel illumination
5	10	LH dipped beam, rear foglight and warning light
6	10	RH dipped beam
7	10	LH main beam, main beam pilot light
8	10	RH main beam
9	25	Radiator cooling fan
10	20	Heater fan
11	20	Heated rear window and warning light
12	10	Cigarette lighter, radio, interior light, clock (full-time feed)
13	10	Hazard warning system
14	20	Horn

*Numbers correspond to those on wiring diagram; fuse box carries symbols instead of numbers

Steering – Strada II and all TC

Front wheel alignment

Toe (unladen):	
All models except TC:	
Up to 1985	1.0 to 3.0 mm (0.04 to 0.12 in) toe-out
From 1985	1.0 mm (0.04 in) toe-out to 1.0 mm (0.04 in) toe-in
105 TC:	
Up to 1983	0 to 4.0 mm (0 to 0.16 in) toe-out
From 1983	0 to 3.0 mm (0 to 0.12 in) toe-out
130 TC:	
Shock absorbers with 2 nuts	1.0 to 3.0 mm (0.04 to 0.12 in) toe-out
Shock absorbers with 3 nuts	3.0 mm (0.12 in) toe-out to 1.0 mm (0.04 in) toe-in
Camber (unladen:)	
1100 and 1300:	
Up to 1985	+1°10' to +2°10'
From 1985	+1°30' to +2°30'
1500:	
Up to 1985	+1°10' to +2°10'

From 1985	+1°15' to +2°15'
105 TC:	
Up to 1983	+1°20' to +2°20'
From 1983	+1° to +2°
130 TC:	
Shock absorbers with 2 nuts	0 to +40'
Shock absorbers with 3 nuts	−50' to +10'
Castor (unladen):	
All models except TC:	
Up to 1985	+1° to +2°
From 1985	+50' to +1°50'
105 TC:	
Up to 1983	+2°10'
From 1983	+50' to +1°50'
130 TC:	
Shock absorbers with 2 nuts	0 to +1°
Shock absorbers with 3 nuts	−5' to +55'

Torque wrench settings

	lbf ft	Nm˙
Steering wheel hub-to-shaft (105 TC and 130 TC)	27	37
Steering heel-to-hub bolts	4	5

Suspension – Strada II and all TC
Rear suspension geometry, unladen

Toe:	
All except 130 TC	0 to 4 mm (0 to 0.16 in) toe-in
130 TC:	
Front shock absorbers with 2 nuts	2 to 4 mm (0.08 to 0.16 in) toe-in
Front shock absorbers with 3 nuts	1 to 5 mm (0.04 to 0.20 in) toe-in
Camber:	
All models except TC:	
Up to 1985	+30' to +1°30'
From 1985	−30' to + 30'
105 TC:	
Up to 1983	−40'
From 1983	−1° to 0
130 TC	−2° to −3°

Wheels

Rim size	4^1/$_2$B x 13 or 5^1/$_2$J x 14

Tyres

Size:		
1100	145 SR 13, 165/70 SR13 or 165/65 SR 14	
1300 and 1500	165/70 SR 13, 165/65 SR 14 or 165/65 R 14 T	
105 TC	165/65 SR 14 or 185/60 HR 14	
130 TC	185/60 HR 14	
Pressures cold, in kgf/cm² (lbf/in²):	**Front**	**Rear**
Normal load:		
1100, 1300 and 1500	1.9 (28)	1.8 (26)
1300 S and 1500 S	2.0 (29)	1.9 (28)
105 TC, 165/65 HR 14 tyres	2.2 (32)	2.2 (32)
105 TC, 185/60 HR 14 tyres	2.0 (29)	2.2 (32)
130 TC	1.9 (28)	1.8 (26)
Full load:		
1100, 1300 and 1500	1.9 (28)	2.2 (32)
1300 S and 1500 S	2.0 (29)	2.2 (32)
105 TC, 165/65 HR 14 tyres	2.2 (32)	2.4 (35)
105 TC, 185/60 HR 14 tyres	2.0 (29)	2.2 (32)
130 TC	2.0 (29)	2.1 (30)

Dimensions and weights
Dimensions – Strada II and all TC

Overall length:	
105 TC up to April 1983	3.937 m (155.00 in)
All Strada II models (including TC):	
Up to 1985	4.014 m (158.04 in)
1985 on	3.993 m (157.2 in)
Overall width:	
105 TC up to April 1983	1.688 m (66.46 in)
105 TC (later models) and 130 TC	1.663 m (65.48 in)
All other Strada II models	1.650 m (64.96 in)
Overall height:	
105 TC up to April 1983	1.400 m (55.12 in)

Under-bonnet view of 105 TC model – air cleaner removed

1 Windscreen washer tube	8 Distributor	15 Engine oil filler
2 Heater control cables	9 Radiator top hose	16 Timing belt cover
3 Windscreen wiper motor	10 Fan shroud	17 Choke cable
4 Ignition ECU	11 Crankcase ventilation hose	18 Coolant temperature sender
5 Expansion tank	12 Carburettor	19 Air cleaner hot air pick-up
6 Ignition coil	13 Alternator	20 Throttle cable end fitting
7 Battery	14 Engine oil dipstick	

Underside front view of 105 TC model

1 Steering tie-rods	4 Oil temperature sender	7 Engine mounting (front)	10 Driveshafts	12 Gearchange linkages
2 Track control arms	5 Engine oil drain plug	8 Radiator cooling fan	11 Engine/transmission	13 Exhaust downpipes
3 Anti-roll bar	6 Radius rod attachments	9 Gearbox	mounting (rear)	14 Exhaust hanger

Underside rear view of 105 TC model

1 Handbrake cable pulleys
2 Fuel tank
3 Handbrake cable equaliser

4 Exhaust pipe
5 Intermediate silencer

6 Handbrake cable exclosed
   sections

7 Rear spring
8 Rear silencer

9 Towing eyes
10 Spare wheel

105 TC (later models) and 130 TC	1.390 m (54.73 in)
All other Strada II models:	
Up to 1985	1.405 m (55.32 in)
From 1985	1.418 m (55.83 in)
Wheelbase:	
105 TC up to April 1983	2.448 m (96.38 in)
130 TC	2.441 m (96.11 in)
All other Strada II models (including 105 TC):	
Up to 1985	2.444 m (96.30 in)
1985 on	2.451 m (96.50 in)

Kerb weights – Strada II and all TC

105 TC up to April 1983	950 kg (2095 lb)
105 TC from May 1983	905 kg (1996 lb)
130 TC	950 kg (2095 lb)
Strada 11, models 60 and 70 up to 1985:	
Three-door	815 kg (1797 lb)
Five-door	840 kg (1852 lb)
Strada II, models 60 and 70 from 1985:	
Three-door	845 kg (1863 lb)
Five-door	860 kg (1896 lb)
Strada II, models 75 and 85 up to 1985*:	
Three-door	825 kg (1819 lb)
Five-door	850 kg (1874 lb)
Strada II, models 75 and 85 from 1985*:	
Three-door	855 kg (1885 lb)
Five-door	870 kg (1918 lb)

*For automatic transmission add 10 to 50 kg (22 to 110 lb) according to model

3 Routine maintenance (later models)

The maintenance schedule for Strada II models is given below. Owners of earlier models may wish to adopt some of the additional tasks, particularly the precautionary renewal of the timing belt.

Weekly, before a long journey or every 250 miles
    Check engine oil level
    Check brake reservoir fluid level
    Check tyre pressures and condition
    Check operation of lights, signals, instruments etc
    Top up washer reservoir(s), check operation of washers and wipers
    Check coolant level

Monthly, regardless of mileage
    Check battery electrolyte level (if possible)

Quarterly, regardless of mileage
    Check automatic transmission fluid level

Every 6000 miles or 6 months, whichever comes first
    Renew engine oil and filter
    Check clutch adjustment
    Check manual gearbox oil level
    Check final drive oil level (automatic transmission)
    Check coolant breaker points condition and gap (when fitted)
    Clean and re-gap spark plugs
    Check ignition timing (contact breaker ignition)
    Check brake lining wear
    Check seat belts for correct operation and security of mountings
    Check idle speed
    Road test

Every 12 000 miles or 12 months, whichever comes first
In addition to, or instead of, the work previously specified
    Renew air cleaner element
    Renew contact breaker points (when fitted)
    Renew spark plugs
    Check timing belt condition
    Check valve clearances
    Check cylinder compression
    Check idle speed and mixture
    Check antifreeze concentration
    Clean battery terminals

    Check charging system output and battery condition
    Check accessory drivebelt(s) for correct tension and condition
    Clean engine and engine bay, rectify fluid leaks
    Check headlight beam alignment
    Check exhaust system condition and security of mountings
    Check fuel line for leakage or corrosion
    Check brake hydraulic pipes and hoses for leakage, corrosion or other damage
    Check condition of brake calipers and wheel cylinders
    Adjust handbrake if necessary
    Check front and rear wheel alignment
    Check driveshaft gaiters for splits
    Check steering and suspension linkages, pivots and balljoints for security and condition
    Lubricate hinges, locks and controls

Every 24 000 miles or two years, whichever comes first
In addition to, or instead of, the work previously specified
    Renew engine coolant
    Renew manual gearbox oil
    Renew brake hydraulic fluid

Every 36 000 miles or three years, whichever comes first
In addition, or instead of, the work previously specified
    Renew automatic transmission fluid, clean or renew filter
    Renew final drive oil (automatic transmission)
    Renew timing belt

4 Jacking and wheel changing (later models)

1 The jack supplied with later models for wheel changing engages with the weld flange under the body sills. Locate the jack head as near to the wheel which is being removed as possible.
2 When the car is being raised by means of a workshop jack, on no account place it under the lower edge of the plastic bumpers.
3 If raising the front end, place the jack with a wooden block as an insulator under the front crossmember.
4 If raising the rear end, place the jack head under the leaf spring clamp.
5 On later models, the spare wheel is no longer located within the engine compartment, but is supported in a cradle under the rear of the car. Use the wheelbrace supplied with the car to lower the cradle until it can be unhooked from the lower end of the threaded screw, and the spare wheel removed (photos).

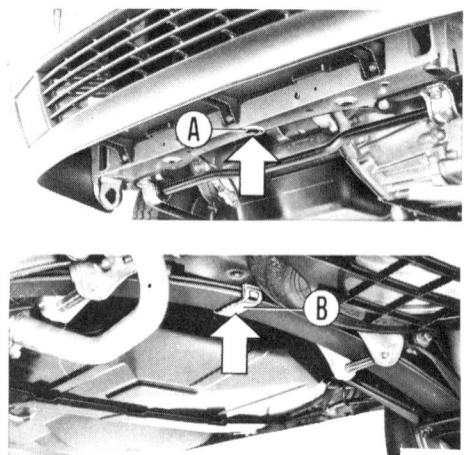

Fig. 13.1 Front and rear jacking points (Sec 4)

A   Crossmember   *B   Leaf spring clamp*

4.5A Spare wheel and carrying cradle

4.5B Wheelbrace engaged to wind down
spare wheel carrier

4.6 Spare wheel cradle screw
(1985 on)

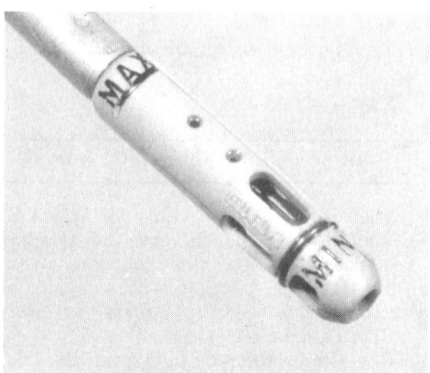

5.3 Oil level sensor type dipstick
markings

6   Access to the cradle lowering and raising mechanism is obtained
by removing the rear bumper (up to 1985) or the trim panel between
the rear lamp clusters (1985 on) – see paragraphs 35 and 36 of Section
19 of this Supplement (photo).

---

5   Engine (all models)

Engine oil – level checking
1   The engine oil level should be checked with the car standing on
level ground.
2   The engine should be cold or should have been switched off for at
least ten minutes.
3   Withdraw the dipstick, wipe it clean, re-insert it and withdraw it for
the second time. The oil level should be between the 'MIN' and 'MAX'
notches. Top up if necessary, but do not fill above the 'MAX' level
(photo).

Engine oil and filter – renewal
4   The engine oil should be drained when the engine is hot.
5   Unscrew the sump drain plug and catch the old oil in a suitable
container.
6   While the oil is draining, unscrew the oil filter cartridge. This may
require the use of an oil filter removal tool (photo). These are
obtainable from most motor accessory stores. Alternatively, a large
screwdriver may be driven through the oil filter and used as a lever to
unscrew it.
7   Smear the rubber seal of the new filter with engine oil and screw it
into place using hand pressure only.
8   Fill the engine with the correct grade and quantity of oil.

5.6 Unscrewing oil filter cartridge

9   Start the engine. It will take a few seconds for the oil warning light
to go out. This is normal and is due to the new filter filling with oil.
10 Switch off the engine, wait ten minutes, then check for leaks, and if
necessary top up the oil level as previously described.

6   Engine (early models, except TC)

Valve stem oil seals – fitting

1   If a protective sleeve is provided with the new oil seals, place it over the stem of each valve and lubricate it before sliding the seal over it. If the seal is tight, use a piece of tube to press it home.

2   When a protective sleeve is not provided, take great care not to damage the oil seal on the cotter seating groove.

Timing belt – renewal

3   It is recommended by the manufacturers that the timing belt be renewed whenever it is removed, even if it is apparently in good condition.

Cylinder head – bolt tightening after refitting

4   After the cylinder head has been refitted and the car has covered between 700 and 1000 miles, the cylinder head bolts should be retightened as follows.

5   On early models (M12 bolts with 19 mm hexagon), slacken off a bolt by approximately one quarter turn, then retighten it to the Stage 3 specified torque (Chapter 1, Specifications). Repeat on each cylinder head bolt in turn, following the sequence given in Fig. 1.8 (Chapter 1).

6   On models where final tightening of the bolts is carried out by angular rotation (M10 bolts with 17 mm hexagon), tighten each bolt without previous slackening through 60° to 90°. Follow the sequence in Fig. 1.8 (Chapter 1) and tighten each bolt the same amount.

Camshaft sprocket and camshaft – removal and refitting

7   Remove the camshaft carrier as described in Chapter 1, Section 4.

8   Remove the camshaft sprocket securing bolt and washer, then remove the sprocket from the camshaft. Recover the alignment dowel if it is loose.

9   Remove the cover plate and gasket from the tail end of the camshaft carrier (except on air conditioned models, where the distributor has already been removed from this location).

10 Withdraw the camshaft from the tail end of the carrier, being careful not to damage the carrier bearing surfaces with the cam lobes.

11 Renew the oil seal at the sprocket end of the camshaft carrier before refitting the camshaft.

12 Lubricate the camshaft bearing surfaces before refitting; be careful not to damage the oil seal or the carrier bearing surfaces when refitting. Use a new gasket on the cover plate.

13 Refit the camshaft sprocket, making sure that it engages with the dowel. Fit the securing bolt and washer and tighten the bolt to the specified torque; use a strap wrench or an old timing belt to restrain the sprocket when tightening the bolt.

14 Refit the camshaft carrier as described in Chapter 1, Section 4.

Camshaft carrier cover plate modification

15 During 1982 the aluminium camshaft carrier cover plate was replaced by a steel one; in consequence a thicker gasket, new studs

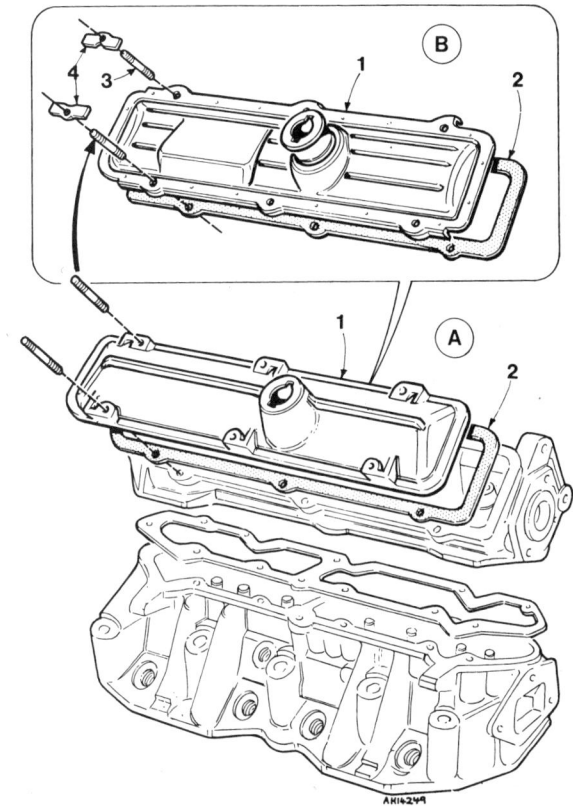

Fig. 13.2 Camshaft cover plates (Sec 6)

A Old type	2 Gasket
B New type	3 Stud
1 Cover	4 Reinforcement plates

and securing plates are used.

16 Early and late parts are not interchangeable.

Piston and bore grade marks

17 It will be noticed from the Specifications that 'standard' size pistons are graded in diameter from A to B, corresponding to variations in 'standard' bore diameters. Gudgeon pins and their bores are likewise graded 1, 2 or 3.

18 The piston markings will be found on the underside, stamped on the connecting rod boss (Fig. 13.3). The corresponding bore grade is stamped on the cylinder block sump mating face (photo). Not all bores in one engine will necessarily be of the same grade. The gudgeon pin grade is stamped on the pin.

19 Only piston grades A, C and E are available as spares. Oversize pistons are not graded.

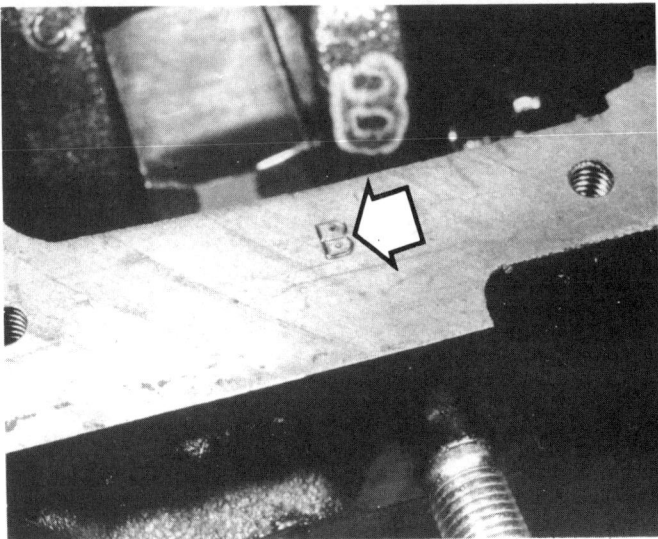

6.18 Cylinder bore grade letter stamped on sump mating face

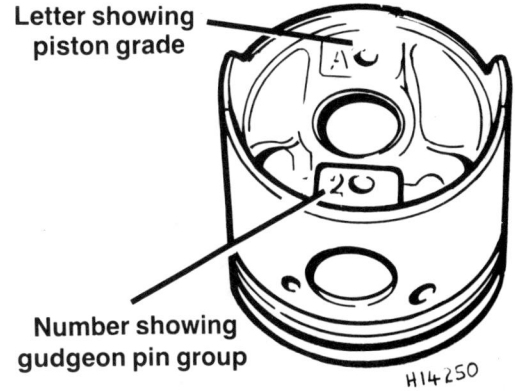

Letter showing piston grade

Number showing gudgeon pin group

Fig. 13.3 Piston grade markings (Sec 6)

7 Engine (Strada II models, except TC)

General description

1   The engines fitted to Strada II models are almost identical to those described in Chapter 1. The design of some peripheral components has changed, and there are considerable specification differences between the 1100 cc and the other engine sizes.

2   For procedures or specifications not given in this Chapter, please refer to Chapter 1 or to Section 5 of this Chapter.

Cylinder head – refitting

3   The cylinder head gaskets provided by the manufacturers are self-polymerizing: this property eliminates the need for head bolt retightening after refitting on most engines. The gaskets are known by the name ASTADUR. To obtain the best results for this type of gasket, the following precautions must be observed:

(a) Do not remove the gasket from its sealed packet until it is about to be used
(b) Do not allow oil or grease to get onto the gasket
(c) Lubricate the head bolt threads and washers with engine oil and allow them to drip for 30 minutes before fitting
(d) Follow the bolt tightening sequence (Chapter 1, Fig. 1.8) and stages (Specifications, this Chapter) accurately

4   Note that cylinder head bolts should be renewed after they have been used four times.

5   The cylinder head on late 1500 cc engines has additional securing bolts (see Fig. 13.4). These should be tightened to the specified torque in the sequence given after the main cylinder head bolts are tight.

Cylinder head – bolt tightening after refitting

6   The only engines on which cylinder head bolt retightening is necessary are 1300 cc up to Nos 4 592 066 or 4 595 636, and 1500 cc up to No 4 592 093. On these engines, follow the procedure in Section 6, paragraph 6.

7   No retightening is necessary on later 1300 cc or 1500 cc engines, nor on any 1100 cc engine.

Timing belt – tensioning procedure

8   The following procedure should be followed when a new belt has been fitted. No subsequent tensioning is permitted.

9   With the new belt fitted and the timing marks aligned, slacken the tensioner centre nut.

10 Turn the crankshaft through two complete revolutions (720°), stopping with the timing marks aligned again.

11 Tighten the tensioner nut to the specified torque. Check that the timing marks are still correctly aligned before refitting the belt cover.

Engine – removal with manual transmission

12 The engine is removed with the transmission from below the car.

13 Proceed as described in Chapter 1, Section 10, paragraphs 1 to 30, making due allowance for the different gearchange linkage (Section 13) and the conventional speedometer cable (if fitted).

Pistons and connecting rods – 1100 and 1100 ES

14 The gudgeon pins in the 1100 cc engine are pressed into position, making an interference fit in the connecting rods.

15 Piston or gudgeon pin renewal, or other work requiring the separation of pistons from rods, should be left to a FIAT dealer or an engineering works.

Piston rings – all models

16 Profiles of the piston rings are shown in Fig. 13.5.

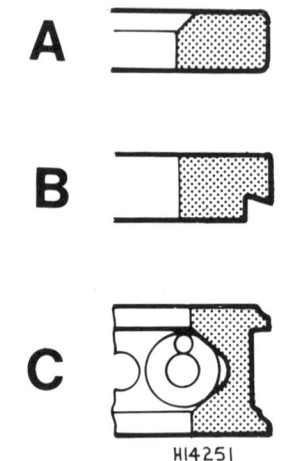

Fig. 13.5 Piston ring profiles (Sec 7)

A   Top compression ring   C   Oil scraper ring
B   Second compression ring

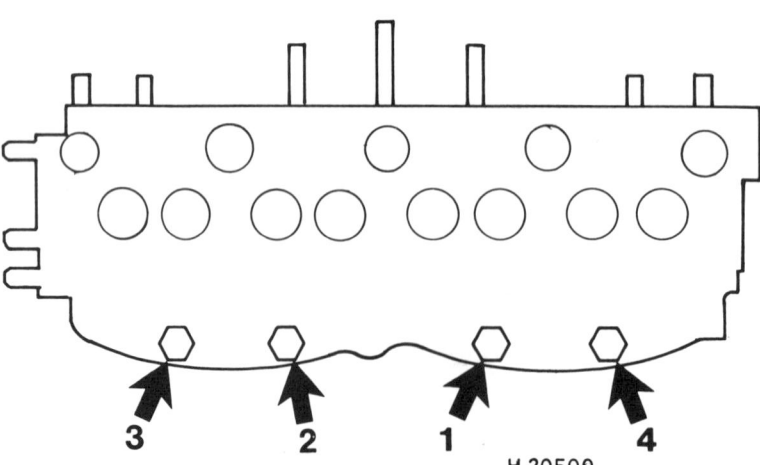

Fig. 13.4 Additional cylinder head bolts on late 1500 cc engines (Sec 7)
Tighten in numerical order

7.18A Eccentric pulley type tensioner pulley

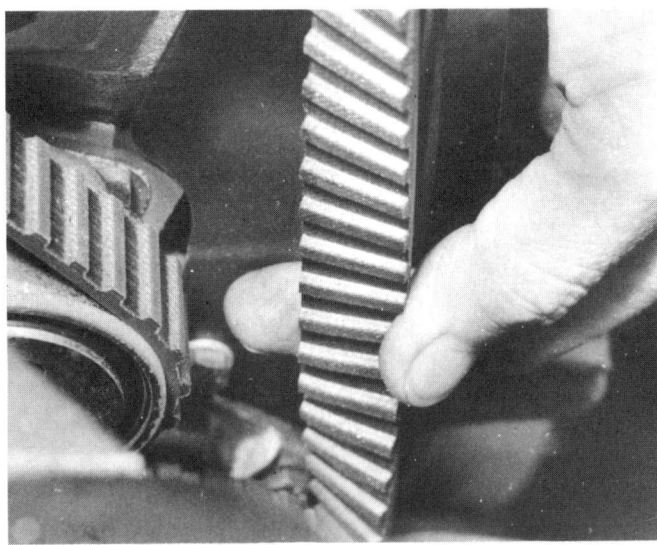

7.18B Checking timing belt tension

8.6A Using a C-spanner to keep the tappet depressed

8.6B Extracting the tappet shim with a pair of pliers

17 The two compression rings carry the word TOP. The ring gaps should be staggered at 120°.

Timing belt tensioner – modified type

18 On 1986 models (1100, 1300, 1500 cc) the spring plunger type of timing belt tensioner is no longer fitted. The eccentric pulley type of tensioner fitted to these models should be adjusted to apply sufficient pressure on the belt so that the belt can just be turned through 90° when twisted between the finger and thumb at the centre of its longest run (photos).

1300 cc engine – modifications

19 As from late March 1984, a 1299 cc version (as opposed to 1301 cc) of the '1300 cc' engine became available. The reduction in capacity is achieved by reducing the stroke from 55.5 mm to 55.4 mm. This is the only difference between the 1299 cc and 1301 cc engines and all procedures and specifications given in Chapter 1 and in this Supplement apply equally to all '1300 cc' engines.

8 Engine (TC models)

General description

1 The engines fitted to TC models have two camshafts – hence the initials TC. One camshaft operates the inlet valves, the other operates the exhaust valves. The engine design is well proven, a similar design having been used for some years in the Lancia Beta.

2 As might be expected, the TC engines differ from their single camshaft counterparts mainly in the cylinder head, valvegear and associated components. The cylinder block, crankshaft, pistons etc are very similar or identical to those found in the 'ordinary' engines.

3 Reference to the Specifications will show that many clearances and tolerances are tighter on the 130 TC than on the 105 TC. Apart from this, the twin cam engines are more or less identical.

4 For procedures not given in this Section, please refer to Chapter 1 or to Section 7 of this Chapter, making due allowances for the differences between single and twin cam engines.

Valve clearances – checking and adjustment

5 The procedure is essentially as described in Chapter 1, Section 34. Inlet valves are towards the front of the car, exhaust towards the rear.

6 In the workshop it was found that a small C-spanner (such as may be found in bicycle or motorcycle tool kits) made a good substitute for the officially prescribed tappet holding-down tool (photos). The camshaft is turned until the tappet is fully depressed. The C-spanner is inserted to bear on the edge of the tappet and the camshaft is turned again to allow removal of the shim.

7 Do not attempt to turn the camshaft with any of the valve adjusting shims removed: it is possible for a cam lobe to jam in a tappet.

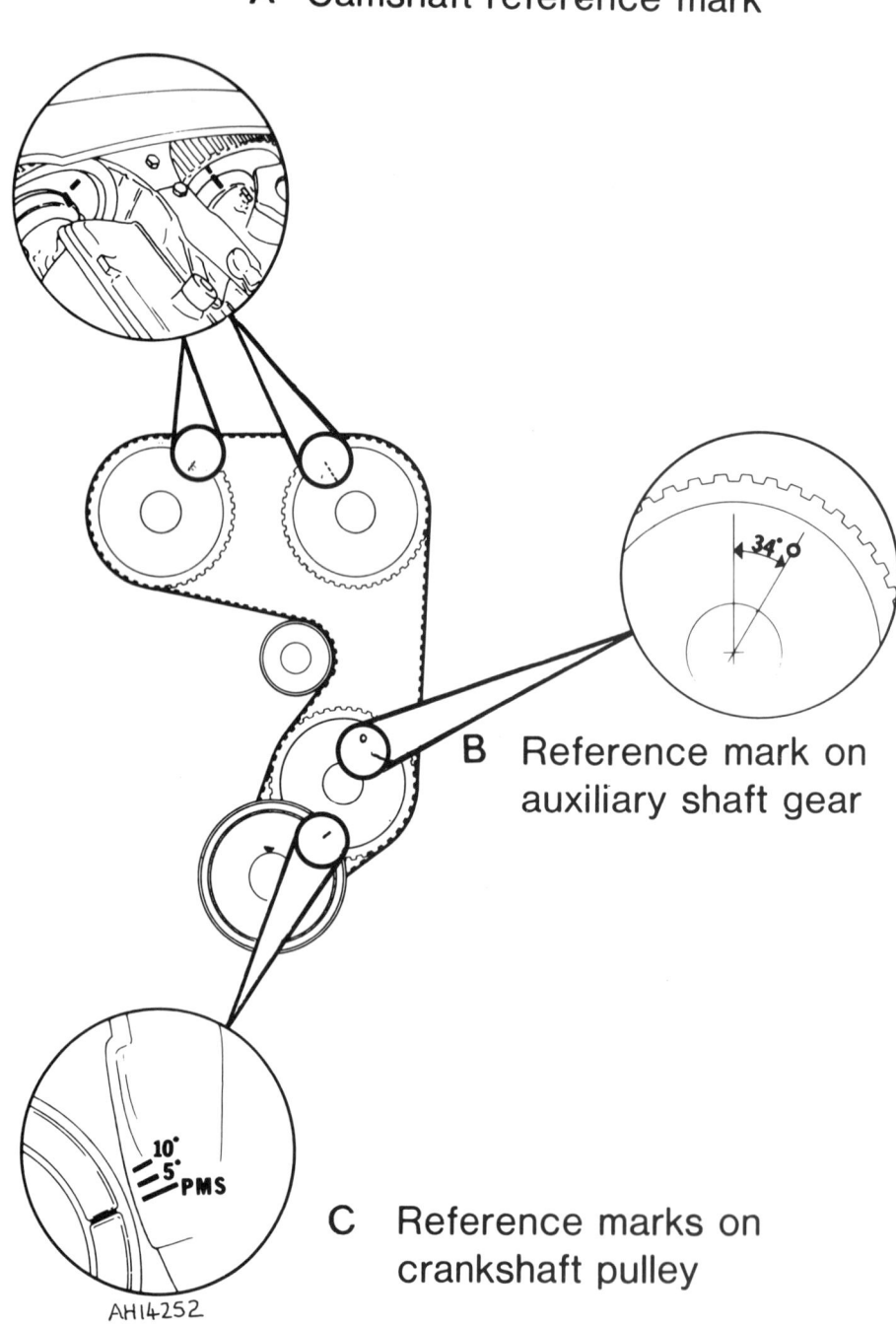

A Camshaft reference mark

B Reference mark on auxiliary shaft gear

C Reference marks on crankshaft pulley

AHI4252

Fig. 13.6 Typical twin cam engine timing marks (Sec 8)

Timing marks – important notes

8   The timing marks as envisaged by the maker are shown in Fig. 13.6. When the marks are aligned as shown. No 1 cylinder (pulley end) is alleged to be at TDC on its firing stroke.

9   The timing marks found on the engine dismantled for this book differed in the following respects:

(a)   The camshaft sprocket marks were holes, not lines (photo)

(b)   The auxiliary shaft mark was a line, not a hole (photo)

(c)   The crankshaft marks were on the flywheel and bellhousing, not on the pulley

(d)   With the marks aligned, No 4 cylinder (flywheel end) was on its firing stroke

8.9A Camshaft sprocket timing hole aligned with pointer

8.9B Auxiliary shaft sprocket timing mark (arrowed)

8.18A Timing belt tensioner roller bolt

8.18B Timing belt tensioner pivot bolt

8.19 Access to crankshaft pulley through right-hand wheel arch

8.38 Coolant expansion tank fixing nuts (arrowed)

10 The reader is advised to establish the location and meaning of the timing marks on the engine being dismantled before the timing belt is removed.

11 Auxiliary shaft timing is necessary to stop the fuel pump cam interfering with No 2 connecting rod.

Timing belt – removal and refitting (engine in car)

12 Remove the right-hand front roadwheel, securely supporting that corner of the car.

13 Remove the air cleaner and (where applicable) disconnect the choke cable at the carburettor end.

14 Remove the alternator drivebelt.

15 Remove the right-hand side shield from the engine bay. It will be necessary to release some of the wheel arch liner screws to gain access to the side shield screws.

16 Remove the timing belt cover (three screws).

17 If not already done, establish the location and meaning of the crankshaft, camshaft and auxiliary shaft timing marks (as previously described).

18 Position the crankshaft so that the desired timing marks are aligned. Slacken the tensioner roller and pivot bolts (photos), lever the tensioner against spring tension to slacken the belt and nip up the bolts to hold it in the slack position.

19 Slip the belt off the sprockets and remove it. There is not much clearance around the crankshaft pulley on any model; on models with Digiplex ignition it will be necessary to turn the crankshaft some distance off TDC to allow the belt to pass between the TDC sensor and the firing pip (photo). When turning the crankshaft with the timing belt disconnected, beware of piston-valve contact.

20 Fit the new belt, being careful not to kink it or contaminate it with lubricant. Make sure that all the timing marks are correctly aligned before engaging the belt teeth with the sprockets.

21 Slacken the tensioner bolts. Turn the crankshaft through two complete rotations, then tighten the tensioner bolts. Do not attempt to apply additional tensioning force.

22 Make sure that all the timing marks are still in correct alignment,

then refit the timing belt cover.

23 Refit the alternator drivebelt. Run the engine and (on models with inductive discharge ignition only) check the ignition timing.

24 Refit the remaining components to complete the operation.

Engine (105 TC up to April 1983) – removal and refitting

25 The engine and transmission are removed together from below the car.

26 Proceed as described in Chapter 1, Section 10, paragraphs 1 to 16 and 18 to 20.

27 Disconnect the automatic choke coolant hoses and secure them out of the way.

28 Disconnect the speedometer cable at the transmission.

29 From below the car, remove the engine/transmission side shields and the alternator shield.

30 Disconnect the driveshafts at the inboard CV joint flanges.

31 Disconnect both front radius rods (see Chapter 11, Section 4).

32 Disconnect the remaining engine mounting.

33 Make sure that all wires, cables and hoses have been detached, then lower the engine/transmission out of the engine bay. Raise the car if necessary and remove the engine/transmission unit.

34 Refit in the reverse order to removal. Use new driveshaft flange screws; tighten all fastenings to their specified torques.

Engine (105 TC from May 1983) – removal and refitting

35 The engine and transmission are removed together by lifting them out of the engine bay.

36 Proceed as described in Chapter 1, Section 10, paragraphs 1, 2 and 4 to 15.

37 Drain the gearbox oil to avoid spillage during removal.

38 Remove the coolant expansion tank and the thermostat housing (photo).

39 Disconnect the earth strap and the speedometer cable or sender from the gearbox.

40 Disconnect the additional electrical leads (eg idle cut-out, crankshaft pulley sensor, oil temperature sensor) from around the

engine/transmission. Label the connectors if necessary for reference when reassembling.

41 Take the weight of the engine/transmission unit on a hoist. Note that when the unit is lifted out, the pulley end of the engine will need to be tilted upwards at a considerable angle.

42 From below the car, remove the engine/transmission side shields (This is not essential, but improves access.)

43 Disconnect the driveshafts at the inboard CV joint flanges.

44 Disconnect the gearchange linkage at the gearbox end.

45 Disconnect the engine centre mounting (see Chapter 1, Section 10, paragraph 20).

46 Although not essential, it is probably advisable to remove the radiator and electric cooling fan.

47 Make sure that the hoist is securely attached, then unbolt the remaining engine mountings and lift the engine/transmission unit out of the engine bay (photo). Be careful not to damage the brake master cylinder or the battery tray, which between them prevent the unit being lifted straight out.

40 Refit in the reverse order to removal. Because of the angle at which the unit must enter the engine bay, a trolley jack or a good selection of wooden blocks will be required to support the transmission while the pulley end of the engine is lowered. If difficulty is experienced in reconnecting the driveshaft flange, try unloading the suspension by taking the weight of the car off its wheels.

49 Use new driveshaft flange screws, and tighten all fastenings to their specified torques.

50 Make sure that the gearchange linkage is in position before refitting the centre mounting, otherwise it will be necessary to split the linkage to pass it over the mounting.

Engine (130 TC) – removal and refitting

51 The procedure is similar to that described for the 105 TC. The additional bracing bars and torque rods fitted around the power unit must also be removed, and the pipes must be disconnected from the oil cooler take-off flange (between the oil filter and the oil filter housing).

Engine (105 TC) – complete dismantling

52 Separate the engine and transmission as described in Chapter 1, Section 11. The fixed driveshaft can be left attached to the engine if wished; to remove it, unbolt its bracket from the engine. If the driveshaft flange prevents access to bracket fastenings, unscrew the bearing retainer plate, release the circlip and drive the shaft and bearing out of the bracket (photo).

53 If not already done, drain the engine oil and clean the outside of the engine.

54 Remove the following ancillary components, referring to the appropriate Chapters as necessary:

    (a) Clutch assembly
    (b) Dipstick and guide tube
    (c) Engine mounting brackets (if not already done)
    (d) Carburettor
    (e) Alternator and drivebelt
    (f) Timing belt cover

55 Remove the coolant distribution pipes from between the camshaft carriers and from the coolant pump.

56 Establish the location and meaning of the timing marks as described earlier in this Section.

57 If not already done, make alignment marks and remove the distributor.

58 Unbolt and remove the camshaft carrier covers.

59 Slacken the timing belt tensioner bolts. Lever the tensioner against its spring to slacken the belt and nip up the tensioner roller bolt to hold it in the slack position.

60 Restrain the flywheel from turning and remove the crankshaft pulley securing nut or bolt. **Note:** *If the pulley is secured by a bolt, that bolt will have a* **left-hand thread** *– ie it is undone in a clockwise direction.* Remove the pulley.

61 On later models, remove the ignition timing sensor from its bracket adjacent to the crankshaft pulley. **Do not** remove or disturb the sensor bracket.

62 Remove the timing belt, crankshaft sprocket and Woodruff key.

63 Restrain the camshaft sprockets from turning and remove their securing bolts. Remove the camshaft timing pointer and the camshaft sprockets.

64 Unbolt and remove the coolant pump pulley, followed by the pump itself. Recover the gasket.

65 Unbolt and remove the timing belt tensioner if it is to be renewed – if not, leave it in place. Its powerful spring must be treated with caution.

66 Unbolt and remove the auxiliary shaft sprocket.

67 Remove the alternator tensioner strap.

68 Unbolt and remove the camshaft carriers, being careful not to scatter the tappets and shims. Identify the tappets and shims if they are to be re-used.

69 Slacken the cylinder head securing bolts progressively, following the reverse of the tightening sequence (Fig. 13.7). Remove the bolts.

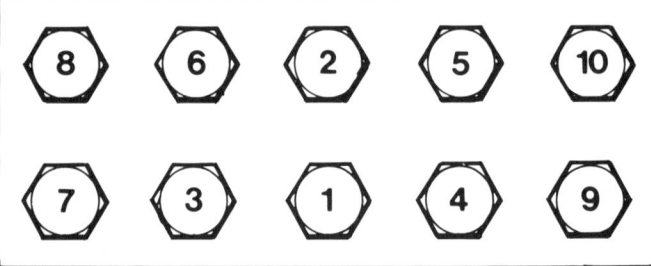

H14253

Fig. 13.7 Cylinder head bolt tightening sequence – TC models (Sec 8)

70 Remove the cylinder head from the block. If it is stuck, rock it free using the manifolds as handles. Recover the cylinder head gasket.

71 Remove the manifolds and their gaskets.

72 Remove the oil breather by extracting its central bolt and releasing its hoses (photos).

73 Remove the fuel pump and spacer.

74 Remove the oil filter, oil filter housing, oil pressure gauge sender and oil pressure switch.

8.47 Removing engine/transmission – note the steep angle necessary

8.52 Removing the driveshaft bracket from the crankcase

8.72 Crankcase oil breather

8.75A Unscrewing distributor drive hole blanking plate nut

8.75B Removing oil pump drivegear spacer from distributor drive hole

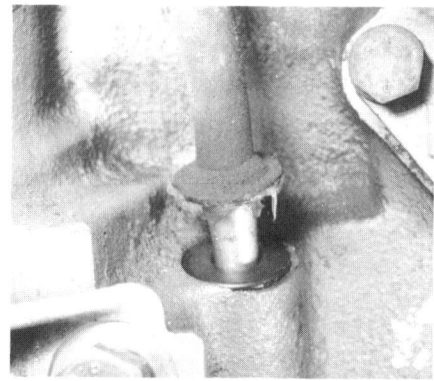

8.94 Jointing compound applied to dipstick guide tube flange

75 Remove the clamp plate and spacer from the distributor drive hole (not used on this engine) (photos).

76 Unbolt and remove the auxiliary shaft endplate and oil seal. Extract the oil pump drivegear (from the unused distributor drive hole) and withdraw the auxiliary shaft.

77 Make alignment marks, then unbolt and remove the flywheel.

78 Unbolt and remove the sump. Recover the gasket.

79 Unbolt and remove the crankshaft oil seal carriers (front and rear) and their gaskets.

80 Unbolt and remove the oil pump and the oil drain pipe.

81 Unbolt and remove the big-end caps, then remove the pistons and connecting rods from the top of the engine. See Chapter 1, Section 14, paragraph 24.

82 Unbolt and remove the main bearing caps. Note the disposition of plain and grooved bearing shells.

83 Lift out the crankshaft and recover the top half main bearing shells, again noting where the plain and grooved shells lie.

84 Dismantling of the engine is now complete.

Engine (130 TC) – complete dismantling

85 The procedure is almost identical to that given for the 105 TC engine, although some of the peripheral components are different.

86 The oil cooler take-off flange can be separated from the oil filter housing after removing the hollow central bolt.

Cylinder head – dismantling, overhaul and reassembly

87 Refer to Chapter 1, Section 15, and to the Specifications at the beginning of this Chapter.

Camshaft(s) – removal and refitting

88 If the engine is in the car, remove the timing belt, the camshaft sprocket and the camshaft carrier cover from the camshaft in question. If it is the inlet camshaft which is being removed, also remove the distributor. Unbolt the camshaft carrier and remove it with the camshaft, taking care not to lose the tappets and shims.

89 Unbolt and remove the distributor mounting or blanking plate from the rear of the camshaft carrier.

90 Remove the camshaft from the rear of the carrier, taking care not to damage the carrier bearing surfaces.

91 Renew the oil seal at the front of the camshaft housing by prising out the old seal and driving in the new one, lip inwards. Fill the lips of the seal with grease.

92 Refit in the reverse order to removal. Oil the camshaft bearing surfaces and be careful not to damage the oil seal. Use a new gasket on the distributor mounting or rear blanking plate.

Engine (105 and 130 TC) – reassembly

93 Reassemble in the reverse order to dismantling, referring to Chapter 1, Sections 26 to 33, for guidance if necessary.

94 If oil leakage has been noticed from the bottom of the dipstick guide tube, use a new seal and coat the guide tube flange generously with jointing compound (photo).

95 Before refitting the cylinder head, refer to Section 7, paragraphs 3 to 5.

96 Tighten the cylinder head bolts in the correct sequence (Fig. 13.7) and in the stages specified. Make or buy a simple disc to measure angular rotation (photo), or make paint marks on the bolt heads.

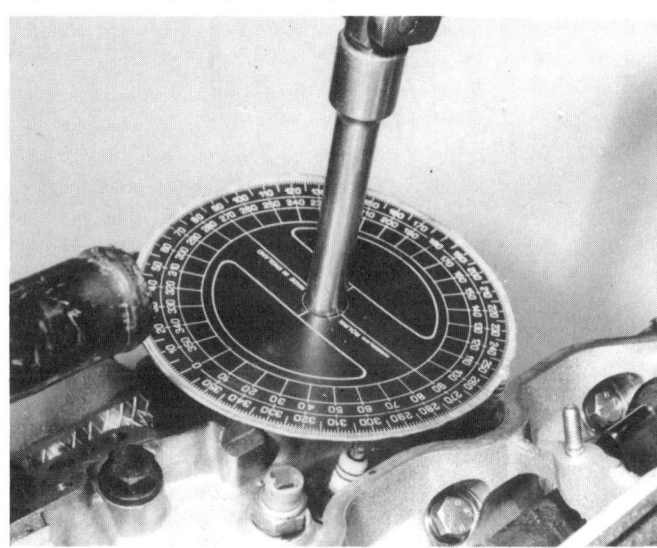

8.96 Using a disc to tighten cylinder head bolts using angular method

Cylinder head – bolt tightening after refitting

97 After the cylinder head has been refitted and the car has covered between 700 and 1000 miles, the cylinder head bolts on 'old' TC models (up to April 1983) should be retightened as described in Section 6, paragraph 5. Refer to the Specifications at the beginning of this Chapter for the Stage 3 specified torque, which should be used even when initial tightening was by angular rotation.

98 On 'new' 105 TC models (from May 1983), and all 130 TC models, there is no need for retightening after refitting.

9 Cooling system

Cooling system (all models) – draining

1 In the event that a radiator drain tap is not provided, the system should be drained by disconnecting the radiator bottom hose.

2 The cylinder block drain plug is located on the rear face of the engine; it may be hidden by the exhaust downpipe.

Cooling system (Strada II, except TC) – filling

3 The expansion tank is now built into the side of the radiator, so there is only one filler cap for radiator and expansion tank.

4 Correct filling level is indicated when the top of the indicator float is flush with the top of the filler neck.

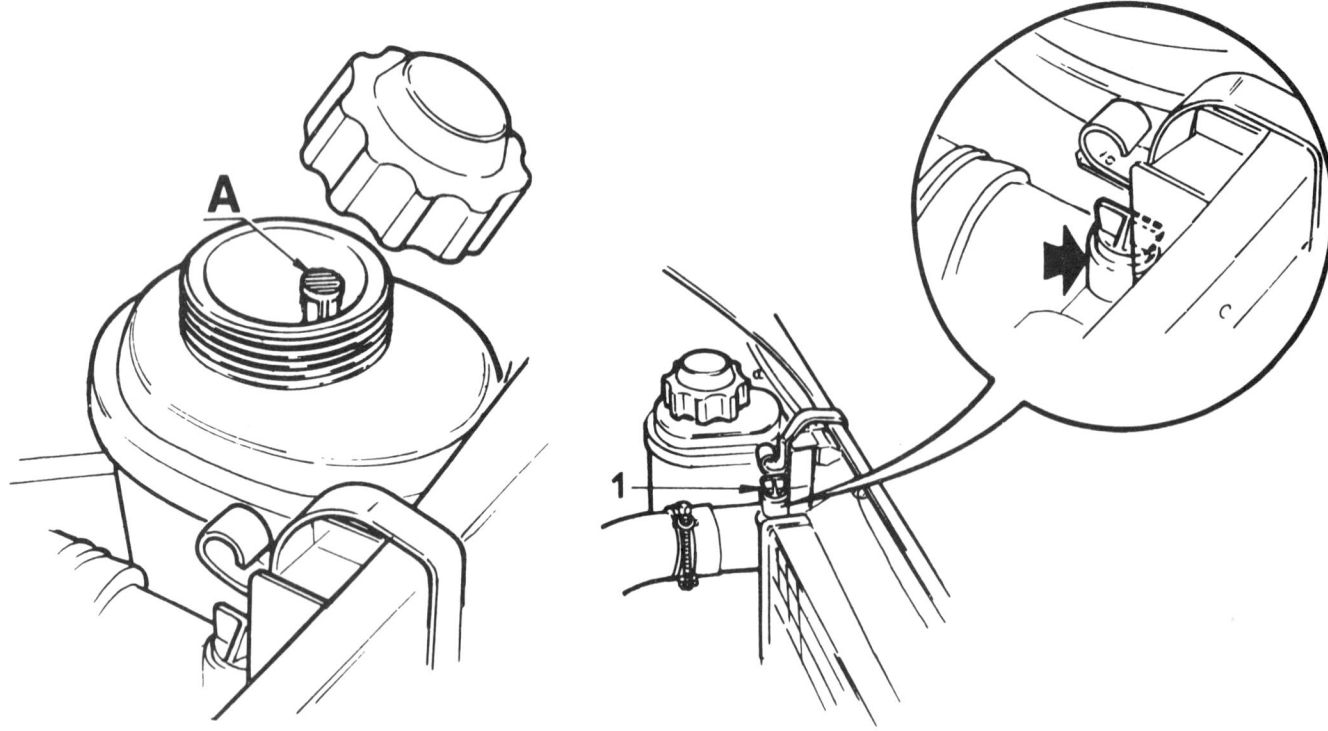

Fig. 13.8 Expansion tank level indicator float (A) (Sec 9)   Fig. 13.9 Cooling system vent plug (1) (Sec 9)

5   Open the vent plug (Fig. 13.9) when refilling; close it when refilling is complete.

Expansion tank (Strada II models) – modifications

6   As from 1985, the integral expansion tank (see paragraph 3) is made of translucent material so that the coolant level is visible.
7   In consequence of this modification, the float is no longer fitted.
8   On TC versions with air conditioning, which have a remotely-sited expansion tank, this too is now made of translucent material.
9   Both types of expansion tank are marked wth a minimum coolant level line.

Thermostat (TC models) – description, removal and refitting

10   The thermostat housing on TC models is not attached to the engine: it is located at the flywheel end, at the junction of the hoses coming from the coolant pump, the cylinder head and the bottom of the radiator.
11   Drain the cooling system, saving the coolant if it is for re-use.
12   Disconnect the hoses from the thermostat housing and remove the housing.
13   The thermostat can be tested by putting it, in its housing, in boiling water and observing the movement of the valve. The thermostat cannot be renewed independently of the housing.
14   Refit in the reverse order of removal, taking the opportunity to renew hoses and hose clips as necessary. The 'sardine can' type of hose clip is particularly liable to cause leaks if it is re-used.

Radiator (Strada II) – removal and refitting

15   Drain the cooling system and disconnect the hoses from the radiator. Unplug the fan wiring connector, and (if fitted) the coolant level sensor.
16   On single cam models, release the spring clips from the top of the radiator. On TC models, unbolt and remove the top securing clamp (photo).
17   Carefully lift out the radiator and fan together. Be careful not to

9.16 Radiator top clamp bolts

lose the rubber mounting bushes (photo).
18   Refit in the reverse order to removal.

Coolant pump (models with air conditioner) – removal and refitting

19   On vehicles with air conditioning, have the system discharged and remove the compressor and its mount before removing the pump (Chapter 2, Section 9).
20   Refit the compressor and have the system recharged on completion.

9.17 Radiator lower mounting rubber bushes

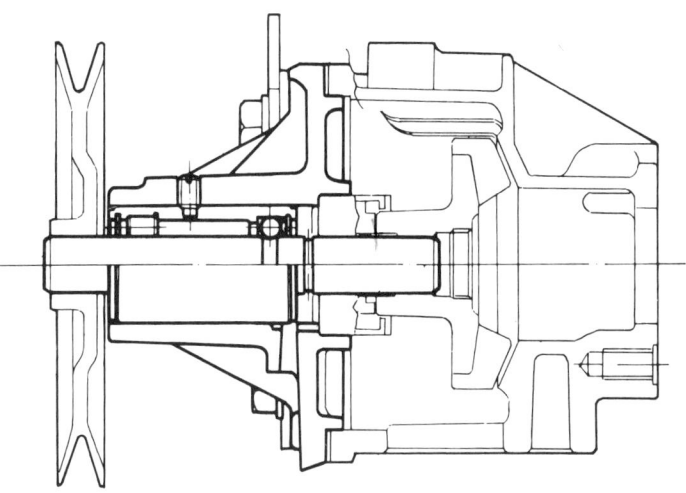

Fig. 13.10 Sectional view of later type coolant pump (except TC) (Sec 9)

Coolant pump (later models except TC) – overhaul

21 From late 1981, the coolant pump fitted at the factory has its bearings permanently attached to the shaft; therefore they cannot be renewed separately.

22 Early and later pumps are interchangeable as complete units, but individual components cannot be interchanged.

Coolant pump (TC models) – removal and refitting

23 Drain the cooling system.

24 Remove the alternator/coolant pump drivebelt.

25 Jam the pump pulley and remove the pulley securing bolts (photo). Remove the pulley.

26 Unbolt the distribution pipe from the rear of the pump.

27 Unbolt the pump from the block and remove it. Access will be easier if the timing belt cover is removed also.

28 Before refitting the pump, check that the clearance between the impeller blades and the casing is as specified (photo). If not, renew the pump.

29 Refit in the reverse order of removal. Use a new gasket between pump and block, and a new O-ring between the distribution pipe and the pump (photo). Tension the drivebelt on completion.

Heater control panel (Strada II) – removal and refitting

TC models

30 Prise off the trim which surrounds the heater control panel.

31 Pull the knobs off the controls with a pair of pliers.

32 Remove the radio from its housing. Remove the radio housing trim to gain access to the heater control panel securing screws; remove the screws.

33 Disconnect the heater control cables. Access is difficult at either end, but it is probably easiest to disconnect them at the heater.

34 Disconnect the fibre optic bundles at the bulbholder. Carefully withdraw the panel into the car.

35 Refit in the reverse order of removal. Check for correct operation before refitting the surrounding trim.

Other models

36 The procedure is similar to that just described, but removal of the surrounding trim may differ.

Heater (Strada II) – removal and refitting

37 Drain the cooling system, then disconnect the heater hoses. They are more easily detached at the engine end.

38 On TC models, unbolt the expansion tank and move it out of the way.

39 Unbolt and remove the split bulkhead which separates the heater from the engine bay. It is secured by two bolts at each end, two in the middle and three along the bottom. Disconnect or move aside wiring etc secured to or passing through the bulkhead.

9.25 Coolant pump pulley jammed for bolt removal

9.28 Checking impeller-to-coolant pump casing clearance

9.29 O-ring seal between coolant distribution pipe and pump

9.40 Heater control valve cable attachment

9.44A Heater fan and motor securing screws

9.44B Removing the heater fan and motor

40 Disconnect the three control cables from the heater, and unplug the fan wiring harness connector (photo).
41 Remove the screws which secure the heater to the body. Remove the heater from the engine bay.
42 Refit in the reverse order to removal.

Heater fan and motor (Strada II) – removal and refitting

43 Remove the right-hand half of the split bulkhead to gain access to the fan.
44 Unplug the wiring harness connector, remove the three screws and special washers and remove the fan and motor together (photos).
45 Do not attempt to separate the fan from the motor: the balance of the assembly may be upset. In any case they are not available separately.
46 Refit in the reverse order to removal.

10 Fuel system

PART A: GENERAL

Manually-operated choke control

1 If a new choke control assembly is being fitted to the steering column shroud, note that the bush (1) in Fig. 13.11 must be pushed into position so that its positioning lug aligns with the notches in the shroud, and the retaining tabs lock behind the shroud.
2 The tabs (3) must then be aligned horizontally so that when they are pushed into the bush (1) they will lock positively.
3 On later models, the bush is modified to ensure that the tabs can only be inserted in one way.

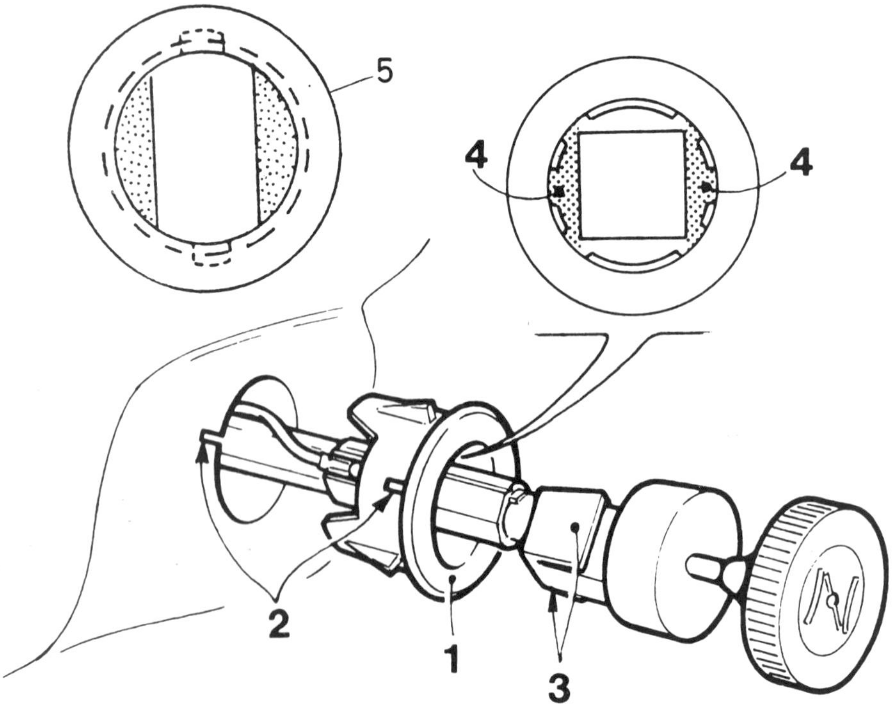

Fig. 13.11 Choke control knob components (Sec 10A)

1 *Plastic bush*
2 *Positioning lug*
3 *Retaining tabs*
4 *Tabs aligned horizontally (early models)*
5 *Modified bush (later models)*

Unleaded fuel

4 Most models can operate on unleaded fuel, but as the octane rating is reduced to 95 RON from the 98 RON of leaded fuel, sudden acceleration and continuous high speed driving should be avoided.

5 Cars with the following engine numbers **should not** be operated on unleaded fuel, and should only be filled with 98 RON (4-star) leaded fuel.

Capacity	Engine No.
1100 cc	*138B1-000*
	138C1-000
1500 cc	*149A5-000*
	149A5-046
2000 cc	*138ARI-000*
	138ARI-046
	138AR2-000

Air cleaner (130 TC) – element renewal

6 Disconnect the hot air pick-up pipe from the top of the air cleaner. Release the spring clips and remove the air cleaner lid.

7 Remove the element and undertray from the air cleaner body. Wipe clean inside the body and lid, being careful not to get dirt into the carburettor throats. Clean the undertray also.

8 Refit the undertray and fit the new element, making sure that it is the right way up. Fit and secure the lid and reconnect the hot air pick-up pipe.

Fuel pump pressure regulation (all models except 130 TC)

9 Fuel pump pressure can be altered by fitting a different thickness of gasket between the pump and its spacer.

10 Gasket thicknesses available are 0.3, 0.7 and 1.2 mm (0.012, 0.028 and 0.047 in). Fitting a thinner gasket increases the pump pressure, and vice versa.

11 The desired fuel pressure is given in the Specifications; suitable pressure gauges can be purchased in motor accessory shops.

Fuel supply system – 130 TC models

12 Unlike the other models in the book, the 130 TC has an electric fuel pump mounted next to the fuel tank.

13 As well as an in-line fuel filter, a fuel pressure regulator is fitted in the fuel supply line, upstream of the filter.

14 Repairs to the pump and regulator are not possible. A defective component must therefore be renewed.

Overrun fuel cut-off system

Description

15 The overrun fuel cut-off (known by the makers as 'idle cut-out device') acts to improve fuel economy by cutting off fuel to the idle circuit when the vehicle is slowing down and the accelerator pedal is released.

16 The components of the system are:

(a) An electronic control unit (ECU)
(b) A solenoid valve which interrupts the idle fuel circuit when de-energised
(c) A 'throttle closed' switch on the idle speed adjustment screw
(d) Associated wiring

17 During deceleration, the ECU cuts off the fuel circuit until the engine speed is approaching idle, when the circuit is restored. (In practice a bypass orifice in the idle circuit keeps the circuit primed by passing a small quantity of mixture; without this bypass the engine would frequently stall after deceleration.)

18 The ECU is also linked to the economy meter so that a signal corresponding to infinite mpg (0 litres/100 km) is sent when the system is operating.

Testing – all models except 85S with Digiplex ignition

19 The most probable causes of faults in this system are;

(a) Poor wiring or earth connections
(b) Cut-off control unit faulty
(c) Incorrect or inadequate information fed from the ignition coil
(d) Faulty throttle butterfly switch at the carburettor

20 Check the cut-off device by connecting up a suitable test lamp between the cut-out switch and a good earth. Connect a tachometer and then start the engine, increasing its speed to between 3000 and

Fig. 13.12 Fuel pressure regulator (1) and filter (2) – 130 TC (Sec 10A)

Fig. 13.13 Overrun fuel cut-off system components on carburettor (Sec 10A)

4 Cut-out supply cable	1 Idle cut-out switch
5 'Throttle closed' cable	3 'Throttle closed' switch

4000 rpm, then release the accelerator. Apart from a brief period when the cut-out is in operation, the test light should remain on, even when the engine is stopped with the ignition switched on.

21 If the above test indicates a fault (the light stays permanently on, or fails to operate at all), check the 'throttle closed' switch is earthed, and that the idle solenoid switch is not open, short circuited or to earth.

22 To check the supply circuit for continuity, detach the wiring multi-connector plug from the control unit then, with the ignition switched on, connect the test lamp between terminal 7 on the connector and earth. The lamp should be on, if not the supply circuit should be checked (a task best entrusted to a Fiat dealer or automotive electrician).

23 To check the 'throttle closed' butterfly switch, first check that the choke is off, then detach the switch cable. Connect a test lamp between the battery positive terminal and the carburettor 'throttle closed' butterfly switch cable. The test lamp should illuminate. Depress the throttle cable a small amount and check that the lamp goes out,

then comes on again when the pedal is released. It faulty, the switch must be renewed. Reconnect the switch cable.

24 To check the circuit between the butterfly switch and the multi-connector, connect the test lamp between the No 4 terminal of the multi-connector and the battery positive terminal. Now depress and release the accelerator pedal. If the lamp fails to illuminate when the butterfly valve is closed, the switch contacts-to-multi-connector circuit is broken and must be renewed.

25 To check the system earth connection, detach the multi-connector at the control unit, then with the ignition switched off, check for continuity between earth and contact No 3 using an ohmmeter. If continuity does not exist, check the vehicle earth connections for security and ensure that they are clean. Similarly check the connector in the engine compartment under the cut-out device.

26 To check that the engine speed signal from the coil to the control unit is satisfactory, detach the cut-out control unit wiring connector. Start the engine and connect a tachometer to the No 2 terminal of the multi-connector and earth. An engine speed reading should be given.

Voltage supply to the cut-off control unit (between terminal 7 and earth)
Continuity between control unit and earth (terminal 3 and battery)
Resistance (or continuity) between control unit and cut-out winding on carburettor (terminal 6 and battery)
Continuity between control unit and 'throttle closed' switch, also efficiency of contacts (terminal 4 and battery)

Citymatic system – ES models
Description
29 This system is fitted to ES models as a device for saving fuel in heavy traffic conditions. The system may be brought into operation by depressing the facia-mounted switch. Whenever the vehicle is then moving below a roadspeed of 5km/h, if the gearchange lever is moved to neutral and the clutch pedal released, the engine will switch off. The engine will re-start once the clutch is fully depressed.

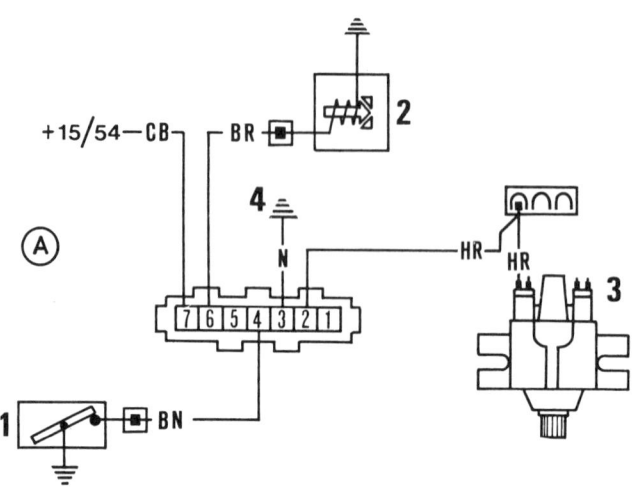

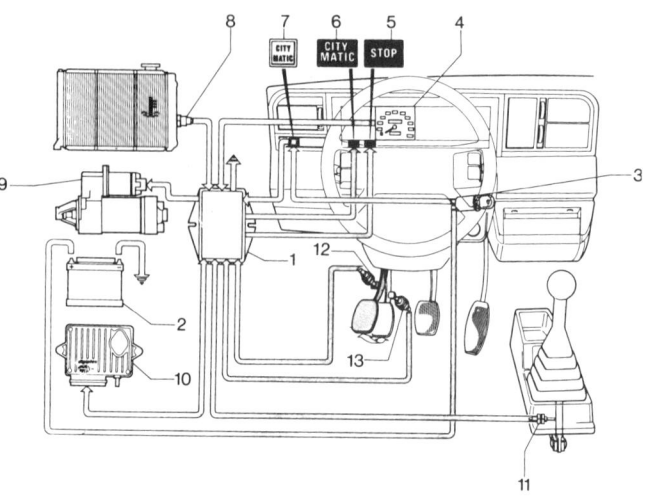

Fig. 13.15 Citymatic system layout (Sec 10A)

1 Electronic control unit
2 Battery
3 Ignition switch
4 Speedometer sensor
5 Engine stopped warning lamp
6 Citymatic system 'ON' warning lamp
7 System on/off switch
8 Coolant temperature sensor
9 Starter motor
10 Digiplex ignition control unit
11 Gearbox neutral switch
12 Clutch pedal released switch
13 Clutch pedal depressed switch

30 Overriding of the re-start control is always available through normal operation of the ignition switch.
31 The device also cuts off fuel supply to the carburettor when the accelerator pedal is released during deceleration. Certain conditions must apply before the engine stop and re-start cycle can occur.

Engine stop conditions:
Engine speed 500 to 1500 rpm
Gearchange in neutral
Clutch pedal released
Roadspeed not exceeding 5 km/h (3 mph)

Engine re-start conditions:
Coolant temperature within specified limits
Clutch fully depressed
Roadspeed not exceeding 10 km/h (6 mph)
Four seconds must have elapsed since previous re-start

32 The main components of the system are shown in Fig. 13.15.
33 Two warning lamps are fitted. The Citymatic lamp indicates that the system is activated, while the lamp marked STOP comes on when the engine switches off and goes out at re-starting.
34 A flashing Citymatic lamp indicates that the system operating conditions are not being met.

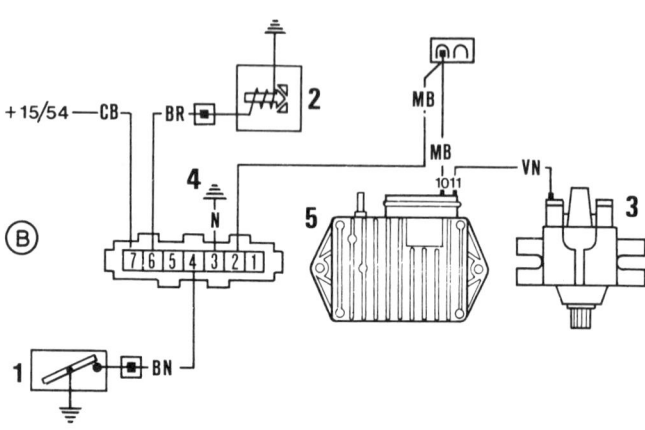

Fig. 13.14 Overrun fuel cut-off system wiring diagrams (Sec 10A)

A All models except 85S with Digiplex ignition
B 85S with Digiplex ignition
1 'Throttle closed' switch
2 Cut-out switch
3 Ignition coil
4 Earth
5 Digiplex control unit

Testing – 855 models with Digiplex ignition
27 Check that the engine speed cable from the coil to the No 10 terminal of the Digiplex control unit is in good condition and securely connected.
28 Detach the cut-off control unit multi-connector and, using a suitable meter, make the following checks.

Fault tracing

35 A fault in the system can be traced by carrying out the following checks.

36 Disconnect the red plugs on the black wire which runs from terminal 13 on the control unit. Using a jump lead from the terminal 13 plug, earth it. Carry out the checks in any order.

37 Switch on the ignition, when the two system warning lamps should come on for two seconds. This proves that the electronic control unit is in good order.

38 Depress and release the clutch pedal. If the clutch switches are operating correctly, then the Citymatic warning lamp should come on for a period of two seconds. If this does not happen, check the cables and switches.

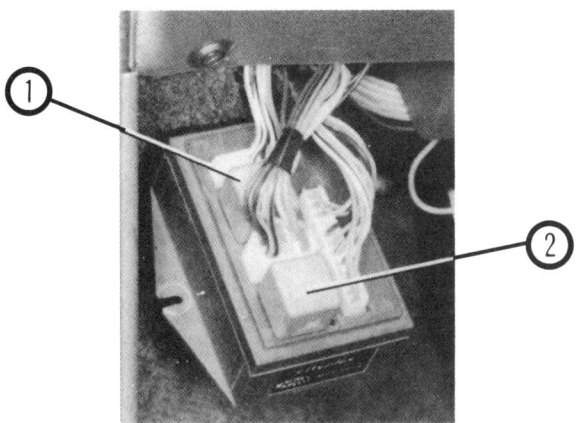

Fig. 13.16 Citymatic control unit showing starter relay (1) and ignition relay (2) (Sec 10A)

39 When moving the gearchange lever from neutral to a gear or *vice versa*, the Citymatic lamp should come on for about two seconds. If this does not happen, check the cables and neutral switch.

40 Each time the accelerator pedal is depressed and released, the Citymatic lamp should come on for two seconds. If this does not

happen, make sure that the choke control is fully off. If it is, then the carburettor switch or cables are at fault.

41 Check the engine rpm signal. The Citymatic warning lamp should flash at a rate proportional to the engine speed. If this does not happen, check out the ignition coil connections, also terminal 10 of the Digiplex ignition control unit (see Section 11 and the brown/white cables at the Citymatic control unit.)

42 To check the roadspeed signal reception, drive the car on the road in excess of 5 km/h (3 mph). The Citymatic warning lamp should flash at a rate proportional to the speed of the car. If this does not happen, check the speed sensor connections.

43 Check the system (Citymatic) control switch. Each time the switch is pressed, the Citymatic warning lamp should come on for a period of two seconds.

44 Renew any faulty components and re-make the original connections at the red connector plugs near the control unit.

45 In addition to the foregoing operational checks, the following symptoms will indicate faults as stated.

46 *Engine fails to start:* Check starter relay and the lead to terminal 50 of the starter motor.

47 *Engine will not switch off:* Check ignition relay and the lead to terminal 8 of the Digiplex ignition control unit (see Section 11).

48 *Citymatic warning lamp flashes* (coolant temperature correct): Check the temperature sensor.

49 *Engine cut-off does not occur:* Check the carburettor switch and the lead to terminal 6 on the control unit.

Fuel degassifier and fuel tank ventilation

50 A fuel degassifier is fitted to later models, being located in the fuel line between the fuel pump and the carburettor. The fuel line connections are shown in Fig. 13.17.

51 The function of the fuel degassifier is to prevent vapour locks in the fuel line at high operating temperatures. It achieves this by allowing the fuel to warm up before it reaches the carburettor, and any excess fuel vapours are returned to the fuel tank.

52 The fuel/vapour return hose has a 1 mm diameter jet and this ensures a suitable residual pressure is maintained to supply fuel to the fuel pump.

53 The fuel tank is fitted with a safety valve which allows air to enter or leave the tank as fuel level varies. This maintains approximately atmospheric pressure within the tank.

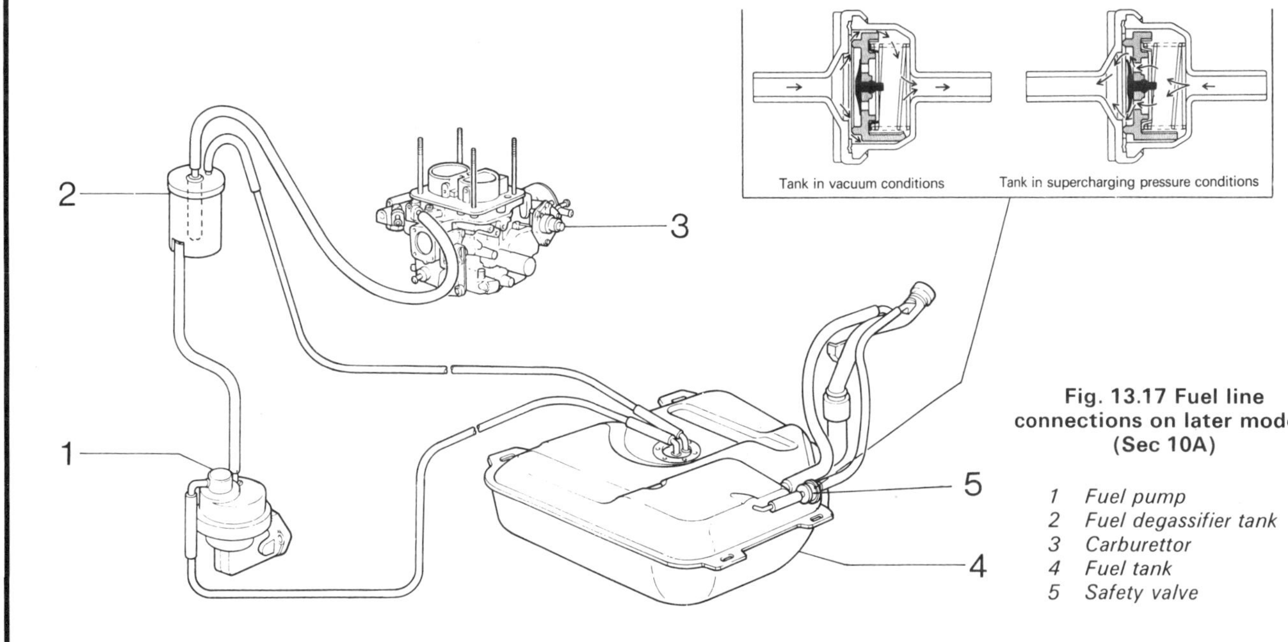

Tank in vacuum conditions   Tank in supercharging pressure conditions

Fig. 13.17 Fuel line connections on later models (Sec 10A)

1 *Fuel pump*
2 *Fuel degassifier tank*
3 *Carburettor*
4 *Fuel tank*
5 *Safety valve*

PART B: CARBURETTORS – ABARTH 130 TC MODELS

Carburettor adjustments – important note

1   When making carburettor adjustments it is probable that one or more adjustment screws will be found to be 'tamperproofed', either by a plug or by a limiter cap.

2   The purpose of tamperproofing is to discourage, and to detect, adjustment by unskilled or unqualified persons. In some territories, including parts of the EEC, it is an offence to drive a vehicle with missing tamperproof seals.

3   Before removing any tamperproof seal or device, satisfy yourself that local regulations do not prohibit this. Do not remove any seals from cars still under warranty. Fit new seals on completion of adjustment where this is required by law.

Weber 40 DCOE

Description

4   This carburettor is fitted to later Abarth 130 TC models as an alternative to the Solex ADDHE carburettor.

5   **Note:** *The following information must be regarded as general and not specific to the Strada due to the fact that at the time of publication, detailed information was not available from Fiat.*

6   The Weber DCOE carburettor has two throttle barrels of equal diameter, each barrel being fitted with similar size venturis, jets and fuel passageways, which are fed from a single float chamber between the two barrels. A single accelerator pump feeds the two accelerator pump jets when the accelerator pedal is depressed, and a single cold starting device feeds fuel into each barrel when brought into action by operation of the choke control.

7   By using two of these carburettors fitted to a manifold with four separate ports connecting the four throttle barrels of the two carburettors to the four inlet ports of the cylinder head, the advantages of one carburettor for each cylinder are obtained. The throttle shafts of the two carburettors are linked and synchronized so that all four throttles operate together.

8   This arrangement gives increased power and torque because the carburettors supply each cylinder individually, and are not restricted by the limitations of a common inlet manifold system.

Idle speed and mixture adjustment

9   Before making any adjustments to the carburettor settings, make sure your reasons for the adjustment are sound and that you only do one at a time. Check the result of each adjustment after it is made. The Weber carburettor is a finely balanced and relatively delicate instrument and can easily be put off tune.

10   Control settings are important. Make sure the operation of the cold start (choke) cable moves the lever easily throughout its full range of movement and returns to its closed position when the control knob is pushed home. Adjustment can be made by repositioning the inner cable relative to the operating arm at the clamping screw. The outer

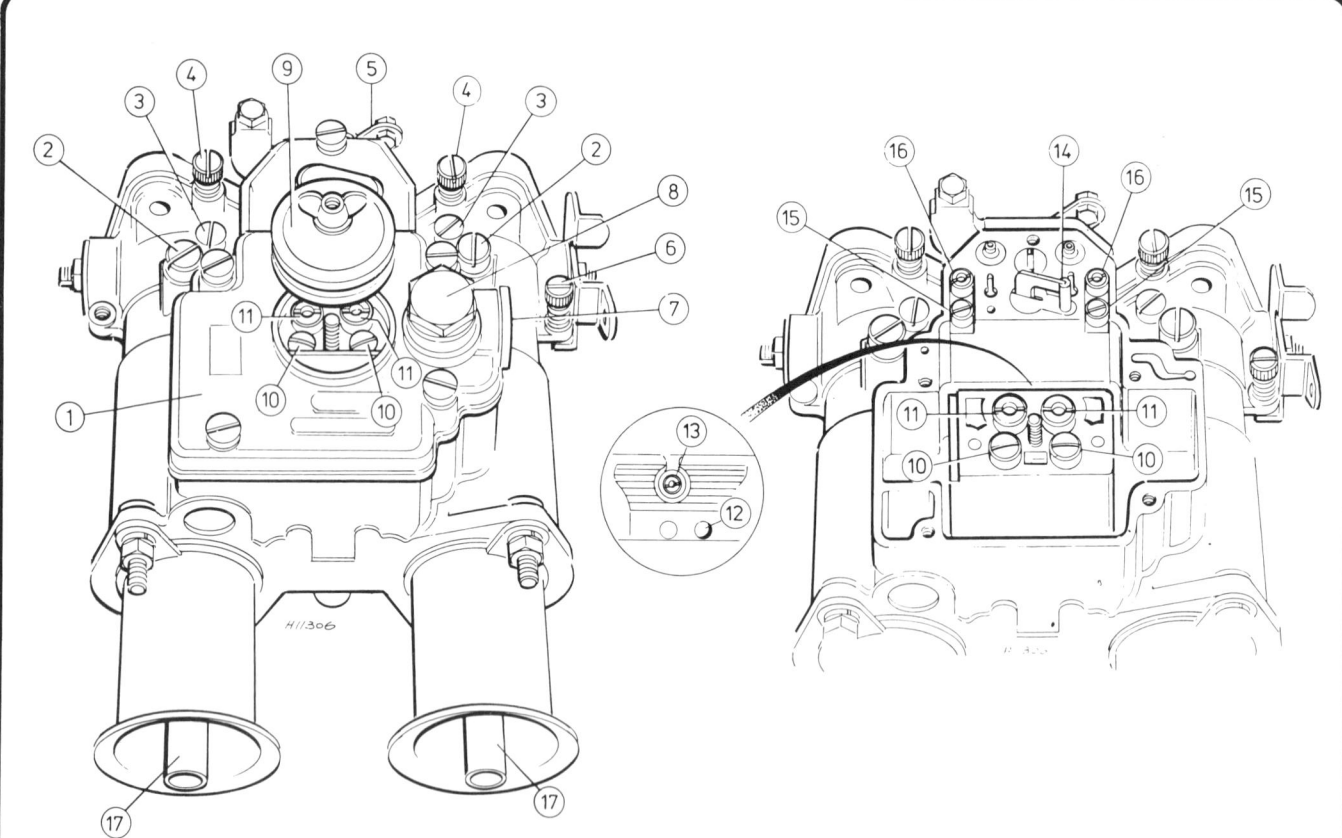

Fig. 13.18 Weber 40 DCOE carburettor with and without top cover (Sec 10B)

1 Float chamber cover	6 Slow running speed adjustment screw	12 Feed holes to well below main and
2 Accelerator pump jets	7 Fuel inlet	slow running jets
3 Progression hole inspection cover	8 Fuel filter cover	13 Accelerator pump inlet valve
screws	9 Removable cover for jet assemblies	14 Accelerator pump
4 Slow running mixture volume control	10 Slow running jet assemblies	15 Accelerator pump outlet valves
screws	11 Main jet-emulsion tube – air	16 Starter jets
5 Cold start device operating lever	correction jet assemblies	17 Small venturi extension

cable can be repositioned as necessary where it clips to the bracket on the carburettor.

11 The throttle cable should also be checked for movement throughout its range. Make particularly sure that when the throttle flap is in the fully open position, the position of the accelerator pedal is as far down as it could possibly be, even with the cable disconnected. Otherwise, pressure on the pedal will impart strain on the cable and more important, on the throttle spindle and bearings. Adjustment should be made at the point where the end of the cable outer is located into the bracket near the carburettor. Slacken the two locknuts and move the outer cable so that when the accelerator pedal is fully depressed, the throttle is just fully open.

12 Referring to Fig. 13.19, slow running adjustment is controlled by the screw (3) between the two carburettors. Clockwise rotation increases the idling speed and anticlockwise rotation decreases it. If, after obtaining the correct idling speed of 1000 rpm, the running appears to be uneven, the carburettors will have to be synchronized.

13 Warm up the engine thoroughly, then remove the carburettor air box. Check the tightness of all manifold and carburettor retaining nuts and bolts to ensure there are no leaks which could cause the uneven running.

14 Screw the mixture control screws (1) lightly onto their seats, then back them off half a turn each. Start up the engine and adjust the throttle stop screw until the engine runs at 1000 to 1200 rpm.

15 Listen, with a suitable length of pipe, at the same point on each air intake. A similar 'hiss' should be heard from each one. If the 'hiss' is different adjust the synchronizing screw (2) until a similar hiss is obtained.

16 Listening to the engine very carefully, or with an assistant in the car watching the tachometer, adjust each mixture control screw by no more than $1/12$th of a turn at a time until the highest engine speed is obtained as each screw is adjusted. Clockwise movement of the screws weakens the mixture and anticlockwise richens it. If there is no response to these adjustments it indicates that there is an air leak either at the inlet manifold gasket or at the joint between the carburettor and the inlet manifold.

17 Finally adjust the slow running to 1000 rpm with the adjustment screw (3). Short out each spark plug in turn and if the adjustments have been done correctly, there should be the same falling off of revs as each plug is shorted out.

18 Refit the air box, and recheck idling speed.

19 A more precise adjustment of the carburettors can be obtained using a carburettor balancer (synchroniser) and an exhaust gas analyser in accordance with the manufacturer's instructions.

Removal and refitting

20 The operations are similar to those described for the Solex 40 ADDHE carburettor in paragraphs 51 to 57.

Overhaul and adjustment

21 Before commencing work, obtain a repair kit which will contain all the necessary gaskets, seals and other renewable items.

22 With the carburettor in position and the air cleaner removed, attention to the jets and floats is quite straightforward. If more extensive dismantling is required, remove the carburettor and clean it externally.

23 Referring to Fig. 13.18 remove the circular cover (9) by undoing the wing nut on its top, and remove the slow running jets (10) and the air correction jets (11).

24 Now remove the two accelerator pump jets (2) and undo the progression hole inspection cover screws (3).

25 Remove the float chamber cover (1) by undoing the five retaining screws and take out the starter jets (16).

26 Undo and remove the fuel filter cover plug (8) from the float chamber cover and take off the gauze filter. Wash it in petrol and dry it with low pressure compressed air, if available.

27 Allow the floats to hang down as low as possible and with compressed air, blow through the fuel feed hole (7) which is normally covered by the filter.

28 Remove all fuel and any dirt or water that may have accumulated from the float chamber and the well below the main jets which is accessible through the small hole (12).

29 Carefully, blow through all the jets previously removed with compressed air. *Do not* under any circumstances use wire or any hard object to clean the jets, as this will enlarge or score them and thereby upset the workings of the carburettor.

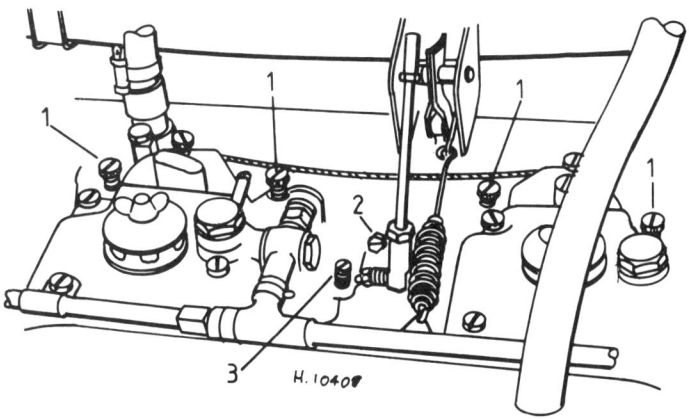

Fig. 13.19 Weber 40 DCOE carburettors – adjustment screws (Sec 10B)

1 *Slow running mixture volume control screws*
2 *Carburettor synchronizing adjustment screw*
3 *Slow running speed adjustment screw*

30 Having cleaned all the jets, refit them in their locations. Before refitting the float chamber cover it is worth checking that the float level is correct.

31 Check the float can move freely on its fulcrum pin. Also, examine the float lever for signs of pitting where it contacts the needle valve. If wear is present, it must be renewed as it can cause faulty operation of the needle valve.

32 Check the needle valve body is screwed tightly into its housing and that the pin ball end of the spring-loaded damping device in the needle valve is not jammed.

33 Hold the float chamber cover in a vertical position so the weight of the float allows the float lever to just contact the needle valve. It must not move the ball end of the needle damper pin. In this position the minimum clearance between the nearest points of the floats to the cover gasket and the surface of the gasket should be 7.0 mm (0.27 in).

34 If the float level is found to be incorrect, bend the lever tab to correct it. Take care when bending the tab to keep its face at right-angles to the needle centre line.

35 Refit the float chamber cover.

Solex 40 ADDHE

Description

36 The Solex carburettor is a twin choke sidedraught instrument. Throttle opening is simultaneous and two carburettors are fitted, so the effect is that of having one single choke carburettor per cylinder.

37 The cold start device (choke) is manually operated, and works by increasing the supply of fuel instead of restricting the supply of air.

Idle speed adjustment

38 If the carburettor balance is satisfactory, adjustments can be made to the idle speed by acting on the master adjustment screw (Fig. 13.22). Provided no other screws are disturbed, the balance of the carburettors will not be much upset.

Balancing and mixture adjustment

39 To enable the idle speed to be adjusted while keeping the carburettors in balance, an accurate tachometer and a bank of four vacuum gauges will be required. For mixture adjustment and exhaust gas analyser, or other proprietary gas analysis device, will be required. Attempts to adjust 'by ear', or with inadequate equipment, are unlikely to prove satisfactory.

40 The engine must be warmed up and in good condition. The air clearance element must be fitted (and serviceable); spark plugs must be in good condition and correctly gapped. Make sure that the choke control is pushed right in.

41 Connect the tachometer to the engine in accordance with its maker's instructions. Connect a vacuum gauge to each carburettor, in place of the crankcase ventilation pipes.

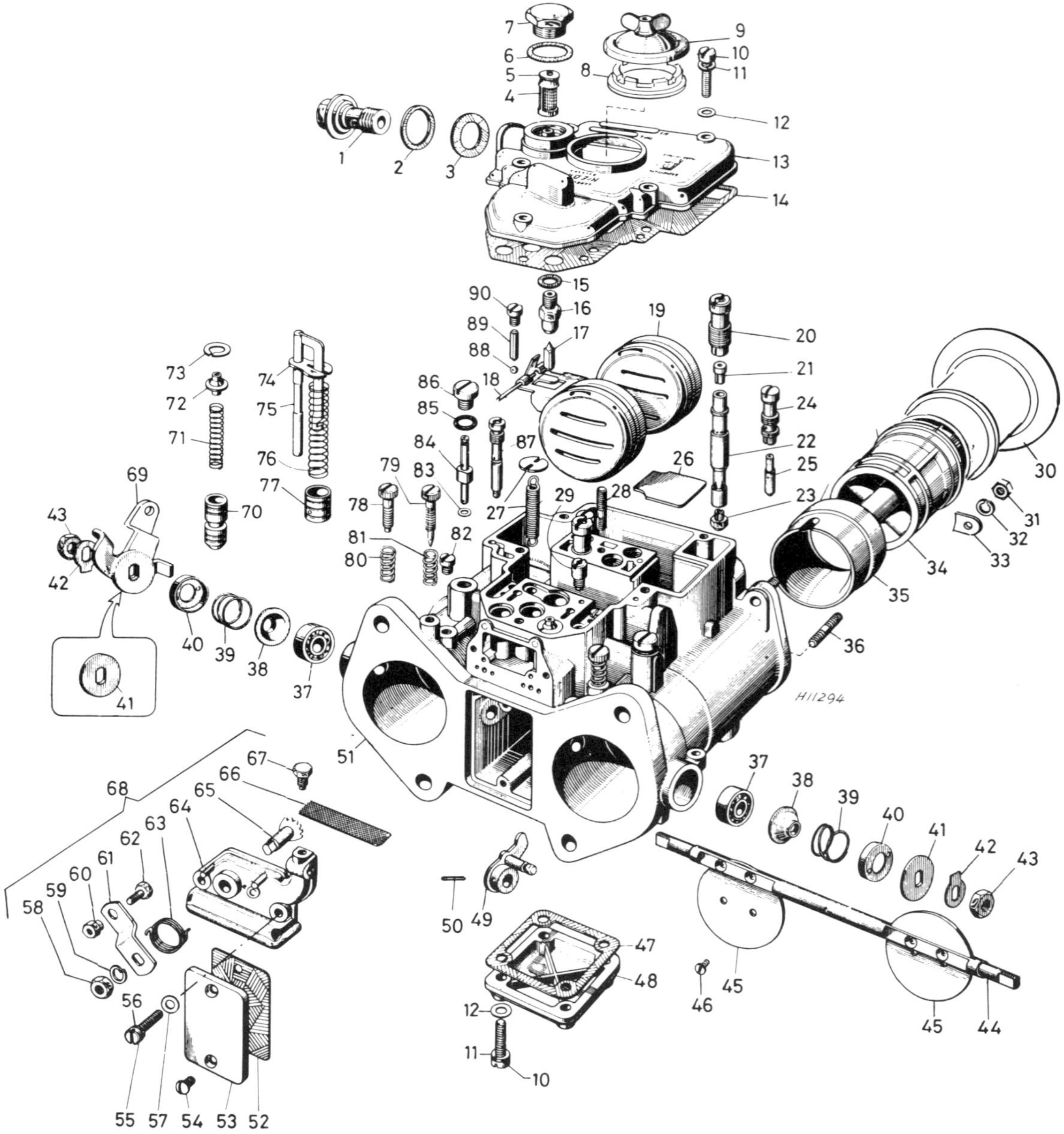

Fig. 13.20 Exploded view of typical Weber 40 DCOE carburettor (Sec 10B)

H11294

1 Fuel inlet union
2 Washer
3 Washer
4 Filter gauze
5 Bushing
6 Washer
7 Filter cover plug
8 Float chamber air vent
9 Jet inspection cover
10 Screw
11 Spring washer
12 Brass washer
13 Float chamber cover
14 Gasket
15 Washer
16 Needle valve body
17 Needle valve
18 Pin
19 Twin floats
20 Emulsion tube holder
21 Air correction jet
22 Emulsion tube
23 Main jet
24 Slow running jet holder
25 Slow running jet
26 Cover plate
27 Spring and anchorage
28 Stud
29 Accelerator pump inlet valve
30 Air inlet
31 Nut
32 Spring washer
33 Plate
34 Auxiliary venturi
35 Large venturi
36 Stud
37 Bearing
38 Dust cover
39 Spring
40 Cover
41 Distance washer
42 Lock washer
43 Nut
44 Throttle spindle
45 Throttle plates
46 Screw
47 Gasket
48 Cover plate

49 Accelerator pump control lever
50 Pin
51 Carburettor body
52 Gasket
53 Cover plate
54 Screw
55 Screw
56 Spring washer
57 Washer
58 Nut
59 Spring washer
60 Choke cable attachment
61 Starter device operating lever
62 Screw
63 Return spring
64 Cold start device body
65 Starter shaft
66 Gauze
67 Screw
68 Cold start device assembly
69 Throttle lever
70 Starter valve
71 Return spring
72 Spring guide and retainer
73 Spring ring
74 Retainer plate
75 Accelerator pump control rod
76 Return spring
77 Piston
78 Slow running adjustment screw
79 Volume control screw
80 Spring
81 Spring
82 Progression hole cover screw
83 Gasket washer
84 Accelerator pump jet
85 Sealing ring
86 Screw plug
87 Starting jet
88 Ball valve
89 Weight
90 Screw

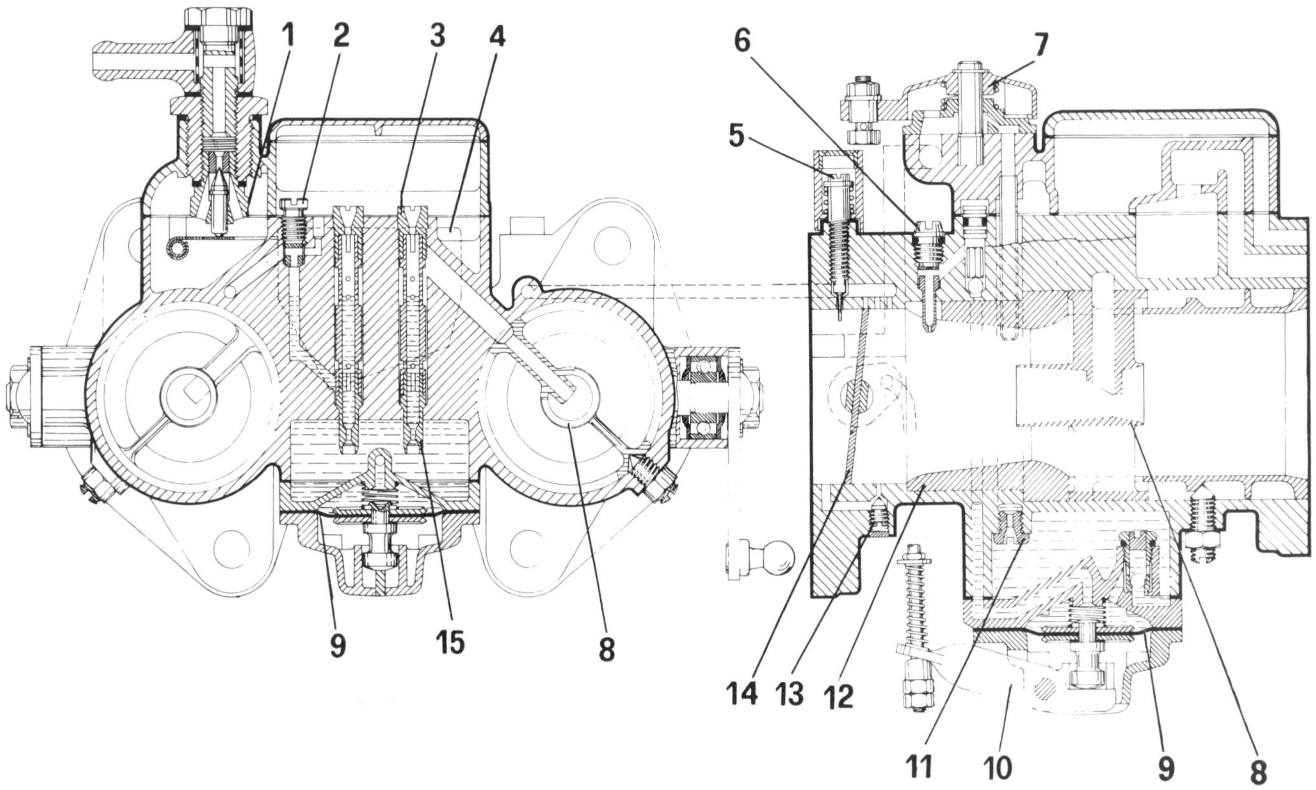

Fig. 13.21 Sectional view of Solex 40 ADDHE carburettor (Sec 10B)

1	Needle valve	5	Idle mixture adjustment
2	Idle jet		screw
3	Air bleed jet	6	Pump injector
4	Float	7	Choke (cold start) unit

8	Auxiliary diffuser	12	Venturi
9	Pump diaphragm	13	Air bypass screw
10	Pump control lever	14	Throttle butterfly valve
11	Choke jet	15	Main jet

42 Start the engine and allow it to idle. Turn the idle speed master adjustment screw (Fig. 3.22) to bring the idle speed within specified limits.

43 If the vauum gauge readings are all the same, proceed to adjust the mixture (if necessary). If a discrepancy exists in one or more readings, proceed as follows.

44 If the readings are different on the same carburettor, act on the air bypass screws (Fig. 13.23) to make them equal.

Fig. 13.22 Idle speed master adjustment screw (arrowed) – Solex 40 ADDHE carburettors (Sec 10B)

Fig. 13.23 Air bypass screws (arrowed) – Solex 40 ADDHE carburettors (Sec 10B)

45 If the readings are different between the two carburettors, act on the synchronizing screw (Fig. 13.24) until they are equal.

46 When all the readings are equal, readjust the idle speed if necessary using the master adjustment screw. Disconnect the vacuum gauges and reconnect the crankcase ventilation pipes.

47 To adjust the idle mixture, an exhaust gas analyser (CO meter) with a probe which can be screwed into the exhaust manifold will be needed. A proprietary gas analysis device which screws into the spark plug holes may be a satisfactory substitute.

48 With the engine running at the specified idle speed, check the mixture in each cylinder in turn. Act on the appropriate idle mixture adjustment screw (Fig. 13.26) to bring the CO level within limits.

49 After each mixture adjustment, check the idle speed and readjust if necessary at the master adjustment screw.

50 Reconnect the vacuum gauge and recheck the carburettor balance; correct it if necessary.

Removal and refitting

51 Remove the air cleaner.

52 Disconnect the choke cable and the throttle linkage and connecting coupling.

53 Disconnect the vacuum hoses from the carburettors.

54 Disconnect the fuel hoses.

55 Unbolt and remove the carburettors.

56 Discard the original flange gaskets.

57 Refitting is a reversal of removal, use new flange gaskets.

Overhaul

58 Refer to Chapter 3, Section 12. Do not separate the carburettors unless absolutely necessary.

Float level adjustment

59 The procedure is the same as that given for the Solex CIC/1 carburettor in Part C of this Section.

Accelerator pump delivery adjustment

60 Fill the float chamber and prime the pump by operating the main throttle lever several times. Take appropriate fire precautions.

61 Position the carburettor over a funnel and measuring glass. Operate the throttle lever ten times, pausing for a few seconds at the end of each stroke.

62 Measure the quantity of fuel delivered and compare it with that specified. Adjust if necessary at the pump lever: screw the nut in to increase delivery, out to decrease it. Tighten the locknut when adjustment is correct.

Initial synchronization

63 If the carburettors have been separated, or their balance has been otherwise disturbed, set them up as follows.

64 With the carburettors secured to their mounting plate, slacken the idle speed master adjustment screw as far as possible.

65 Act on the synchronizing screw until all the throttle valves are closed.

66 Screw in the master adjustment screw until it comes into contact with the operating lever, then back it off one whole turn.

67 Screw each idle mixture adjustment screw home, being careful not to force it into its seat, then back it off between five and seven whole turns. Make the same adjustment on each screw.

68 If the bypass screws have been disturbed, treat them similarly to the mixture adjustment screws.

69 Final adjustment must be made on the car, as described earlier.

Fig. 13.24 Synchronising screw (arrowed) – Solex 40 ADDHE carburettors (Sec 10B)

Fig. 13.25 Exhaust manifold plugs (arrowed) for exhaust gas analyser probe (Sec 10B)

Fig. 13.26 Idle mixture adjustment screws (arrowed) on Solex 40 ADDHE carburettors (Sec 10B)

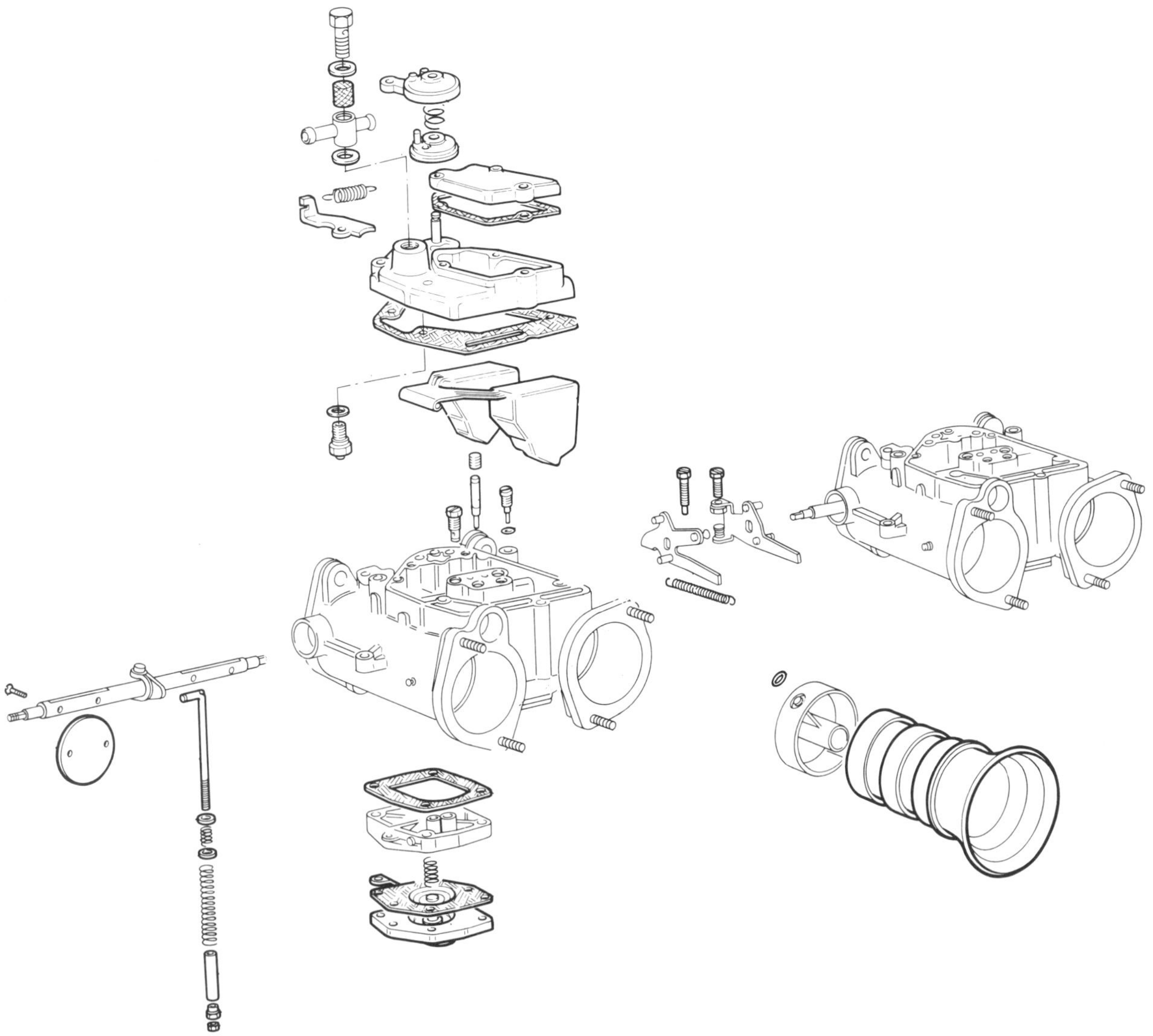

Fig. 13.27 Exploded view of Solex 40 ADDHE carburettor (Sec 10B)

Fig. 13.28 Adjusting accelerator pump delivery – Solex 40 ADDHE carburettor (Sec 10B)

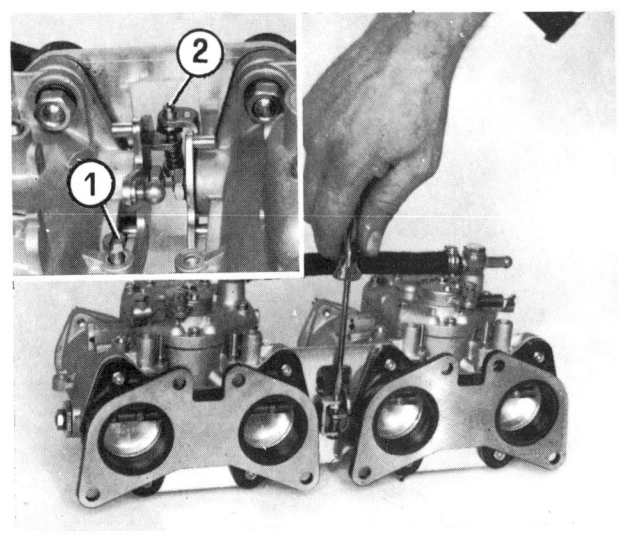

Fig. 13.29 Initial synchronisation of Solex 40 ADDHE twin carburettors (Sec 10B)

1   Idle speed master adjustment screw

2   Synchronizing screw

PART C: CARBURETTORS – MODELS EXCEPT ABARTH 130 TC

Carburettor adjustments – important note

1   When making carburettor adjustments it is probable that one or more adjustment screws will be found to be 'tamperproofed', either by a plug or by a limiter cap.

2   The purpose of tamperproofing is to discourage, and to detect, adjustment by unskilled or unqualified persons. In some territories, including parts of the EEC, it is an offence to drive a vehicle with missing tamperproof seals.

3   Before removing any tamperproof seal or device, satisfy yourself that local regulations do not prohibit this. Do not remove any seals from cars still under warranty. Fit new seals on completion of adjustment where this is required by law.

Weber 32 1CEV 51/250

Description

4   This carburettor is a single choke downdraught instrument. The cold start device (choke) is of the strangler type, mechanically operated with a vacuum unloader (anti-flooding device).

Idle adjustment

5   Refer to Chapter 3, Section 10 and to Fig. 13.30.

Removal and refitting

6   Refer to Chapter 3, Section 11.

Overhaul

7   Refer to Chapter 3, Section 12.

Other adjustments

8   Refer to Chapter 3, Section 13, for float level and choke unloader adjustments.

9   To check accelerator pump delivery, place the carburettor over a measuring cylinder with the float chamber full of fuel. Take appropriate fire precautions. Operate the throttle lever ten times over its full stroke, pausing at the beginning and end of each stroke. Measure the quantity of fuel delivered and compare it with the value given in the

Specifications.

10   If adjustment is necessary, act on the nut at the bottom of the control lever. Unscrew the nut to reduce delivery, or screw it up to increase it.

11   For initial adjustment after overhaul, set the adjustment nut so that it is just touching the control lever with the throttle gap as shown (Fig. 13.31).

12   Make sure that the pump discharges vertically, and not against the venturi or auxiliary venturi.

Solex C32/DISA/12

Description

13   This Solex carburettor is the equivalent of the Weber ICEV, which it closely resembles.

Idle adjustment

14   Refer to Chapter 3, Section 10 and to Fig. 13.32.

Removal and refitting

15   Refer to Chapter 3, Section 11.

Overhaul

16   Refer to Chapter 3, Section 12.

Other adjustments

17   Refer to Chapter 3, Section 14, and to Figs. 13.33 and 13.34. There is no need for a vacuum source when checking the choke valve opening: the operating rod can be pushed with a screwdriver to produce the same effect.

18   For accelerator pump adjustment, proceed as described for the Weber ICEV carburettor.

Weber 30 DMTE

Description

19   The DMTE carburettor is fitted to 1100 ES models. It is very similar to the DMTR series, with the refinement that the idle cut-off solenoid is also used to cut off fuel on the overrun.

20   Adjustment and overhaul procedures are as described for the DMTR series. Testing of the overrun fuel cut-off is considered separately (see Part A of this Section).

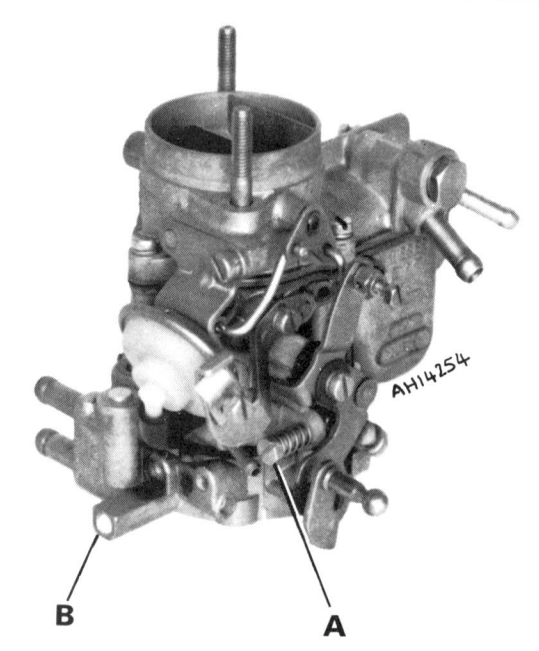

Fig. 13.30 Adjustment screws on Weber 32 ICEV 51/250 carburettor (Sec 10C)

A   Idle speed screw

B   Mixture screw with tamperproof plug

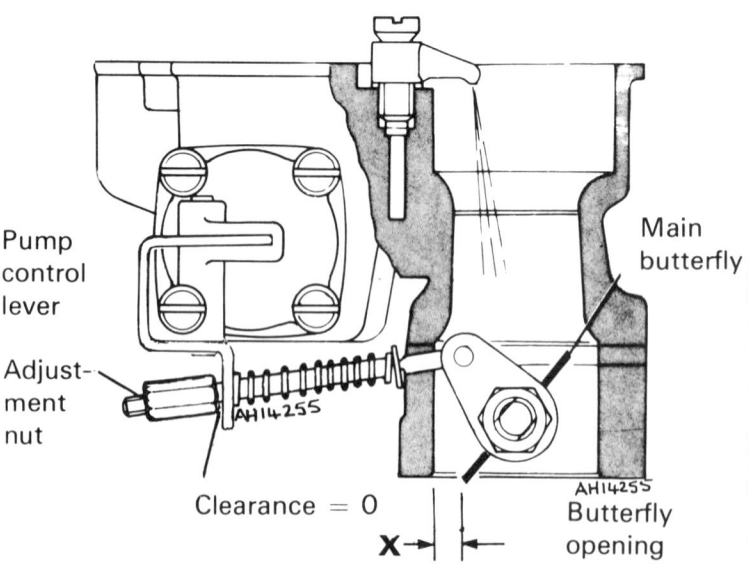

Fig. 13.31 Accelerator pump initial adjustment – Weber 32 ICEV 51/250 carburettor (Sec 10C)

X = 3.5 mm (0.138 in)

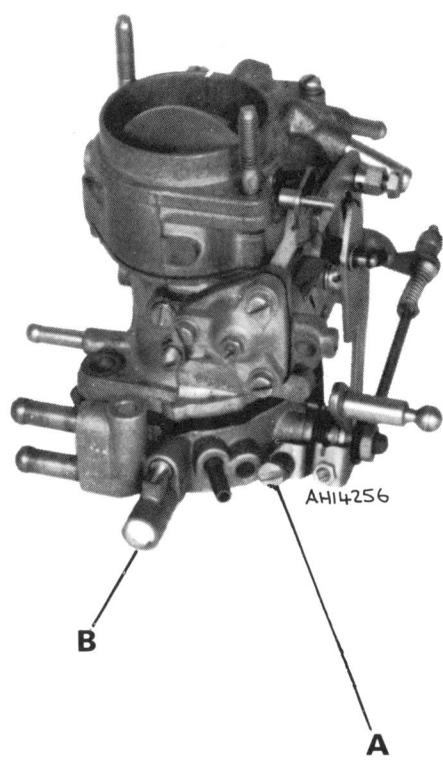

AH14256

B

A

Fig. 13.32 Adjustment screws on Solex C32 DISA/12
carburettor (Sec 10C)

A Idle speed screw   B Mixture screw with
                               tamperproof plug

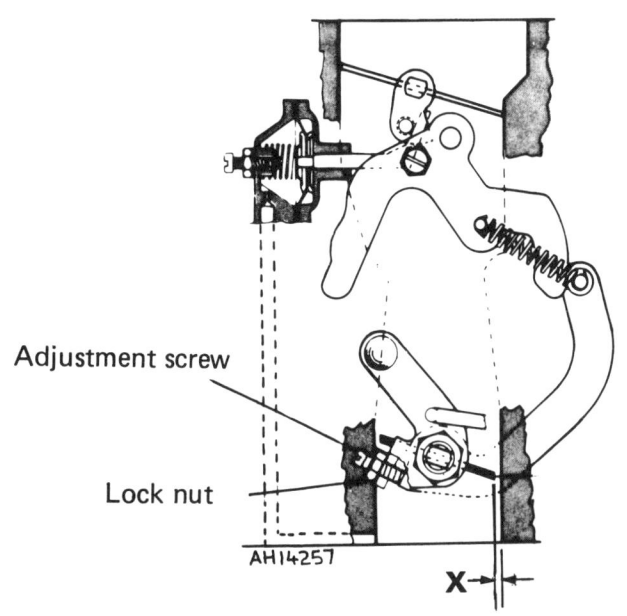

Adjustment screw

Lock nut

AH14257

X

Fig. 13.33 Fast idle adjustment – Solex C32 DISA/12
carburettor (Sec 10C)

X = 0.9 to 1.0 mm
       (0.035 to 0.039 in)

Fig. 13.34 Checking the choke valve opening – Solex C32
DISA/12 carburettor (Sec 10C)

AH14258

A   B

Fig. 13.35 Weber 30 DMTE carburettor (Sec 10C)

A Cut-off solenoid   B 'Throttle closed' switch

Weber DMTR series

Description

21 The DMTR carburettor is a twin choke downdraught instrument. Throttle opening is sequential and mechanically controlled. The cold start device is of the strangler type and is manually controlled; the offset of the strangler flap and a vacuum unloader prevent flooding after the engine is started on full choke (photos).

22 Some carburettors are fitted with a solenoid valve which interrupts the idle mixture supply when the ignition is switched off. This prevents the engine running on (photo).

Idle adjustment

23 Refer to Chapter 3, Section 10; the adjusting screws are located as shown (photos).

Removal and refitting

24 Refer to Chapter 3, Section 11.

Overhaul

25 Refer to Chapter 3, Section 12; the same principles apply.

26 Note that the strangler operating rod is secured by a small split pin (photo). After removing this split pin and the cover screws, the cover can be removed by lifting and twisting through 90° to free the operating rod.

27 With the cover removed, most parts of the carburettor are accessible for overhaul (photos). If it is simply wished to clean or renew the idle jets, main jets or emulsion tubes, these can be unscrewed without removing the cover.

28 Before refitting the overhauled carburettor, carry out the checks and adjustments detailed below.

29 These adjustments are not routine operations; they may be necessary after carburettor overhaul.

Float level adjustment

30 The float level is measured with the carburettor cover vertical. The

10C.21A Weber DMTR carburettor – vacuum unloader arrowed

10C.21B Weber DMTR carburettor – crankcase ventilation hose arrowed

10C.22 Weber DMTR carburettor – idle cut-off solenoid arrowed

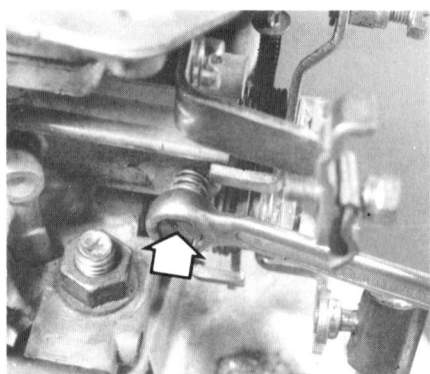

10C.23A Idle speed adjusting screw (arrowed) – Weber DMTR carburettor

10C.23B Idle mixture adjusting screw – Weber DMTR carburettor

10C.26 Split pin securing choke valve plate (strangler) operating rod – Weber DMTR carburettor

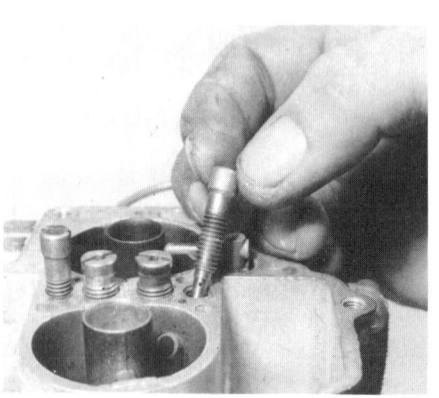

10C.27A Removing primary idle jet – Weber DMTR carburettor

10C.27B Removing the primary main jet and emulsion tube – Weber DMTR carburettor

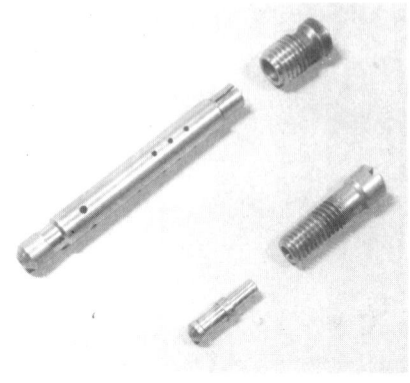

10C.27C Jets and holders – Weber DMTR carburettor

10C.30 Measuring the float level – Weber DMTR carburettor

10C.37 Measuring primary throttle valve fast idle opening – Weber DMTR carburettor

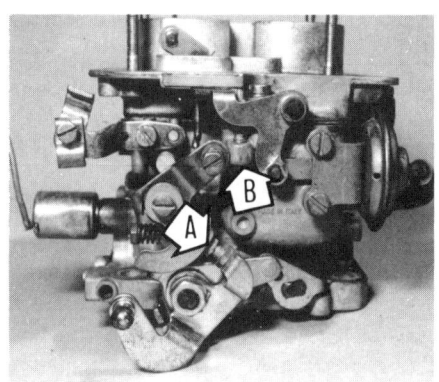

10C.38 Fast idle adjusting screw (A) and choke vacuum unloader adjusting screw (B) – Weber DMTR carburettor

dimension specified is between the top of the float and the gasket (photo).

31 If adjustment is necessary, bend the float arm so that with the dimension correct, the arm lug just touches the needle valve ball.

Accelerator pump delivery adjustment

32 Arrange the carburettor over a funnel and measuring glass, and fill the float chamber with fuel. Take appropriate fire precautions.

33 Operate the throttle lever fully ten times, pausing at the beginning and end of each stroke. Measure the quantity of fuel delivered and compare it with the value given in the Specifications.

34 No adjustment of the accelerator pump is possible. If the delivery is outside acceptable limits, check the pump diaphragm, spring and delivery passages.

35 The spray from the pump delivery tube should be vertical, and not strike the venturi or auxiliary venturi.

Fast idle adjustment

36 Operate the choke (strangler) lever fully, so that the choke valve is closed.

37 Measure the primary throttle valve opening, using a gauge rod or

twist drill (photo). The desired opening is given in the Specifications.

38 If adjustment is necessary, act on the fast idle adjusting screw and locknut (photo).

Choke unloader adjustment

39 Close the choke valve fully by means of the operating lever.

40 Press down on the vacuum unloader operating lever so that the choke valve opens a small distance. Measure the opening with a gauge rod or drill shank (photo). The desired opening is given in the Specifications.

41 If adjustment is necessary, act on the adjusting screw (item B in photo 10C.38).

42 On 30/32 DMTR and 30 DMTE carburettors, check that with the choke lever still in the fully closed position the choke valve can be opened to the gap specified (mechanical unloading). Bend the choke control lever stop to adjust if necessary; check after adjustment that the choke valve will still close fully.

Throttle valve partial opening adjustment

43 Slowly operate the throttle lever until the secondary throttle valve is about to start opening. In this position, measure the opening of the primary throttle valve and compare it with the value specified.

10C.40 Measuring the choke valve plate (strangler) opening – Weber DMTR carburettor

Fig. 13.36 Checking throttle valve partial opening – Weber DMTR carburettor (Sec 10C)

X See Specifications

44 If adjustment is necessary, carefully bend the linkage as shown (Fig. 13.37).

Solex CIC/1 series
Description
45 This carburettor is almost identical to the Weber DMTR.

Idle adjustment
46 Refer to Chapter 3, Section 10 and to Fig. 13.38.

Overhaul
47 Refer to Chapter 3, Section 12.

Float level adjustment
48 The float level is measured with the carburettor cover horizontal, so that the needle valve is closed by the weight of the float. The gasket should be in place.
49 Adjustment is effected by changing the thickness of the washer under the needle valve seat, or by carefully bending the float arm.

Accelerator pump delivery adjustment
50 Proceed as described for the Weber DMTR, but note that the pump stroke can be adjusted if delivery is incorrect.

Fast idle adjustment
51 Proceed as described for the Weber DMTR, referring to Fig. 13.40.

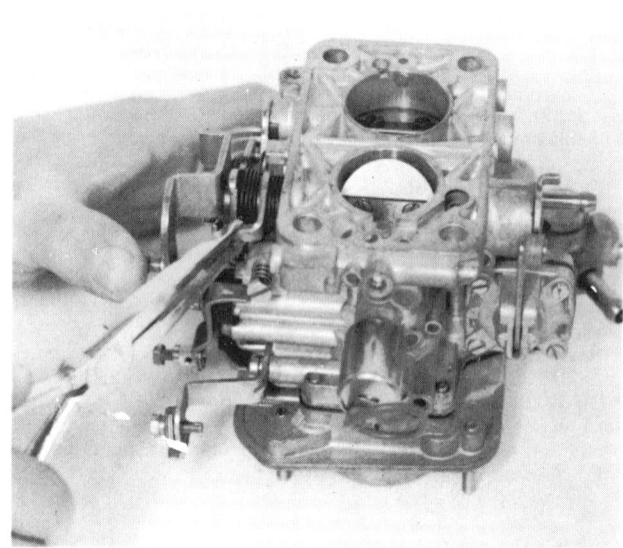

Fig. 13.37 Adjusting throttle valve partial opening – Weber DMTR carburettor (Sec 10C)

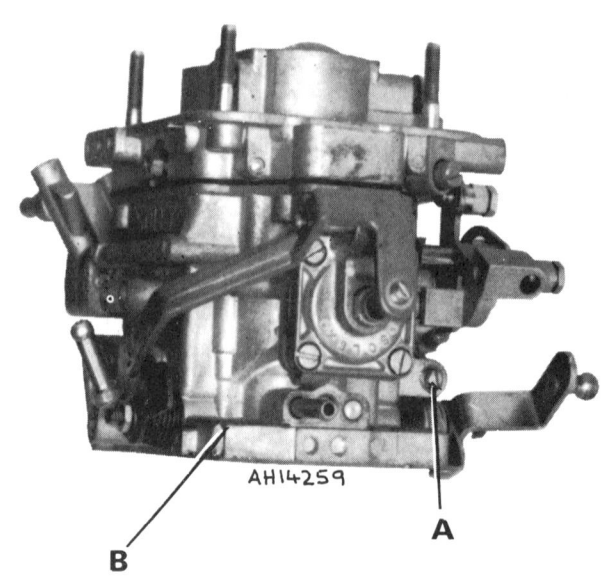

Fig. 13.38 Adjustment screws on Solex CIC/1 carburettor (Sec 10C)

A   Idle speed screw   B   Mixture screw with tamperproof plug

Fig. 13.39 Adjusting accelerator pump stroke – Solex CIC/1 carburettor (Sec 10C)

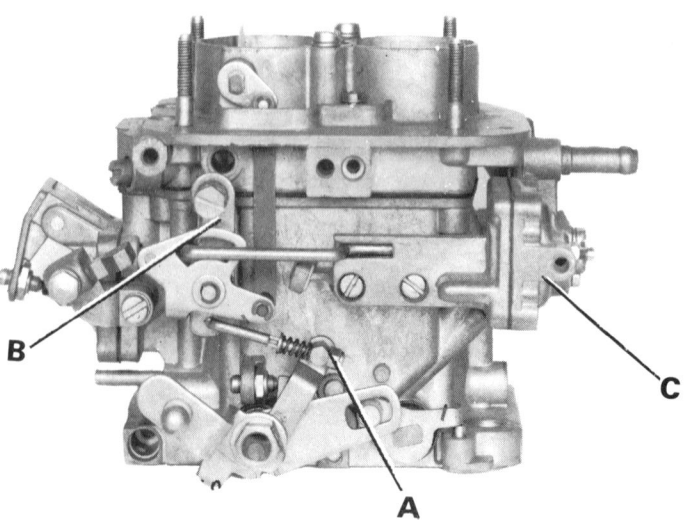

Fig. 13.40 Fast idle adjustment nut (A) – Solex CIC/1 carburettor (Sec 10C)

B   Choke control lever   C   Choke unloader

Note also that the throttle valve gap is measured on the side away from the progression holes, ie nearest the centre-line.

Choke unloader adjustment

52 Proceed as described for the Weber DMTR, referring to Figs. 13.41 and 13.42.

Weber 34 DAT
Description

53 The Weber 34 DAT is a twin choke downdraught instrument. Throttle opening is sequential. The cold start device (choke) is automatic, responding to coolant temperature.

54 In many respects this carburettor resembles the Weber 28/30 DHTA described in Chapter 3.

Idle adjustment

55 Refer to Chapter 3, Section 10 and to Fig. 13.43.

Overhaul

56 Refer to Chapter 3, Section 12, noting the following points.

57 Before dismantling the automatic choke cover, make alignment marks (if none are present) so that the components can be refitted in the same relative position.

58 Renew the automatic choke cover every 30 000 miles (48 000 km).

Float level adjustment

59 Refer to Chapter 3, Section 15.

Fast idle throttle valve opening adjustment

60 With the automatic choke cover removed, close the choke valve completely and position the fast idle screw on the highest cam step.

61 Measure the opening of the primary throttle valve, using a twist drill or gauge rod. If it is outside the specified limits, adjust by turning the fast idle screw.

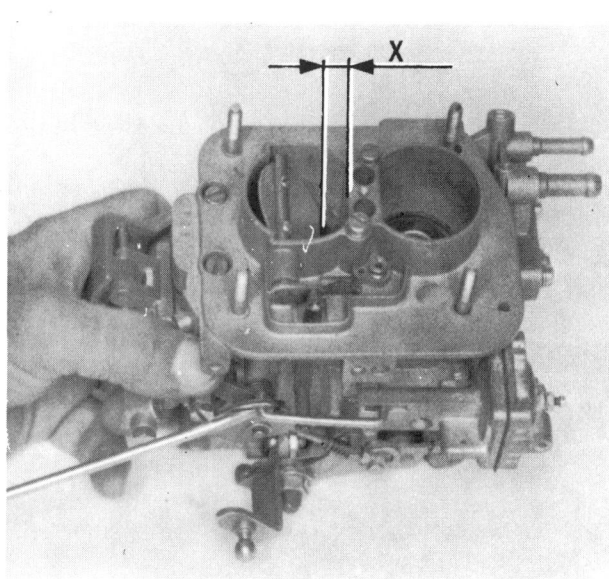

Fig. 13.41 Checking choke unloader – Solex CIC/1 carburettor (Sec 10C)

X See Specifications

Fig. 13.42 Adjusting choke unloader – Solex CIC/1 carburettor (Sec 10C)

Fig. 13.43 Idle mixture adjustment screw (arrowed) on Weber 34 DAT carburettor. Idle speed adjustment screw is on throttle linkage (Sec 10C)

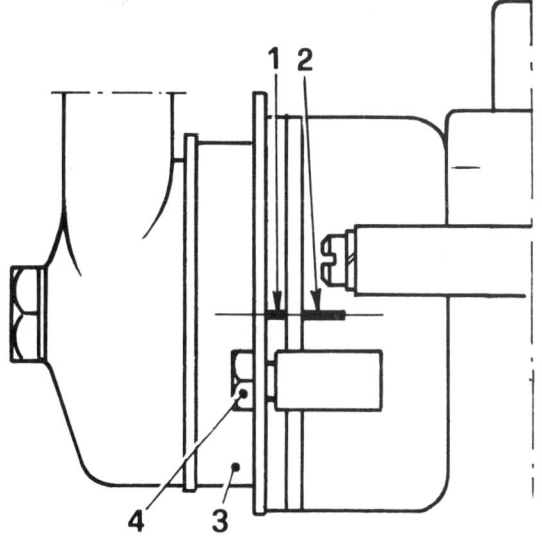

Fig. 13.44 Automatic choke housing and cover alignment marks on Weber 34 DAT carburettor (Sec 10C)

1 and 2 Alignment marks   4 Flange screw
3 Case

Choke unloader adjustment
62 Refer to Chapter 3, Section 15.

Fast idle cam intermediate setting adjustment
63 Refer to Chapter 3, Section 15, but note that gap C should be 5.75 to 6.25 mm (0.226 to 0.246 in).

Choke unloader minimum opening adjustment
64 Refer to Chapter 3, Section 15, but note that gap D should be 4.5 to 5.5 mm (0.177 to 0.217 in).

Weber 32/34 TLDE/150
Description
65 This carburettor is of twin venturi downdraught type, with a manually-operated choke (cold start) device (photos).

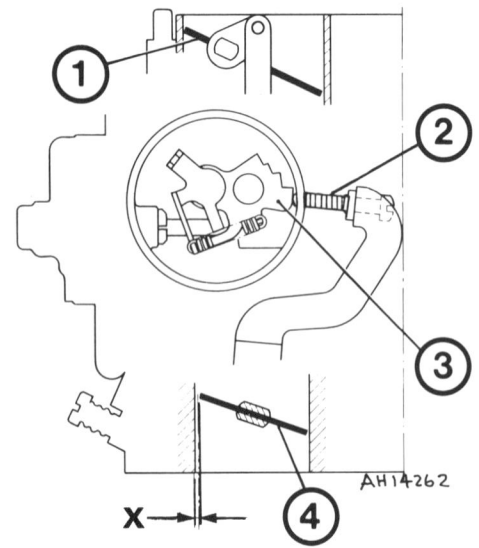

Fig. 13.45 Fast idle throttle valve opening – Weber 34 DAT carburettor (Sec 10C)

1 Choke butterfly valve plate
2 Fast idle screw
3 Cam
4 Primary throttle butterfly valve
X = 0.9 to 1.0 mm (0.035 to 0.039 in)

10C.65A Weber 32/34 TLDE carburettor viewed from accelerator pump side

A Accelerator pump   B Mixture screw with tamperproof cap

66 An anti-run-on (anti-diesel) solenoid valve is fitted, and also a solenoid valve for the fuel cut-off device. This device cuts off fuel to the idle circuit during overrun (deceleration) conditions as a means of fuel economy and reduced exhaust emission. Additional components of the fuel cut-off system are a control unit (located adjacent to the Digiplex ignition control unit on the engine compartment rear bulkhead) and a primary 'throttle closed' switch – see Part A of this Section.

Fig. 13.46 Cut-off device control unit (arrowed) (Sec 10C)

10C.65B Weber 32/34 TLDE carburettor showing rubber insulating block (A) and idle speed screw (B)

10C.65C Weber 32/34 TLDE carburettor showing idle cut-off (anti-diesel) solenoid valve (A) and fuel cut-off (overrun) solenoid valve (B)

10C.65D Top view of Weber 32/34 TLDE carburettor. Top cover fixing screws and bolts arrowed

Idle speed and mixture – adjustment

67 The engine must be at normal working temperature with all electrical accessories switched off.

68 Turn the throttle speed screw until the engine idle speed is at the specified level – see Specifications at the start of this Chapter.

69 The mixture screw is located under a tamperproof plug in the carburettor bottom flange. The mixture is set in production and should not normally require adjustment; however, where this is necessary, prise out the plug and turn the screw in to weaken the mixture or out to enrich it. It is recommended that an exhaust gas analyser is used, in accordance with the manufacturer's instructions, to set the mixture precisely.

Removal and refitting

70 Remove the air cleaner after disconnecting the cold and hot air intake pipes and the crankcase vent hose, unscrewing its bracket nut from the camshaft cover and unscrewing the casing retainer on top of the carburettor (photos).

71 Disconnect the choke cable by unscrewing the trunnion pinch screws (photo).

72 Disconnect the throttle cable. Do this by swivelling the cable cam sector and releasing the cable end nipple. Pull out the throttle cable adjuster clip and push the rubber bush out of the support bracket to enable the throttle cable to pass through the slot in the bracket (photos).

73 Disconnect the electrical leads, the earth wire and the vacuum hoses (photos).

74 Disconnect and plug the fuel hoses. It is recommended that the cap of the fuel tank is unscrewed to reduce the pressure in the fuel supply pipe.

75 Unscrew the mounting nuts and washers, noting which nut secures the earth wire (photo).

76 Lift the carburettor from the manifold, noting the rubber insulating block with sealing gasket on which the carburettor is mounted.

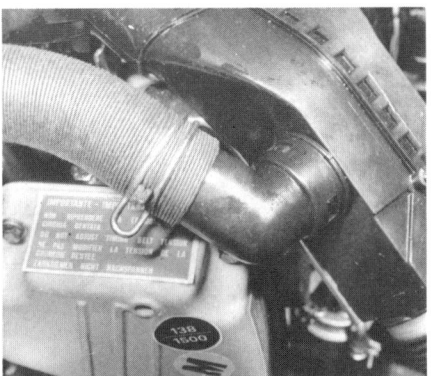

10C.70A Air cleaner hot air intake duct

10C.70B Crankcase vent hose attached to air cleaner

10C.70C Air cleaner support bracket

10C.70D Air cleaner lid fixing nuts

10C.70E Air cleaner casing retainer plate, spacers and nuts (arrowed)

10C.71 Choke cable and trunnions – Weber 32/34 TLDE carburettor

10C.72A Releasing throttle cable from cam sector on Weber 32/34 TLDE carburettor

10C.72B Throttle cable adjuster clip (arrowed)

10C.72C Releasing throttle cable rubber bush from support bracket

10C.72D Throttle cable passing through slot in bracket

10C.73A Electrical power and earth terminals on Weber 32/34 TLDE carburettor

10C.73B Fuel and vacuum hoses connected to Weber 32/34 TLDE carburettor – note fuel line connection markings

10C.75 Unscrewing carburettor mounting nut

10C.79A Removing fuel union

10C.79B Extracting gauze filter

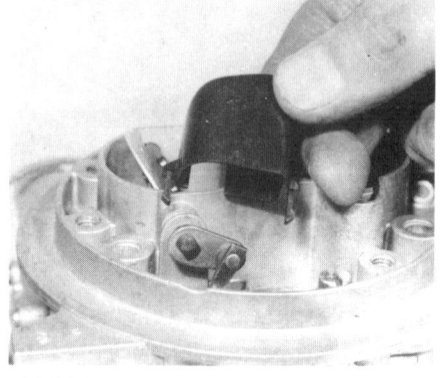

10C.82A Extracting plastic cover

10C.82B Choke link rod circlip (arrowed)

10C.82C Fast idle link rod and spring clip

77 Refitting is a reversal of removal, but set the throttle cable so that it is slightly slack by moving the clip to a suitable groove in the cable outer sleeve.

78 Check that full throttle can be obtained.

Maintenance and overhaul

79 Regular maintenance is minimal and should be restricted to keeping the outside of the carburettor clean, and cleaning the fuel filter gauze by disconnecting the fuel return hose, unscrewing the union pipe stub, extracting the filter gauze and cleaning it (photos).

80 Overhaul should be limited to the following operations. If more extensive dismantling is required (renewal of venturis, valve plates etc), purchase a new or factory reconditioned unit.

81 With the carburettor removed as described earlier, clean dirt and grease from its external surfaces.

82 Remove the top cover. To do this, unscrew the two screws and then the four bolts. The latter also secure the rubber insulating base. Extract the choke cable support bracket fixing screws. Remove the plastic cover, extract the small circlip and disconnect the choke valve

plate link rod. Withdraw the spring clip and disconnect the fast idle link rod. Lift the top cover from the carburettor body (photos).

83 The jets located on both sides of the top cover may be unscrewed and blown through with air from a tyre pump. Never probe a jet with wire, or its calibration will be ruined (photos). Do not overtighten the jets when refitting.

84 The twin floats may be removed after carefully tapping out the pivot pin (photos).

85 Withdraw the fuel inlet valve needle. If its tip is scored or damaged, unscrew the valve body and renew the body and needle as an assembly. Tighten the valve body to ensure a positive seal. Leakage of fuel here will cause flooding from the float chamber.

86 Renew the top cover gasket and refit the floats and pivot pin. Now check the float setting. Due to the lip on the top cover, the specified distance between the surface of the gasket and the nearest point on the floats (when the top cover is held vertically with the float arm just touching, not depressing the needle ball) cannot be measured, so it must be calculated in the following way.

87 With the top cover held vertically and the floats hanging down,

10C.83A Top cover jets (arrowed)

10C.83B Accelerator pump jet withdrawn

10C.84A Float pivot pin withdrawn

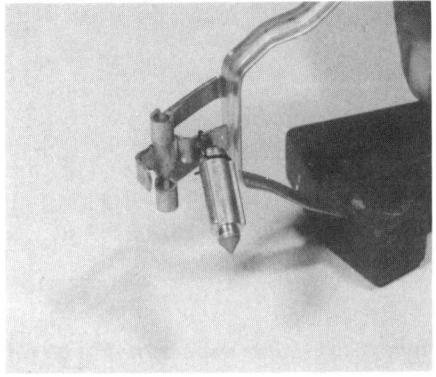

10C.84B Spring clip used to attach fuel inlet needle to float arm tab

10C.87A Float measurement in full extended position

10C.87B Float measurement in retracted position

move the floats to the full extent of their travel (maximum stroke) and measure from the surface of the top cover gasket to the furthest point of the float. Now allow the float arm to rest against the needle valve ball without depressing it and measure again as previously described. Subtract the second dimension from the first to give the float setting. If this is not as specified, carefully bend the float arm tab (photos).

88 The throttle valve block can be removed by inverting the carburettor and extracting the two securing screws. Dismantling the throttle butterfly valves is not recommended; wear should be rectified by renewing the valve block complete (photo).

89 The solenoid valves can be unscrewed and removed, and air pressure applied to their passages in the carburettor body to clear them. When refitting the valves, do not overtighten them.

90 Refit the top cover, reconnect the link rods and fit the choke cable support bracket.

11 Ignition system – Strada II and all TC models

Conventional ignition system – contact breaker adjustment

1 The contact breaker gap is adjusted from outside the distributor, using a 3 mm Allen key (Fig. 13.47).

10C.88 Throttle valve block (carburettor inverted). Fixing screws arrowed

Fig. 13.47 External adjustment of contact breaker points (Sec 11)

2   The contact breaker gap should only be set using a feeler gauge as an initial measure when the contact breaker set has been removed. Thereafter adjustment should be made using a dwell meter – see Chapter 4, Section 2. Adjustment can be made with the engine running.
3   Do not attempt to clean 'pip and crater' wear off the contact breaker point faces, as this will almost certainly shorten their life. As long as the dwell angle can be brought within limits, the pip and crater can be ignored.
4   Always check the ignition timing after adjusting the dwell angle.

Conventional ignition system – contact breaker renewal

5   The contact breaker set is renewed complete with baseplate, distributor shaft top bush and adjuster mechanism.
6   Remove the distributor cap, rotor arm and anti-flash shield.
7   Disconnect the electrical leads from the contact breaker set. Unhook the vacuum advance link and lift the set out of the distributor.
8   Apply a drop of engine oil to the bush in the centre of the new contact breaker set before fitting. Connect the vacuum advance link and the electrical leads.
9   Set the contact breaker gap using feeler gauges, then refit the anti-flash shield, rotor arm and distributor cap.
10   Check the dwell angle and adjust it if necessary, then check the ignition timing.

Conventional ignition timing system – ignition timing adjustment

11   The ignition timing marks are on the flywheel and the flywheel housing. The marks are 0° (TDC) 5° and 10° BTDC on the housing, and a dot on the flywheel (photo).
12   Proceed as described in Chapter 4, Section 4, referring to the Specifications at the beginning of this Chapter for the desired timing values.
13   Static timing (with the engine stationary) should be regarded only as a preliminary measure. Once the engine will run, the timing should be set at idle speed using a stroboscopic timing light.

Inductive discharge ignition system – description and maintenance

14   The inductive discharge ignition system is fitted to early 105 TC models. For all practical purposes it is the same as the breakerless system described in Chapter 4, to which reference should be made.

Digiplex ignition system – description and maintenance

15   The Marelli Digiplex ignition system is fitted to 1100 ES, 105 TC and 130 TC Strada II models. It may well be fitted to other models in future.
16   The system uses no contact breaker or mechanical advance components. The function of the distributor is simply to distribute HT voltage to the appropriate plug. Firing points are determined by a crankshaft pulley sensor (TDC sensor); ignition advance is determined by an electronic control unit (ECU), based on information received from the rpm sensor mounted near the flywheel and from the manifold vacuum sensor. The ECU provides the optimum amount of advance under all speed and load conditions.
17   Ignition timing cannot be 'set' in the accustomed way with this system; the only possible cause of incorrect timing (apart from an ECU fault) is displacement or distortion of the TDC sensor or its bracket.
18   Apart from periodic spark plug renewal, maintenance is limited to checking the system wiring and vacuum connections for security and good condition. Clean and inspect the distributor cap, rotor arm and HT leads at time of spark plug renewal.

Digiplex ignition system – precautions

19   The electronic components in the ignition system must be protected against electrical damage by observing the precautions prescribed for the alternator (Chapter 9, Section 6).
20   Always switch off the ignition before disconnecting or reconnecting the ECU.
21   If the vehicle is to be subject to temperatures in excess of 80°C (176°F) – eg in a paint drying oven – remove the ECU beforehand.
22   Do not crank the engine or otherwise energise the ignition system

11.11 Flywheel and bellhousing timing marks

with any HT leads disconnected, unless the ECU has first been disconnected.
23   Take great care to avoid receiving personal electric shocks from the HT system.

Digiplex ignition system – distributor removal and refitting

24   Remove the distributor cap.
25   Scribe alignment marks between the distributor flange and the camshaft carrier.
26   Remove the securing nuts and washers and remove the distributor. Recover the gasket.
27   When refitting, note that the drive dog is offset so there is no possibility of incorrect fitting. The slots in the distributor flange are not for adjusting the timing, but simply for aligning the rotor arm tip with respect to the contacts in the distributor cap. If fitting a new distributor, align the rotor arm tip with the scribed line (photo) with No 4 cylinder at TDC on the firing stroke.
28   If the camshaft has been removed, it may be found that the distributor will not sit on its flanges. Do not try to pull the distributor down with its nuts, but remove it and strike the rear of the camshaft a few times to take up the endfloat.

Digiplex ignition system – sensor removal and refitting

TDC sensor

29   Disconnect the sensor wiring plug, remove the screws which hold the sensor to its bracket and remove the sensor (photo). **Do not** disturb the bracket mounting screws (they will probably be tamper-proofed in any case).
30   Refit in the reverse order to removal. Check that the gap between the sensor face and a firing pip is within the limits given in the Specifications; carefully bend the bracket if necessary to correct the gap.

RPM sensor

31   Disconnect the sensor wiring plug and unbolt the sensor from the flywheel housing. Remove the sensor (photo).
32   Refit in the reverse order to removal. The gap between the sensor and the flywheel teeth is important for correct functioning, but it cannot be adjusted and is unlikely to be incorrect unless the wrong components have been fitted.

Digiplex ignition system – ECU removal and refitting

33   On TC models, remove the coolant expansion tank.
34   Disconnect the multi-plug and the vacuum hose from the ECU (photo).
35   Unbolt the ECU and remove it from the bulkhead.
36   Refit in the reverse order to removal.

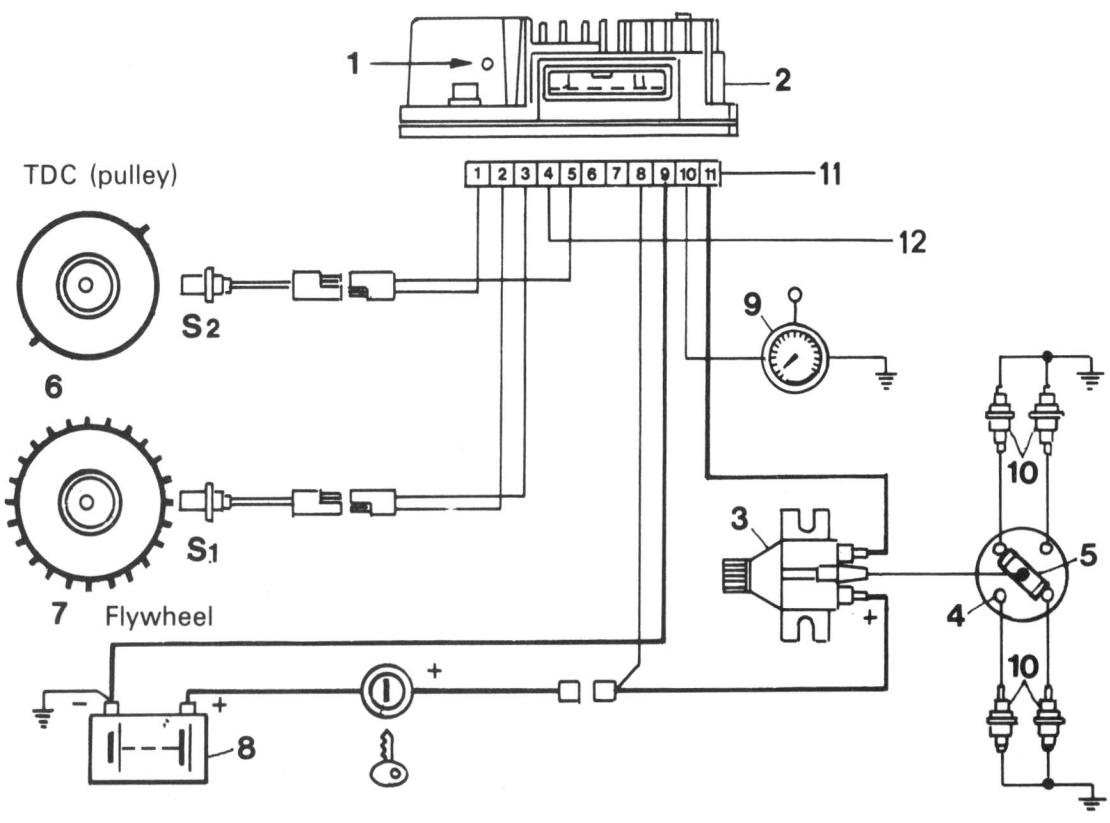

Fig. 13.48 Schematic diagram of Digiplex ignition system (Sec 11)

1 Vacuum connection	4 Distributor cap	8 Battery	12 To economy meter
2 Electronic control unit	5 Rotor arm	9 Tachometer	(when fitted)
(ECU)	6 Crankshaft pulley	10 Spark plugs	51 RPM sensor
3 Coil	7 Flywheel	11 Multi-plug	52 TDC sensor

11.27 Scribed line on distributor body rim (arrowed) denoting No 4 firing point

11.29 TDC sensor adjacent to crankshaft pulley

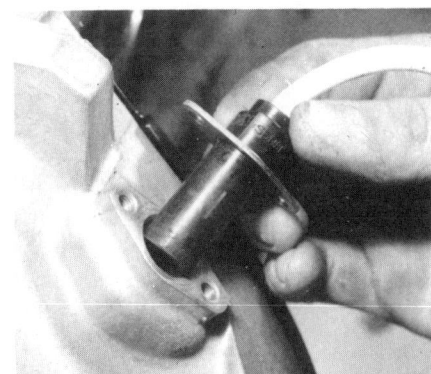

11.31 Rpm sensor on flywheel housing

Digiplex ignition system – fault diagnosis

37 If an ignition system fault is suspected, first make sure that all connections are clean and tight. Also check the security and the fitted gaps of the TDC and rpm sensors.

38 If an ohmmeter is available, check the winding resistances of the sensors and the ignition coil (see Specifications).

39 Disconnect the ECU multi-plug with the ignition switched off. Using a voltmeter or a low wattage test lamp, check the voltage across terminals 9 and 11 of the multi-plug (ignition on). If battery voltage is

not present, either the coil primary winding is open-circuit, or the wiring to or from the coil is broken.

40 Similarly check across terminals 8 and 9. If battery voltage is not present, either the feed (terminal 8) or the earth (terminal 9) connection is defective. Switch off the ignition and reconnect the multi-plug.

41 During all tests, take great care not to splay female connectors, as this can cause fresh problems on reconnection.

42 The HT side of the system can be checked as described in Chapter

4, Section 14; *note however that HT leads must not be disconnected with the engine running.*
43 Furthermore fault diagnosis should be by substituting known good units, preferably after taking specialist advice.

Breakerless electronic ignition system – description

44 Where this system is used on later models, an impulse generator type distributor is fitted. This distributor is fitted with a centrifugal mechanical device to regulate the ignition advance in accordance with engine speed. It also has an automatic advance vacuum unit which increases the engine ignition advance at low engine speeds.
45 The main visual difference of this type is that it has an electrical control unit, complete with heat dissipater plate and spacer, attached on the outside of the distributor casing (Fig. 13.49 and 13.50).

Breakerless electronic ignition system – timing

46 Follow the procedure given in Chapter 4, Section 4, for the stroboscopic method. Use the timing figure given in the Specifications for this Chapter.
47 Access to the crankshaft pulley and timing chest marks can be gained by removing the side shield from the wheel arch on the right-hand side.

---

12 Clutch

Clutch pedal – adjustment

1 On later models (1986 on), the clutch cable should be adjusted to give the following pedal travel:

All models except Abarth 130 TC: 140 to 150 mm (5.5 to 5.9 in)
Abarth 130 TC: 150 to 160 mm (5.9 to 6.3 in)

Clutch cable renewal – TC models

2 Proceed as described in Chapter 5, Section 3, but note that it will be necessary to remove the heat shield from the steering gear in order to gain access to the cable quadrant (photo).

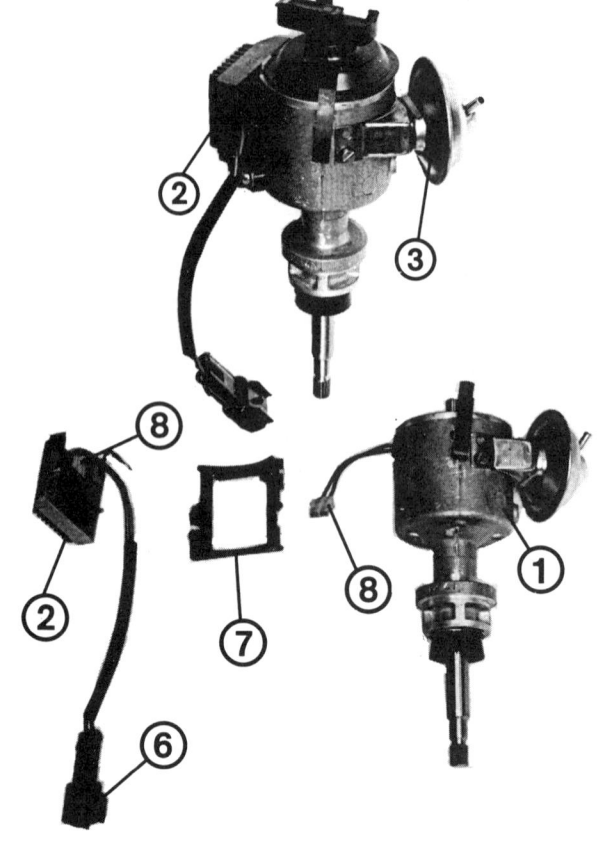

Fig. 13.49 Breakerless electronic distributor, with impulse generator (Sec 11)

1 Distributor casing	6 Connector (to coil)
2 Electronic control unit (ECU)	7 Spacer
3 Vacuum advance unit	8 Connectors (to ECU)

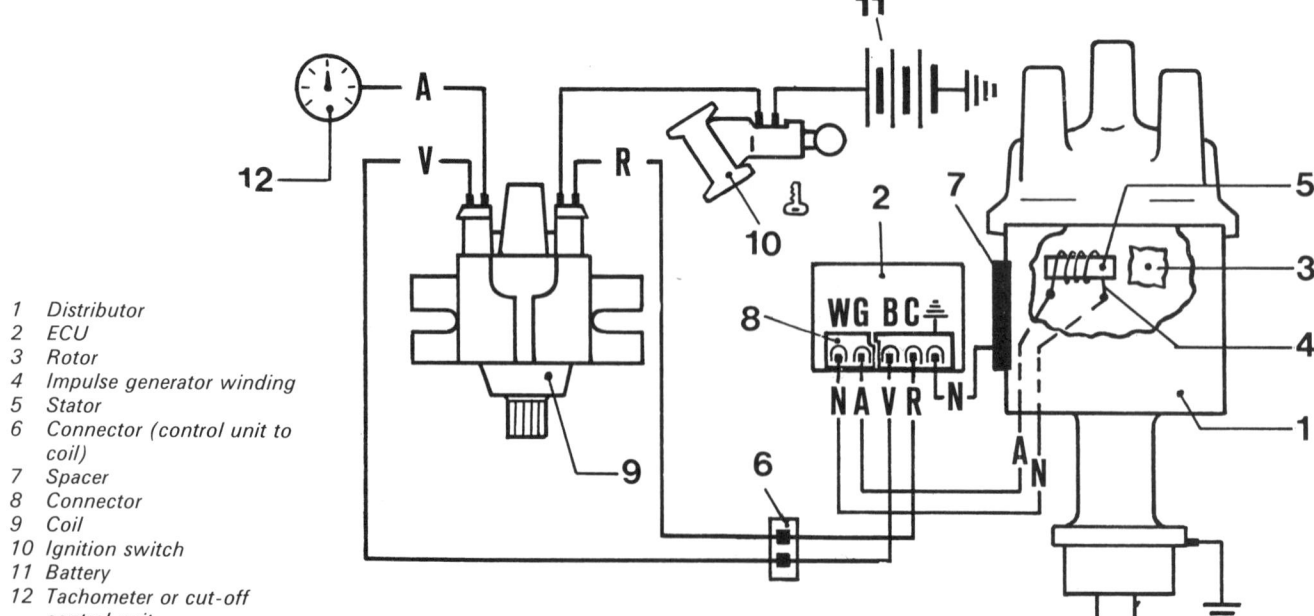

1   Distributor
2   ECU
3   Rotor
4   Impulse generator winding
5   Stator
6   Connector (control unit to coil)
7   Spacer
8   Connector
9   Coil
10   Ignition switch
11   Battery
12   Tachometer or cut-off control unit

Fig. 13.50 Schematic diagram of Marelli breakerless ignition system (Sec 11)

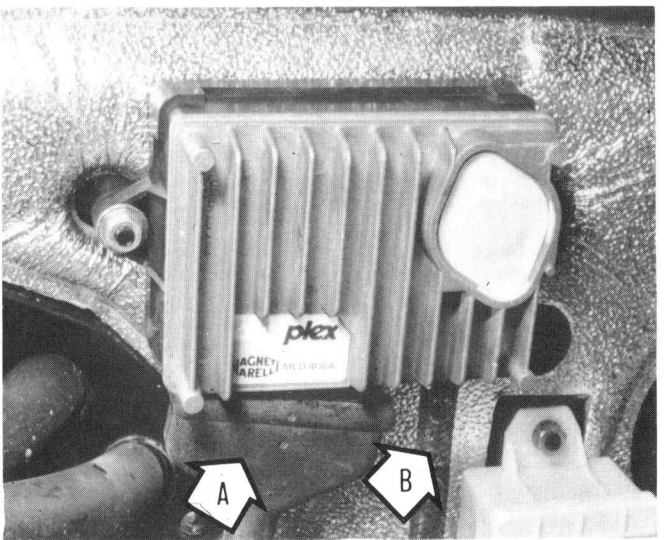

11.34 Digiplex ECU
A   Multiplug   B   Vacuum hose

13 Manual transmission

ZF transmission (130 TC) – general
1   No overhaul data for the ZF transmission was available at the time of writing.

Input shaft bearing/oil seal retainer modification
2   During 1982 the old type bearing/oil seal retainer was replaced by a type which does not require a gasket. The retainer securing screws, and the bellhousing itself, have also been modified.
3   Old and new parts are not interchangeable. The new type retainer should be fitted using silicone sealant on its mating face.

Gearchange linkage – later models
4   At the end of 1981 the single rod gearchange linkage was replaced by a twin rod system (Fig. 13.52). A more elegant version of the twin rod system is fitted to Strada II models (Fig. 13.53).
5   From 1985, the gearchange linkage was further modified to improve gear selection (photos).
6   No adjustment is required for these later linkages. Unsatisfactory performance, if not due to clutch or gearbox problems, will probably be caused by worn bushes or distorted components. Component renewal is self-explanatory on inspection.

12.2 Clutch cable quadrant above steering gear

13.5A Front end of gearchange linkage (1985 on)

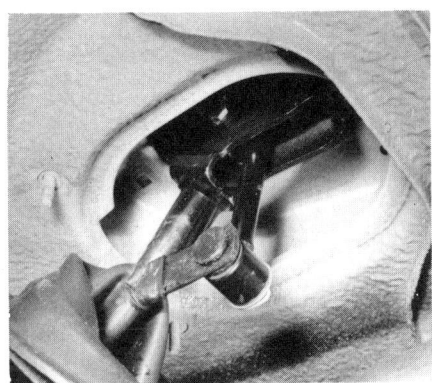

13.5B Rear end of gearchange linkage (1985 on)

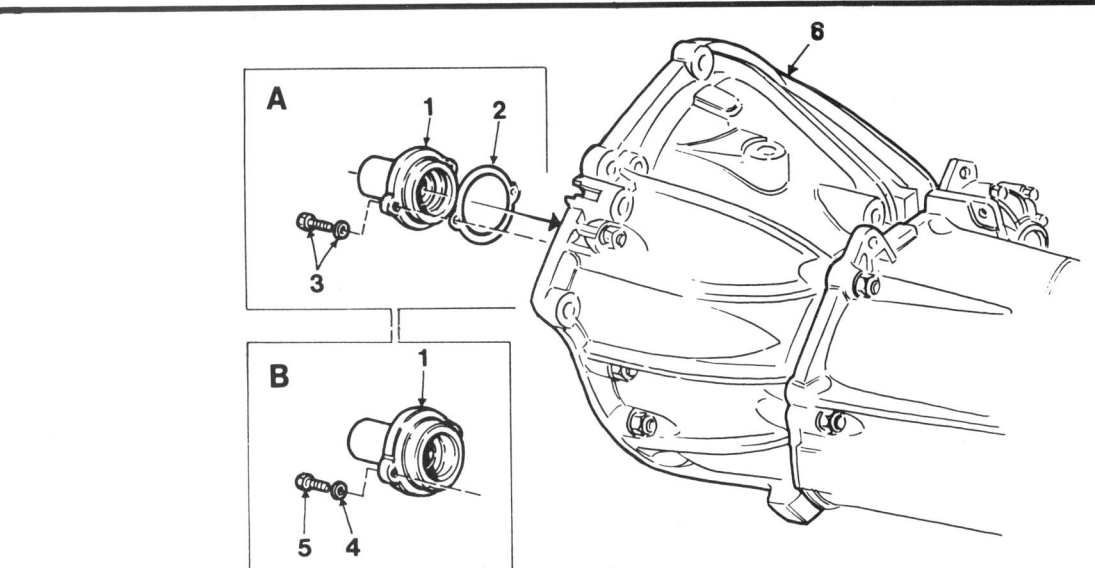

Fig. 13.51 Input shaft bearing/oil seal retainer early (A) and later (B) types (Sec 13)

1   Retainer
2   Gasket
3   Screw and washer
4   Washer
5   Screw
6   Bellhousing

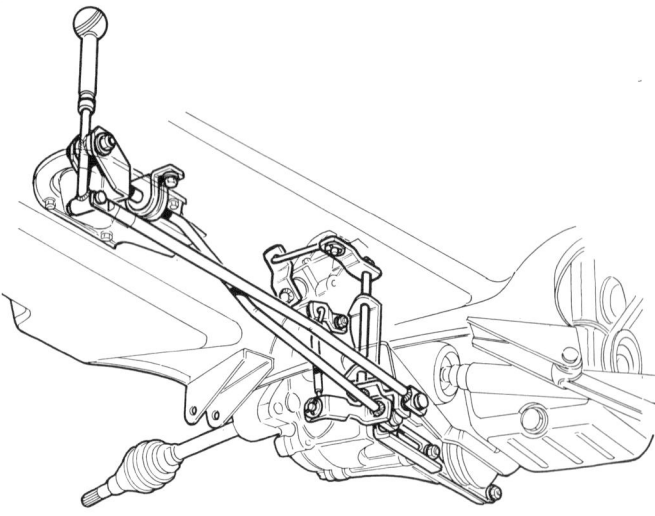

Fig. 13.52 Twin rod gearchange linkage – 1981 to 1983 (Sec 13)

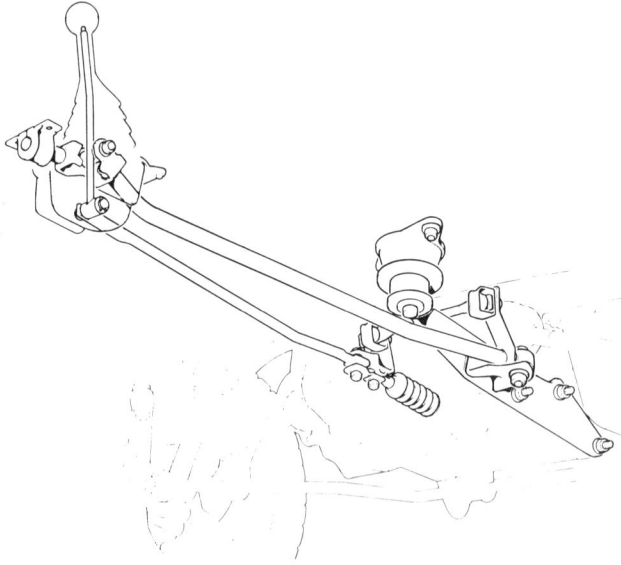

Fig. 13.53 Twin rod gearchange linkage – 1983 to 1985 (Sec 13)

14 Driveshafts (later models)

Description

1   One-piece driveshafts with Tripode inner joints are fitted to most later models (except TD and Automatic).

2   Removal, refitting and overhaul procedures are as given in Chapter 7. For models with Tripode inner joints, follow the instructions for old 65 models; with double CV joints, follow the instructions for old 75 models.

3   From 1987 modified driveshafts are fitted to all models except Abarth 130. The new shafts are fitted with redesigned boots at the inboard end which incorporate a bearing in addition to the seal.

4   No parts are interchangeable between old and new driveshaft assemblies.

5   When fitting a new boot bearing to the driveshaft use a tube to drive it on until it is the following distance from the inboard end of the shaft.

Right-hand driveshaft: 133 mm (5.24 in)
Left-hand driveshaft: 108 mm (4.25 in)

15 Braking system

Brake pads (105 TC from May 1983) – removal and refitting

1   Slacken the front wheel bolts, raise and securely support the front of the car and remove the front wheels.

2   Using two spanners, remove the caliper top mounting bolt, holding the nut on the bracket side stationary. Similarly slacken, but do not remove, the bottom mounting bolt (photo).

3   Pivot the caliper forwards to expose the pads. Be careful not to strain the hydraulic hose (photo).

4   Lift out the pads, disconnecting the wear warning wire from the inboard pad. Clean the caliper and its bracket, being careful not to inhale the dust.

5   Depress the caliper piston into its bore to make room for the increased thickness of the new pads. Be prepared to draw off some brake fluid from the reservoir if necessary.

6   Fit the new pads with their friction surfaces against the disc with the wear warning light contact on the inboard side (next to the piston). Refit and secure the caliper, tightening the bolts to the specified torque.

7   Repeat the operations on the other caliper, then depress the brake pedal several times to bring the new pads up to the disc.

8   Refit the roadwheels, lower the car and tighten the wheel bolts.

15.2 Slackening brake caliper bottom mounting bolt

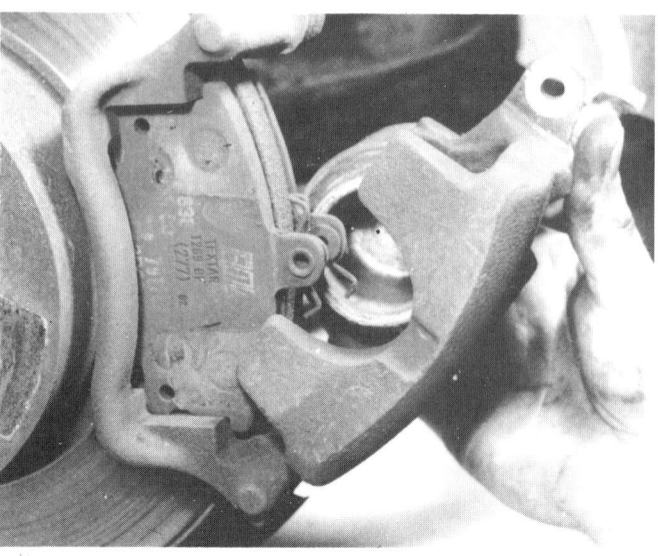

15.3 Caliper pivoted to remove disc pads

*Brake caliper (105 TC from May 1983) – removal,
overhaul and refitting*
9   Proceed as described for pad removal, but also disconnect the
flexible hose at its bracket and remove the bottom mounting bolt.
10 With the caliper itself removed, the mounting bracket may be
unbolted from the steering knuckle.
11 Overhaul is basically as described in Chapter 8, Section 5. Refer
also to Fig. 13.54.

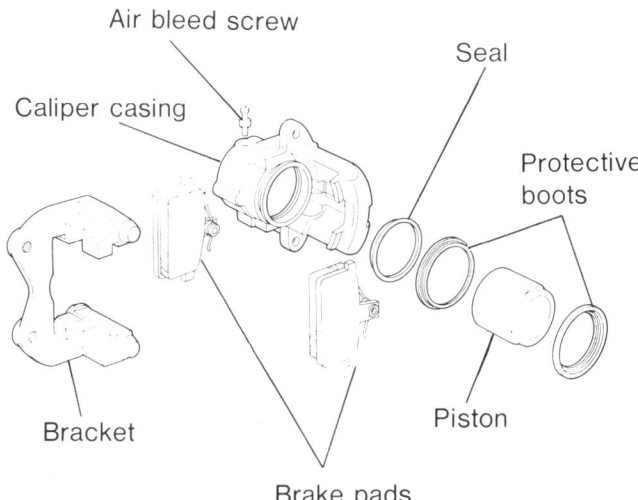

Fig. 13.54 Exploded view of brake caliper fitted to later 105
TC models (Sec 15)

12 Renew the rubber boots on the caliper bracket if necessary.
13 Bleed the hydraulic system on completion.

Brake shoe removal and refitting – all models
14 Note that the two milled areas have been provided in the hub
flange (Fig. 13.55) to make easier the passage of the self-adjusters.

Rear brake self-adjusters – later models
15 The self-adjusters are now renewed with the shoes; they cannot be
dismantled or renewed separately.

Rear wheel cylinder – union thread change
16 Towards the end of 1982 the thread pitch on the rear wheel
cylinder hydraulic unions was changed (from M10 x 1.25 to M10 x 1).
17 The new wheel cylinders are identified by blue paint marks on the
body; the new pipe union is identified by a step on its hexagon (Fig.
13.56).
18 Old and new components cannot be mixed, and old pattern
cylinders are no longer supplied; if renewing an old cylinder, therefore,
a new union must be purchased as well.

Handbrake (Strada II) – adjustment and cable renewal
19 Handbrake adjustment is still carried out as described in Chapter 8,
Section 13.
20 Cable renewal is similar to the procedure in Chapter 8, Section 14,
but there are now four pulleys to remove instead of one (Fig. 13.57).

*Pressure differential regulator (early UK models) –
adjustment*
21 The adjustment procedure in Chapter 8, Section 10, has been
superseded. The new procedure requires special tools unlikely to be
available to the home mechanic.
22 Adjustment of the regulator should therefore be left to a FIAT
dealer.

Pressure differential regulator (Strada II) – adjustment
23 If the operation of the regulator is suspect, or after a new unit has
been fitted, it should be adjusted as follows.
24 Position the car on a flat surface with its weight on its wheels. Load
the luggage area with ballast as follows:

*105 TC and 130 TC – 100 kg (220.5 lb)
Other three-door models – 130 kg (286.7 lb)
Five-door models – 120 kg (264.6 lb)*

25 Refer to the Specifications and inspect the rear brake components
to determine the calibration load required.
26 Slacken the regulator bracket bolt, apply the specified calibration
load downwards to the spring eye, then tighten the bracket bolt
(photo). A spring balance is probably the best tool for applying the
load.

Fig. 13.55 Hub flange cut-outs (arrowed) to provide
clearance for shoe adjusters (Sec 15)

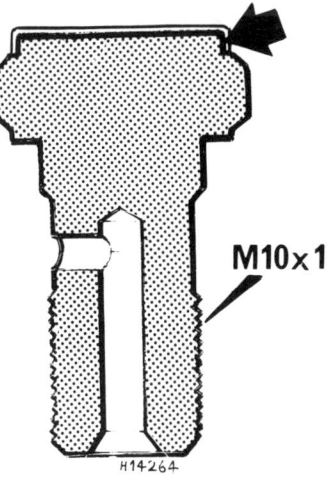

Fig. 13.56 New type of hydraulic union is identified by step
on hexagon (arrowed) (Sec 15)

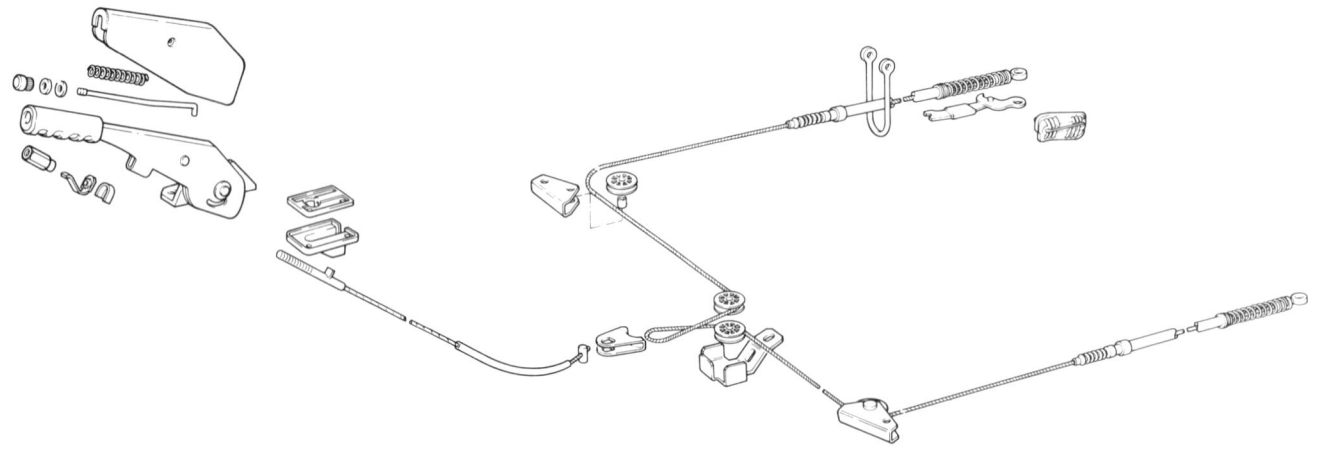

Fig. 13.57 Handbrake linkage on Strada II models (Sec 15)

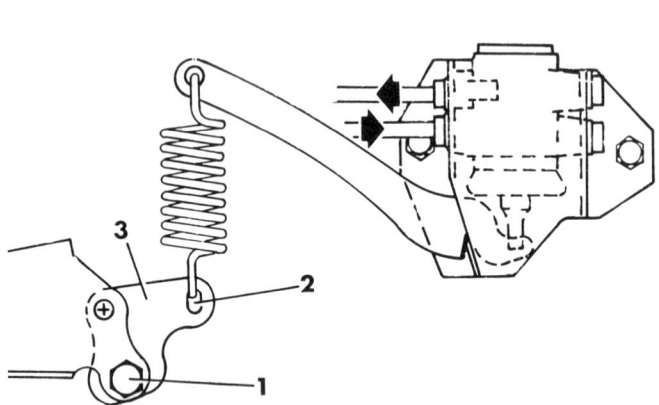

**Fig. 13.58 Later type pressure differential regulator.
Arrows show direction of fluid flow (Sec 15)**

    1   Bracket bolt
    2   Spring eye
    3   Bracket

15.26 Pressure differential regulator adjustment
A Slackening bracket bolt
B Load on eye

16 Electrical system

Battery maintenance (all models)

1 Batteries fitted as original equipment to later models, and as replacements on earlier models, are likely to be of the 'low-maintenance' or 'maintenance-free' types.

2 If the battery has a removable cover, it is wise to check the electrolyte level periodically as described in Chapter 9, Section 2. Some batteries are completely sealed, so that checking or topping up the electrolyte is not possible.

3 If it is necessary to recharge a sealed battery by external means, the charging current (in Amps) must not exceed one tenth of the battery capacity (in Amp-hours). Thus, a 50 Ah battery may be charged at not more than 5A. On no account subject a sealed battery to 'boost' charging; there is a risk of electrolyte loss and even explosion.

4 On all types of battery, keep the terminals clean and their connectors tight.

Starter motor overhaul – 105 TC

5 The Ducellier starter motor fitted to some 105 TC models has its solenoid secured by Torx screws.

6 When removing or refitting these screws, it is wise to use the correct tool (Torx 20, or equivalent) to avoid damage to the screw head.

Fusible link – description

7 When fitted, the fusible link protects all the electrical circuits except for the starter motor and alternator. It may be mounted on the front bulkhead (photo) or below the fuse box (see Chapter 9, photo 13.1B).

8 If the fusible link fails, all electrical systems will become inoperative. It is important that the short-circuit which caused the failure be found before the link is renewed.

Headlight bulb (later models) – renewal
Main headlight

9 Open the bonnet, pull the cover from the rear of the light unit and unplug the connector. Release the spring clips by turning them anti-clockwise and remove the bulb. Do not touch the bulb glass with the fingers (photos).

10 Fit the new bulb in the reverse order to removal.

Auxiliary headlight

11 Proceed as for the main headlight but note that a different type of

spring clip secures the bulb. As the bulb is of the halogen type, the glass must not be touched with the fingers.

Parking lamp bulb (later models) – renewal

12 The sidelight (parking) bulb is housed in the main headlight reflector on later models.
13 Open the bonnet, unplug the connector and twist and pull the bulbholder to withdraw it.
14 Renew the bulb and refit in the reverse order to removal.

Number plate light bulb (Strada II) – renewal

Up to 1985
15 Remove the rear light cluster lens on the side concerned.
16 Unhook the number plate light lens from its surround to expose the bulb (photo).
17 Renew the bayonet fitting bulb and refit the lenses.

1985 on
18 The twin number plate lamps are located under the lip of the

number plate recess. Extract the fixing screws and withdraw the lamp downward (photo).

Interior lamps (Strada II) – bulb renewal

19 To renew the festoon bulb in the front roof-mounted light, carefully prise out the lens to expose the bulb (photo).
20 To renew the map reading bulb, remove the lens as just described and remove the two retaining screws from the centre of the light unit. Pull the unit from its location and remove the bulbholder by twisting and pulling (photo).
21 The glovebox lamp bulb is accessible after prising out the lens. If the wires are too short, disconnect them when changing the bulb (photo).
22 The bulb in the inspection lamp can be renewed after prising off the lens/reflector assembly from the front. The bulb is of bayonet fitting type (photo).

Light unit lens retaining screw (all models) – removal

23 Many of the retaining screws used on light unit lenses have

16.7 Fusible link mounted on bulkhead

16.9A Headlamp wiring connectors

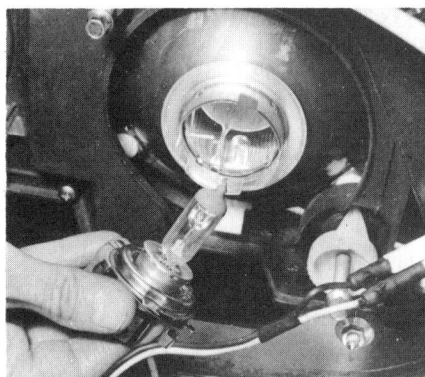
16.9B Headlamp halogen bulb

16.16 Rear number plate lamp lens removed (up to 1985)

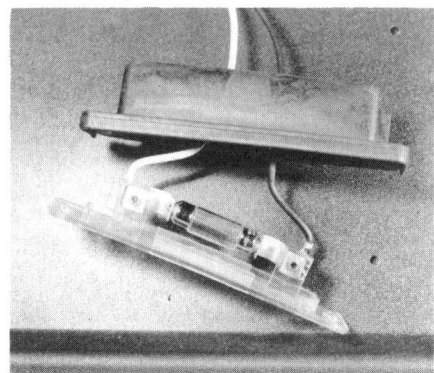
16.18 Rear number plate lamp withdrawn (1985 on)

16.19 Interior lamp festoon bulb

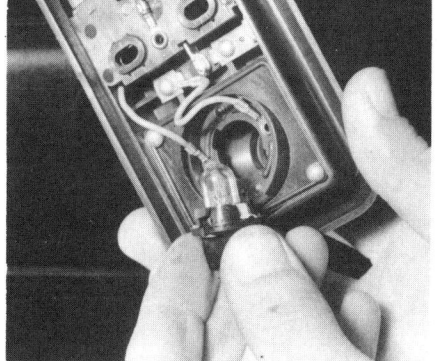
16.20 Interior map reading lamp bulb

16.21 Glovebox lamp partly removed

16.22 Inspection lamp bulb

coloured plastic heads. If such a head breaks, the screw can be removed as follows.

24 Heat the tip of a screwdriver in a gas flame, then press it into the remains of the plastic head. Allow to cool, then use the newly formed head to remove the screw. Renew the screw as soon as possible.

Fibre optic light source – bulb renewal

25 Two special bulbs provide illumination for the fibre optic bundles which illuminate the heater controls and some of the switches (photo).
26 If bulb renewal is necessary, first remove the instrument panel. Follow the bundles to their source behind the heater control panel. Separate the bundle carrier from the bulbholder and extract the bulb.
27 Refit in the reverse order to removal. Take care not to damage the fibre optic bundles, as they cannot be repaired.

Ignition switch (Strada II) – renewal

28 The ignition/starter switch can be renewed independently of the steering column lock. Proceed as follows.
29 Disconnect the battery earth lead.
30 Remove the steering column shrouds.
31 Insert the ignition key and turn it to the STOP position.
32 Unplug the two connectors from the ignition switch.
33 Turn the key to position MAR. Remove the switch, releasing its retaining lugs with a screwdriver.
34 Align the reference marks on the cam and baseplate of the new switch (Fig. 13.59). Press the switch into position until the lugs are home.
35 Turn the key to STOP and refit the electrical connectors.
36 Reconnect the battery and check the operation of the switch, then refit the column shroud.

Instrument panel switches (later models) – removal and refitting

37 Pull off the trim from around the switches.
38 Gain access to the rear of the switches, either by removing the instrument panel or by prising out the blanking plate (when fitted) to the right of the switch cluster.
39 Push out the switch from behind. Unplug the electrical connectors and the fibre optic bundle and remove the switch (photo).
40 Refit in the reverse order to removal.

Instrument panel (later models) – removal and refitting

41 Disconnect the battery earth lead.
42 Remove the instrument panel securing screws (five on TC models, two on other models).
43 On all except TC models, remove the steering wheel.
44 Carefully withdraw the instrument panel. Unplug the electrical connectors, making notes if necessary to avoid confusion on reassembly; on models so equipped, disconnect the speedometer cable.
45 Refit in the reverse order to removal.

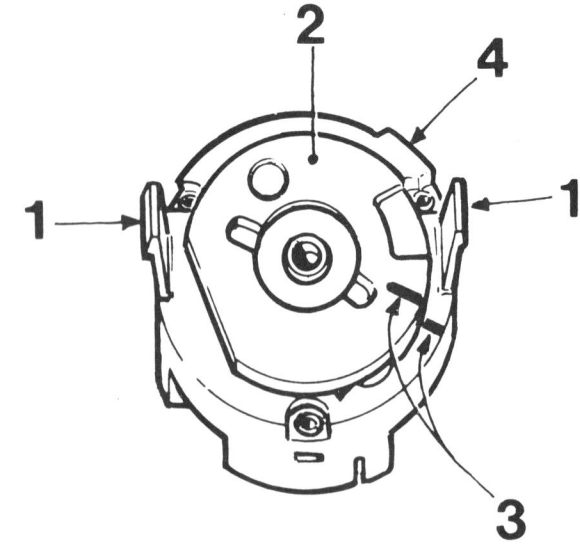

Fig. 13.59 Ignition switch unit (Sec 16)

1	Lugs	3	Reference marks
2	Cam	4	Locating tab

Instrument panel (later models) – dismantling and reassembly

46 On TC models, free the instrument panel from its surround (five screws) and release the glass and frame by depressing the retaining tabs.
47 On all models, the instruments can now be removed after undoing the appropriate retaining screws or nuts. Be very careful not to damage the printed circuit.
48 Illumination and warning light bulbs are removed from the rear of the panel by turning the bulbholder 90° and pulling it out. Some types of bulb are wedge based and can be pulled out of the holder for renewal; other types cannot be separated from their holder (photo).
49 Reassemble in the reverse order to dismantling.

Economy meter (ES models) – description and testing

50 The economy meter integrates information on vehicle speed, engine speed and manifold vacuum to display to the driver the approximate instantaneous fuel consumption. An LED in the instrument face illuminates when changing up a gear would improve fuel economy.
51 If a fault develops in the economy meter, this may be due to a fault in the ignition ECU, the overrun cut-off ECU or in the meter or its control unit. Note that the economy meter will not work if the speedometer is not working, and the LED will not function until the engine has warmed up.

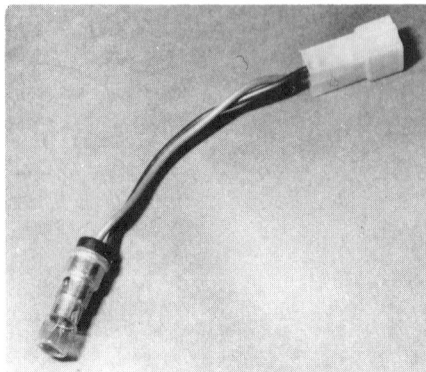

16.25 Fibre optic bulb, holder and wiring

16.39 Removing an instrument panel switch

16.48 Instrument panel bulb and holder removed

52 With the instrument panel removed and the economy meter disconnected, check for battery voltage at the light blue/white cable of the multi-plug (ignition on). If voltage is not present, the fault is in the meter power supply.

53 If an accurate voltmeter is available, measure the voltage between the light blue cable at the multi-plug and earth (ignition on, engine stopped). On models up to 1985 a reading of 0.7 to 0.9 volts is in order, on later models the reading should be 0.6 to 0.8 volts; any other reading suggests a fault in the vacuum transducer of the ignition ECU or its associated wiring.

54 Check that the vacuum pipe from the inlet manifold to the ECU is secure and in good condition.

55 If the above checks do not explain a malfunction, seek expert advice.

Check system – description

56 Fitted to some models from 1981, the check system warns the driver of low oil or coolant levels, brake pad wear, low brake fluid level, and failure of certain bulbs.

57 The 'brain' of the check system is the power module behind the instrument panel; this module receives information from various sensors and from the lighting circuits. Warnings are displayed on the monitor panel.

58 The brake fluid and coolant level sensors are magnet-operated reed switches; when the fluid level is correct, the contacts are closed. The brake pad wear sensor is a loop of wire embedded in the lining: when the loop is earthed, the pad wear warning is triggered during braking. If the loop is broken, the warning is shown continuously.

59 The engine oil level sensor is incorporated in the dipstick. This makes the dipstick more fragile than usual and it should be treated carefully. The sensor contains a bimetallic strip and a heating element: when a current is passed through the heating element, the heat generated will be dissipated in the oil if the oil level is correct. If the oil level is low, the heat will cause the bimetallic strip to bend and close the contact which activates the low level warning. Oil level is not monitored once the engine is running.

60 Bulb failure monitoring is based on the principle that pairs of bulbs are unlikely to fail simultaneously. (If they do, no warning will be displayed.) False warnings may be given if bulbs of different wattage are fitted. For the same reason, expert advice should be sought if it is proposed to connect a trailer wiring socket.

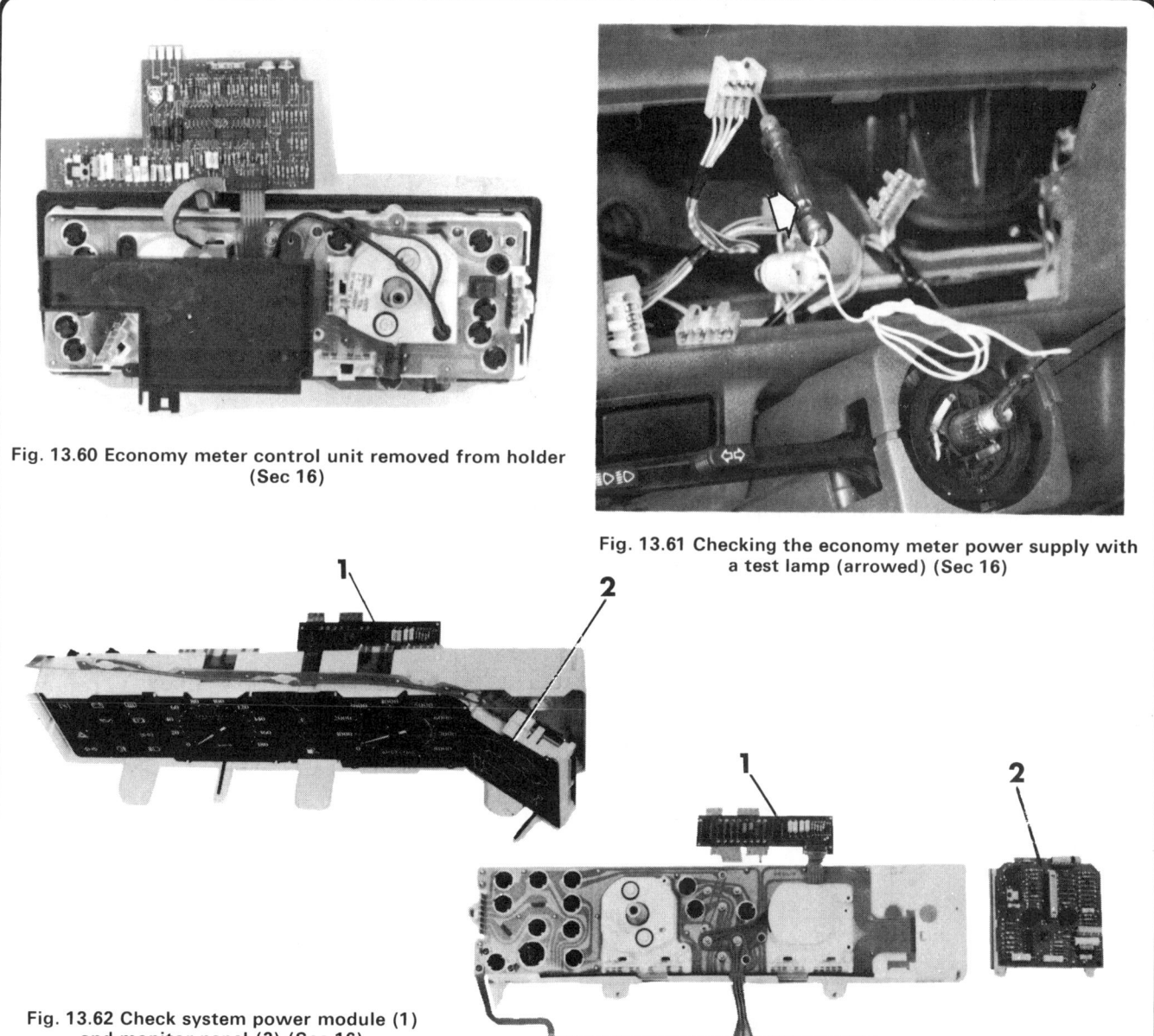

Fig. 13.60 Economy meter control unit removed from holder (Sec 16)

Fig. 13.61 Checking the economy meter power supply with a test lamp (arrowed) (Sec 16)

Fig. 13.62 Check system power module (1) and monitor panel (2) (Sec 16)

Check system sensors – testing

61 Before suspecting a sensor fault, make sure that the appropriate wiring is intact and that the connectors are not loose or corroded.

62 To check the coolant level sensor, drain the cooling system and remove the sensor from the radiator. Check the contacts, with the float in 'full' and 'empty' positions, using an ohmmeter. The contacts should be closed when the level is correct and open when it is low.

63 The brake fluid level sensor can be tested in the same way after removing the reservoir cap.

64 If the oil level sensor is suspected of giving false alarms, unplug the dipstick connector and substitute a 12 ohm resistor (Fig. 13.64). Switch off the ignition, then switch on again: if a 'low level' warning is given with the resistor in place, the power module is defective. If no warning is given with the resistor, and false warnings were given with the sensor connected, the sensor is defective.

65 Do not short-circuit the oil level sensor cables together, as damage may result.

66 Further testing of the check system should be left to a competent auto electrician.

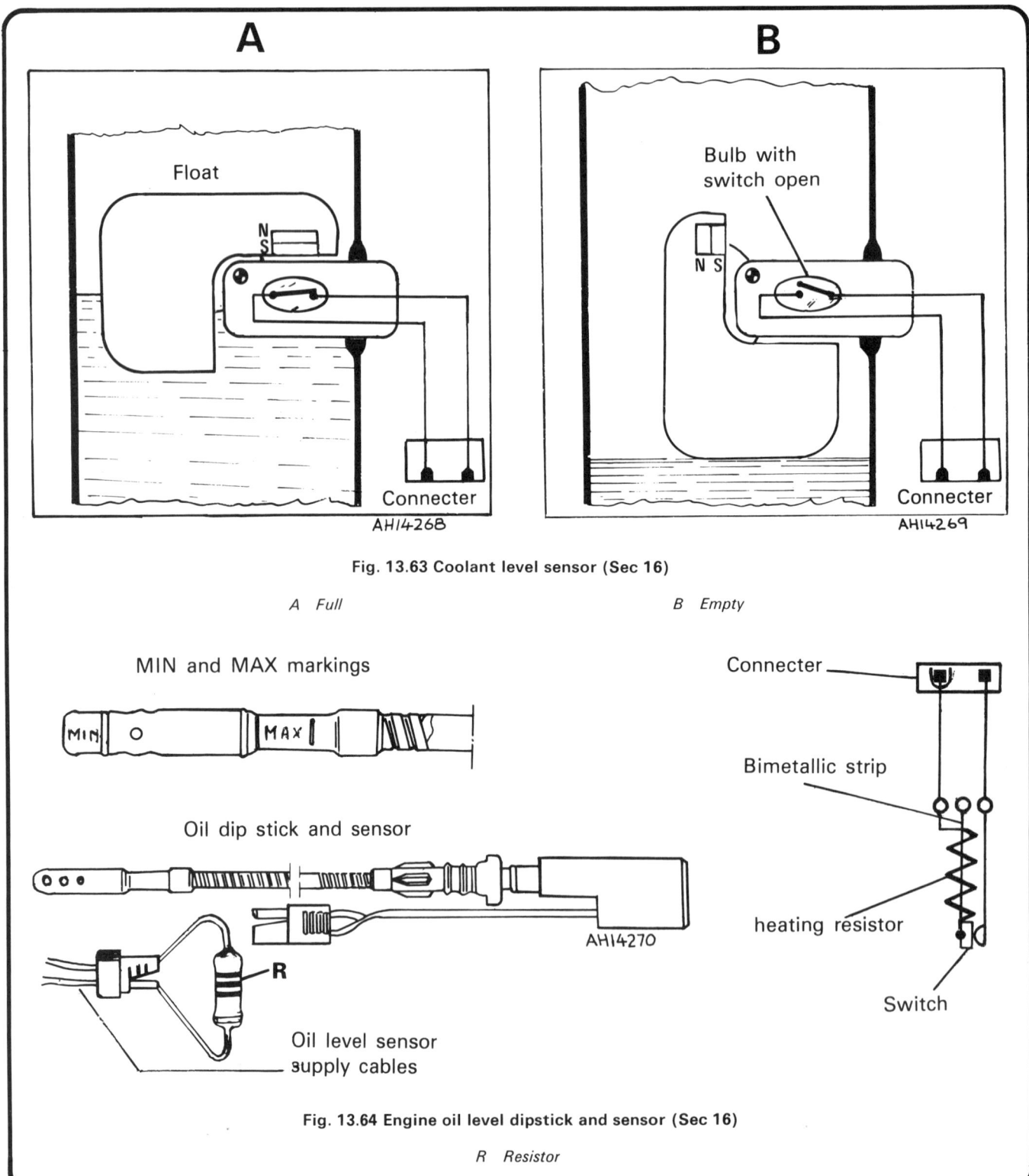

Fig. 13.63 Coolant level sensor (Sec 16)

A Full   B Empty

Fig. 13.64 Engine oil level dipstick and sensor (Sec 16)

R Resistor

Oil temperature sender – removal and refitting

67 When fitted, the oil temperature sender is screwed into the side of the sump (photo).

68 Unplug the electrical connector from the sensor. Place a drain pan beneath the sump, then unscrew and remove the sensor. Be prepared for oil spillage.

69 When refitting the sender, smear a little sealant on the threads. Tighten the sender to the specified torque, refit the electrical connector and top up the engine oil.

Oil pressure gauge and warning light senders – TC models

70 On TC models the oil pressure senders are screwed into the oil filter bracket. The gauge sender is the larger of the two (photo).

Fuses and relays (Strada II) – general

71 The main fuse box is located below the glovebox. The lid is removed by turning the plastic knob at its base and freeing it from its clips at the top.

72 The fuses are of the blade type; a symbol above each fuse indicates its main function. Spare fuses are carried at the bottom right-hand corner. The numbers on the fuses denote their continuous current rating (photo).

73 The fuse box also carries two or three relays. From top to bottom they are for the horn, the heated rear window and the radiator cooling fan. On some models a bridge is fitted instead of the horn relay.

74 On earlier models, the direction indicator flasher unit and the headlight relay are located next to the fuse box. On later models, the flasher and power window relays are located under the right-hand side of the facia panel (photo). Alternatively, an additional fuse and relay board may be found under the facia panel. See Fig. 13.66.

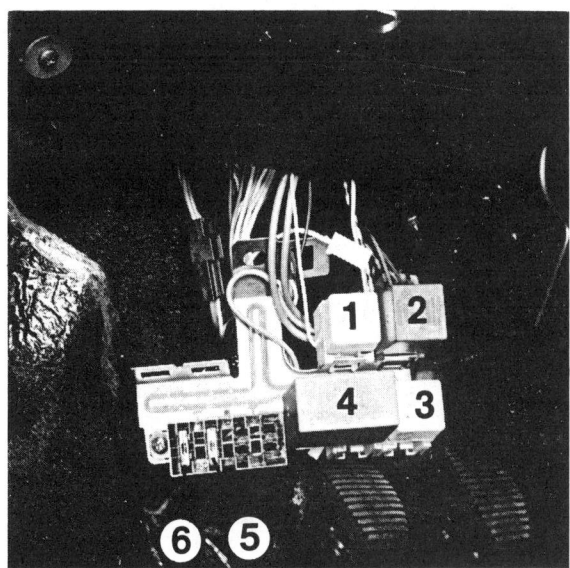

Fig. 13.66 Additional fuse and relay board (Sec 16)

1 Headlamps main beam relay
2 Indicators and hazard warning flasher
3 Power windows relay
4 Central locking system relay
5 Central locking system fuse
6 Power windows fuse

Radio (Strada II) – removal and refitting

75 On later models the radio supplied as original equipment is quickly detachable. Press the tab below the front face of the radio and lift the radio out (photo).

76 When refitting the radio, slide it gently into its housing, then press it home until the locating tab clicks into place.

Digital clock – removal and refitting

77 Remove the instrument panel complete with central air vents and clock.

78 Remove the instrument cluster (five screws) and the control vent/clock assembly (four screws).

79 Remove the cover from the rear of the clock. On the car examined for this book, the cover was glued in place and had to be cut free.

80 Depress the spring clips at the sides of the clock and remove it from the front of the panel. The clips are not easily released; if the clock is to be renewed, it will be easier to drill out the rivets which secure the clips to the back of the clock (photos).

81 Refit the clock in the reverse order of removal, making sure it is the right way up before engaging the spring clips.

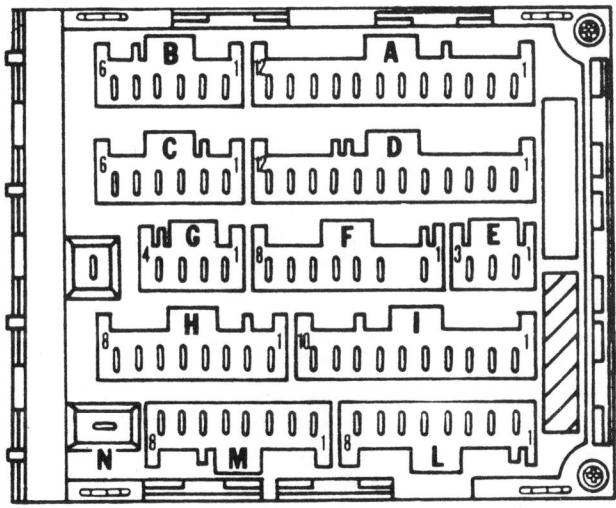

Fig. 13.65 Fuse box connectors. Letters correspond with those used in wiring diagrams (Sec 16)

16.67 Engine oil temperature sender

16.70 Oil pressure sender

16.72 Main fuse/relay block

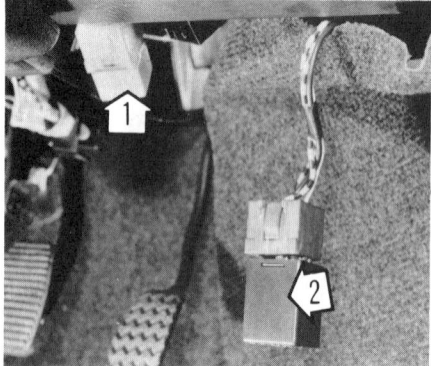

16.74 Relays under facia panel
1 Power-operated windows relay
2 Flasher relay

16.75 Pressing radio retaining tab

16.80A Removing clock from vent grille

16.80B Clock spring clip rivets (arrowed)

16.82 Unscrewing wiper motor mounting bolt

16.88 Supplementary fuses under left-hand side of facia panel

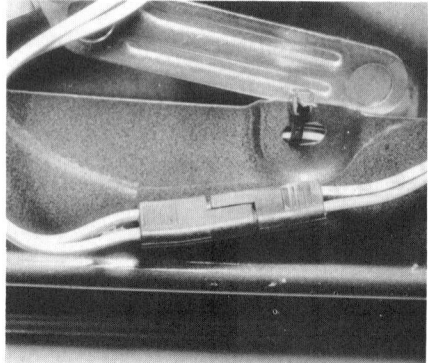

16.90A Power-operated window wiring plug

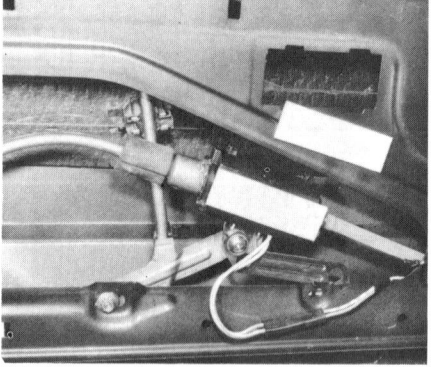

16.90B Power-operated window motor and drive cable

Windscreen wiper motor (Strada II) – removal and refitting

82 The procedure is similar to that described in Chapter 9, Section 21, but the motor mountings are slightly different (photo).

Rear screen wiper motor (later models) – removal and refitting

83 Refer to Chapter 9, Section 22, but note that on some models a cover must be removed from the inside of the tailgate to expose the motor. This cover is retained by ten plastic plugs, some of which will almost certainly be broken when prising them free.

Fault diagnosis (all models) – warning

84 Semiconductor devices are found in increasing numbers in modern vehicles, including the Strada. Such devices include the alternator voltage regulator, electronic ignition control unit and some instrumentation.

85 Semiconductors are electrically fragile: they are easily destroyed by excessive, or wrong polarity, voltage or current. For this reason it is most unwise to use a test lamp for electrical fault tracing, except when stated in the text. Checking for the presence of voltage by 'flashing' wires to earth is also not recommended. Ideally a multi-meter of sensitivity not less than 10 000 Ω/V should be used. If using an ohmmeter, the voltage at the probes must not exceed 2.5, nor the current 2mA.

Power-operated windows

86 Electrically-operated front door windows are fitted to some models.

87 The facia-mounted switches operate the left-hand and right-hand windows once the ignition key has been turned to the MAR position.

88 If the windows fail to operate, first check the fuse and relay. The 30 A fuse is located under the left-hand side of the facia, whilst the relay is positioned adjacent to the flasher relay under the right-hand side of the facia panel (photo). Alternatively, the fuse and relay may be mounted

on an additional board under the tacia panel (see Fig. 13.66).

89 Access to the electric motor is obtained after removing the door trim panel (see Section 19).

90 Disconnect the wiring plug, then remove the fixing screws and bolts which secure the motor and cable drive (photos).

91 Release the cable drive from the bottom of the glass. To do this, pinch the anchor tabs of the connecting plastic pin which passes through the hole in the glass, and then pull the lifter block from the glass.

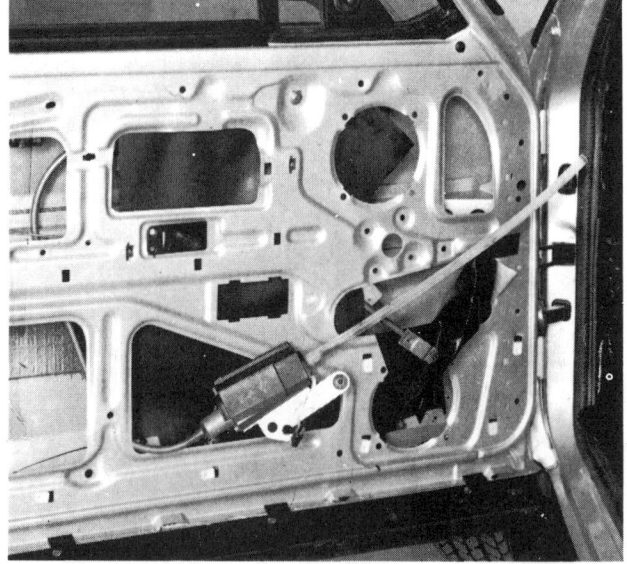

Fig. 13.67 Withdrawing window lift motor/cable assembly (Sec 16)

92 Withdraw the motor/cable drive assembly from the lower centre aperture in the door panel.

93 Refitting is a reversal of removal.

Central door locking system

94 This is fitted to some top of the range models. The system operates irrespective of the ignition key position by either turning the key in an exterior door lock or by depressing or lifting an interior door sill button.

95 The door locks are actuated by a solenoid switch located within each door cavity (photo).

96 The circuit is protected by a 20 A fuse, located adjacent to the one for the power-operated windows – see paragraph 88.

97 A door locking motor may be removed after taking off the door trim panel (see Section 19). Have the door glass fully raised.

98 Disconnect the wiring plug and the lock link rod (photo).

99 Unbolt the solenoid switch from the door frame and withdraw it. It may be necessary to release the window lift motor and turn it slightly to provide sufficient space for removal of the door locking motor.

100 Refitting is a reversal of removal.

Tailgate contact block

101 On later models, contact blocks are used to transmit power to the heated tailgate window and to the wiper motor.

102 The fixed block on the body or the spring-loaded plunger block on the tailgate may be removed by prising their ends with a screwdriver (photos).

Headlight unit (later models) – removal and refitting

103 A headlight unit can be removed by firm pressure from behind, releasing the ball ends of the mounting/adjusting screws from their sockets. Be careful not to eject the unit onto the floor (photo).

16.95 Central door locking system solenoid switch

16.98 Door lock link rod

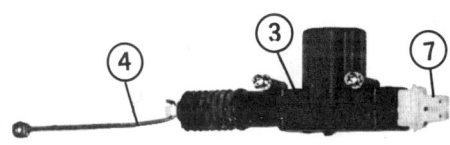

Fig. 13.68 Centre door lock solenoid switch (Sec 16)

3 Solenoid body
4 Lock control rod
7 Wiring connector plug

16.102A Tailgate fixed contact block

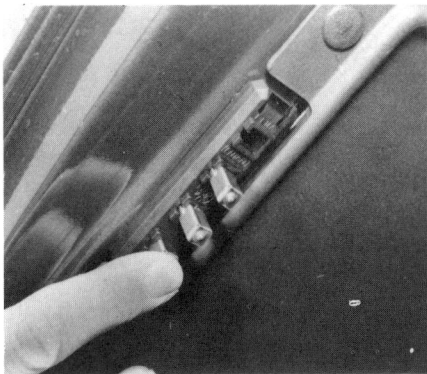

16.102B Tailgate spring-loaded plunger block

16.103 Releasing a headlamp from its ball-studs (1985 on)

104 A more controlled method of removing a headlamp is described in the following paragraphs. Disconnect the wiring plug before starting work.

Up to 1985

105 Refer to Section 19 and remove the radiator grille, then release the retainers one by one squeezing with pliers (photos).
106 In either case, refit the headlight by offering it to its mountings and pressing it home.

1985 on

107 Remove the radiator grille complete with the four headlamps as described in Section 19 of this Supplement.
108 Extract the screws which hold the headlamp frames to the grille. Pull the headlamp frame from its positioning lug and its spring clip (photos).
109 Giving the lamp unit a sharp jerk release it from its ball-stud sockets.
110 The outer headlamps incorporate the parking lamp bulbs (photo).
111 Refit the headlamp and frame and then refit the radiator grille.

Front foglight (later models) – removal and refitting

112 It is necessary to remove the light unit for bulb renewal. Reach up behind the light and remove the two nuts which secure the rear cover. Remove the cover, pull the light unit out forwards and unplug the connectors after freeing the bulb cover.
113 Release the bulb by undoing the spring clip. Do not touch the bulb glass with the fingers (photos).
114 Fit the new bulb and clip it into place. Refit the light unit in the reverse order of removal. The electrical connectors are inhibited, so they cannot be fitted the wrong way round.
115 If beam adjustment is necessary, this is done using the screw which protrudes from the base of the light unit.

Headlamp beam load adjustment device (Strada II)

116 At the back of each main headlamp is a knurled knob, accessible from under the bonnet, for altering headlamp alignment when heavy loads are carried in the rear of the vehicle (photo).
117 For normal use the adjuster lug should be at the top; when laden, both adjusters should be turned 90° to lower the beam.

16.105A Releasing a headlamp retainer (up to 1985)

16.105B Headlamp retainer released (up to 1985)

16.108A Headlamp frame-to-grille screws

16.108B Headlamp frame-to-grille screw and spring clip

16.110 Parking lamp bulb in headlamp

16.113A Front foglamp bulb spring clip

16.113B Front foglamp bulb withdrawn

16.116 Headlamp beam load adjuster
A   Normal load   B   Heavy load

Headlamp dim-dip system

118 In order to comply with current legislation, 1986 and later models are equipped with a headlamp dim-dip system.
119 This system provides a headlamp brightness between that of sidelamps and normal dipped beam headlamps. The system functions when the light switch is in the ON position, and the ignition is switched on, and it is designed to prevent the vehicle from being driven with sidelamps only.

Horns

120 Some models are equipped with twin horns which are located behind the front grille just above the foglamps (if fitted) or blanking plates in the front bumper (photo).

16.120 Horn location behind radiator grille

Wiring diagrams commence overleaf

Key to wiring diagrams 13.69 and 13.70 – Super 85 models

Location of connectors
1 Engine bay near battery
2 Under dashboard near key switch
3 Under dashboard near key switch
4 Under dashboard at centre switch
5 Under dashboard RH side near glovebox light switch
6 Under dashboard LH side
7 Under dashboard near digital clock
8 Under dashboard at centre
9 Under dashboard at centre near heater controls
10 Under dashboard near heater controls
11 Under dashboard near key switch
12 Engine bay near LH sidelight
13 Engine bay near LH sidelight
14 Under dashboard near fuse and relay box
15 Boot near RH lamp
16 Engine bay near RH sidelight
17 Engine bay near RH sidelight
18 Boot near LH lamp
19 Engine bay below wiper motor
20 Under steering column cover near key switch
21 Engine bay below washer reservoir
22 Engine bay near radiator
23 Engine bay near radiator
24 Engine bay near radiator
25 Under dashboard at centre near heater
26 Under dashboard near key switch
27 Engine bay near washer reservoir
28 In tailgate LH side
29 Under dashboard at centre near cigar lighter
30 Under dashboard LH side near fuse and relay box
31 Boot under LH quarter panel near boot light
32 Under dashboard near key switch
33 Engine bay near battery
34 Boot near LH lamp
35 Engine bay near washer reservoir
36 Engine bay near radiator
37 In front RH door
38 Fuse and relay box
39 Under dashboard near instrument panel
40 In front RH door
41 Boot under LH quarter panel near boot light
42 Under dashboard at centre near power window switches
43 Engine bay near battery
44 Engine bay below battery
45 Engine bay RH side near alternator
46 Under dashboard near key switch
47 Under dashboard near instrument panel
48 Instrument panel
49 Under dashboard near key switch

Location of units
50 Engine coolant temperature gauge transmitter fitted to cylinder head
51 Engine oil low pressure warning light switch fitted to crankcase
52 Engine coolant gauge sensor fitted to overflow tank
53 Engine oil gauge sensor fitted to crankcase
54 Boot light near rear screen washer reservoir
55 Instruments light rheostat
56 Duplex flasher for direction indicators and hazard warning lights under dashboard near key switch
57 Radiator fan thermal switch fitted to radiator
58 Heater fan speed control resistor in engine bay near heater duct
59 Air inlet and fan control lever (1st speed)
60 Two-position switch (2nd/3rd speeds)
61 Ventilation fan motor under dashboard
62 Parking and marker light switch optic fibre cable light
63 Heater symbols optic fibre cable light
64 Switch panel optic fibre cable light
65 Windscreen washer pump in engine bay passenger's side
66 Wiper delay switch in engine bay on driver's side near shunt box
67 Rear screen washer pump on driver's side in boot
68 Courtesy light switch on front door pillar
69 Front interior light with switch
70 Glovebox light
71 Glovebox light switch
72 Key switch light
73 LH brake pad wear sensor
74 RH brake pad wear sensor
75 Brake fluid low level warning light switch
76 Stoplight switch near brake pedal
77 Handbrake switch
78 Digital clock
79 Gearlever pattern light
80 Starting and reversing inhibitor switch
81 Power window motors
82 RH power window switch
83 LH power window switch
84 Reversing light switch on gearbox bellhousing

Ground points
A Engine bay under air intake casing near RH mounting
B Boot on low LH side
C Windscreen wiper motor mounting
D Under windscreen washer reservoir
E Engine bay under LH headlight
F Engine bay under RH headlight

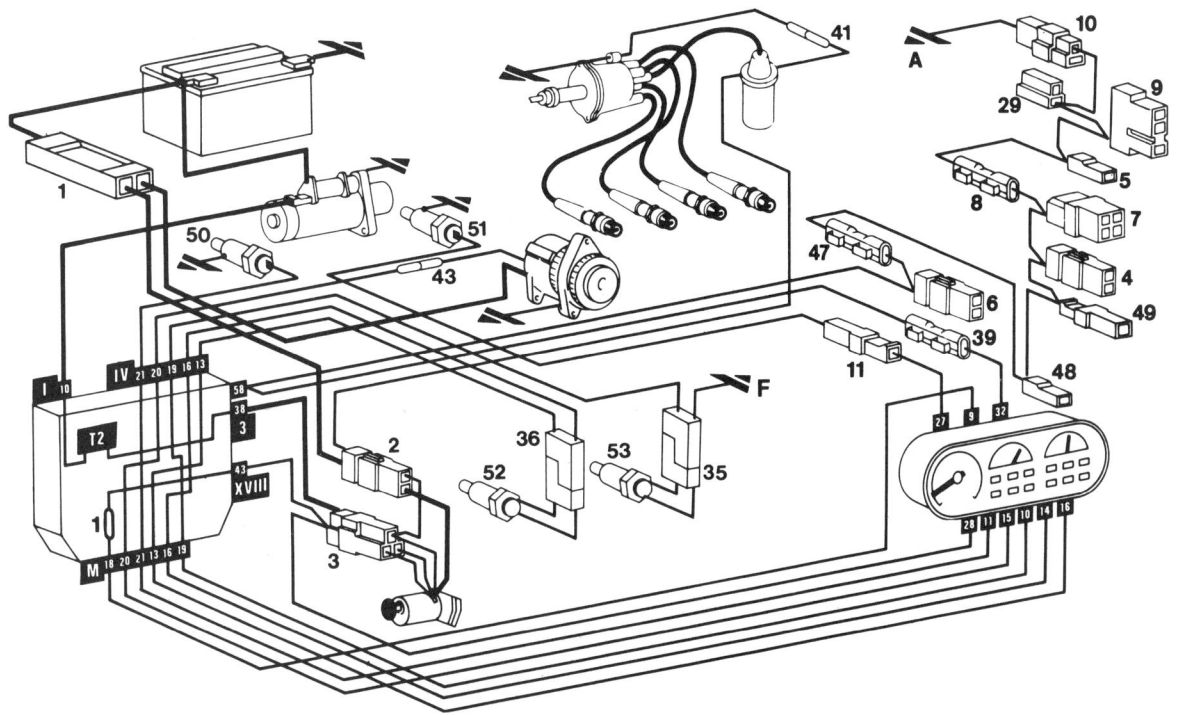

Fig. 13.69A Wiring diagram – ignition, charging, starting, oil pressure, oil level, coolant temperature and level (early Super 85 models)

For key see page 268

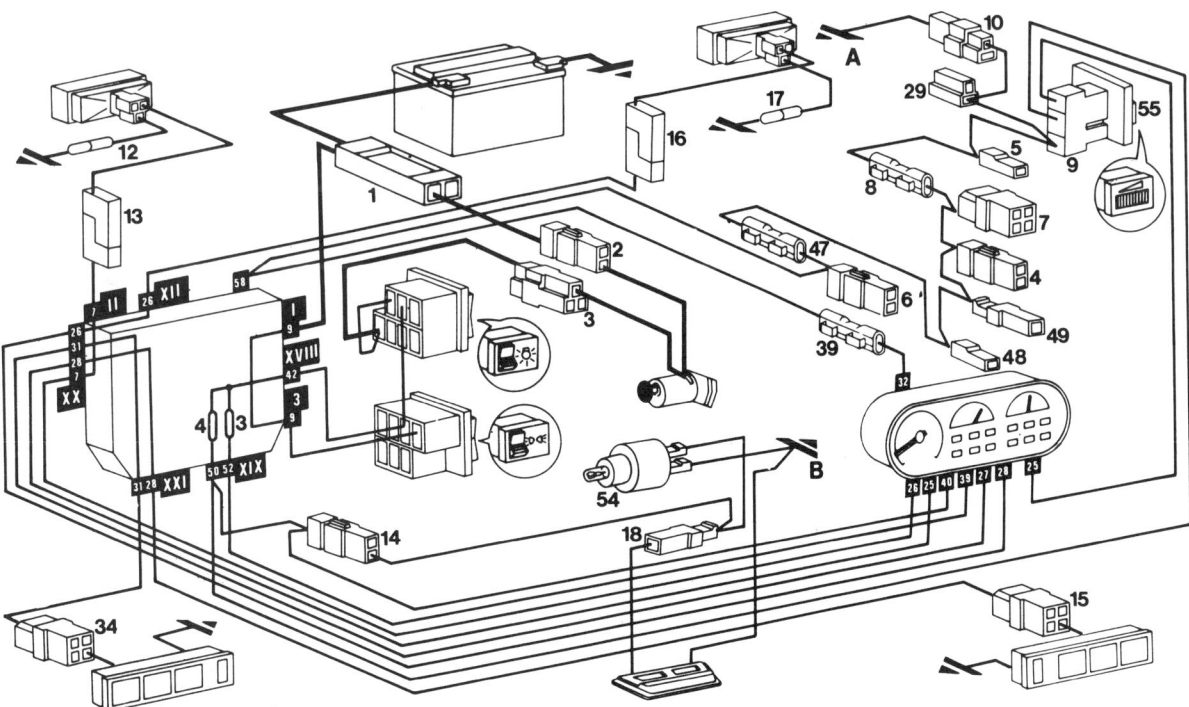

Fig. 13.69B Wiring diagram – parking lamps, side marker lamps, rear number plate lamps. instrument panel, tailgate (early Super 85 models)

For key see page 268

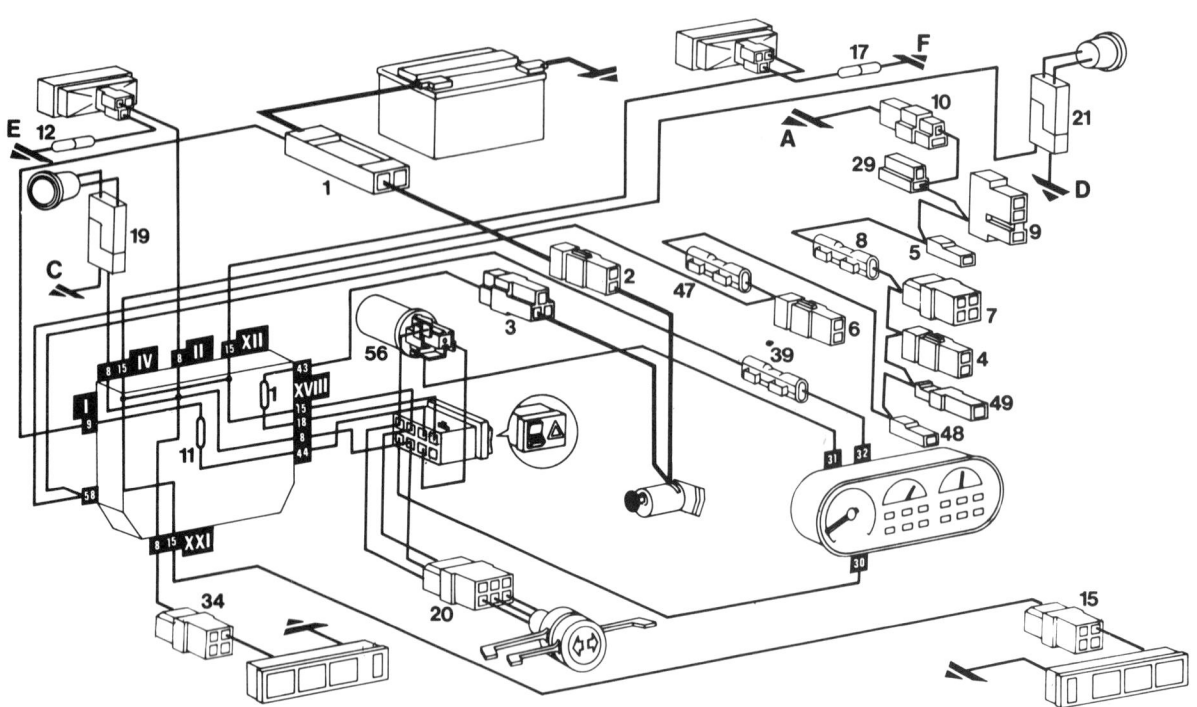

Fig. 13.69C Wiring diagram – direction indicator and hazard warning lights (early Super 85 models)

For key see page 268

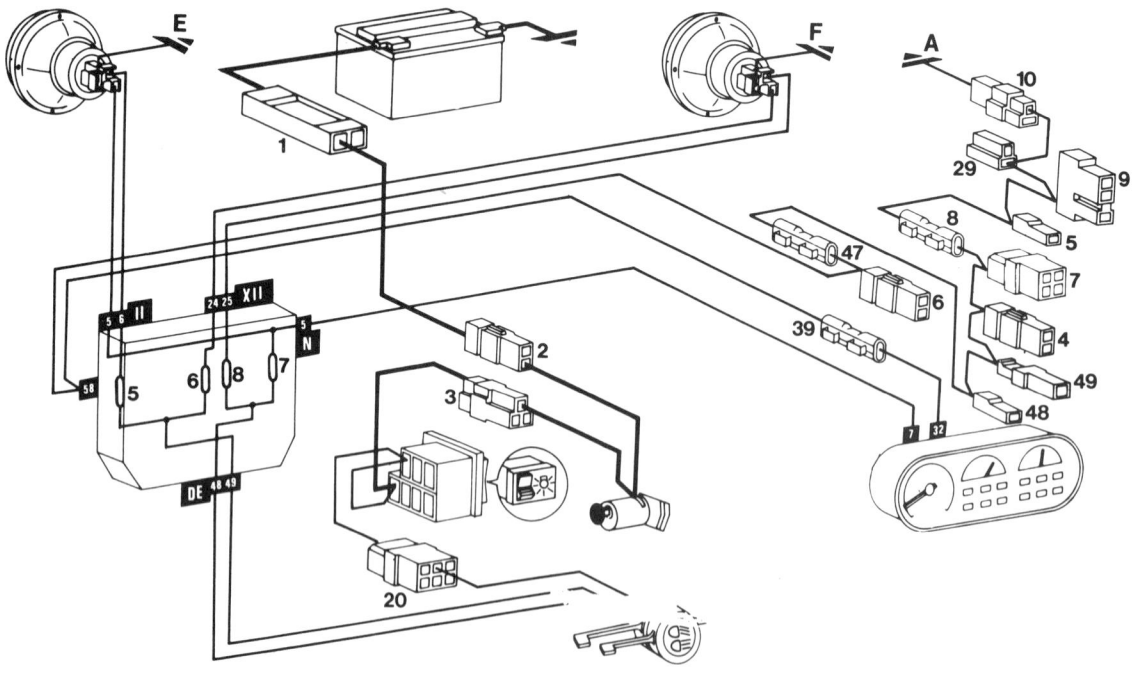

Fig. 13.69D Wiring diagram – headlamp main and dipped beam (early Super 85 models)

For key see page 268

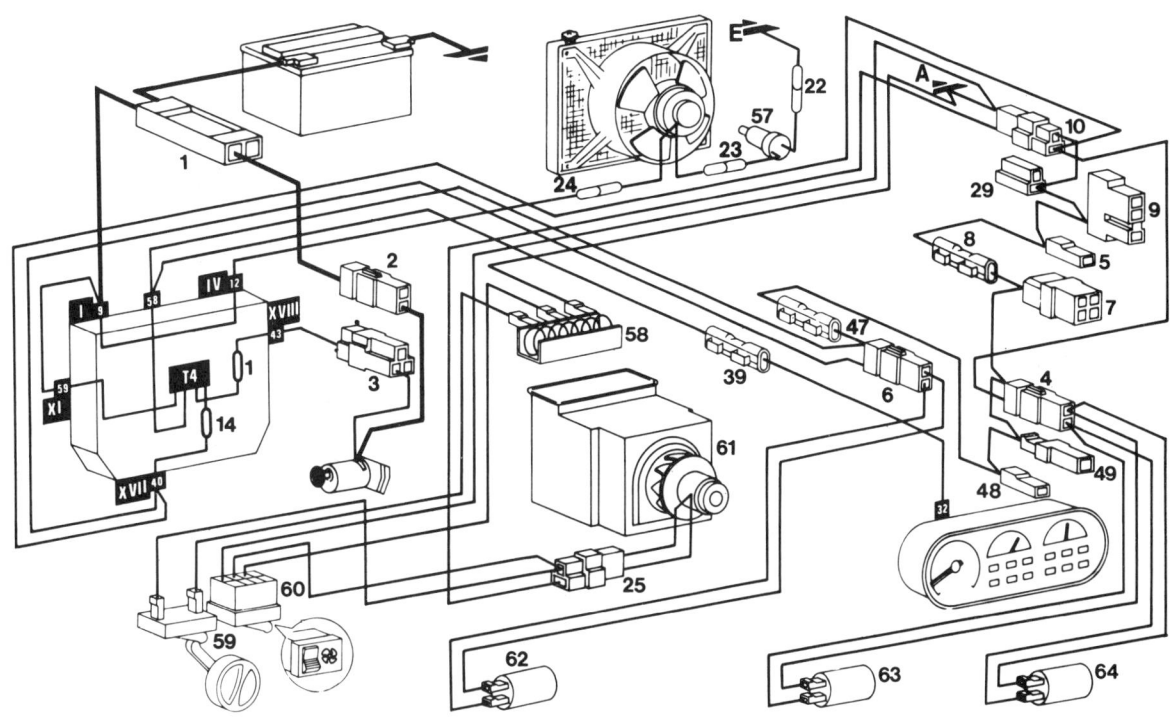

Fig. 13.69E Wiring diagram – radiator fan, heater, heater illumination, switch and switch panel illumination (early Super 85 models)

For key see page 268

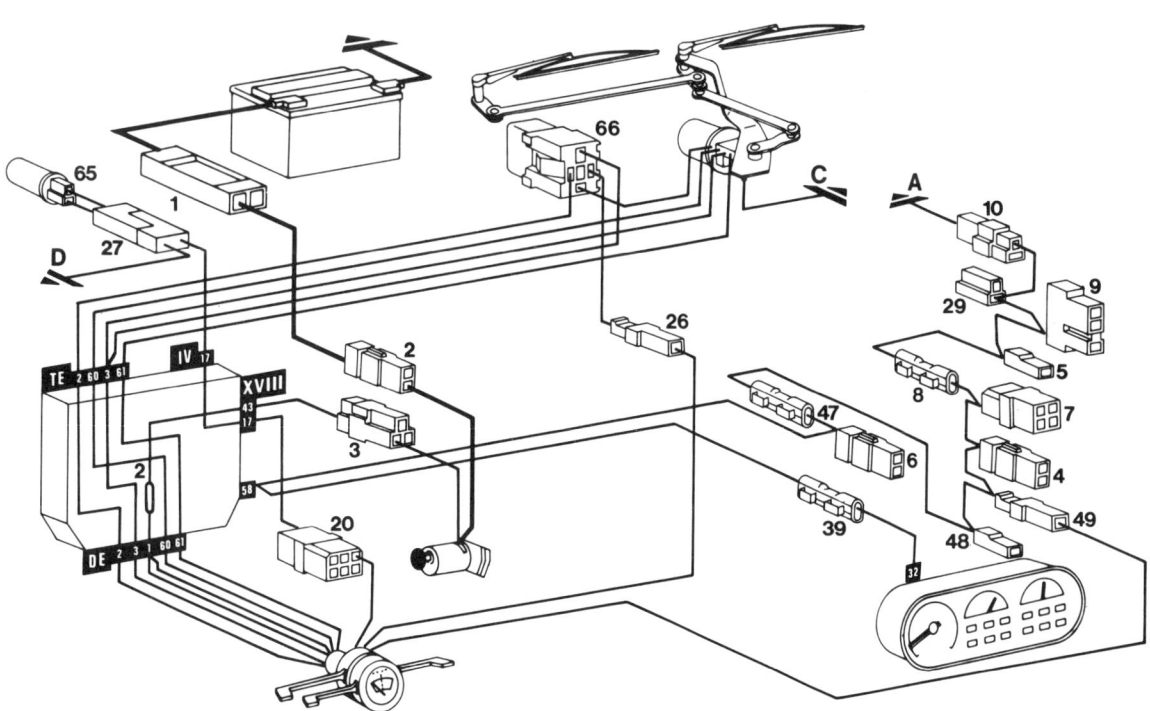

Fig. 13.69F Wiring diagram – windscreen wash/wipe (early Super 85 models)

For key see page 268

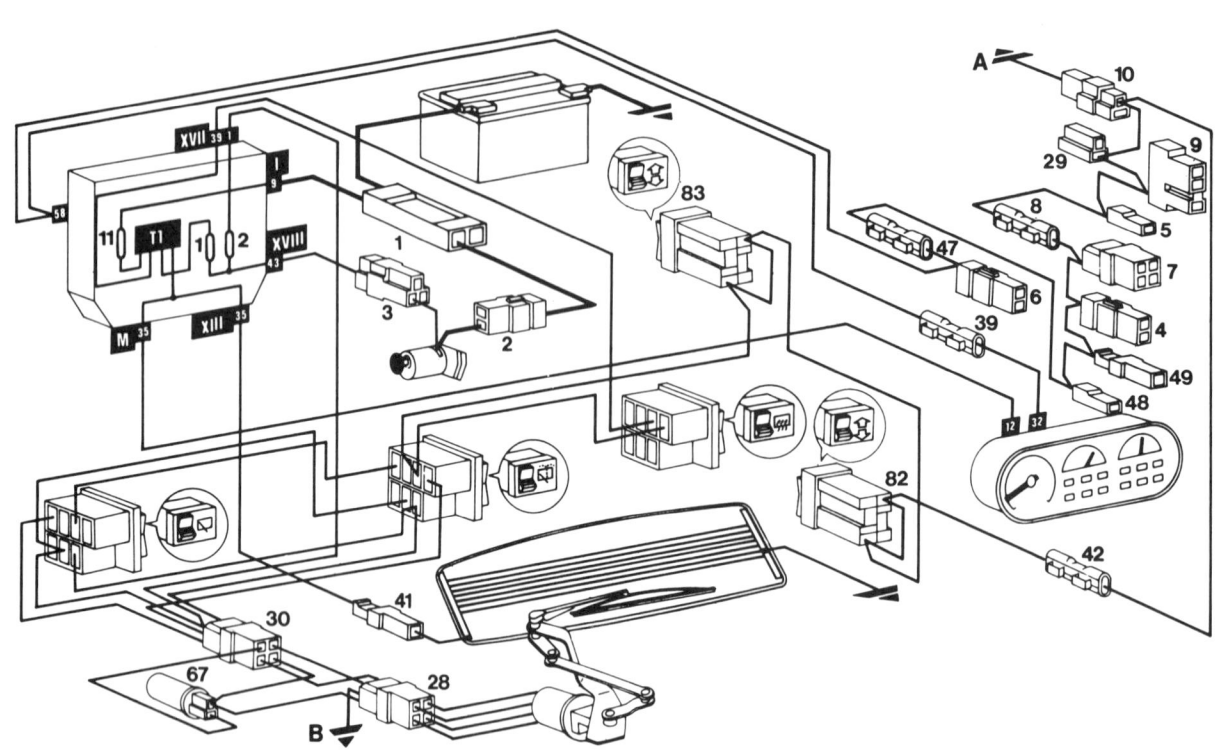

Fig. 13.69G Wiring diagram – heated tailgate screen, rear wash/wipe (early Super 85 models)

For key see page 268

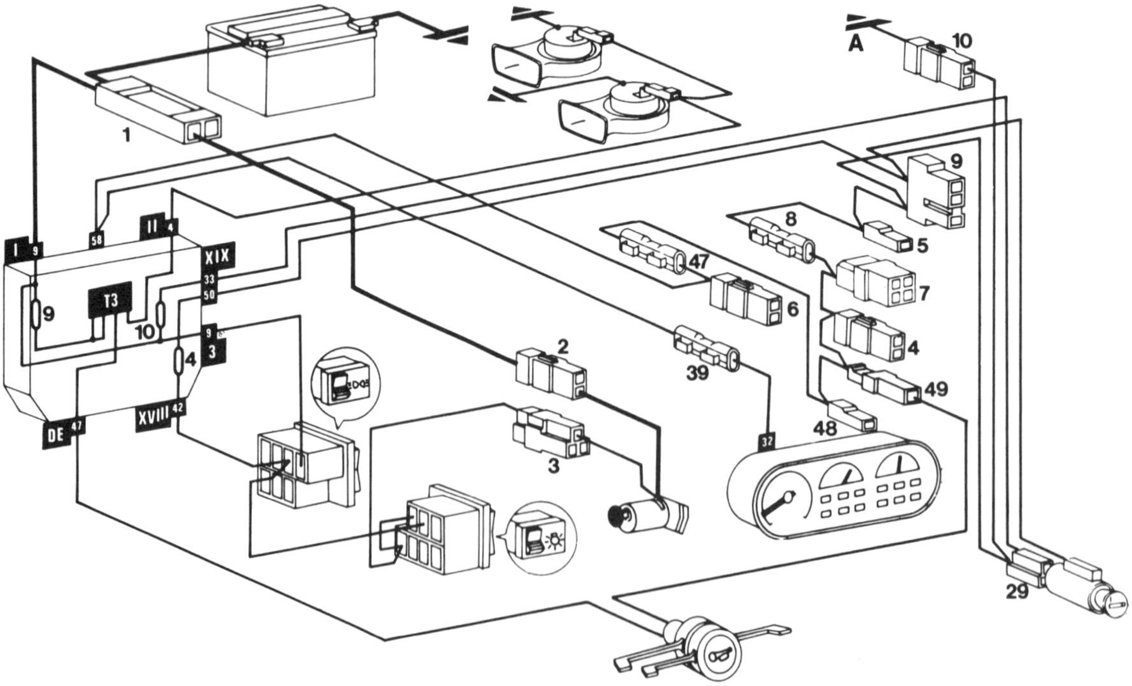

Fig. 13.69H Wiring diagram – horn and cigar lighter (early Super 85 models)

For key see page 268

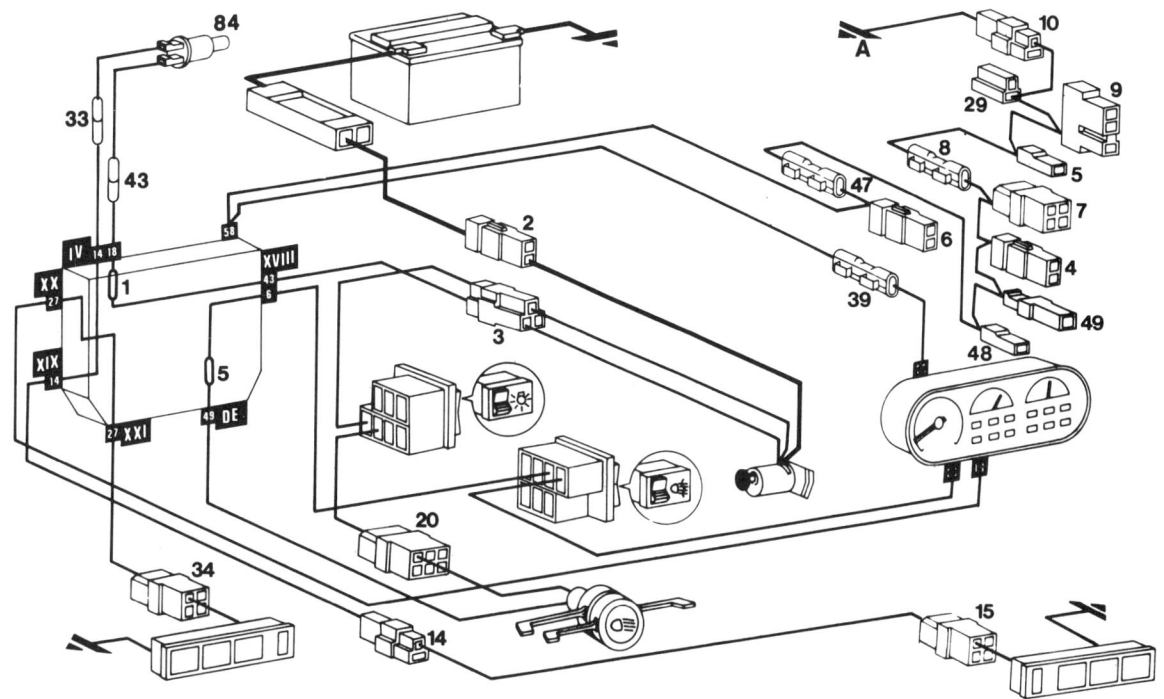

Fig. 13.69J Wiring diagram – fuel gauge/reserve, interior lamps (early Super 85 models)

For key see page 268

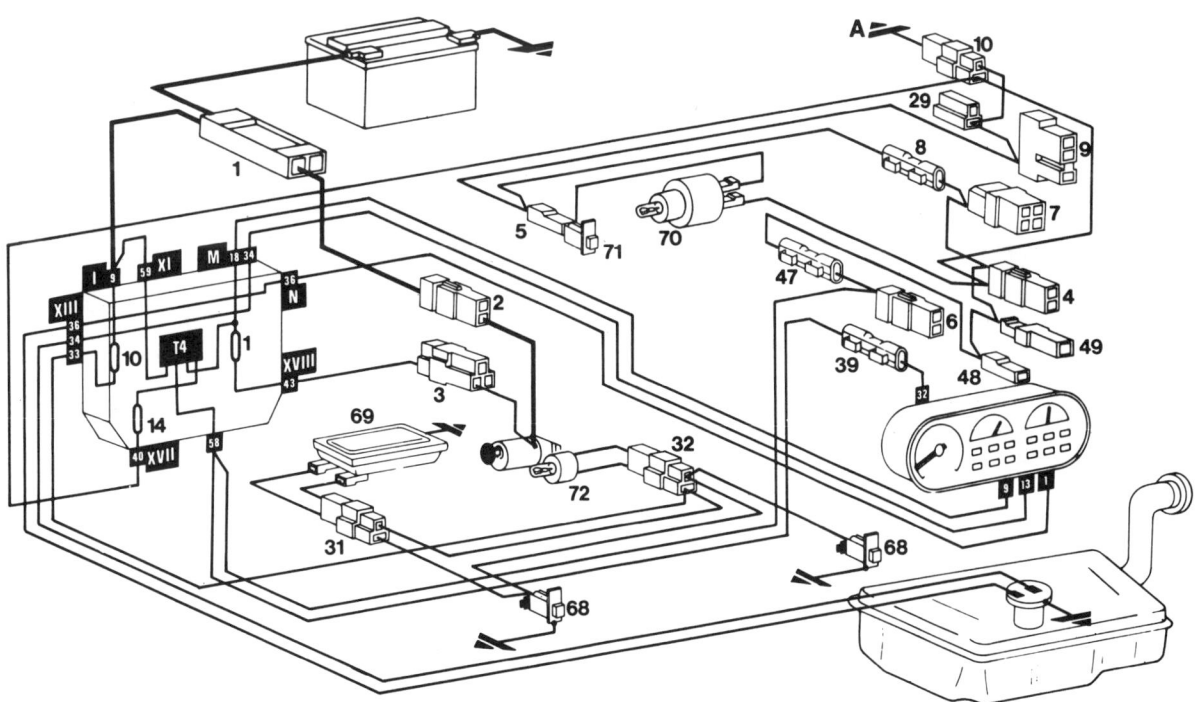

Fig. 13.69K Wiring diagram – reversing and rear foglamps
(early Super 85 models)

For key see page 268

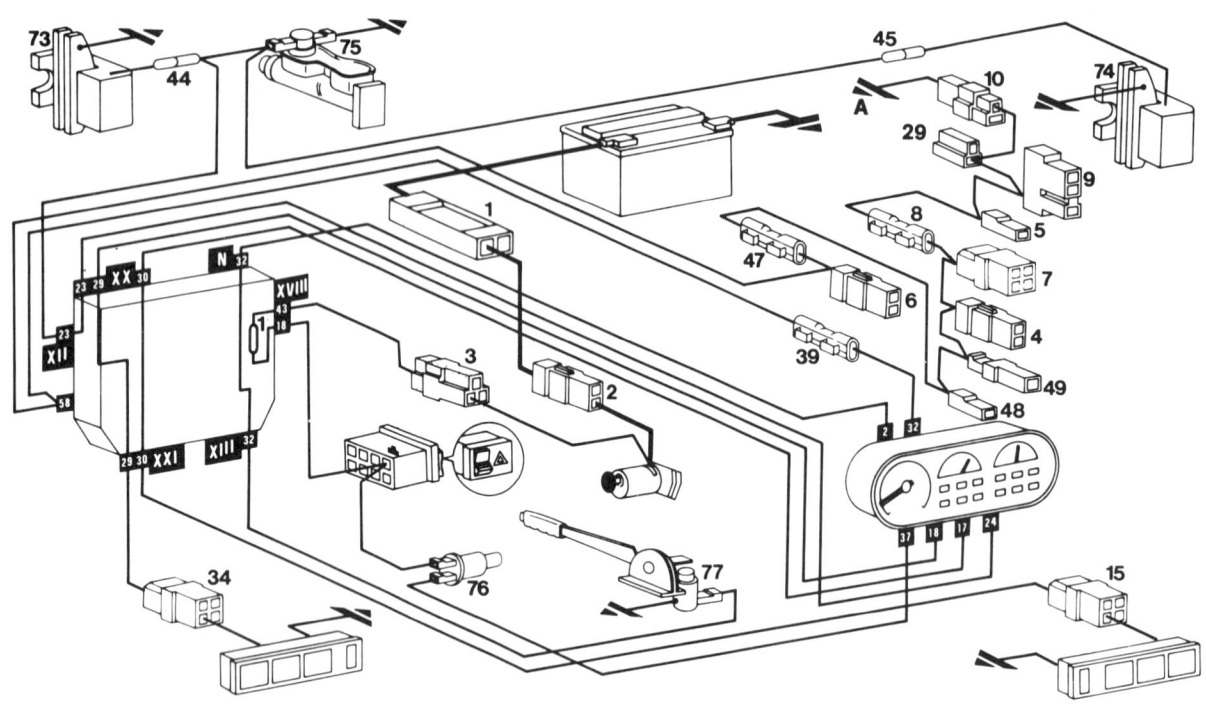

Fig. 13.69L Wiring diagram – stoplamps, low brake fluid level, handbrake 'on' and disc pad wear sensors
(early Super 85 models)

For key see page 268

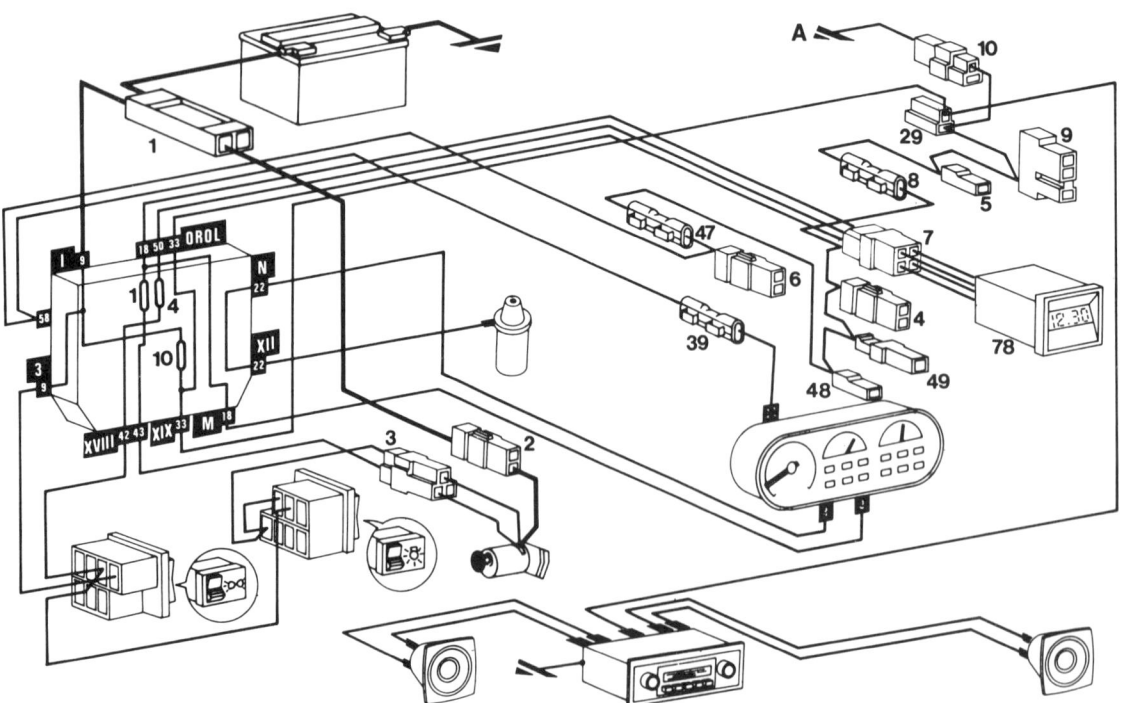

Fig. 13.69M Wiring diagram – radio, electronic rev counter, digital clock (early Super 85 models)

For key see page 268

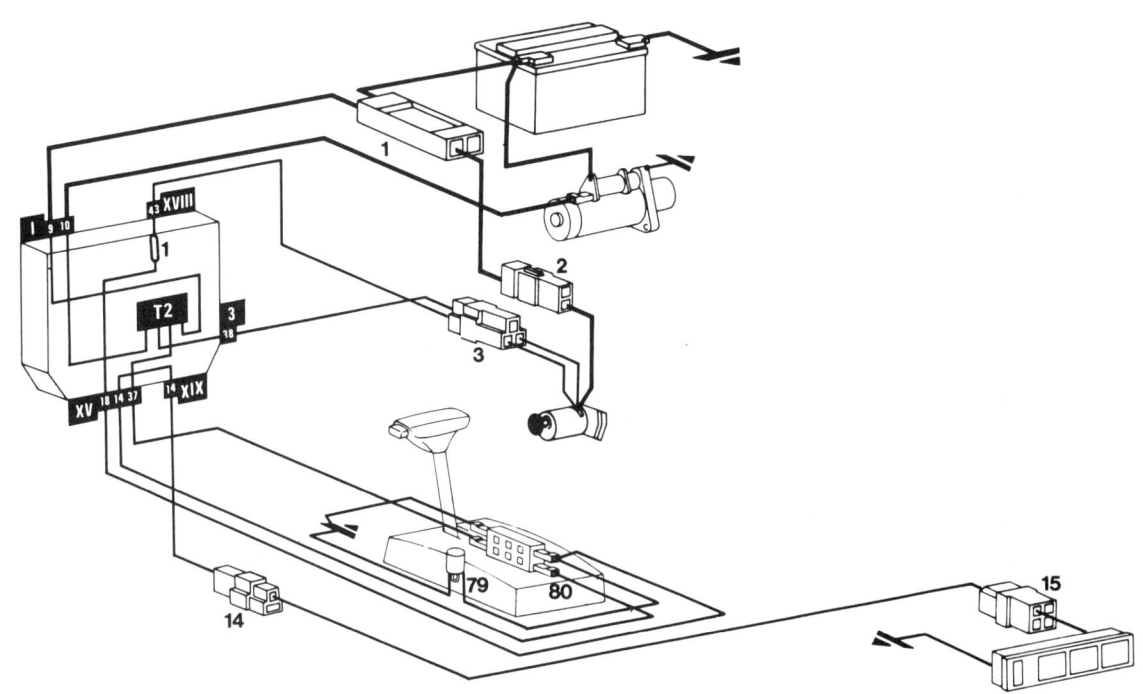

Fig. 13.69N Wiring diagram – automatic transmission (early Super 85 models)

For key see page 268

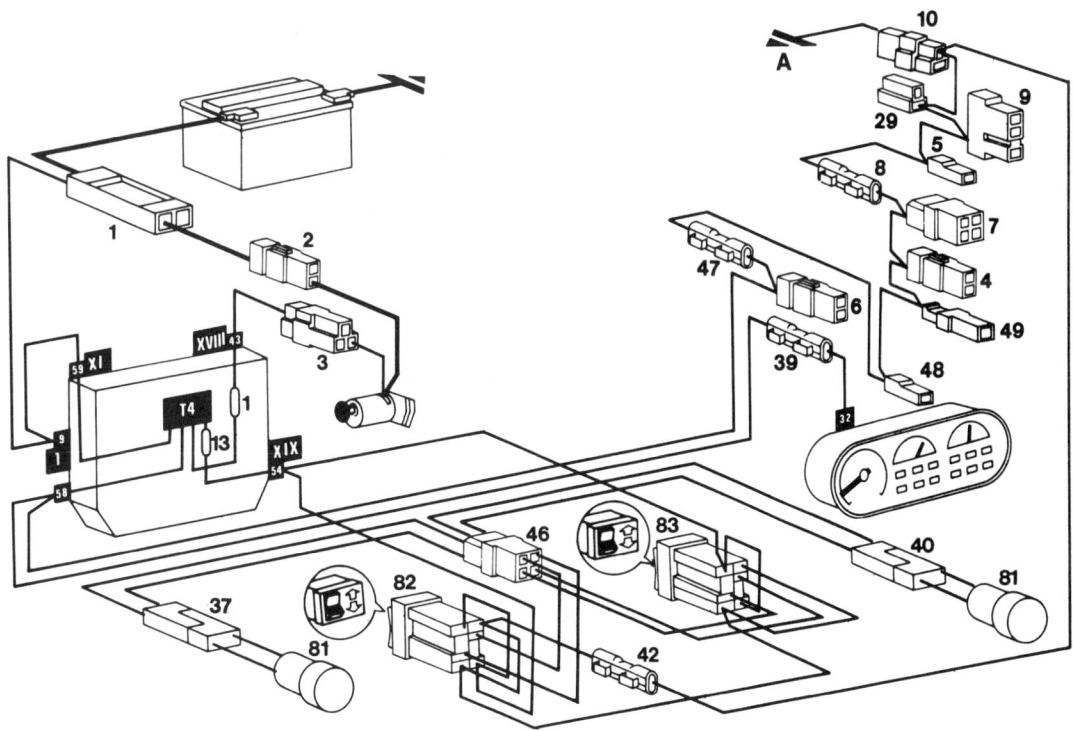

Fig. 13.69P Wiring diagram – power-operated window (early Super 85 models)

For key see page 268

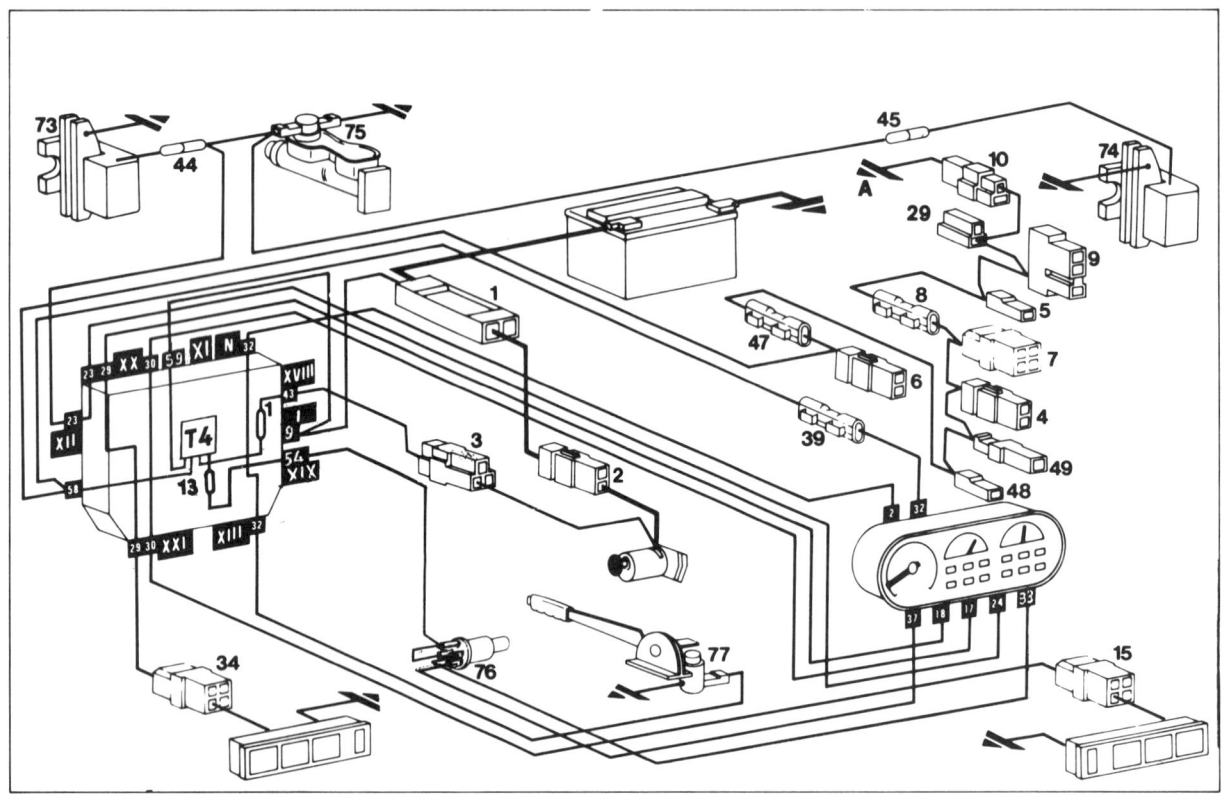

Fig. 13.70 Wiring diagram – stoplamps, low brake fluid level, handbrake 'on' and disc pad wear sensors
(later Super 85 models)

For key see page 268

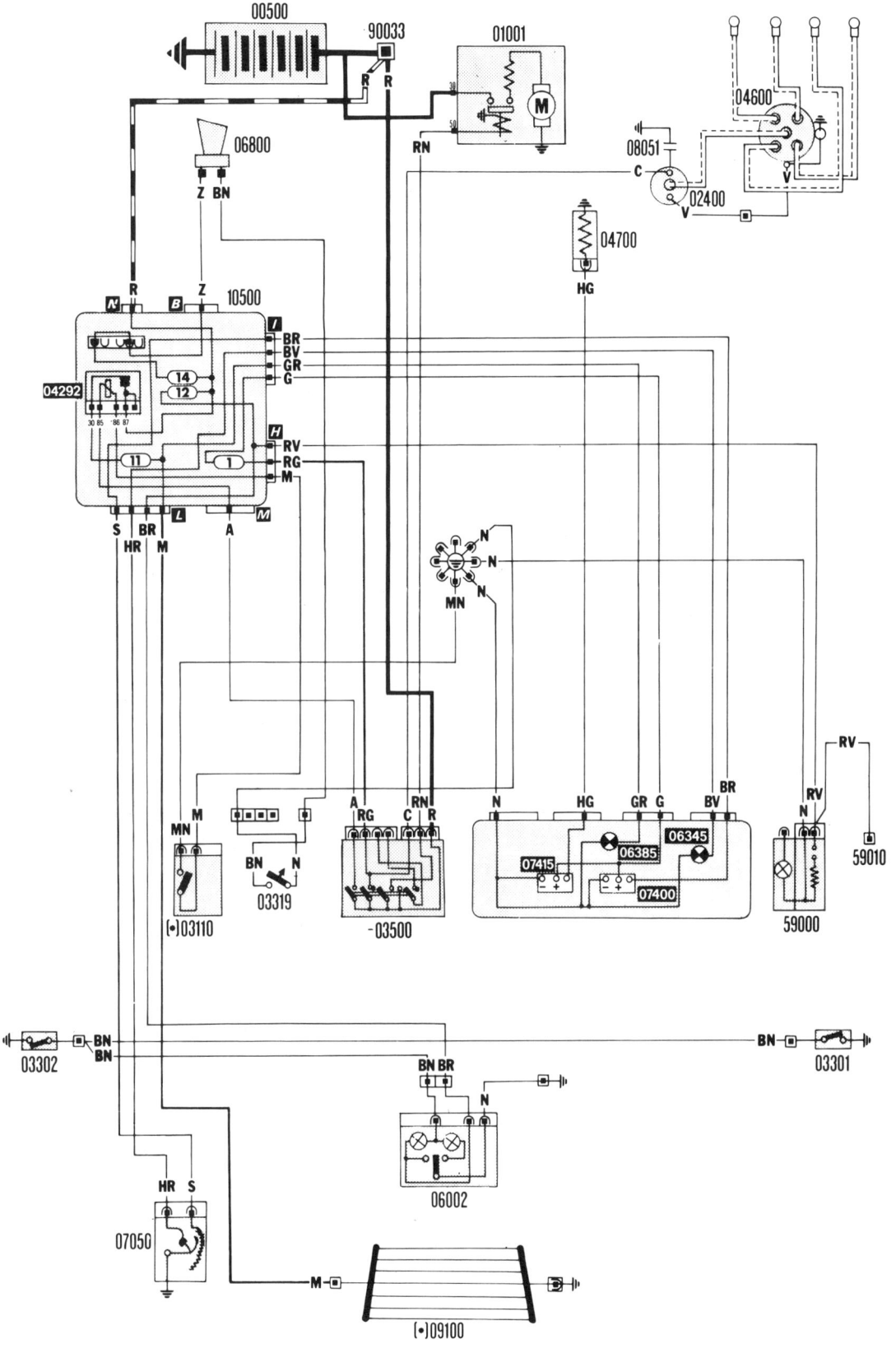

Fig. 13.71A Wiring diagram – starting, ignition, heated tailgate screen, horn, cigar lighter, fuel gauge/reserve, courtesy lamp/map reading lamp, coolant temperature warning lamp (Strada II except Super and TC models)

For key see page 305

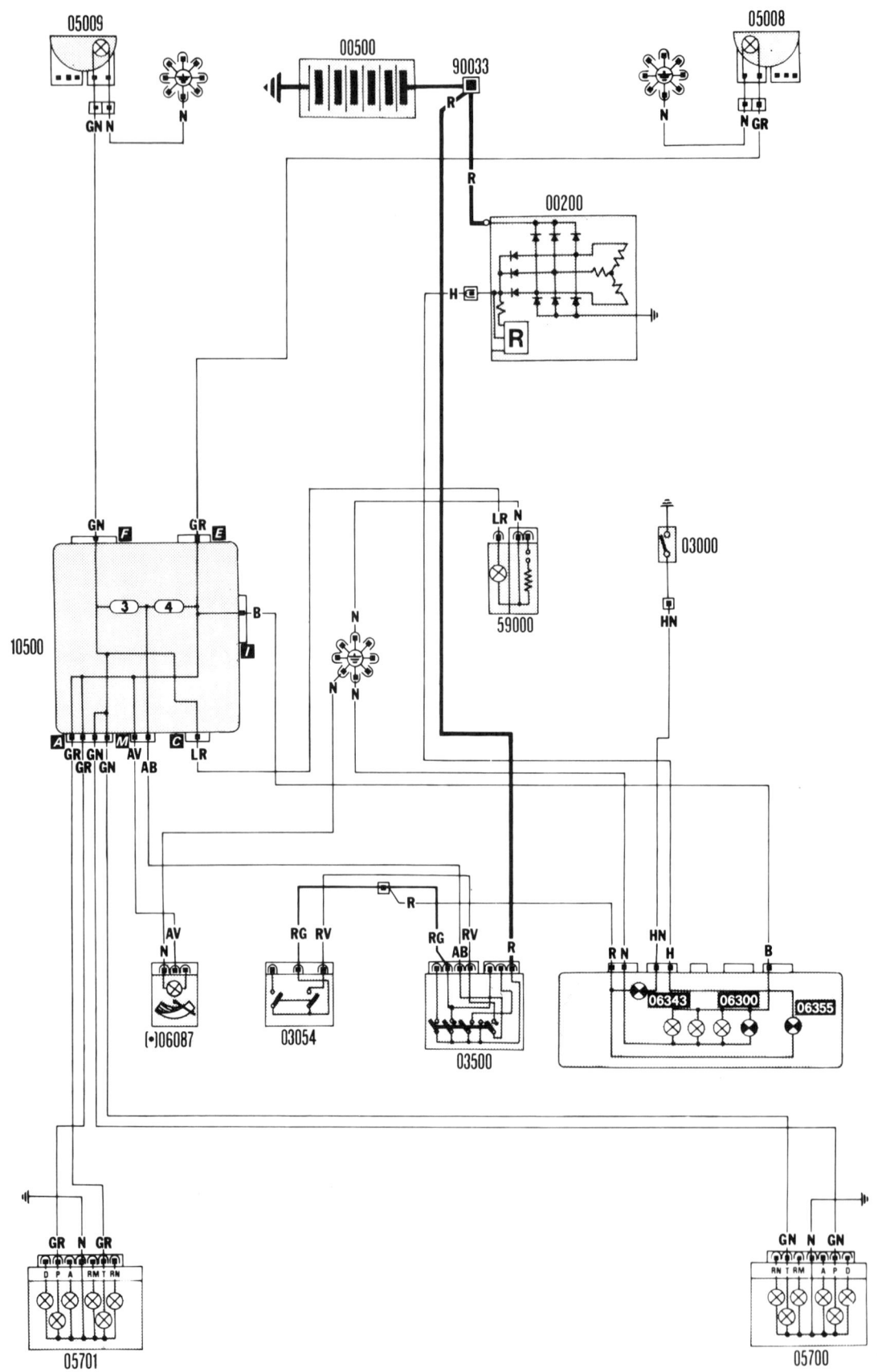

Fig. 13.71B Wiring diagram – charging, oil pressure warning lamp, rear number plate lamp
(Strada II except Super and TC models)

For key see page 305

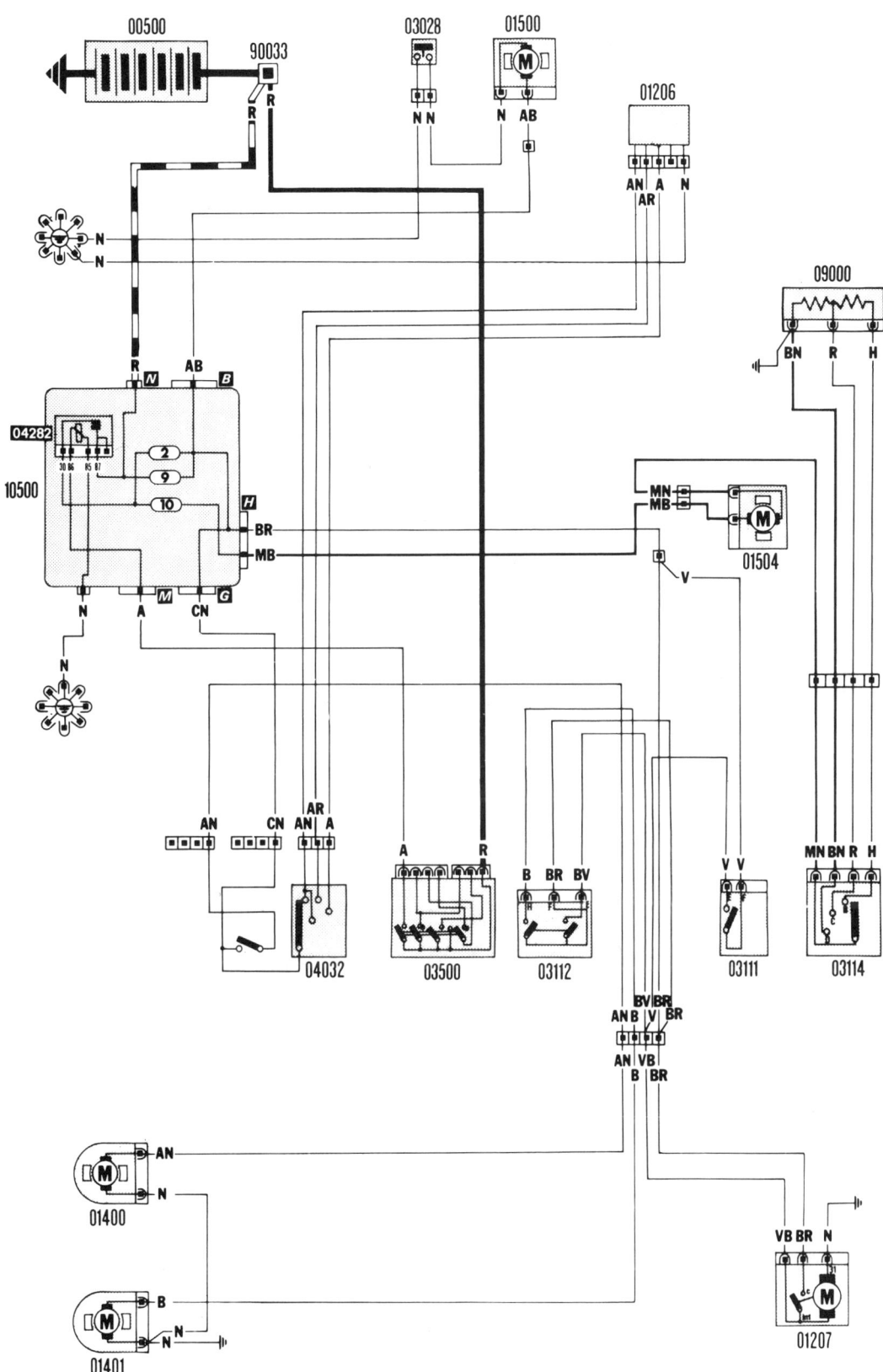

Fig. 13.71C Wiring diagram – radiator fan, heater, windscreen wash/wipe, tailgate wash/wipe
(Strada II except Super and TC models)

For key see page 305

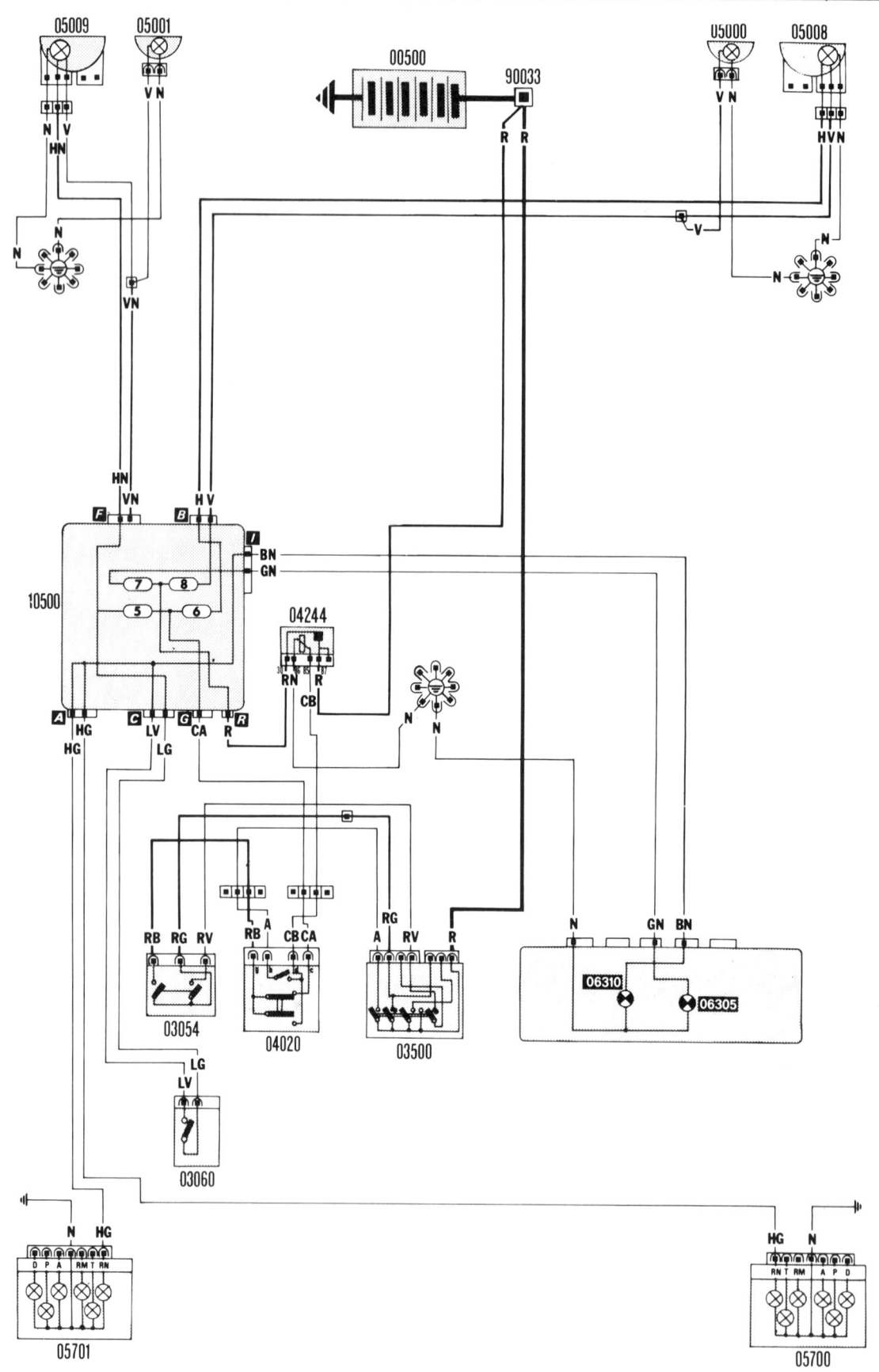

Fig. 13.71D Wiring diagram – headlamp main and dipped beam, spotlight and rear foglight
(Strada II except Super and TC models)

For key see page 305

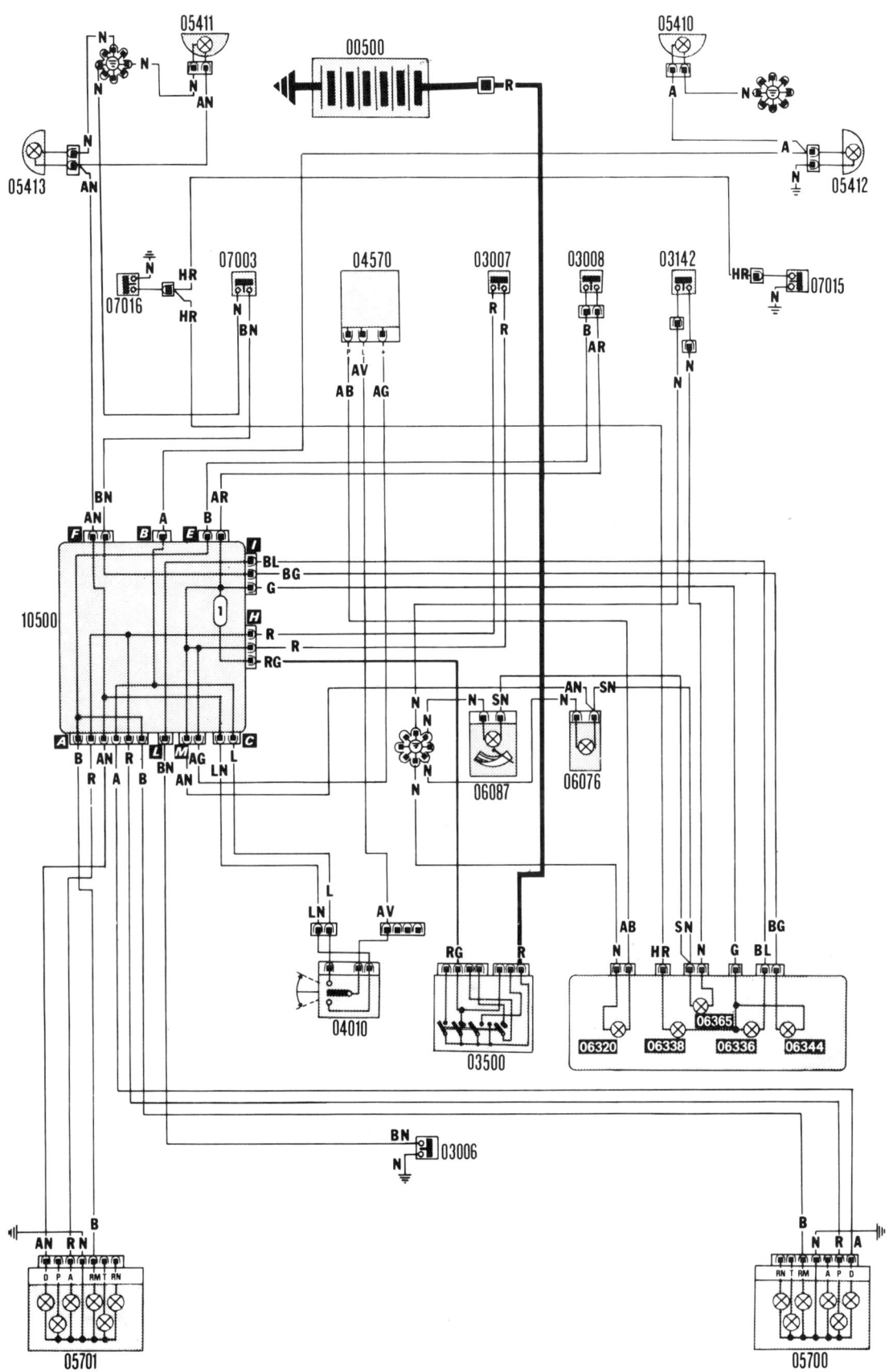

Fig. 13.71E Wiring diagram – direction indicators, stop lamps, choke warning lamp, reversing lamps, brake fluid low level lamp, disc pad wear sensor, handbrake 'on' warning lamp, ideogram illumination (Strada II except Super and TC models)

For key see page 305

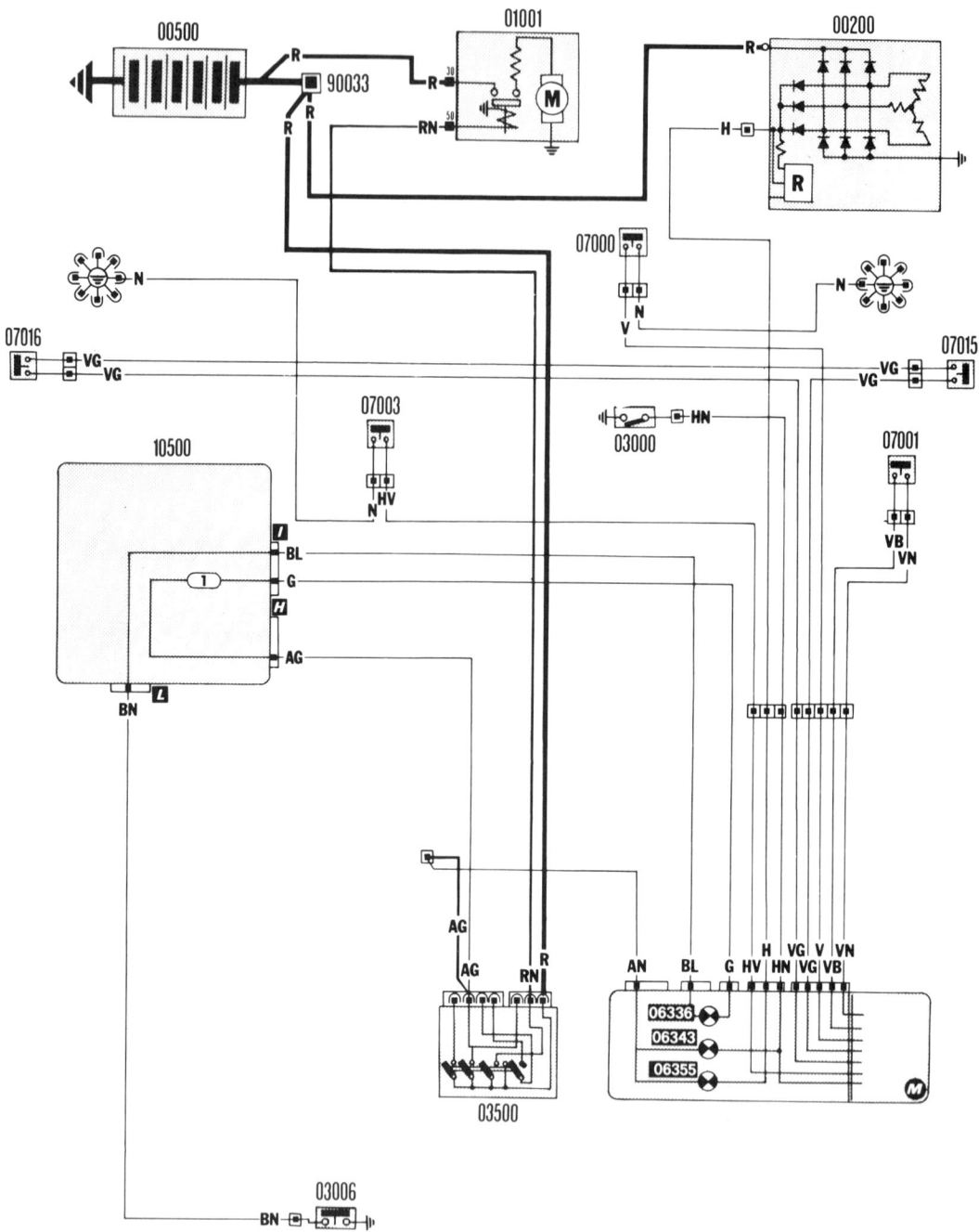

Fig. 13.72A Wiring diagram – starting, charging, low oil pressure, oil level, low coolant level, low brake level, handbrake 'on' warning lamps, disc brake pad wear sensor (Strada II Super models)

For key see page 305

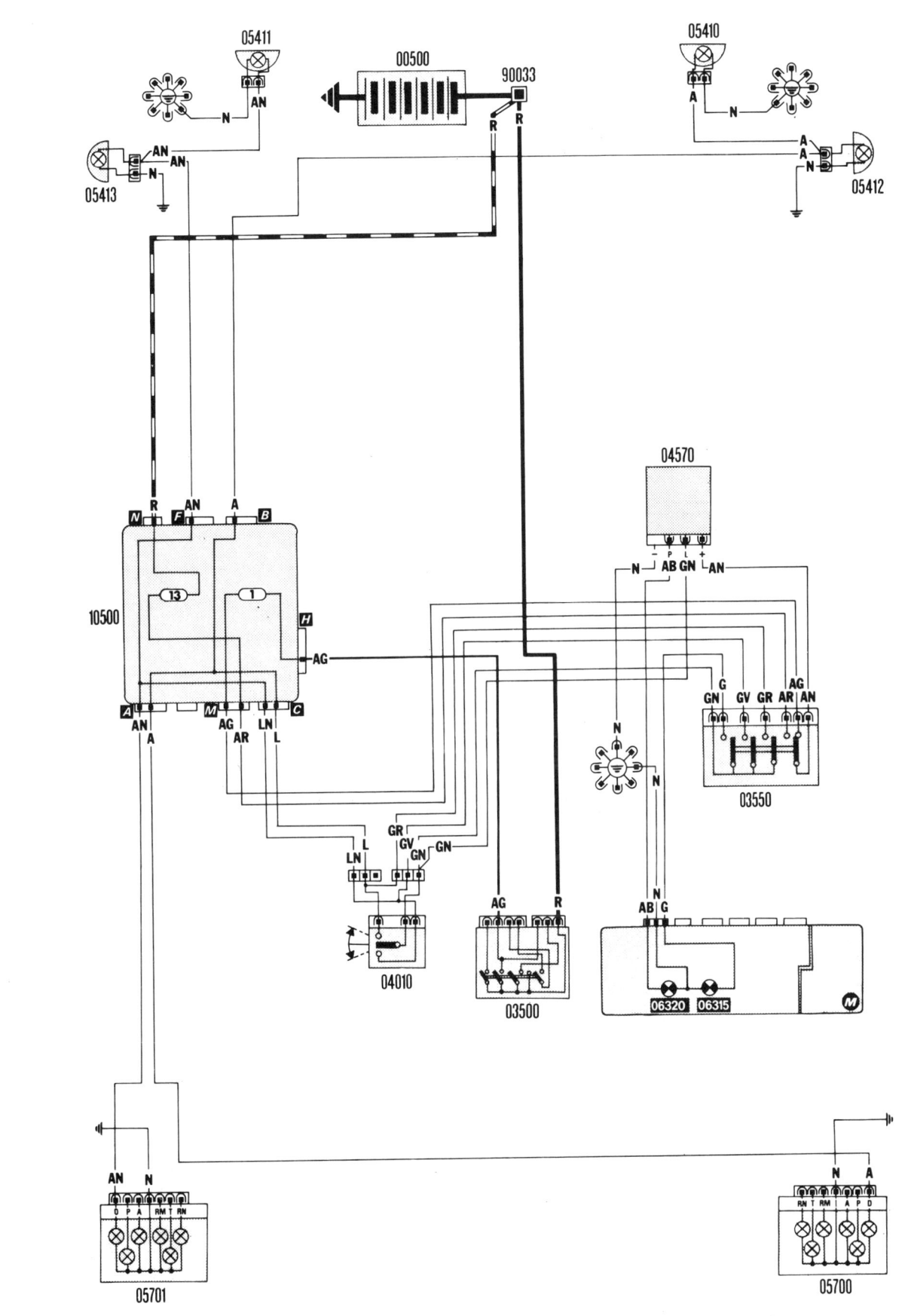

Fig. 13.72B Wiring diagram – direction indicators, hazard warning lamps (Strada II Super models)

For key see page 305

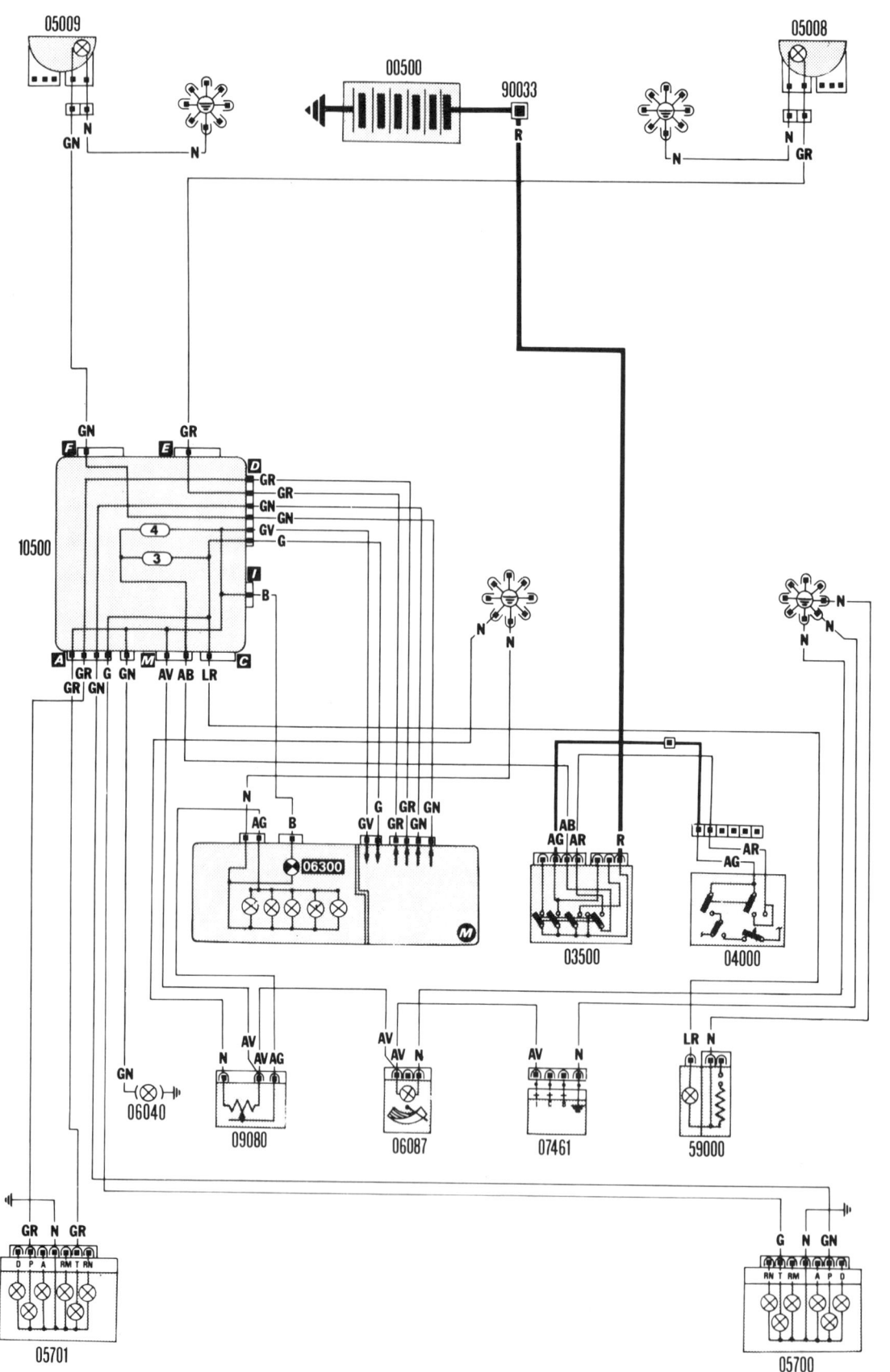

Fig. 13.72C Wiring diagram – front parking lamps, rear number plate, lamps, digital clock, ideogram lamp adjuster, economy meter (Strada II Super models)

For key see page 305

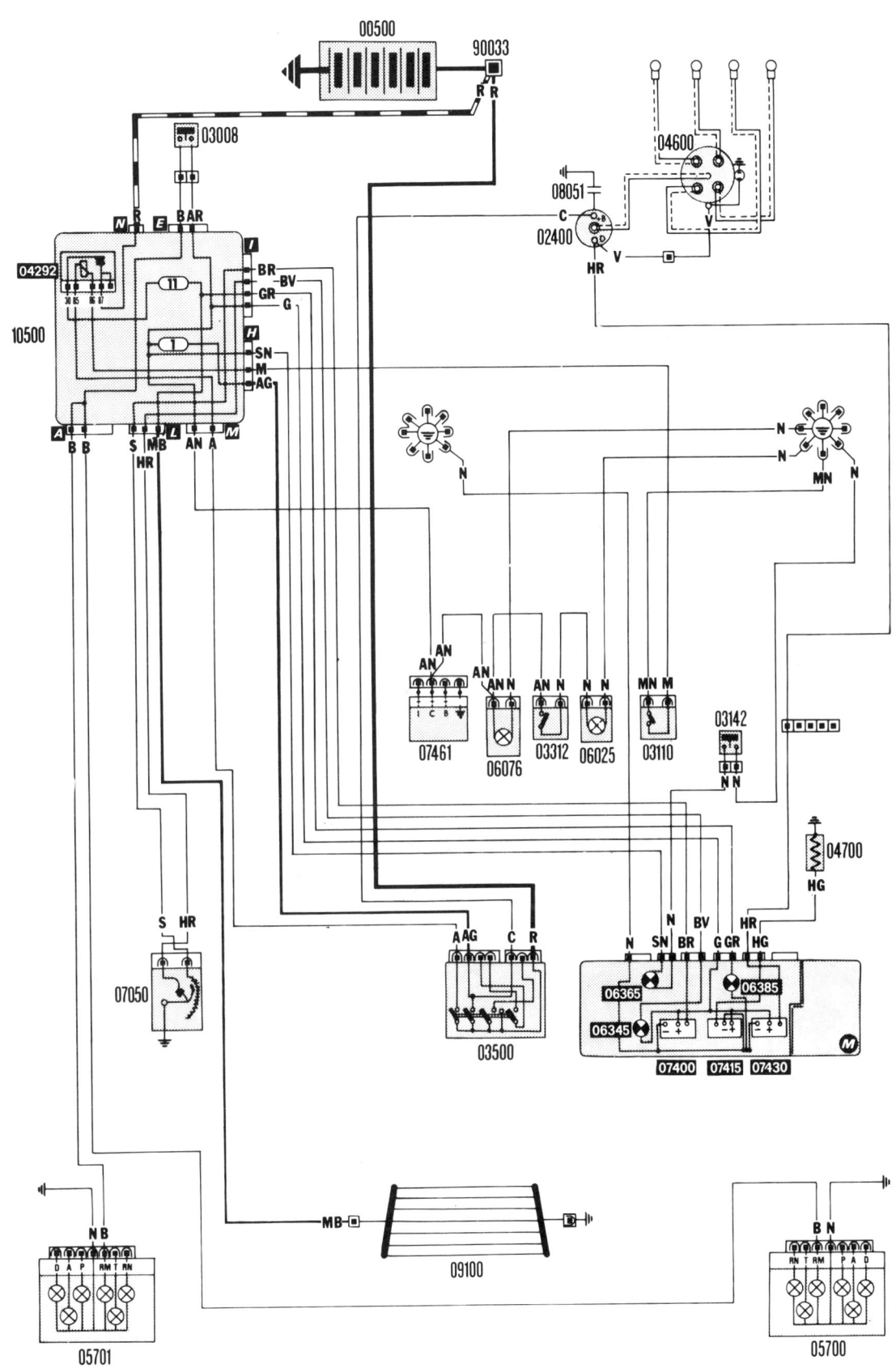

Fig. 13.72D Wiring diagram – ignition, reversing lamps, coolant temperature gauge, ideogram and glovebox illumination, heated tailgate screen, fuel gauge/reserve, choke warning lamp (Strada II Super models)

For key see page 305

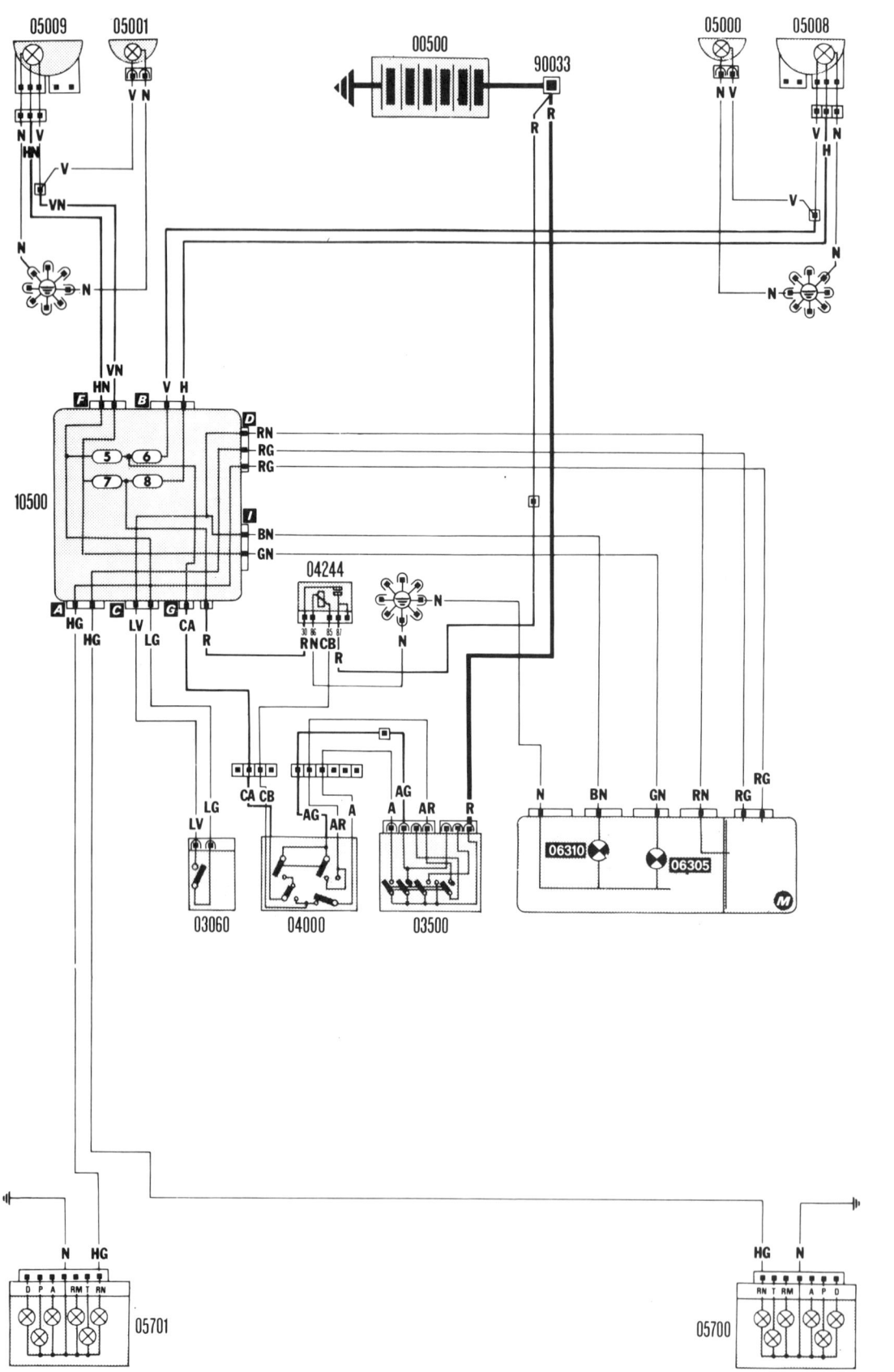

Fig. 13.72E Wiring diagram – headlamp main and dipped beam, spotlamps, rear foglamps (Strada II Super models)

For key see page 305

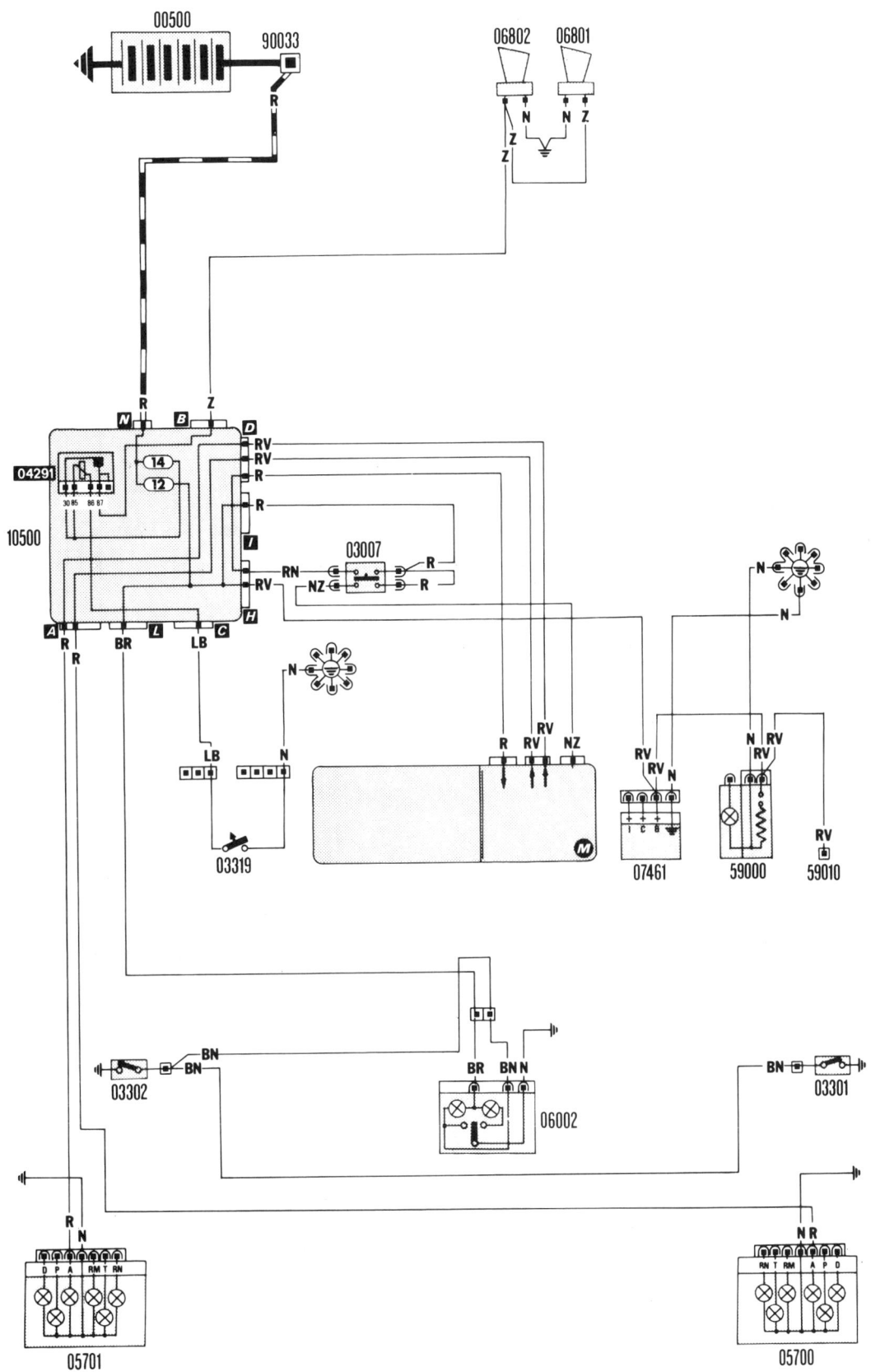

Fig. 13.72F Wiring diagram – courtesy lamp/spotlamp, horn, digital clock, cigar lighter, radio and stop lamps (Strada II Super models)

For key see page 305

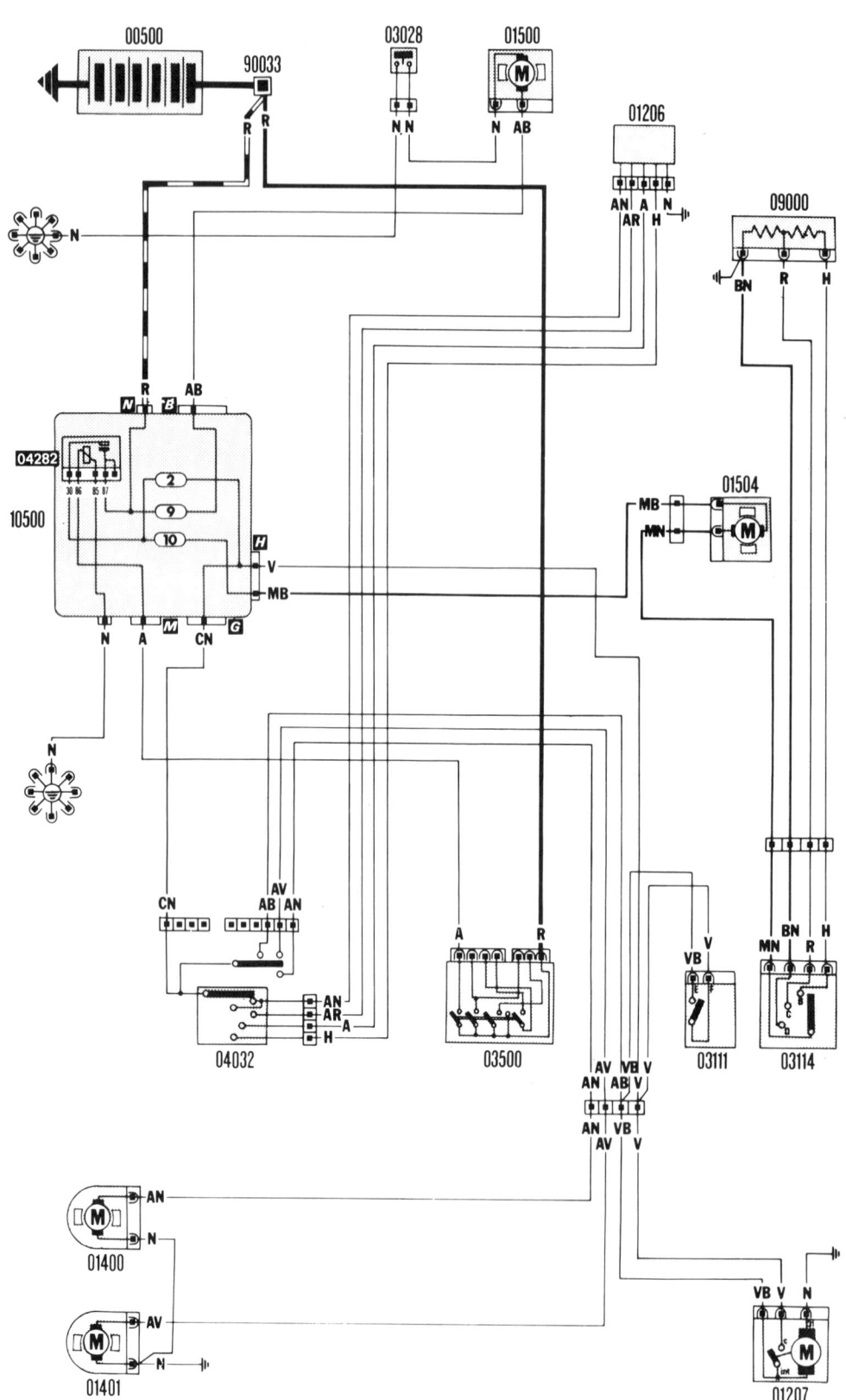

Fig. 13.72G Wiring diagram – radiator fan, heater, tailgate wash/wipe, windscreen wash/wipe (Strada II Super models)

For key see page 305

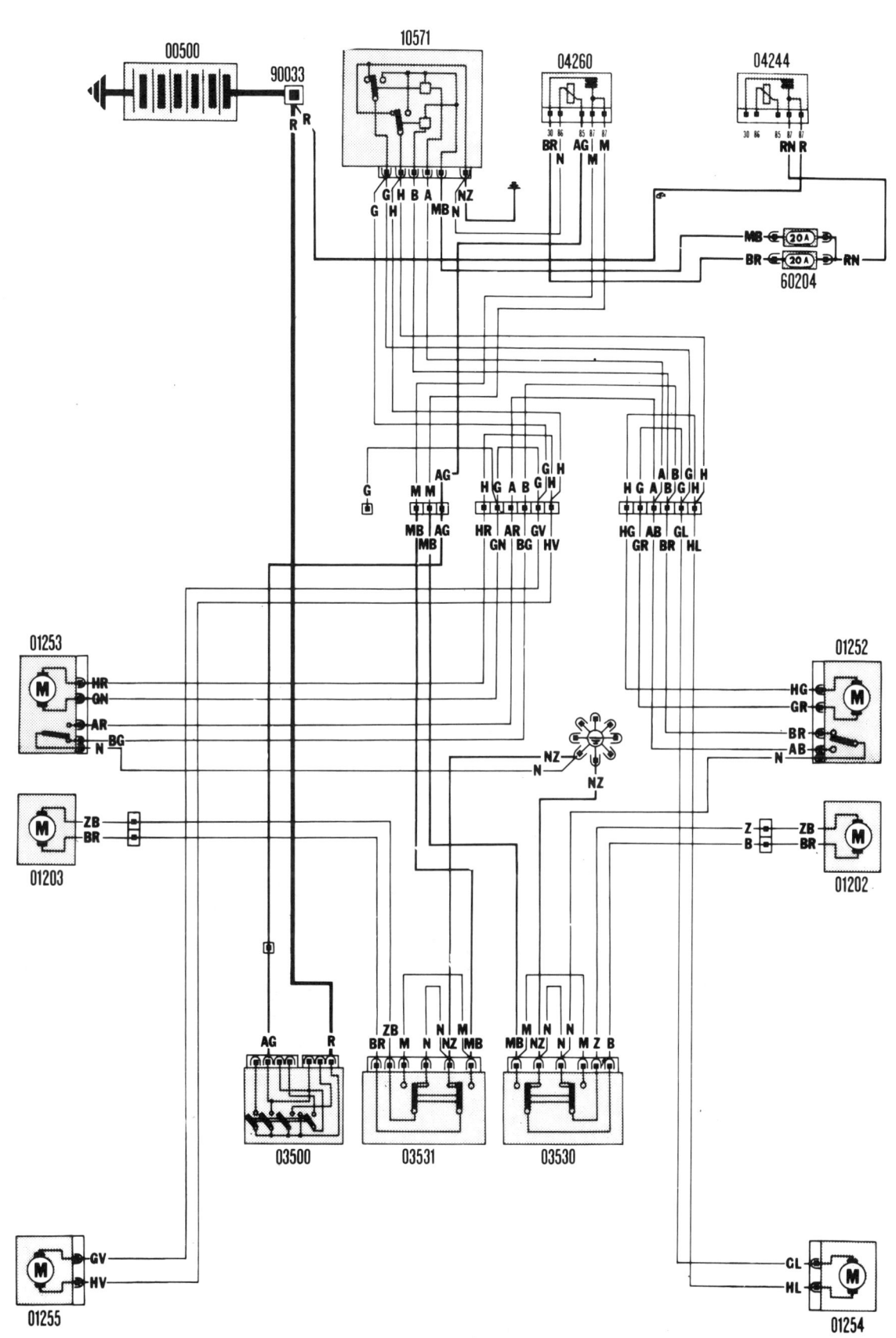

Fig. 13.72H Wiring diagram – central door locking, power-operated windows, bonnet locking (Strada II Super models)

For key see page 305

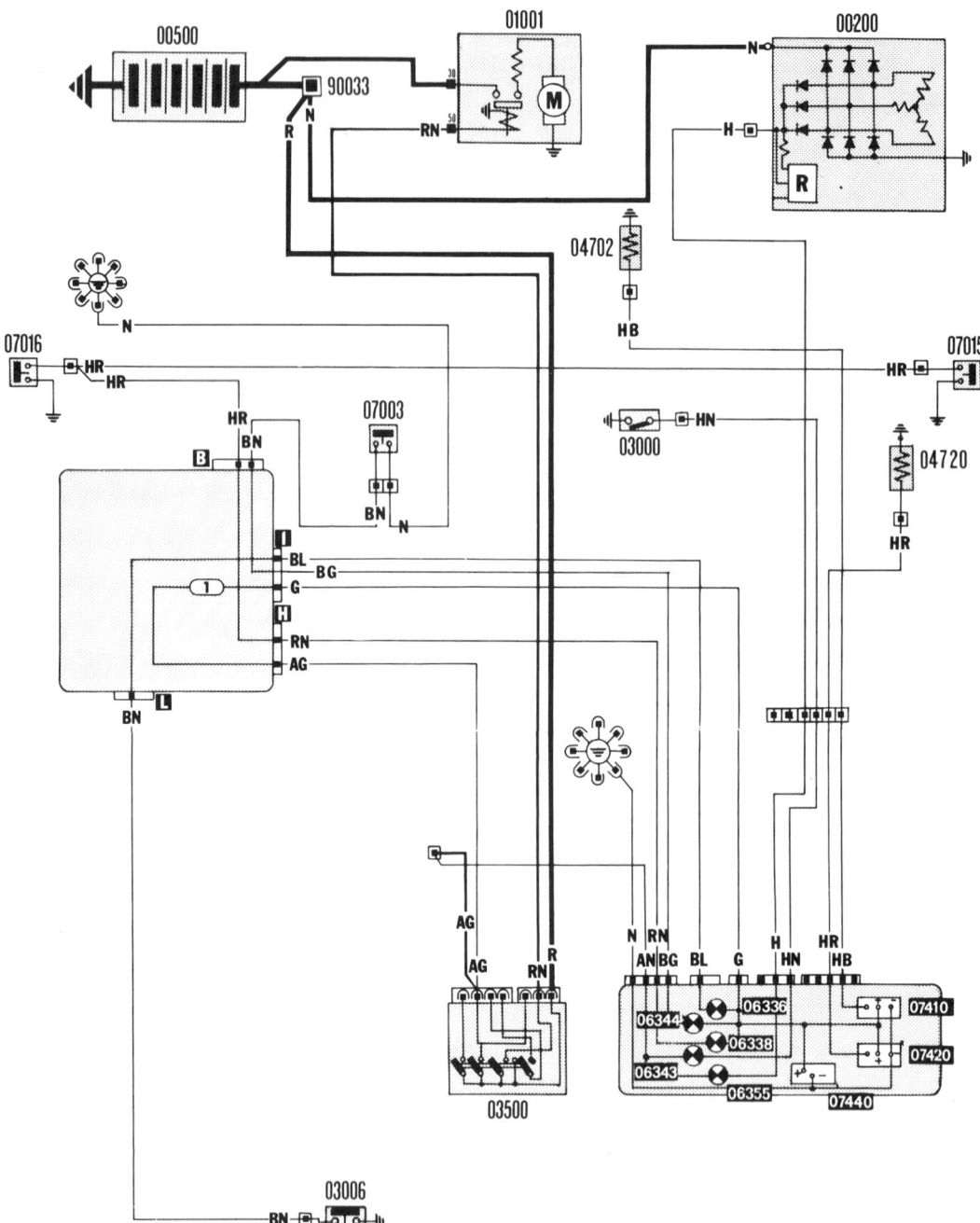

Fig. 13.73A Wiring diagram – starting, charging, battery condition indicator, oil pressure warning lamp, brake fluid low level, handbrake 'on' and disc pad wear warning lamps (105 TC models)

For key see page 305

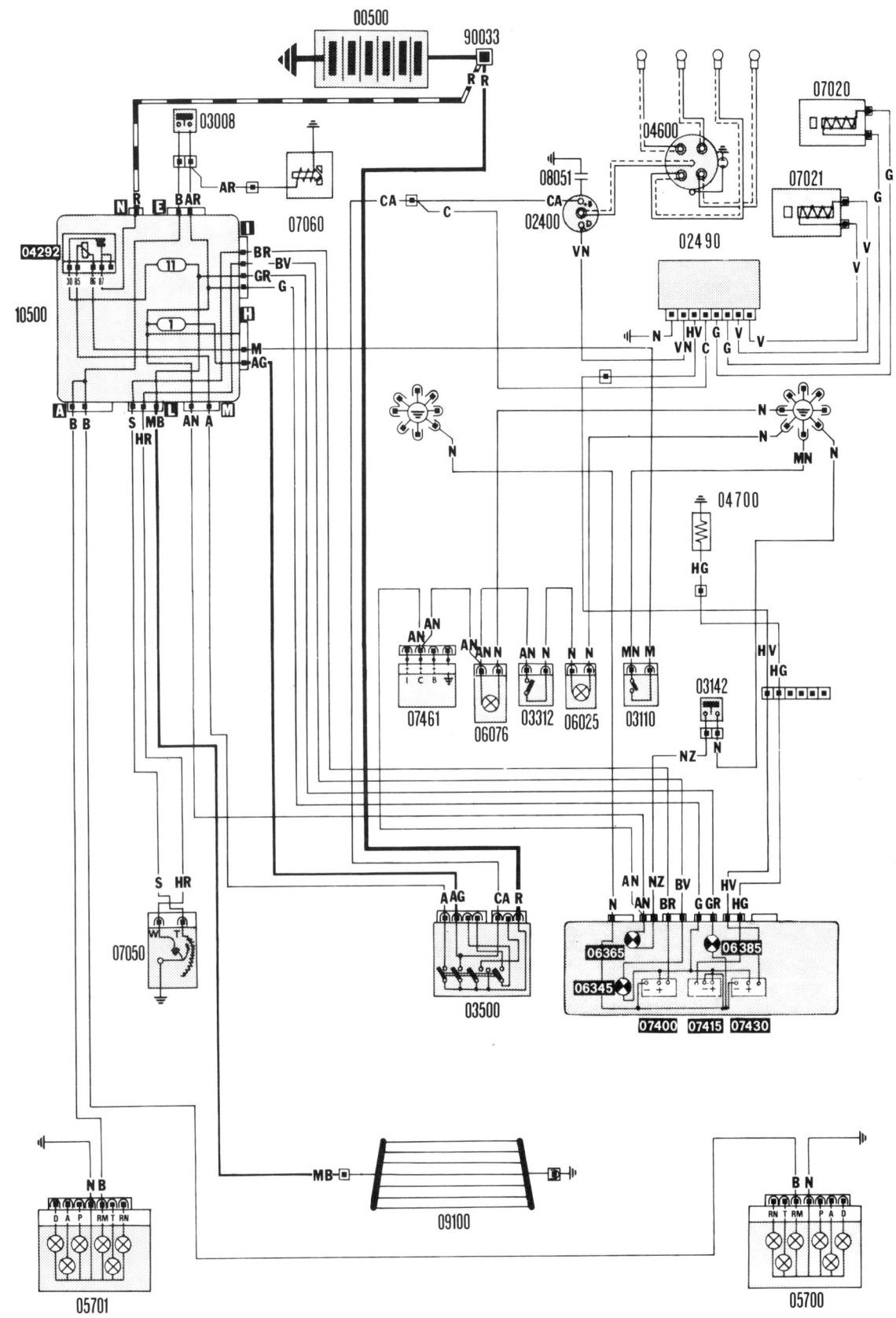

Fig. 13.73B Wiring diagram – ignition, reversing lamps, idle cut-out (overrun) device, static advance electronic ignition, coolant temperature gauge, ideogram illumination, glovebox lamp, heated tailgate screen, fuel gauge/reserve, choke warning lamp (105 TC models)

For key see page 305

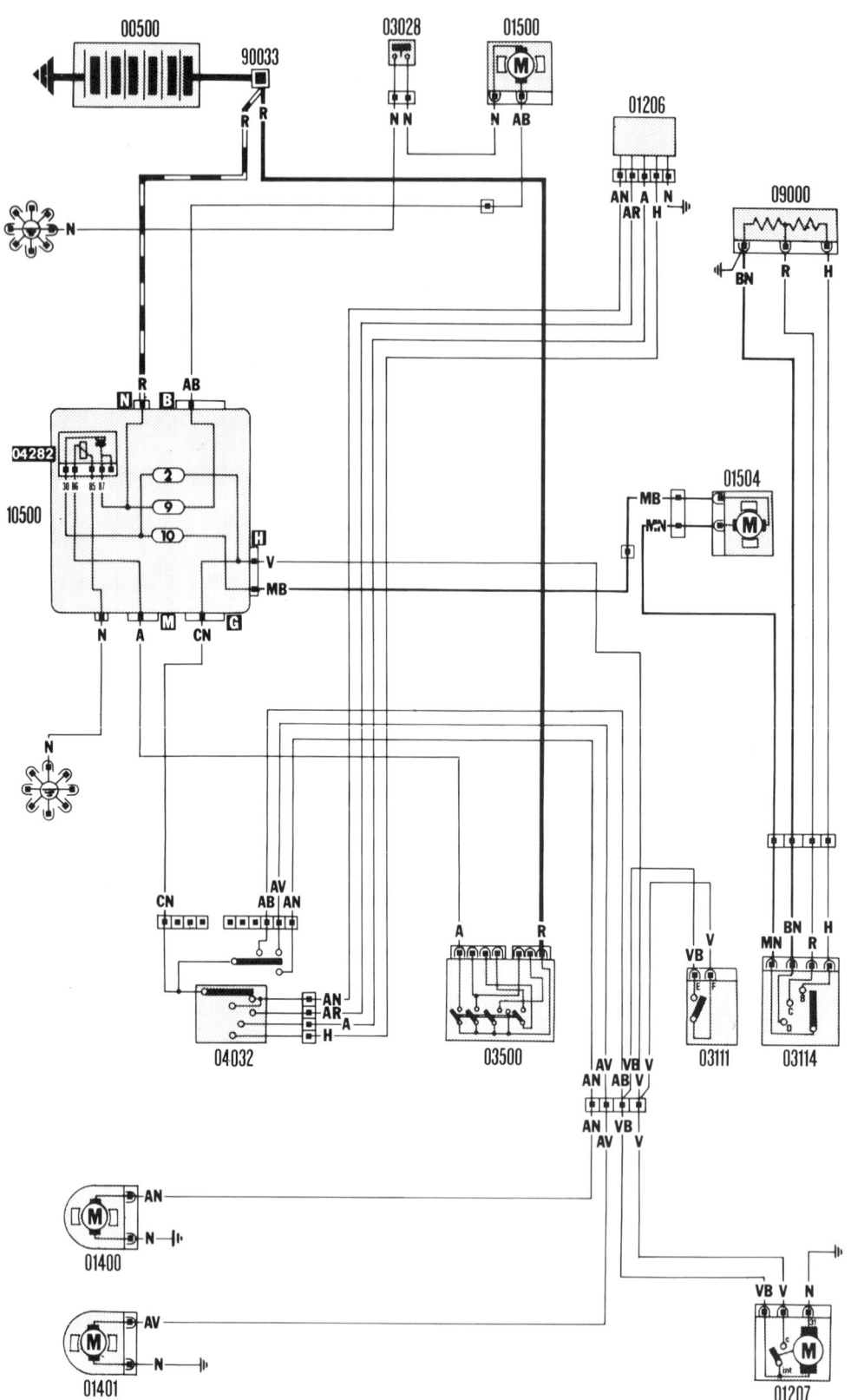

Fig. 13.73C Wiring diagram – radiator fan, heater, windscreen wash/wipe, tailgate wash/wipe (105 TC models)

For key see page 305

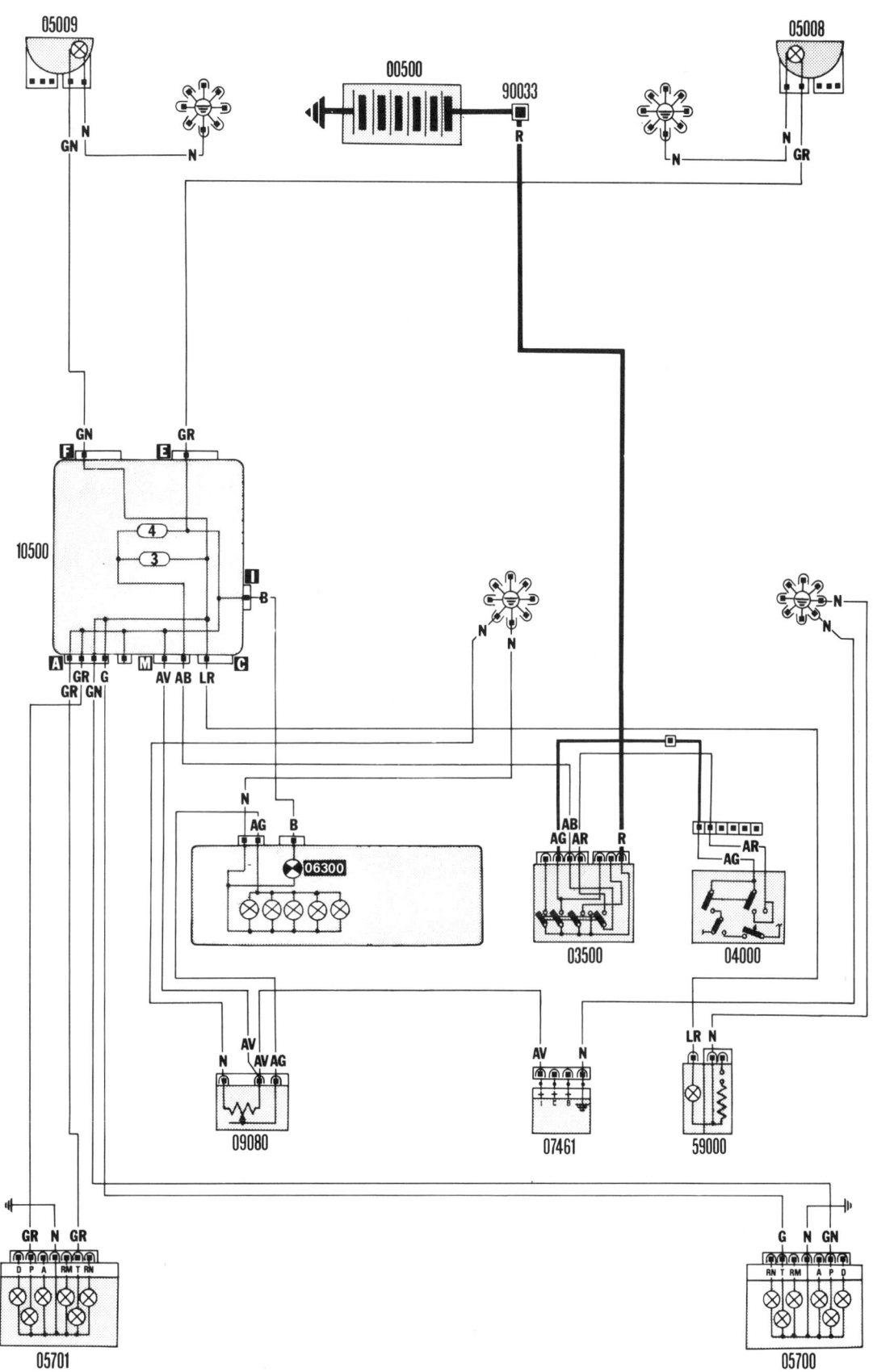

Fig. 13.73D Wiring diagram – front parking lamps, rear number plate lamps, digital clock and cigar lighter illumination, ideogram illumination rheostat (105 TC models)

For key see page 305

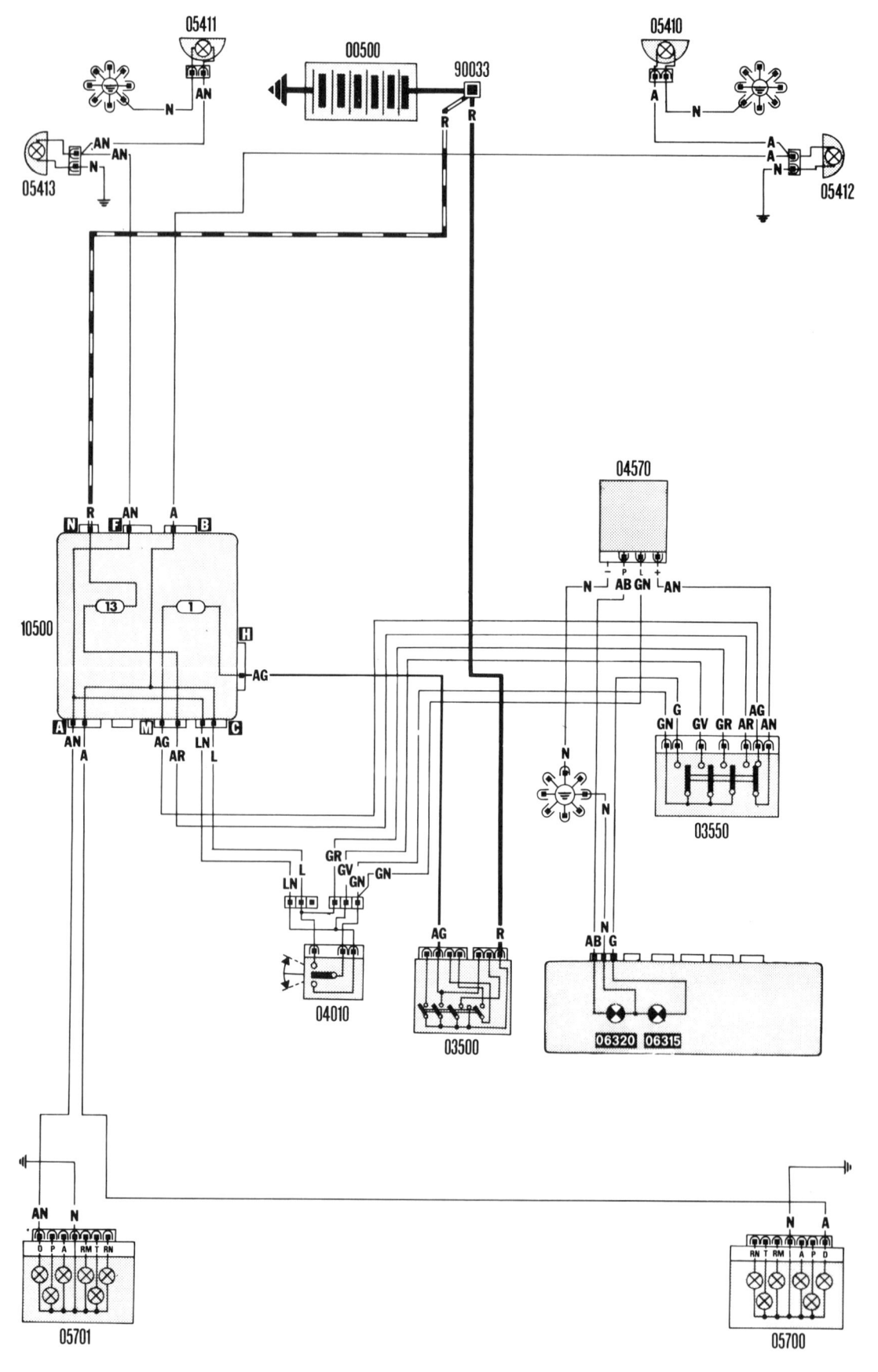

Fig. 13.73E Wiring diagram – direction indicators, hazard warning lamps (105 TC models)

For key see page 305

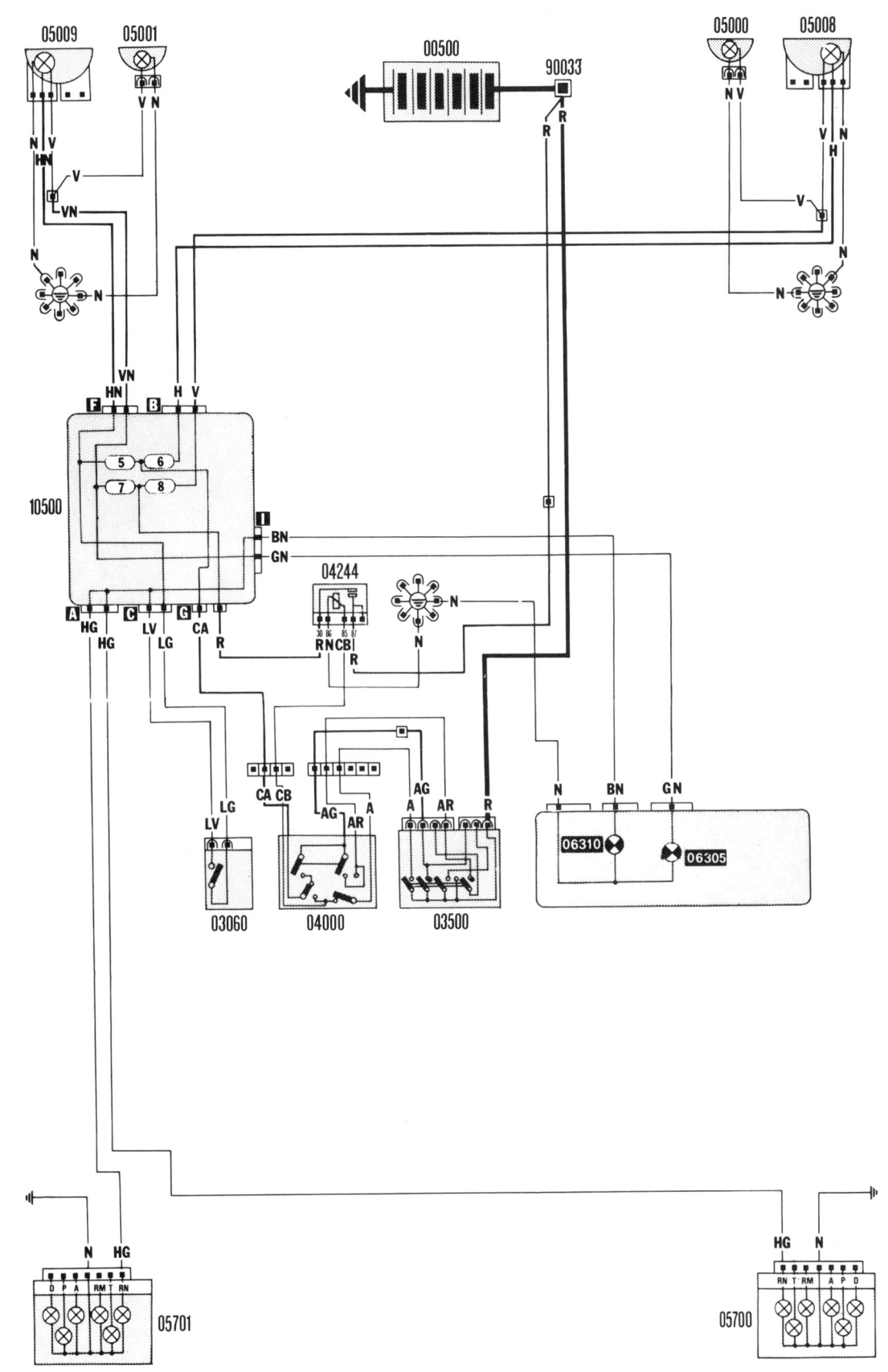

Fig. 13.73F Wiring diagram – headlamp main and dipped beam, spotlamps, rear foglamps (105 TC models)

For key see page 305

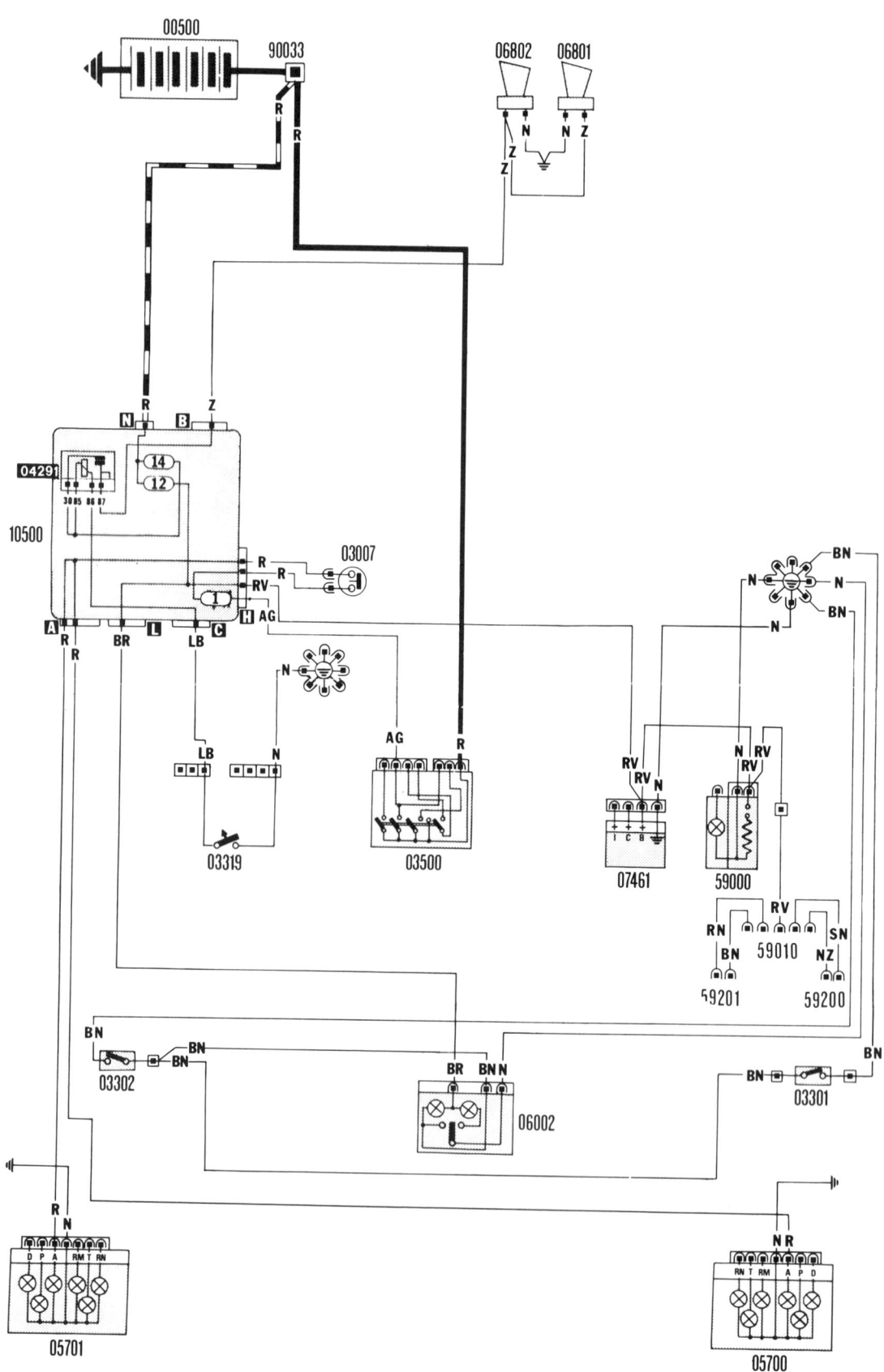

Fig. 13.73G Wiring diagram – courtesy lamp/map reading lamp, horn, digital clock, cigar lighter, radio, stop lamps (105 TC models)

For key see page 305

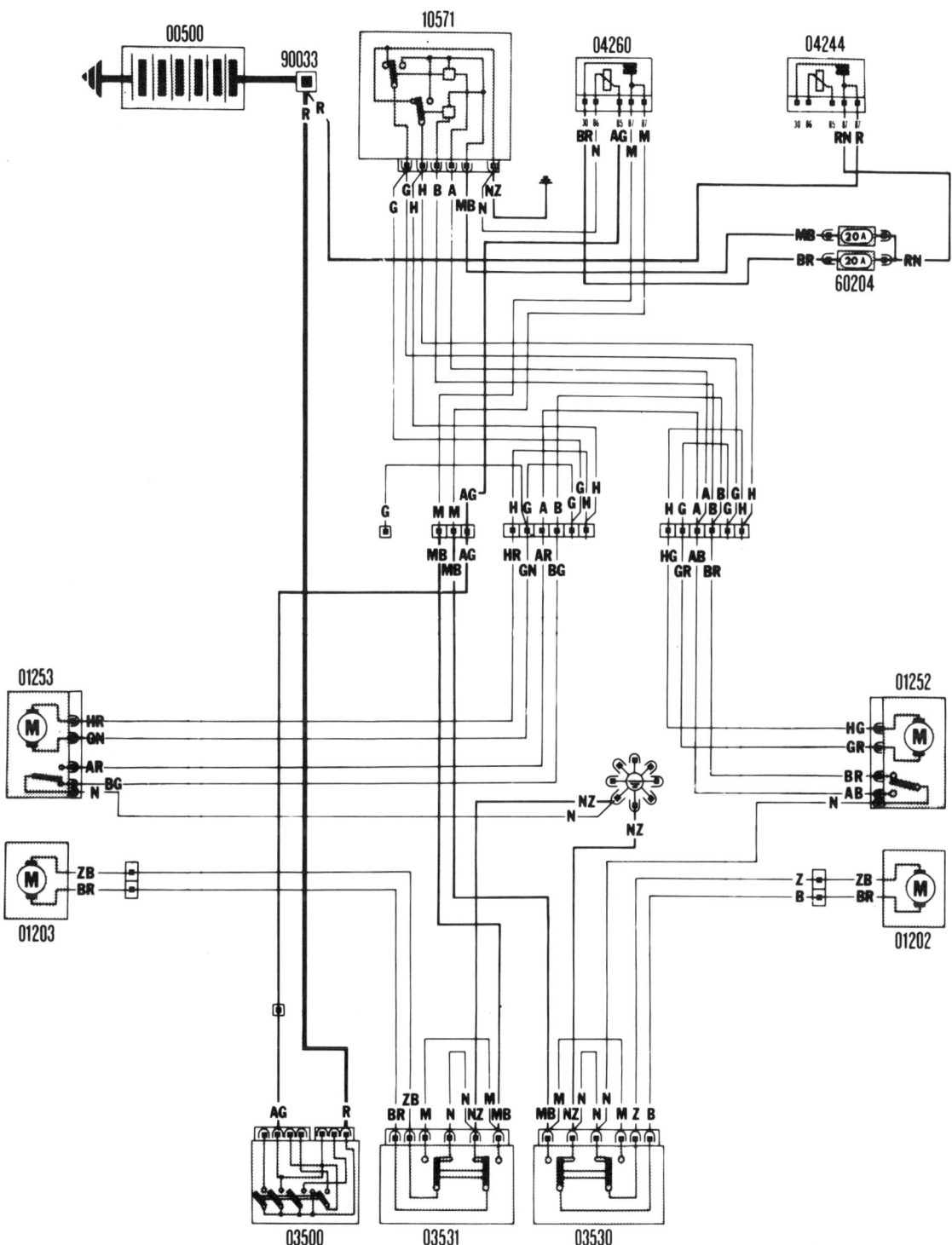

Fig. 13.74A Wiring diagram – central door locking, power-operated front door windows (130 TC models)

For key see page 305

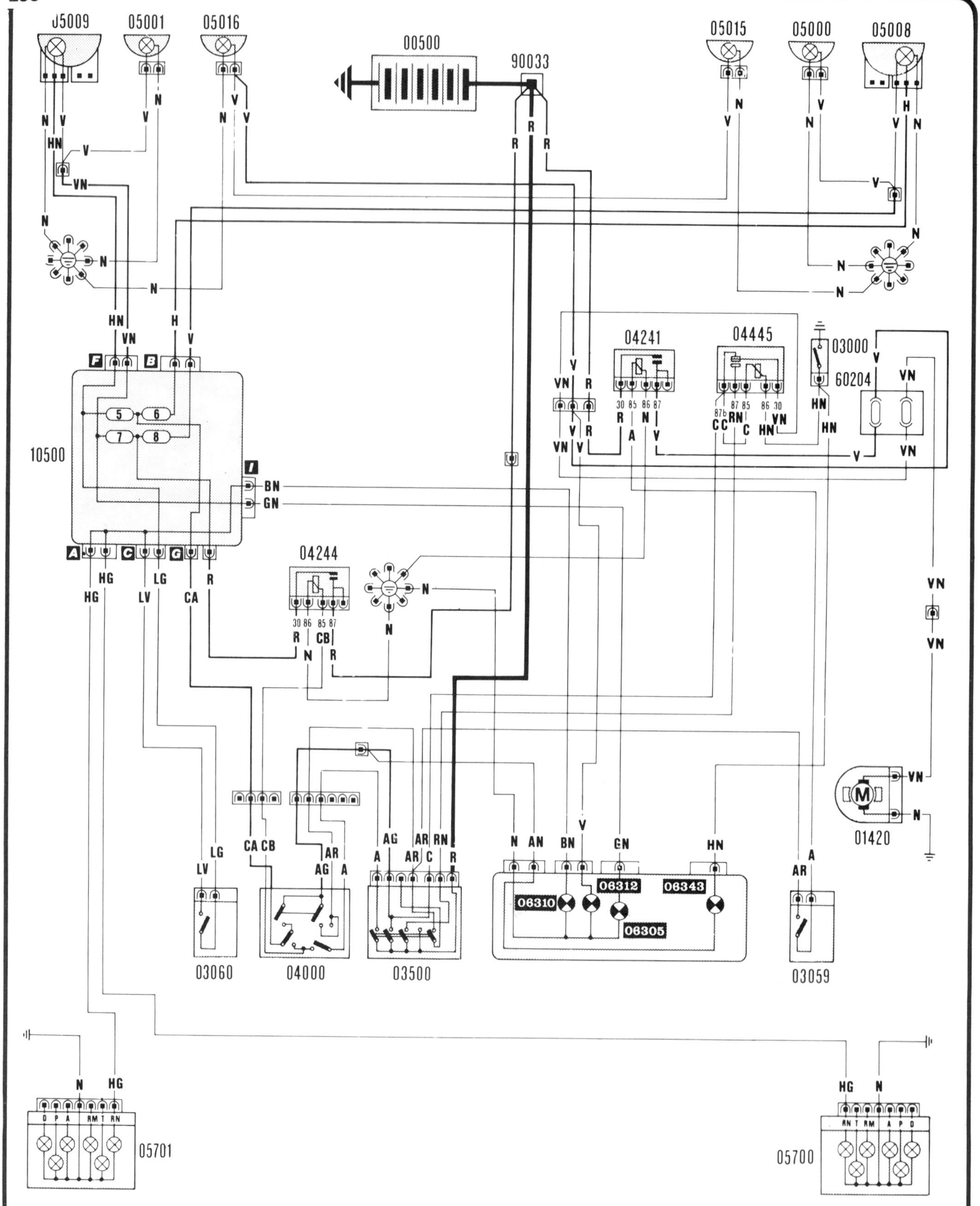

Fig. 13.74B Wiring diagram – headlamp main and dipped beam, spotlamps, front and rear fog lamps, electric fuel pump (130 TC models)

For key see page 305

For other circuits see wiring diagram 13.73

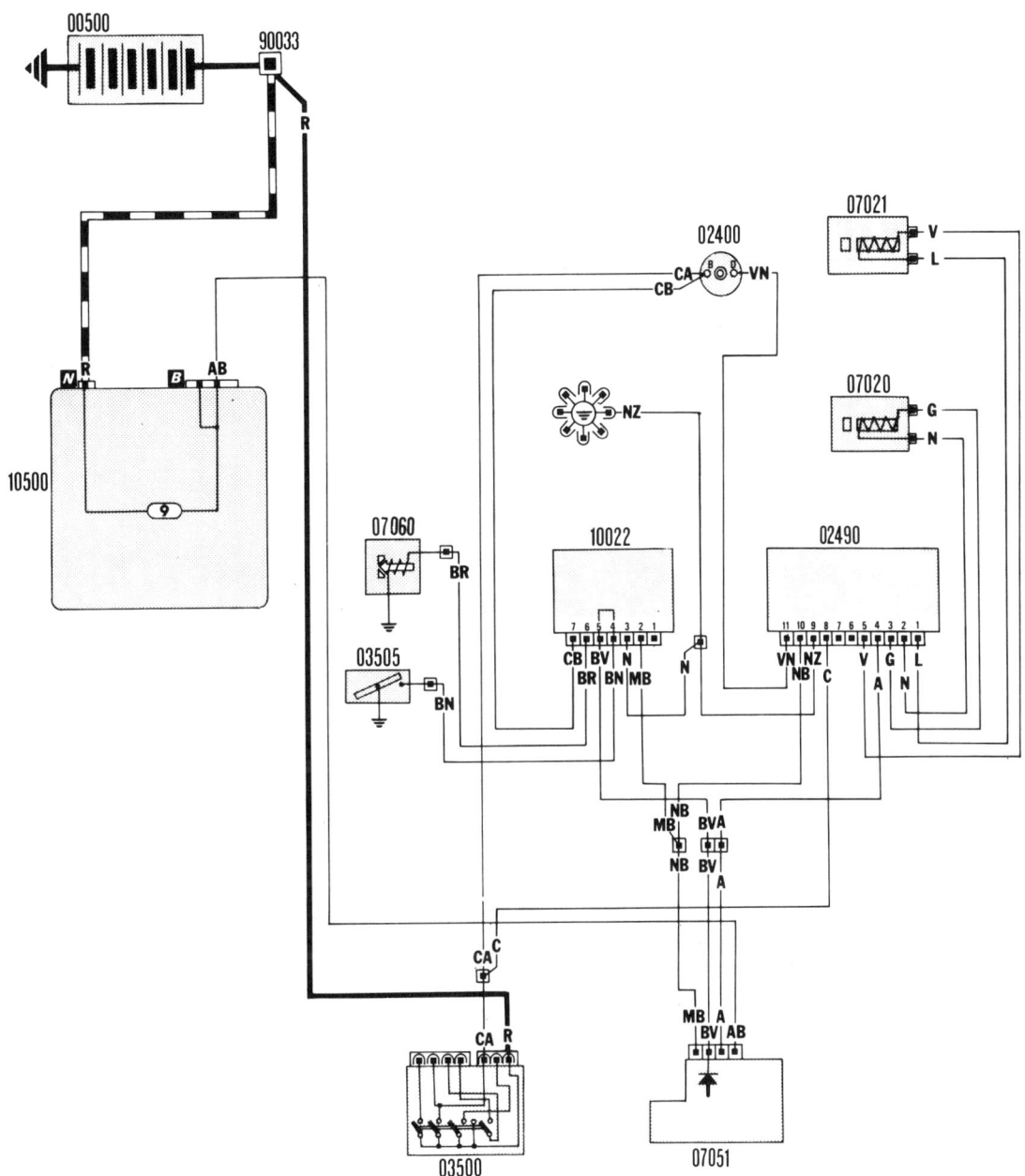

Fig. 13.75 Supplementary wiring diagram – electronic ignition, idle cut-out device, economy meter (ES models)

For key see page 305

CONNECTION DIAGRAM

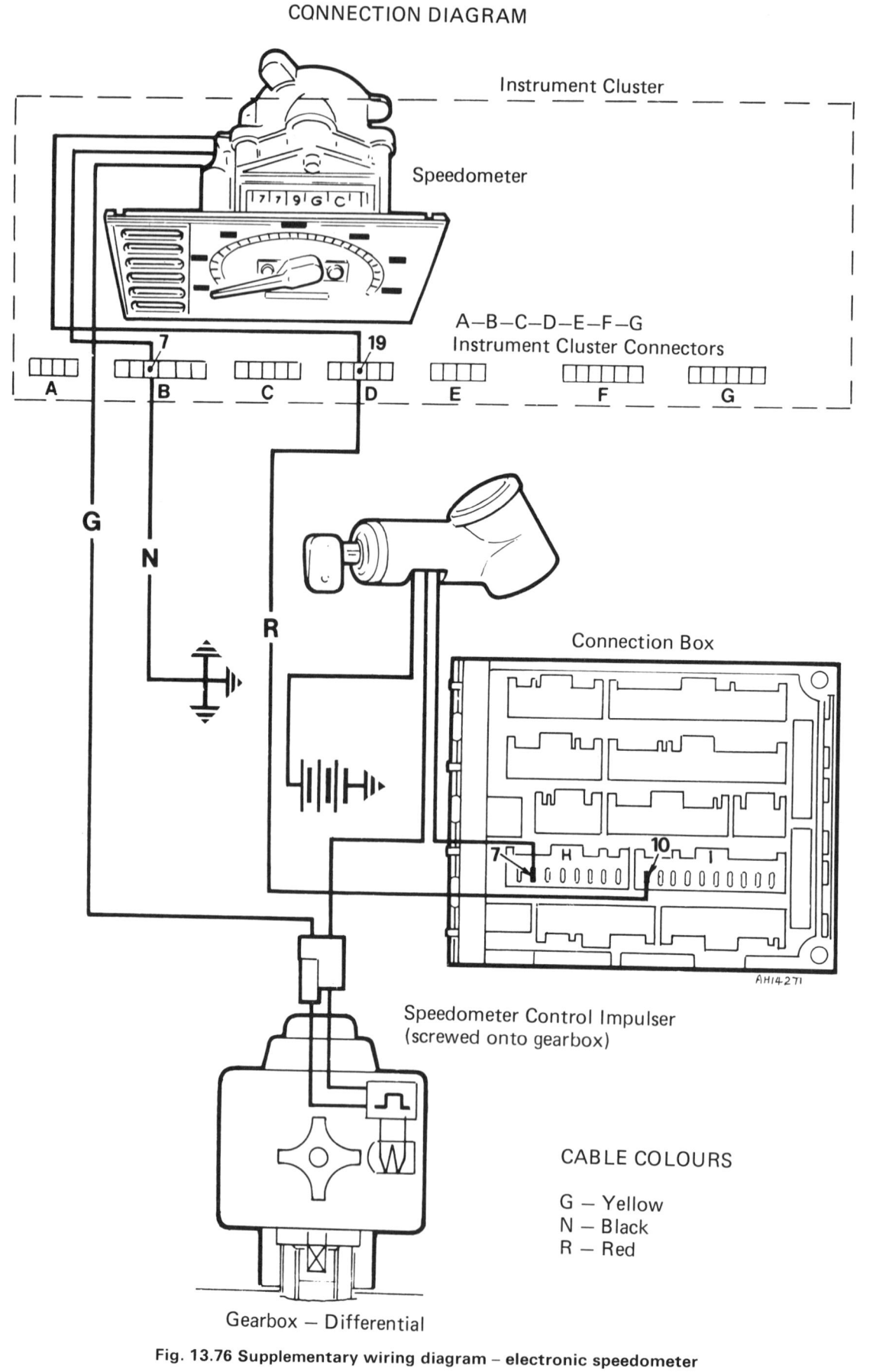

Instrument Cluster

Speedometer

A–B–C–D–E–F–G
Instrument Cluster Connectors

A B C D E F G

G

N

R

Connection Box

Speedometer Control Impulser
(screwed onto gearbox)

CABLE COLOURS

G – Yellow
N – Black
R – Red

Gearbox – Differential

Fig. 13.76 Supplementary wiring diagram – electronic speedometer

For key see page 305

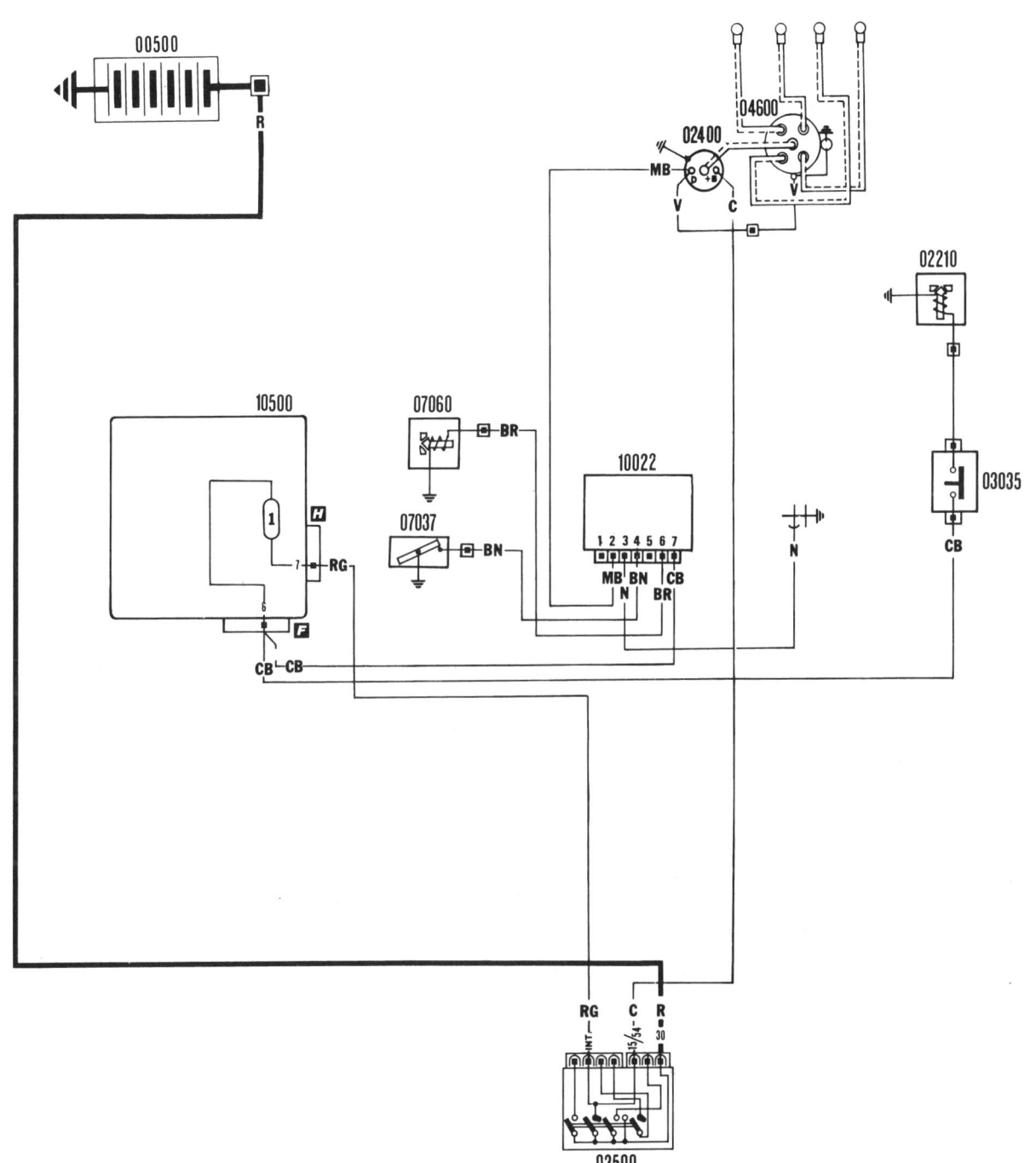

Fig. 13.77 Supplementary wiring diagram – fuel cut-off systems (60 L and 60 CL models from 1985)
For key see page 305

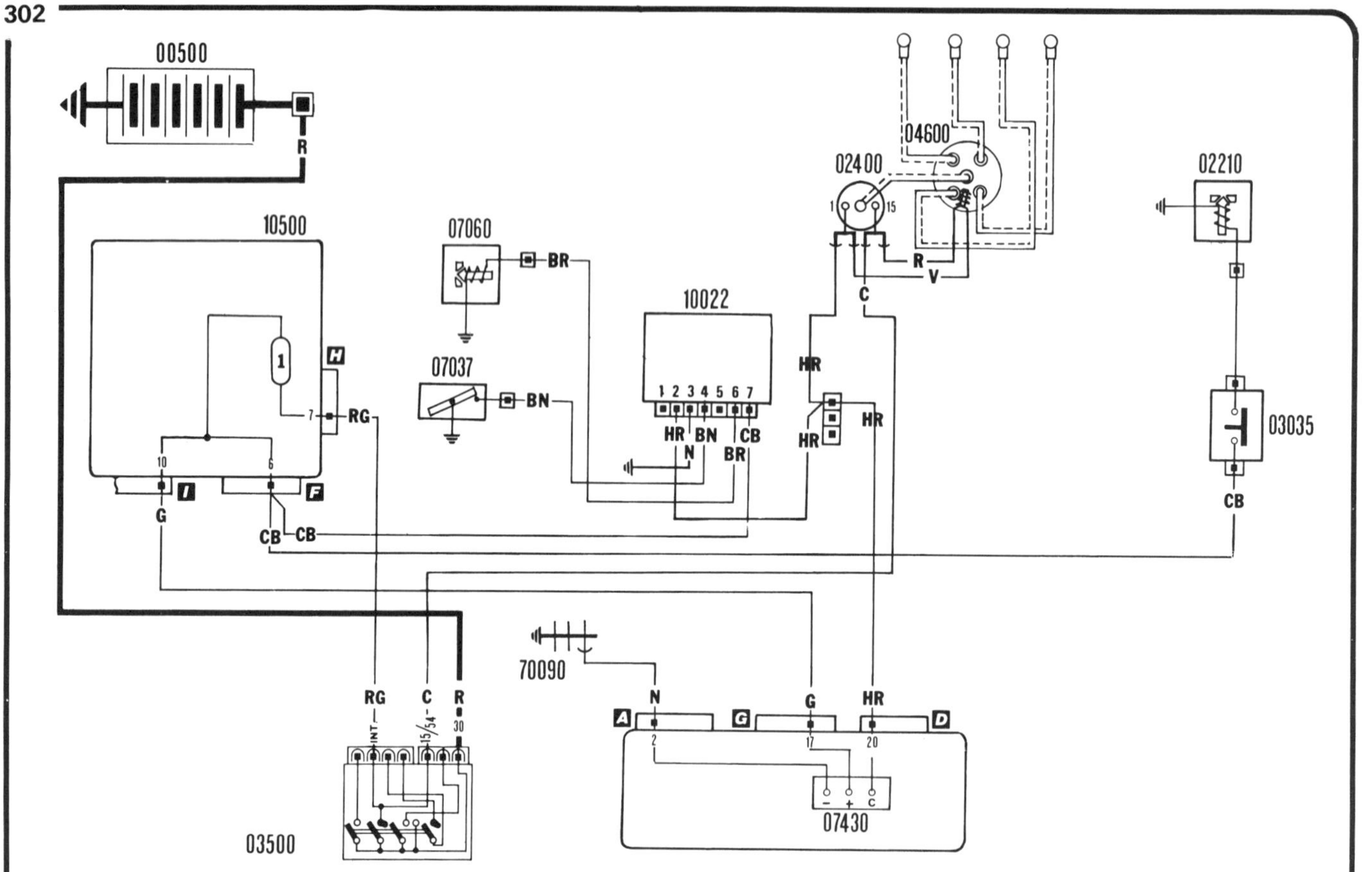

Fig. 13.78 Supplementary wiring diagram – breakerless ignition, fuel cut-off systems and tachometer (70 CL and 70 S models from 1985) For key see page 305

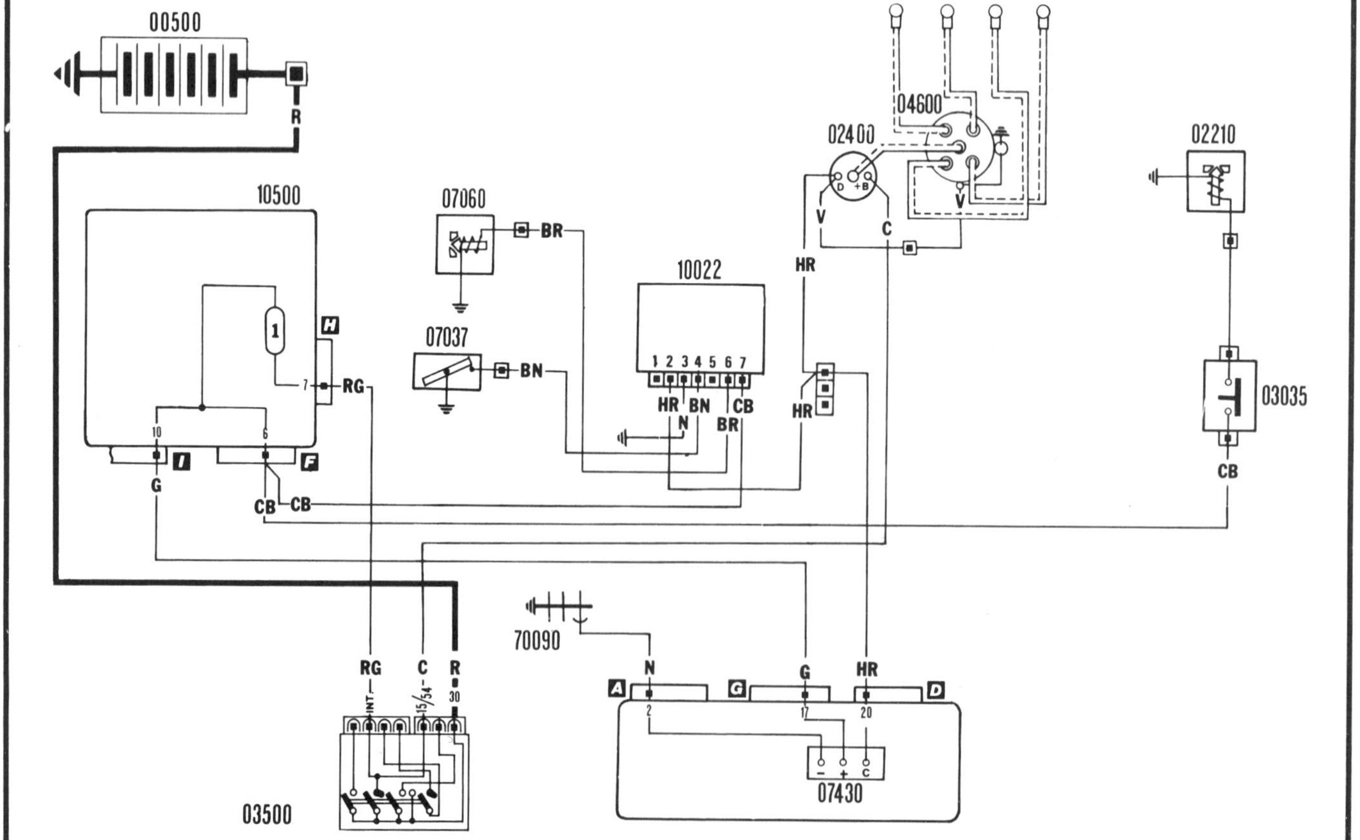

Fig. 13.79 Supplementary wiring diagram – ignition, fuel cut-off systems and tachometer (60 S models from 1985)
For key see page 305

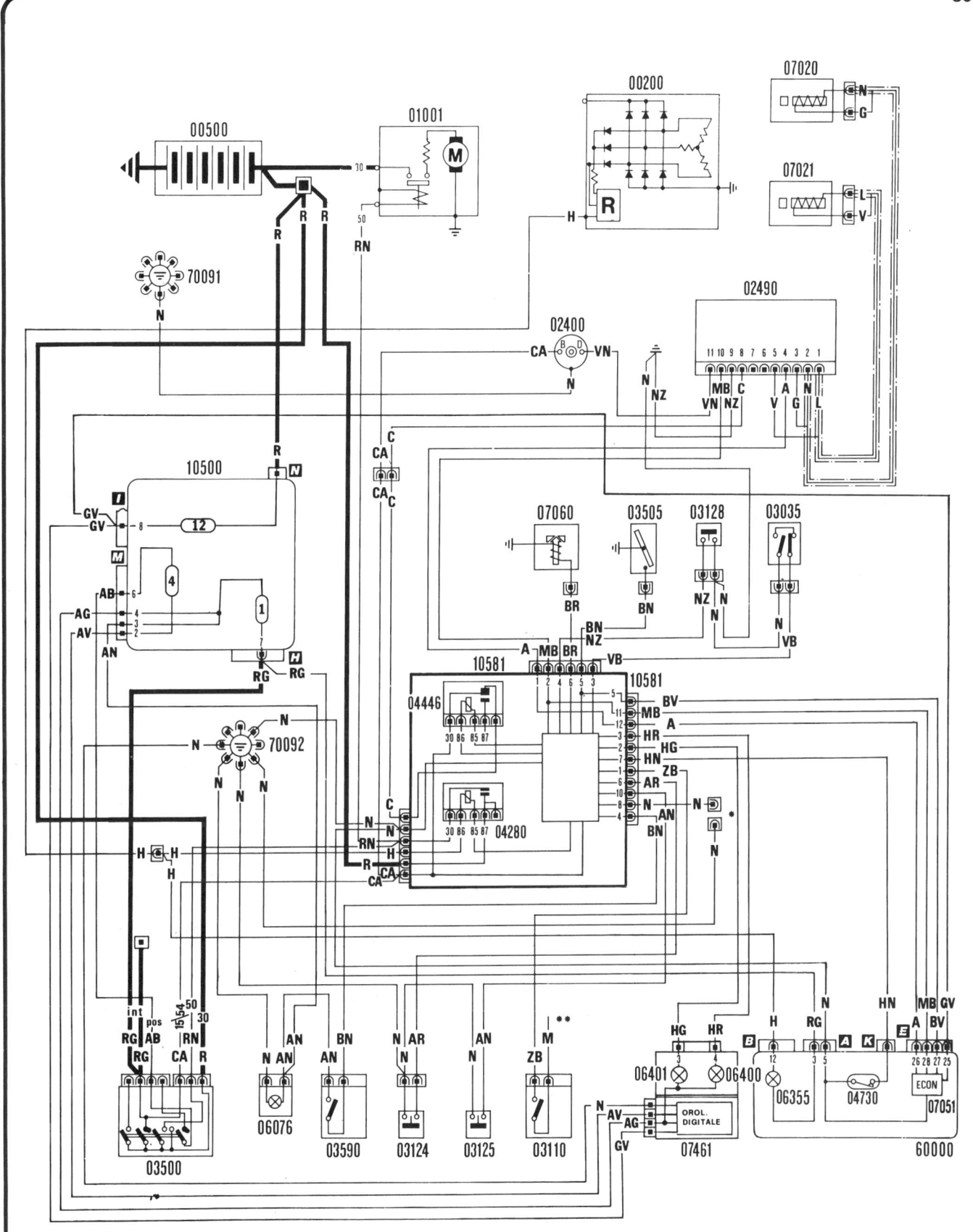

Fig. 13.80 Supplementary wiring diagram – Digiplex ignition, Citymatic and digital clock (ES models from 1985)
For key see page 305

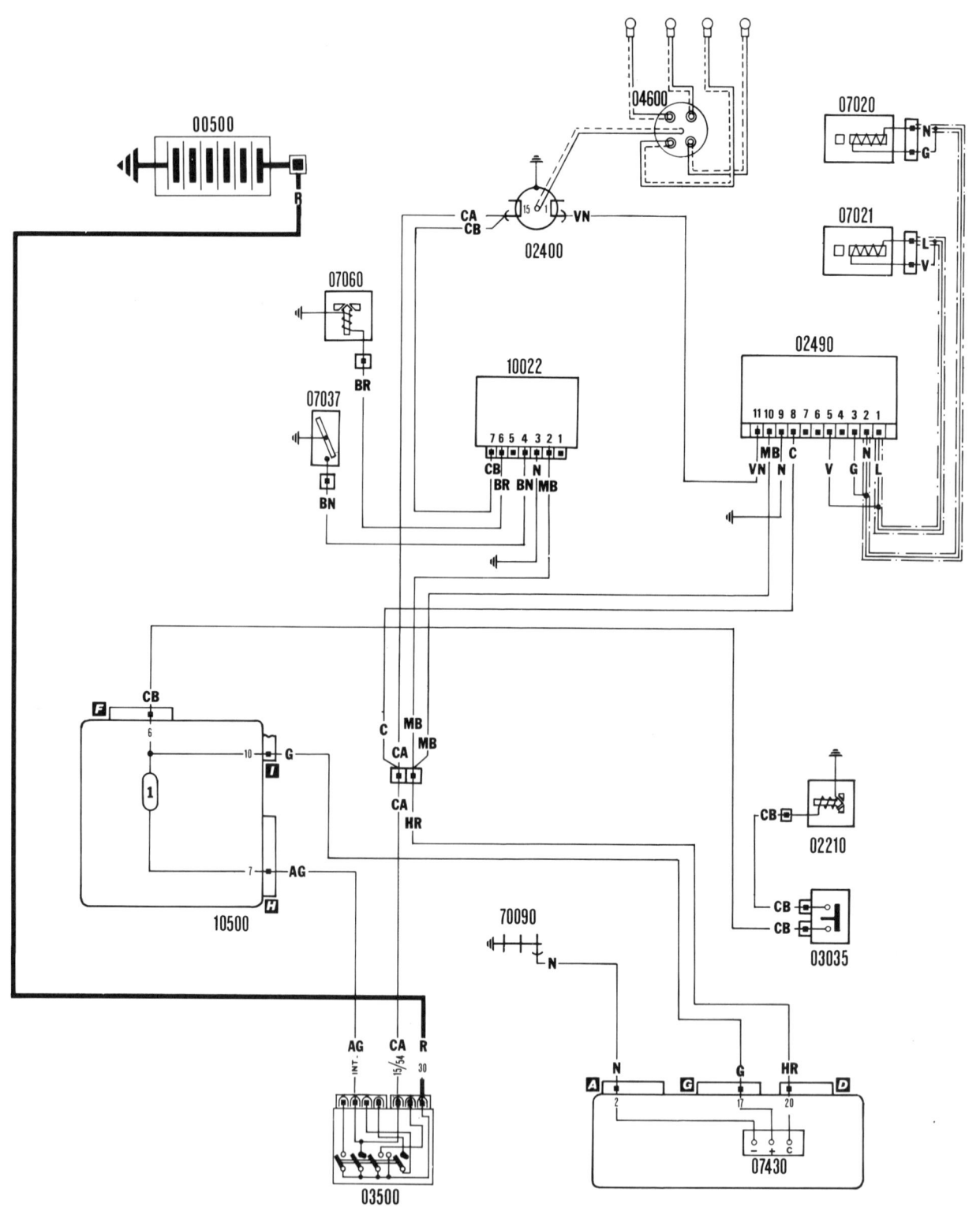

Fig. 13.81 Supplementary wiring diagram – Digiplex ignition, fuel cut-off systems and tachometer (85 S models from 1985)
For key see page 305

Key to wiring diagrams 13.71 to 13.81

00200	Alternator with built in regulator
00500	Battery
01001	Starter motor
01202	Right front electric window
01203	Left front electric window
01206	Windscreen wiper motor
01207	Rear screen wiper motor
01252	Right front door locking motor
01253	Left front door locking motor
01254	Right rear door locking motor
01255	Left rear door locking motor
01400	Windscreen washer electric pump
01401	Rear screen washer electric pump
01420	Electric fuel pump
01500	Engine cooling electric fan
01504	Heater electric fan
02001	Engine cut-out solenoid on injection pump
02210	Solenoid cut-out valve in accelerator pump outlet opening on carburettor
02400	Ignition coil
02490	Static advance ignition control unit
02510	Heater plug
03000	Insufficient engine oil pressure switch
03006	Handbrake warning light switch
03007	Brake light switch
03008	Reversing light switch
03028	Radiator thermal switch
03035	Thermal switch for solenoid cut-out valve in accelerator pump outlet opening on carburettor
03054	External lights switch
03059	Foglights switch
03060	Rear foglamp switch
03110	Heated rear windscreen switch
03111	Rearscreen wash/wipe control
03112	Rearscreen washer control
03114	Heater fan switch
03124	Clutch pedal depressed switch
03125	Clutch pedal released switch
03128	Gear lever in neutral switch
03142	Choke warning light switch
03301	Push button on right front door for courtesy light
03302	Push button on left front door for courtesy light
03312	Glove compartment light
03319	Horn control
03500	Ignition switch
03505	Butterfly valve cut-off switch
03530	Right front electric window switch
03531	Left front electric window switch
03550	Hazard warning lights switch
03590	Citymatic control switch
04000	Steering column switch unit
04010	Steering column switch unit, direction indicators
04020	Steering column switch unit, headlamps, main beam and dipped
04032	Steering column switch unit, windscreen wash/wipe
04225	Engine cooling fan relay
04241	Foglights relay
04244	Main beam headlamps relay
04260	Electric windows motor relay
04280	Starter relay
04282	Heater fan relay
04291	Horn relay
04292	Heated rear windscreen relay
04445	Fuel pump switch
04446	Ignition cut-out switch
04570	Direction indicators – hazard warning lights flasher unit
04600	Distributor
04700	Coolant temperature sender unit
04702	Oil temperature sender unit
04720	Oil pressure sender unit
04730	Vehicle speed signal impulse generator
05000	Right additional driving lamp
05001	Left additional driving lamp
05008	Right headlamp, main beam and dipped with sidelight
05009	Left headlamp, main beam and dipped with sidelight
05015	Right foglight
05016	Left foglight
05410	Right front direction indicator
05411	Left front direction indicator
05412	Right front side direction indicator
05413	Left front side direction indicator
05700	Right rear light cluster: side light, direction indicator, brake light, number plate light, reversing light, rear foglamp
05701	Left rear light cluster: sidelight, direction indicator, brake light, number plate light, reversing light, rear foglamp
06002	Courtesy light with adjustable map
06025	Glove compartment light
06040	Luggage compartment light
06076	Ideogram fibre optic light
06087	Vacuum gauge light
06300	Sidelights warning light
06305	Main beam headlamps warning light
06310	Rear foglamps warning light
06315	Hazard warning lights warning light
06320	Direction indicators warning
06336	Handbrake warning light
06338	Brake pad wear warning light
06343	Insufficient engine oil pressure warning light
06344	Brake fluid level warning light
06345	Fuel reserve warning light
06355	Recharging warning light
06365	Choke warning light
06367	Heater plugs warning light
06385	Heated rear windscreen warning light
06400	Citymatic engaged warning light
06401	Engine stopped warning light
06800	Horn
06801	Right horn

Key to wiring diagrams 13.71 to 13.81 (continued)

06802	Left horn
07000	Insufficient coolant level sensor
07001	Insufficient engine oil level sensor
07003	Insufficient brake fluid level sensor
07015	Right front brake pad wear sensor
07016	Left front brake pad wear sensor
07020	Speed signal sensor
07021	TDC sensor
07037	Closed carburettor butterfly sensor
07050	Fuel gauge
07051	Instant fuel consumption gauge (econometer)
07060	Idle cut-out device
07400	Fuel level gauge
07410	Oil temperature gauge
07415	Coolant temperature gauge
07420	Engine oil pressure gauge
07430	Rev counter
07440	Voltmeter
07461	Digital clock
08051	Ignition coil condenser

08475	Fuse for engine cooling fan
09000	Additional resistor for varying heater fan speed
09008	Resistor for two speed cooling fan
09080	Ideogram illumination rheostat
09100	Heated rear windscreen
10022	Cut-off device electronic control unit
10101	Pre-heating system control box
10500	Control box
10571	Central locking control unit
10581	Citymatic device control unit
59000	Cigar lighter
59010	Radio power lead
59200	Right front speaker
59201	Left front speaker
59204	4-place fusebox
60204	Fusebox
70092	Earth plate
90033	Connector block
M	Electronic control unit

Colour code

A	Light blue	AV	Light blue/Green	HR	Grey/Red
B	White	BG	White/Yellow	LB	Blue/White
C	Orange	BL	White/Blue	LG	Blue/Yellow
G	Yellow	BN	White/Black	LN	Blue/Black
H	Grey	BR	White/Red	LR	Blue/Red
L	Blue	BV	White/Green	LV	Blue/Green
M	Brown	BZ	White/Violet	MB	Brown//White
N	Black	CA	Orange/light blue	NZ	Black/Violet
R	Red	CB	Orange/White	RB	Red/White
S	Pink	CN	Orange/Black	RG	Red/Yellow
V	Green	GL	Yellow/Blue	RN	Red/Black
Z	Violet	GN	Yellow/Black	RV	Red/Green
AB	Light blue/White	GR	Yellow/Red	SN	Pink/Black
AG	Light blue/Yellow	GV	Yellow/Green	VB	Green/White
AN	Light blue/Black	HG	Grey/Yellow	VN	Green/Black
AR	Light blue/Red	HN	Grey/Black	VR	Green/Red

17 Steering

Steering gear (TC models) – removal and refitting
1   Proceed as described in Chapter 10, Section 8, but note that the heat shield will have to be removed from the pinion area before removing the steering gear, and refitted afterwards.

Steering damper (105 TC) – removal and refitting
2   A steering damper is fitted to some later models.
3   To remove the damper, unbolt the heat shield, then unscrew the damper fixing nuts and bolt from the rack and housing (photos).
4   Refitting is a reversal of removal.

Steering wheel (adjustable rake type)
5   This type of steering wheel can be tilted after pulling the clamp lever towards the driver.
6   If the steering column is being overhauled, the clamp can be removed by unscrewing its self-locking nut and withdrawing the lever, bushes and spacer (photo).
7   When reassembling the clamp, locate the lever in the clamped position and tighten the self-locking nut until the steering wheel is firmly held. Check that the wheel is released when the clamp lever is pulled towards the driver. Slightly loosen or tighten the self-locking nut if necessary, to give smooth and positive operation of the lever.

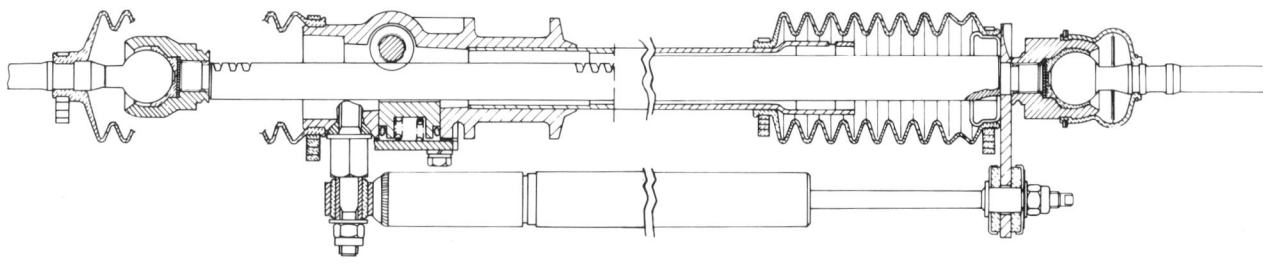

Fig. 13.82 Sectional view of steering gear with damper (Sec 17)

17.3A Steering gear heat shield top bolt (arrowed)

17.3B Steering gear heat shield lower bolts (arrowed)

17.3C Steering damper eye (arrowed)

17.3D Steering damper rod connecting nut (arrowed)

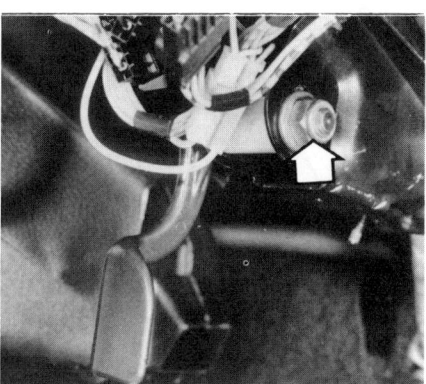

17.6 Steering wheel rake adjusting clamp lever self-locking nut arrowed

Fig. 13.83 Steering wheel rake adjuster clamp lever (Sec 17)

1   Locked   2   Released

18 Suspension

Front strut mountings – later models

1   During 1983, the number of front strut upper mounting points was increased from two to three. In consequence most steering and suspension angles were altered – see Specifications for details (photo).
2   Removal, refitting and overhaul procedures are essentially unchanged.

Front anti-roll bar (TC models) – removal and refitting

3   The anti-roll bar is secured by four clamps and bushes (photo).
4   To remove the anti-roll bar, simply unbolt the clamps.
5   Refit in the reverse order to removal, using new bushes if necessary.

Front track control arm – overhaul

6   If the control arm balljoint is worn or damaged, the complete arm must be renewed.
7   The rubber bush can be renewed, having first removed the old one by drilling out the peened end of its spacer and pressing it out. Have the new bush and spacer pressed in and secured by a FIAT dealer. Special press tools are required to secure the bush.

Front hub bearing (later models) – renewal

8   On later models the front hub bearing is retained by a circlip, not a ring nut as described in Chapter 11.
9   Bearing renewal should be delegated to a FIAT dealer, or other competent specialist, having suitable press facilities. Attempts to drive bearings in or out of the hub will probably result in damage.

Rear suspension strut mountings

10 As from 1985, the rear suspension strut rubber mountings are of modified type to improve suspension response characteristics.

Rear suspension components (all models) – refitting

11 The weight of the car must be on its wheels, and the car must be laden with the equivalent of five passengers plus 50 kg (110 lb), when final fastening is carried out.
12 Always tighten nuts and bolts to the specified torque.

Roadwheel trim

13 On certain later models, the roadwheel trim is secured by three of the four wheel bolts.
14 When refitting a roadwheel, locate it on its positioning spigot, and then screw one wheel bolt into the hole closest to the tyre valve.
15 Offer up the wheel trim so that the larger bolt hole passes through the head of the bolt just fitted. The other large hole in the trim will then align with the tyre valve (photo).
16 Screw in the remaining three wheel bolts which will secure the trim.

18.1 Front strut top mounting (later models)

18.3 Front anti-roll bar mounting clamp

18.15 Roadwheel trim

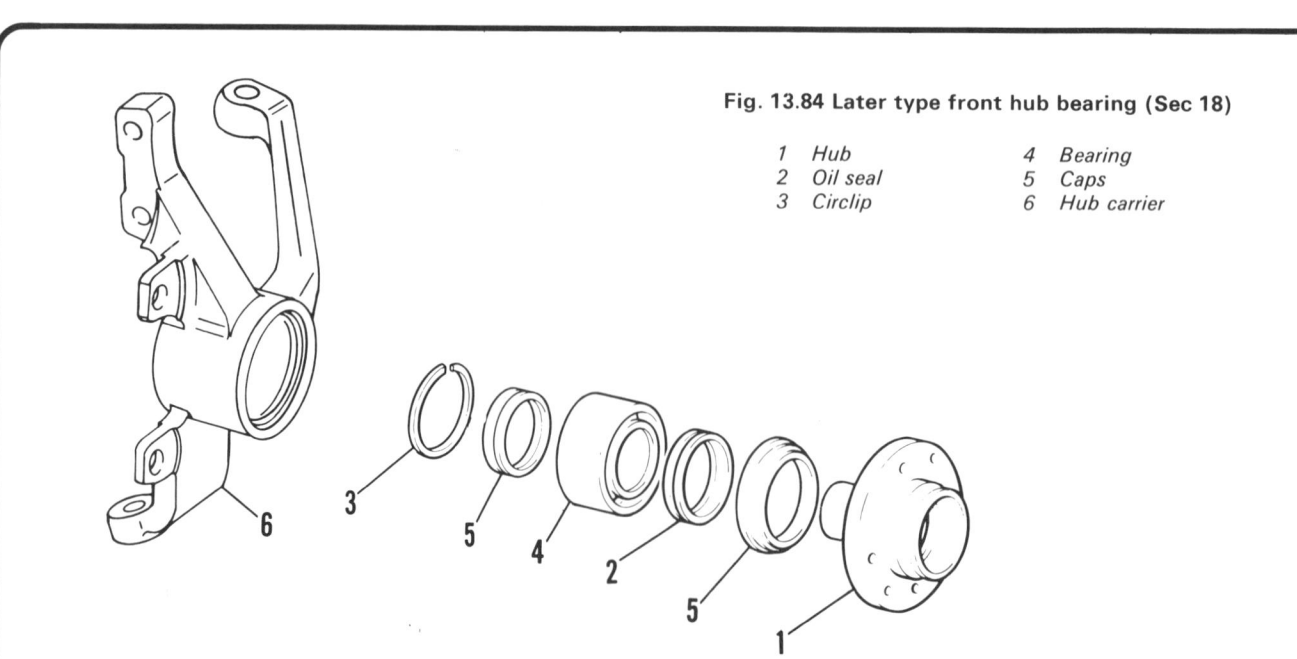

Fig. 13.84 Later type front hub bearing (Sec 18)

1   Hub
2   Oil seal
3   Circlip
4   Bearing
5   Caps
6   Hub carrier

19 Bodywork and fittings

Front grille (Strada II) – removal and refitting

Up to 1985

1   Remove the four screws from around the headlights on each side of the grille (photo).
2   Prise out the two plastic clips which secure the top of the grille (photo). The grille can now be withdrawn.
3   Refit in the reverse order of removal.

1985 on

4   Open and support the bonnet and then extract the top two grille fixing screws (photo).
5   Disconnect the wiring plugs from the four headlamps.
6   Working inside and at each side of the grille, unscrew the three fixing nuts (photo).
7   Withdraw the grille complete with headlamps (photo).
8   Refitting is a reversal of removal.

Front wings – 130 TC

9   During 1984, plastic front wings were fitted instead of metal ones.
10 Should repair of the wing or attention to its paintwork be required, consult a FIAT dealer or other competent body specialist.
11 Metal wings are still available as spares.

19.1 Removing grille fixing screw (up to 1985)

19.2 Grille retaining clip (up to 1985)

19.4 Extracting radiator grille top fixing screw (1985 on)

19.6 Unscrewing a grille fixing nut (1985 on)

19.7 Withdrawing grille/headlamp assembly (1985 on)

Inner wing reinforcements (Strada II) – renewal
12 If for any reason it is necessary to renew the inner wing reinforcements (Fig. 13.85) note that they are bolted and glued in place.
13 The glue specified for this application is a two-component epoxy resin, which should be applied in accordance with its maker's instructions.

Rear spoiler (ES and 105 TC) – removal and refitting
14 The rear spoiler is secured by two side brackets, which are secured to the body, and by glue.
15 Remove the side brackets and rubber pads and carefully pull off the old spoiler. Should the glue be too strong, try the effect of moderate heat (hot water or hot air – not a naked flame). Be careful not to damage the paintwork.
16 Thoroughly clean the mounting areas on the body with a safe degreasing solvent.
17 Warm the spoiler, in an oven or under a lamp, to between 40° and 50°C (104° and 122°F). Maintain this temperature for 10 to 15 minutes.
18 Remove the protective liner from the spoiler and offer the spoiler to the body, starting at one side and working across. Apply light hand pressure to seat the spoiler, then apply sustained pressure of approx 1 kg (2 lb) until the glue has set.
19 Fit and secure the side brackets and rubber pads.

Front bumper (Strada II) – removal and refitting
Up to 1985
20 Remove the three screws from the front of the bumper panel.
21 Remove the single bolt on each side which secures the angled bracket to the body.
22 Support the bumper and remove the single nut on each side which secures the steady bar to the bumper.
23 On models so equipped, disconnect the front foglamps or auxiliary driving lamps.
24 Remove the bumper; retrieve lights, brackets etc, if it is to be renewed.
25 Refit in the reverse order of removal.

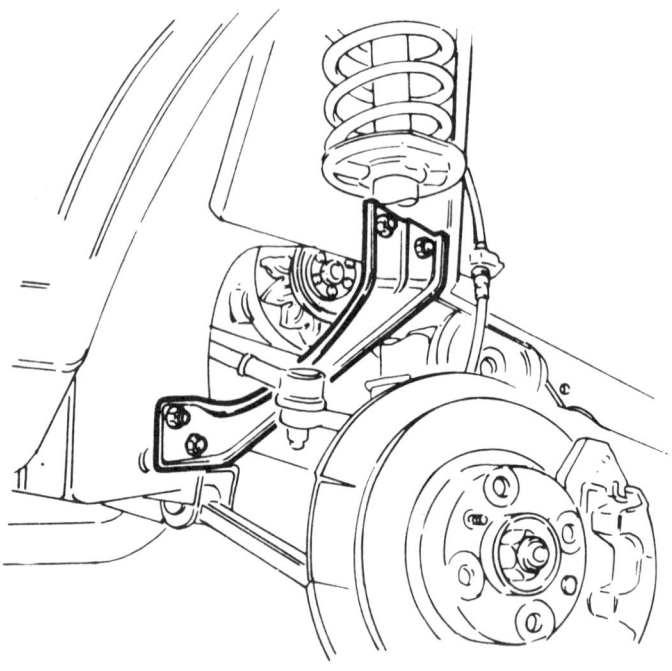

Fig. 13.85 Inner wing reinforcement (Sec 19)

1985 on
26 Remove the foglamps or blanking plates (two self-tapping screws) from the front bumper.
27 Unscrew the fixing nuts which are located above the foglamp or

Fig. 13.86 Front bumper fixings (arrowed) – up to 1985 (Sec 19)

19.27 Using a spanner to unscrew a front bumper nut

19.28A Front bumper bracket fixing screws

19.28B Front bumper bracket fixing screws

19.29A Underwing protective shield and screws

19.29B Front bumper side fixing

19.35 Unscrewing an outer trim panel nut

blanking plate apertures (photo).

28 Unscrew and remove the screws from under the lower edge of the bumper. These screws hold the bumper and brackets to the body (photos).

29 Peel back the underwing protective shield from the front edge of the wings and then unscrew the bumper side fixing nuts (photos).

30 Refitting is a reversal of removal.

Rear bumper (Strada II) – removal and refitting
Up to 1985

31 Remove the rear light clusters and the number plate.

32 Remove the eight nuts and bolts which secure the rear bumper to the body. Remove the bumper.

33 Refit in the reverse order of removal.

1985 on

34 Open the tailgate.

35 Working inside the luggage area, unscrew the two nuts which secure the outer trim panel, which is located between the two rear lamp clusters. The nuts are in the two deeply recessed holes (closest together) in the interior trim panel. Use a box spanner or long socket to reach them (photo).

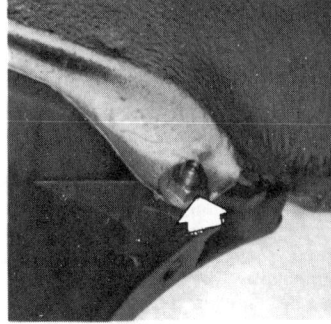

Fig. 13.87 Rear bumper fixings (arrowed) – up to 1985 (Sec 19)

Inset – location of side fixing nuts

19.36 Outer trim panel locating tab and slot

19.37 Withdrawing a rear lamp cluster

19.38A Rear bumper upper fixing screw

19.38B Rear bumper lower fixing screw

19.39 Rear bumper side fixing

19.40 Rear bumper fixing bolt with earth wire

36 Squeeze the exterior trim panel upper and lower edges towards each other to disengage the locating tabs and remove the panel (photo).

37 Withdraw both rear lamp clusters. Two of the cluster fixing nuts are located in deeply recessed holes (furthest apart) in the interior trim panel, and a box spanner or long socket will again be required to remove them (photo).

38 Extract the fixing screws from the bumper upper and lower edges (photos).

39 Unscrew the bumper side fixing nut from the near edge of each rear wing (photo).

40 Working inside the luggage area, unscrew the two bumper fixing bolts. Note the earth wire connections underneath their heads (photo).

41 Remove the bumper.

42 Refitting is a reversal of removal.

Seat belts

43 Check the condition of the seat belts regularly. If there is evidence of fraying or other damage, or if the belts have been subjected to strain as the result of a collision, then they should be renewed.

44 The belts may be cleaned using warm water and detergent. Keep the belts extended until dry. Never use a solvent of any kind to clean a belt as it may affect the strength of the belt material.

45 If a seat belt is removed, make sure that when refitting it, the original sequence of anchor plate components (plate, spacer, wave washer) is maintained.

46 On certain later models, rear seat belts are fitted as standard equipment, the inertia reels being bolted to the sides of the luggage compartment (photo).

Plastic components

47 With the use of more and more plastic body components by the vehicle manufacturers (eg bumpers, spoilers, and in some cases major body panels), rectification of damage to such items has become a matter of either entrusting repair work to a specialist in this field, or renewing complete components. Repair by the DIY owner is not really feasible owing to the cost of the equipment and materials required for effecting such repairs. The basic technique involves making a groove

along the line of the crack in the plastic using a rotary burr in a power drill. The damaged part is then welded back together by using a hot air gun to heat up and fuse a plastic filler rod into the groove. Any excess plastic is then removed and the area rubbed down to a smooth finish. It is important that a filler rod of the correct plastic is used, as body components can be made of a variety of different types (eg polycarbonate, ABS, polypropylene).

48 If the owner is renewing a complete component himself, he will be left with the problem of finding a suitable paint for finishing which is compatible with the type of plastic used. At one time the use of a universal paint was not possible owing to the complex range of

19.46 Rear seat belt inertia reel

Fig. 13.88 Facia panel fixing screws (arrowed) on Strada II models (Sec 19)

plastics encountered in body component applications. Standard paints, generally speaking, will not bond to plastic or rubber satisfactorily. However, it is possible to obtain a plastic body parts finishing kit which consists of a pre-primer treatment, a primer and coloured top coat. Full instructions are normally supplied with a kit, but basically the method of use is to first apply the pre-primer to the component concerned and allow it to dry for up to 30 minutes. Then the primer is applied and left to dry for about an hour before finally applying the special coloured top coat. The result is a correctly coloured component where the paint will flex with the plastic or rubber, a property that standard paint does not normally possess.

Facia panel (later models) – removal and refitting
49 The procedure is as described in Chapter 12, Section 15, noting the different locations of the securing screws (Fig. 13.84).

Grab handles
50 Prise back the end covers using a small screwdriver and remove the screws now exposed (photo).

Doors – dismantling and reassembly
Up to 1985
51 The procedure is similar to that described in Chapter 12, Section 17. When a door pocket is fitted, unscrew it to remove the trim.
52 The new type door lock handle can be removed by depressing its retaining clip. Pull the handle out and twist it to withdraw it (photos).
53 Before refitting the window winder handle, make sure that the spacer plate is in position.

1985 on
54 To remove the door trim panel, first withdraw the frame from the lock remote control handle. To do this; pull the upper edge of the frame slightly out and then push it downwards (photo).
55 Prise out the plugs from the armrest, extract the fixing screws and remove the armrest (photos).
56 Extract the screws from the door tidy bin and remove it (photo).
57 If a window winder handle is fitted, remove it as described in Chapter 12, Section 17.

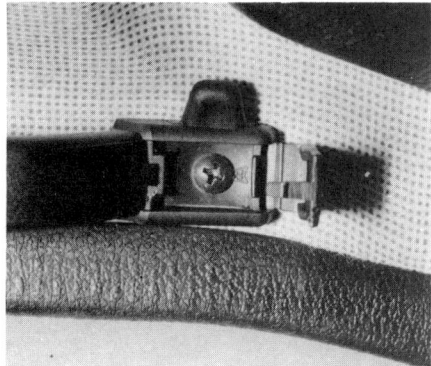

19.50 Grab handle fixing screw

19.52A Door lock handle retaining clip (up to June 85)

19.52B Disengaging the door lock remote control handle (up to June 1985)

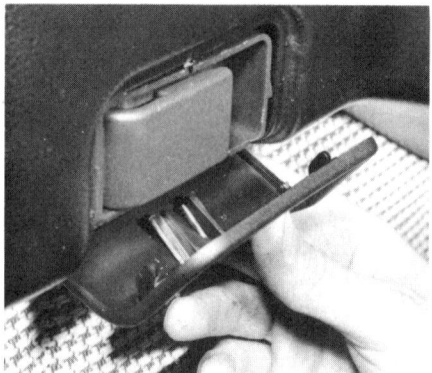

19.54 Removing door lock remote control handle frame (July 1985 on)

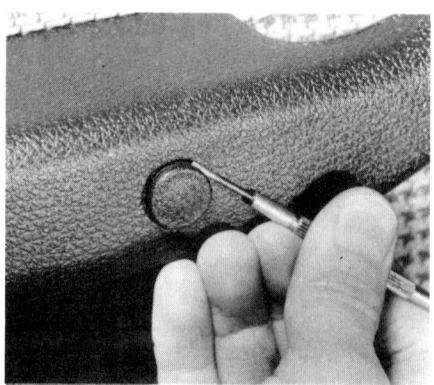

19.55A Prising out an armrest plug

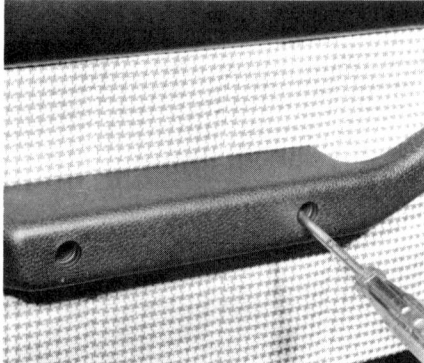

19.55B Extracting an armrest screw

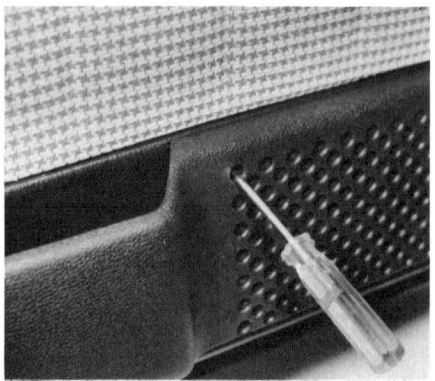

19.56 Extracting a door tidy bin fixing screw

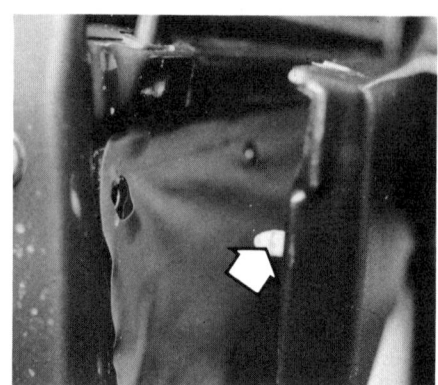

19.58 Door trim panel fixing clip

19.59 Peeling away door waterproof sheet

58 Insert the fingers under the lower edge of the door interior trim panel and give a sharp jerk to release the securing clips (photo).

59 Peel away the waterproof sheet (photo).

60 If manually-operated locks and windows are fitted, the assemblies can be unbolted and removed as described in Chapter 12 (photo).

61 If central door locking or power-operated front door windows are fitted, the components can be removed from the door as described in Section 16 of this Supplement.

62 A location for radio speakers in the doors is provided, but when the speakers are fitted (not factory supplied as standard equipment) the door trim panel will have to be cut.

63 If the later type rectangular exterior door handle must be removed while the trim panel is off, extract the screw from the door edge and slide the handle frame towards the front of the car. Withdraw the handle and disconnect the ball socket type of link rod (photos).

Rear view interior mirror – removal and refitting

64 The dipping type of interior rear view mirror can be removed in the following way.

65 Unscrew but do not remove the exposed screw. Push the screw fully inwards and hold it depressed, then pull the mirror sharply to release it from it 'safety' shear type socket (photo).

66 When refitting, again keep the screw fully depressed while the mirror bracket is pushed firmly onto its mounting base. Tighten the screw which will tighten the wedge nut and expand the retaining fingers inside the socket cup (photo).

Exterior mirror (internally adjustable type) – removal and refitting

67 Pull the rubber cover from the adjusting knob to expose the large ring nut.

19.60 Remotely-operated door lock handle

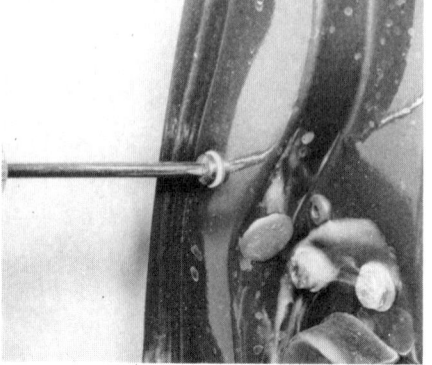

19.63A Door exterior handle fixing screw (1985 on)

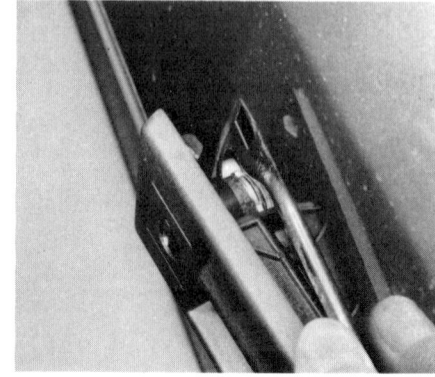

19.63B Removing door exterior handle (1985 on)

19.63C Exterior door handle link rod

19.65 Rear view mirror wedge nut (arrowed)

19.66 Connecting mirror stem to mounting base

68 If there is a screw securing the mirror backing plate to the mirror base, remove it. On TC models there is no screw fitted.
69 Unscrew the ring nut, using a peg spanner or a small hammer and a drift. Support the mirror and remove the nut.
70 Remove the mirror and recover the mounting components and backing plate. Note the position of any washers.
71 No spares are available for repair of the mirror head or articulating system.
72 Refit in the reverse order of removal. Check for correct operation of the mirror before refitting the rubber cover.

Cabriolet hood – care and maintenance
73 The hood fitted to Cabriolet models must be looked after if it is to give satisfactory service. Observe the following points:

   (a) Clean the hood regularly with water and a soft brush. Do not use powerful detergents, solvents or stain removers; do not use an automatic car wash
   (b) Do not lower the hood when it is dirty, or when it is covered with snow or ice
   (c) Do not raise or lower the hood when the car is in motion
   (d) Do not switch on the heated rear window when the hood is lowered
   (e) Always fit the cover over the folded hood

74 Oil the joints of the hood frame occasionally; wipe off surplus oil immediately to avoid staining the hood.
75 Apart from the opening and closing instructions which follow, no other information is available concerning the hood.

Cabriolet hood – lowering
76 Open the boot lid and free it from its attachment to the bottom of the hood.
77 Open the zip across covers on both sides of the rear window and undo the zips.
78 Inside the car, release the two catches which secure the front of the hood to the windscreen pillars.
79 With the aid of an assistant if possible, fold back the hood by pressing upwards and then rearwards on the crossbar. Do not apply pressure to any other part of the frame.
80 Lift the crossbar slightly and tuck in the material, then push the crossbar down firmly.
81 Stow the hood in the boot and fit the boot lid. Make sure that no objects in the boot will chafe against the heated rear window elements. Also check that no fabric is trapped by, or outside, the lid.
82 Fit the hood cover, securing it with the eyes, press studs and straps provided.

Cabriolet hood – raising
83 Remove the hood cover.
84 Open and free the boot lid.
85 With the help of an assistant, lift the hood by means of the crossbar. Settle the rear part of the frame on the roll bar and pull the crossbar towards the windscreen.
86 Secure the two front catches by pushing down on the outside of the hood with one hand and pulling the hook into place with the other.
87 Close the rear window zips, locating the zip tabs on the boot lid arm, and secure the zip covers.
88 Refit the boot lid, making sure that the bottom edge of the hood lies above the top edge of the lid. Secure the two flaps at the bottom of the rear window.

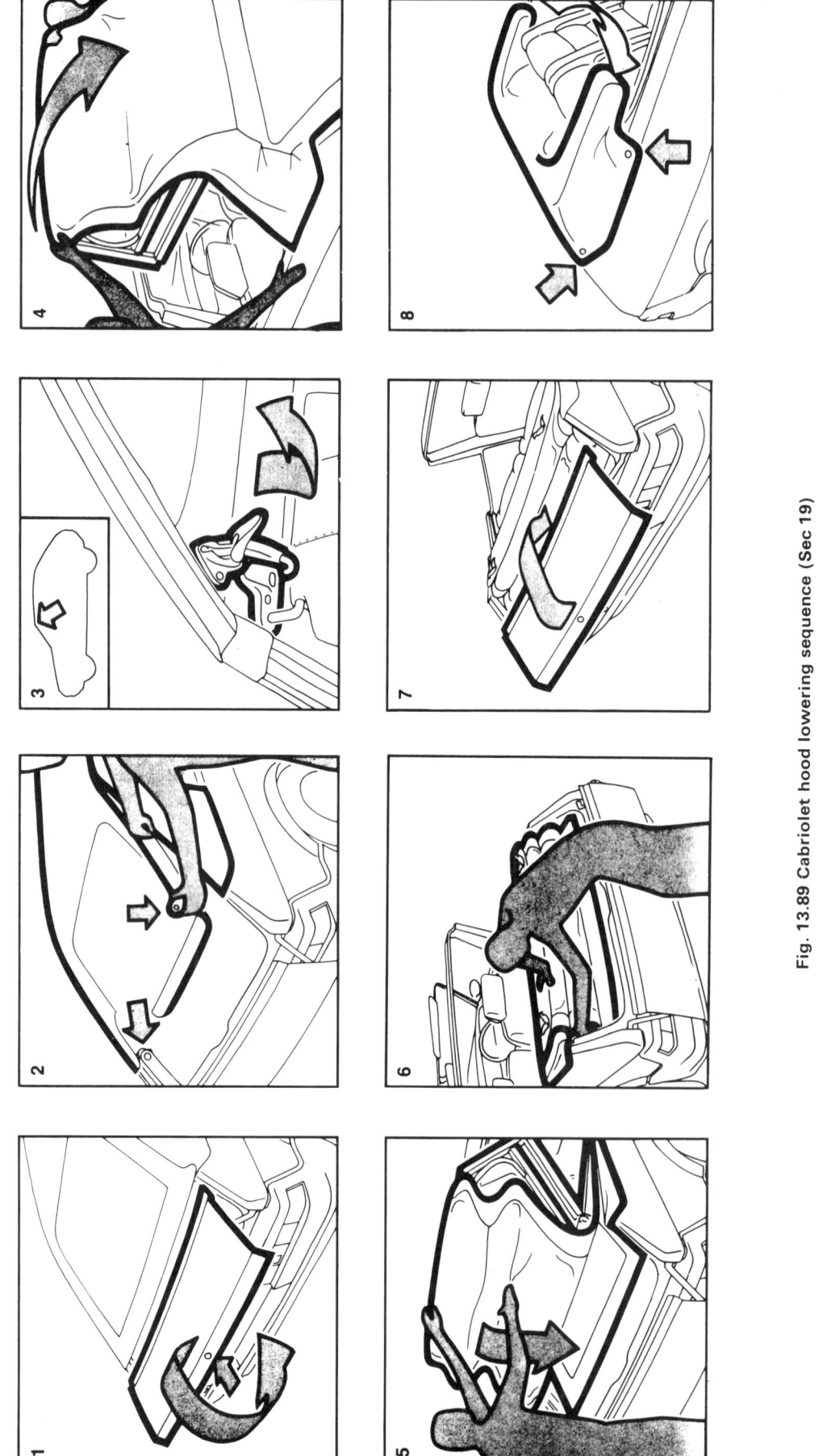

Fig. 13.89 Cabriolet hood lowering sequence (Sec 19)

1 Release boot lid
2 Unzip rear window
3 Release catches
4 Fold back
5 Tuck in
6 Stow in boot
7 Secure boot lid
8 Fit cover

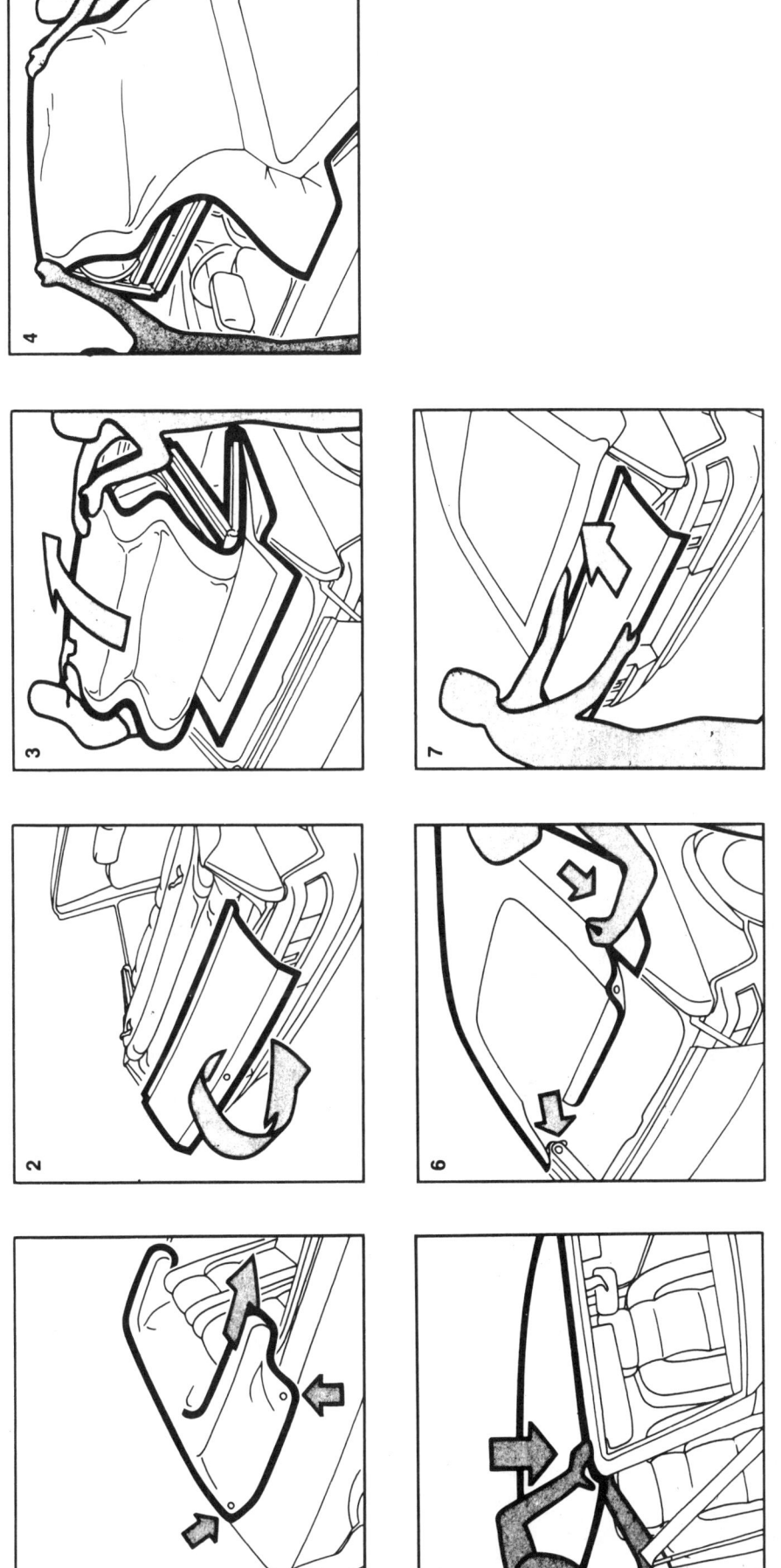

Fig. 13.90 Cabriolet hood raising sequence (Sec 19)

1 Remove cover
2 Release boot lid

3 Lift up
4 Fold forwards

5 Secure catches
6 Zip up window

7 Secure boot lid

Conversion factors

Length (distance)
Inches (in)	X	25.4	= Millimetres (mm)	X	0.0394	= Inches (in)
Feet (ft)	X	0.305	= Metres (m)	X	3.281	= Feet (ft)
Miles	X	1.609	= Kilometres (km)	X	0.621	= Miles

Volume (capacity)
Cubic inches (cu in; in³)	X	16.387	= Cubic centimetres (cc; cm³)	X	0.061	= Cubic inches (cu in; in³)
Imperial pints (Imp pt)	X	0.568	= Litres (l)	X	1.76	= Imperial pints (Imp pt)
Imperial quarts (Imp qt)	X	1.137	= Litres (l)	X	0.88	= Imperial quarts (Imp qt)
Imperial quarts (Imp qt)	X	1.201	= US quarts (US qt)	X	0.833	= Imperial quarts (Imp qt)
US quarts (US qt)	X	0.946	= Litres (l)	X	1.057	= US quarts (US qt)
Imperial gallons (Imp gal)	X	4.546	= Litres (l)	X	0.22	= Imperial gallons (Imp gal)
Imperial gallons (Imp gal)	X	1.201	= US gallons (US gal)	X	0.833	= Imperial gallons (Imp gal)
US gallons (US gal)	X	3.785	= Litres (l)	X	0.264	= US gallons (US gal)

Mass (weight)
Ounces (oz)	X	28.35	= Grams (g)	X	0.035	= Ounces (oz)
Pounds (lb)	X	0.454	= Kilograms (kg)	X	2.205	= Pounds (lb)

Force
Ounces-force (ozf; oz)	X	0.278	= Newtons (N)	X	3.6	= Ounces-force (ozf; oz)
Pounds-force (lbf; lb)	X	4.448	= Newtons (N)	X	0.225	= Pounds-force (lbf; lb)
Newtons (N)	X	0.1	= Kilograms-force (kgf; kg)	X	9.81	= Newtons (N)

Pressure
Pounds-force per square inch (psi; lbf/in²; lb/in²)	X	0.070	= Kilograms-force per square centimetre (kgf/cm²; kg/cm²)	X	14.223	= Pounds-force per square inch (psi; lbf/in²; lb/in²)
Pounds-force per square inch (psi; lbf/in²; lb/in²)	X	0.068	= Atmospheres (atm)	X	14.696	= Pounds-force per square inch (psi; lbf/in²; lb/in²)
Pounds-force per square inch (psi; lbf/in²; lb/in²)	X	0.069	= Bars	X	14.5	= Pounds-force per square inch (psi; lbf/in²; lb/in²)
Pounds-force per square inch (psi; lbf/in²; lb/in²)	X	6.895	= Kilopascals (kPa)	X	0.145	= Pounds-force per square inch (psi; lbf/in²; lb/in²)
Kilopascals (kPa)	X	0.01	= Kilograms-force per square centimetre (kgf/cm²; kg/cm²)	X	98.1	= Kilopascals (kPa)
Millibar (mbar)	X	100	= Pascals (Pa)	X	0.01	= Millibar (mbar)
Millibar (mbar)	X	0.0145	= Pounds-force per square inch (psi; lbf/in²; lb/in²)	X	68.947	= Millibar (mbar)
Millibar (mbar)	X	0.75	= Millimetres of mercury (mmHg)	X	1.333	= Millibar (mbar)
Millibar (mbar)	X	0.401	= Inches of water (inH₂O)	X	2.491	= Millibar (mbar)
Millimetres of mercury (mmHg)	X	0.535	= Inches of water (inH₂O)	X	1.868	= Millimetres of mercury (mmHg)
Inches of water (inH₂O)	X	0.036	= Pounds-force per square inch (psi; lbf/in²; lb/in²)	X	27.68	= Inches of water (inH₂O)

Torque (moment of force)
Pounds-force inches (lbf in; lb in)	X	1.152	= Kilograms-force centimetre (kgf cm; kg cm)	X	0.868	= Pounds-force inches (lbf in; lb in)
Pounds-force inches (lbf in; lb in)	X	0.113	= Newton metres (Nm)	X	8.85	= Pounds-force inches (lbf in; lb in)
Pounds-force inches (lbf in; lb in)	X	0.083	= Pounds-force feet (lbf ft; lb ft)	X	12	= Pounds-force inches (lbf in; lb in)
Pounds-force feet (lbf ft; lb ft)	X	0.138	= Kilograms-force metres (kgf m; kg m)	X	7.233	= Pounds-force feet (lbf ft; lb ft)
Pounds-force feet (lbf ft; lb ft)	X	1.356	= Newton metres (Nm)	X	0.738	= Pounds-force feet (lbf ft; lb ft)
Newton metres (Nm)	X	0.102	= Kilograms-force metres (kgf m; kg m)	X	9.804	= Newton metres (Nm)

Power
Horsepower (hp)	X	745.7	= Watts (W)	X	0.0013	= Horsepower (hp)

Velocity (speed)
Miles per hour (miles/hr; mph)	X	1.609	= Kilometres per hour (km/hr; kph)	X	0.621	= Miles per hour (miles/hr; mph)

Fuel consumption*
Miles per gallon, Imperial (mpg)	X	0.354	= Kilometres per litre (km/l)	X	2.825	= Miles per gallon, Imperial (mpg)
Miles per gallon, US (mpg)	X	0.425	= Kilometres per litre (km/l)	X	2.352	= Miles per gallon, US (mpg)

Temperature
Degrees Fahrenheit = (°C x 1.8) + 32   Degrees Celsius (Degrees Centigrade; °C) = (°F - 32) x 0.56

*It is common practice to convert from miles per gallon (mpg) to litres/100 kilometres (l/100km),
where mpg (Imperial) x l/100 km = 282 and mpg (US) x l/100 km = 235

Index

Printed by
J H Haynes & Co Ltd
Sparkford Nr Yeovil
Somerset BA22 7JJ England